HOUGHTON MIFFLIN

WE·THE PEOPLE

Discover Our Heritage

WE·THE
PEOPLE

Discover Our Heritage

Sarah Bednarz
Catherine Clinton
Michael Hartoonian
Arthur Hernandez
Patricia L. Marshall
Pat Nickell

The City of Olvera in Andalusia, Spain

HOUGHTON MIFFLIN   BOSTON · MORRIS PLAINS, NJ

California · Colorado · Georgia · Illinois · New Jersey · Texas

AUTHORS

Sarah Bednarz
Assistant Professor
Texas A&M University
College Station, TX

Arthur Hernandez
Associate Professor
Division of Education
College of Social and
Behavioral Sciences
University of Texas at
San Antonio
San Antonio, TX

Catherine Clinton
W.E.B. Du Bois Institute
Fellow
Harvard University
Cambridge, MA

Patricia L. Marshall
Assistant Professor
Department of Curric-
ulum and Instruction
College of Education
and Psychology
North Carolina State
University
Raleigh, NC

Michael Hartoonian
Professor and Director
Carey Center
Hamline University
St. Paul, MN

Pat Nickell
Director
High School Curriculum
and Instruction
Fayette County Schools
Lexington, KY

Susan Buckley General Editor

Acknowledgments appear on page 753.

Copyright © 2003 by Houghton Mifflin Company. All rights reserved.
No part of this work may be reproduced or transmitted in any form or by any means, electronic or mechanical, including photocopying and recording, or by any information storage or retrieval system without the prior written permission of the copyright owner, unless such copying is expressly permitted by federal copyright law. With the exception of nonprofit transcription in Braille, Houghton Mifflin is not authorized to grant permission for further uses of copyrighted selections reprinted in this text without the permission of their owners as identified herein. Address requests for permission to make copies of Houghton Mifflin material to School Permissions, Houghton Mifflin Company, 222 Berkeley Street, Boston, MA 02116.

Printed in the U.S.A. ISBN: 0-618-20661-2   23456789-VH-07 06 05 04 03 02

CONSULTANTS

Felix D. Almárez, Jr.
Department of History
University of Texas
San Antonio, TX

Manley A. Begay, Jr.
John F. Kennedy School
of Government
Harvard University
Cambridge, MA

William Brinner
University of California
Berkeley, CA

Phap Dam
Director of World
Languages
Dallas Independent
School District
Dallas, TX

Philip J. Deloria
Department of History
University of Colorado
Boulder, CO

Jorge I. Domínguez
The Center for
International Affairs
Harvard University
Cambridge, MA

Kenneth Hamilton
Department of History
Southern Methodist
University
Dallas, TX

Charles Haynes
Freedom Forum First
Amendment Center
Vanderbilt University
Nashville, TN

Shabbir Mansuri
Founding Director
Council on Islamic
Education
Susan Douglass
CIE Affiliated Scholar

Roberta Martin
East Asian Institute
Columbia University
New York, NY

Acharya Palaniswami
Editor
Hinduism Today
Kapaa, HI

Linda Reed
Department of History
Princeton University
Princeton, NJ

Dahia Ibo Shabaka
Director of Social Studies
Detroit Public Schools
Detroit, MI

Ken Tanaka
Institute of Buddhist
Studies
Graduate Theological
Union
Berkeley, CA

Ling-chi Wang
Department of Asian
American Studies
University of California
Berkeley, CA

TEACHER REVIEWERS

Kindergarten/Grade 1: Wayne Gable, Langford Elementary, Austin Independent School District, TX • **Donna LaRoche,** Winn Brook School, Belmont Public Schools, MA • **Gerri Morris,** Hanley Elementary School, Memphis City Schools, TN • **Eddi Porter,** College Hill Elementary, Wichita School District, KS • **Jackie Day Rogers,** Emerson Elementary, Houston Independent School District, TX • **Debra Rubin,** John Moffet Elementary, Philadelphia School District, PA

Grade 2: Rebecca Kenney, Lowery Elementary School, Cypress-Fairbanks School District, TX • **Debbie Kresner,** Park Road Elementary, Pittsford Central School District, NY • **Karen Poehlein,** Curriculum Coordinator, Buncombe County School District, NC

Grade 3: Bessie Coffer, RISD Academy, Richardson School District, TX • **Shirley Frank,** Instructional Specialist, Winston-Salem/Forsyth County Schools, NC • **Elaine Mattson,** Aloha Park Elementary, Beaverton School District, OR • **Carmen Sanchez,** Greenbrier Elementary, Fort Worth School District, TX • **Irma Torres,** Galindo Elementary School, Austin Independent School District, TX

Grade 4: Patricia Amendariz, Lamar Elementary, El Paso Independent School District, TX • **Lenora Barnes,** Duncan Elementary, Lake County School District, IN • **Dianna Deal,** Park Hill Elementary, North Little Rock School District, AR • **Karen Dodson,** Martin Elementary, Alief Independent School District, TX • **Linda Johnson,** Memorial Drive Elementary, Spring Branch School District, TX • **Marina Lopez,** Hillside Elementary, El Paso Independent School District, TX • **Becky Murphy,** Butler Elementary, Springfield School District, IL • **Ann Powell,** Austin Independent School District, TX • **Sumner Price,** Legion Park Elementary, Las Vegas City School District, NM • **Sara Stultz,** Richland Elementary, Richardson Independent School District, TX • **Jim Wilkerson,** Glenoaks Elementary School, Northside Independent School District, TX

Grade 5: Pat Carney-Dalton, Lower Salford Elementary School, Souderton School District, PA • **Janice Hunt,** Dearborn Park Elementary, Seattle Public Schools, WA • **Debbie Ruppell,** Dover Elementary, Dover Union Free School District, NY • **Jon Springer,** Bethany Elementary, Beaverton School District, OR • **Nancy Watson,** Weeks Elementary, Kansas City School District, MO • **Gloria Wilson,** Forest Park Elementary, Little Rock School District, AR

Grade 6: Marcia Baynes, The Longfellow School, Middlesex County Schools, MA • **Diane Bloom,** Steelman School, Eatontown School District, NJ • **Hillary Callahan,** Coordinator of Language Arts, Roanoke City Schools, VA • **Tom Murphy,** Carusi Elementary, Cherry Hill School District, NJ • **Mark Newhouse,** A.T. Morrow School, Central Islip School District, NY • **Dot Scott,** Meadow Creek Elementary, Hurst-Euless-Bedford Independent School District, TX

CONTENTS

UNIT 3 The Spread of Civilization
THEME: GROWTH AND CHANGE

UNIT 4 Global Exchanges

THEME: CONTACT AND INTERACTION

UNIT 7 Asia and Australia in the Modern Age

THEME: CHALLENGES AND OPPORTUNITIES

UNIT 8 Central and South America in the Modern Age

THEME: UNION AND INDIVIDUALITY

UNIT 9 North America and the Caribbean in the Modern Age

THEME: MOVEMENT AND TRANSFORMATION

Chapter 24   North America and the Caribbean: Patterns of Living   **642**

FEATURES

★ CITIZENSHIP ★

THINK LIKE A GEOGRAPHER

MAPS

Skills Workshop

LITERATURE

We·the People

American Voices

"*Here is not merely
a nation but a teeming
nation of nations.*"

Walt Whitman

" *Do justice, that you may live long upon earth.*"

King of Heracleopolis, c. 2135 B.C.

" *The basis of a democratic state is liberty.*"

Aristotle

" *To none will we sell,
to none deny or delay,
right or justice.*"

Magna Carta, 1215

*" Men are born
and remain free
and equal in
rights . . ."*

**Declaration of the
Rights of Man, 1789**

" *We could not have known of your Declaration of Independence and not elected to join in the struggle to guarantee the people life, liberty, and the pursuit of happiness.*"

Nelson Mandela

" *Where, after all,
do universal
human rights
begin? In small
places, close to
home . . .*"
Eleanor Roosevelt

We are the

Spirit of America!

Learning About Our World

"A journey of a thousand miles must begin with a single step."

Lao-tzu

Patterns in Diversity

❝*Learning about other cultures either across the country or on the other side of the world can help us understand how other people live so we will all get along.*❞

Caity Brodeur, Sixth Grade
Waitsfield, VT

The world is beautiful and complicated, and we are forever trying to make sense of it. People who study the earth are called geographers. They understand the land by finding patterns in landforms, climates, or even languages. To understand people, we study their culture — the characteristics of a group of people that make them alike. We find patterns in the ways people live, and we come to know them better as a result. So begins a journey to understand our world.

Theme Project

Exploring Geography and Culture

Pick two places in the world and compare and contrast them with each other.

- Make a compare/contrast poster that lists the similarities and differences between the two places.
- Create a travel poster for each place that highlights the features that would attract tourists to that place.
- Draw a map of each place and label the major geographic features.
- Write a one-page description of life in each place.

RESEARCH: Look up facts about the history of each place you are studying.

◀ The city of Olvera in Andalusia, Spain.

WHEN & WHERE
ATLAS

Studying the history and geography of the world is not an easy task. Apart from thousands of historical events, there are a multitude of peoples, religions, and languages to sort through. As you can guess, just keeping all the countries straight can be difficult.

Understanding geography and culture can make the task easier. Knowing the geographic features of an area or the culture of the people who live there can help you make sense of the history and geography of that area.

In this unit, you will learn more about geography and culture. You will read about the techniques geographers use to study physical and human geography. You will learn how studying culture can help shed light on history. By the end of the unit, you will know why geography and culture are essential tools for understanding world history.

Unit 1 Chapters

150°W

NORTH
AMERICA

ROCKY MTNS.

Mississippi R.

30°N

Tropic of Cancer

PACIFIC

OCEAN

0°

SOUTH
AMERICA

30°S

N
W   E
S

60°S

150°W   120°W   90°W

Unit Timeline

| 3,500 B.C. | 2,400 B.C. | 1,300 B.C. |

Incan Roads

This rocky road is more than 500 years old, and people still use it. *Chapter 1, Lesson 1*

Marshall Islands

Find out how Marshall Islanders mapped the ocean. *Chapter 1, Lesson 1*

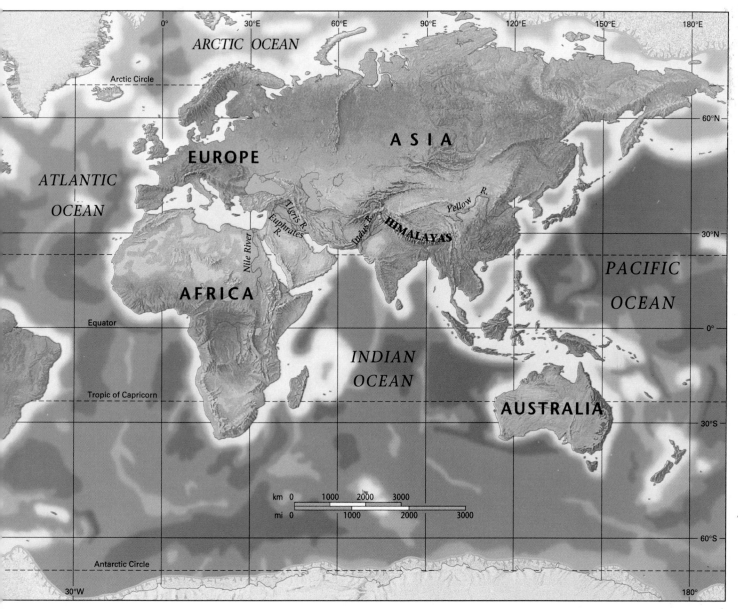

ARCTIC OCEAN

Arctic Circle

EUROPE

ASIA

ATLANTIC
OCEAN

60°N

Tigris R.

Euphrates
R.

Nile River

Indus R.

HIMALAYAS

Yellow R.

30°N

AFRICA

PACIFIC
OCEAN

Equator

0°

INDIAN
OCEAN

Tropic of Capricorn

AUSTRALIA

30°S

km 0   1000   2000   3000
mi 0   1000   2000   3000

60°S

Antarctic Circle

30°W

180°

0°   30°E   60°E   90°E   120°E   150°E   180°E

200 B.C.   A.D. 900   A.D. 2000

Landforms

What four landforms do you see here? *Chapter 1, Lesson 2*

Family Life

Families spending time together in many ways — that's culture. *Chapter 2, Lesson 1*

An Archaeological Dig

Hidden in the earth, past cultures are waiting to be found. *Chapter 2, Lesson 2*

CHAPTER 1

The Shape of the Earth

Chapter Preview: *People, Places, and Events*

| 3500 B.C. | 2400 B.C. | 1300 B.C. |

Captain James Cook

A bold explorer and geographer, he was one of the first to map the Pacific. *Lesson 1, Page 16*

Satellite Maps

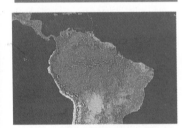

Maps like these help geographers and other scientists learn about the world. *Lesson 1, Page 16*

Early Mapping

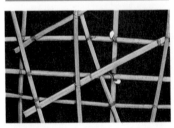

How did early people use maps like these to find their way? *Lesson 1, Page 19*

Exploring Our World

Main Idea Geographers study the world by asking questions about it, measuring it with scientific tools, and making maps.

Key Vocabulary
atmosphere
biosphere
geography
thematic map
reference map

The earth's six billion people share a planet that is 24,902 miles around — so large a supersonic jet would take more than 30 hours to circle it at top speed. Its surface area is over 196 million square miles. About 70 percent is underwater, mostly in vast oceans. These seas are so deep a two-pound steel ball would take over an hour to sink to their deepest point. All this water provides food, quenches thirst, and creates weather — making life on our amazing planet possible.

Without protection from the sun's harmful rays and from the airless chill of space, all life on the earth would cease to exist. Fortunately, the earth is cloaked by a mixture of gases called the **atmosphere**. The atmosphere reaches about 310 miles above the earth's surface, then fades into space. Beneath this shield lies the **biosphere**, which includes the earth's surface and all the things that live on it. It is within the biosphere that **geography** — the study of the earth and its people — begins.

◀ The earth, photographed from space.

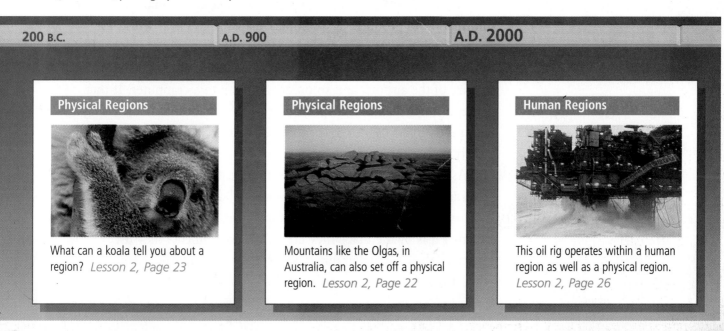

200 B.C.   A.D. **900**   A.D. **2000**

Physical Regions

What can a koala tell you about a region? *Lesson 2, Page 23*

Physical Regions

Mountains like the Olgas, in Australia, can also set off a physical region. *Lesson 2, Page 22*

Human Regions

This oil rig operates within a human region as well as a physical region. *Lesson 2, Page 26*

How Geographers See Our World

Focus *How do geographers study the world?*

Geographers study the biosphere — its heights and depths, its plants and animals, its people and environments, its regions and climates. They find ways to display what they have learned.

To understand what it is that geographers do, it is important to know the kind of questions they ask. Geographers look at a particular location on the earth's surface and ask: Where is it in relation to other places? What is it like there? When was it formed? How did it get to be that way? By asking these questions, geographers learn about the earth and how humans interact with it.

Just like any other scientist, geographers use tools to get the job done. Maps are one of the geographer's most important tools. Maps display information about the world. Throughout history, people all over the world have made many kinds of maps. Some civilizations built maps right into their cities. In South America, the ancient Inca capital of Cuzco (KOOZ koh) was a kind of map. Its buildings were laid out in lines that showed the movement of the sun. The map on the right shows how Inca roads made a kind of map of their empire.

High Tech Tools

Today, geographers use the latest technology to create maps. Satellites miles above the earth take photographs that become detailed maps. These maps can show a city, a continent, the whole planet, or even other planets. Satellites also produce maps that show such things as weather, surface temperature, elevation, and vegetation.

Computers play a role in mapmaking, too. By using Geographic Information Systems (GIS), computers can coordinate many layers of information to produce very complex maps. A GIS is at work, for instance, when a computer makes a map of how a noisy airport affects a neighborhood. Data about noise levels, the shape of the neighborhood, the size of the airport, and so on are all fed into a computer. It then makes a single map that displays all this information at once. Using a GIS, geographers can analyze more information and make maps more swiftly than ever before.

As important as they are, maps are just one of many tools geographers use. Equally important are the special devices that allow them to learn such things as water temperature, elevation, latitude, and longitude. Whether it is by the maps they create, the instruments they use, or the questions they ask, geographers want to learn about the earth — both what it is like now and how it got that way.

James Cook

Captain James Cook was one of the most adventurous — and successful — geographers in history. Beginning in 1768, Cook commanded three voyages of discovery. Through his careful mapmaking, Cook expanded human knowledge of the limits of the Pacific Ocean. He was also first to use a chronometer, a very accurate clock, to find his exact position at sea. Cook died at the hands of Hawaiian Islanders on a voyage in 1779.

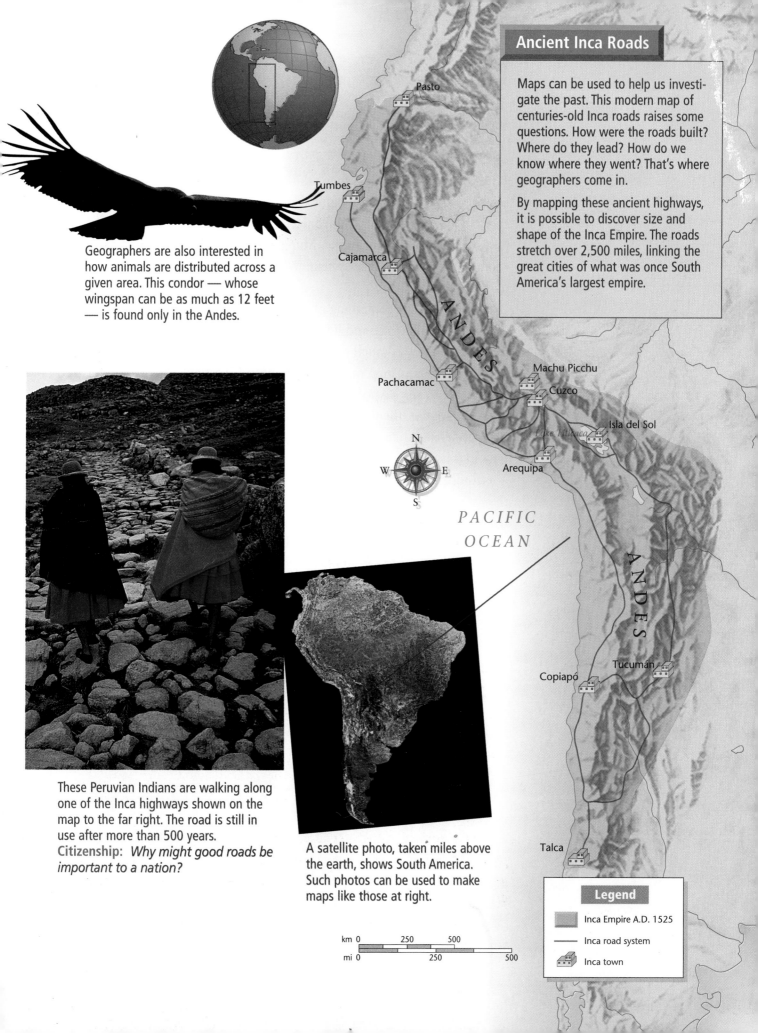

Ancient Inca Roads

Maps can be used to help us investigate the past. This modern map of centuries-old Inca roads raises some questions. How were the roads built? Where do they lead? How do we know where they went? That's where geographers come in.

By mapping these ancient highways, it is possible to discover size and shape of the Inca Empire. The roads stretch over 2,500 miles, linking the great cities of what was once South America's largest empire.

Geographers are also interested in how animals are distributed across a given area. This condor — whose wingspan can be as much as 12 feet — is found only in the Andes.

Pasto

Tumbes

Cajamarca

ANDES

Pachacamac

Machu Picchu
Cuzco

Isla del Sol

Lake Titicaca

Arequipa

PACIFIC OCEAN

ANDES

Tucumán

Copiapó

These Peruvian Indians are walking along one of the Inca highways shown on the map to the far right. The road is still in use after more than 500 years.
Citizenship: *Why might good roads be important to a nation?*

A satellite photo, taken miles above the earth, shows South America. Such photos can be used to make maps like those at right.

Talca

km 0   250   500
mi 0   250   500

Using Maps as a Window on Our Past

Focus *How did people in the past use maps to describe the world?*

When people make maps, they take information they've learned and present it to others. For example, if you make a map showing the location of everything in your room, someone else can look at the map and get an idea of what your room is like. Maps can show something as small as a room or as large as a star system. Whatever the subject, maps describe a part of our world.

Maps also say something about the mapmakers, who decide what information to include and how to present it. In this way, maps from long ago can tell us much about people who lived then.

In the 900s, a map made for European Christians showed Paradise somewhere to the east of Asia. Even though no living person had ever been to Paradise, the mapmakers believed it existed. They included it on the map. A map like this is called a **thematic map** because it has a theme to it — in this case, life after death.

Another kind of map is called a **reference map**, which shows where things are located. A reference map might show you how to get from one town to another, or it might show the layout of your neighborhood. A reference map around 5,800 years old is shown below. This map shows an area in ancient Mesopotamia.

This clay map from Mesopotamia is almost 6,000 years old. The illustration at left shows a translation of the ancient symbols.

This map shows the estate of what must have been a rich Mesopotamian.

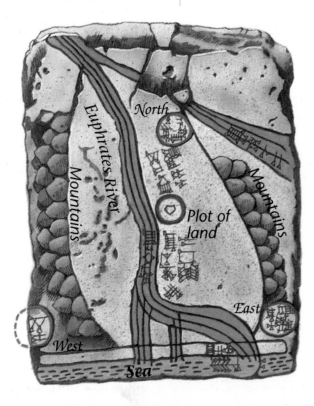

Maps with Special Uses

People can use both reference and thematic maps to express their knowledge of the world. The Aztecs, an ancient people of Mexico, made reference maps showing the land and trees. They marked the roads by drawing footprints. The Aztecs also made thematic maps that showed how they viewed their place in the universe. The Aztecs based these maps on their religious beliefs.

Traveling long distances calls for a special kind of reference map, the navigational map. The navigational map on this page was made by people of the Marshall Islands in the South Pacific. It is made of strips of wood tied together with coconut fiber, and uses shells to stand for islands. Although it may seem simple at first, it is actually a very complex map that shows many levels of important information. In addition to showing the relative position of the islands, the sticks indicate the direction and location of ocean currents and prevailing winds. When islanders set out on their voyages, they relied on maps like this one to guide them safely.

Our world is vast. It is made up of many areas, each with its own history and character. Just as different students in a class have things in common, so it is with places on the earth. Maps help make us aware of the patterns shared by different areas. As you are about to learn, finding these common patterns can help clarify the world's complexity.

Marshall Islanders used swift canoes to sail between islands.

A Micronesian sailing chart of the Marshall Islands. **Geography:** *What does a map like this say about the people who made it? What might it tell a geographer?*

Lesson Review: Geography

1. **Key Vocabulary:** Use the following words in a sentence: **atmosphere, biosphere, geography.**

2. **Focus:** How do geographers study the world?

3. **Focus:** How did people in the past use maps to describe the world?

4. **Critical Thinking: Comparing Then and Now** How might people have mapped the world long ago?

5. **Geography:** What would a map of your neighborhood have in common with a Marshall Islands stick map?

6. **Citizenship/Art Activity:** Draw a map of the route you take to school. In a group with two or three other students, compare your maps. How are they similar? How are they different?

Comparing Map Projections

Flattening the Earth

What's similar about an orange and the planet Earth? They're both spheres. If you've ever peeled an orange and flattened out the peel, you'll know the problem mapmakers have when drawing the curved surface of the earth on flat paper. It's impossible to do without changing the shape.

Mapmakers have found many ways to view the earth. These are called **map projections**. Each type of projection changes the shape of, or distorts, some part of the earth's surface. However, each projection serves a purpose.

1 Here's How

Study the map projections on these pages.

- Find the name of each type of projection. In an atlas, the name often appears near the map legend.

- If there is no projection label, ask yourself: Are the longitude lines straight as in a Mercator projection? Do they curve as in equal-area projections? Are the latitude lines in circles as in polar projections?

- Compare the maps to a globe to find distortions in the size or shape of continents.

- Compare continents on the map projections. For example, how do Greenland and Africa compare in size in each projection?

2 Think It Through

How would Mercator, equal-area, and polar projections help you plan a trip? What kind of information would each map give?

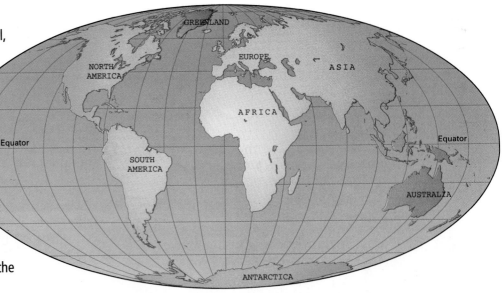

Equal-area projections divide the earth into equal areas. This allows you to accurately measure land area, but, as you can see, it creates distortions, especially near the edges of the map.

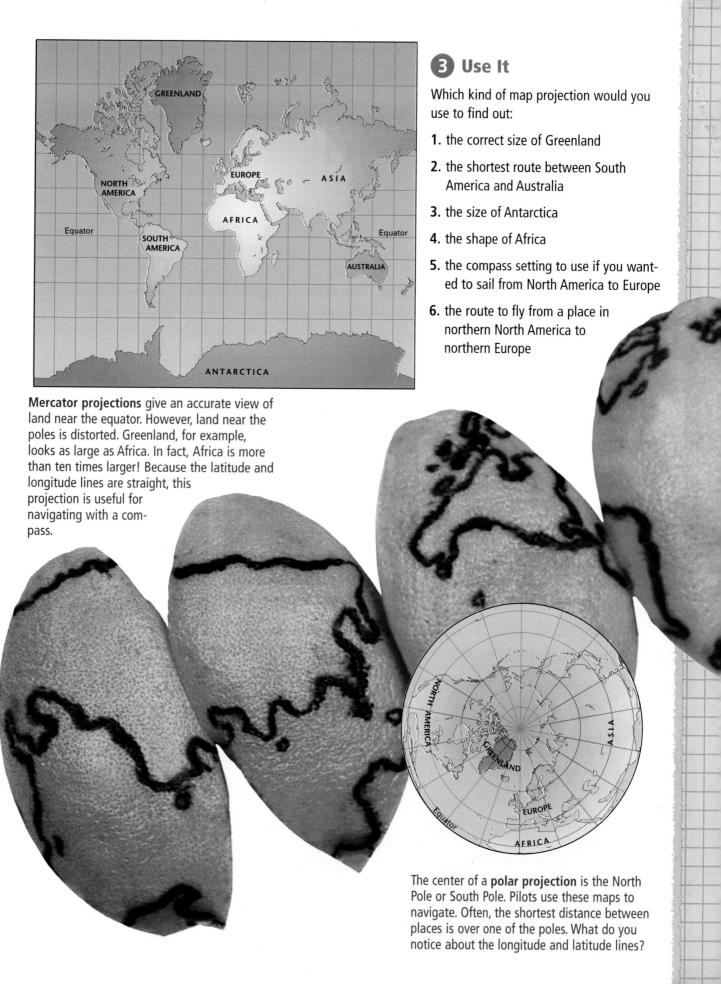

Which kind of map projection would you use to find out:

1. the correct size of Greenland

2. the shortest route between South America and Australia

3. the size of Antarctica

4. the shape of Africa

5. the compass setting to use if you wanted to sail from North America to Europe

6. the route to fly from a place in northern North America to northern Europe

Mercator projections give an accurate view of land near the equator. However, land near the poles is distorted. Greenland, for example, looks as large as Africa. In fact, Africa is more than ten times larger! Because the latitude and longitude lines are straight, this projection is useful for navigating with a compass.

The center of a **polar projection** is the North Pole or South Pole. Pilots use these maps to navigate. Often, the shortest distance between places is over one of the poles. What do you notice about the longitude and latitude lines?

The Shape of the Earth   **21**

Regions of Our World

Main Idea Geographers divide the world into regions in order to understand its complexity.

Key Vocabulary

region
landform
steppe
tundra
climate
savanna

In the fall of 1989, German students scrambled on top of a large concrete wall in Berlin. For years, the wall had divided their city. Now it was coming down. Tearing down the Berlin Wall meant the end of two regions — the countries of East and West Germany. These regions were not separated by mountains or rivers or even language. They were divided instead by politics. When the wall fell, so did the artificial barrier between the two nations. By 1990, Germany had become one again.

Physical Regions

Focus *How do geographers define physical regions?*

A **region** is any area on the planet's surface that has a single common feature. Regions can be defined by physical characteristics, like mountains, or by the political allegiance or cultural identity of the people who live there.

Dividing the earth into physical regions is one way to make sense of the natural world's incredible diversity. Physical regions are defined by one or more physical features such as landforms, animals and vegetation, or climate.

Landforms

One of the main building blocks of physical regions is the landform. A **landform** is a feature of the earth's surface. There are four types of landforms: mountains, valleys, plateaus, and plains. You can see what each of these landforms looks like in the illustrated diagram at the bottom of the opposite page.

German students wave the flag of a united Germany on the Berlin Wall. East German soldiers stand in the background.

A plateau (pla TOE) is a large, flat area that rises like a tabletop above the land around it. One large landform region is the Colorado Plateau; it stretches across parts of Colorado, Utah, New Mexico, and Arizona. A plain is a low, flat area of land that can cover thousands of miles. The Great Plains in the Midwest cover several states, making them one of this country's largest landform regions.

Animals and Vegetation

Sometimes animals define a region. The koala, the kangaroo, and the wallaby are all members of the same family of animal, the marsupial. A pouch-bearing mammal, the marsupial is found almost exclusively on the continent of Australia. In this way, the presence of a type of animal helps set off Australia as a kind of physical region. Other animals, such as deer or mice, are found in certain areas on several continents.

Vegetation — the plants that grow in a certain area — can also define a region. One vast plain covers part of Europe and Asia. This plain, called a **steppe**, was once completely covered with wild grasses. These grasses are what determines whether a given plain is a steppe. Similarly, Canada has huge regions covered with forests. Along the Arctic Circle is the **tundra**, a region with few or no trees.

This koala and its baby are members of a family of animals that appear almost solely on the continent of Australia.

The four types of landforms, shown below, are:

1 mountains
2 plains
3 valleys
4 plateaus

The Amazing Deep

Deep beneath the waves lie dramatic landforms that would dwarf those on dry land.

A few of these are indicated on the map at right.

1 The Marianas Trench — 36,198 feet deep

2 Mauna Kea — 33,480 feet tall

3 Mid-ocean ridge — more than 30,000 miles long

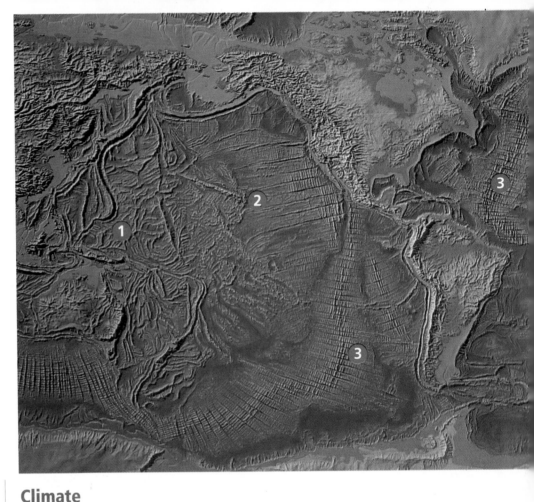

Curious Facts

The wettest place on the planet is Mount Waialeale, Hawaii, where an average of 460 inches of rain falls every year. That's almost twice the annual rainfall of a tropical rain forest!

Climate

Climate, or the typical weather condition of a given area, produces another pattern of regions. Two examples of regions defined by climate are deserts and savannas. Desert regions are extremely dry areas that receive less than 10 inches of rain per year. The Sahara, a desert in Africa, can get as little as one inch per year in some places. Temperatures there can easily jump past 100° F in the summer. At the same time, a **savanna** can get up to 60 inches of rain in a year, while being as hot as a desert. Because of the difference in rainfall, one area is practically barren while the other can be lush and green.

The chart on the next page can give you an idea of how regions can be determined by climate, composed of temperature and precipitation. Looking carefully at the photographs next to the chart, you can also see how dramatically rainfall, or its absence, can affect a region. Note the differences in the plant and animal life in the two images.

In addition, any location can belong to more than one type of physical region. A town in northern Maine might be considered part of a mountainous region in terms of landforms and part of a temperate region in terms of climate. At the same time, there are different types of desert or savanna depending on how much rain they get or how high their temperatures are. The type of savanna shown at right, for example, is a tropical savanna.

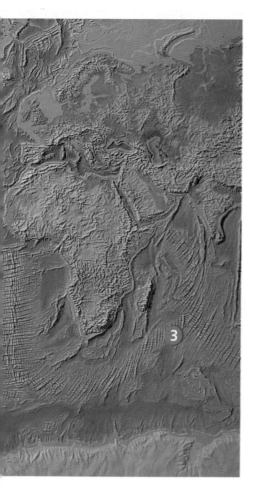

The Ocean Floor

The map at left shows regions we can't see because they are below the ocean. Just like dry land, the ocean floor can be divided into physical regions. For example, the deep crevices in the ocean floor are regions known as trenches. One such trench, the Marianas, plunges more than seven miles below the surface of the Pacific Ocean. In the same ocean, the Hawaiian mountain Mauna Kea, if measured from base to peak, is taller than Mount Everest, the highest peak on land. The mid-ocean ridge, an underwater mountain chain, snakes more than 30,000 miles from the Arctic Ocean through the Atlantic, across the Pacific to the west coast of North America. This, too, is a physical region.

Physical regions — whether based on landforms, vegetation, animals, or climate — are just one one way of dividing up the earth's area. Another equally important type of region is the human region.

Below, the top photograph shows the Sahara. It has so little rainfall that almost nothing grows over most of the desert.

The bottom photograph shows the savanna. As hot as the desert, the savanna receives large amounts of rain on a regular basis. **Chart Skill:** *What climate factor changes between these two regions? What factor stays the same?*

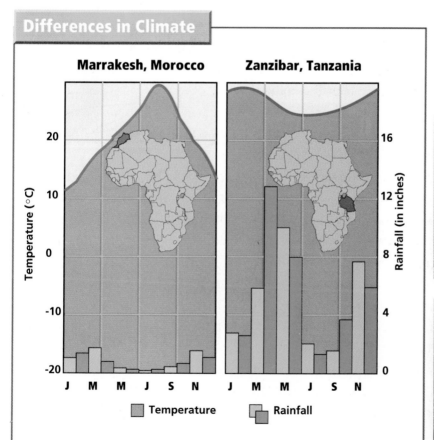

Differences in Climate

Marrakesh, Morocco   Zanzibar, Tanzania

Temperature (°C): 20, 10, 0, -10, -20

Rainfall (in inches): 16, 12, 8, 4, 0

J M M J S N

■ Temperature   ■ Rainfall

Human Regions

Focus *How do people organize the world into human regions?*

A human region is an area defined by human activity. Whether it is an area in which people share a government, a language, a belief, or a culture, human regions are a vital part of geography.

You're probably familiar with one common human region: a nation. The world has almost 190 nations. But nations can be broken down into even smaller human regions, such as a state, county, and town.

A human region can also be larger than a nation. About 12 European countries have formed an alliance called the European Union (EU). More than 300 million people share a set of laws and close economic ties. Because Europeans also lead similar lifestyles, the EU can be said to share other connections, too.

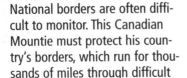

National borders are often difficult to monitor. This Canadian Mountie must protect his country's borders, which run for thousands of miles through difficult terrain and climate.

Human regions can easily change. **Map Skill:** *How many years does this map cover?*

Changing Regions

Human regions can change over time. The map below traces the Ottoman Empire as it shrank into what is now the modern nation of Turkey. Note that, as the borders of this empire dwindled, new nations sprang into being, while others increased in size. See, too, how the borders seemed to shift without regard to the physical features of the land. This is because borders were set according to political situa-

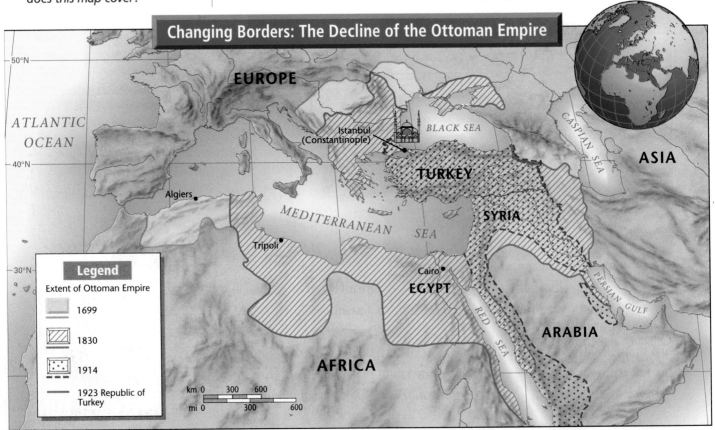

Changing Borders: The Decline of the Ottoman Empire

EUROPE

ATLANTIC OCEAN

Istanbul (Constantinople)

BLACK SEA

CASPIAN SEA

ASIA

TURKEY

Algiers

MEDITERRANEAN SEA

SYRIA

Tripoli

Cairo

EGYPT

PERSIAN GULF

RED SEA

ARABIA

AFRICA

Legend

Extent of Ottoman Empire

1699

1830

1914

1923 Republic of Turkey

km 0   300   600
mi 0   300   600

tions, national identities, or language differences of populations. Overlooking these important differences when setting national boundaries is a frequent source of conflict among peoples.

No area of the globe is without political division of some kind. Even the high seas — symbol of freedom and adventure — are the subject of constant international squabbles. As countries look to the ocean for food, oil, and other natural resources, the question of who owns the sea and its riches becomes ever more fiercely debated.

Ultimately, how regions are defined depends on who defines them and what they wish to accomplish. Defining regions helps geographers study the world. But defined regions are also necessary for nations and the people who live in them. The ability to keep track of how the earth's natural treasures are divided up depends on borders that can be made clear and distinct. Finally, and perhaps most importantly, defining human regions can also help us look at small groups of people and see the forces that shape their lives. This helps us to understand others.

Now you should have a little better understanding of world geography. You're going to be a geographer, too, by studying the world's lands and people. You'll read how people lived in the past, how that history affects us today, and how you just might live tomorrow.

The contest for control of the ocean's bounty has gone on since the first fishers set out to sea in rafts. Today, platform rigs like this one in the savage North Sea vie for the oil deep beneath the ocean floor.

Lesson Review: Geography

1. **Key Vocabulary:** Write a sentence about geography for each of these words: **region, landform, steppe, tundra, climate,** and **savanna.**

2. **Focus:** How do geographers define physical regions?

3. **Focus:** How do people organize the world into human regions?

4. **Critical Thinking: Classify** Name or describe two regions — one physical and one human — that include your town.

5. **Theme: Patterns in Diversity** Regions can have many different things in common. What are some things regions might have in common that aren't mentioned in the text?

6. **Citizenship/Art Activity:** Make a collage about what makes the human region of the United States different from other human regions, and what it has in common with them.

The Shape of the Earth   27

THINK LIKE A
GEOGRAPHER

Places and Regions

How Was the Soviet Union a Nation of Many Regions?

For most of the twentieth century, the Union of Soviet Socialist Republics (U.S.S.R.) — also known as the Soviet Union — was the largest country in the world. Stretching some 6,000 miles (9,656 kilometers) from east to west, the U.S.S.R covered 11 time zones and made up more than one seventh of the world's total land area.

Studying the regions of the Soviet Union clearly illustrates what a complex place it was. When viewed as a country, the U.S.S.R. could be considered a single region. But it actually contained dozens of overlapping human and physical regions. For example, each of the country's 15 republics was a separate political region. Each republic had different ethnic regions inside it. Because the U.S.S.R. spanned two continents, it also contained a European region and an Asian region. In addition, the U.S.S.R. contained many natural regions, including tundra, steppe (grasslands), mountains, and forests.

1 Latvia

A Latvian Woman
The U.S.S.R. contained more than 100 different ethnic groups. When it broke up in 1991, many groups that had been minorities in the U.S.S.R. — like Latvians — were the majority in the new countries.

The natural geography of the U.S.S.R. contained great contrasts — from the mountains of Kazakhstan to the frozen plains of Siberia.

UNION OF SOVIET SOCIALIST REPUBLICS

Language Arts Connection

In the U.S.S.R., as in many other countries, regional divisions contributed to differences in language. There were four major language groups in the country, and many smaller ones. While most of the population used Russian at least part of the time, many also spoke other languages, like Ukrainian, Armenian, or Kazakh. What are some different languages spoken by people in the United States?

The Former Soviet Union, 1995

ARCTIC OCEAN

(RUSSIA) ESTONIA
LITHUANIA LATVIA St. Petersburg
BELARUS
Moscow
Kiev
MOLDOVA
UKRAINE
Volga River
BLACK SEA
GEORGIA
ARMENIA AZERBAIJAN
Baku
AZER.
CASPIAN SEA
UZBEKISTAN
TURKMENISTAN
TAJIKISTAN
Tashkent
KYRGYZSTAN

RUSSIA
Novosibirsk
Lake Baikal
Vladivostok
Arctic Circle
KAZAKHSTAN
ARAL SEA

50°N
40°N
30°N
PACIFIC OCEAN

km 0 500 1000
mi 0 500 1000
40°E 60°E 70°E 80°E 90°E

Legend
— Boundary of former Soviet Union

When the U.S.S.R. broke up in 1991, it created some unusual problems. Many people who considered themselves Russian found that they were living in a different country. **Map Skill:** *After Russia, which of the 15 new nations was the largest?*

Research Activity

The U.S.S.R was so big that each part of it could be divided into many smaller regions.

1 Choose a new country in the U.S.S.R. that interests you.

2 Make a list of that area's regions. Label the regions on your list as either physical regions or human regions.

3 Give an oral report about that area and its regions to the class. Explain how knowing about that area's regions can help you understand it better.

2 Moscow

A Densely Populated City
The population of the U.S.S.R. was not evenly distributed. More than two-thirds of the people lived in the European region. What regions of the United States are the most densely populated?

The Shape of the Earth   **29**

Languages

Language is an important part of every culture. Language can unify people, but it can also divide them. Often a "stranger" is identified by the way he or she speaks. It's not likely that there will ever be just one language used everywhere on earth, but think how many problems could be solved if people everywhere were able to speak and understand the same language. Many people think that eventually, everyone on earth will be able to use and understand basic English.

Indo-European
Sino-Tibetan
Black African
Malayo-Polynesian
Afro-Asian
Dravidian
Japanese and Korean
Uralic and Altaic
Mon-Khmer
Other Languages

This map shows the chief language groups and where they are most widely spoken. Almost half the world's peoples speak Indo-European languages. This group originated among peoples living in the area from northern India to Europe.

The world's people speak between 4,000 and 5,000 languages and dialects (local variations of a language). About 845 of these languages are spoken in India. The language spoken by the greatest number of people in the world is Mandarin Chinese. English is spoken in more countries than any other language. All languages change so long as people speak them. New words are added, others fall out of use. In a few hundred years, a language can change greatly. A language that is no longer spoken is called a dead language.

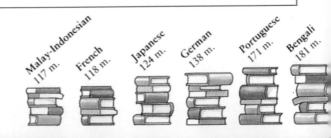

Malay-Indonesian 117 m. French 118 m. Japanese 124 m. German 138 m. Portuguese 171 m. Bengali 181 m.

ALPHABETS

An alphabet is a collection of letters or signs that stand for sounds in speech. Alphabets were developed from ancient picture-writing systems. The oldest letter is "O," unchanged in shape since it was used by the Phoenicians over 3,000 years ago.

Russian

АБВГДЕЖЗИЙКЛМНОПРСТУФХЦЧ
ШЩЪЬЫ ЬЭЮЯ

Greek

ΑΒΓΔΕΖΗΘΙΚΛΜΝΞΟΠΡΣΤΥΦΧΨΩ

Arabic

ابتثجحخدذرزسشصضطظغغفقكلمنهو يلا

Bengali

আমাদের পোস্টমাস্টার কলিকাতার ছেলে । জলের
মাছকে ডাঙ্গায় তজলিলে যেরষ অবস্থা হয় এই গণ্ডু
ধগরামের মধ্যে আসিয়া পোস্টমাস্টারেরও সেই দশা

Egyptian hieroglyphs or picture-signs are about 5,000 years old. The earliest signs represented objects.

THE WORLD'S MAJOR LANGUAGES

Mandarin, or standardized northern Chinese, is spoken by more people than any other language. English is the language spoken in the most countries (Australia, Canada, the Caribbean, Ireland, New Zealand, the U.K., and the U.S.A.). English is also widely used in parts of Africa and Asia. Hindi is the most widely spoken language of India. Spanish and Portuguese are spoken in Latin America, as well as in Spain and Portugal.

Millions of persons

Arabic 192 m.
Russian 291 m.
Spanish 331 m.
Hindi 338 m.
English 485 m.
Chinese 845 m.

900
800
700
600
500
400
300
200
100
0

Response Activities

1. **Compare Words and Places** How might looking at a globe showing the world's landforms help you understand why different languages formed?

2. **Informative: Write a History** Choose a present-day language. Research its history, then tell the story of where that language began and how it became a modern tongue.

3. **Geography: Draw a Map** Make your own fantasy map showing language regions. Include symbols showing how mountains, seas, or other obstacles divided off your regions. If you like, label your map with made-up names.

Chapter Review

Summarizing the Main Idea

1 Copy the chart below and fill in the missing information to compare how different types of regions are defined.

Region Defined By:	Human or Physical?	Examples
Landforms		
Vegetation		
Language		
National boundaries		
Climate		

Vocabulary

2 Using at least five of the following terms, write a letter to a geographer, explaining why you are qualified to be his or her assistant.

atmosphere (p. 15)   region (p. 22)   tundra (p. 23)

biosphere (p. 15)   landform (p. 22)   climate (p. 24)

geography (p. 15)   steppe (p . 23)   savanna (p. 24)

Reviewing the Facts

3 What is the difference between the atmosphere and the biosphere?

4 What is the geographer's job, and how is it accomplished?

5 What is the difference between a thematic map and a reference map? Give some examples of each.

6 What is a region? Why do geographers divide the world into regions?

7 Name three ways physical regions can be defined, and give examples of each.

8 Define climate.

9 Describe some of the unique features of the ocean floor.

10 Name three ways human regions can be defined, and give examples of each.

Skill Review: Map Projections

11 What are the three map projections you learned about, and why are none of them completely accurate?

12 If you were a sea captain, which map projection would you use?

Geography Skills

13 Look at the map of the ancient Inca roads on p. 17. The Inca Empire was a human region. Why do you think it had the shape it did?

14 Name three physical and two human regions that the area you live in belongs to.

Critical Thinking

15 **Predict** Describe what you think the world would be like if there were no oceans.

16 **Cause and Effect** Human regions are constantly changing. What do you think would cause physical regions to change?

17 **Problem Solving** You are a geographer and must divide your school into regions, both physical and human. How will you go about it?

Writing: Citizenship and Economics

18 Many nations are arguing over who owns the sea. Should the oceans belong to everyone? Or should they belong just to the nations whose coastlines border them? Write a letter to the United Nations and express your opinion.

Activities

Geography/Research Activity
Many kinds of maps are mentioned in the chapter: temperature, navigational maps, and so on. Do research to find out what other kinds of maps there are. Bring in copies of different maps to share with the class.

Culture/Arts Activity
Create a thematic map that reflects your personal or cultural heritage. This map can be a reflection of your own life, or a representation of your ancestry.

Internet Option

Check the **Internet Social Studies Center** for ideas on how to extend your theme project beyond your classroom.

THEME PROJECT CHECK-IN

As you begin your theme project, use information you learned in this chapter about the things geographers study to understand places.
• What kind of maps will best represent your two locations?
• In what physical regions are these places located? What unique landforms, animals, and vegetation do they have?
• What is the climate in each place?
• In what human regions are these places located?

CHAPTER 2
A World of People

Chapter Preview: *People, Places, and Events*

3500 B.C.	2400 B.C.	1300 B.C.

Elements of Culture

What do you like to eat? Play? Read? Every day you take part in a culture. *Lesson 1, Page 36*

An Apache Ritual

How do the Apache people celebrate the passage to adulthood? *Lesson 1, Page 38*

A Jewish Ritual

What is a *bar mitzvah?* How is it celebrated? *Lesson 1, Page 39*

Defining Culture

Main Idea Culture is all the things that distinguish one group of people from another.

> **"I**n the shelter of each other, the people live.**"**
>
> (Gaelic proverb)

All humans share similar needs. From the earliest times — whether they lived in the Arctic, in tropical jungles, or in high mountains — people have had to find food, clothing, and shelter. They have also needed the love and security provided by family and relationships.

As those basic needs are being met, people can bring meaning to their lives through religion, art, stories, music, and dance. All of these things together form **culture**: the whole way of life of a group of people.

Banding together in groups has made human survival possible. People all over the world live in communities that create their own customs and codes of behavior. Today, some cultures are also nationalities. But unlike a nation, there are no real boundaries to a culture.

◀ Children the world over take part in culture.

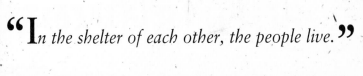

200 B.C.	A.D. 900	A.D. 2000

Books Through Time

Books have been around for thousands of years. How has their look changed? *Lesson 2, Page 46*

Anthropologist at Work

Like geographers, anthropologists use questions to do their jobs. *Lesson 2, Page 46*

Sutton Hoo

Archaeologists dig things up to learn about the past. *Lesson 2, Page 48*

What Is Culture?

Focus *What elements make up a culture?*

The term culture includes all the ways that a group of human beings has learned to interact, both among themselves and with their environment. The elements of a culture can take many forms and go through many changes. Such things as houses, music, clothing, and art can be unique to a particular culture. And yet each of these things changes over time.

How people in a culture raise their children is another major element of culture — the family. Families shape and preserve culture, as parents provide their children with models of behavior and ways of viewing the world.

Another important element that shapes and preserves culture is a group's **beliefs** — the system of ideas by which people live. Because beliefs tend to change less over time than other aspects of culture, what people

· Tell Me More ·

Elements of Culture

Family:

Families are a basic building block of culture. Even in the simple act of sharing meals people are shaped by their families. It is within the family unit that you experience many other aspects of culture for the first time. Your parents and other family members are, in a sense, your first teachers.

Beliefs:

Religion and personal beliefs are at the very foundation of culture. No matter what these beliefs may be, they are often taught to us when we are young and affect the way we live our lives.

believe in is, in a sense, the foundation of culture. These beliefs are often reflected in traditions. The basic traditions people share are remembered and passed on through repeated ceremonies, called **rituals**. Rituals usually develop from beliefs.

The language we speak and the many ways we express our ideas in music, art, books, and movies are a vital part of culture. From literature to popular entertainment, words and music tell us who we are by giving voice to human emotions. In reading a book, watching television, visiting a museum, or going on vacation, we are taking part in our culture.

Economics and politics are also cultural expressions. When we buy things or vote for political leaders, we add a bit of ourselves to that expression. Being a part of our own culture helps us share things with those around us, and helps build a community that can function, deal with change and disaster, and ultimately survive.

Ask Yourself

What are some ways your family preserves the culture or traditions of earlier generations?

? ? ? ? ? ? ? ? ? ? ? ? ?

Government/Education/Art:

Art and music are an extremely valuable part of culture. Whether through playing in a school band or writing poetry, you can take part in culture. How people order their societies is an aspect of culture. Government shapes culture by creating and enforcing laws — such as the law that requires that you attend school. The education that takes place in school and at home is another part of culture. Cultures preserve themselves by teaching each generation the values of the one before.

Economy:

The way people earn their money and what they choose to buy with it reflects a culture. You are participating in the economy any time you earn or spend money.

One World, Many Peoples

Focus *How are cultures alike and different?*

Families are basic to culture. When people marry, raise children, or work to support their families, they are participating fully in their culture. Through rituals associated with the family and the raising of children, cultures mark births, marriages, and deaths. They also celebrate natural changes like the change of seasons.

Cultures stay alive by handing their traditions down from one generation to another. Education is important to culture. What people decide to teach their young will ultimately be the things we find most important for a good life. Also important are the traditions surrounding the passage from childhood to adulthood. These "coming of age" customs ensure the survival of a culture's most essential beliefs.

Each culture celebrates the passage into adulthood in its own way. Such special occasions as high school and college graduations are one way of recognizing this important event. The coming of age ceremonies practiced by the Apache and Jewish people *(see below and above, right)* show that, while there are differences in dress, language, and meaning, both rituals declare one thing: A child has become an adult.

Culture, then, is many things, all growing out of a common soil.

Apache "Changing Woman" Ceremony

Apache girls participate in a four-day ceremony attended by family and friends (there is a similar ritual for boys). During the ceremony, the girl dances and runs, symbolizing different stages of her life.

Jewish Bar Mitzvah

When he reaches the age of 13, a Jewish boy has completed a long period of study and is ready for his *bar mitzvah*. The ritual includes prayers and passages read from a holy book called the Torah. Girls have a similar ceremony, the *bat mitzvah*.

People all around the world share similar needs. They also share the urge to create, to express feelings and ideas. These creations — in the form of books, music, movies, and other works of art — cross borders and affect other cultures. People also move from one cultural area to another. In these ways, cultures are shared among people and are constantly changing.

Learning about other cultures helps us to understand both ourselves and others better. Just as two individuals may have different tastes in clothes and movies, so each culture has its own preferences. The more we know about those other preferences, the richer our lives become.

Lesson Review

1 **Key Vocabulary:** Write a paragraph about culture, using the words **culture**, **beliefs**, and **ritual**.

2 **Focus:** What elements make up a culture?

3 **Focus:** How are cultures alike and different?

4 **Critical Thinking: Classifying** Give examples of rituals that you think are important. Explain what they mean and why you chose them.

5 **Theme: Patterns in Diversity** What are some of the ways in which different cultures have touched your life?

6 **Citizenship/Writing Activity:** Write a description of a favorite tradition or custom that you know about from another culture. Share it with the class.

CITYMAZE!

A Collection of Amazing City Mazes

Nonfiction

by Wendy Madgwick

illustrated by Dan Courtney, Nick Gibbard, Dean Entwistle, and John Fox

Cities all around the world reflect cultural and geographical differences. In past ages, just getting to a distant city was a huge problem. Advances in transportation have changed that, but finding your way around in a strange city can still be a challenge, even for the modern traveler. Ready for an adventure?

LONDON • A ROYAL CITY

The ancient city of London, the capital of the United Kingdom, was founded by the Romans in A.D. 43. An international center of banking and commerce, London is also home to the British royal family and houses the seat of government. A popular tourist center, thousands of visitors flock to the city from all over the world to see London's cultural heritage: the great buildings, art collections, and museums, as well as the ancient traditions and pageantry, such as the Changing of the Guard at Buckingham Palace. The River Thames, once the main means of transport, snakes through London in elegant, sweeping curves. It is now crossed by numerous road bridges — six between the Houses of Parliament and the Tower of London alone, including the famous Tower Bridge.

Two Americans who have arrived at Victoria (**A**) are to meet some friends as St. James's Palace (**B**). They hail a London taxicab to take them there, and the driver promises to show them some of the famous sights on their way. Can you find the one clear route the taxi driver took?

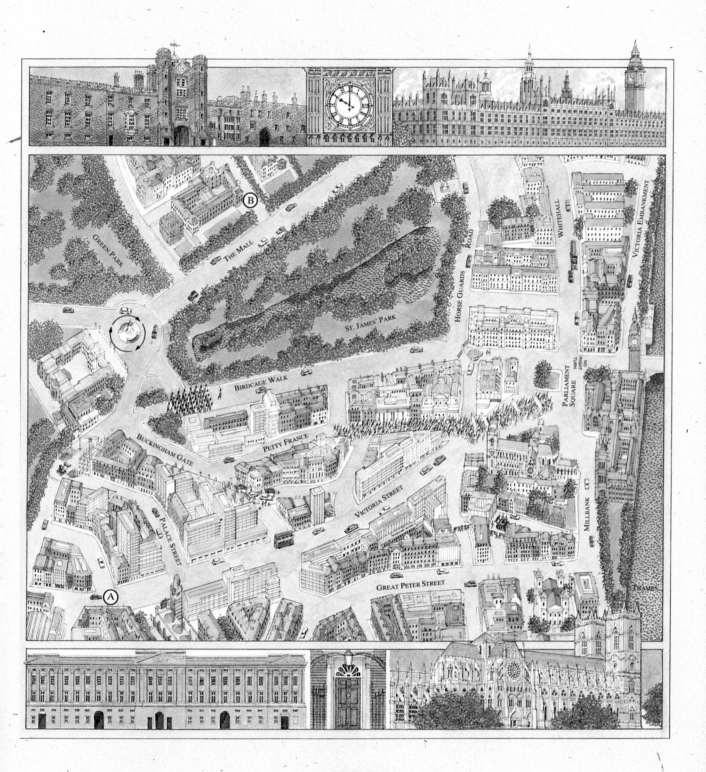

LONDON

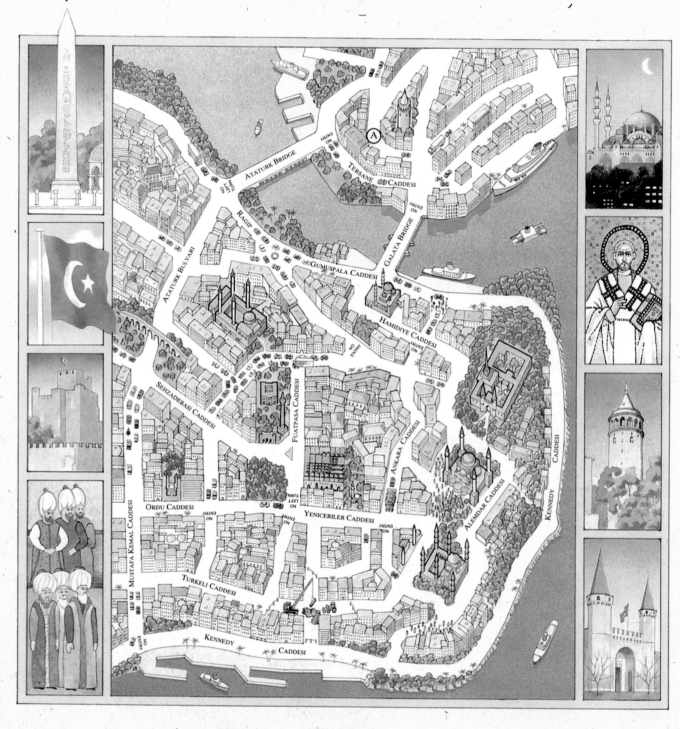

ISTANBUL

ISTANBUL • CITY OF TWO CONTINENTS

Istanbul, Turkey's largest city, straddles the Bosporus at the entrance to the Black Sea. Founded about 660 B.C. by the Greeks, it is the only city in the world that is built on two continents — Europe and Asia. Formerly known as Byzantium and then Constantinople, Istanbul was the capital of the Byzantine Empire for more than 1,000 years and of the Ottoman Empire for 500 years. The skyline is dominated by the domes and minarets of the ancient mosques that crown and decorate Istanbul's seven hills. A busy, bustling port, Istanbul is a major link between East and West. The city has a wealth of ancient monuments and historic sights, including the Topkapi Palace (once home to the Ottoman Emperors), Hagia Sophia (a Byzantine church), and numerous beautiful domed minarets.

There are so many sights to see that a guided tour is the best way to view this amazing city. A circular tour from the Galata Tower (**A**) will take our tourists past most of the ancient monuments in Old Istanbul. However, the streets are very busy, and a lot of them are one-way systems. Can you trace the only clear circular route that the bus driver took?

Meet the Author

Wendy Madgwick loves to take a nonfiction subject and make it fun and interesting. She has written a number of other books, including Animaze! A Collection of Amazing Nature Mazes.

Additional Books to Read

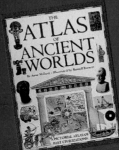

The Atlas of Ancient Worlds, by Dorling Kindersley. Enjoy this visual encyclopedia.

People, by Peter Spier. An illustrated view of the varieties of people on earth.

Why We Study Culture

Main Idea Studying culture can help us understand how others live.

The term **global village** was first used around 1960 by a Canadian writer named Marshall McLuhan. His idea was that radio, television, computers, and telephones would shrink the vast distances that can separate the people of different cultures. More and more, the world becomes like a small village, where news passes quickly between the members of different populations that share many of the same concerns. The timeline below shows the speed with which methods of communication have changed. As science fiction writer Isaac Asimov wrote a decade after McLuhan, "There are no boundaries in the global village."

Learning About Cultures

Focus *Why do we study other cultures and our own?*

The map on the opposite page shows migration to the United States. **Map Skill:** *What movements of peoples are not shown on the map? Why might that be?*

When people move from one part of the world to another, they bring their cultures with them. Sometimes many people from one culture move, or migrate, at one time. In the last two centuries, millions of people have come from every part of the globe to live in the United States. The map and pie chart on the next page show where they came from and what percentage are from each country. This migration has shaped American culture, as each additional culture has changed our country's overall picture.

This timeline shows the quickening pace of change. **Technology:** *What communications technology arrived in your parents' lifetime?*

Communication Revolution Timeline

Cave paintings
15,000 B.C.

15,000 B.C.   10,000 B.C.

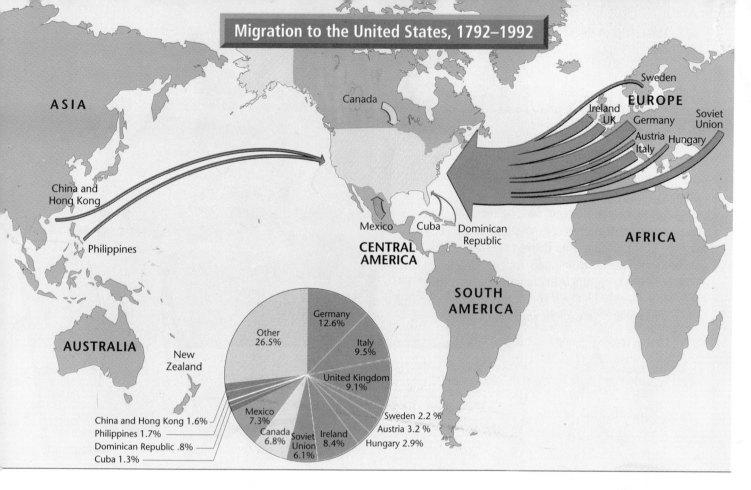

Migration to the United States, 1792–1992

ASIA

Canada

EUROPE
Sweden
Ireland
UK
Germany
Austria
Italy
Hungary
Soviet Union

China and Hong Kong

Philippines

Mexico Cuba Dominican Republic

CENTRAL AMERICA

AFRICA

AUSTRALIA

New Zealand

SOUTH AMERICA

Germany 12.6%

Other 26.5%

Italy 9.5%

United Kingdom 9.1%

China and Hong Kong 1.6%
Philippines 1.7%
Dominican Republic .8%
Cuba 1.3%

Mexico 7.3%

Canada 6.8%

Soviet Union 6.1%

Ireland 8.4%

Sweden 2.2 %

Austria 3.2 %

Hungary 2.9%

As modern technology and migration bring people together, it becomes all the more important to learn about the cultures of other places. By understanding the customs and habits of people far away, we can become more at ease with change that happens nearer to home. Often cultural differences become the root cause of violent conflict between separate groups. The more comfortable we become with differences and change, the less likely these fights become.

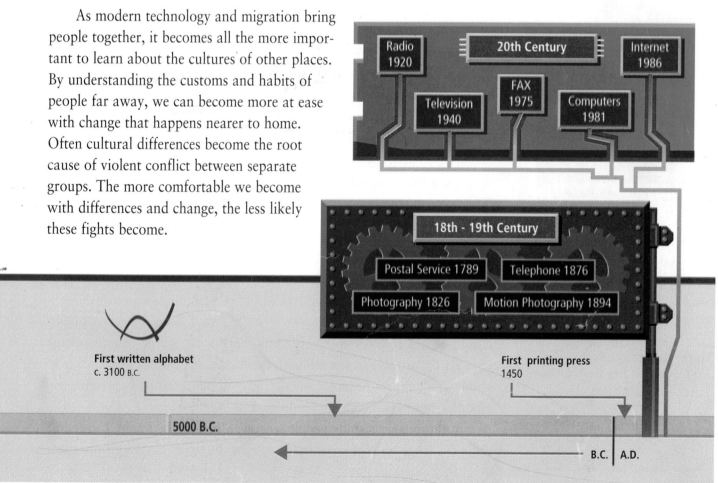

Radio 1920

20th Century

Internet 1986

Television 1940

FAX 1975

Computers 1981

18th - 19th Century

Postal Service 1789

Telephone 1876

Photography 1826

Motion Photography 1894

First written alphabet
c. 3100 B.C.

First printing press
1450

5000 B.C.

B.C. | A.D.

Cultures Change Over Time

While people have written and read books since ancient times, the appearance of books has changed throughout history. The design and shape of objects that cultures use can evolve, just like language and styles of dress. Despite the change, many objects retain their original purpose. In ancient Egypt, people used books to record stories and cultural information. Today, in modern society, books serve the same function. What do you think it would be like if computers took over the job of books? How might your life change?

1 Chinese scroll, Diamond Sutra, from A.D. 868

2 The Gutenberg Bible, printed in 1455

3 A modern paperback

Dr. Jane Beck

Dr. Jane Beck is a folklorist. This means she studies the stories, songs, traditions and superstitions of a culture. As state folklorist for Vermont Dr. Beck spends time studying that state's traditions, as well as interviewing older members of local communities. Born in New York in 1941, Beck now lives in Vermont.

How We Study Culture

Focus *How do we study culture?*

Many different professions are devoted to the study of people and their cultures. Sociologists study how people interact with each other. Geographers examine how and why people settle in a given place.

Culture — both past and present — is the focus of anthropologists and archaeologists. **Anthropologists** study the interactions of people and their cultures, while **archaeologists** study the remains of past civilizations. Both types of scientists go about their jobs in different ways.

Anthropologists

A cultural anthropologist discovers, explains, and preserves culture by learning the local language and sharing in the daily life of the people that he or she studies. Anthropologists learn how a culture functions by observing, by interviewing, and by recording oral histories — the stories a culture passes down by word of mouth. Folklorists, a type of anthropologist, are particularly concerned with these stories and what they say about a culture. Anthropologists also learn about a culture's customs, ceremonies, holidays, family life, politics, and belief systems.

Anthropologists study people wherever they can be found. Cities are a big challenge for these scientists, as many different cultural groups can be found living side by side. In one part of New York City that was recently studied by an urban anthropologist, there are residents of 120 different nationalities. In fact, this part of the city, called Queens, is considered to be more diverse than any other county in America.

What an anthropologist wants to discover is how the people in a given area live. In the case of Queens, the scientist asks, "What kind of resources do they have? How do they bring their own culture to the city? How does the city affect the way they live? How do they change the city?"

Queens has bakeries, restaurants, clubs, cafes, grocery stores, clothing shops, and houses of worship from cultures around the globe. Along the main subway route live immigrants from Afghanistan, Argentina, Bangladesh, China, Colombia, the Dominican Republic, India, Ireland, Korea, Mexico, Pakistan, Peru, the Philippines, Romania, Thailand, and Uruguay. Because urban anthropologists are concerned with language, studying the way the members of all these different cultures communicate is very important. Whether they spend time in cafes in Queens or in the jungles of the Amazon, anthropologists study people.

These archaeologists are using tools like those below — a trowel, a pick, a whisk broom, a paint brush, a notepad, and a strainer.

Archaeologists

Archaeologists reconstruct past cultures by gathering clues. Bones are one kind of clue. Other clues include artifacts and fossils. **Artifacts** are objects from the past, usually made by people. **Fossils** are impressions or remains of plants and animals that have turned to stone. Archaeologists begin to collect this evidence at a spot where people might have lived and worked. At that spot, scientists begin to clear away layers of earth to find signs of human civilization. Archaeologists call this spot a **site**, or dig.

Archaeologists remove each layer by hand, using all kinds of tools, from shovels to dental instruments. They work slowly because they do not want to damage the delicate artifacts and fossils buried in the soil. Workers sift the dirt and rubble through a sieve. They look for such things as bits of pottery, tools, weapons, seeds, and bones.

Archaeologists record the precise location of every item they find. Then they use high-tech devices to discover

This helmet was used by Anglo-Saxons, who settled in Britain in the fifth and sixth centuries. It was rebuilt from pieces found at Sutton Hoo. **Technology:** *Why do you suppose it has a metal face?*

This Norse-style buckle was also found at Sutton Hoo. **Cultures:** *How would this knowledge help an archaeologist?*

each item's age. To identify artifacts, archaeologists must know as much as possible about past cultures.

The artifacts at left are part of a treasure found in Britain. The items show the influence of Roman, Middle Eastern, and Scandinavian cultures. Known as Sutton Hoo, the site was discovered in 1939 and contains the remains of an Anglo-Saxon funeral ship that was buried almost 1,400 years ago. The photo above shows all that remains of the ship. Instead of actual timbers, what you see is the hard-packed earth that filled the space left as the boat rotted away.

Near where the men are squatting, archaeologists discovered beautifully carved gold jewelry, like the buckle shown at left. They also found a jeweled helmet, once worn by the tomb's occupant.

Culture is common to everyone on earth. By studying a variety of cultures, we stand a much better chance of understanding our own place on earth and in history. The exciting journey to other worlds and other ways of thinking begins here.

Lesson Review

1 **Key Vocabulary:** Write a paragraph about culture using at least three of these words: global village, anthropologist, archaeologist, artifact, fossil, site.

2 **Focus:** Why do we study other cultures and our own?

3 **Focus:** How do we study culture?

4 **Critical Thinking: Classify** How does the work of an anthropologist differ from

that of an archaeologist? Is either job more important?

5 **Theme: Patterns in Diversity** How does studying culture help us understand the world?

6 **Citizenship/Research Activity:** Become an anthropologist for a week. Plan to study your school or neighborhood. Write a report of your findings and present it to the class.

Skills Workshop

Using the Internet

A World of Resources

You want to do a report on the culture of Korea. How can you locate information? One way to find information is through the Internet. The Internet is a network of computers that connects people, businesses, and institutions all over the world. Most libraries and schools have computers with access to the Internet. You may also have Internet access on a home computer.

1 Here's How

- Click into the computer's Internet access.

- Choose a search engine and type in the broad topic you wish to search, such as "Korea."

- You can narrow your search by adding more specific key words or phrases, such as "sports" or "music." Your computer will suggest resources, or Web sites, containing information on the topics.

- Go to the Web sites that you think will provide the most helpful information and read them. If they are useful, print them out or take notes on them.

2 Think It Through

What do you think are the advantages and disadvantages of using the Internet for research?

3 Use It

1. Choose a subject that interests you. List the broad subject and several key words you will use to search the Internet for information on the subject.

2. Search the Internet with the words you've chosen. If the search with these words does not provide the information you want, try other key words or phrases.

3. As you find information of use to you, be sure to write down the name of the Web site and the day on which you found the information. Because Web sites change over time, it is important to record where and when you find information.

Resolving Conflicts

What Are Rules For?

Some people enjoy conflict. Others try to avoid it. One thing is sure: Conflict is a fact of life. Politics is about resolving conflicts over who takes part in government, how much power government has, and how it uses its power. The case study below describes the conflict and compromise that led to the Constitution of the United States. As you read it, think about how people can resolve conflict with compromise.

Case Study

Compromise Forges a Constitution

In 1787, freed from Britain's rule, the United States needed better rules of government. So a group of men from 12 of the 13 original states met that summer in Philadelphia to write those rules — the United States Constitution. They elected George Washington to lead the meetings.

Washington faced a conflict. Those from large states argued that states with more people and more land should have more power to make laws. Small states protested and threatened to leave. They wanted each state to have the same amount of power. Finally, they all compromised. Congress would have two law-making chambers. In the Senate, each state would have two votes. In the House of Representatives, states would receive votes according to their population.

> " *We the people of the United States, in order to form a more perfect Union, establish justice, insure domestic tranquility, provide for the common defense, promote the general welfare, and secure the blessings of liberty to ourselves and our posterity, do ordain and establish this Constitution for the United States of America.* "
>
> Preamble to the Constitution

Take Action

The Preamble to the Constitution (on the previous page) states reasons why the United States needed a new government. The Bill of Rights was added to the Constitution in 1791. It states many basic rights, a few of which are listed below. Now it is your turn to write a constitution and bill of rights. Use the Preamble and Bill of Rights as your model.

Constitutional Amendments

 I

You May...
Gather, Worship, Write, Speak, and Assemble

Congress shall make no law respecting an establishment of religion, or prohibiting the free exercise thereof; or abridging the freedom of speech, or of the press; or the right of the people peaceably to assemble...

 IV

You Have...
Individual Rights

The right of the people to be secure in their persons, houses, papers, and effects, against unreasonable searches and seizures, shall not be violated...

 VI

You May...
Have a Trial by Jury

...the right to a speedy and public trial, by an impartial jury...

VIII

You Have...
Human Rights

Excessive bail shall not be required, nor excessive fines imposed, nor cruel and unusual punishments inflicted.

1 In small groups, list what you think are some of the purposes of school. Then create a list of the rights and responsibilities of the "citizens" of the school.

2 Use this information to write a constitution. Begin it like the Preamble, filling in your own words where needed: "We the people of _____ , in order to form a more perfect _____ , establish _____ , insure_____ ," and so on.

3 Share your constitutions. How are they the same? How are they different? Do you wish to adopt one for the year?

Tips for Resolving Conflicts

- Make sure the rules are clear and specific.
- Rules need to allow for disagreements between people.
- A document that works to prevent or end conflict will provide ways for people to work out disagreements.
- Make sure people have specific tasks and that they know what is expected of them.

Research Activity

America had democratic governments before the Pilgrims and other English settlers arrived. Find out about the Algonquin Indian nations or other Native American groups of that time. How did they govern themselves?

Chapter Review

Summarizing the Main Idea

1 Copy the chart below and fill in the missing information.

Aspect of Life	Example of Culture
Housing	*apartments, houses in U.S.A.*
Clothing	
Transportation	
Art/Music	
Entertainment	
Holidays	
Rituals	

Vocabulary

2 You are a scientist studying an ancient people.
Write a journal entry using at least five of the following terms.

culture (p. 35)	global village (p. 44)	artifact (p. 47)
beliefs (p. 36)	anthropologist (p. 46)	site (p. 47)
rituals (p. 37)	archaeologist (p. 46)	

Reviewing the Facts

3 What is culture?

4 What are the differences between a nationality and a culture?

5 How do families shape and preserve culture?

6 Why are beliefs the foundation of a culture?

7 How is the world becoming more like a village?

8 Why is it important to study other cultures?

9 How do anthropologists study the interactions of people and their cultures?

10 How do archaeologists study the remains of past civilizations?

Using the Internet

11 Write down a culture or country that you would like to find out more about. Then list at least five subjects related to the culture or country that you could look at in an Internet search engine.

12 Use the Internet to research one of the subjects from question 11. Copy down the address (URL) and date of at least three Web sites on that subject.

Geography Skills

13 How do you think geography influences a culture's development?

14 Study the map on page 45, "Migration to the United States, 1792–1992." What do you think happens to a culture that developed in one geographic area when it is transplanted to a completely different geography?

Critical Thinking

15 **Classify** What are some of the things you do that are part of our shared American culture? What are some things you do that are part of your family's culture? Do any overlap?

16 **Interpret** An archaeologist digging at a site finds a tool that is much older than the site being excavated. What might this mean?

Writing: Citizenship and Cultures

17 **Citizenship** Write a letter to a pen pal in another country. Write about what you did during the last week, and describe the type of culture we have in the United States. Be sure to ask questions about your pen pal's culture.

18 **Culture** Invent your own culture. What if a group of people lived on a deserted island, for instance? Write about the traditions they develop, and about how they entertain themselves.

Activities

Culture/Art Activity
Suppose a new people has just been discovered on an unknown continent. Invent their culture. Create a piece of art or an artifact from that culture.

National Heritage/Research
Be a cultural anthropologist. Interview and record the oral histories of your parents and grandparents. Ask them what life was like when they were your age. Combine your findings with your classmates' as a larger oral history project.

Internet Option

Check the **Internet Social Studies Center** for ideas on how to extend your theme project beyond your classroom.

THEME PROJECT CHECK-IN

To complete your theme project use the information in this chapter. Ask yourself these questions as you work on the project components:
• What is the culture like in each place? How are the cultures alike and different?
• What are some of the beliefs and rituals of each culture?
• How have these cultures changed over time?
• What things would attract a tourist to these places?

2 The Rise of Civilizations

"Ancient times were the youth of the world."

Francis Bacon

· T H E M E ·

Lasting Beginnings

❝ *It's important to study the earliest civilizations so the past doesn't repeat itself, and so we can learn from others' mistakes and their successes.* **❞**

Tyler Runnells, Sixth Grade
Topeka, KS

Human beings existed for tens of thousands of years before ever writing down so much as a game of tick-tack-toe. Then, about 5,500 years ago, people started writing. From the Middle East to India and China, from Africa to the Americas, cities grew, systems of government developed, and people worked to better themselves. Religions appeared, and amazing technologies grew from the most barren soils. Every day we use things these people invented thousands of years ago.

Theme Project

Create a Civilization

Plan and create your own civilization by completing the following tasks:

- Construct a timeline that indicates the major events in your civilization's history.
- Create a diagram that illustrates your civilization's system of government.
- Write a description of the beliefs of your civilization.
- Draw different aspects of the culture of your civilization (clothing, architecture, and so on).

RESEARCH: Read more about the civilization in this unit that most closely resembles your civilization.

◀ The Great Wall of China at Huang Ya Guan.

WHEN & WHERE
ATLAS

When people think of ancient history, they often picture people leading simple lives — surviving by hunting and gathering. But as the map illustrates, as long as 4500 years ago, large and complex civilizations existed in many parts of the world. How did these civilizations come to be? What were they like? Why did they decline? Historians have been studying these questions for centuries.

In this unit, you will learn how early peoples lived and how agriculture changed the lives of many of these people. You will also read how, after the introduction of farming, more complicated societies began to develop in different parts of the world. Finally you will learn more about the geographies, cultures, and histories of some of these civilizations.

Unit 2 Chapters

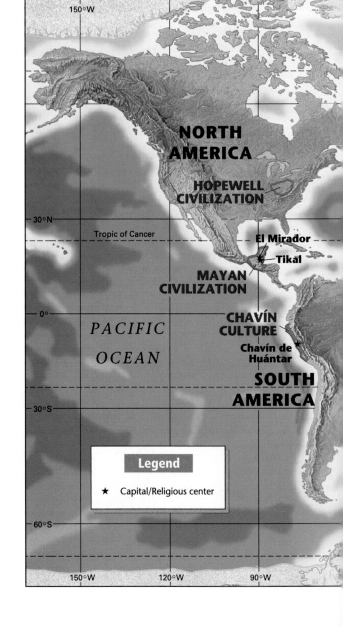

NORTH AMERICA

HOPEWELL CIVILIZATION

150°W

30°N

Tropic of Cancer

El Mirador

★ Tikal

MAYAN CIVILIZATION

0°

PACIFIC OCEAN

CHAVÍN CULTURE

Chavín de Huántar

SOUTH AMERICA

30°S

Legend

★ Capital/Religious center

60°S

150°W   120°W   90°W

Unit Timeline

30,000 B.C.	23,600 B.C.	17,200 B.C.

Ziggurats   3000–2000 B.C.

This early civilization built a "stairway to Heaven." Who were they?
Chapter 3, Lesson 3

Tutankhamun   c. 1300 B.C.

The boy-king ruled one of the greatest civilizations of the ancient world.
Chapter 4, Lesson 2

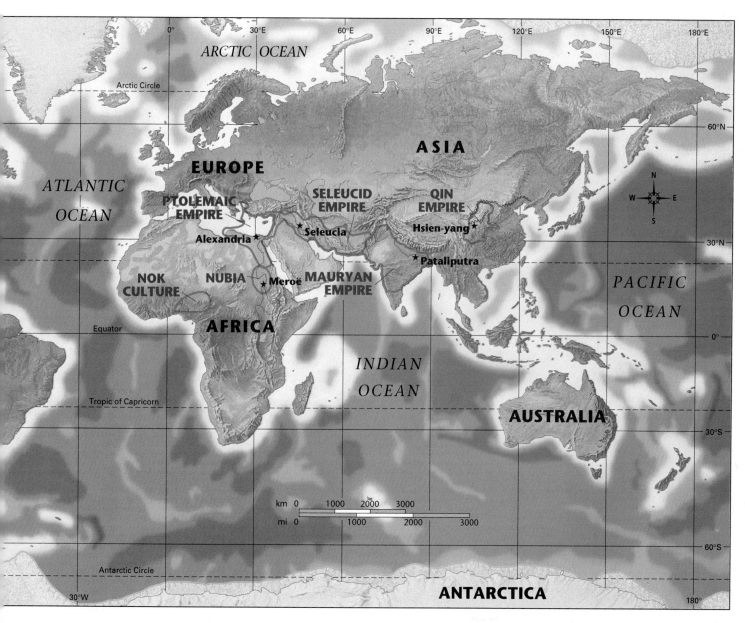

ARCTIC OCEAN

Arctic Circle

ATLANTIC OCEAN

EUROPE

ASIA

PTOLEMAIC EMPIRE

SELEUCID EMPIRE

QIN EMPIRE

Alexandria ★

★ Seleucia

Hsien-yang ★

★ Pataliputra

NOK CULTURE

NUBIA

★ Meroë

MAURYAN EMPIRE

PACIFIC OCEAN

Equator

AFRICA

INDIAN OCEAN

Tropic of Capricorn

AUSTRALIA

km 0   1000   2000   3000
mi 0   1000   2000   3000

Antarctic Circle

ANTARCTICA

10,800 B.C.   4,400 B.C.   A.D. 2000

Scholars Rule 124 B.C.

In Han Dynasty China, people had to take tests to gain government positions. *Chapter 5, Lesson 4*

Machu Picchu 300 B.C.

This stone city is located high up in the Andes. Who lived there? *Chapter 6, Lesson 2*

Niger River

This river has supported life and civilization in Africa for thousands of years. *Chapter 7, Lesson 1*

The Dawn of Civilization

Chapter Preview: *People, Places, and Events*

30,000 B.C.	24,000 B.C.	18,000 B.C.

Cave Painting   28,000 B.C.

The first artists drew the world around them on the walls of caves. *Lesson 1, Page 60*

Euphrates River

Why did the first civilizations develop in this river valley in the Middle East? *Lesson 2, Page 66*

Fierce Warriors   1350 B.C.

The Assyrians were a powerful military force. Learn how they built their empire. *Lesson 3, Page 74*

Early Human Life

Main Idea Traces left by prehistoric people suggest that they gradually moved from searching for food to growing crops and taming animals.

Key Vocabulary

prehistoric
Homo sapiens
hunter-gatherer
agriculture
domestication

Key Events

Before 3,000 B.C.
The Stone Age

28,000 B.C. Ardèche
cave paintings
created in France

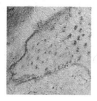 Cries of wonder rang out in the vast, dark cave. The three explorers stumbled forward, shining their flashlights on the rough stone walls. They looked in awe at the pictures of daily life some 30,000 years ago painted in colors of yellow, red, and black.

On the walls and ceilings of this cave were pictures of prowling and leaping animals. Some drawings were smaller than the actual size of the animals. Others were huge — up to 13 feet long. The flickering flashlights caught a hyena, a red bear, a reindeer, and more.

One scene showed a group of 50 woolly rhinos. Another showed a mysterious figure that was only half animal: It had a bison's head and shoulders and a man's legs. In another scene, a horse lifted its head, mane flying, while a mammoth walked on round feet. Mammoths, large elephants with long tusks and thick hair, are now gone from the earth. They lived during the time when ice covered large areas of the earth. The explorers discovered this site in the Ardèche (ar DESH) region of southern

◀ Like many ancient civilizations, the Persians left behind fine works of art.

| 12,000 B.C. | 6,000 B.C. | B.C. | A.D. |

The Exodus

"Let my people go!" Moses cried. How did the Israelites find freedom? *Lesson 4, Page 78*

The Temple at Jerusalem

King Solomon built the first temple at Jerusalem. It became the center of Jewish life. *Lesson 4, Page 81*

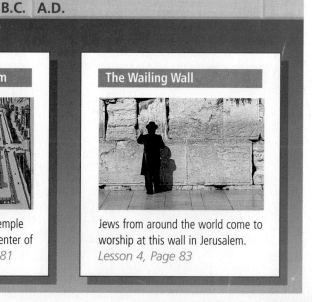

The Wailing Wall

Jews from around the world come to worship at this wall in Jerusalem. *Lesson 4, Page 83*

Most of the figures on the cave walls at Ardèche *(above)* were simple outline sketches made with charcoal. In some cases the figures were filled in with paint by the prehistoric artists. These paintings and the ones at Lascaux, France *(above right),* showed animals important to early people.

Scientists examine the fossil remains of early humans in Africa. The study of fossils reveals clues about human history.

France in December 1994. They found hundreds of paintings on the walls of the 1,500-yard-long cave. Scholars believe that the paintings were made approximately 30,000 years ago. The explorers also found footprints of humans and bears. Traces, or marks, were left by campfires, and a bear's skull was carefully placed on a rock, resembling an altar.

Prehistoric People

Focus *What do we know about people who lived before history was written down, and how do we know it?*

The three explorers were thrilled by the paintings at Ardèche because they provided clues about what prehistoric people were like and how they lived. The term **prehistoric** means "before history was written down." Because there are no written records, scientists learn about prehistoric people by studying what they left behind. Some of the first **Homo sapiens** (HO mo SAY pee ehnz), people with the same skull structure and other physical characteristics that we have today, left behind their bones. The oldest bones ever found were in Africa and are 120,000 to 130,000 years old. From them scientists conclude that Homo sapiens first lived in warmer Africa, then later migrated to many other parts of the world.

In addition to fossilized remains, tools and other objects left by prehistoric people

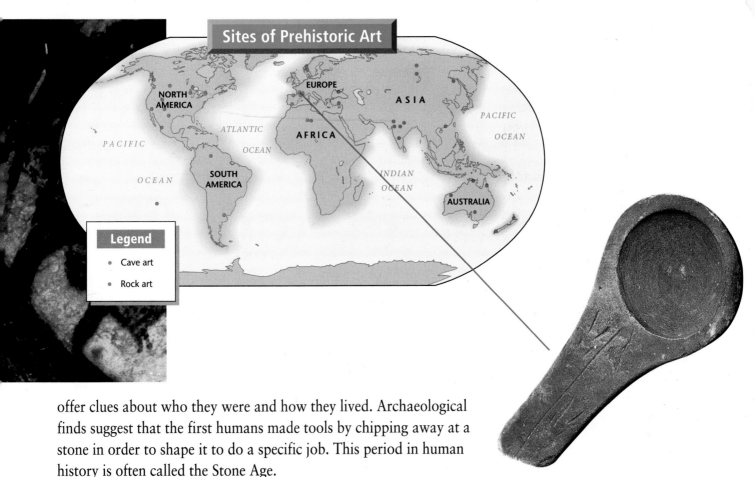

Legend
- Cave art
- Rock art

Artists at Lascaux probably painted cave walls by light from burning lumps of fat placed in stone lamps like this one.

offer clues about who they were and how they lived. Archaeological finds suggest that the first humans made tools by chipping away at a stone in order to shape it to do a specific job. This period in human history is often called the Stone Age.

During the Stone Age, people used stone tools in many different ways. Instead of just picking up any stone and throwing it at an animal they were stalking, people made stones with sharp points for hunting. Stone knives were used for killing animals and cutting up skins for clothing. Stone scrapers were made for cleaning the hides, and stone awls, or thick needles, were used for poking holes for rawhide laces to hold the skins together. The stone lamp on this page was made by using one stone to shape another.

New Ways of Life

Focus *What important changes took place when Stone Age people settled in one place?*

Clues suggest that the earliest humans were **hunter-gatherers,** people who lived off wild game and any plants, fish, fruit, seeds, and honey that they could find. This does not mean that they wandered about, finding something to eat only if they were lucky. Remains of campfires and tools suggest that small groups returned to the same areas at certain times of the year. They might spend warmer months near fields of wild grain. Then, in winter, they might move to a spot where animals were plentiful.

Slowly a change took place. Instead of moving in search of food, people began to settle in one place and grow their own food right there.

Many species of animals were domesticated from their wild ancestors. **Chart Skill:** *When was the horse domesticated?*

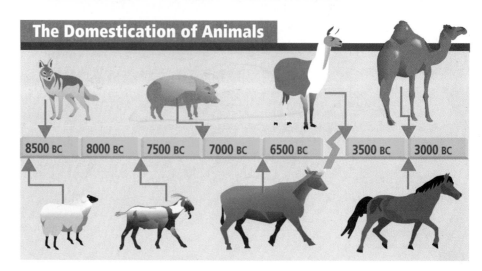

The Domestication of Animals

8500 BC	8000 BC	7500 BC	7000 BC	6500 BC	3500 BC	3000 BC

Curious Facts

Dogs were among the first animals to be domesticated. Wolves were probably the wild ancestors of the dog, although fossil evidence for this is scarce. Some early evidence of domesticated dogs comes from present-day Israel. Soon after early farmers began taming dogs, canines were used to herd and guard animals.

Agriculture, working the land in order to grow plants on it, took the place of gathering food. **Domestication,** the taming and raising of wild animals, gave people a steady supply of meat and milk. Leather, fur, and wool from these animals were also used for clothing. The chart above shows when particular animals were domesticated.

There are many possible reasons why this new, more settled way of life evolved. Perhaps as more people were born into bands of hunter-gatherers, competition for food increased. It may have become impossible to live entirely on what was found in the wild. Then, as agriculture took hold, early humans spent more time near their fields. In addition, changes in climate may have made winters colder and summers hotter and drier. If so, people needed to store away food for times when it was not easily found. Whatever the reason, when humans settled down in one place, they paved the way for a dramatic change in history.

Lesson Review

30,000 B.C.	10,000 B.C.

28,000 B.C.
Ardèche cave paintings created in France

Before 3000 B.C.
The Stone Age

1 **Key Vocabulary:** Write a paragraph about early people, using these words: **prehistoric, Homo sapiens, hunter-gatherer, agriculture, domestication.**

2 **Focus:** What do we know about people who lived before history was written down, and how do we know it?

3 **Focus:** What important changes took place when Stone Age people settled in one place?

4 **Critical Thinking: Decision Making** Which do you think would be more challenging: hunting wild animals or caring for domesticated ones? Why?

5 **Theme: Lasting Beginnings** Look at the chart on this page. How are these animals used today?

6 **Geography/Art Activity:** Make a "cave painting" that shows places, animals, and objects that would have been important to early humans.

Measuring Time

Arranging the Past

You are a time traveler. First you stop in the eighth century B.C. to see the Olympic Games in Greece. Then you zoom further back, jumping across a break in the timeline. You stop at 28,000 B.C. to visit the Ardèche caves. As you have traveled back into time B.C., the numbers have grown larger, not smaller as in A.D. time. How is measuring time A.D. different from the way time is measured B.C.? How is it the same?

Events in History

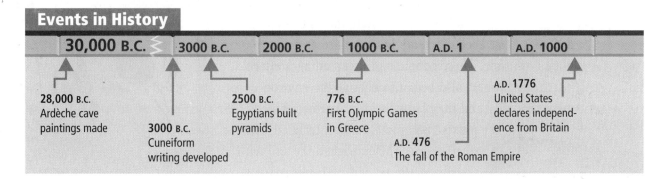

30,000 B.C. | 3000 B.C. | 2000 B.C. | 1000 B.C. | A.D. 1 | A.D. 1000

28,000 B.C.
Ardèche cave
paintings made

3000 B.C.
Cuneiform
writing developed

2500 B.C.
Egyptians built
pyramids

776 B.C.
First Olympic Games
in Greece

A.D. 476
The fall of the Roman Empire

A.D. 1776
United States
declares independ-
ence from Britain

1 Here's How

- Look at the timeline above. The broken section means that a long period of time was not included.

- Read the events and dates. Notice in which era, B.C. or A.D., each event occurred.

- Calculate how many years passed between events. For two A.D. or B.C. dates, subtract the smaller number from the larger number. For a B.C. date and an A.D. date, add the two together. For example, add 776 + 476 to find the number of years that passed between 776 B.C. and A.D. 476.

- Centuries are numbered the same way in B.C. and A.D. For example, the first century B.C. refers to the years 1 to 100 B.C., and the first century A.D. refers to the years A.D. 1 to 100. The second century B.C. includes the years 101 to 200 B.C., and so on.

2 Think It Through

How does finding the number of years that passed between events help you better understand these events? Why might some periods of time not be included on a timeline?

3 Use It

1. How many years passed between the development of cuneiform and the building of the pyramids?

2. In what centuries do the years 452 B.C., 1872 B.C., 2 B.C., and A.D. 476 occur?

3. How many years passed between the first Olympic Games and the declaration of U.S. independence from Britain?

GEOGRAPHER

Environment and Society

In What Ways Did Farming Change the Environment?

By picking wild plants and hunting wild animals, ancient hunter-gatherers used their environment. They did not change it very much. They traveled from place to place, using available resources and then moving on.

Gradually, people realized that if they put the seeds of certain plants in the ground, food would be available when they came back later on. Eventually, people in different places began to stay in one place and grow plants full time. These people had invented agriculture.

Early farmers also began to change the environment that they and the plants lived in. Farmers killed plants and animals that interfered with their crops. They enriched the soil with fertilizers. Some early farmers made sure their crops had enough water by irrigating their fields.

1 Mexico

Avocado, squash, & chilies
Early Mexican farmers began to grow crops about 8,500 years ago. They developed their most important food, maize (or corn), about 3,000 years later, around 3,500 B.C.

This rice field in Indonesia has been terraced and irrigated. Land that is terraced has been shaped into many flat levels to make a good surface for plants to grow.

This woman in Malaysia is gathering wild plants in the rain forest. She is using her environment without changing it.

Wheat, dates, & chickpeas
The Egyptians farmed the flood plains of the Nile River more than 5,000 years ago. They used irrigation to water fields away from the Nile.

Science Connection

Early farmers realized that some plants produced more or better food than others. One way to grow better plants is to replant only seeds of the most successful plants. Gradually, the plants began to change in ways that benefited people. Think of different breeds of a fruit, like apples. Why are there so many varieties?

Early Centers of Farming

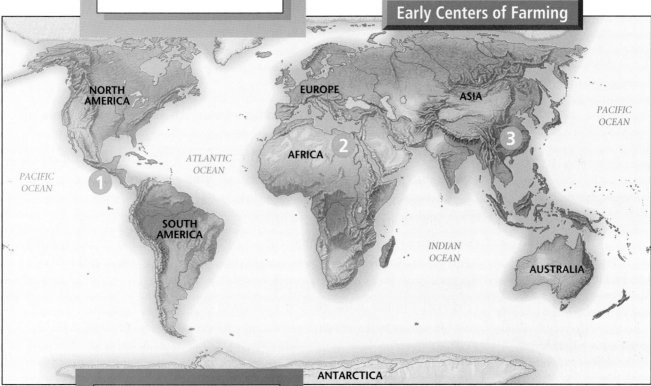

3 China

The importance of rice
About 4,800 years ago, Chinese farmers began to grow rice. Growing rice took organization and cooperation. But rice became the main food crop for more than half the world's people.

The map shows three places where farming developed independently. Early farmers grew different plants in all three places. But they all changed their environments to help their plants grow. **Map Skill:** *What ocean is between Africa and Australia?*

Research Activity

1 Choose one of the crops shown in the boxes.

2 Do research to find out about that crop. Where was it first grown? Where is it grown now? How has it changed since ancient times?

3 Share your findings with the class.

The Geography of the Fertile Crescent

Key Vocabulary

silt

irrigation

surplus

specialization of labor

civilization

Key Places

Tigris River

Euphrates River

Fertile Crescent

The map on the following page shows the area of the Fertile Crescent. **Map Skill:** *Judging from the map, how do you think the Fertile Crescent got its name?*

Main Idea Geography, especially the location of rivers, determined where early civilizations grew.

On a hot afternoon in the Middle East about 7,000 years ago, a 12-year-old girl walks through her father's fields. All around her, locusts and other insects keep up a low, drowsy humming. The nearby river has shrunk in its banks, exposing mud flats. There, water birds lower their beaks into puddles in search of food. The family's sheep and goats nibble on wild grass. It is midsummer, and there has been no rain for months.

Still, the fields are thick with barley and vegetables. River water, delivered to the fields through a series of ditches, keeps the plants healthy and green. In a few weeks, the crops will be harvested. There will be grain for the winter, with some to spare. The girl's mother will keep enough for the family to use, while the remainder will be sold.

In spring, the rain will come, and new crops will be planted. By next summer, the girl will again walk through fields ripe for harvest.

Geography changes. In ancient times, the Tigris and Euphrates rivers did not follow the same courses they do today.

Life Along the River

Focus *Why did an agricultural society emerge in the Fertile Crescent?*

The girl lived in the Fertile Crescent, an area where the Tigris (TY grihs) and Euphrates (yoo FRAY teez) rivers flow into the Persian Gulf. Fresh water and fish first drew people to the rivers, which also supplied reeds and mud for building homes and boats and for making baskets and pottery. The rivers also provided some of the richest soil in the ancient world.

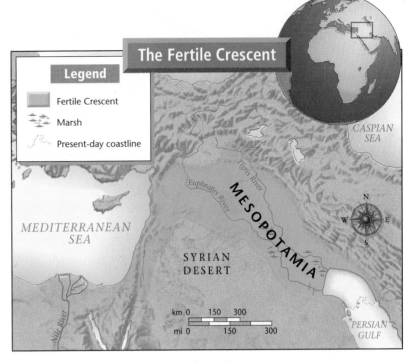

The Fertile Crescent

Legend
- Fertile Crescent
- Marsh
- Present-day coastline

The Tigris and Euphrates rivers began as streams in the mountains of Armenia. Every fall rains fed the streams. Through winter and early spring, the rivers on their way to the Persian Gulf swelled from melting snow and rain. As they flowed, their waters picked up **silt**, fine particles of soil, from the lands they passed through. In the late spring, both rivers poured over their banks onto the plain of the Fertile Crescent. When the water went down at the beginning of summer, it deposited the silt, leaving a thick layer of rich soil on the flood plain. (The diagrams below show what the Tigris or Euphrates might have looked like at various times of the year.) The greatest amount of soil was deposited closest to the river's normal channel. Gradually the banks of the Tigris and Euphrates grew higher than the plains on either side.

During summer, the Fertile Crescent is hot and almost rainless. **Irrigation** developed there when farmers realized that they could break through riverbanks and direct water to their fields, through a system of ditches. Hot weather, rich soil, and irrigation produced plentiful harvests.

The Flooding Cycle

The rivers of the Fertile Crescent changed with the seasons.

1. In winter and early spring, the rivers began to swell with rain and melting snow in the mountains.

2. In late spring, the waters overflowed their banks onto the plains of the Fertile Crescent.

3. As the summer went on and temperatures rose, water evaporated, and the rivers began to shrink.

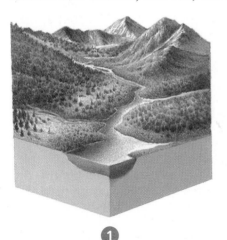

1

2

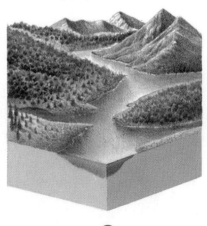

3

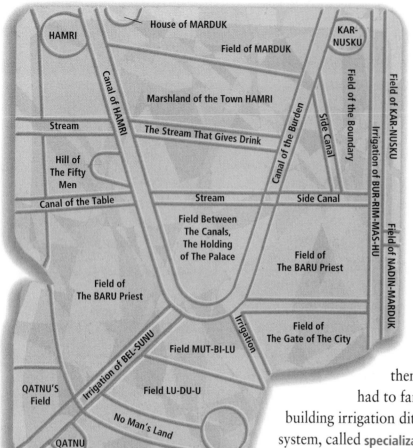

This map made on a clay tablet *(right)* in 1300 B.C. shows farmland and irrigation ditches outside the Mesopotamian city of Nippur. The English translation of the map is on the left. **Map Skill:** *Why might the king have owned the land between the canals?*

Farmers could now produce a **surplus** of food, far more than they needed for themselves. A surplus meant that not everyone had to farm. Instead, some workers spent their time building irrigation ditches. Others cared for animals. Under this system, called **specialization of labor**, people became skilled at specific jobs that helped the entire community.

Gradually complex societies, called **civilizations**, developed in the Fertile Crescent. People working together needed a government and a system of recordkeeping. Different social classes, groups of people who shared similar economic and social conditions, emerged. Artists began producing beautiful items, and writers recorded the stories of their people in literature. Organized religion developed. The most important civilizations to evolve in the Fertile Crescent were those in an area called Mesopotamia, from a Greek word meaning "between two rivers."

Lesson Review: Geography

1. **Key Vocabulary:** Use the following terms to describe life along a river in the Fertile Crescent: **silt, irrigation, surplus.**

2. **Focus:** Why did an agricultural society emerge in the Fertile Crescent?

3. **Critical Thinking: Generalize** What are the advantages and disadvantages of settling near a major river?

4. **Citizenship: Geography** Compare the map of the Fertile Crescent on page 67 with a map of modern political states in the Atlas at the back of this book. What countries or parts of countries occupy the Fertile Crescent today? List them.

5. **Geography/Science Activity:** Using material from reference books at your library, create a model of a flood plain of a river. Write a paragraph about how rivers change with the seasons.

Ancient Mesopotamia

Main Idea Cultures that developed in ancient Mesopotamia strongly influenced cultures of the present day.

The wall painting below tells about daily life in ancient Mesopotamia. You can see people doing various jobs — milking cows, churning cream into butter, tending animals in a cowshed. Just as running a business today involves a number of workers and skills, so did the tasks of daily life thousands of years ago. Life back then was similar to our life in other ways, too. Here is a father writing to his son:

> **"Y**ou who wander about in the public square, do you want to be successful? Go to school, it would do you some good. . . . Because I was tired of dealing with you, I avoided you and your problems and excuses. I was angry with you — yes, angry — because of your endless complaining. . . . Your grumblings have worn me down, and have made me feel like giving up. **"**

Some battles between parents and children haven't changed in 5,000 years!

Key Vocabulary

city-state
cuneiform
class
polytheistic
ziggurat
empire

Key Events

C. 2900 B.C.
Development of cuneiform

C. 1750 B.C. Code of Hammurabi

C. 1350-600 B.C. Assyrian Empire

The Sumerians domesticated animals such as goats and cows. This panel from a temple shows workers and dairy cows. **Economics:** *How does this panel illustrate specialization of labor?*

Mesopotamian Culture Begins

Focus *What was the culture of Mesopotamia like?*

The map on the opposite page shows a region called Sumer (SOO mur) in the southern part of Mesopotamia. There, between 3000 and 2000 B.C., self-governing cities, with names like Kish, Adab, and Ur, grew and prospered. Called **city-states**, they were independent political units that controlled areas of surrounding farmland. These city-states were the first known civilizations.

Writing

Harvests were large on irrigated land of the Fertile Crescent, and there was a surplus of food. Sumerians now needed a way to keep records of the kind and amount of surplus they produced, as well as the goods and services they traded their products for. The earliest human records were made by drawing pictures on damp clay tablets. Gradually signs took the place of pictures. Each sign was made up of wedge-shaped marks. The signs stood for specific words and ideas, as well as for letter sounds. **Cuneiform** (KYOO nee uh form), or wedge-shaped writing, contained over 800 signs. The chart below shows how some of those signs developed.

Besides agriculture and trading, there were many other uses for writing. People set down in clay everything from doctors' prescriptions to songs and stories. Those who could write, called scribes, established schools where they taught others to read and write.

Social Classes and Government

As Sumerian communities grew more complex, people needed a permanent leader. Someone had to organize the workers in specialized tasks. Necessary jobs, such as building and maintaining irrigation systems, had to be

Cuneiform script developed over thousands of years. At first, word-pictures were used to represent ideas. Later signs changed to represent letter sounds as well as objects and ideas.

The Development of Cuneiform Script

Pictographic sign c. 3100 B.C.						
Cuneiform sign c. 2400 B.C.						
Cuneiform sign c. 700 B.C.						
English word	god, sky	day, sun	water, stream	food	to eat	to walk, to stand

carried out. In many Sumerian city-states, leaders who acted like kings were called *lugals,* a Sumerian word that means "big man."

In the city-states, the lugal governed a society that had distinct classes. A **class** is a group of people who make about the same amount of money and hold the same social position in society. In Sumer, the small upper class was mostly made up of priests, government officials, and very wealthy landowners. Most people were in the middle class, which included farmers, craftsmen, traders, scribes, and all kinds of laborers. The lower class was made up of enslaved people. Human societies have generally been divided into classes like these ever since.

Religion

The people of Sumer were **polytheistic** (pol ee thee IS tik), that is, they worshipped many gods. Sumerian stories and legends included gods of the sun, the moon, darkness, and the air. There were also less important gods of daily objects, such as building tools, for example.

According to Sumerian religion, gods lived in a society that was very much like the Sumerian city-states. Important gods belonged to the highest class. Sumerians believed they should worship the gods and carry out the gods' will on earth. This close relationship with the heavenly powers played a major role in the lives of the Sumerians — and later, in the lives of all the peoples influenced by the Sumerians.

All social classes, from the highest to the lowest, worshipped the gods and brought them offerings. Leaders of the city-states believed it was their job to lead their people in worshipping the gods. They paid skilled craftsmen to make statues of the gods and build elaborate temples to house the statues. These temples were huge pyramid-shaped structures called **ziggurats** (ZIHG uh rats) that rose in a series of stories toward the sky. You can read about the features of a ziggurat on the next page.

The Empires of Mesopotamia

CASPIAN SEA

TAURUS MTS

ASSYRIAN EMPIRE • Nineveh

Euphrates R.

BABYLONIAN EMPIRE Assur •

ZAGROS MOUNTAINS

SUMERIAN EMPIRE

MEDITERRANEAN SEA

Tigris R.

Babylon •

KINGDOM OF ISRAEL Jerusalem •

Modern shoreline

EGYPT

Ur •

PERSIAN GULF

Nile R.

RED SEA

km 0   300
mi 0   300

Legend

▬	Sumerian Empire, 2500 B.C.	▬	Kingdom of Israel, 922 B.C.
▬	Babylonian Empire, 1595 B.C.	▬	Assyrian Empire, 660 B.C.

The map above shows the important empires of Mesopotamia.
Map Skill: *Which empire might have been the most difficult to control? Why?*

A Glorious Temple

Mesopotamians believed that the ziggurat served as a staircase or ladder to connect earth and heaven. These temples, some more than 200 feet tall, were first built in about 2000 B.C. Archaeologists working in Mesopotamia have found remains of more than 30 ziggurats.

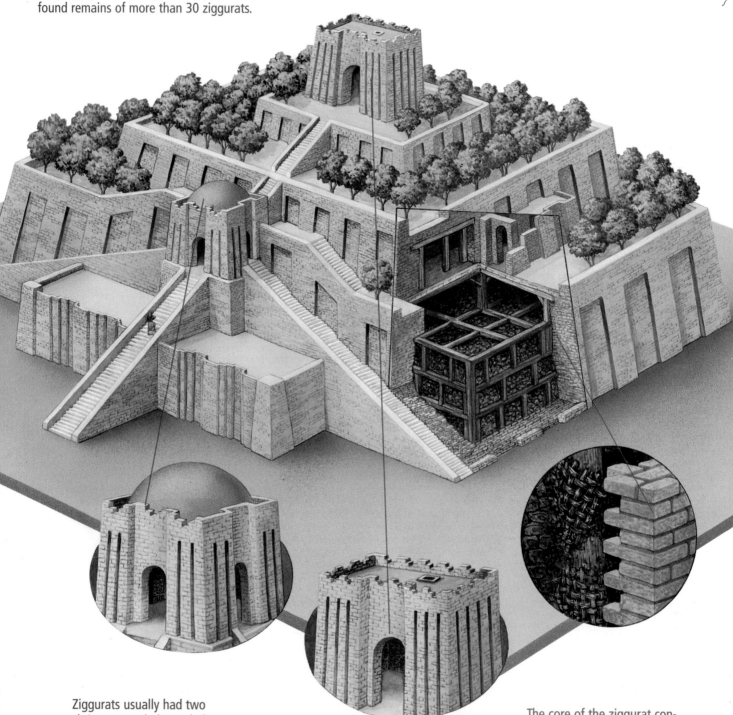

Ziggurats usually had two shrines, sacred places dedicated to a god or goddess. Mesopotamians believed gods or goddesses would descend from heaven and greet worshippers in this lower shrine.

At the top of the ziggurat was a second shrine, designed to welcome the god or goddess when he or she first descended from heaven.

The core of the ziggurat consisted of mud bricks placed in an excavated hole. Baked bricks covered the inner structure.

Babylon: The Rule of Law

The Sumerian city-states were eventually overrun by outside invaders. Some of the invaders settled in Babylon (BAB uh lon), which became the capital of the next great civilization after Sumer in the Fertile Crescent. (Locate Babylon on the map on page 71.) Here King Hammurabi (ham uh RAH bee) came to power in about 1792 B.C. and ruled for 42 years. He ruled far longer than most people of the time lived.

Hammurabi built his kingdom by setting up a strong and effective government in Babylon. The group of 282 laws that governed this civilization are known as The Code of Hammurabi. (A code is a collection of laws.) This was not the first code of laws written by the people of the region. Archaeologists have discovered fragments of much earlier laws. The Code of Hammurabi is the best known because it is the best preserved. A stone stele (STEE lee), a column on which the laws are carved, has survived intact.

The laws that made up the Code of Hammurabi set down different punishments for different crimes, depending on the social class of the people involved. For example, one law reads, "If a freeman has knocked out the tooth of another freeman, they shall knock out his tooth. . . . If he has knocked out a common person's tooth, he shall pay one-third mina of silver." Under this code, male slaves who left their masters and pretended to be free could have an ear cut off when they were caught.

Many of the laws protected the rights of women and children. For example, if a woman became ill, her husband was required to keep her in his house and care for her and their children, even if he took another wife.

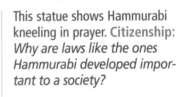

This statue shows Hammurabi kneeling in prayer. **Citizenship:** *Why are laws like the ones Hammurabi developed important to a society?*

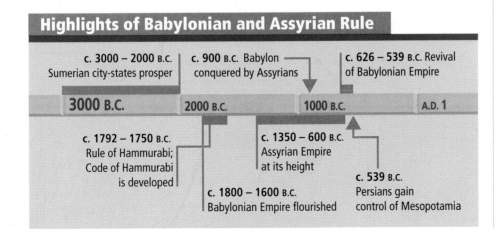

Highlights of Babylonian and Assyrian Rule

c. 3000 – 2000 B.C. Sumerian city-states prosper

c. 900 B.C. Babylon conquered by Assyrians

c. 626 – 539 B.C. Revival of Babylonian Empire

3000 B.C.   **2000 B.C.**   **1000 B.C.**   **A.D. 1**

c. 1792 – 1750 B.C. Rule of Hammurabi; Code of Hammurabi is developed

c. 1350 – 600 B.C. Assyrian Empire at its height

c. 539 B.C. Persians gain control of Mesopotamia

c. 1800 – 1600 B.C. Babylonian Empire flourished

This panel shows an Assyrian king and his soldiers escaping from their enemies across the Euphrates River in 878 B.C. Technology: *How are they able to breathe underwater? How can we breathe underwater today?*

Ask Yourself

Sumer was divided into a number of small city-states. Its political influence was weak, but Sumerian culture spread throughout the Fertile Crescent region.

Do you think Sumerian culture would have spread farther if Sumerian city-states had been stronger politically?

The Struggle for Empire

Focus *Why were the Assyrians so successful in building their empire?*

Like Sumer, the rulers of the Babylonian Empire struggled to keep control of other peoples. Around 1350 B.C., the Assyrians, who lived north of Babylon, broke free of Babylonian rule. Assyrians successfully conquered lands around them, including Babylon, by about 900 B.C.

The Assyrians built an **empire,** a state in which a single ruler controls several kingdoms or territories, through powerful military force and new methods of waging war. Assyrian soldiers traveled by horseback or by horse-drawn chariots and attacked their enemies with iron weapons. Assyrian archers filled the air with deadly, whistling arrows. Crowds of foot soldiers used iron-tipped battering rams to knock down city walls. Writings and art from the period suggest that Assyrians showed little mercy to people they conquered.

Mesopotamian Inventions

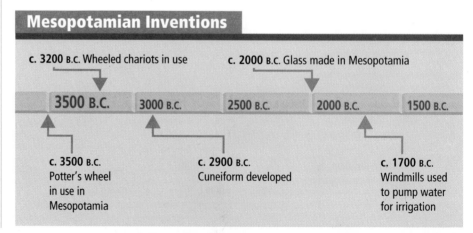

c. 3200 B.C. Wheeled chariots in use   c. 2000 B.C. Glass made in Mesopotamia

| 3500 B.C. | 3000 B.C. | 2500 B.C. | 2000 B.C. | 1500 B.C. |

c. 3500 B.C. Potter's wheel in use in Mesopotamia

c. 2900 B.C. Cuneiform developed

c. 1700 B.C. Windmills used to pump water for irrigation

The Assyrian rulers did not always destroy the societies they conquered. They also created laws and improved cities. Rulers kept in touch with their large empires, using a system of message-relay stations. Assyrian rule remained harsh, however. Around 650 B.C., some conquered cities rebelled, and invaders rushed into the empire. As the Assyrian Empire broke apart, the Babylonians recaptured power.

Under King Nebuchadnezzar II (nehb uh kuhd NEHZ ur), the Babylonians built another empire in the Fertile Crescent. Nebuchadnezzar also made Babylon into a city of great wealth and beauty.

The new Babylonian Empire didn't last long, however. Around 539 B.C., it was conquered by a group of people called Persians, who came from the area that is now Iran. The Persians would control the Fertile Crescent for more than a century.

Gifts from Mesopotamia

Focus *What are some of the major achievements of the Mesopotamian civilizations?*

The Mesopotamians made many discoveries and invented many things that are still used today. For example, cars, buses, and bikes all roll along on something that may have been invented by Sumerians: the wheel. The potter's wheel, a flat, round stone that turns while the potter shapes clay on it, was used in Mesopotamia as early as 3500 B.C. Wheeled chariots were in use by 3200 B.C. Ancient drawings also show wheeled carts used for hauling. These are our earliest records of a civilization on wheels.

Mesopotamians invented instruments to measure time by dividing an hour into 60 minutes and a minute into 60 seconds. They also invented a way to melt bronze and pour it into large molds. With these molds, they created statues of their gods.

Over the centuries, Mesopotamians studied the night sky. They kept records of the movement of constellations, or groups of stars. They also made calendars based on the movement of the sun and the moon.

Curious Facts

For 3,000 years, cuneiform was used by many different peoples. It was especially useful in political life. Assyrians and Babylonians both adopted the script from Sumerians. Cuneiform, which had hundreds of signs, was abandoned about 900 B.C. for another language, Aramaic, which had only 22 letters and was much easier to write.

Fact File

Mesopotamian Inventions
Soap
Musical notation (a system of writing down music so that any person who knows the system can play the notes)
Potter's wheel
Sailboat
A method for pouring melted bronze to make statues
Wheel

A Mesopotamian carving of Gilgamesh.

Literature

Writings from Mesopotamia range from short sayings of everyday advice to long poems about the adventures of gods and heroes. One saying reads:

> "He who has much silver may be happy;
> he who has much grain may be glad;
> but he who has nothing can sleep."

Do you agree with the idea that poor people have fewer things to worry about than rich people?

The most famous poem tells of a king named Gilgamesh. Gilgamesh fights a wild half-man, half-beast named Enkidu but ends up becoming friends with him. Gilgamesh and Enkidu share many adventures together. Before they can, Enkidu must be "tamed," he must learn many things: "Enkidu learned to sit on a chair and to wash his hands before eating. He learned how to care for animals, to make plants grow, and to build with mud and brick and reeds. He learned to play on a flute. He ate bread . . . His face shone, he rejoiced; he sang." Enkidu learned what the Mesopotamians had learned — the benefits of civilization.

Lesson Review

3000 B.C.	2000 B.C.	1000 B.C.

c. 2900 B.C.
Development of **cuneiform**

c. 1750 B.C.
Code of **Hammurabi** developed

1350 B.C.–600 B.C.
Assyrian empire comes to power

1 Key Vocabulary: Write a paragraph describing ancient Mesopotamia using the words city-state, cuneiform, class, polytheistic, ziggurat, and empire.

2 Focus: What was the culture of Mesopotamia like?

3 Focus: Why were the Assyrians so successful in building their empire?

4 Focus: What are some of the major achievements of the Mesopotamian civilizations?

5 Critical Thinking: Problem Solving If you had been Hammurabi, what laws would you write to govern your people?

6 Theme: Lasting Beginnings Compare how early civilizations measured time with how we measure time today.

7 Geography/Research Activity: Is soil in the ancient Fertile Crescent region still rich? Find the answer at your library and write a report explaining your research.

The Birth of Judaism

Main Idea Judaism is a system of religious beliefs that began in the Fertile Crescent and continues today all over the world.

Often we describe ourselves in terms of where we live or where we come from: "I'm Cambodian." "I'm from Phoenix." We use geography to help define who we are.

How would you feel if you were told:

> **"G**o forth from your native land and from your father's house to the land that I will show you.**"**

Such a move would require a lot of faith and courage.

According to the collection of religious writings called **The Bible**, God spoke these words to Abram, a herdsman living in the Fertile Crescent sometime around 2000 B.C. "Raise your eyes," Abram was told, "and look out from where you are . . . for I will give all the land that you see to you and your offspring forever." The Bible says God and Abram made an agreement, called a **covenant**. God promised to help Abram and his descendants if they in return would worship only God. Abram's name was then changed to Abraham, meaning "father of many nations."

Key Vocabulary

- The Bible
- covenant
- nomad
- monotheism
- Diaspora
- rabbi
- synagogue

Key Events

- **c. 2000 B.C.** Abraham's journey to Canaan
- **c. 1250 B.C.** Moses brings Israelites the Ten Commandments
- **c. 1200 B.C.** Israelites control Canaan

This scene from the Arch of Titus in Rome, Italy, shows Roman soldiers taking away Jewish religious treasures after Jerusalem was destroyed in A.D. 70. The men are carrying a menorah, or candelabra.

The Founding of Judaism

Focus *What is Judaism, and how did it start?*

Sometime after 2000 B.C., Abraham left his homeland and went into Canaan (KAY nuhn), the land in the western part of the Fertile Crescent that God had promised him. He and his family became **nomads**, herders who moved to find good grazing land. Wandering people who hoped to settle down in an area were not always welcomed by those already there.

According to the Bible, Abraham had a son, Isaac, and a grandson, Jacob (also called Israel). Jacob had 12 sons of his own. Each great-grandson of Abraham became the founder of one of the 12 tribes known as the Israelites. People who can trace their roots back to the Israelites are called Jews. Their religion is called Judaism.

During Jacob's lifetime, widespread crop failure in Canaan forced him to move his people to Egypt. They lived there for centuries, their numbers growing. Then the Egyptians enslaved the Israelites, forcing them to build cities and temples. According to the Bible, a leader named Moses led the Israelites out of Egypt — and out of slavery — with God's help. Their journey from Egypt was called the Exodus.

For 40 years Moses and the Israelites wandered in the wilderness, moving back toward the homeland in Canaan that God had promised Abraham. Early in the journey they came to Mount Sinai, where, the Bible says, God gave Moses the Ten Commandments. These were a set of laws that explained how to worship and honor God and how to behave toward other people. The first commandment is still central to Jewish belief:

The Dead Sea Scrolls were found in clay jars deep inside caves in the Middle East. They are religious writings of an early Jewish group. Below is a small piece of one of the scrolls. History: *Why might these scrolls be important to historians and religious scholars?*

"I *the Lord am your God. You shall have no other gods besides Me.* **"**

The commandment emphasizes **monotheism**, the worship of one all-powerful god. Other commandments basic to Judaism include:

"Honor your father and your mother," "You shall not steal," "You shall not murder." **"**

As the Israelites moved toward their homeland, Moses had a difficult time holding the group together. Temptations came from other groups who had established civilizations and who worshipped many other gods. However, the Israelites remained a people who worshipped one god. Moses himself died before the Israelites reached Canaan.

The first five books of the Bible record the history of the Jewish people up to the death of Moses. These books, which include the additional laws that God gave the Jews later, together are called the

The page *(above)* is from a Jewish book that describes the Exodus in pictures and Hebrew writing. The picture shows Egyptians drowning in the Red Sea. According to the Bible, the Israelites escaped from the Egyptians when God parted the waters of the sea, allowing them to cross. Once they were on the other side, the sea swept over the Egyptians. Below is a map of some of the possible routes of the Exodus. **History:** *Why might scholars disagree on which route the Israelites followed?*

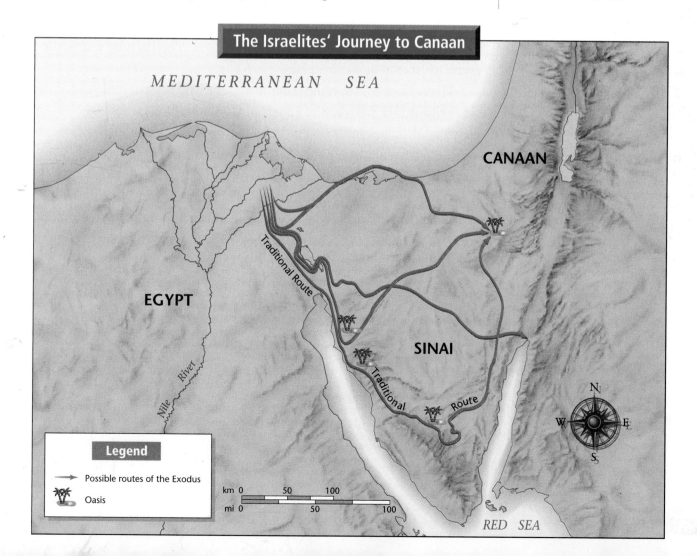

The Israelites' Journey to Canaan

MEDITERRANEAN SEA

CANAAN

EGYPT

Traditional Route

SINAI

Traditional Route

Nile River

Legend

→ Possible routes of the Exodus

🌴 Oasis

km 0   50   100
mi 0   50   100

N W E S

RED SEA

Torah, a word meaning "instruction." The Torah remains today the center of Jewish beliefs.

A Homeland Gained and Lost

Focus *What kind of homeland did the Israelites create in Canaan?*

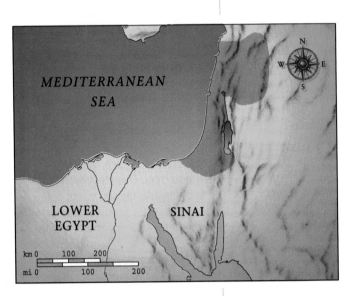

The land of Canaan was located in the western part of the Fertile Crescent. **Map Skill:** *Why might Canaan have been a desirable place for Abraham and his family to settle?*

Around 1200 B.C., the tribes of Israel fought their way back into Canaan and conquered city after city. Early Israelite leaders, called judges, helped create governments based on the teachings of the Torah. (You can read about Deborah, one of these judges, on the next page.) Threats to their land by invaders with large armies finally led the Israelites to choose one strong leader. Their first king was Saul. Later came King David, and then his son, Solomon.

King David united the tribes of Israel. A wise commander, he was also a musician and a poet. His songs are found in the Book of Psalms in the Bible. His son, King Solomon, built the first Temple in Jerusalem. Here, finally, was a permanent place to house the Ark of the Covenant, the small chest containing the Ten Commandments given to Moses at Mount Sinai. The Temple became the center of Israelite life and worship.

When King Solomon died, the 12 Israelite tribes separated. Ten of the tribes formed the kingdom of Israel, and the other two formed the kingdom of Judah. In 722 B.C., the huge Assyrian army, still known for its fierce, effective fighting, swept in from the desert and destroyed the kingdom of Israel. The tribes that had formed the northern kingdom of Israel were broken apart and scattered. Judah remained.

Judah was conquered by the Babylonians in 597 B.C. Eleven years later, Nebuchadnezzar, who restored Babylon to glory, burned the Temple in Jerusalem. Many citizens were killed, and about a quarter of the

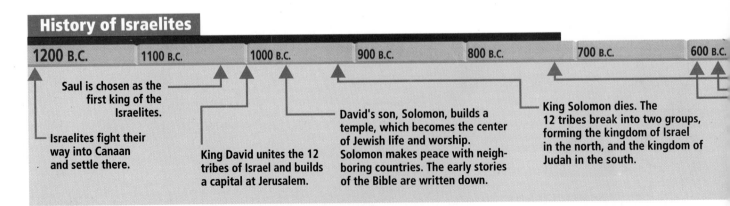

History of Israelites

| 1200 B.C. | 1100 B.C. | 1000 B.C. | 900 B.C. | 800 B.C. | 700 B.C. | 600 B.C. |

Saul is chosen as the first king of the Israelites.

Israelites fight their way into Canaan and settle there.

King David unites the 12 tribes of Israel and builds a capital at Jerusalem.

David's son, Solomon, builds a temple, which becomes the center of Jewish life and worship. Solomon makes peace with neighboring countries. The early stories of the Bible are written down.

King Solomon dies. The 12 tribes break into two groups, forming the kingdom of Israel in the north, and the kingdom of Judah in the south.

population was taken to Babylon as slaves. So began what is referred to today as the **Diaspora** (dy AS pehr eh), the scattering of Jews around the world.

Now came a great test of the Jewish faith. How could Jews keep their religion alive when they had no temple for worship? How could they maintain their identity when they had no country?

Jews saved their faith by carrying it within themselves. They kept their tradition of study and worship. Religious scholars, called **rabbis**, took leadership roles. Over the ages, rabbis wrote volumes of interpretations about the words of the Bible and collected their interpretations in a book called the Talmud. Wherever Jews settled, they built places for worship and study, called **synagogues**. In this way, Judaism lives within every Jew, everywhere.

The Jews were able to rebuild the Temple in Jerusalem around 515 B.C. But it was destroyed again, this time by the Romans, in A.D. 70. *(You can read about the Romans in Chapter 9.)*

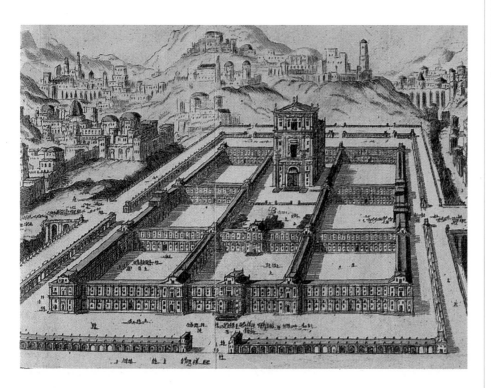

The Temple in Jerusalem was rebuilt about 515 B.C. This etching was made over 2,000 years later, in A.D. 1700, by an artist named Petrus Cunus.

500 B.C.	400 B.C.	300 B.C.	200 B.C.	100 B.C.	B.C.	A.D.	A.D. 70

Assyrians conquer the kingdom of Israel. The 10 tribes of Israel are forced to move to other lands. They mix with other cultures and disappear. They are now referred to as the 10 lost tribes.

Judah is captured by the Babylonians. Many of its leading citizens are taken to Babylon.

Babylonians conquer Jerusalem. Nebuchadnezzar burns down the temple in Jerusalem.

The Persians conquer Babylon, and the Jews are allowed to return to Judah. The Jews build a second Temple in 515 B.C.

The Romans destroy the second Temple.

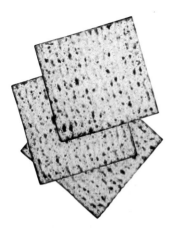

Matzo is a brittle, flat cracker. It is eaten by Jews at Passover as a symbol of the unleavened bread Jews ate during the Exodus.

Modern Judaism

Focus *How do modern Jews hold on to their traditions?*

Not only have Jews kept their faith alive, they have made it stronger. Judaism endured and grew for almost 1900 years, during which time the faithful had no temple and no homeland. In 1948, the modern nation of Israel was created in part of the area that had once been the ancient kingdoms of Israel and Judah. Today, more than 18 million Jews of all nationalities live throughout the world. They share many basic beliefs, even though they might practice their religion in different ways.

Like most religious groups, Jews observe holy days — holidays — throughout the year. Rosh Ha-Shanah is the Jewish New Year, which falls in the autumn. Yom Kippur is 10 days later. It is a day of fasting and prayer, when Jews ask for forgiveness of their sins.

The Seder Plate

Each type of food on the Seder plate is a symbol to help Jews remember the meaning of the Exodus. One special plate is set up for the table's center.

Green vegetable: Often parsley or celery, the green vegetable symbolizes spring and rebirth. It is dipped in salt water, which symbolizes the tears the Israelites shed under slavery.

Roasted egg: The spherical shape of the egg, with no beginning or end, symbolizes eternal life and the cycles of nature.

Haroset: A mixture of chopped nuts, apples, wine, and spice, haroset symbolizes the mortar that the slaves made to hold together the bricks.

Bitter herbs: Bitter herbs, sometimes freshly ground horseradish or romaine lettuce, stand for the bitterness of slavery.

Lamb bone: The roasted lamb bone is a symbol of the lamb sacrificed as the Israelites were preparing to leave Egypt.

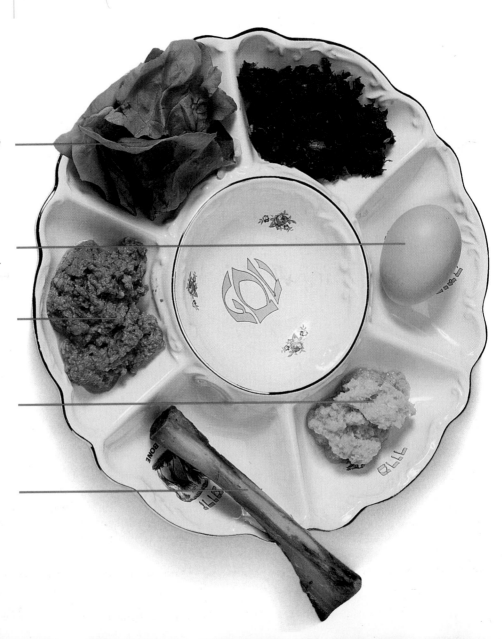

A favorite holiday is Passover, when Jewish families hold a special religious feast called a Seder. In Hebrew, Passover is also called "the season of our liberation." The holiday is a time for Jews to remember how their ancestors were freed from slavery. It is a reminder that no matter how difficult life can seem, there is always hope.

During the Seder, families and friends read and discuss a book called the Haggadah (hah gah DAH), a Hebrew word that means "telling." The book tells the story of Moses and the Exodus. It helps Jews of all ages understand why the journey to freedom is still important today. Part of it says: "In every generation, each person should feel as though she or he were saved from Egypt. . . . For the Holy One saved not only our ancestors; He saved us with them."

As the Exodus story is told, people at the Seder eat special foods. Each dish helps them remember something about the Exodus. The picture on the previous page shows what the various foods symbolize.

Children have a special part in the dinner. Near the beginning of the meal, the youngest child at the table asks the traditional "Four Questions." He or she says: "Why do we eat unleavened bread on this night? Why do we eat bitter herbs on Passover? Why do we dip green vegetables into salt water and bitter herbs into haroset? Why do we sit in a reclining position at the Seder?"

The reading of the Haggadah answers all these questions. It links today's families with the world of thousands of years ago, preserving important Jewish traditions.

Then & Now

The Wailing Wall in the city of Jerusalem is an ancient stone structure. Also called the Western Wall, it is all that remains of the Second Temple destroyed by the Romans in A.D. 70. Today, Jews from around the world travel to Jerusalem to visit and pray there.

Lesson Review

2000 B.C.	1500 B.C.	1000 B.C.
c. 2000 B.C. Abraham's journey to Canaan	**c. 1250 B.C.** Moses brings Israelites the Ten Commandments	**c. 1200 B.C.** Israelites control Canaan

1 **Key Vocabulary:** Write a paragraph about Judaism using The Bible, covenant, monotheism, Diaspora, rabbi, and synagogue.

2 **Focus:** What is Judaism, and how did it start?

3 **Focus:** What kind of homeland did the Israelites create in Canaan?

4 **Focus:** How do modern Jews hold on to their traditions?

5 **Critical Thinking: Interpret** What are the advantages and disadvantages of using a religious text as a source to learn about history?

6 **Theme: Lasting Beginnings** How did Judaism change after the destruction of the Temple in Jerusalem?

7 **Geography/Art Activity:** Make a map that shows some of the important places in the history of Judaism.

Biography

DAVID

by Barbara Cohen

In ancient times, there were many kings and rulers in the area now called the Middle East. Among them all, David, King of Israel, is one of the most important. He was a great leader, a brilliant general, and a talented musician and poet. Most of the Psalms in the Bible were written by David, including the 23rd Psalm, which begins, "The Lord is my shepherd; I shall not want."

But David was not born into a royal family. He spent his boyhood years tending his father's flocks in the rugged hill country. A prophet had once told David that God had chosen him to do important things, but still, David kept on working as a shepherd. Then, in a single day in the year 1020 B.C., David's life changed forever.

In the spring of David's twentieth year, war broke out between the Israelites and the Philistines. That was no surprise; it happened every spring. Only this year the troops faced each other on hills lining the valley of Elah in the territory of Judah. And this year, the Philistines had a new champion, a man called Goliath, a giant from the city of Gath. He was nearly nine feet tall. He wore a bronze helmet and a scaly bronze breastplate weighing more than one hundred twenty-five pounds. His legs too were covered with bronze armor, and a javelin was slung across his shoulders. The shaft of his spear was as thick as the trunk of a small tree, and its iron head alone weighed at least fifteen pounds!

Every day Goliath marched up and down the valley of Elah, calling out to the Israelites camped on the hillside. "We don't need an enormous battle between our two armies," he shouted. "Choose just one man, and let him come down to fight me. If he kills me, we'll be your slaves. But if I kill him, you'll be our slaves. I challenge Israel. Get me a real man, and we'll fight it out." When King Saul and his soldiers heard these words, they shook with terror. Not one of them dared face a giant nine feet tall.

Goliath repeated his challenge every day for forty days. Among those who heard it every day for forty days were David's brothers Eliab, Abinadab, and Shammah, who had enlisted in Saul's army. In ancient times, battles weren't fought just for the sake of expanding or defending national territory. They had a more direct economic function: the victors seized anything valuable from the bodies of the dead and from the towns they conquered. It was in hope of such riches that men joined armies. A successful warrior could become a wealthy man.

Furthermore, the central command didn't supply soldiers with food. They lived off the land. Saul's army had been at Elah so long, it had probably exhausted local supplies. Back in Bethlehem, Jesse and Nazbit were beginning to worry about their sons.

"Listen, David," Jesse ordered, "take some food up to your brothers in the army. When you come back, tell us how they're doing."

Nazbit packed dried grain and loaves of bread for her sons. She sent

ten cheeses along as a gift for their captain. Early the next morning David left a servant in charge of the flock, took the food, and set out for the valley of Elah. At the camp David rushed to greet his brothers. They'd barely said two words to one another when Goliath came out into the valley. With his own eyes and ears David saw and heard the giant's sneering challenge. He saw the blood drain from the soldiers' faces. He turned to one of them and said, "Is there a reward for the man who kills that Philistine? Someone has to do it, or the whole world will call Israel coward."

"Oh, they say the king will make him a rich man," the soldier answered. "They say he'll marry the king's daughter, and his family won't have to pay taxes anymore."

Eliab seized David by the shoulder and shook him. "What did you come down here for, David?" he scolded. "What's going on in that tricky little head of yours? Your business is sheep, not war."

"I was only asking," David said. "Where's the harm in that?" He asked the same question of many others, and from all he received the same answer. Finally, even Saul heard about the young man and his questions, and ordered that he be brought before him.

David knelt before the king. "My lord king, don't be afraid," he said. "I'll fight the Philistine."

Saul couldn't help smiling at such nerve. "You can't fight him," he said. "You're very young, and he's been a warrior for years."

"I watch my father's flocks," David replied. "When a lion or bear attacks the sheep, I kill it. God, who saved me from wild animals, will save me from the Philistine. Goliath will end up just as dead as those lions and bears."

Saul figured he had little to lose. "Well," he said, "do as you please. May the Lord be with you."

The king ordered David dressed in a helmet, breastplate, and sword. After clanking around for a few minutes, David complained, "I can't move in these things. I'm not used to them." He took off the armor and the sword. Carrying only his stick and his sling, he climbed down to the valley. The streambed, or wadi, was full of water from the winter rains. David knelt down at the edge and carefully selected five smooth stones, put them in his shepherd's bag, and walked out into the open field.

Meanwhile, preceded by his shield bearer, Goliath marched toward David. When he came close, he saw that David was only a boy. "Am I a dog," he shouted, "that you attack me with a stick? Come here, pretty little boy, and I'll give your flesh to vultures and lions."

David was neither surprised nor frightened by Goliath's words. In an effort to break their enemy's spirit, warriors taunted one another, flaunting their own strength. David had his reply well prepared. He was convinced that God was with him. He was convinced he was taking the first step toward the goal God had in mind for him.

"You come against me with spear and javelin," David cried, "But I come against you in the name of the Lord God of Israel. I'll cut off your head and feed *it* to vultures and lions. The Lord can give victory to a boy who carries neither spear nor sword. The battle is His, and He will deliver you into our hands."

David reached into his bag, drew out a stone, and slung it. His aim was true; the stone struck Goliath in the forehead and he fell to the ground.

Meet the Author

Barbara Cohen wrote more than 35 books for children and young people. Her special interest in David grew out of her own Jewish heritage. David was the final book of her twenty-year writing career. She died in 1992.

Additional Books to Read

Rain Player, by David Wisniewski. Read about a Mayan warrior and a legendary sports contest.

Sundiata: Lion King of Mali, by David Wisniewski. Discover the life and exploits of an ancient African king.

Response Activities

1. **Predict** What do you think will happen to David after he has killed Goliath?

2. **Narrative: Write a Story** Try writing the story of David and Goliath from the point of view of a member of the Philistine army. What do you think about David's chances? How does Goliath's defeat affect you?

3. **History: Research** The text says people in ancient times sometimes fought for different reasons than they do today. Look up as much information as you can about warfare in early times, then prepare a brief report on why the Israelites and Philistines might have gone to war every spring.

CHAPTER 3 Chapter Review

Chapter Review Timeline

| 30,000 B.C. | 24,000 B.C. | 18,000 B.C. | 12,000 B.C. | 6,000 B.C. | B.C. | A.D. |

1350 – 600 Assyrian Empire

After c. 1200 Israelites control Canaan

c. 28,000 Ardèche cave paintings in France

c. 2000 – 1550 Abraham's journey to Canaan

1750 Code of Hammurabi

Summarizing the Main Idea

1 Copy the chart below and fill in the missing information to compare the civilizations of ancient Mesopotamia and ancient Israel.

	Mesopotamia	Israel
Religion	*polytheism*	*monotheism*
Government		
Law		
Literature		

Vocabulary

2 Create a crossword puzzle using at least eight of the following terms. First create the answers to the puzzle by hooking the words together. Then write a list of clues defining the terms you use.

prehistoric (p. 60)
hunter-gatherer (p. 61)
domestication (p. 62)
irrigation (p. 67)

surplus (p. 68)
specialization of labor (p. 68)
civilization (p. 68)
cuneiform (p. 70)

ziggurat (p .71)
covenant (p. 77)
monotheism (p. 79)
synagogue (p. 81)

Reviewing the Facts

3 How do scientists learn about prehistoric people? Give some examples.

4 How did agriculture and domestication of animals change the lives of hunter-gatherers?

5 What is specialization of labor, and how did it lead to the development of civilizations?

6 Describe the origin of cuneiform writing.

7 What was the Code of Hammurabi?

8 How did Judaism begin?

9 What are the Bible, the Torah, the Talmud, and the Haggadah?

Timelines

10 Look at the timeline on page 73. How much time went by between the development of the earliest Sumerian city-state and the start of the Assyrian Empire?

11 Find the timeline on pages 80 and 81. How many years were there between the building of the first Temple in Jerusalem by Solomon and the destruction of the second Temple by the Romans?

Geography Skills

12 Look at the map of Mesopotamian cities and empires on page 71. Do you think there was much travel or trade between the independent cities? Why or why not?

13 Suppose you were part of Abraham's household. Describe your journey to Canaan, and what you found there.

Critical Thinking

14 **Interpret** Since there are no written records, how do scientists know what the prehistoric artifacts they find were used for?

15 **Cause and Effect** Why might hunter-gatherers have moved on?

16 **Generalize** Look at the list of Mesopotamian inventions on page 75. How would life today be different if Mesopotamian civilization had never existed, and these inventions never invented?

Writing: Citizenship and Cultures

17 **Citizenship** The Sumerians developed writing, which was then used for everything from record keeping to writing stories. Do you think it is important for everyone in a culture to learn how to read and write? Write a paragraph explaining why this might or might not be important.

18 **Cultures.** Reread the letter from the father to his son on p. 69. Write a letter in response, explaining the son's side of the story.

Activities

Culture/Art
Animals are the main subject of prehistoric cave paintings. Look at some paintings and carvings of animals in cultures today in which animals are important. How are the animals similar to prehistoric art? How are they different?

History/Research
Ancient people mentioned in the chapter included King Hammurabi, Nebuchadnezzar II, Abraham, Moses, Deborah, King Solomon, and others. Choose one and research and write a report about his or her life.

Internet Option

Check the **Internet Social Studies Center** for ideas on how to extend your theme project beyond your classroom.

📁 THEME PROJECT CHECK-IN

To begin your theme project, use the information in this chapter about early civilizations. Think about these questions as you create your civilization:
• What geographic features determined where this civilization developed?
• What were some of this civilization's early beliefs and traditions?
• What natural resources were available to this civilization? How did they use them?
• What early technologies did they develop? How did these affect the civilization?

Chapter Preview: *People, Places, and Events*

3500 B.C.	2800 B.C.	2100 B.C.

Nile River

The Nile River creates a long strip of green, fertile land in the desert.
Lesson 1, Page 92

Life Along the Nile

Can you tell what this person is doing? *Lesson 1, Page 93*

Egyptian Life

Egypt had a well-developed civilization and left many records of daily life. *Lesson 2, Page 96*

The Geography of the Nile

Main Idea Conditions along the Nile River were ideal for the development of the ancient Egyptian and Nubian civilizations.

Key Vocabulary
delta
cataract

Key Places
Nile River
Egypt
Nubia

Two Egyptian hunters stand motionless in their boat. Before them stretches the vast expanse of the Nile, the world's longest river. A source of many things, the Nile provides food, water, and the reeds used to make paper, furniture, and building materials. It is also a watery highway that transports people and goods.

The two hunters wait in their boat. From the nearby reeds, birds rustle and call. Fish dart through the sparkling waters. Yesterday, the hunters easily caught some of both. Today, they have their sights set on something far more dangerous.

At last, they spot him! The enormous hippopotamus surfaces suddenly, threatening to upset the fragile craft with his thrashing. Their spears at the ready, the hunters launch their attack. The battle is on!

◄ This golden mask is from the tomb of Tutankhamun, the boy pharaoh.

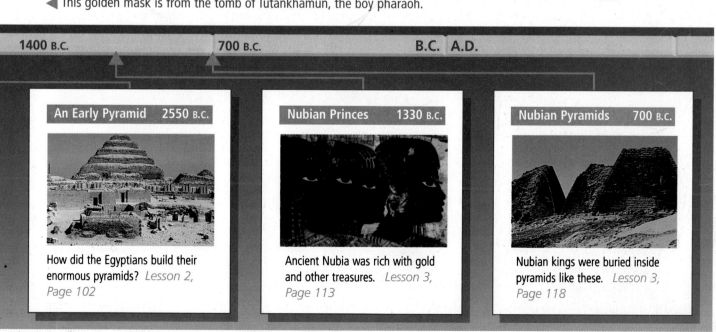

1400 B.C.　　　700 B.C.　　　B.C. A.D.

An Early Pyramid 2550 B.C.

How did the Egyptians build their enormous pyramids? *Lesson 2, Page 102*

Nubian Princes 1330 B.C.

Ancient Nubia was rich with gold and other treasures. *Lesson 3, Page 113*

Nubian Pyramids 700 B.C.

Nubian kings were buried inside pyramids like these. *Lesson 3, Page 118*

A River Through the Desert

Focus *What are the special features of the Nile Valley?*

This scene could have happened 5,000 years ago in ancient Egypt or Nubia, which were located in northeastern Africa. This area was mostly dry and forbidding, with one important exception. Flowing through the arid desert valleys was the mighty Nile River.

The Nile flowed down from its source in the mountains of central Africa, running north to its mouth at the Mediterranean Sea. Every year in July at the start of central Africa's rainy season, the river swelled. As its water level rose, the Nile flooded, depositing a rich layer of silt on the surrounding land.

In September, the rainy season ended, and a wide ribbon of fertile soil was left on each side of the river. This soil was then plowed and planted. Harvests were plentiful in the Nile Valley. Watered by the river, vegetables, fruits, and grains grew well.

Because of the desert to the east and west, travel in Egypt went mainly downstream with the Nile's current (north) and upstream against the current (south). Winds in this area generally blow from north to south. If an Egyptian needed to travel north from Thebes to Giza, his boat would be carried by the current, moved faster by the work of rowers. Coming south to get home, he would put up the sails on his boat. Wind would push the boat upstream, against the current, back to Thebes. You can trace the traveler's route using the map to the left.

The city of Thebes was in a region known as Upper Egypt, farther south on the river. Giza was in Lower Egypt. At the mouth of the river, at sea level, was the Nile's **delta**, a triangular area of fertile land formed by silt that the river deposited.

The soil of the Nile River Valley was rich and fertile. The land away from the Nile was a vast desert. **Map Skill:** *What geographic features kept visitors and invading armies out of Egypt?*

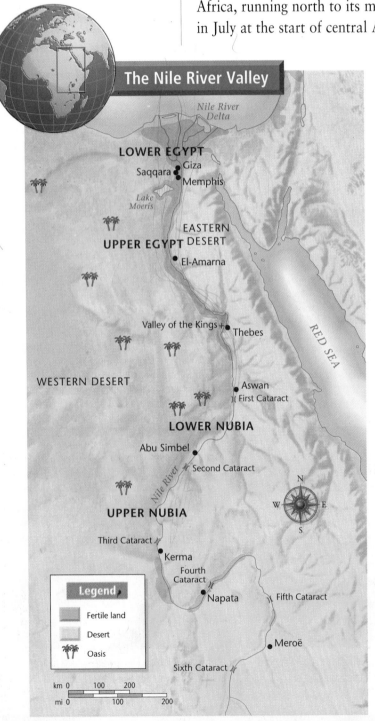

The Nile River Valley

Nile River Delta

LOWER EGYPT

Giza
Saqqara
Memphis

Lake Moeris

EASTERN DESERT

UPPER EGYPT

El-Amarna

Valley of the Kings
Thebes

RED SEA

WESTERN DESERT

Aswan
First Cataract

LOWER NUBIA

Abu Simbel

Second Cataract

UPPER NUBIA

Third Cataract

Kerma

Fourth Cataract

Napata

Fifth Cataract

Meroë

Sixth Cataract

Legend

Fertile land

Desert

Oasis

km 0   100   200
mi 0   100   200

Scenes from Life Along the Nile

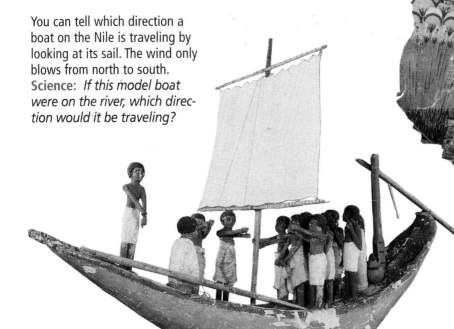

You can tell which direction a boat on the Nile is traveling by looking at its sail. The wind only blows from north to south. **Science:** *If this model boat were on the river, which direction would it be traveling?*

Egyptians hunted birds in the reeds along the river's edge. **Science:** *How many different animals can you identify? If you wanted to make more detailed identifications, how would you go about doing the research?*

Along the Nile River to the south of Egypt lay Nubia. It, too, was divided into an upper and lower region. South of Aswan, the Nile had a series of six dramatic turns and rocky rapids called **cataracts** which were extremely difficult to navigate. The first of these cataracts served as a natural border between Egypt and Nubia. The Nile did not flood in Nubia as much as it did in Egypt. As a result, Nubia's land was far less fertile than Egypt's.

Lesson Review: Geography

1. **Key Vocabulary:** Write a description of the Nile Valley, using the following terms: **delta, cataract.**

2. **Focus:** What are the special features of the Nile Valley?

3. **Critical Thinking: Interpret** As far as historians know, the language of the ancient Egyptians contains no word for "bridge." What does this tell us about life along the Nile in ancient Egypt?

4. **Theme: Lasting Beginnings** How did the geographic features of the Nile Valley encourage settlement in Egypt and Nubia?

5. **Geography/Art Activity:** Make a map for a river traveler in ancient Egypt and Nubia. Outline the northern coast of Africa and the path of the Nile River. Mark the locations of towns and cities the traveler might wish to visit.

Ancient Egypt

Main Idea The Egyptians developed a complex civilization that lasted for many centuries.

Key Vocabulary

nomad

pharaoh

dynasty

papyrus

hieroglyphics

afterlife

Key Events

3100 B.C. Egypt united under one king

2650 B.C. First pyramid built in Egypt

The palace of the Egyptian king was alive with the sounds of the many people who had been called to serve the royal family. Scribes arrived to record faithfully their accounts of daily life in the court. Sculptors were summoned to produce works of art from ivory, wood, bronze, gold, and turquoise. Cooks and bakers worked hard preparing royal meals. Long after these people came and went, the palace remained full of officials busily attending to the needs of their king.

Royal life was far from being all work and no play. It also included sports and entertainment. The king enjoyed hunting, fishing, and riding in chariots, two-wheeled vehicles pulled by horses. He provided an enthusiastic audience for wrestling matches between his soldiers and Egyptian slaves.

In this scene, the queen offers the king a small jar of oil or perfume. **Arts:** *How can you tell that these people are royalty?*

Life Along the Nile

Focus *What was life like for Egyptian rulers and common citizens?*

Egypt was not always organized into well-run cities ruled by kings and officials. Around 7000 B.C., **nomads,** people who moved from place to place in search of food and water, lived in small camps in the Nile Valley. They hunted animals, fished, and gathered the plentiful wild fruits and vegetables of the area.

Later, the Egyptians began farming and domesticating animals. These small farms grew into village communities that eventually became part of two separate kingdoms called Upper and Lower Egypt. Legend says that in about 3100 B.C., more than 5,000 years ago, the two regions were united by King Menes (MEE neez), the ruler of Upper Egypt. This was the first time that a national government was formed anywhere.

Egyptians believed that their kings received power directly from the gods. In this statue, the king is receiving power from the hawk god, Horus, a sky god who had the power to overcome evil.

Ancient Egyptian Government

Throughout most of its history, Egypt was ruled by kings. These kings were thought to be representatives of the gods. Using the king's name directly was considered disrespectful, so people referred to him by his residence. They called him the "per aa," or **pharaoh,** which meant "great house" in Egyptian. (You can read about famous pharaohs in the article that begins on page 106.)

The union of Upper and Lower Egypt under one pharaoh marked the start of the kingdom's first dynasty. A **dynasty** is a group of rulers over several generations descending from the same family. Thirty-one different dynasties ruled Egypt for nearly 3,000 years. Historians divide the dynasties into periods, which are listed in the Fact File below. During periods called the Old Kingdom, the Middle Kingdom, and the New Kingdom, Egypt prospered. The First and Second Intermediate periods were times of unrest.

The pharaohs controlled every aspect of life in Egypt. The pharaoh was considered the kingdom's most important high priest. He was also a lawmaker and a leader in battle. Officials called viziers (vih ZIHRS) were selected by the pharaoh to act as judges, mayors, and supervisors of tax collectors. Next highest in rank was the chief of the treasury, who managed the tax money.

Fact File:

Dynasty	Period	Approximate Date {B.C.}
I–II	Archaic	3100–2686
III–VI	Old Kingdom	2686–2181
VII–XI	First Intermediate	2181–1991
XII–XIII	Middle Kingdom	1991–1786
XIV–XVII	Second Intermediate	1786–1567
XVIII–XX	New Kingdom	1567–1085
XXI–XXVI	Late (including Kushite)	1085–525
XXVII	First Persian Period	525–404
XXVIII–XXX	Late Period	404–343
XXXI	Second Persian Period	343–332
Greek	Ptolemaic	332–30
	Romans conquer Egypt	30

In ancient times, Egyptians had many dental problems, the most common of which was worn-down teeth. Sand and grit got into the flour they used to make bread, possibly because it was ground outside. When people chewed the baked bread, the sand and grit wore away their teeth.

Egyptians used cattle and oxen to help them farm. This man is plowing his field. A farmer's wealth was measured largely by the number of cattle he owned. *Arts: Why would a large number of cattle indicate wealth?*

The death of a pharaoh was mourned by his people. It was usually his son (or, occasionally, his daughter) who took over as the next ruler. In this way, the royal family continued.

Daily Life of Citizens

It is morning, and an Egyptian nobleman is already out the door of his home, thinking ahead to the plans for the temple he is designing. As he leaves, he passes the family's servants entering the home and heading back to the kitchen, ready to be assigned their daily tasks.

Heading off to the temple classroom for his first day of school, the nobleman's four-year-old son is ready to learn to read and write as he begins his training as a scribe. His parents are proud — after all, this is one of the most respected occupations in Egypt. If he excels at his lessons, the boy can go on to become an official scribe for the court. He could even become the pharaoh's vizier one day. His older sister remains at home where she will learn cooking, sewing, and other household skills.

The children's mother has no time to waste. There is grain to be ground and bread to be baked. She will oversee the preparation of this evening's meal. The family will dine on beef, a variety of vegetables, such as onions, leeks, beans, chickpeas, radishes, spinach, and carrots, and fruits, such as figs, grapes, dates, and pomegranates.

After the servants have served and cleared dinner, the family may spend the evening at home. The parents can relax over a board game called senet, and the children may play leapfrog or outdoor games. Or the family might decide to take to the streets and enjoy the music of harp players. Or they could go for a swim in the Nile before the sun sets on their busy day.

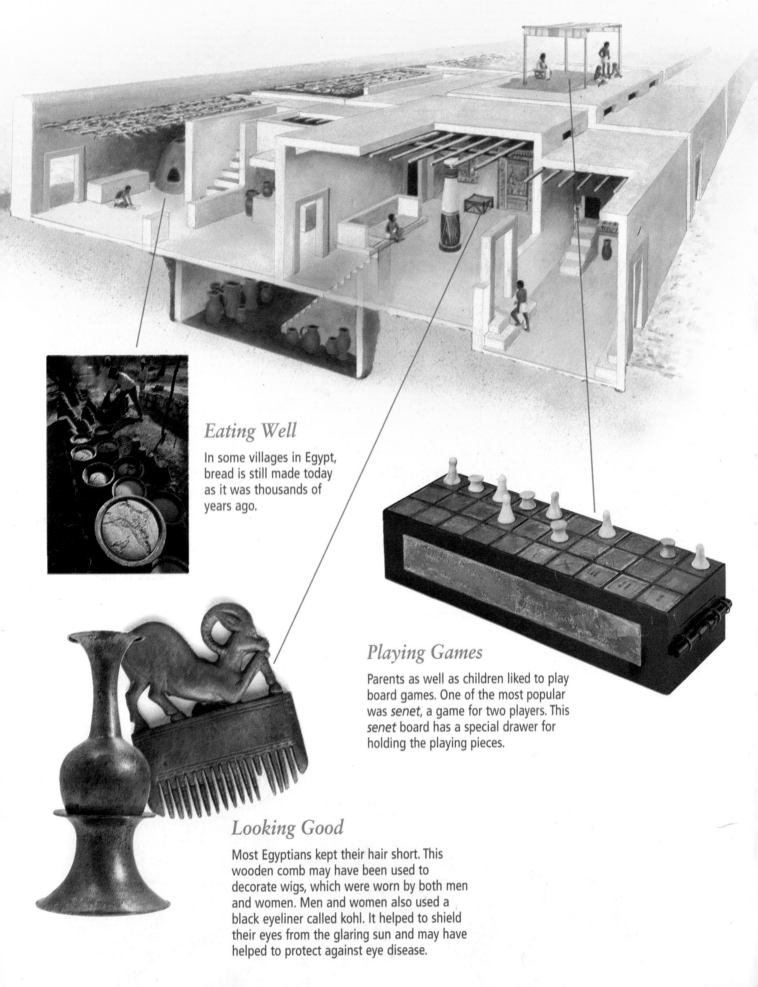

Eating Well

In some villages in Egypt, bread is still made today as it was thousands of years ago.

Playing Games

Parents as well as children liked to play board games. One of the most popular was *senet*, a game for two players. This *senet* board has a special drawer for holding the playing pieces.

Looking Good

Most Egyptians kept their hair short. This wooden comb may have been used to decorate wigs, which were worn by both men and women. Men and women also used a black eyeliner called kohl. It helped to shield their eyes from the glaring sun and may have helped to protect against eye disease.

Families like this one belonged to Egypt's upper class. The kingdom also had a middle and lower class. Merchants, manufacturers, and craftspeople made up the middle class. Poor farmers and unskilled workers were part of the lower class. In the bottom-most class were prisoners who had been enslaved at war and brought to Egypt.

Cultural Contributions

Focus *What were some of the key achievements of ancient Egypt?*

Pyramids, the 365-day calendar, reed boats. What do these things have in common? They were just a few of the Egyptians' many accomplishments. The Egyptians also taught themselves how to set broken bones. They invented sails and established many libraries to house scrolls that covered a wide range of subjects.

From River Plants to Paper

Before they had paper, people in ancient times usually wrote on clay tablets or stone chips. While they served the purpose, these tablets and stones were heavy and hard to carry around. In about 3000 B.C., the Egyptians came up with the idea of making a kind of paper from the papyrus (puh PY ruhs) plants that grew along the Nile. Papyrus sheets were used for writing books in the form of scrolls, letters, and legal documents. The word "paper" comes from the word "papyrus."

Writing with Pictures

For the Egyptians, writing was important. There were accounts to be kept, directions to write, and marks of ownership to be noted. In addition, scribes recorded events from everyday life and wrote religious texts. Many professions required a knowledge of reading and writing. If you wanted to amount to anything in Egyptian society, the first thing you had to do was acquire these skills.

How Papyrus Sheets Were Made

The papyrus stalks were cut, peeled, and sliced.

The thin slices were laid closely side by side. Another layer was placed on top at a right angle to the first layer. The strips were pounded as they dried.

To make long rolls, sheets could be glued together side by side.

Hieroglyphic writing

Hieratic script

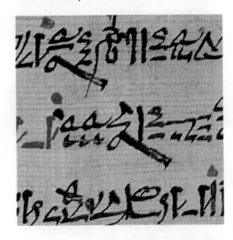

The Egyptian method of writing, hieroglyphics (hy ehr eh GLIF iks), was based on hieroglyphs, or pictures that stood for sounds, objects, or ideas. For example, a hieroglyph might stand for the sound of the letter "T." Or it might be a picture of writing tools, which meant "scribe." Anyone who wanted to read and write had to master more than 700 signs in the hieroglyphic system. These pictures were time consuming to draw and were mainly used for carvings on monuments and in tombs. For everyday writing, a simpler cursive form called *hieratic script* (hy uh RAT ihk) was used. It was written with a reed pen on sheets of papyrus.

Egyptians used hieroglyphics for almost 4,000 years. Centuries later, people had forgotten how to read hieroglyphics. Then, in 1799, an important link with the past was found near the town of Rosetta in Egypt. It was a partially broken stone carved with a message written in three different languages. One of those languages was ancient Greek,

Jean François Champollion
(1790–1832)

· **Tell Me More** ·

How Did Champollion Break the Code?

Jean François Champollion was a nine-year-old in France the year the Rosetta Stone was found. As an adult, he joined the ranks of those trying to crack the Egyptian hieroglyphic code. Champollion began working with cartouches (kar TOOSH ez), which are hieroglyphs enclosed in an oval representing the names of Egyptian kings and queens. Other historians had already determined which cartouches stood for the names Ptolemy (TAHL uh mee) and Cleopatra. Champollion was able to figure out which hieroglyphs in Ptolemy's cartouche stood for which sounds. The lion symbol, for example, stood for an "L" sound. Comparing Ptolemy's cartouche with Cleopatra's, he found the same symbols for the same sounds. For example, the lion hieroglyph is repeated in Cleopatra's cartouche. He went on to decipher all the images in the hieroglyphic code.

The Rosetta Stone

Cleopatra's cartouche

C L E O P A T R A

Ptolemy's cartouche

P T O L E M Y

Egyptian gods often assumed human, or part-human, forms. To the left is Anubis, the god of mummification. To the right is Isis, the goddess of magic.

Then & Now

Ramesses II, who ruled in the 1200s B.C., built more temples and statues than any other Egyptian king. His largest temple was built in a sandstone cliff. In the 1960s, the Aswan High Dam almost flooded this temple. People all over the world sent money to move it to higher ground. The huge temple was entirely rebuilt 215 feet above its original site.

which people could still read. Thinking that the other two languages repeated the same message, scholars set to work trying to decode these Egyptian hieroglyphics. In the box on the previous page, you can read more about Jean François Champollion (sham paw lee AWN), the man who unlocked the mystery.

Gods and the Afterlife

Focus *What were the Egyptians' religious beliefs, and how did these beliefs affect daily life?*

Like the Mesopotamians, the ancient Egyptians were polytheists. They prayed to hundreds of gods and goddesses. Each village had its own major god, in addition to several minor gods. There were also some gods and goddesses that all Egyptians worshipped. Pictures and statues of these gods and goddesses showed them in various forms. Some looked like humans; others were shaped like creatures that lived in the Nile Valley. Still others were combinations of the two.

Osiris was an important god. Egyptians believed that he had ruled as the Egyptian king until he was murdered by his jealous brother, Seth. According to the Egyptians' beliefs, Osiris was brought back to life by his wife Isis and became the king who ruled over the dead in the underworld. Horus, the son of Osiris and Isis, challenged and defeated his wicked uncle Seth. Horus then took over as ruler of Egypt.

One of the major Egyptian gods was Ra, the sun god. He was sometimes portrayed as a young falcon god; at other times, he took the shape of a wise, old man. During the New Kingdom Period, Egyptians wrote a hymn to Ra and inscribed it on a stone monument:

H*ail to you Ra . . .*
   You stir to rise at dawn,
   and your brightness opens the eyes of the flock;
   you set in the western mountain,
   and then they sleep as if in death.

The Egyptians built numerous temples. Each temple was thought to be the home of a particular god or goddess. Sometimes, temples were dedicated to the memory of a pharaoh. The king was believed to be a god come to earth in a human form or the physical son of a god. Inside the temple, only the high priests were allowed to approach the god or goddess, who was often represented by a gold statue. The priests washed, dressed, and decorated the statue with jewels before making daily offerings of food and drink.

Ordinary Egyptians were not allowed to enter the temples, so they prayed at home to their favorite gods and goddesses. The only time the people might have caught a glimpse of the god or goddess was when priests carried the statue through the streets during festivals.

Life After Death

The Egyptians hoped that Osiris, the god who rose from the dead, would grant them life after death, too. Burial practices reflected this wish.

Egyptians believed that they were born with a *ka*, a spirit or life force that stayed with them throughout the course of their lives. They thought that the *ka* had an **afterlife**, that is, it continued to live after death. They believed that it remained in the tomb with the body. Priests and relatives of the dead person gave the *ka* daily offerings of food. Tombs were often filled with a variety of items considered necessary for the afterlife: furniture, scrolls, games, clothing, and jewelry.

The Egyptians also thought that it was important for the *ka* to recognize its former body. To keep the body unchanged in its appearance and intact for the next life, the Egyptians developed a system of preservation

How Mummies Were Made

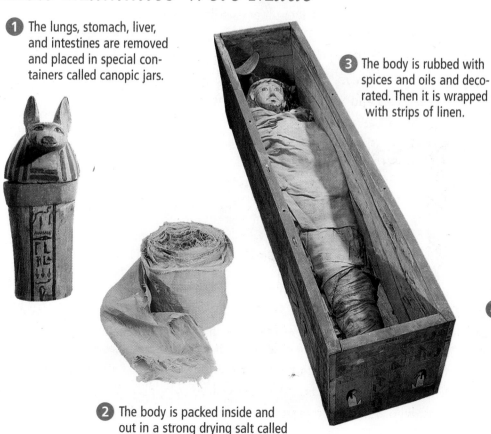

1 The lungs, stomach, liver, and intestines are removed and placed in special containers called canopic jars.

2 The body is packed inside and out in a strong drying salt called natron so that it does not rot.

3 The body is rubbed with spices and oils and decorated. Then it is wrapped with strips of linen.

4 One or more coffins are made, usually out of wood. In royal burials, the coffin then fits inside a large stone coffin called a sarcophagus.

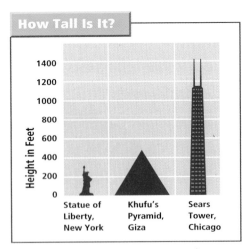

For thousands of years, the pyramids of Egypt were the tallest structures on Earth. **Math:** *What other tall buildings could you add to this chart?*

known as mummification. (You can read about mummy making at the bottom of the previous page.) Some mummies were so well preserved that their teeth, hair styles, and even facial expressions are still intact. Modern scientists can learn about diseases, causes of death, and other facts of Egyptian life from these ancient bodies.

Pyramids

In very early times, Egyptians had simply surrounded their dead with the food, clothing, and weapons they would need in the afterlife and buried them in the sand. But this simple burial offered no protection against sandstorms or roving animals. For this reason, Egyptian kings and nobles began to build burial places that were more long lasting.

• Tell Me More •

How Did They Build the Great Pyramid?

Built by the pharaoh Khufu during the Old Kingdom period, the Great Pyramid was originally 481 feet high. Its tremendous base covered an area of about 13 acres. It was constructed of about 2.3 million enormous limestone blocks, some as tall as 5 feet. All together, the stones in the pyramid weighed about 7 million tons.

When the blocks arrived from nearby quarries by boat, workers unloaded them onto sledges, wooden sleds with runners. Using ropes made from palm fibers, teams of men then pull the blocks to the pyramid site.

Layer by layer, the stones were put into place. As the pyramid grew higher, workers built ramps around the structure so they could drag stones to each new level. As the pyramid went up, they constructed passageways and a room that would be the pharaoh's burial chamber. They then added more

In approximately 2650 B.C., Imhotep (ihm HOH tehp), an architect and statesman, built the first pyramid. This structure, which is still standing, was a tomb for the pharaoh Djoser (DZOH suhr). It is referred to as a step pyramid because it was constructed as a series of terraces that resembled steps. The first smooth-sided pyramid was built about 2600 B.C. It still stands today at Medum. The pyramid's shape was thought to imitate the sun's rays as they shone down from the heavens.

Before building these tombs, architects had to choose a suitable location. They found a rock plateau, a flat elevated stretch of land, located near the Nile. Other decisions had to be made: which direction the pyramid would face, how steeply the pyramid's side would slope. River rafts then brought blocks of stones directly from quarries to the building site. Once these blocks arrived, thousands of workers could begin building.

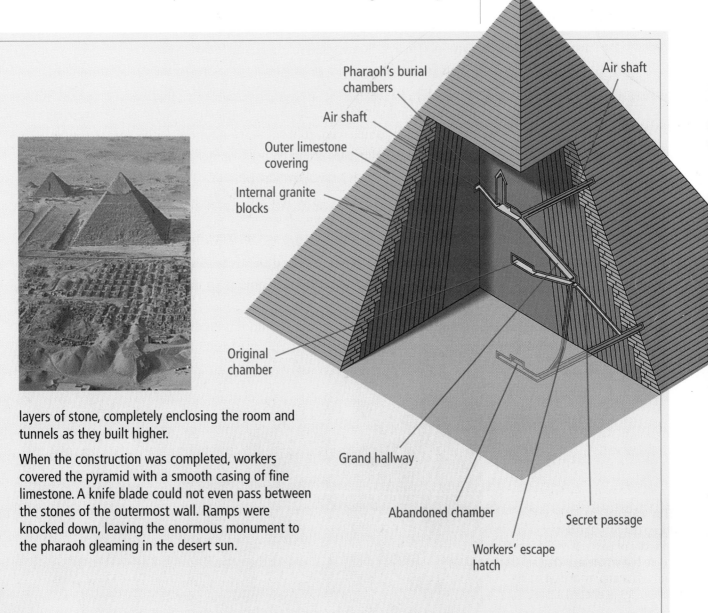

Pharaoh's burial chambers

Air shaft

Air shaft

Outer limestone covering

Internal granite blocks

Original chamber

Grand hallway

Abandoned chamber

Workers' escape hatch

Secret passage

layers of stone, completely enclosing the room and tunnels as they built higher.

When the construction was completed, workers covered the pyramid with a smooth casing of fine limestone. A knife blade could not even pass between the stones of the outermost wall. Ramps were knocked down, leaving the enormous monument to the pharaoh gleaming in the desert sun.

This pendant is from the tomb of the young King Tutankhamun (toot ahng KAH muhn), now called King Tut. The treasure of King Tut's tomb, found in 1922, captured the interest of people all over the world. It gave rise to Egyptian fashions in clothing, jewelry, and architecture.
Cultures: *In what other ways might an archaeological discovery influence people?*

In Giza in Lower Egypt, three of the largest pyramids remain standing. Ancient travelers considered the tallest of the pyramids, the Great Pyramid, one of the Seven Wonders of the Ancient World. You can read about the construction of the Great Pyramid on the previous pages.

Long after their pharaoh was laid in his pyramid, the Egyptians liked to think that their ruler's good favor continued to shine down on them. Still considered a god after he had died, the pharaoh was buried as he had lived: surrounded by possessions, jewelry, and treasure.

Grave Robbing and the Valley of the Kings

The pharaohs of the Old Kingdom spent a huge amount of Egypt's wealth to build their pyramids. Over the centuries, these enormous tombs were easy targets for thieves, who robbed them of their treasures. To better hide their tombs, the pharaohs of the New Kingdom carved their tombs deep into cliffs in the Valley of the Kings, across the Nile from the city of Thebes. Some scholars think the location was chosen because it contained a huge rocky peak similar in shape to the earlier pyramids.

This royal cemetery was used for over four hundred years, and more than 60 tombs have been discovered there. Over time, however, even these hidden tombs were robbed. Starting in the 1500s, many people believed that mummies could be used as medicine. Hundreds of tombs were robbed at that time. Powdered mummy was a popular medicine until the 1700s, especially in Europe, where people used it to treat bruises, wounds, and even stomachaches!

Today, scientists can learn much about people in ancient times by carefully studying mummies and the treasures of tombs. Many museums preserve fragile remains and rare objects so that people will be able to study and admire them in the future. Some people, however, think that mummies and their treasures should not be disturbed or even displayed in

The Valley of the Kings was a deep gorge in the desert near the city of Luxor. Many kings were buried there, including King Tutankhamun, who died at the age of 19 in about 1325 B.C.

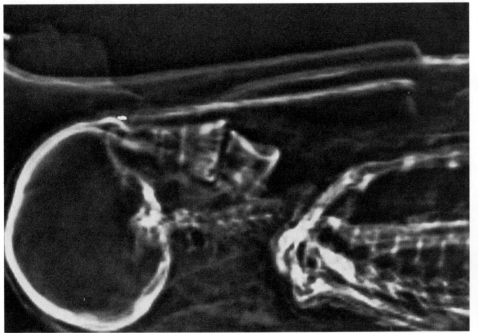

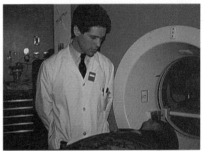

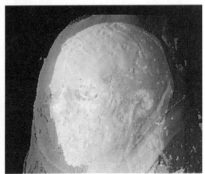

museums. They believe that this is disrespectful to the memory of the dead. The Egyptian Museum in Cairo, Egypt, removed its collection of mummies from public view for more than a decade because of the controversy. The mummies are now back on display.

Exciting discoveries are still being made in Egypt. One of the largest Egyptian tombs ever found was discovered in the Valley of the Kings in the spring of 1995. It contains the tombs of some of Ramesses II's 52 sons. Archaeologists were exploring the site because the area was supposed to become a parking lot. You can read more about it in the *TIME* magazine article "Secrets of the Lost Tomb," which begins on the next page.

Today, scientists can study mummies without unwrapping or damaging them. At top right, a medical device called a CAT scanner is used to study the remains of a mummy. At far left, a cross section shows the outline of the coffin and the skeleton.
Technology: *Why is it better to study mummies without unwrapping them?*

Lesson Review

4000 B.C.	3000 B.C.	2000 B.C.

3100 B.C.
Egypt united under one king

2650 B.C.
First pyramid built in Egypt

1. **Key Vocabulary:** Use these vocabulary words in a paragraph: **pharaoh, hieroglyphics, dynasty, afterlife.**

2. **Focus:** What was life like for Egyptian rulers and common citizens?

3. **Focus:** What were some of the key achievements of ancient Egypt?

4. **Focus:** What were the Egyptians' religious beliefs, and how did these beliefs affect daily life?

5. **Critical Thinking/Interpret** Make a chart of the advantages and disadvantages of dynastic rule.

6. **Theme: Lasting Beginnings** Why might Egyptian culture have lasted for so many centuries?

7. **Citizenship/Writing Activity:** You are a scribe in the court of the pharaoh. Make a record of a day in the king's life.

FROM THE PAGES OF

TIME

The New NRA: Venom Pays

TIME

SECRETS OF THE LOST TOMB

The discovery of a crypt fit for 50 princes sheds new light on the epic life of Ramesses the Great

Secrets of the Lost Tomb

A mammoth mausoleum uncovered in Egypt may hold up to 50 sons of the greatest of the pharaohs

by Michael D. Lemonick

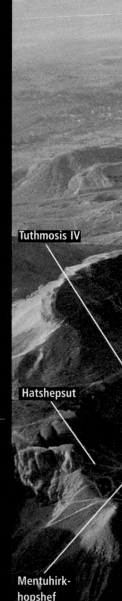

Tuthmosis IV

Hatshepsut

Mentuhirk-hopshef

Egyptologists had long since lost interest in the site of Tomb 5, which had been explored and looted decades ago, and was about to give way to a parking lot. But for that parking lot, in fact, no one would have ever known the treasure that lay only 200 ft. from King Tut's resting place, just beyond a few rubble-strewn rooms that previous excavators had used to hold their debris.

Wanting to be sure the new parking facility wouldn't destroy anything important, Dr. Kent Weeks, an Egyptologist with the American University in Cairo, embarked in 1988 on one final exploration of the old dumping ground. Eventually, he was able to pry open a door blocked for thousands of years — and last week announced the discovery

of a lifetime. "We found ourselves in a corridor," Weeks remembers. "On each side were 10 doors, and at the end there was a statue of Osiris, the god of the afterlife." Two more corridors branched off from there, with 16 more doors on each one.

Although the tomb is mostly unexcavated and the chambers are choked with debris, Weeks is convinced that there are more rooms on a lower level, bringing the total number to more than 100. That would make Tomb 5 the biggest and most complex tomb ever found in Egypt — and quite conceivably the resting place of up to 50 sons of Ramesses II, perhaps the best known of all the pharaohs, the ruler believed to have been Moses' nemesis in the book of

Valley of The Kings

GOD OF AFTERLIFE The statue of Osiris lies deep within the tomb. Its missing face may lie in the rubble below.

Tuthmosis III

Seti II

Tuthmosis I

Twosret

Siptah

Royal Tombs

Maherpra

Amenhotep II

Userhet

Ramesses III

Amenemopet

Amenmesses

Horemheb

Ramesses X

Seti I

Ramesses VI

Ramesses I

Merneptah

Smenkhkare

Tutankhamun

Ramesses IX

Ramesses II

TOMB 5

Ramesses XI

Yuya and Tuya

Ramesses IV

A TOMB FIT FOR 50 SONS

Tomb 5 contains at least 62 chambers and was intended as the burial place for many of Ramesses II's sons. Evidence of stairways and some collapsed columns suggest that there is a lower level of rooms where mummies may be entombed.

Statue of Osiris

Possible lower layer of rooms

Pillared Hall

Area explored by James Burton in 1820

10 m (33 ft.)

North

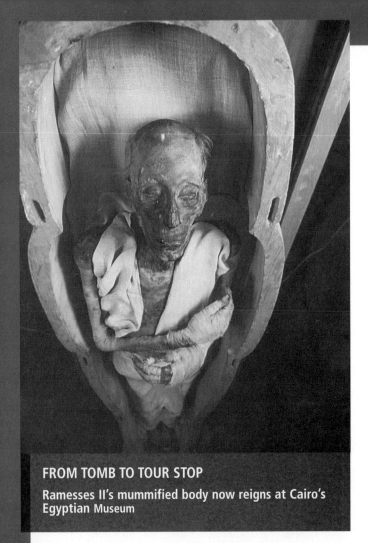

FROM TOMB TO TOUR STOP
Ramesses II's mummified body now reigns at Cairo's Egyptian Museum

Exodus. Says Emily Teeter, an Egyptologist with Chicago's Oriental Institute Museum: "To find large tombs is one thing, but to find something like this, that's been used for dozens of burials, is absolutely amazing." The cheeky London *Daily Mail* carried this headline: PHARAOH'S 50 SONS IN MUMMY OF ALL TOMBS.

"Egyptians do not call him Ramesses II," Sabry Abd El Aziz, director of antiquities for the Qurna region, told TIME correspondent Lara Marlowe last week, as she and photographer Barry Iverson became the first Western journalists to enter the tomb since the new discoveries were announced. "We call him Ramesses al-Akbar— Ramesses the Greatest."

No wonder. During his 67 years on the throne, stretching from 1279 B.C. to 1212 B.C., Ramesses could have filled an ancient edition of the *Guinness Book of Records* all by himself: he built more temples, obelisks and monuments; took more wives (eight . . .) and claimed to have sired more children (as many as 162, by some accounts) than any other pharaoh in history. And he presided over an empire that stretched from

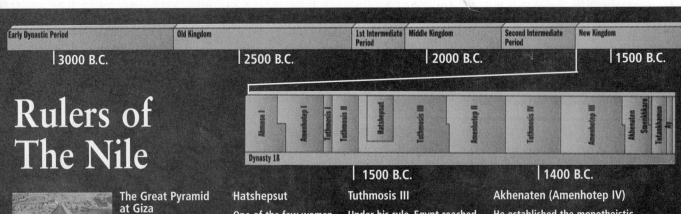

| Early Dynastic Period | Old Kingdom | 1st Intermediate Period | Middle Kingdom | Second Intermediate Period | New Kingdom |

| 3000 B.C. | 2500 B.C. | 2000 B.C. | 1500 B.C. |

Rulers of The Nile

Dynasty 18: Ahmose I, Amenhotep I, Tuthmosis I, Tuthmosis II, Hatshepsut, Tuthmosis III, Amenhotep II, Tuthmosis IV, Amenhotep III, Akhenaten, Smenkhkare, Tutankhamun, Ay

| 1500 B.C. | 1400 B.C. |

The Great Pyramid at Giza

One of the seven wonders of the ancient world, it was built by the 4th Dynasty pharaoh Khufu (also known as Cheops). It covers 13 acres and contains more than 2 million blocks of stone.

The Great Sphinx and the Second Pyramid were built at Giza by Khafre, Khufu's son. The Sphinx is thought to be a likeness of Khafre, and is the oldest known large-scale royal portrait.

Hatshepsut

One of the few women to rule Egypt, she took power during the reign of her stepson Tuthmosis III while he was a child. The outstanding monument erected under her direction was her mortuary temple at Deir el-Bahari.

Tuthmosis III

Under his rule, Egypt reached the height of its power. Now known as the Napoleon of ancient Egypt, he led military campaigns into western Asia and brought Palestine, Syria, and Nubia into his empire. During the last 10 or so years of his reign, Egypt was settled and prosperous.

Akhenaten (Amenhotep IV)

He established the monotheistic cult of the sun god Aten and forced the Egyptians to abandon all other gods. He also moved the capital from Thebes to Akhetaten (now el-Amarna). He is often depicted with a misshapen skull, a stoop, and broad hips; some scholars think he suffered from a tumor of the pituitary gland. Images of his queen, Nefertiti, attest to her great beauty.

present-day Libya to Iraq in the east, as far north as Turkey and southward into the Sudan.

Because of his marathon reign, historians already know a great deal about Ramesses and the customs of his day. But the newly explored tomb suddenly presents scholars with all sorts of puzzles to ponder. For one thing, many of the tombs in the Valley of the Kings are syringe-like, plunging straight as a needle into the steep hillsides. For reasons nobody yet knows, says Weeks, this one "is more like an octopus, with a body surrounded by tentacles."

The body in this case is an enormous square room, at least 50 ft. on a side and divided by 16 massive columns. Anyone who wants to traverse the chamber has to crawl through a tight passage, lighted by a string of dim electric light bulbs, where the dirt has been painstakingly cleared away. "It's like crawling under a bed," says TIME's Marlowe, "except that it goes on and on, and the ceiling above your head is studded with jagged outcroppings of rock that are in danger of caving in."

At the end of this claustrophobic journey lies the door Weeks found, and the relatively spacious corridors beyond. It is here, as well as in two outermost rooms, that . . . artifacts were discovered — most of them broken. "Clearly," says Weeks, "the tomb was pretty well gone over in ancient times."

Additional artifacts could lie buried if, as Weeks believes, the tomb had an unusual split-level design. The ceilings of the corridors to the left and right of the statue of Osiris slope downward and then drop abruptly about 4 ft. — strong evidence of stairways. Says Weeks: "I think there are more rooms on the lower level." Moreover, while the doors that line the corridors all lead to identical 10-ft. by 10-ft. chambers, the openings themselves are only about 2 1/2 ft. wide, too narrow to accommodate a prince's sarcophagus. That suggests to Weeks that the rooms weren't burial chambers but rather "chapels" for funeral offerings. And cracks in these rooms and in four of the massive pillars in the larger chamber are clues that the floors are unsupported — that hollow areas lie below. Could they contain intact sarcophagi

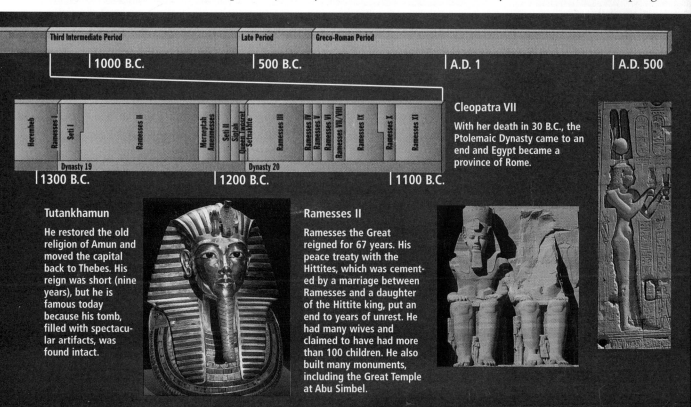

Third Intermediate Period | Late Period | Greco-Roman Period

1000 B.C. 500 B.C. A.D. 1 A.D. 500

Horemheb | Ramesses I | Seti I | Ramesses II | Merneptah Amenmesses | Seti II Siptah Queen Twosret Sethnakhte | Ramesses III | Ramesses IV Ramesses V | Ramesses VI Ramesses VII/VIII | Ramesses IX | Ramesses X | Ramesses XI

Dynasty 19   Dynasty 20

1300 B.C. 1200 B.C. 1100 B.C.

Cleopatra VII

With her death in 30 B.C., the Ptolemaic Dynasty came to an end and Egypt became a province of Rome.

Tutankhamun

He restored the old religion of Amun and moved the capital back to Thebes. His reign was short (nine years), but he is famous today because his tomb, filled with spectacular artifacts, was found intact.

Ramesses II

Ramesses the Great reigned for 67 years. His peace treaty with the Hittites, which was cemented by a marriage between Ramesses and a daughter of the Hittite king, put an end to years of unrest. He had many wives and claimed to have had more than 100 children. He also built many monuments, including the Great Temple at Abu Simbel.

with mummies inside? "I'm hoping," says Weeks.

"It's unique," asserts Weeks. "We've never found a multiple burial of a pharaoh's children. And for most pharaohs, we have no idea at all what happened to their children." Archaeologists either have to assume that Ramesses II buried his children in a unique way, Weeks says, or they have to consider the possibility that they've overlooked a major type of royal tomb. "It's very obvious," he says, "that there are whole areas that have to be looked at more closely, and not just in Luxor."

Before that happens, though, there is still an enormous amount of work to do in Tomb 5. Archaeologists still haven't resolved many basic questions — when the tomb was built, for example, and over what period of time was it used.

Some answers could pop up as the excavations progress. Says Kenneth Kitchen, a professor of Egyptology at the University of Liverpool in England: "Let's hope the tomb yields a whole lot of new bodies. Then the medicos can get to work on them and find out what these princes were like, whether they had toothaches, how long they lived."

And what happened to Ramesses' dozens of daughters? Were they buried in a similar mausoleum, perhaps in the Valley of the Queens, a few miles to the southwest? That is where many pharaohs' wives and princesses and some princes are buried. "Why not?" asks the Oriental Institute Museum's Teeter. "The daughters of pharaohs were certainly important. The Valley of the Queens hasn't been as thoroughly explored as the Valley of the Kings, so there

could be a lot of surprises there."

Weeks' team, meanwhile, plans to return to Tomb 5 for the month of July. Their goal is to get far enough inside to explore the staircases and lower level. Weeks estimates that it will take at least five years to study and map the entire tomb, protect the decorations, install climate controls and electricity and shore up the precarious sections. Says Abdel Halim Nur el Din, secretary-general of Egypt's Supreme Council of Antiquities: "We're in no hurry to open this tomb to the public. We already have 10 or 12 that they can visit."

The recent find gives scholars hope, though, that more can

be discovered even in this most-explored of Egypt's archaeological sites. Notes the antiquities department's Abd El Aziz: "We still haven't found the tombs of Amenhotep I or Ramesses VIII," he says. "We have 62 tombs in the Valley of the Kings, but in the Western Valley, which runs perpendicular to it, we have discovered only two tombs."

The pharaohs would be pleased to know they have held on to a few of their secrets. After all, they dug their tombs deep into hillsides, where the crypts would be safe, they hoped, from the rabble and robbers. What they never counted on was the need for parking lots.

EXACTING EXCAVATION

Egyptologist Weeks was the first to discover how huge the tomb is, with many corridors beyond the entrance shown above.

Response Activities

1. **Predict** Predict what effect the discovery of the tomb of the sons of Ramesses II will have on our knowledge of ancient Egypt and on the economy of modern-day Egypt.

2. **Narrative: Write a Report** Suppose you are Dr. Weeks and have just discovered the tomb described in the article. Write a report for the Egyptian government about why your find is so important.

3. **History: Draw a Diagram** Make a diagram of the tomb. Label areas and features that suggest to archaeologists that another layer of chambers may exist below the one already found.

Analyzing Points of View

Voices from the Past

When you want to understand an event from the past, it helps to read or hear the words of the people who experienced the event. It also helps to find out what's been written by people who weren't there, but who have studied the facts. To understand the devastating famines of ancient Egypt, for example, you can read one account by the King of Sumer and another by a modern historian. It's important to recognize that every source — sometimes even a secondary source — has its own point of view.

① Here's How

Read the two accounts of a seven-year famine in ancient Egypt.

- Study each source. Does the author directly state feelings, beliefs, or opinions? Or does the account include only or mostly facts?

- Are there particular words that might be a clue to the author's feelings or beliefs?

- How is the information in each source the same or different? Are facts left out of one source? Does that tell you anything about the author's point of view?

② Think It Through

How is reading more than one point of view valuable in learning about events?

③ Use It

1. List the words in the primary source that show it is a personal point of view.

2. List the facts in the secondary source.

3. Find a news article that is an example of a primary source, or eyewitness account. What is the author's point of view? How do you know?

Primary Source

These excerpts are from the Amarna Letters, ancient Egyptian clay slabs found over a century ago.

" The sons, the daughters, have come to an end . . .Give me something to feed them. . . I have nothing. . . There is no grain for our support. What shall I say to my peasants? . . . There is nothing to give for deliverance. . . . "

Secondary Source

" This famine overshadowed all other events of that time; the mark of hunger was impressed on the entire period. . . . The famine was so great that children were sold for bread. After the sons and the daughters had been sold into slavery to save them and the remnants of the population from starvation, the implements of the households also went in exchange for food. . . . "

Ancient Nubia

Main Idea Nubian culture reflected the unique achievements of its people as well as an exchange of ideas with Egypt.

What people, according to the Romans, could carve an entire temple from a single stone? Who were "the most just of men; the favorites of the gods," according to Homer, a famous Greek poet? Whom did the Greek historian, Herodotus, describe as being "the tallest and most handsome of men?" Answer: the Nubians, some of the earliest known inhabitants of what is now the country of Sudan in Africa.

The Nubians were respected throughout the ancient world. Their soldiers were so well known for their talent with a bow and arrow that Egyptians called Nubia "Ta-Seti" (ta SEE tee), which meant "land of the bow." The Nubians developed a successful trade with Egypt and other neighbors. They were also skillful artists and craftspeople. Their civilization continued for 5,000 years, outlasting the Egyptian empire.

Crossroads of Cultures

Focus *Why was Nubia an important center of trade?*

As you read in Lesson 1, Egypt and Nubia were connected by the Nile River. The Nubians, unlike their Egyptian neighbors, did not have uninterrupted stretches of smooth waters and fertile land along the river banks. Upstream from Aswan, the Nile was full of twists and turns. It

Key Vocabulary

caravan

ore

smelting

Key Events

1500 B.C. Egypt conquers Nubia

724 B.C. Nubia conquers Egypt

270 B.C. Golden Age of Meroë begins

Four princes from Nubia are shown on this wall painting from a tomb in Thebes.

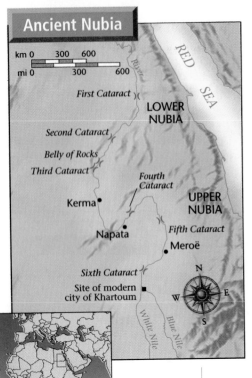

km 0 | 300 | 600
mi 0 | 300 | 600

First Cataract
LOWER NUBIA
Second Cataract
Belly of Rocks
Third Cataract
Fourth Cataract
Kerma
UPPER NUBIA
Napata
Fifth Cataract
Meroë
Sixth Cataract
Site of modern city of Khartoum
White Nile
Blue Nile
RED SEA

The map above shows the major cities of Nubia. **Map Skill:** *Why do you think a separate culture developed at the southern end of the Nile River?*

In this fragment from a Nubian tomb painting, the man at center holds a bunch of giraffe tails in his left hand. The man at right carries the skin of a leopard (*shown above*). Live baboons are at his feet and on his shoulder. Nubians also traded elephant tusks, ostrich eggs, and feathers. The man at far left carries gold, shaped into rings. **Economics:** *Why might the gold have been shaped into rings?*

churned over large boulders at its six cataracts. One particular stretch was so dangerous that the local people called it the "Belly of Rocks."

The area between the First and Second cataracts was called Lower Nubia. Upper Nubia began at the Second Cataract and ended near the location of the modern-day city of Khartoum.

Travelers heading south, or upstream, from Egypt often had to stop at the cataracts, take their boats out of the water, and carry them around the rapids. At the places where they stopped, people began trading. In time, communities grew up there.

Another common means of transport in Nubia was the cara-van, a group of people and camels moving across the desert. Camels were well suited to desert travel because they could walk for long distances without having to stop for water. The caravans allowed people to avoid the dangers of navigating the Nile. Also, going by land instead of by water could mean a shorter distance to travel. Meroë (MEHR oh ee), one of Nubia's southern cities, became a busy meeting place for desert caravan travelers.

As use of desert trade routes grew, so did Nubia's wealth. The Nubians charged Egyptian traders a fee as they passed through Nubia. In addition, the kingdom's resources were in great demand in Egypt and the

Middle East. Gold, granite, iron ore, ivory, ebony, vegetable oils, and leopard and panther skins were plentiful in Nubia. They brought great riches to the kingdom when they were traded.

Nubia's gold became so famous that the kingdom soon became known as "the land of gold." In fact, some historians think that the word "Nubia" comes from the Egyptian word for gold. The kingdom was also referred to as Kush — which was originally the Egyptian name for Upper Nubia — in the Egyptian, Assyrian, Persian, and Hebrew languages. Historians still do not know what name the Nubians gave themselves.

The Nubian Empire

Focus | *How and why did Nubian culture change over time?*

Throughout its long history, different kingdoms flourished in various regions of Nubia. Three of the most important capital cities were Kerma (KER mah), Napata (NAH pah tah), and Meroë.

Kerma

From 2000 B.C. to 1550 B.C., one of the first and greatest Nubian kingdoms prospered. The kingdom was named for its capital, Kerma, which was located south of the Third Cataract. Its territory included much of what we now call northern Sudan, as well as parts of southern Egypt. Kerma was wealthy: Its gold trade with Egypt was brisk. The Nubians built forts in order to protect their trade routes, and they began charging the Egyptians more for Nubian goods. Some Egyptian traders even settled in Kerma.

Curious Facts

Images of elephants have been found throughout the Nubian city of Meroë. The people of Meroë may have believed that elephants were gods. One story suggests that the palace at Meroë was built on a wheeled platform and pulled by elephants. There might even have been a school for training elephants for use by the army.

Crocodiles circle around this clay vessel from Meroë. The wood-and-rawhide bed at left is a reconstruction of a bed found at a royal Kerma burial site. The bed is decorated with animals carved from ivory.

Biography

King Taharqa

Taharqa was the only Nubian king whose name is specifically mentioned in the Bible. He ruled Nubia from around 690 B.C. to 664 B.C. Much of that time was spent warding off attacks from the Assyrians. Within Nubia, Taharqa concentrated his efforts on construction. He was considered the greatest builder of the Kushite dynasty and left many monuments and temples in both Egypt and Nubia.

This Nubian gold earring of the ram-god Amun is from the sixth century B.C.

With stability and wealth, the Nubians were able to spend time creating art. Kerma craftspeople were particularly skilled at making pottery. Their delicate, elegant pots were often black on top and dark red below with a gray band running around the center.

Another sign of Kerma's wealth was the lavish burials given to royalty. The kings were not mummified. Instead, they were buried under large circular mounds of earth the size of a football field. At the center of the mounds, inside the most impressive of many tomb chambers, the kings' bodies were placed on gold-covered beds. The tombs were brightly colored and filled with ivory, bronze, and gold objects. Records show that as many as 400 servants were buried alive with their king!

The Napatan Period

In 1550 B.C., the Egyptian armies began a war against Kush which lasted about 50 years. Kerma was destroyed, and Egypt took control over all of Nubia. Ahmose I (akh MOH zuh), the Egyptian pharaoh, sent a governor to whom he gave the title of the "King's Son of Kush" to rule Nubia. Nubian princes were taken back to Egyptian royal courts to learn the ways and culture of Egypt.

Although Nubians opposed these policies, Egypt continued to rule Nubia for more than four hundred years. Gradually, Egyptian customs became accepted in Nubia. Kings were mummified and buried in small pyramids. The Nubians began using hieroglyphics and built Egyptian-style temples. Egyptians held higher-level jobs; they were priests, army officers, and merchants. Nubians worked as laborers, soldiers, and police.

In 724 B.C., the balance of power in the area shifted. Egyptian rulers grew weak. The Kushite King Piye (PEE yeh) took power in Nubia and conquered Egypt. For the next 60 years, the Nubians ruled Egypt. New temples were built and decorated; old ones were restored. Art and literature flourished, and many old Egyptian books were copied and saved. During this period, the two Nubian capitals were in Napata and Thebes. This time in Nubian history is called the Napatan Period.

The reign of the Nubian kings is known as the Twenty-fifth Dynasty in Egyptian history. Kushite rule over Egypt ended in 660 B.C. when the Assyrians invaded Egypt and forced the Nubians back into Nubia, south of the First Cataract.

The Power of Amun

The Egyptians had long worshipped the god, Amun (AH muhn). This god became very important to the Nubians, who portrayed him as having the body of a man and the head of a ram. The temple at Jebel

Barkal became the center for the worship of Amun. The power of the priests there increased greatly, because they acted as spokesmen for the god. If the priests did not like a king, they could say that Amun had commanded the king to give up his throne. Then they would issue Amun's command about who would rule instead.

This continued until the third century B.C., when King Arkamani (ark ah MAH nee) ruled Kush. One day, King Arkamani was told by the priests that Amun had ordered the king to commit suicide. The king refused to obey. Instead, he headed to the temple and killed the priests.

After this, King Arkamani moved the royal court and his home to the city of Meroë on the eastern bank of the Nile River. Some historians suggest that the king wanted to separate himself from the temple and priests. The religious capital continued to be Napata but royal burials took place at Meroë.

• Tell Me More •

Nubian Queens

Women played an important role in governing the Nile kingdom.

Women were very important in Nubian culture. In particular, the king's sister played a major role in determining who would be the next ruler. Usually, a child of the king's sister was chosen to be the new queen or king.

Many women ruled Nubia during its long history. Some queens from the time of Meroë are shown on temples as warriors holding swords. These powerful warrior queens are believed to have led their own troops in battle. In other images, the Nubian queens are shown covered with jewelry and wearing ornate robes and headdresses.

The silver mask shown here (upper right) shows the queen Malakaye (Mah lah KAY ah), who ruled Nubia in the 500s B.C. The drawing (right) is a researcher's copy of an Egyptian temple painting. It shows Kemsit (KEHM ziht) (seated, right), the Nubian queen of Egyptian Pharaoh Mentuhotep II (mehn too HOH tehp), and the queen's servant.

Heiroglyph	Cursive	Sound
𓆃	𐦀	a
𓄿	𐦁	e
𓀀	𐦂	i
𓃀	𐦃	o
𓏼	///	y
𓏤	𐦅	e
𓃭	𐦆	b
𓊖	𐦇	p
𓃀	𐦈	m
≈	𐦉	n
𓏥	𐦊	ne
⬭	∽	f

The people of Meroë stopped using Egyptian hieroglyphs and developed their own alphabet. It had 23 symbols that could be written in hieroglyphs or in cursive script. In this writing system, dots are used to separate words. The sound of each letter is known but no one yet has been able to read the language.

These ruins of Nubian pyramids are at Meroë's northern cemetery. The lighter color stone shows the work of modern restoration.

The Golden Age of Meroë

Focus *What were some of the key achievements of Meroë?*

With Meroë as its capital, Nubia's Golden Age had arrived. Trade was brisk and highly profitable. The Nubians built grand structures of stone and produced beautiful gold jewelry. They stopped using Egyptian hieroglyphics and developed their own alphabet.

Daily life for many Nubians meant working on their farms and raising cattle. Tomb carvings tell us that Nubians enjoyed wrestling. One of the gods they worshipped during this period was the lion-god, Apedemak (ah PEHD eh mak). He was the god of war and was usually shown wearing his armor.

Nubian Pyramids

Tombs were first built for Nubian rulers during the Napatan Period. After the capital moved to Meroë, the Nubians built an enormous burial ground east of the city. Nobles were buried in small pyramids and kings in larger ones. About 40 of these structures are still standing today.

The Nubian pyramids were smaller and had steeper sides than the ones built in Egypt. Servants were often sacrificed and buried with their kings. Sometimes, even a king's favorite horse was buried at the entrance to the tomb. Robbers looted many of the Nubian pyramids by cutting off their tops. Archaeologists are still searching the ruins at Meroë to learn more about the civilization.

Gold work from Nubia is among the most beautiful in the ancient world. This hinged bracelet is made of gold and enamel.

Iron Making and Jewelry Making

The Nubians crafted tools and other objects from iron at a time when few other people knew how. The land around Meroë was rich in iron ore. **Ore** is rock that contains a mixture of a metal (in this case iron) and other minerals. The Nubians heated this ore to high temperatures in wood-fueled furnaces. During this process called **smelting,** the other minerals were burned away, leaving pure iron. Archaeologists have found ruins of iron-making factories and furnaces but very few iron tools and weapons. Most have rusted away.

Jewelry produced at this time shows that the Nubians were skillful crafts people. Gold, bronze, semiprecious stones, and enamel were all used in the process. The jewelrymakers produced ornaments for both men and women, who wore necklaces, rings, bracelets, and anklets. Much of this jewelry survives today and is a reminder of Meroë's rich culture.

Ask Yourself

Archaeologists cannot yet read Meroitic writing. They have to study the objects left behind to figure out what life might have been like for ancient Nubians. What artifacts from your daily life would give future archaeologists an accurate picture of your world?

? ? ? ? ? ? ? ? ? ? ? ? ? ?

Lesson Review

| 2000 B.C. | | 1000 B.C. | | B.C. | A.D. | |

1500 B.C.
Egypt conquers Nubia.

724 B.C.
Nubia conquers Egypt

270 B.C.
Golden Age of Meroë begins

1 Key Vocabulary: Describe Nubian trade using the following words: caravan, ore, and smelting.

2 Focus: Why was Nubia an important center of trade?

3 Focus: How and why did Nubian culture change over time?

4 Focus: What were some of the key achievements of Meroë?

5 Critical Thinking: Conclude What conditions had to exist for Egypt to fall and for Nubia to conquer and rule it?

6 Theme: Lasting Beginnings If you were a Nubian during the Napatan Period, which Egyptian customs would you want to borrow? Why?

7 Geography/Writing Activity: Select two locations on the map of Nubia on page 114. If you were on a journey between the two, what sights would you see? Write a journal recording the events of your trip.

Making Decisions

If You Found It, Should You Keep It?

Have you ever found something valuable and wondered what to do with it? As a good citizen, is it your responsibility to return it to its rightful owner? Or is it all right to keep it or sell it? Throughout history, people have had to make this decision. The case study below shows how one man dealt with this issue. Do you think he did the right thing?

Case Study

Treasures Taken from the Pyramids

In the 1800s, many people became treasure hunters. They went to ancient sites, searched for lost artifacts, and sold them for profit.

Giuseppe Ferlini (joo SEHP ee fehr LEE nee) was one such treasure hunter. In 1834, he dug under the pyramid of Amanishakheto (ah mah nuh shah KEE toh) in Meroë, near the Nile River. After two months of digging, he found a chamber filled with beautiful items of gold, silver, bronze, and many more treasures. Ferlini returned to Europe with the treasure and sold it in Germany, where it can still be seen in museums.

Today, many people believe that these artifacts, like the findings of other treasure hunters, should be returned to the countries in which they were found.

Take Action

Communities today must still decide what to do with ancient artifacts. Suppose your town were building a new library and found some artifacts that had been created by early settlers. What should the town do? Keep the artifacts and display them in the library? Return them to the descendants whose ancestors created them? Are there other alternatives? Here are some steps that you can take to make this decision.

1 In small groups, write down some of the items that might have been found. Then create a list of the possible actions your town could take.

2 Have each person choose one action and list its pros and cons.

3 Discuss all the pros and cons and decide which action is best.

4 Present your decision to the class. Compare your decision and your reasons for making it with the decisions of the other groups.

Tips for Making Decisions

- Decide what problem needs to be solved.
- Think about your goals.
- Try to come up with several possible solutions before deciding on one.
- List the pros and cons for each possible solution.
- Decide which choice will best help you reach your goals.

Research Activity

Find out if over the last 100 years any artifacts from past settlements have been found in or near your community. You could contact a local museum, archaeologist, librarian, town planner, or city building representative for information. What were the artifacts? Where were they found? What did your community do with them?

Chapter Review

Chapter Review Timeline

| 3500 B.C. | 2800 B.C. | 2100 B.C. | 1400 B.C. | 700 B.C. | A.D. |

2650 First pyramid built in Egypt

724 Nubia conquers Egypt

3100 Egypt united under one king

1500 Egypt conquers Nubia

270 Golden Age of Meroë begins

660 Assyrians invade Egypt

Summarizing the Main Idea

1 Copy the chart below and fill in the missing information to compare the civilizations of ancient Egypt and Nubia. (The first row has been filled in.)

	Egypt	Nubia
Land	Fertile soil on the banks of the Nile	Much less fertile land than Egypt's.
Government		
Religion		
Daily Life		

Vocabulary

2 Using at least eight of the following terms, write a record of a journey taken by a trader in ancient Egypt.

delta (p. 92)
cataract (p. 93)
nomad (p. 95)
pharaoh (p. 95)

dynasty (p. 95)
papyrus (p. 98)
hieroglyphics (p. 99)
afterlife (p. 101)

caravan (p. 114)
ore (p. 119)
smelting (p. 119)

Reviewing the Facts

3 Name four geographic features of the Nile River Valley.

4 What was the pharaoh's role in ancient Egypt?

5 How did Champollion solve the mystery of the hieroglyphics on the Rosetta Stone?

6 Briefly describe the ancient Egyptian religion.

7 What happened to the treasures that were buried in Egyptian tombs?

8 How did Nubia become a center for trade?

9 What were some of Nubia's cultural achievements?

10 For how many years did Nubian civilization continue?

Skill Review: Analyzing Point of View

11 In your local newspaper, read an account of a recent event. Is the account a primary source or a secondary source? How can you tell?

12 Describe a typical day in the life of an American student. Is your description a primary account or a secondary account? Why?

Geography Skills

13 Look at the map of the Nile River Valley on page 92. Why was it difficult to sail directly from Memphis to Kerma? What did ancient people do about this problem?

14 You are a travel guide in ancient Egypt. Prepare a travel guide for visitors to the Nile River Valley. Include information about transportation, climate, and historical landmarks.

Critical Thinking

15 **Cause and Effect** How did the pharaoh's power influence the way the pyramids were built?

16 **Comparing Then and Now** Compare the daily life of an ancient Egyptian family with your family's daily life. How are your lives similar? How are they different?

17 **Predicting Outcomes** Ancient Nubians were known for their skill in iron making. Think about the tools that can be made with iron. How do you think iron making helped Nubia compete with other cultures?

Writing: Citizenship and History

18 **Citizenship** Is displaying ancient Egyptian mummies in museums disrespectful to the dead? Write a persuasive letter explaining what you think.

19 **History** You are an archaeologist who has just discovered the tomb of an Egyptian pharaoh. Write a journal entry about your discovery.

Activities

History/Research Activity
The Great Pyramid at Giza is one of the Seven Wonders of the Ancient World. Find out what the other six wonders were and read more about them. What, if anything, do these wonders have in common?

Culture/Art Activity
Find out more about Egyptian hieroglyphics. Learn the symbols for the sounds in your own name. Using these symbols, create your own cartouche. Share your cartouche with your classmates.

Internet Option

Check the **Internet Social Studies Center** for ideas on how to extend your theme project beyond your classroom.

THEME PROJECT CHECK-IN

Answer the following questions to see how you have used information about ancient Egypt and Nubia in your theme project.
• What kinds of clothing designs became typical in your civilization?
• What kinds of children's games did you develop?
• What has been the most challenging part of this project?

CHAPTER 5 Ancient India and China

Chapter Preview: *People, Places, and Events*

2500 B.C.	1900 B.C.	1300 B.C.

Indus Valley Civilization

Who was this man? Find out about the people of ancient India. *Lesson 1, Page 126*

Young Buddhist Monks

Buddhism arose in India to become a major world religion. *Lesson 2, Page 132*

Asoka's Stupa

What is a stupa? Who built it? *Lesson 2, Page 135*

The Geography of Ancient South Asia

Main Idea Complex civilizations arose in ancient India and China.

The soldiers struggled through the snow, dwarfed by the rock wall that rose above their heads. In places these mountains soared more than 25,000 feet above sea level. This was the Hindu Kush (HIN doo KUSH), the westernmost range in a chain of mountain ranges that includes the 1,500-mile-long Himalayas (him uh LAY uhz). While these mountains had **passes** — gaps through which people could travel — they could be deadly.

The tiny figures weaving through the mountain pass were the troops of Alexander the Great. The year was 327 B.C., and Alexander, one of the most successful generals the world has ever known, had come all the way from Greece, conquering every land he came to. He and his army were braving the fierce, freezing winds and deep river gorges to extend their conquest to the Indian **subcontinent** — a vast area of land that forms a major part of a continent. But Alexander was not India's first invader.

Key Vocabulary

pass
subcontinent
monsoon

Key Places

Himalayas
Indian subcontinent
Indus River
Mohenjo-Daro

◀ The towering peaks of the Himalayas.

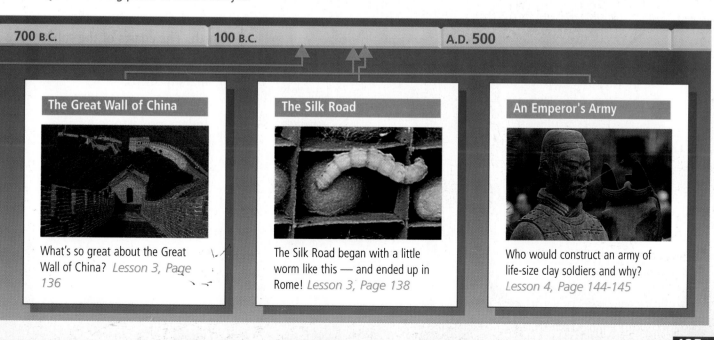

700 B.C.　　　100 B.C.　　　A.D. 500

The Great Wall of China

What's so great about the Great Wall of China? *Lesson 3, Page 136*

The Silk Road

The Silk Road began with a little worm like this — and ended up in Rome! *Lesson 3, Page 138*

An Emperor's Army

Who would construct an army of life-size clay soldiers and why? *Lesson 4, Page 144-145*

These beautifully carved stone seals were used by Indus Valley traders. **Science:** *What animals do these seals show?*

Map Skill: *Can you find where the trade route uses a pass?*

River Valley Civilization

[Focus] *How did India's river valleys give rise to civilization?*

Just as in Egypt and Sumer, the valleys that gave birth to India's civilization were formed by great rivers. The Ganges and Indus rivers emerge from the Himalayas and flow out across the plains of northern India. If you trace each of these rivers with your finger on the map below, you will find that the Ganges continues its journey east into the Bay of Bengal, while the Indus heads west to the Arabian Sea. The mouths of these rivers form deltas with excellent growing soil.

During the rainy season, from early summer to late fall, a moist wind blows off the Indian Ocean. This wind creates a weather condition known as the **monsoon**. As the monsoon winds blow, rains blanket the subcontinent. The Indus and the Ganges overflow their banks. These floods can cause devastation. They also spread badly needed nutrients across the fields, helping crops grow.

As you can see from the map, the Indian subcontinent is nearly diamond-shaped. The pointed top is crowned by a spiky mountain range.

One of those spikes, Mount Everest in the Himalayas, soars almost as high as a cruising passenger jet. At 29,035 feet above sea level, it is Earth's highest mountain.

Most of southern India is covered by the rocky Deccan Plateau. The valleys that gave rise to Indian civilization are nestled between this plateau and the mountains to the north. The coasts of the subcontinent are narrow, marshy strips.

Little is known about India's prehistoric inhabitants. They may have come through those same treacherous passes that Alexander took — as many as 10,000 years before the conqueror made his journey. What is known is that

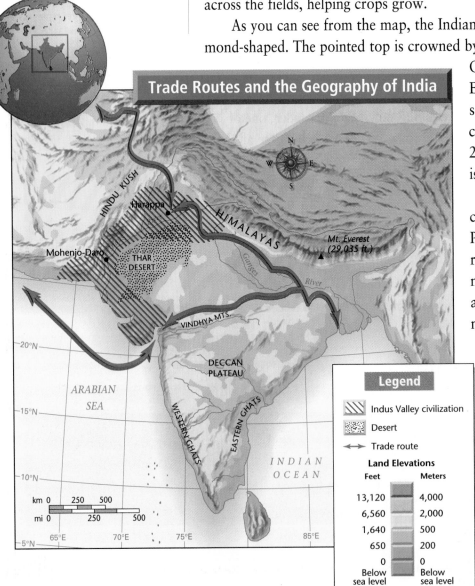

Trade Routes and the Geography of India

HINDU KUSH

Harappa

HIMALAYAS

Mohenjo-Daro

THAR DESERT

Mt. Everest (29,035 ft.)

Ganges River

VINDHYA MTS.

DECCAN PLATEAU

ARABIAN SEA

WESTERN GHATS

EASTERN GHATS

INDIAN OCEAN

20°N

15°N

10°N

5°N

65°E   70°E   75°E   85°E

km 0   250   500

mi 0   250   500

Legend

Indus Valley civilization

Desert

Trade route

Land Elevations

Feet	Meters
13,120	4,000
6,560	2,000
1,640	500
650	200
0	0
Below sea level	Below sea level

around 2500 B.C. — more than 2,000 years before Alexander — an extensive farming civilization arose in the Indus River valley. At its height, this civilization covered nearly half a million square miles — more than Egypt and Sumer put together. Unlike those powerful empires, however, the Indus Valley people were only loosely knit together by a common culture and similar religion. Their primary concern was trade, which they pursued as far as Mesopotamia, both by land and by sea. The map on the previous page shows the major routes used by the Indus Valley traders, including the pass through the dangerous Hindu Kush.

Mohenjo-Daro's streets were straight and well planned. The simple buildings had few windows, and those were on upper stories. They may have been designed this way to keep the owners safe from thieves and wild animals. **Cultures:** *Why do you think there are few great monuments from this civilization?*

Life in Mohenjo-Daro

The ruins of two major centers of Indus Valley trade and government, Mohenjo-Daro (mo HEN jo DAHR oh) and Harappa (huh RAP uh), provide most of what we now know about ancient India. Life in Mohenjo-Daro had some features that were remarkably modern for the period. An advanced plumbing system allowed its residents to take showers and helped keep the city clean and healthy — a necessity in the valley heat, which often reached 120° F. Merchants, whose ranks included women, used the decimal system just as we do today.

As well ordered as it was, Indus Valley life was destined to change. After nearly a thousand years of relative calm along the river, a new and very different people were headed for the subcontinent.

Lesson Review: Geography

1 **Key Vocabulary:** Use subcontinent and monsoon in a paragraph about farming in ancient India. Use passes in a sentence about the Himalayas.

2 **Focus:** How did India's river valleys give rise to civilization?

3 **Critical Thinking: Interpret** Explain the meaning of this statement: The Hindu Kush is like a wall with cracks in it.

4 **Theme: Lasting Beginnings** How did the monsoon help Indian civilization start?

5 **Geography/Art Activity:** Design your own blueprints for Mohenjo-Daro. Remember to use a grid layout for the streets and to include markets and government buildings.

The Culture and Religions of Ancient India

Main Idea Migrating people brought changes to Indian culture — new oral traditions, belief systems, and art forms.

An ancient Indian poem called the *Bhagavad-Gita* (bah guh vahd GEE ta), or Lord's Song, describes the experiences of superhero Prince Arjuna (AHR juh nuh), a fearless warrior. Arjuna rides into battle on a swift war chariot. Neither the chariot that bore the prince nor the poem that described it had been known to the people of the Indus Valley civilization. Who brought these things to the subcontinent, and why?

The Aryan Migration

Focus *What effect did Aryan migration have on Indian culture?*

About 4,000 years ago, Mohenjo-Daro and the other Indus Valley cities fell into decay. Perhaps the Indus River had shifted course, either leaving their communities high and dry or flooding them. Whatever the case, about 250 years after this decline, a new people appeared on the plains of India. They were the Aryans.

Much less is known about the Aryans than about more settled, agricultural peoples. They led lives of constant movement, and left behind no monuments or buildings. What is known is that the Aryans came from the plains northwest of India. There they must have lived like other nomadic inhabitants of that region,

following herds of cattle from one grazing area to another. These nomads crossed the great grassy plain of central Asia as if it were a sea and their horses and chariots, ships. Such nomads would play an important role in the spread of culture and trade across Asia, between the West and the East. The Aryans, however, broke off from them. Like Alexander the Great over a thousand years later, they struggled through the difficult mountain passes to the fertile lands of the Indian subcontinent.

Change in the Indus Valley

The word Aryan means "the Noble Ones." These proud invaders brought with them a new way of life, galloping across the river plains in their horse-drawn chariots. You can imagine the shock and fear of the Indus Valley people as these swift-moving foreigners charged into their villages. They had never seen anything faster than a lumbering mule cart.

Besides horses and chariots, the Aryans brought livestock. At first the Aryans lived much as they had on the steppe, wandering the hills and valleys in search of grazing land, and raiding villages to steal cattle.

In time they saw the advantages of settling down. Over the centuries, the Aryans became farmers, using fire to clear the land. Aryan religion also began to develop within this period of gradual change. By about 800 B.C., the Aryans had developed a stable agricultural society that would influence the subcontinent for centuries to come.

Curious Facts

Many of our words come from the ancient Indus Valley. Our word *pedal* is related to the Sanskrit word *pets,* meaning foot. *Father* is related to the Sanskrit *pitar.* Roughly half the people on earth speak a language that comes from Indo-European roots.

The painting above shows a scene from the Bhagavad-Gita.

Model ox carts like the one at left were popular toys for Indus Valley children. This example is made from terra cotta, a kind of clay. Research: *Find out as much as you can about the history of toymaking.*

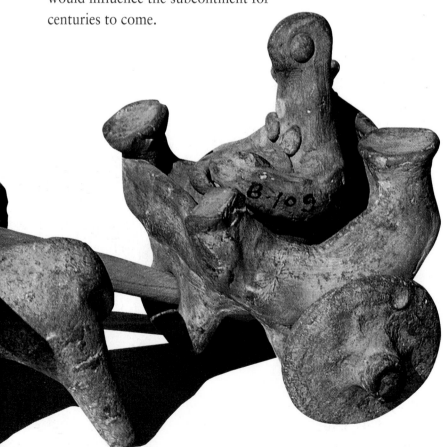

Hinduism

Focus *What are the main teachings of Hinduism?*

We might never have known about the Aryans if religion had not been so important to them. Sometime between 1500 B.C. and 1000 B.C., Aryans in the Indus Valley began composing over a thousand hymns, and other writings in praise of their gods. These writings, known as the Vedas (VAY duh), are the most ancient and sacred of Hindu religious texts.

Along with their ancient gods, the Aryans also brought a new way of organizing society — the **caste** system. Originally there were four castes, or levels of society: priests, warriors, merchants, and peasants. In time there were hundreds of castes, all interacting in a complex way. Eventually these Aryan beliefs, blended with those of the Indus Valley people, would flower into the powerful and lasting religion called Hinduism.

"Where are we born, where do we live, and where are we going?"

Hindu shrines like this can be found all across India. **Culture:** *How is this temple like other houses of worship you have seen?*

• Tell Me More •

Siva: Creator and Destroyer

Hinduism has many gods. The god Siva is shown in this bronze, dancing. For Hindus, Siva's dance is all life — he is the creator of the universe, its preserver and its destroyer.

1 Siva's head: His expression is calm, symbolizing his role as the "unmoved mover."

2 Siva's Arms: His back right hand holds a drum, a symbol of his power of creation. Siva's front right hand is raised in a gesture that means "fear not." His back left hand holds a blazing flame — his power of destruction — while his front left hand points to his foot, which stands for grace.

3 The Arch of Flames: This represents the cycle of creation, destruction, and rebirth.

4 The Demon: Siva stands on a dwarf-like demon while doing a dance intended to free the world of illusion.

These questions are what the Hindu writings called the Upanishads (oo PAN uh shadz) try to answer. The last Upanishads were written about 200 years after the Vedas. In many ways they show what happened to the early Aryan religion celebrated in the Vedas. Over the centuries, their rituals and hymns became more complex. By the time of the Upanishads, the basic Hindu beliefs were worked out.

For the early Aryans of the Vedas, rituals and sacrifice had been everything. As time passed and Hinduism grew, a new kind of spirituality was born. This new thinking made proper living more important than ritual.

In this painting, the Hindu god Krishna appears standing and wearing a crown, below the tall figure with outstretched arms.

A Universal Force

The goal in life according to the Hinduism of the Upanishads is to free the individual soul, or atman, by joining it with brahman, or the universal life force. Hindus believe it takes more than one lifetime to free the soul. Thus a soul must be reborn into another body, passing through as many of these rebirths as it takes until it reaches the highest level of spiritual understanding. Known as **reincarnation,** this process of rebirth can mean coming back in the form of either a human or an animal. Knowing this, many Hindus take care to practice ahimsa – not injuring any living thing.

To gain the perfect understanding that leads to the freedom of the soul, Hindus may practice various forms of yoga. **Yoga** is a form of exercise that is both physical and mental. Fasting and religious pilgrimages are also important for Hindus seeking oneness with the universe.

Hinduism Today

After thirty-five centuries Hinduism thrives. In modern-day India there are hundreds of thousands of Hindu holy men, known as sadhus and swamis. Poems from the Vedas may be recited at family occasions. On certain holidays children reenact the stories of heros from ancient epics. Children also take part in Diwali, or the Festival of Lights, when they place hundreds of tiny lamps around their homes. Today Hinduism remains a vital part of life for over 760 million people — over 900,000 of them living in the United States.

? Ask Yourself

What are your thoughts about the practice of ahimsa? How do you think such a practice might be adapted into a form of protest?

? ? ? ? ? ? ? ? ? ? ? ? ? ?

Buddhism

Focus What are the main teachings and practices of Buddhism?

Around 2,600 years ago, some people living in the Ganges River valley grew dissatisfied with the Hindu religion. They questioned the truth of the sacred Veda texts. A religious movement was born. One of its leaders was Siddhartha Gautama (sih DAHR tah GAW tuh muh).

Most of what we know about Siddhartha is based on accounts that were carefully handed down by word of mouth for four centuries, then put into writing. Several accounts say he was born around 540 B.C. as prince of a kingdom. His father wanted him to be a warrior and ruler. Even as a young man, Siddhartha grew tired of his life of luxury and began to search for a more meaningful existence. While driving his chariot beyond the castle walls, Siddhartha was stunned to see a man who was very sick, another man who was old and frail, and a third man who had died. These

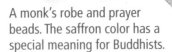

A monk's robe and prayer beads. The saffron color has a special meaning for Buddhists.

• Tell Me More •

The Buddha: Enlightened One

Artists have made many pictures and sculptures of the Buddha over the centuries. The Buddha can be shown in many different postures. Each posture represents an event in the Buddha's life or an aspect of his teachings. In this stone carving from the late 800s, the wise man sits in meditation beneath a sacred tree.

1 The small bump, or topknot, on the Buddha's head represents his enlightenment. Some stories say he grew a second brain to contain his enlightened wisdom. The topknot covers this second brain.

2 This posture is called "touching the earth." While the Buddha meditated, Buddhist tradition says, he was attacked by a god called Mara, the Tempter. The Buddha touched the earth and asked it to be a witness to his goodness. This helped him defeat Mara.

three encounters filled the prince with despair. From that day forward, Siddhartha decided to lead a religious life.

Siddhartha abandoned the luxury and power. For six years, he fasted and thought deeply in an attempt to let go of the world. His ribs poked from his chest and his weary eyes sank into their sockets, but no great spiritual realization came. Eventually, Siddhartha gave up his life of hardship in favor of a middle path rejecting both luxury and self-denial.

Awakening

Then, when he was 35 years old, Siddhartha sat down under a Bodhi tree and began to meditate. Early one morning, his mind was filled with a deep understanding about the nature of suffering and the way to overcome it. This experience was the Great Enlightenment, which transformed him into the Buddha, or "Enlightened One."

Young monks like these are a common sight in Buddhist countries.

The great religion of Buddhism sprang from the experiences of Siddhartha. Buddhists believe in rebirth, but not in a permanent soul or in the caste system. They believe selfish desire causes human suffering.

The ultimate goal in Buddhism is to let go of greed, hatred, and ignorance. Achieving this goal leads to a serene state of mind known as nirvana. This blissful state is eternal. Nirvana is realized while a person is still alive, but lasts beyond death.

Over the centuries Buddhism spread from India to the rest of Asia. There are many different forms of Buddhism, some of which are found mainly in certain countries. Zen Buddhism, for instance, is found chiefly in Japan. Zen stresses the quest for a state of spiritual bliss called satori.

Buddhism Today

Although Buddhism declined in India, it today has over 300 million followers worldwide, including more than 200,000 in the United States.

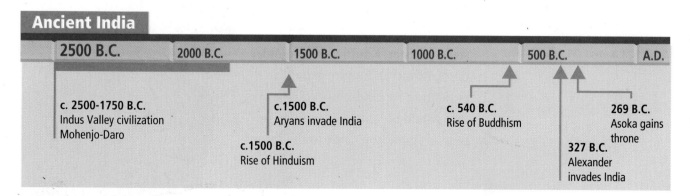

Ancient India

2500 B.C.	2000 B.C.	1500 B.C.	1000 B.C.	500 B.C.	A.D.

c. 2500-1750 B.C.
Indus Valley civilization
Mohenjo-Daro

c.1500 B.C.
Aryans invade India

c.1500 B.C.
Rise of Hinduism

c. 540 B.C.
Rise of Buddhism

269 B.C.
Asoka gains throne

327 B.C.
Alexander invades India

Every year, usually in the spring, Buddhists around the world celebrate a holiday known in this country as Buddha's Birthday. In Japan, children celebrate this day by building a canopy of flowers over a statue of a baby Buddha, then pouring sweet tea over the statue. Throughout the year, Buddhist holy men and women throughout the world still practice the ancient disciplines of poverty, meditation, and study.

Rise of the Mauryan Empire

Focus | *What role did Buddhism play in the Mauryan Empire?*

Shortly after Alexander the Great swept through the Hindu Kush and invaded India in 327 B.C., a young man named Chandragupta (chuhn druh GUP tuh) rose to the throne of the most brilliant and long-lasting Indian dynasty—the Mauryan (MOR ee uhn) Empire.

Little is known about Chandragupta's origins. Some sources say he began in poverty, others say he was a noble. One story even says that he met Alexander, who used the occasion to make fun of him.

What is known is that Chandragupta was a brilliant, ruthless ruler. When Alexander left India, the young Indian swiftly pounced on the weak regime the conqueror had left behind. By 305 B.C. Chandragupta had met and defeated Alexander's representative in battle. In one stroke the man Alexander the Great had joked about had become India's first emperor.

Under Chandragupta's strong rule, India was fairly peaceful and prosperous. Chandragupta also supported scholars and poets in his court. With the advice of his stern minister, Kautilya, the founder of the Mauryan Empire gained a reputation for cold-blooded efficiency that would become his family legacy — until his grandson came to the throne.

Sculptures of four lions standing back to back were a favorite symbol of Asoka's. The wheel on the statue's base is a symbol of Buddha. The whole carving was once mounted on a tall pillar that proclaimed Asoka's laws. **Citizenship:** *How might posting his laws on pillars have helped Asoka govern?*

Asoka

When Chandragupta's grandson Asoka (ah SHO kuh) became emperor, the Mauryan empire was at its largest, covering most of the Indian subcontinent. At first Asoka behaved as ruthlessly as the earlier emperors. Then his behavior suddenly changed. After witnessing a bloody military campaign that caused thousands of deaths, the ruler began to stress a different aspect of Buddhist philosophy than his grandfather had. Asoka ordered new laws, or **edicts**, erected on stone pillars throughout the empire. Rock Edict II stated simply:

A stupa is a bell-shaped monument made of masonry, meant to be used as a Buddhist shrine. Some of those from the time of the Mauryan Empire can still be found in India.

> **"A**ll men are my children. Just as I seek the welfare and happiness of my own children in this world and the next, I seek the same things for all men. **"**

With his vast power Asoka swiftly spread Buddhism throughout the subcontinent. He built thousands of stupas, which are dome-shaped shrines commonly found in Buddhist countries. His representatives spread Buddhism throughout Southeast Asia. Today Asoka is considered by many to have been one of India's most influential and successful leaders.

Lesson Review

2500 B.C.	1500 B.C.	500 B.C.

2500–1750 B.C.
Indus Valley Civilization After several hundred years civilization in the Indus Valley dissolves.

1500 B.C.
The Aryans Sweeping through the Hindu Kush, Central Asian horsemen bring new gods to India.

540 B.C.
Buddha is Born With Siddhartha Gautama's birth in approximately this year a great religion begins.

1. **Key Vocabulary:** Use caste, reincarnation, and yoga to write a paragraph about Hinduism.

2. **Focus:** What effect did Aryan migration have on Indian culture?

3. **Focus:** What are the main teachings of Hinduism?

4. **Focus:** What are the main teachings and practices of Buddhism?

5. **Focus:** What role did Buddhism play in the Mauryan Empire?

6. **Critical Thinking: Compare** How did Asoka's Buddhism differ from Chandragupta's?

7. **Theme: Lasting Beginnings** How do Indians still maintain ancient religions?

8. **Citizenship/Art Activity:** Make a chart comparing Hinduism and Buddhism.

LESSON 3

The Geography of Ancient China

Main Idea Rugged terrain both protected and isolated ancient China.

Thousands of miles long, the Great Wall took generations to build. *Citizenship: Do you think the wall was worth spending lives for?*

Key Vocabulary

- basins
- species
- bronze

Key Places

- Great Wall of China
- Yangtze River
- Yellow River

When orbiting astronauts pass over China, they can see a wriggling gray ribbon that zigzags from China's eastern coast to Gansu (gahn soo) Province in the north — the distance from Baltimore to Denver. Although the ribbon seems to bend and twist like a great river, it is not a river or a natural feature at all. It was built by humans.

What the astronauts see is the Great Wall of China. The Chinese began building this barrier of earth and stone more than 2,000 years ago to defend China against possible invasion from the north. For parts of its length, it follows China's great Yellow River, hugging the edges of the mountains and valleys in its path. A massive structure, if pulled into a straight line the Great Wall would extend for over 4,000 miles — roughly the distance from New York to San Francisco and back again as far as Dallas!

For centuries the wall's solid presence discouraged invasion from the north, while great mountains and oceans protected China's other borders. The longest continuous construction project in history, the wall's first sections were probably built in the 400s B.C. Work was still being done as late as the A.D. 1600s.

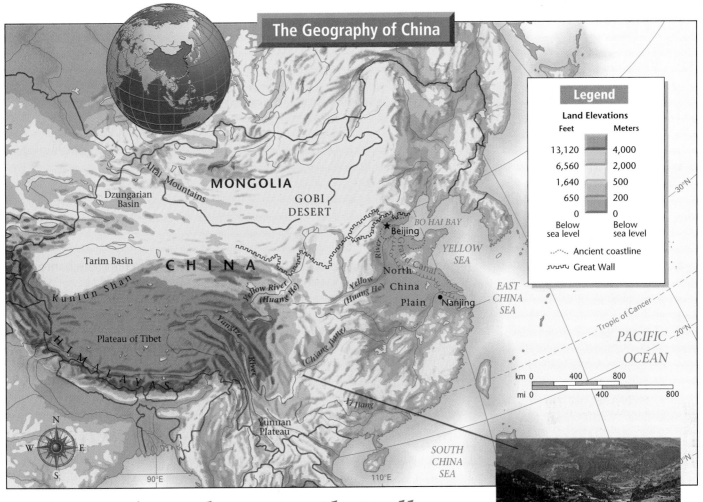

The Geography of China

Legend

Land Elevations

Feet	Meters
13,120	4,000
6,560	2,000
1,640	500
650	200
0	0
Below sea level	Below sea level

.... Ancient coastline

᠅᠊᠅᠊ Great Wall

Natural Borders, Fertile Valleys

Focus *How did China's geography affect people in ancient times?*

For centuries the people of China believed they were living at the center of the world, or at least the center of civilization. They called their country Zhonghua (joong gwoh), which means "middle country." Stretching for millions of square miles across Asia, this middle land was protected on three sides. To the south and east lay the Pacific, the largest ocean in the world. In the west stood the earth's highest mountains and one of its widest, most deadly deserts. Only in the north was there a gap — a broad grassy lowland called the North China Plain. Horsemen from Central Asia could easily gallop across this flat land and invade, as they had done in India. This was the gap the Great Wall was built to close.

Find China's mountain chains in the map above. As you can see, almost half of China is mountainous. Many of the mountains surround huge, bowl-shaped plateaus or **basins,** such as the Tarim (TAH reem) Basin in the northwest. This vast landform contains one of Asia's driest deserts. Today these vast, barren areas are a productive part of modern China. They were useless to the ancient Chinese. Only about 10 percent of the land that is now China could support crops. For this reason, Chinese civilization sprouted in the fertile river valleys to the east.

Farmland in Guizhou Province. Why do you suppose the land is carved into steps? **MAP SKILL:** *What river flows through this area?*

China's high mountain walls were a mixed blessing. Although the mountains kept out invaders, they also prevented easy trade and cultural exchange with other countries. China's extreme isolation had fascinating results in the natural world. Whole **species,** or varieties, of plants and animals are unique to China. Among these is the giant panda.

The Silk Road

Despite China's impressive natural barriers, as early as the second century B.C. the ancient Chinese did succeed in establishing trade with countries as far away as Rome. The route this trade took is known as the Silk Road. This was not an actual road. Rather, it was a series of different merchants trading from one to the other along a route that covered thousands of miles. Chinese merchants would trade silk and spices for the big, strong horses owned by the nomads of the north. The nomads, in turn, would trade the silk farther west as they crossed Central Asia's grassy sea to Mesopotamia. Eventually the silk would reach Rome, though no single individual at the time knew exactly how it got there!

Silk was not China's only product. A great deal of farming took place in early China's wet and fertile river valleys. The valleys provide a variety of crops, including rice, wheat, and soybeans. Because parts of South China are tropical, pineapples, bananas, and oranges can be grown there.

On the map on the previous page, trace the path of the Yangtze (yang DZEE), which runs from west to east through central China. It twists and turns around a series of basins. Connecting the interior of the country with the Pacific Ocean, the Yangtze is China's longest river. Its tributaries provide China with a huge transportation network. The Huang He, or Yellow River, is the second largest river in China. It gets its name from the yellowish clay it picks up as it cuts through valleys on its seaward journey

Many types of animals — such as this giant panda — can be found in China and nowhere else in nature. GEOGRAPHY: *Why do you think this is so?*

A fertile valley in mountainous China. The pillars in the background are actually the limestone remains of washed away mountains.

Tonglushan Copper Mine

Mines like this provided tons of copper ore, which could then be refined and mixed with tin to make bronze.

1. First a shaft would be dug to the bottom of a seam of copper – over 150 feet down.

2. Next, horizontal shafts would be dug along the seam so ore could be mined.

3. Deep vertical shafts were used to send up ore and ground water.

4. Winches like this were used to haul the loads up.

5. Heavy planks lined the shafts.

from the Kunlun mountains.

Even more than most countries, China's geography was a kind of recipe for its history, with mountains as the major ingredient. Shut off from the world — except for its contact with Central Asia's nomads — China developed on its own. It had all the farmland it needed, and plenty of copper for making a useful metal, called **bronze**. Protected by barriers both natural and man-made, and possessing enough resources to support a growing nation, Chinese civilization blossomed.

Mines like the one at Tonglushan provided copper to make bronze for weapons, ritual vessels, and artwork.

Lesson Review: Geography

1. **Key Vocabulary:** Use **basin** and **species** to describe the geography of China.

2. **Focus:** How did China's geography affect people in ancient times?

3. **Critical Thinking: Conclude** Why might the nomads of Central Asia have been very important to the development of China?

4. **Citizenship:** Today China has a difficult relationship with western countries. How might China's past have influenced modern China's politics?

5. **Citizenship/Art Activity:** Make a drawing that shows China's major regions. Decide on a symbol to illustrate each region.

The Culture and Philosophy of Ancient China

Key Vocabulary

- mandate
- civil war
- bureaucrat

Key Events

221 B.C. Unification

87 B.C. Height of the Han dynasty

Main Idea Chinese culture survived intact for thousands of years.

For centuries China's earliest dynasty, the Shang, was considered a myth. Even in the sixth century B.C., Confucius, the great Chinese philosopher, doubted the existence of the Shang dynasty. "How can we talk about their ritual?" he once asked. "There is a lack of both documents and learned men."

It was not until 1899 that documents and learning came together by chance in a hospital room. When a Chinese scholar visited a friend in the hospital, he discovered his friend was being treated with a medicine made from tortoise shells. Picking up one of the shells, the scholar made a stunning discovery – the shell was covered with ancient writing. In time, the men discovered where the shells had come from, and the mystery of the Shang dynasty began to unravel. Thousands of shells and bones covered with ancient writing were found in the years that followed. Eventually their purpose became clear. The shells had been used to tell fortunes!

Tortoise shells like this were used by ancient Chinese to tell fortunes.

Early Chinese Inventions

2000 B.C.	1500 B.C.	1000 B.C.

Shang: c. 1700 – 1050 B.C.
Beautifully cast bronzes like this elephant, used as a container for wine, were typical of the Shang dynasty.

Zhou: 1050 – 221 B.C.
Compasses like this helped Chinese as early as the Zhou dynasty to find their way on land and sea.

Early Cultural Achievements

Focus *What were the earliest cultural achievements of ancient China?*

China's long rise from the early settlements that grew up along its river valleys to the great empires that began with the Shang dynasty took many centuries. Tropical jungles had to be cleared, enemies had to be defeated, and new ways of tilling the soil had to be invented. The basis of Chinese culture, however, was formed at an early date. People in China invented a great many tools and systems of thought centuries before the rest of the world. Chinese values, scholarship, and family life grew to become lasting traditions. These traditions were encouraged and sometimes enforced by China's many dynasties.

By the time China's first dynasty, the Shang, began around 1700 B.C., stone tools were being replaced by bronze, marking the end of the Stone Age. The civilization that grew up on the plains of the Yellow River boasted powerful warriors. These men fashioned armor and shields and used powerful bows made from horns. Like the Aryans, they rode into battle on two-wheeled chariots. They also had sharp axes to fling at their enemies.

During the Shang dynasty, the independent lives of villages gave way to a system of landowners and slaves. A capital was built for the king and other officials. There was still no strong central government, but the king controlled many important duties. He was supported by noble families made up of his relatives and local chiefs. The family was valued. Young people respected their elders. People worshipped their ancestors, asking for their advice through religious rituals.

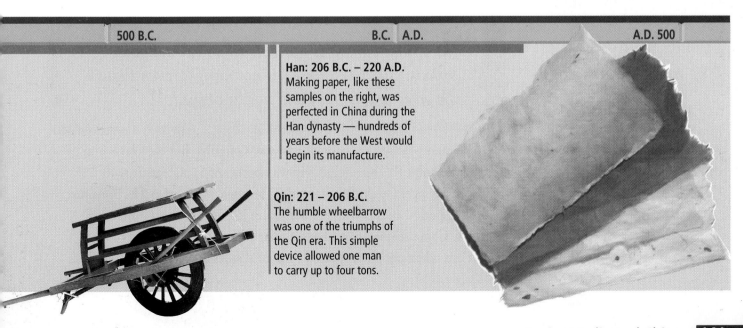

500 B.C.		B.C.	A.D.		A.D. 500

Han: 206 B.C. – 220 A.D.
Making paper, like these samples on the right, was perfected in China during the Han dynasty — hundreds of years before the West would begin its manufacture.

Qin: 221 – 206 B.C.
The humble wheelbarrow was one of the triumphs of the Qin era. This simple device allowed one man to carry up to four tons.

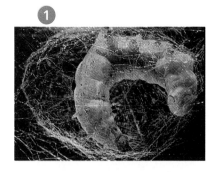

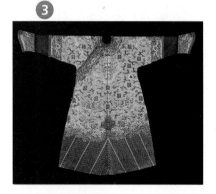

Silkmaking

① First the silk worm creates a cocoon of silk threads.

② Next, the silk threads are spun onto spools.

③ Finally, the spun silk is woven to create a finished garment. The example above is from the Han dynasty.

China Evolves

About 3,000 years ago the Shang dynasty was swallowed up by warlike people from the west known as the Zhou (SHOO). Throughout history cultures have flourished only to be destroyed by enemies. Instead of wiping out the Shang's accomplishments, however, the Zhou dynasty preserved and strengthened them. In many ways, they merely picked up where the Shang had left off.

The Zhou marched their armies throughout north China and the Yangzi valley, bringing Shang culture with them. They controlled their lands by putting them under the rule of warriors who commanded large armies. Once the Zhou were firmly in control of a region, they organized communities by dividing the land into squares and assigning them to peasants. Aside from working their own plots, the peasants also worked together to cultivate a central piece of land for the warrior lords of the region. During the Zhou dynasty, iron tools were invented, and agriculture increased. Iron-tipped plows drawn by oxen allowed farmers to raise more crops. They grew wheat, rice, beans, and fruit.

According to the Zhou, heaven had given them a **mandate**, or permission to rule. This idea became known as the "heavenly mandate." Those in heaven who gave permission were said to be the ancestors of the ruling class. By the eighth century B.C. the authority of the Zhou was being questioned. By the fifth century, the open rebellion of the Zhou's own warrior states drove the Zhou from power. The fighting over supreme rule of China would go on for almost 200 years. This time would come to be known as the Warring States period.

Confucius and Lao-tzu

Focus *What are the main teachings of Confucianism and Taoism?*

> **"I**f a ruler himself is upright, all will go without orders. But if he himself is not upright, even though he gives orders, they will not be obeyed.**"**

The man who wrote these words was Kongfuzi, but we know him as Confucius (kuhn FYOO shuhs). He was born in 551 B.C. in a small Chinese province. Confucius wanted to be a teacher, yet he was born just before the period of the Warring States, a violent time more suited to warriors. China seemed to be falling apart. Confucius dreamed of a former era when people respected their ancestors and followed their leaders. Was there a way, he wondered, to restore a spirit of honesty?

With this goal in mind, Confucius created a philosophy, known to us as Confucianism, that would affect China for centuries to come.

The cornerstone of his philosophy was to treat others as you would like to be treated. Confucius wanted peace. He imagined a government in which the ruler behaved as a loving father and all the people obeyed. He reasoned that if the man at the top behaved well, everyone under him would become good by example. According to Confucius' principle of the Five Relationships, there is a correct relationship between ruler and subjects, parent and child, elder and younger brother, husband and wife, and friend and friend. The principle stresses polite, respectful behavior and a high regard for learning.

Confucius' ideas have survived, even though China's current government discourages interest in his teachings. His commonsense sayings are still quoted by parents to their children, and scholars all over the world still study him.

Lao-tzu and Taoism

Around the time of Confucius another philosopher saw the world very differently. His name was Lao-tzu (low dzuh), and his belief was that order and harmony come not from society but from nature. His advice to those seeking calm and reason would be to go up into the hills and watch the clouds, or sit near a babbling stream.

Lao-tzu urged those seeking order to follow the Way, or Tao. Animals follow the Tao naturally, claimed Lao-tzu. Only humans argue about the big questions of right and wrong. In Taoism, people pull back from the world of humans and learn from observation of nature not to seek after useless things or create unnecessary argument. Like Confucianism, Taoism would become an influential philosophy for hundreds of years to come.

Confucius was often shown as a aged, bearded scholar. **CULTURE:** *Why would it make sense to show Confucius as a kind of father figure?*

Lao-tzu is shown in this bronze. The bull on which he sits stands for the natural world he loved.

Age of Empires, Age of Scholars

Focus *How did the rise of scholars help Chinese civilization?*

In 221 B.C. the Warring States period was finally brought to a close. Calling himself Shihuangdi (shur hwahng dee), or "first great emperor," one man brought the divided states under the rule of his own dynasty – the Qin (CHIN). Forever after, all of China would be named after this dynasty. The word "China" comes from the word "Qin."

China would not find the road to unification easy. Having conquered all the so-called Warring States, Shihuangdi declared himself China's total master. He took land away from noble families and organized their holdings into 36 provinces. He established a standard system of coinage, then standardized weights and measures. Even the distance between cart wheels was standardized. Then Shihuangdi began to build. He built roads, canals, and irrigation systems. The emperor next looked to the north, saw the threat of a nomad invasion, and directed the building of the Great Wall. This project nearly ruined the first generation that worked on it, as thousands of people were forced to spend their entire lives in hard labor.

During the Qin dynasty China absorbed other lands until the empire stretched from Southern Manchuria in the east to the Yellow River in the

Ask Yourself

Emperor Shihuangdi unified China, but he also passed a law calling for the burning of books. How do you feel about this law? Do you think destroying books means something more than destroying other kinds of property? Why?

? ? ? ? ? ? ? ? ? ? ? ? ? ?

• Tell Me More •

An Emperor's Tomb

The Find of a Lifetime

When archaeologists uncovered the Qin emperor Shihuangdi's tomb in the 1970s, they knew they were making history. Standing in three enormous pits was an enormous army of clay soldiers — over 5,000 strong!

1 The first pit contained over 1,000 fully excavated, life-size terra cotta clay warriors.

2 Each figure's face was unique. This was done by mixing and matching pre-made noses, moustaches and beards!

3 The soldiers were originally set up in orderly ranks, in real battle formation. Each man held an actual weapon.

4 Each warrior needed to be carefully restored.

west. Keeping order in the empire was expensive and difficult. Shihuangdi had to raise taxes and force people to serve in his large army. He considered the ideas of Confucius and other philosophers dangerous to his rule and tried to suppress all ideas except those spread by the government. It is said that the emperor was so anxious to maintain power that he sometimes disguised himself as a commoner and went traveling, making notes about every law he saw being disobeyed. In 213 B.C. he issued a law calling for the burning of all books not approved by him.

By the end of Shihuangdi's reign, many common people hated him for forcing them into the army or to work on the Great Wall. Nobles resented the power he had taken from them. Scholars hated him for burning books. He began to carry a sword as he sat on the throne. Legend has it that several times he used the weapon to defend himself against assassins. Finally, **civil war** — fierce fighting within a single nation — broke out. The Qin dynasty crumbled.

Ancient & Modern Chinese Characters

	Ancient	Modern
Sun		日
Mountain		山
Tree		木

Over thousands of years Chinese writing has changed remarkably little. The words, or characters, above show just how little.

The Scholars Govern

During the civil war, a rebel leader from a poor family named Liu Bang seized power. In 202 B.C. he declared himself emperor and founded the Han dynasty. This dynasty would reverse the Qin's policies against Confucianism. It would promote Confucian philosophy as a powerful tool of the government.

The age of the first Han dynasty, which lasted about 200 years, was the age of scholars. The great Imperial Library, which had been destroyed during the rule of the Qin, was restored. Books on literature, philosophy, poetry, math, medicine, and war were collected.

In 124 B.C., an official school, known as the Imperial Academy, was created. It taught only the philosophy of Confucius and his many followers. By spreading the ideas of Confucianism, the Han created an empire that was more stable than the Qin Empire had been. Anyone who wished to play a part in ruling the empire went through a series of exams. Aside from needing to know how to write, the exam taker had to have memorized most of the sayings of Confucius and other philosophers. Those who passed these difficult exams were in a position to acquire power through politics. This meant that even a man of little wealth who managed to learn to read and write might some-day rise in the ranks of Chinese society.

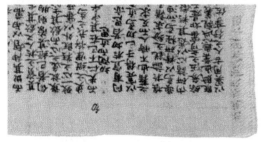

In the painting above, would-be bureaucrats take the exam that will decide their futures. The exam was seen as so important that some people risked the punishment of death and cheated. The handkerchief below the painting was used in just such a way over 2,000 years ago.

These scholars spread Confucius' ideas of respect and order throughout the empire. Their positions were clearly defined to work together in a complicated way. They formed a vast bureaucracy, which is a government with a large set of roles, rules, and levels of power. The main duties of the scholar **bureaucrats** were taking the census and registering land for taxation. But they also handled local justice and education and built roads, parks, and public buildings. The bureaucracy turned China from a society that had been divided between poor farmers and nobles into one that was divided between the educated and the uneducated. For the first time, scholars formed a part of the government.

The Mighty Han

By about 87 B.C., China had extended its boundaries almost to what they are today. Enemies could hardly resist the Chinese. During the Han dynasty, the Chinese had invented a crossbow that was more powerful and accurate than any other weapon at the time. Also during the Han dynasty, China began to have more contact with the rest of the world. The dynasty traded with its nomadic neighbors who carried Chinese silk and other goods as far as Rome. By the third century B.C., large numbers of people and merchandise found transport on a newly built waterway, known as the Magic Canal, which linked two major Chinese rivers.

Developed under the Han rulers, the Chinese system of bureaucracy, controlled by strict rules of behavior in the spirit of Confucius, kept China together for over a thousand years. Even when governments fell and new groups struggled for power, Chinese society remained stable, certain that it understood right from wrong.

It was not until the mid–100s A.D. that China's proud Han dynasty first quavered and then began to crack. Nevertheless the Han period is the one that the Chinese have most identified with over time. In fact, in Chinese, their country is not called China, but Han.

An ancient earthquake warning system. When a tremor began, a bronze ball would drop into the mouth of the nearest frog!

Lesson Review

2000 B.C.	1000 B.C.	B.C.	A.D.	

1700 B.C.
The Shang China's first dynasty established.

221 B.C.
China Unified Shihuangdi founds Qin dynasty, declares himself emperor.

87 B.C.
Height of the Han By this date China had almost reached its modern shape.

1 Key Vocabulary: Use the words mandate, civil war, and bureaucrat in a paragraph about the rule of scholars in China.

2 Focus: What were the earliest cultural achievements of ancient China?

3 Focus: What are the main teachings of Confucianism and Taoism?

4 Focus: How did the rise of scholars help Chinese civilization?

5 Critical Thinking: Conclude How might the Qin dynasty have avoided civil war?

6 Theme: Lasting Beginnings What Chinese inventions do we still use today?

7 Citizenship/Research Activity: Research the role scholars have played in the history of our own government.

Forming Hypotheses Using Parallel Timelines

Two Roads

If the Shang dynasty had not had two-wheeled chariots, do you think it would have become as powerful in China as it did? How did chariots contribute to the collapse of the Indus Valley civilization?

Parallel timelines can help answer these questions. These are time-lines that let you compare events in two or more different places during the same period. When you read parallel timelines, you can develop a hypothesis, a possible explanation for why events happened. You can test your hypothesis by researching other sources.

Ancient India and Ancient China 2,500 B.C. - 1,500 B.C.

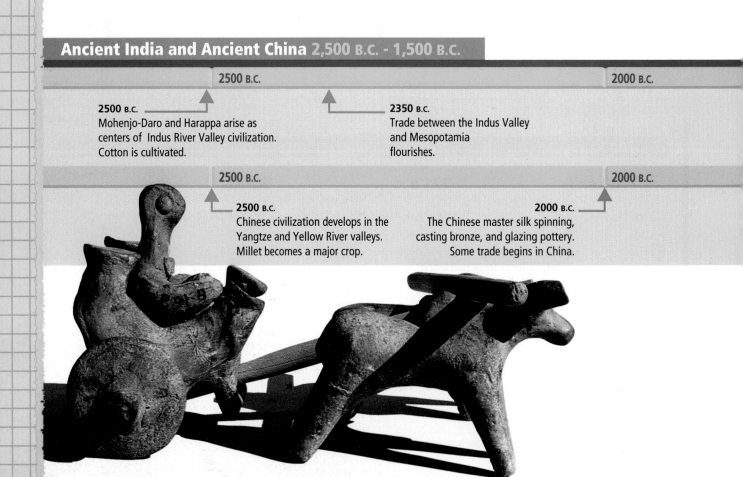

2500 B.C.   2000 B.C.

2500 B.C.
Mohenjo-Daro and Harappa arise as centers of Indus River Valley civilization. Cotton is cultivated.

2350 B.C.
Trade between the Indus Valley and Mesopotamia flourishes.

2500 B.C.   2000 B.C.

2500 B.C.
Chinese civilization develops in the Yangtze and Yellow River valleys. Millet becomes a major crop.

2000 B.C.
The Chinese master silk spinning, casting bronze, and glazing pottery. Some trade begins in China.

1 Here's How

Below are parallel timelines showing events in the development of ancient China and ancient India.

- Read the timelines, looking at all the events listed. Notice that the main idea of both is the development of ancient cultures. One shows ancient India, and the other shows ancient China.

- Compare events in both places at roughly the same time. For example, in 1500 B.C., in both China and India, the two-wheeled chariot played a role in changing the civilization.

- Look at events that lead up to the last date on each timeline. Notice that before the arrival of two-wheeled chariots in India, the Indus Valley civilization was declining. In China, the Shang dynasty was developing.

- Form a hypothesis about events that led to changes in both civilizations. For example, you might look at the arrival of two-wheeled chariots and decide what effect this may have had in both India and China.

- Check reference sources in your library to find out if your hypothesis is correct.

2 Think It Through

How does seeing parallel timelines help you see similarities and differences between two cultures?

3 Use It

1. Study the timelines. Make a list of similarities and differences between the two civilizations at different times.

2. Form a hypothesis about the development of these two cultures. Use library sources to see if you can find evidence for your explanation.

1500 B.C.   **1000 B.C.**

1750 B.C.
Indus Valley
civilization declines.

1500 B.C.
Aryans use two-wheeled
chariots to dominate the
Indus Valley.

1500 B.C.   **1000 B.C.**

1750 B.C.
The Shang dynasty uses two-wheeled
chariots to gain power in China.

Chapter Review

CHAPTER 5

Chapter Review Timeline

| c. 1700-1000 B.C. Shang dynasty | c. 1000-500 B.C. Zhou dynasty | c. 500 B.C. Rise of Buddhism | 221 B.C.- A.D. 206 Qin dynasty | A.D. 206-250 Han dynasty |

| 2500 B.C. | 1950 B.C. | 1400 B.C. | 850 B.C. | 300 B.C. | A.D. 250 |

c. 2500-1500 B.C.
Indus Valley civilization

c. 1500 B.C.
Aryans invade India; rise of Hinduism

c. 269 B.C.
Asoka gains throne

Summarizing the Main Idea

1. Copy the chart below and fill in the missing information to compare the civilizations of ancient India and China.

	India	China
Geography		
Dynasty or People		
Important Ruler		
Religion or Philosophy		
Cultural Achievement		

Vocabulary

2. Use at least eight of the following terms to write the biography of a leader, political or religious, of ancient India or China.

passes (p. 125)   reincarnation (p. 131)   species (p. 138)
subcontinent (p.125) yoga (p. 131)   mandate (p. 142)
monsoon (p. 126)   edict (p. 135)   civil war (p. 145)
caste (p. 130)   basin (p. 137)   bureaucrat (p. 146)

Reviewing the Facts

3. How were the monsoons important to ancient India's civilization?

4. How did the Aryans change life in the Indus Valley?

5. What was the caste system?

6. How did China's geography affect its history?

7. What were some Chinese inventions, and in which dynasty were they invented?

8. What were some of the steps Shihuangdi took to unify his empire?

9. What were the qualifications for becoming a part of the Han dynasty bureaucracy?

Skill Review: Forming a Hypothesis Using Parallel Timelines

10 Using information in the parallel timelines on pages 148–149, what might you hypothesize about the value of a chariot as a military weapon?

11 What major geographical feature aided the rise of civilization in both India and China?

12 How might seeing the similarities and differences between two civilizations aid your understanding of both of them?

Geography Skills

13 Study the map of India on page 126 and the map of China on page 137. What similarities do you see? What are some of the differences?

14 You are the Royal Engineer of the Qin dynasty, and you've just completed a survey of the nation's natural defenses. Write a report to Emperor Shihuangdi on your position on the need to build the Great Wall.

Critical Thinking

15 **Generalize** Why do you think so many early civilizations formed near major rivers?

16 **Conclude** Why would little be known about India's prehistoric inhabitants?

17 **Compare** Develop a chart to describe some of the similarities between Hinduism, Buddhism, Confucianism, and Taoism.

Writing: Citizenship and History

18 **Citizenship** Write a help wanted ad for leaders to help run the Han dynasty. Include the qualities you would want in an administrator.

19 **History** If you were alive during Shihuangdi's reign, what would you have thought of him? Write a letter to a friend describing your feelings about his actions, and how you plan to respond.

Activities

History/Research
Several historical figures, both religious and political, are mentioned in the chapter. Do research to find out more about Siddhartha Gautama, or the Buddha, Chandragupta, Asoka, Confucius, Lao-tzu, or Shihuangdi.

Culture/Literature
Four great Asian religions or philosophies are discussed in the chapter. Each has many religious writings. Find examples of these writings and share them with the class.

Internet Option

Check the **Internet Social Studies Center** for ideas on how to extend your theme project beyond your classroom.

THEME PROJECT CHECK-IN

Consider these questions as you create the details of your civilization:
- What was the climate like there? How did this affect the civilization?
- Did the civilization have any religions? If so, what role did they play?
- Did your civilization try to increase its land and power? If so, why and how did it do this?

The Ancient Americas

Chapter Preview: *People, Places, and Events*

500 B.C.	200 B.C.	A.D. 100

Clovis People   10,000 B.C.

These spear points come from some of the earliest North Americans.
Lesson 1, Page 154

Olmec Head   1500 B.C.

For centuries the meaning of these giant stone heads has been a mystery. *Lesson 1, Page 157*

Snake Mound   A.D. 500

Where in the United States can these mysterious mounds be found?
Lesson 3, Page 164

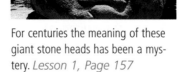

Geography of Ancient America

Main Idea The geography of the Americas gave rise to complex cultures.

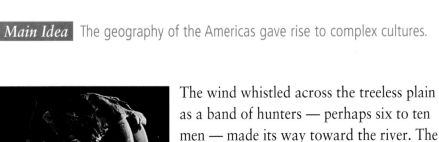

The wind whistled across the treeless plain as a band of hunters — perhaps six to ten men — made its way toward the river. The river's banks were lined with rich grasses and willow shrubs, ideal food for the big game the hunters were after. Perhaps they would find a woolly mammoth, an enormous, lumbering ancestor of the modern elephant. Mammoths had dense coats of matted hair, covering a hide that one expert has described as "tough as an eight-ply truck tire." Or perhaps the hunters would find a giant steppe bison, with its seven-foot horn span. Or a saber-toothed tiger, like the one whose skull appears above, might find the hunters!

Scientists believe that hunters like these, together with their families, were the first humans to reach the Americas. Probably in search of new hunting grounds, they came from northern Asia and followed game across a land bridge to what is now called Alaska.

Key Vocabulary
glacier

isthmus

maize

Key Places
Beringia

Rocky Mountains

Andes

Mesoamerica

Yucatan

◀ A ceremonial knife of the Inca.

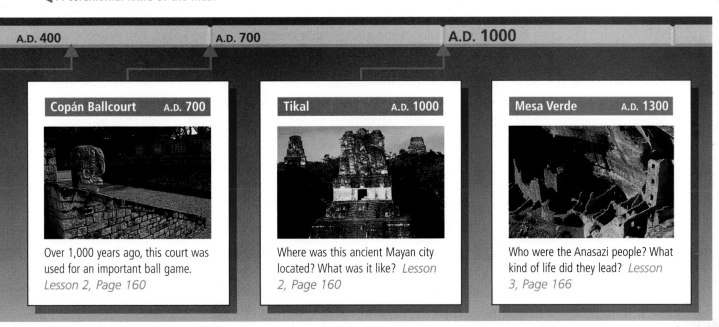

A.D. 400   A.D. 700   A.D. 1000

Copán Ballcourt A.D. 700	Tikal A.D. 1000	Mesa Verde A.D. 1300
Over 1,000 years ago, this court was used for an important ball game. *Lesson 2, Page 160*	Where was this ancient Mayan city located? What was it like? *Lesson 2, Page 160*	Who were the Anasazi people? What kind of life did they lead? *Lesson 3, Page 166*

The World's Longest Land Mass

Focus *What are the main geographic features of North, Central, and South America?*

The land bridge that ancient hunters crossed — probably around 13,000 B.C. — has been called Beringia, after the Bering Sea, which now covers it. Beringia was formed by the freezing of much of the earth's water in vast ice sheets called glaciers. During these periods, known as ice ages, so much water froze that sea levels dropped and new lands emerged.

Some scientists argue that the first humans came to America not by land but by sea, in canoes made from animal skins. Others believe that humans arrived by land during an even earlier ice age, between 45,000 and 75,000 years ago. So far there is no firm evidence for either theory.

Humans soon spread throughout America. By at least 9000 B.C., they had reached the southernmost tip of South America. By that time, people had spread from the Pacific coast to the Atlantic.

The map on the next page shows the main features that early Americans encountered on their great journeys. Trace with your finger the continental backbone of the Rocky Mountains which eventually merges into the Andes to extend down to the tip of South America. Find the Great Lakes. They were holes gouged out by glaciers that later flooded when the glaciers melted at the end of the last ice age. Finally, locate the isthmus, or narrow neck of land, that connects North and South America.

Early Civilizations in the Americas

Focus *What geographic factors contributed to ancient American civilizations?*

The melting of the glaciers that created the Great Lakes also raised sea levels — once again Beringia lay underwater. Asia and America were separated. The warming of the earth's climate also made North America extremely dry. Grass became sparse, and most of the big game died out. America's first inhabitants were forced to adapt to this change or become extinct like the animals they hunted. New tools had to be developed for hunting the smaller animals that had survived the warming. Faced with this challenge, some early peoples turned from a diet of meat to one of fruits and vegetables. They became more skillful at fishing and at gathering nuts, berries, and roots. Most important for their survival, they discovered how to cultivate plants. By at least 4,500 years ago — and perhaps as far back as 7,000 years ago — some groups of early Americans had domesticated beans, squash, and maize, or corn. The hunters were becoming farmers.

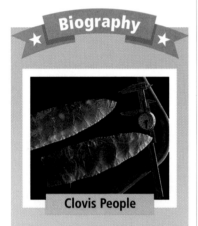

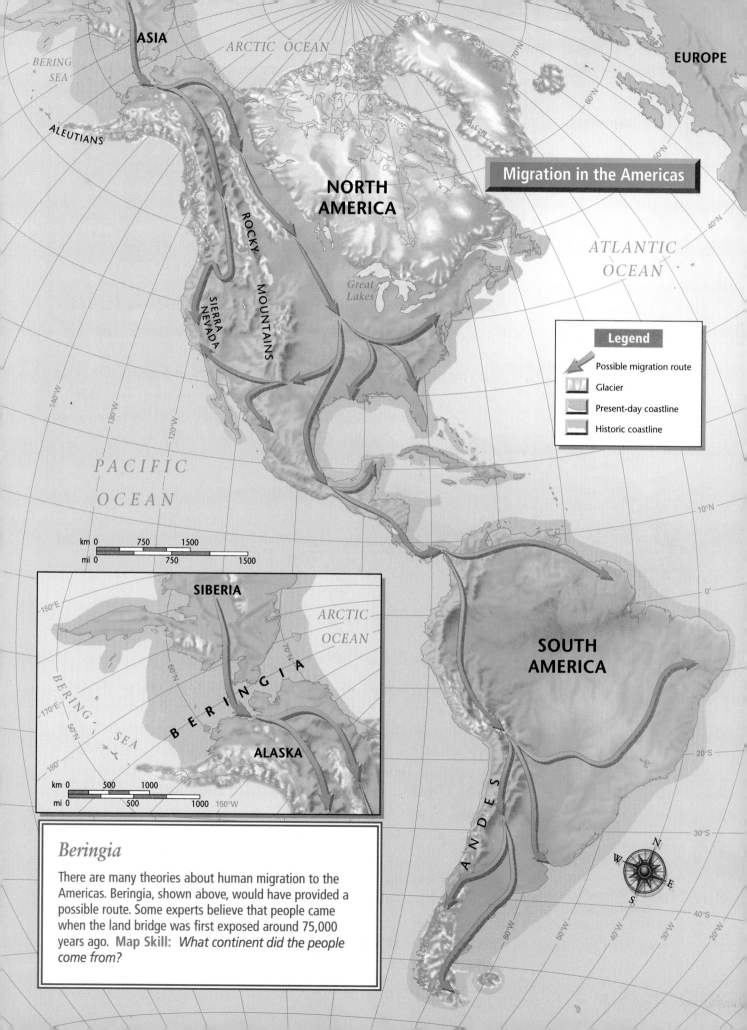

ASIA

ARCTIC OCEAN

EUROPE

BERING SEA

ALEUTIANS

NORTH AMERICA

ROCKY MOUNTAINS

SIERRA NEVADA

Great Lakes

ATLANTIC OCEAN

PACIFIC OCEAN

Migration in the Americas

Legend

- Possible migration route
- Glacier
- Present-day coastline
- Historic coastline

SOUTH AMERICA

ANDES

km 0   750   1500
mi 0   750   1500

SIBERIA

ARCTIC OCEAN

BERING SEA

BERINGIA

ALASKA

km 0   500   1000
mi 0   500   1000   150°W

Beringia

There are many theories about human migration to the Americas. Beringia, shown above, would have provided a possible route. Some experts believe that people came when the land bridge was first exposed around 75,000 years ago. **Map Skill:** *What continent did the people come from?*

Ancient American Civilizations

Legend							
☐ North America					Mississippian		
☐ Mesoamerica				Anasazi			
☐ South America			Hopewell				
	Olmec		Teotihuacán		Aztec		
		Maya					
	Chavín					Inca	
		Moche					

2000 BC	1500 BC	1000 BC	500 BC	BC	AD	AD 500	AD 1000	AD 1500

Many cultures arose in the Americas. This chart shows some major ones. **Chart Skill:** *Which three groups lasted the longest?*

A warrior's ear ornament, made by the Moche of South America. This "ear spool" was worn just as it was by the miniature warrior. **Arts:** *How many separate parts do you think this piece has?*

Corn soon became the leading crop. Ancient Americans also grew many other foods: tomatoes, peppers, peanuts, pumpkins, and 3,000 different kinds of potatoes. They made chocolate from the bean of the cacao tree. They even raised a few animals for their own use — including alpacas, llamas, guinea pigs, turkeys, and ducks. By planting corn, these early Americans had planted the seeds of civilization.

Mother Cultures

Farming in the ancient Americas seems to have begun in two separate places, spreading outward from both. One early farming culture took root in Mesoamerica which includes present-day Mexico, Belize, Guatemala, Honduras, and El Salvador, as well as the jungle peninsula called the Yucatan (yook uh TAN). Another group of people began farming in South America, high in the Andes. Both of these complex farming cultures became civilizations in their own right, with still mightier civilizations as their descendants.

The Olmec people of Mesoamerica thrived from about 1500 B.C. to 900 B.C. While their existence was unknown to scholars until the beginning of this century, the Olmec have since come to be seen as the "mother culture" of all of Mesoamerica. Olmec accomplishments paved the way for the still more impressive civilizations that succeeded them, from the Maya to the Aztec. Cultivation of corn, pyramid architecture, religious practices, even the development of a calendar and writing system — all had their origins in Olmec culture.

Most famous for their monumental sculptures — huge stone heads have been discovered throughout the Olmec region of Central America — the Olmec were also gifted architects and mathematicians. Just as the cultures that followed would do, the Olmec held religious rites in large stone temples, set in clearings carved from the surrounding jungle.

Little is known about the exact nature of Olmec worship, but the Olmec left many intriguing hints. Some Olmec relics were deliberately buried by the Olmec themselves. Why this was done is puzzling, but from the surrounding evidence it seems that these burials were an important aspect of Olmec life. It appears that one grouping of small statues was dug up by the Olmec themselves 100 years after its burial, as if they wanted to check on it. The statues were immediately reburied.

Meanwhile, in South America, the Chavín (shah VEEN) civilization of Peru flourished from about 1000 B.C. to 200 B.C. Like the Olmec, the Chavín farmed maize and were noted for their architecture and sculpture. They built large urban centers with carefully planned streets and homes. They also erected vast step pyramids to honor their gods, and impressive tombs for their dead leaders and nobles. Together with another, later group, the Moche (moh SHAY), Peru's Chavín people would eventually give rise to an even more spectacular civilization — that of the Inca.

Huge Olmec heads like this one could be as tall as 10 feet and weigh as much as 20 tons. **Culture:** *Why do you think these mysterious heads were made?*

Lesson Review: Geography

1 **Key Vocabulary:** Use **glacier, isthmus,** and **maize** in a paragraph about how early hunters developed into farmers.

2 **Focus:** What are the main geographic features of North, Central, and South America?

3 **Focus:** What geographic factors contributed to ancient American civilizations?

4 **Critical Thinking: Interpret** Why do you think the "seeds of civilization" might be planted through the process of farming?

5 **Theme: Lasting Beginnings** Why might change be good for an early culture? Why might stability be good?

6 **Geography/Science Activity:** Research and create a diagram that shows how the glaciers formed the Great Lakes.

LESSON 2

Mayan and Incan Civilizations

Main Idea Great civilizations arose in Mesoamerica and South America.

Key Vocabulary

plaza

glyph

Key Events

300 B.C.– A.D. 900
Height of Mayan civilization

c. A.D. 500
Teotihuacán flourishes

c. A.D. 1520
Inca high point

Teotihuacán was a model Mesoamerican city. **Map Skill:** *Which colored squares would show the temples? Which would show the suburbs?*

The city stretched for miles through the Valley of Mexico. By A.D. 500, it was home to as many as 200,000 people making it the sixth-largest city in the world. Its name was Teotihuacán (teh oh tee hwah KAHN), "the place of the gods." The main street, called the Avenue of the Dead, was studded with massive temples. Towering above the other temples stood the mighty Pyramid of the Sun. Some 20 stories high, it was made of earth and brick. Drums boomed as priests climbed its steep staircase to the altar on its flat top. There they performed the rituals of human and animal sacrifice that were the cornerstone of Mesoamerican religion.

Teotihuacán was both a city and a nation, a unique Mesoamerican civilization that began around A.D. 50. This city-state was a manufacturing and commercial hub as well as a religious center, exporting tools, weapons, and beautiful orange pottery to regions hundreds of miles away. Then, about A.D. 750, most of the city was destroyed by fire. Eventually, this locale would become the capital of the fabulous Aztec Empire, about which you can read more in Chapter 12. But first another civilization — the Maya — would take center stage.

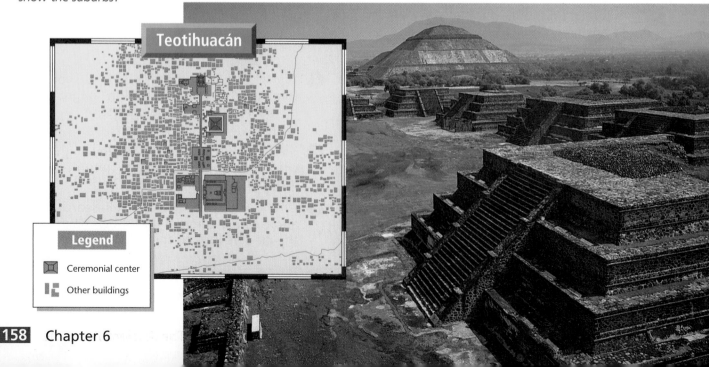

Teotihuacán

Legend

Ceremonial center

Other buildings

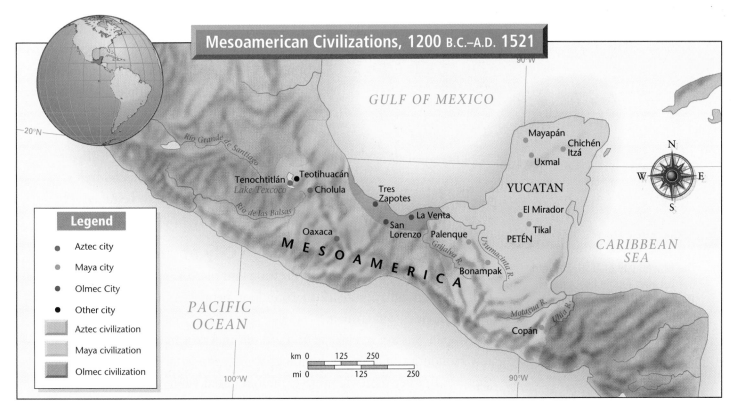

GULF OF MEXICO

20°N

Río Grande de Santiago

Mayapán
Chichén Itzá
Uxmal
YUCATAN

Tenochtitlán • Teotihuacán
Lake Texcoco • Cholula
Tres Zapotes
El Mirador
Tikal
PETÉN

Río de las Balsas

La Venta
San Lorenzo
Palenque

Oaxaca

M E S O A M E R I C A

CARIBBEAN SEA

Grijalva R.
Usumacinta R.
Bonampak

PACIFIC OCEAN

Motagua R.
Ulúa R.

Copán

Legend

• Aztec city
• Maya city
• Olmec City
• Other city
Aztec civilization
Maya civilization
Olmec civilization

N
W E
S

km 0   125   250
mi 0   125   250

100°W

90°W

The Maya and Mesoamerica

Focus *What did the Maya have in common with other Mesoamerican civilizations?*

Although the Maya had a typical Mesoamerican civilization, theirs lasted longer than any other, spanning the time between the end of the Olmec and the rise of the Aztec. Even today, echoes of the ancient Mayan tongue can be heard in the voices of Mexicans in the Yucatan region.

The early Maya modeled themselves after the achievements of the Olmec. Later, the Maya were inspired by the Teotihuacán civilization. Eventually, other Mesoamerican peoples would model themselves after the Maya. Each Mesoamerican empire consisted of a number of city-states. A city-state is a center of political power that includes an urban area and surrounding farmland. The classic Mesoamerican city was built around a plaza, or public square. In front of the plaza was the city's largest structure, a flat-topped pyramid with a temple on top.

In most Mesoamerican cities, warrior kings ruled over a society that was divided into two classes: nobles and peasants. Typically, these cities fought each other in order to win prisoners for sacrifice to the gods. Mesoamericans worshiped many gods, with the sun god usually considered the most powerful. The Maya in particular believed that the will of the gods was shown in the movements of heavenly bodies. As a result, their priests spent a great deal of time studying the sky. Eventually, this interest — and the need to set accurate dates for sacrifice — led to the development of the calendar.

As can be seen from the map, the regions that gave rise to Mesoamerican civilization were very close together. **Map Skill:** *Which one of the cities shown above is neither Mayan, Aztec, nor Olmec?*

The Mayan city of Tikal. Set into the Yucatan jungle like a jewel, Tikal was a center of commerce.

Farming was the main Mayan occupation in Mesoamerica. Both in raising crops and building cities, these people used stone tools rather than metal ones. Although they knew about the wheel, it may have been of little use to them in their difficult terrain. They used it solely on children's toys. If something needed to be taken somewhere, it traveled by human back.

A Jungle City of the Maya

During its height, the Mayan civilization embraced some 200 city-states with a total population of 12 to 16 million people. Among the most important cities was Copán.

Copán was a gorgeous sight. Laid out in a rich river valley in what is now Honduras, many of its buildings were hewn from pale green volcanic rock rather than the more commonly used white limestone. The use of this beautiful stone was intentional, for Copán was the cultural capital of the Mayan Empire. The staircase of just one of its temples was like a history book in stone. Its 72 steps were carved with 1,250 stone **glyphs,** or word pictures, telling the deeds of Copán's divine kings. Red-painted stone statues of these rulers stood at the city's center. Monuments bore dates in a special Mayan calendar. Known as the Long Count, this calen-

·Tell Me More·

The Mayan Ballcourts
A game of life and death

Of all the Mayan rituals, one of the most important was the ball game. In one form or another this game was played throughout ancient Mesoamerica. The rubber ball at far right ❹ was used by the Olmec 3,000 years ago. It still smells of rubber! The ballcourt at Copán ❸ was situated near the center of the city. Like most Mesoamerican courts, it was shaped like the capital letter I and had sloping stone side walls.

Just as the rules of modern sports change over time, so the ball ritual changed and evolved. At Copán, the point of the game was simply to keep the ball aloft without using hands or feet. Players

dar dated time from what they considered the creation day of the world — August 11 in the year 3114 B.C. — by our calendar.

Copán was especially active on market days, when farmers from miles around crowded into the city to sell goods in the public bazaar. In addition to food, farmers sold craftwork, such as paper or embroidered cotton cloth. Each kind of item was sold in a different section of the marketplace. There were also areas for jewelers and image makers. Image makers were popular with farmers. Farmers liked to bury clay likenesses of the corn god or the rain god to ensure a good crop. The Maya did not use money, but bartered for their purchases with cacao beans, sea salt, or other goods.

Copán was a place of beauty, power, and wealth. Its merchants did business throughout Mesoamerica. In fact, the city's glory hastened its end. The trouble began in the late 700s. First, there was a population boom. By that time, much of the best farmland at the bottom of the valley was taken by temples and palaces. Farmers were forced to cultivate the mountain slopes. The more forest they cleared, the more the soil eroded. In time, the farmers could no longer feed the population. People grew weak. Disease spread. In addition, warfare between Copán and its neighbors grew constant. By A.D. 1000, most of Copán's inhabitants had left the valley, and the city was abandoned to the jungle.

A jaguar of the Yucatan. The worship of these jungle cats was common to many Mesoamerican cultures, including the Maya, the Olmec and the Aztec. **Science:** *Why do you suppose the jaguar has spotted fur?*

3

4

used hips, shoulders, and elbows to keep the ball bouncing in a symbolic representation of the order of the universe. In some versions, the losing team was sacrificed to the gods.

The game was always played fast and hard. Heavy padding of wood and leather (shown on the Mayan clay figure at left ❶), protected the players.

On some courts, players could score by passing the ball through a hoop. The ring shown here ❷ is from the ballcourt at the Mayan city of Chichén Itzá, which was built hundreds of years after Copán. A player who got the ball through the ring could win the clothing and jewels of the spectators!

Chocolate Feasts

The tradition of drinking chocolate may go back further than you think. The very word for the bean we make chocolate from, cacao, is Mayan. It means "bitter juice." No one knows how long ago the Mayans cultivated cacao beans, but they were definitely drinking their bitter, unsweetened chocolate by Columbus's arrival in 1492.

1 A Mayan chocolate pot.

2 Cacao beans, from which chocolate is made.

3 The glyph for chocolate (which literally means "sour water").

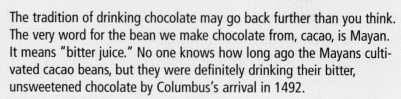

The Inca and South America

Focus *How did the Incan Empire compare to Mesoamerican civilizations?*

While Mesoamerica thrived, civilizations were also developing to the south, along the rugged Andes. First, the Chavín people appeared in South America, perhaps as early as 1000 B.C. Like the Olmec to the north, these early farmers worshiped jaguar gods, of whom they made exquisite carvings. Later, another people, called the Moche, arose and became the dominant group, building on the achievements of the declining Chavín.

The Incan town of Machu Picchu, below, was built high in the Andes. The site went undiscovered by outsiders until 1911. In the photo at right, the splendid Incan stonework can be seen, together with llamas, the Inca's chief means of transport.

Just as the Maya were inspired by the Olmec, so the Inca of Peru followed the Chavín and the Moche cultures. Conquering the remnants of these earlier peoples, in less than 200 years the Inca expanded from a simple chiefdom to become the single largest empire in the Americas.

Like the Mesoamerican empires, the Inca had a highly structured society in which all authority was in the hands of a single ruler. Human sacrifice to ensure good crop yields was also a common feature of Incan life. However, the Inca could be benevolent conquerors. Rather than simply enslaving or sacrificing defeated opponents, the Inca brought them into their empire, extending them privileges of citizenship in exchange for heavy taxes.

In time, the empire became a sprawling network of states, each paying tribute to the Incan capital at Cuzco. Their empire was built on military might and an excellent road system. Training their young nobles as warriors, the Inca built a powerful standing army and used it to subdue neighboring states. Their road system allowed the army to move swiftly to any trouble spots. (A map of this road system appears in Chapter 1, page 17.) In addition to being good road builders, the Inca were fantastic architects.

Whether they arose in Mesoamerica or South America, the early civilizations of these regions achieved great things. With simple tools and careful planning, they erected cities and monuments that still stand today. At the same time, through the mastery of farming, they created strong societies that endured for thousands of years.

This ritual knife, called a *tumi*, was made from pure gold and bits of turquoise. The handle shows a wealthy Inca, with his massive ear spools. **Culture:** *What does this figure have in common with the one on page 156?*

Lesson Review

500 B.C.	A.D. 500	A.D. 1500
300 B.C.–A.D. 900 Height of Mayan civilization	**c. A.D. 500** Teotihuacán flourishes	**c.A.D. 1520** Incan high point

1 **Key Vocabulary:** Use plaza in a sentence about life in ancient Copán.

2 **Focus:** What did the Maya have in common with other Mesoamerican civilizations?

3 **Focus:** How did the Incan Empire compare to Mesoamerican civilizations?

4 **Critical Thinking: Compare Then and Now** Can you draw any parallels between the decline of Copán and present-day ecological problems?

5 **Geography:** How did the Andes pose a challenge to the Inca people?

6 **Writing/Citizenship Activity:** Imagine you are writing a journal that describes life in Copán. Describe a typical day.

Early North American Cultures

Key Vocabulary

mesa

pueblo

Key Events

200 B.C.– A.D. 500
The Hopewell culture

A.D. 900 Founding of Cahokia

c. A.D. 900 Anasazi build cliff dwellings

This half-mile-long earthen snake was built by Mound Builder people in what is now Ohio. **Culture:** *Why might it have been made?*

Main Idea Extensive trade shaped much of early North American cultures.

For centuries, the ancient mounds of eastern North America have left viewers awestruck. In the 1800s, people believed the massive earthworks at such sites as Poverty Point, Louisiana, and Cahokia, Illinois, were the work of a race of giants. Some of the mounds are simply huge. Monk's Mound in Cahokia covers three more acres than the Great Pyramid at Giza. Other mounds are ornate, representing animals in designs so large they can only be recognized from the air. While the mounds' purpose remains a mystery, more is known about their builders.

The Mound Builders

Focus *How did trade affect North America's early cultures?*

The Mound Builders lived in the eastern half of what is now the United States. While there were many mound-building groups living in this region, the two most important were the Hopewell and the Mississippian.

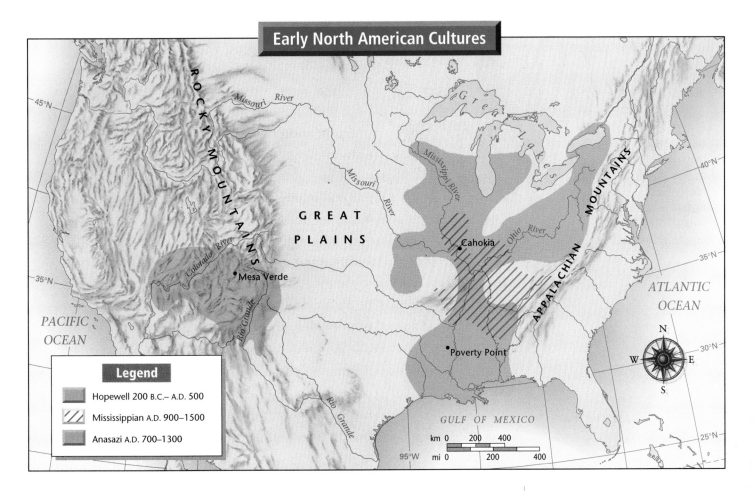

Early North American Cultures

Legend
- Hopewell 200 B.C.– A.D. 500
- Mississippian A.D. 900–1500
- Anasazi A.D. 700–1300

The Hopewell

The Hopewell culture was centered in present-day Ohio. It flourished from about 200 B.C. to A.D. 500. Mostly hunters and gatherers, the Hopewell people lived simply and in small villages. Surprisingly, they were also brilliant and energetic builders. They left behind elaborate earthen mounds, some in the shape of animals. Some mounds were used for burials. Whether circles or squares, these earthen tombs were only for nobles, whose bodies would be placed in log rooms deep in the mound. Treasures were usually added: pearl beads, copper jewelry, wooden masks, and finely carved stone pipes. Finally, millions of baskets of dirt were piled on top.

When these tombs were first discovered, their contents revealed something interesting about Hopewell culture. Many of the materials that appeared in the burials could not be found locally. So, this group must have developed an extensive trading network. On foot and by canoe, Hopewell merchants traveled as far north as the Great Lakes and down the length of the Mississippi, Missouri, Tennessee, and Ohio rivers.

The Mississippians

The Mississippian culture started later than the Hopewell, beginning around A.D. 900 and lasting almost until the arrival of the first Europeans

Map Skill: *Which two cultures overlap each other?*

Curious Facts

What common factors link pyramids in the Americas, Egypt, and elsewhere in the world? Many were built around the same time, of similar materials. Experts think that building a pyramid may well be simply the easiest way to create a very large monument.

Ears of corn like this one were the staple crop of civilizations in both North America and Mesoamerica. **Science:** *Over the centuries, ears of corn became larger. Why was this?*

at the start of the 1500s. The culture really began to develop when the knowledge of how to cultivate corn and beans spread north from Mesoamerica. Once they got the knack of farming, the Mississippian population boomed. People built towns and even — near what is now Cahokia, Illinois — a large, bustling city.

With 30,000 inhabitants, ancient Cahokia was the largest community in North America. Seventeen earthen pyramids — some as tall as 100 feet — dotted the skyline. At the base of these great monuments was a large plaza where Mississippians held public events. Several of the pyramids were used as temples, still others as tombs or dwellings. One pyramid supported the palace of Cahokia's chief. Outside a stout wooden wall stood more mounds and a circle of posts. Their precise locations helped Cahokia's priests track the stars.

The Pueblo

Focus *How did the Anasazi cope with the harsh desert environment?*

In the winter of 1888, two cowboys, Richard Wetherill and Richard Mason, were rounding up some stray cattle on their Colorado ranch. What they discovered that day made history. While riding across a **mesa**

The skull of an Anasazi woman from the 1300s. The spear point that killed her can be clearly seen.

Pueblo Pottery

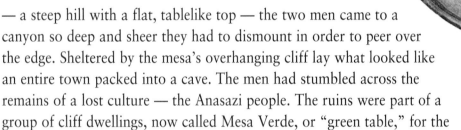

The Pueblo people were accomplished potters, as this bowl shows. The painting on it probably shows a man and woman from the Mimbres region of the Southwest. The woman is on the left, the man on the right.

This bowl has a special significance. It is called a "killed" bowl, because of the hole in the center. Bowls and pots like these were made for use in funeral rituals, in which the ceremonial dish — painted with the likeness of the deceased — would have a hole punched through it to release the spirit of the dead.

Most Pueblo pottery was decorated with painting, as Pueblo artisans appear not to have known of — or cared to use — the glazes used by Mesoamerican cultures.

— a steep hill with a flat, tablelike top — the two men came to a canyon so deep and sheer they had to dismount in order to peer over the edge. Sheltered by the mesa's overhanging cliff lay what looked like an entire town packed into a cave. The men had stumbled across the remains of a lost culture — the Anasazi people. The ruins were part of a group of cliff dwellings, now called Mesa Verde, or "green table," for the forests on the mesa's top.

The Anasazi culture appeared around A.D. 200. By that time, people in the Southwest had learned from Mesoamericans how to cultivate beans and corn. At first the people lived in pit houses, dug partly under ground. Later, they moved aboveground into **pueblos,** or villages of flat-roofed adobe houses. These houses shared adjoining walls and were built on many levels, in a step pattern. In this way the roof of each level provided a terrace for the one above. The former pit houses became *kivas*, or religious centers. Later still, around A.D. 900, the people built their famous cliff dwellings.

The Anasazi adapted to their harsh desert environment. They designed their buildings to be cool during the day and warm at night. They irrigated their fields with rainwater. In addition to being fine architects, the Anasazi were good farmers. But it was difficult to feed a growing population in the desert. So they added to their diet in other ways. They hunted rabbit, deer, and bighorn sheep,

This detail from a larger painting is from the wall of an Anasazi *kiva*. It shows the vibrant style their artists favored.

using everything from bows and arrows to nets woven from human hair.

The Anasazi also established a trading system. For example, the Anasazi site of Chaco Canyon, New Mexico, is the hub of a 400-mile web of roads. One thing Anasazi traders were after was corn. Other imports included such luxury goods as seashells from the Pacific and copper bells and macaw feathers from Mesoamerica. The main export was bright blue turquoise, which the Anasazi also made into jewelry and religious objects for their own use. The actual trading was carried on at fairs during which thousands of people crowded into Chaco.

The Anasazi flourished for about 900 years. Then, during the 1100s, a period of drought set in. Crops failed, and life became increasingly difficult. In addition, the Anasazi had cut down so many trees to use for building material and fuel that the soil began to erode. By 1300, the people had abandoned most of their settlements and moved away. As with other ancient North American peoples, in time only their impressive architecture remained.

Lesson Review

500 B.C.	A.D. 1000

200 B.C.–A.D. 500
The Hopewell culture

c. A.D. 900
Founding of Cahokia
Anasazi build cliff dwellings

1. **Key Vocabulary:** Write a paragraph about the Anasazi using **mesa** and **pueblo.**

2. **Focus:** How did trade affect North America's early cultures?

3. **Focus:** How did the Anasazi cope with the harsh desert environment?

4. **Critical Thinking: Problem Solving** What might the Maya have learned from the Anasazi about overcoming an overpopulation problem?

5. **Geography:** How did early North Americans use the physical geography for trade?

6. **History/Arts Activity:** Chart out a trade network for one group of North American Mound Builders.

Using Periodicals as a Source

Cracking Codes

Did you know that when he was just 11, David Stuart became one of the first people to read Mayan hieroglyphics? If you want to learn about his recent discoveries and about the newest developments in this field, look up an article on Mayan writing.

Newspapers, magazines, and journals are all **periodical literature**. They are published in regular intervals — daily, weekly, monthly, and so on — and contain up-to-date information on almost any topic. You can find your way to the periodical you want by looking in the *Readers' Guide to Periodical Literature*, which is published monthly.

READERS'
GUIDE
TO
PERIODICAL
LITERATURE

1992

52

① Here's How

- Identify a subject (example: the Maya).

- Narrow your subject (Mayan writing). List words to describe your subject (writing, Maya, hieroglyphics).

  • Look up your subject words in the *Readers' Guide to Periodical Literature*.

  • Choose the articles that interest you and write down their titles. Include the names and dates of the periodicals and the page numbers of the articles.

  • Ask a librarian if the article is on microfilm or in the periodical itself.

  • Find the periodical, then the specific issue by using the date. Locate the article by using the page number.

  • Take notes on relevant information.

  • Record the source (title of article, author, publication, date, page numbers). Include the source in any report you write.

② Think It Through

How is information in a periodical different from information in an encyclopedia or a nonfiction book? How can you use these sources together?

Article Title   Narrowed Subject   Periodical

...oul. [Dos Pilas site; research by Arthur Dema...
olger. il *Discover* 13:59-60 Ja '92
Writing
Deciphering the Maya [cover story] B. Bower. il *Science News* 141:40-2 Ja 18 '92
MAYAS IN DRAMA
Coping with change, the Maya discover the play's the thing. P. Breslin. bibl (p117) il *Smithsonian* 23:78-84+ Ag '92
... HALL (BERKELEY, CALIF.)

Page Numbers   Date

③ Use It

1. What do the numbers written with colons (141:40-2) mean?

2. Using the *Readers' Guide to Periodical Literature*, write down names of articles that will give you information about Mayan writing. Include article titles, names and dates of the periodicals, and page numbers.

Chapter Review

Chapter Review Timeline

500 B.C.	200 B.C.	A.D. 100	A.D. 400	A.D. 700	A.D. 1000

200 B.C. - A.D. 500
Hopewell culture

A.D. 900
Founding of Cahokia

300 B.C. - A.D. 900
Height of Mayan civilization

C. A.D. 500
Teotihuacán flourishes

C. A.D. 900
Anasazi build cliff dwellings

Summarizing the Main Idea

1 Choose four of the following civilizations: Olmec, Chavín, Maya, Inca, Hopewell, Mississippian, Anasazi. Copy and complete the chart below, filling in the missing information to compare the civilizations you chose.

	People 1	People 2	People 3	People 4
Dates of civilization				
Site today (country or state)				
Geography				
Major city or place lived				
Cultural achievement				

Vocabulary

2 Using the six words below, write a description of life in the ancient Americas.

glacier (p. 154)   maize (p.154)   mesa (p. 166)

isthmus (p. 154)   plaza (p. 159)   pueblo (p. 167)

Reviewing the Facts

3 How did America's first inhabitants adapt to the changing climate in their new home?

4 Why are the Olmec considered the "mother culture" of Mesoamerica?

5 What was life like in the city of Teotihuacán?

6 Why did the Maya invent the calendar?

7 What caused the downfall of Copán?

8 How did the Inca people increase the size of the empire?

9 Who were the Mound Builders, and what were the mounds they built?

10 Describe the three different kinds of homes the Anasazi lived in at one time or another.

Skill Review: Using Periodicals as a Resource

11 What advantages might a periodical have over an encyclopedia when it comes to getting fresh information?

12 Why is it important to narrow your subject before beginning the search for articles?

13 Why do you suppose the *Readers' Guide to Periodical Literature* was developed?

Geography Skills

14 Study the map of the Americas on page 155, and review the two main theories of how the first people arrived there. Which theory do you think is correct? Why?

15 You are a travel agent living in the year 13,000 B.C. Write and decorate a travel brochure advertising the Americas, that will attract early humans to this new land.

Critical Thinking

16 **Predict** After the Ice Age, water levels around the world rose, creating the oceans and coastlines we know today. If the world's ice caps continued to melt, the oceans would rise even more. How would the United States and the community where you live be affected if that happened?

17 **Compare then and now** What modern sports do the Mayan ball games resemble? How are they similar? How are they different?

Writing: Citizenship and Cultures

18 **Citizenship** You are an Incan diplomat. Write a speech explaining why it is better to let conquered enemies become citizens in your empire than to enslave them.

19 **Cultures** You are living during the time of the Maya. Write a letter to a pen pal in another land describing your daily life.

Activities

History/Science
The Maya's excellent astronomical skills helped them create a calendar. Find out more about the origins of astronomy and the calendar. What other cultures made calendars? Share your findings with the class.

Economics/Math
The Maya culture did not use money, but instead used a barter system, using such things as cacao beans, and salt. Develop your own barter system. Decide on the value of various objects, and give examples of how your system works.

Internet Option

Check the **Internet Social Studies Center** for ideas on how to extend your theme project beyond your classroom.

THEME PROJECT CHECK-IN

As your civilization grew, it would have come into contact with others. This would have affected it in many ways. Ask yourself these questions as you work on your project:
• What did your culture have in common with other civilizations?
• How important was trade to your civilization?
• How did the civilization adapt to its environment?

Ancient Africa

| 1000 B.C. | 500 B.C. | B.C. | A.D. |

Ancient Rock Paintings

What do these rock paintings tell us about West Africa? *Lesson 1, Page 173*

African Wildlife

Why is this cheetah smiling? *Lesson 1, Page 176*

Nok Culture   500 B.C.

Find out about the Nok culture in West Africa. *Lesson 2, Page 178*

The Geography of Ancient West Africa

Main Idea The geography of ancient West Africa greatly influenced the lives of people in that area.

Key Vocabulary

savanna

sorghum

freshwater

extinction

Key Places

Sahara

sub-Sahara

As soldiers on camelback rode through a dry riverbed of the Sahara, the great desert of northern Africa, in 1933, their leader noted something on the rock walls. He halted the patrol and moved closer to the rocks to investigate. What he found astounded him. Cut into the rock were pictures of wild animals! Elephants marched with their trunks raised and rhinoceros appeared ready to attack. According to one report, the patrol leader thought he was dreaming. He was not.

Thousands of ancient rock pictures, like the one shown at the left of this page, have been discovered in the Sahara. What makes these drawings so amazing is that they include animals no longer found there. Today, the Sahara is hot and dry, with little to support such animals.

◀ This brass head of a female ruler (c. A.D. 1000–1100) clearly shows the high level of culture of ancient African societies.

A.D. 500   A.D. 1000   A.D. 1500

Life in a Village

African villagers lived in an enclosed area called a corral, or kraal. *Lesson 2, Page 181*

Ancient Ghana   A.D. 800

Where did the ancient kingdom of Ghana get its wealth? *Lesson 3, Page 184*

Trade Routes in Africa

Camel caravans carried many kinds of goods. *Lesson 3, Page 186*

West Africa's Ancient Geography

Focus *How did West Africa's ancient geography shape the lives of people living there?*

Continental geography — the physical features of Africa itself — has always affected the lives of the people living there. One of the continent's most important physical features is the Sahara. As the Sahara changed, so did the way people lived.

Ancient rock paintings, fossils, and other archaeological evidence have led scientists to conclude that between 3,000 and 8,000 years ago, the Sahara was green and productive. Wild animals, from rabbits to giraffes, roamed across the land. Cattle grazed as ancient people farmed the fertile fields. Scientists believe that a drier climate developed and the moist, green region slowly turned gray-brown, or "Sahara." The grasses and plants gradually died and the animals and humans moved on, leaving the sandy and rocky wasteland of the Sahara behind.

West African geography — especially the sub-Saharan region south of the Sahara — became very important to people. This sub-Saharan region still includes mountains, grasslands, lakes, rivers, and forests.

Dry, grassy areas known as **savannas** cover nearly half of Africa. The savanna area was very important to people in ancient times. Here they could plant rice and **sorghum**, a grain that can be ground into flour for cooking. The wild grasses of the savanna were used to feed domesticated animals, such as cattle and goats. Most sub-Saharan forests, though, were difficult to clear for farmland. Only the forests' edges were planted. In those places, farmers were able to plant yams and palm trees.

Mountains formed barriers for people moving from one area to another. Rivers became important "highways" in sub-Saharan Africa. Find the Niger River on the map on page 175. The Niger River is longer than the Mississippi River. It starts 150 miles inland from the Atlantic Ocean and wanders 2,600 miles before it empties into the Atlantic Ocean. People used these rivers for transportation, fishing, and for raising crops on the fertile soil along the river banks.

Find the Niger River on the map on page 175.

For thousands of years, African people fished and transported goods along the Niger River. **Geography:** *What ocean does the river flow into?*

The Vegetation of Africa

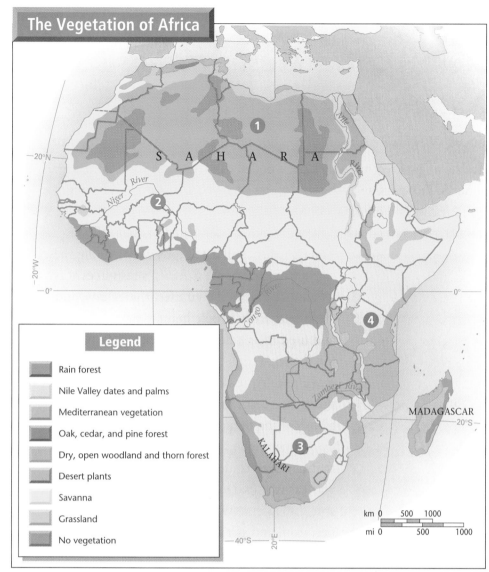

Legend

	Rain forest
	Nile Valley dates and palms
	Mediterranean vegetation
	Oak, cedar, and pine forest
	Dry, open woodland and thorn forest
	Desert plants
	Savanna
	Grassland
	No vegetation

SAHARA

Niger River

Congo River

Nile

Zambezi River

KALAHARI

MADAGASCAR

km 0   500   1000
mi 0   500   1000

1 **Sahara:** The Sahara is the largest desert in the world. It stretches across the northern part of Africa from the Atlantic Ocean to the Red Sea. A dry belt along the fringes of the Sahara is called the Sahel.

2 **Niger River:** The major rivers in western Africa include the Niger, Benue, Volta, and Senegal. Early people settled near rivers. Why do you think so?

3 **Savanna:** The savanna grasslands cover half of Africa. Tall grasses, bushes, and small trees grow where rainfall is plentiful. Shorter grasses and some bushes are found on the fringes of the savanna.

4 **Mountains:** The highest mountains are located in the eastern part of Africa. Mt. Kilimanjaro, the highest peak, is more than 19,000 feet above sea level.

How Ancient West Africans Used Natural Resources

The pictures show a herd of wild animals in present-day Africa and a rock painting of animals that lived long ago.

Focus *What were some of the major resources in ancient West Africa?*

Archaeologists recently dug up a wooden canoe used in West Africa about 8,000 years ago. The canoe was probably for trade and fishing.

Africa has more kinds of **freshwater** fish (fish that live in non-saltwater rivers and lakes) than any other continent — about 2,000. Today, fishers still catch tons of fish along these rivers. Another of West Africa's resources was its animals, including giraffes, rhinoceros, and elephants. Early people hunted them for food and used their hides to make clothing and huts for shelter. People also used elephant tusks to make jewelry and furniture. At that time, elephants were not in danger of **extinction**, or completely dying out, as they are today.

Mineral goods are another African resource that has been traded over the centuries. Gold was easily found in many of the area's rivers and streams. Ancient West Africans also mined copper, iron, and salt for trade. Early people made good use of all of West Africa's resources and built successful societies. In the next lessons you will learn more about their way of life.

Lesson Review: Geography

1. **Key Vocabulary:** Use the terms savanna, freshwater, and extinction in a paragraph about West African geography.

2. **Focus:** How did West Africa's ancient geography shape the lives of people living there?

3. **Focus:** What were some of the major resources in ancient West Africa?

4. **Critical Thinking: Interpret** What can the paintings of ancient artists tell us about their lives?

5. **Citizenship: Economics** Your community discovers a new natural resource in its area and puts you in charge. Using gold or some other mineral as an example, how could you make sure everyone benefits?

6. **Geography/Art Activity:** Collect pictures or draw original ones of what the sub-Saharan area looks like now.

Skills Workshop

Recording Information About Sources

Borrowing Ideas

Whether you're writing a report on the animals that used to roam the Sahara, or the geography of West Africa, you must give credit to the sources of all information and ideas that aren't your own. **Footnotes**, which are at the bottom of the page, credit quotations and paraphrases. A **bibliography**, which is at the end of the report, lists all the sources you used for your research. Using footnotes and bibliographies, writers can be sure to give credit where credit is due.

1 Here's How

- Record details about each source you read. Include the author, title, publisher, publication date and city of publication. Write down the page numbers of any quotations or paraphrases.

- When you include a quotation or paraphrase in your report, write a footnote at the bottom of the page. Use the style shown on the right.

- Put a small number after a quotation or paraphrase. Begin the footnote with the same number (*as shown on the right*).

- At the end of your report, write a bibliography. Arrange your sources in alphabetical order by author. Use the same style as for footnotes, but without the page numbers.

Different types of antelope used to roam the Sahara Desert. They "existed in quite large numbers until about 1900."[1] After this date,

———————

1. Twist, Clint. <u>Deserts</u>. New York: Dillon Press, 1991. p. 33.

2. Author. <u>Title of Book</u>. City of Publication: Publisher, Year of publication. Page number of reference.

-1-

2 Think It Through

What would you think of a report with no footnotes or bibliography? Would you trust its author? Why is it important to give credits?

3 Use It

Use the information below to write a footnote and bibliography entry.

<u>The Sahara and Its People</u> by Simon Scones.
New York Thomson Learning 1993

The Rise of West African Cultures

Main Idea Both the use of iron tools and the migration of Bantu-speaking people influenced the development of West African cultures.

Key Vocabulary

kinship
matrilineage
patrilineage

Key Events

500 B.C. Nok culture begins

Thousands of years ago, near a place in West Africa called Nok, an artist made a clay head. It was heated at a high temperature, creating terra cotta, or "baked earth," pottery. Centuries later, in 1931, miners digging for tin near Nok found the clay head — and more just like it.

When first shown the pottery pieces, archaeologists were baffled. No ancient civilization was known to have existed in the area. They began to dig and found more artifacts, proving that Nok was the site of one of Africa's oldest societies. Archaeologists were able to fit another piece into the giant puzzle of the history of African civilization.

The Nok People

Focus *What contributions did Nok culture make to African history?*

A clay head created by the Nok culture.

As archaeologists continued to dig in the area around Nok, more and more terra cotta objects were unearthed. Iron tools and objects were also found. Soon researchers began to realize that these artifacts were clear evidence of a culture that stretched across parts of West Africa between 500 B.C. and A.D. 200. The Nok culture, as it is now called, flourished along the valleys of the Niger and Benue rivers. *(See the map.)*

After studying the evidence, archaeologists believed that the art of Nok must have influenced the work of artists in Ife (EE fay), a later, nearby culture. The experts also determined that the Nok people were some of the earliest Africans to use iron.

Who were these mysterious people, whose art was beautiful and whose technology was advanced for the times? Unfortunately, we may never know much more about them. Because they did not keep written records, only their art and other artifacts can tell us their history.

Legend

Possible routes of
Bantu speakers

to 300 B.C.

300 B.C. to A.D. 400

A.D. 1000 to A.D. 1100

Bantu speakers migrat-
ed to other parts of
Africa. Many of them
traveled on the Congo
River. **Map Skill:** *In
what directions did
the Bantu speakers
migrate? Why didn't
they go north?*

The Migration of Bantu Speakers

Focus *What skills did Bantu speakers take and learn as they migrated to other parts of Africa?*

Studying ancient Africa, like studying most ancient peoples, is detective
work. Another clue to this history are the languages spoken by Africans
today. Today Bantu-speaking people make up a large part of the population of Africa. In fact, of the more than 1,000 languages spoken in
Africa, approximately 350 fall into a category called Bantu languages. By
carefully mapping where Bantu speakers now live, researchers have
learned about the movements of these people during ancient times. Trace
the areas on the map where Bantu speakers lived.

About 2,000 years ago, Bantu-speaking people lived in what is today
the country of Nigeria, near the Nok region. These people probably lived
by fishing and farming. They had iron tools that helped them produce
enough food for the growing population. Eventually they needed more
space to house their people. Where could they go? The Sahara was a
desert, so they could not go north. Traveling in the forests to the south

Curious Facts

When the Bantu-
speaking people
migrated, they
brought with them
the ability to digest
milk as adults. Among
many populations
around the world,
people lose the ability
to digest milk and milk
products after infancy.
However, Bantu-
speaking adults had a
chemical in their
bodies that allowed
them to drink milk.
Milk was an important
part of the Bantu diet.

Ancient Africa   **179**

In the original language of the Bantu-speaking people, the word for "person" was mantu and the word for "people" was bantu. Compare the words for "person" and "people" in the present-day languages shown below.

Language	person	people
Ganda	omuntu	abantu
Herero	omundu	ovandu
Luba	muntu	bantu
Swahili	mtu	watu
Zulu	umuntu	abantu

The table shows how various African people say the word "person," both as singular and plural words. **Chart Skill:** *How are the words for each language alike? Different?*

was difficult. The Bantu speakers found that the best direction to travel was down the Congo River. From the basin of the Congo, they branched out in new directions. Over the centuries, Bantu speakers migrated across the Zambezi River, east to the shore of the Indian Ocean. Locate forests, rivers, deserts, and grasslands on the map on page 175.

With their iron weapons and farming tools, the Bantu speakers met little resistance along the way. Many of the people they met may have freely adopted the agriculture methods and language of the Bantu.

The Bantu speakers in turn learned from the people they met in East Africa how to raise cattle and to grow crops that had been brought from Asia. Some time after A.D. 300, Bantu speakers began growing bananas, new kinds of yams, rice, coconuts, and sugar cane. These new crops may have spread across Africa within only a few hundred years.

New crops allowed the Bantu-speaking population to grow. By A.D. 1500, much of sub-Saharan Africa belonged to the Bantu-speaking people.

Life in an Enclosed Village

Focus *How did raising cattle shape the lives of Bantu villagers?*

In some areas of Africa, life was centered around cattle. Cows not only provided meat, milk, and hides, they were also used in ceremonies to celebrate a marriage or the birth of a child. Ownership of many cattle represented wealth and power. A man with a large herd of cattle often had a large family that included many children. His cattle gave him the means to provide for his family.

The illustration on the next page shows how villages were designed to protect not only people, but their cattle as well. Each community was surrounded by a fence, often made from thorn bushes. Every evening, villagers brought their cattle into the enclosed corral, or *kraal*, to protect the herd from hungry wild animals and other invaders.

Family Ties

Family ties, or kinship, were important in African villages, where people with common ancestors lived together. The group had authority over the land and the cattle of their group members. Each member owed allegiance to others in the group — to defend and protect them against outsiders, to share resources, and to help pay off one another's debts.

Some Africans traced their ancestry through their mothers to identify themselves. By naming the mother's mother, and the mother's mother's mother, and so on, that person could trace his or her ancestry back through time. This kind of kinship tracing is called matrilineage. The chart

1. **Cattle: The Center of Village Life**
The villagers used their cattle in many ways. They made clothing from cowhide and drank cows' milk and cows' blood. They avoided killing cattle for food, except for feasts on special occasions like births and deaths. If a man wanted to marry, he had to give the most valuable gift he possibly could to the father of the bride: cattle.

2. **An Uncluttered Life** Villagers had very few belongings. They had only what they needed in order to live. A hut might contain a spear, a hoe, and a few skins for clothing.

3. *Kraals* Each village was surrounded by a fence, sometimes made of jagged thorn bushes. It formed an enclosed area called a *kraal.* Every night, villagers brought their cattle into the *kraal* to protect them from hungry lions or other dangerous animals.

4. **Home, Sweet Home** Bantu villagers lived in simple huts shaped like cones. A wooden frame supported the hut. Over the frame was thatch, or grasses. The inside wall was plastered with clay, which came from the ground or sometimes from anthills. The floor was also made of clay and smoothed over with cow dung.

The chart shows how a king or chieftain might be selected under the matrilineal system. **Chart Skill:** *Design a chart to show how a king might be selected under the patrilineal system. How do both charts compare?*

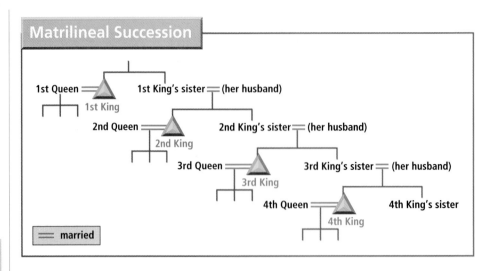

Matrilineal Succession

1st Queen ══ 1st King — 1st King's sister ══ (her husband)

2nd Queen ══ 2nd King — 2nd King's sister ══ (her husband)

3rd Queen ══ 3rd King — 3rd King's sister ══ (her husband)

4th Queen ══ 4th King — 4th King's sister

══ married

Ask Yourself

Today, many people trace their genealogy, a study of family histories, to learn more about their past. Much of the tracing can be done with the use of computers and genealogy research libraries. Why do you think it may be important to trace one's ancestry? What can you learn from a past generation?

? ? ? ? ? ? ? ? ? ? ? ? ? ?

above shows how a new king or chieftain might be selected under the matrilineal systems.

Other Africans identified themselves by naming their fathers. They traced their ancestry by naming their father's father, and the father's father's father, and so on. This is called **patrilineage**.

Tracing ancestors was important to villagers because they believed that relatives who had died still had power over the living. The spirits of the dead must be treated with respect or they might cause trouble. They also believed that ordinary objects like trees and rocks had spirits that lived within them.

Lesson Review

600 B.C.	400 B.C.

500 B.C.
Nok culture begins

1 Key Vocabulary: What is the difference between **matrilineage** and **patrilineage**?

2 Focus: What contributions did Nok culture make to African history?

3 Focus: What skills did Bantu speakers take and learn as they migrated to other parts of Africa?

4 Focus: How did raising cattle shape the lives of Bantu villagers?

5 Critical Thinking: Generalize How can we use language to follow migration patterns?

6 Geography: Economics What food products could the United States export to West Africa?

7 Theme:Lasting Beginnings/Chart Activity: Make a family tree. List your own ancestry or a famous person's ancestry as far back as possible.

The Ancient Kingdom of Ghana

LESSON 3

Main Idea Ghana was a rich trading center in sub-Saharan Africa.

Key Vocabulary
Sahel
monopoly

Key Events
A.D. **1076** Ghana is overrun

A traveler passing through the kingdom of Ghana about 1,000 years ago reported: "The kingdom of Ghana is of great importance and [is next to] the land of the gold mines. [The people who have the gold] have traced out a boundary that no one who sets out to them ever crosses. When the merchants [from across Africa] reach this boundary, they place their wares and cloth on the ground and then depart, and so the people . . . come bearing gold, which they leave beside the merchandise, and then depart. The owners of the merchandise then return, and if they are satisfied with [the amount of gold] they have found, they take it. If not, they go away again, and the people return and add to the price until the bargain is concluded."

Today the area of the ancient kingdom of Ghana is in the countries of Mali and Mauritania in a region known as the Sahel. **Sahel** means "shore," but the kingdom was not on the African coastline. In earlier times, geographers thought of the Sahara as an ocean of sand, and the Sahel as the southern "shore" of the desert.

Gold nuggets are shown in the picture on the left. The map shows the ancient kingdom of Ghana. **Map Skill:** *How would you get from Ghana to Egypt?*

ATLANTIC OCEAN

SAHARA

GHANA

Kumbi Saleh

GOLD FIELDS

King Kanissai of Ghana was known as "one of the lords of the gold." One report about him says that he owned 1,000 horses. Each of the horses was tied with a silken rope, slept on a mattress, and had three servants of its own! According to the report, the king met his subjects every night. First he lit a huge fire, burning a thousand bundles of wood. Then he sat on "a balcony of red-gleaming gold" while his servants brought food for ten thousand people. These stories were probably exaggerated, but Kanissai must have been very rich – and he must have put on quite a show!

A Kingdom Built on Trade

Focus *What were the sources of Ghana's wealth?*

Ancient Ghana sat on the northern borders of the gold-filled Niger and Senegal river valleys. We know about the ancient kingdom, sometimes called the "land of gold," from written reports. For example, in about A.D. 1067–1068, the geographer al-Bakri reported that the king was a powerful ruler with an army of 200,000 men, "more than 40,000 of whom are bowmen, or archers." According to al-Bakri, the king's doors were guarded by dogs "who wear collars of gold and silver," and the king owned "a nugget as large as a big stone."

The king controlled some gold mines. He knew that if there was less gold available to buy, people would want it more. They would be willing to pay a higher price to get it. He kept the large pieces of gold, selling only a few at a time so that he could control the price of gold. In this way, he made sure the price of gold stayed high.

The king's real wealth and power came from trade. Traders brought goods across the Sahara, through the kingdom of Ghana to gold country, and then back again. Each time a trader passed through the kingdom, the trader had to pay a tax to the king. Because Ghana was located between the Sahara and gold country, traders from the north were forced to travel through the kingdom and pay the tax. As a result, the kingdom had a monopoly on the trade route for gold. A **monopoly** is when one group has complete control over a business activity.

What goods brought all the way across the Sahara and through Ghana were as valuable as gold? The main item traders brought was salt, an essential mineral for the human body. Salt was also important for preserving foods. Traders from north of the Sahara had salt and they wanted gold; people southwest of Ghana had gold, and they needed salt. You can see how Ghana got rich by being in the middle. On page 185, you can discover more about salt — where it comes from and what it is used for.

A Town for Traders

The traders had their own town, Kumbi-Saleh (KOOM bee SAH lay). It was a few miles away from al-Ghaba, the capital of the kingdom of Ghana. In Kumbi-Saleh, people built two-story stone houses.

Muslim traders brought the religion known as Islam to Kumbi-Saleh. In the town, estimated to have a population of 30,000 people, there were many places of worship. *(To learn more about Islam, see page 255.)*

Ghana was captured by the Almoravids (Al MAWR ah vihds), people from northwest Africa, around A.D. 1076. The kingdom crumbled. Trade in gold and salt, however, continued to make later empires rich.

Salt: Worth Its Weight in Gold

Salt is an important mineral in human diets. Your body has about half a pound of salt in its cells and tissues. Salt helps muscles to move, food to be digested, and cells to receive nutrients. In very hot climates like that of the Sahara, the body loses a great deal of water and salt through perspiration.

People living in hot climates need to have a daily intake of salt to replace the salt used up in perspiration. If they are eating the meat of wild animals, whose bodies also contain salt, they get all of the mineral they need. If they are living off freshwater fish and grain, the way some Africans did, they need to get the mineral in some other way. That is why salt was traded in Western Africa for gold. Although salt is important in the diet, too much of it may lead to high blood pressure, according to scientists. Find out how much salt you eat in your daily diet. Are you eating too much or too little?

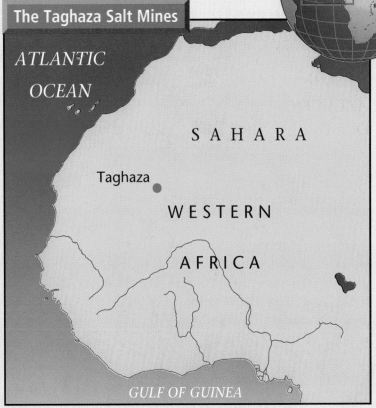

The Taghaza Salt Mines

ATLANTIC
OCEAN

SAHARA

Taghaza

WESTERN

AFRICA

GULF OF GUINEA

The journey that merchants made across the Sahara to trade was dangerous. Still, they felt that the benefits outweighed the risks. What items — food, clothing, or other articles — are so important to you and your family that you would be willing to put yourself in danger to get them?

? ? ? ? ? ? ? ? ? ? ? ? ?

The map shows trade routes in Africa. **Map Skill:** *Why were there only a few east-to-west trade routes?*

Trade Routes Across the Desert

Focus *What difficulties did traders face crossing the Sahara to and from Ghana?*

The Sahara is about the size of the United States. Traders had many routes across this great desert, as you can see from the map below. The trade routes stretched from the border of Ghana and other kingdoms to the shore of the Mediterranean Sea. This is similar to the distance from Mexico to Canada. For example, one route led from Sijilmasa (See jee MAH sah), on the northern edge of the desert, through Taghaza (Tahj ah ZAH), where the salt mines were located. It went on to Timbuktu, an important city on the southern edge of the Sahara.

Desert traders carried many other goods in addition to gold and salt. Archaeologists have found loads lost by traders bound for the Sahel around A.D. 1100. The traders also dealt in dates (the fruit of palm trees), pottery, oil lamps, cotton cloth, beads, swords, knives, and copper.

When traders returned from the south, they brought more than just gold. They sometimes had ostrich feathers, ivory, hides, or kola nuts — the kind used to flavor cola drinks today. At times, the traders also

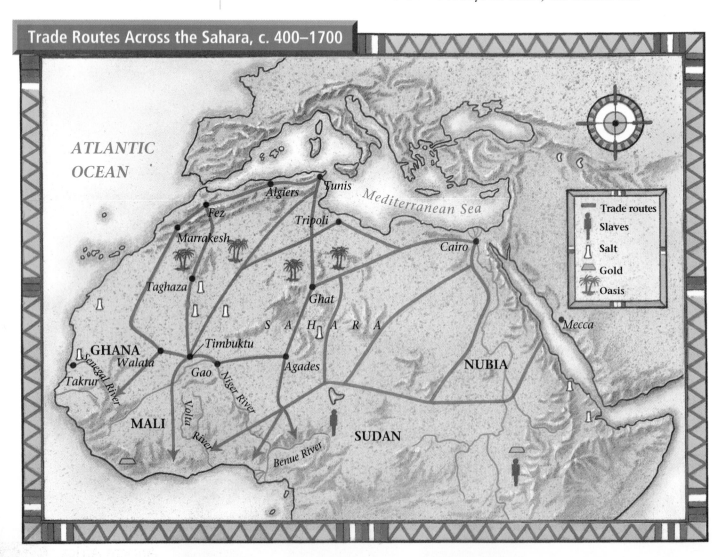

Trade Routes Across the Sahara, c. 400–1700

The Ship of the Desert

The head: The eyes of the camel are protected by long, curly eyelashes that keep out blowing sand. Eyelids and eyebrows keep out glare from the sun.

The hump: The camel's hump consists mostly of fat, which provides the animal with energy. When food is scarce, the animal uses the energy stored in its hump.

The legs and feet: Powerful muscles in the camel's upper legs allow it to carry heavy loads for long distances. Some camels can carry as much as 1,000 pounds. Camels can travel about 25 miles a day at a speed of about three miles an hour.

brought enslaved people, who were bought and sold like merchandise.

The long trip through the desert was full of horrible dangers. Howling sandstorms could spring up and blind or bury the travelers. A sudden thunderstorm caused dry riverbeds to fill suddenly with roaring waters that could drown the traders. Ruthless robbers might attack without warning. To help themselves and each other deal with these risks, the desert traders traveled in huge groups called caravans. The desert animal that made all this Sahara travel and trade possible was the camel, "the ship of the desert."

Lesson Review

A.D. 1000   **A.D. 2000**

A.D. 1076
Ghana is overrun

1. **Key Vocabulary:** Write a journal entry about a trip to ancient Ghana using **Sahel** and **monopoly.**

2. **Focus:** What were the sources of Ghana's wealth?

3. **Focus:** What difficulties did traders face crossing the Sahara to and from Ghana?

4. **Critical Thinking: Cause and Effect**
Explain how trade in Ghana was likely to strengthen the power of the king.

5. **Geography:** Why might the old trans-Saharan trade routes not be used today?

6. **Citizenship/Writing Activity:** You are a trader who is crossing the Sahara as part of a caravan. Keep a journal of your experiences.

CHAPTER 7 Chapter Review

Chapter Review Timeline

1000 B.C.	500 B.C.	B.C.	A.D.	A.D. 500	A.D. 1000	A.D. 1500

500 B.C.
Nok culture begins

A.D. 1076
Ghana is overrun

Summarizing the Main Idea

1 Copy the chart below and fill in the missing information to compare two civilizations of ancient Africa.

	Bantu-speaking peoples	Kingdom of Ghana
Present-day country		
Geography		
Economy		
Cultural achievement		

Vocabulary

2 You are a trader in ancient Africa. Using at least five of the vocabulary words below, write a page in your diary about one of your treks.

savanna (p. 174)   patrilineage (p. 182)   monopoly (p. 184)

kinship (p. 180)   Sahel (p. 183)

Reviewing the Facts

3 How was the Sahara different 3,000 to 8,000 years ago from the way it is today?

4 How were the savanna areas important to the ancient Africans?

5 How were the rivers used by the people of the sub-Sahara?

6 What were some of the uses the people of West Africa found for the wild animals of the area?

7 What is the source of our knowledge about the Nok people?

8 How were the Bantu-speaking people able to travel over so much of Africa?

9 In what ways were cattle important to the early Africans?

10 Why was salt so important in ancient times?

Skill Review: Recording Information About Sources

11 Developing a bibliography is an important part of writing a report. A bibliography is a list of books or articles about a subject. It is found at the end of a report and lists all sources used for research. Gather sources for a report about the people who lived in the Sahara. Use a variety of sources such as books, newspapers, encyclopedias, and atlases. Create a bibliography. List all of the sources you might use for your research.

Geography Skills

12 Look at the map of Africa on page 179. Why do you think the Bantu-speaking people moved in the direction shown on the map?

13 You are a member of a caravan moving over the Sahara. Write a letter to a friend about what you encounter.

Critical Thinking

14 **Compare** Study the map of Africa on page 175. Look at different regions: the Sahara, the savanna, the mountains. How does the geography of Africa compare to that of the United States? Are there similar geographical areas? Name those that are similar.

15 **Conclude** Consider the differences between a matrilineage system and a patrilineage system. Why might one be preferable to another?

16 **Decision Making** Traders would have to weigh the risks and benefits of their dangerous treks across the desert. List some of the factors you think they would consider, and why.

Writing: Citizenship and Economics

17 **Citizenship** Kinship was extremely important in African villages. What part does kinship play in American society? Write a few paragraphs describing the importance of families in American life today.

18 **Economics** Traders in ancient Africa would travel hundreds of dangerous miles to exchange gold, salt, and other goods. Write a conversation between two traders, each trying to make a profit from the exchange.

Activities

Geography/Science Activity
Choose one of the geographic features mentioned in the chapter — such as the Sahara, one of Africa's rivers, or Mount Kilimanjaro — and do research to find out more about it. Create a model or picture of the feature.

Economics/Math Activity
Find out the current prices of gold, salt, and other trading items mentioned in the chapter. Make a chart that shows their relative value. How much gold, for instance, would one have to trade today for an equal value of salt?

Internet Option

Check the **Internet Social Studies Center** for ideas on how to extend your theme project beyond your classroom.

THEME PROJECT CHECK-IN

To complete your theme project, use the information in this chapter to finish creating your civilization. These questions will help you:
• What kinship system did your civilization have?
• What skills and customs did they pass on to other civilizations?
• What forms of transportation did they use and where did they travel?

3

The Spread of Civilization

"Civilization is a movement and not a condition, a voyage and not a harbor."

Arnold Toynbee

· T H E M E ·

Growth and Change

" Instead of relying on the gods to make decisions, people in ancient civilizations started making their own laws and rules. "

Arthur Phrachanphang, Sixth Grade
Fort Smith, AR

People who lived in ancient times led complicated lives. They thought as we do, were as busy as we are, and even went to work and school as we do. Civilizations took a long time to develop, but once they did, they spread rapidly. In a few hundred years, the ideals of Greece and Rome were known from the North Sea to the Indian Ocean. Millions of people became citizens of political and spiritual empires. Some countries invited these new ideas, while others deliberately shut them out.

Theme Project

The Lasting Impact of Civilizations

Choose an ancient civilization and show how it has left a legacy to the world.

- On a world map show areas influenced by the civilization you chose.
- Make a scrapbook showing examples of recent architecture inspired by this ancient civilization.
- Report on a major idea or belief system from this civilization that still has an impact on the world today.

RESEARCH: Find out how modern languages were influenced by the language of the ancient civilization you chose.

◀ The Parthenon, Athens, Greece

191

UNIT 3

WHEN & WHERE
ATLAS

Some ancient civilizations grew to become mighty empires. For example, as the map shows, the Roman Empire included the whole Mediterranean area and beyond. As these civilizations spread, their cultures began to influence distant parts of the world. This influence can still be seen in modern religions, political systems, and languages. In fact, modern societies often contain cultural elements from several of these civilizations.

In this unit, you will read about the history and legacy of ancient Greece. You will also learn about the rise and fall of the Roman Empire. You will read about the growing influence of the world's major religions. Finally, you will learn how some areas of the world accepted and others resisted the influence of other civilizations.

Unit 3 Chapters

Unit Timeline

1,000 B.C.	500 B.C.	B.C.	A.D.

Delphi 800 B.C.–A.D. 393

Ancient Greek culture spread around the Mediterranean and beyond. Find out why. *Chapter 8, Lesson 3*

The Pantheon 27 B.C.

The Roman Empire was the largest political unit the world had ever known. *Chapter 9, Lesson 2*

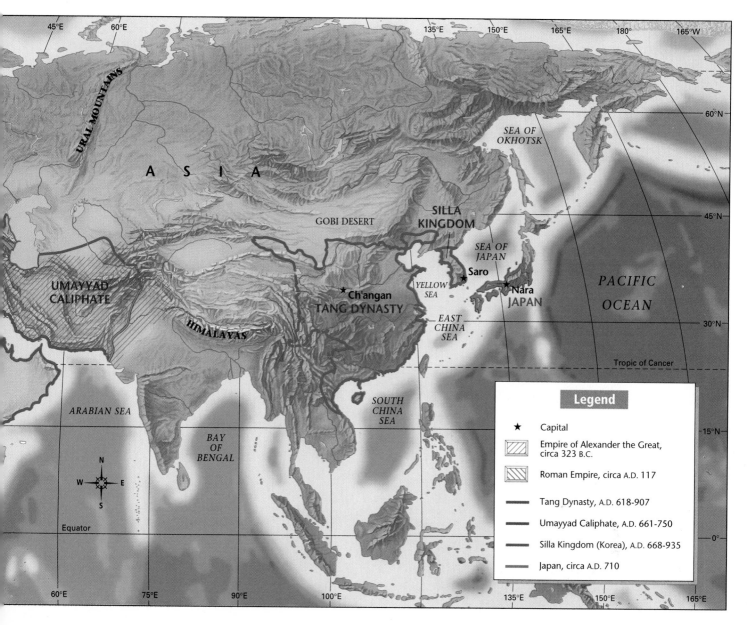

ASIA

URAL MOUNTAINS

GOBI DESERT

UMAYYAD
CALIPHATE

HIMALAYAS

★ Ch'angan
TANG DYNASTY

SILLA
KINGDOM

SEA OF
OKHOTSK

SEA OF
JAPAN

★ Saro

YELLOW
SEA

★ Nara
JAPAN

EAST
CHINA
SEA

PACIFIC
OCEAN

ARABIAN SEA

BAY
OF
BENGAL

SOUTH
CHINA
SEA

N
W   E
S

Equator

Tropic of Cancer

Legend

★ Capital

▨ Empire of Alexander the Great, circa 323 B.C.

▨ Roman Empire, circa A.D. 117

— Tang Dynasty, A.D. 618-907

— Umayyad Caliphate, A.D. 661-750

— Silla Kingdom (Korea), A.D. 668-935

— Japan, circa A.D. 710

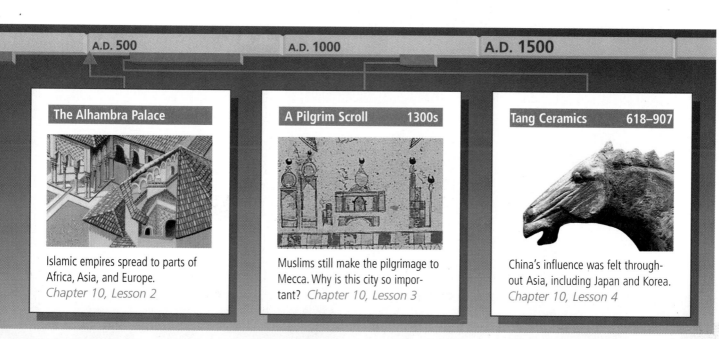

A.D. 500   A.D. 1000   A.D. **1500**

The Alhambra Palace

Islamic empires spread to parts of Africa, Asia, and Europe. *Chapter 10, Lesson 2*

A Pilgrim Scroll   1300s

Muslims still make the pilgrimage to Mecca. Why is this city so important? *Chapter 10, Lesson 3*

Tang Ceramics   618–907

China's influence was felt throughout Asia, including Japan and Korea. *Chapter 10, Lesson 4*

CHAPTER 8

Ancient Greece

Chapter Preview: *People, Places, and Events*

1000 B.C.	720 B.C.	440 B.C.

The Rise of City-States 900 B.C.

Ancient Greek vases tell tales of everyday life. *Lesson 2, Page 199*

The Greek World 500 B.C.

The Greek civilization reached all around the Mediterranean Sea. *Lesson 1, Page 196*

Warriors and Heroes 490 B.C.

Democracy at risk: the Greeks face the Persians and later fight each other. *Lesson 2, Page 202*

The Geography of Ancient Greece

Main Idea Geography influenced the development of Greek civilization.

The storms raged all around Odysseus (oh DIHS yoos). He knew the journey home to Greece would not be an easy one. What he did not know was that his voyage would last for 10 long years, bringing him many adventures and narrow escapes.

This brave sailor was actually the hero of the *Odyssey* (AHD ih see), a poem by the Greek poet Homer. This long adventure poem, or **epic**, tells the story of the vast assortment of creatures and monsters that Odysseus met on his way home from war. The Cyclops (SY klahps), a one-eyed monster, devoured some of Odysseus' men. Others were lost to the murderous whirlpool Charybdis (kuh RIHB dihs). At last, Odysseus made it back to his homeland. There it was as he had dreamed of it, warmed by the sun and lapped by the Mediterranean Sea — Greece.

◀ Ancient Greek woman working with wool.

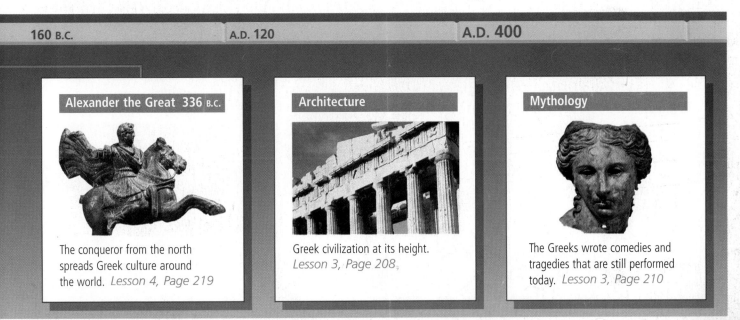

160 B.C.　　　　　A.D. 120　　　　　A.D. 400

Alexander the Great 336 B.C.

The conqueror from the north spreads Greek culture around the world. *Lesson 4, Page 219*

Architecture

Greek civilization at its height. *Lesson 3, Page 208*

Mythology

The Greeks wrote comedies and tragedies that are still performed today. *Lesson 3, Page 210*

A Rugged Land

Painting on pottery was very common in Greece. This drinking cup shows Dionysus, the god of wine, in a boat with a grapevine tangled around the mast. Economics: *Why were grapes and the sea so important to the Greeks?*

The map shows Greek colonies established by the 500s B.C. Map Skill: *Which settlements were the farthest from Greece?*

[Focus] *What role did geography play in the growth of ancient Greek civilization?*

Greece has high mountains, narrow valleys, and a jagged coastline with many harbors. Most of Greece is a **peninsula**, land surrounded on three sides by water. Its geography varies from fertile plains to barren highlands. Mountains made travel slow in ancient times. It could take a week to travel just 60 miles. This rough landscape kept communities separated from each other.

Summers are hot and dry, and winters are often cool and wet. In fact, about three-quarters of the rainfall comes in winter. Ancient farmers produced olives for oil and grapes for wine. With only about one-quarter of their land suitable for growing crops, the ancient Greeks were forced to travel abroad, trading what they had grown for what they needed. Greek ships, loaded with olive oil, wine, and wheat, traveled and traded throughout the Mediterranean region.

As ancient Greek cities grew, land and jobs at home became scarce. Voyaging and trading abroad, the Greeks founded **colonies**, or foreign settlements in distant lands ruled originally from home. On the map below, you can see how many settlements the Greeks had by the 500s B.C. In what modern country was the westernmost Greek settlement?

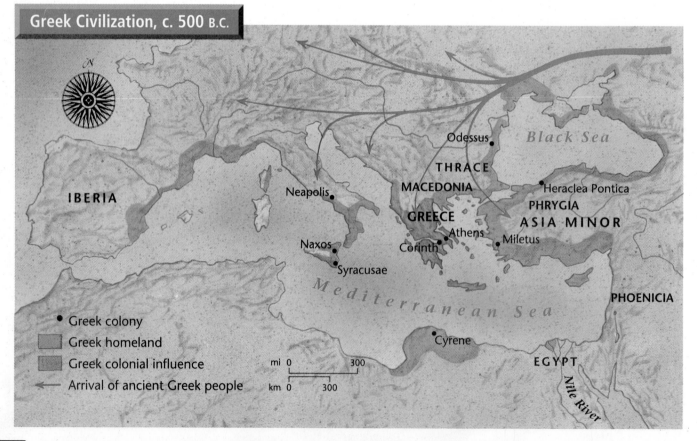

Greek Civilization, c. 500 B.C.

Odessus
Black Sea
THRACE
MACEDONIA
Heraclea Pontica
Neapolis
PHRYGIA
GREECE
ASIA MINOR
Athens
Miletus
Naxos
Corinth
Syracusae
IBERIA
Mediterranean Sea
PHOENICIA
Cyrene
EGYPT
Nile River

- Greek colony
- Greek homeland
- Greek colonial influence
- ← Arrival of ancient Greek people

mi 0   300
km 0   300

Seagoing Ancestors

Focus *How did the sea help create wealth for the early Greeks?*

The very first people to inhabit the area around the Aegean (ih JEE uhn) Sea also developed a **maritime**, or sea-based, culture. These were the ancestors of the ancient Greeks, the Minoans (mih NOH uhns). From about 3000 B.C. until 1400 B.C., the Minoans ruled the island of Crete (KREET). Find Crete on a map. In what direction would you travel to get there from Greece? The Minoans were skilled sailors and became wealthy through trading.

At this time, southern Greece was ruled by the city of Mycenae (my SEE nee). The Mycenaeans (my suh NEE uhns) learned seafaring skills from the Minoans. This enabled the Mycenaeans to become successful traders, like the Minoans.

The Mycenaeans conquered Crete about 3,500 years ago. Continuing their conquests, the Mycenaeans sailed to Asia Minor (modern-day Turkey).

Roughly 300 years later, around 1200 B.C., Mycenae itself collapsed. Greeks, however, felt its influence for centuries to come.

Greeks still make a living from the sea. This harbor on the island of Santorini provides a home for fishing boats and a destination for tourists. Once, it would have seen ancient fishing boats and vessels loaded with grapes and olives to trade. **Economics:** *How are goods transported in your community?*

Lesson Review: Geography

1. **Key Vocabulary:** Use the following terms to describe the geography of Greece: peninsula, colony, maritime.

2. **Focus:** What role did geography play in the growth of ancient Greek civilizations?

3. **Focus:** How did the sea help create wealth for the early Greeks?

4. **Critical Thinking: Interpret** If Greece had been a country of flat, fertile land, far from the sea, how might life have been different for the ancient Greeks?

5. **Theme: Growth and Change** Apart from material goods, like wheat and timber, what else might traders have brought back to Greece from abroad? What effect would this have had?

6. **Citizenship/Writing Activity:** You are a leader in a Greek city that has too little land to support its people. Write and deliver a speech to persuade people to go abroad and start new settlements.

Greek Politics and Society

Main Idea Greek self-government took shape more than 2,500 years ago.

Key Vocabulary

- polis
- aristocracy
- sponsor
- democracy
- spartan
- tyrant

Key Events

594 B.C. Reforms of Solon

490 B.C. Persian invasion

480 B.C. Second Persian invasion

431-404 B.C. Peloponnesian Wars

The blind poet, Homer, created his epics, the *Iliad* (IHL ee uhd) and the *Odyssey*, 2,500 years ago. They told the tale of the terrible 10-year Trojan War and its many heroes. While the ancient Greeks thought of these stories as true, few modern readers thought of them as real.

Heinrich Schliemann (SHLEE muhn) had read the works of Homer as a child. He was convinced that Troy had existed. Using the geographical clues in the *Iliad*, he traced the possible site of Troy to a place in modern-day Turkey. In 1871, he began an archaeological dig. Soon he came across a large buried trading city, with a treasure trove of golden jewelry. He had found Troy: The city that everyone thought was imaginary was real after all.

The map shows Greece about 450 B.C. **Map Skill:** *How do you think most people would have traveled to Olympia?*

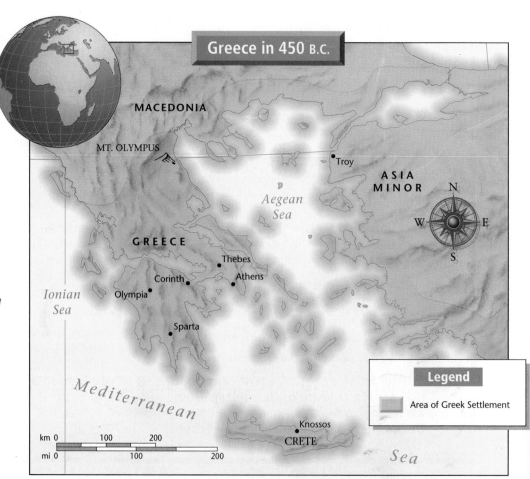

Greece in 450 B.C.

MACEDONIA

MT. OLYMPUS

Troy

ASIA MINOR

Aegean Sea

GREECE

Thebes

Corinth   Athens

Ionian Sea   Olympia

Sparta

Mediterranean

Knossos

CRETE

Sea

km 0   100   200
mi 0   100   200

Legend

Area of Greek Settlement

The Rise of City-States

Focus *What were Greek city-states, and how did they function?*

After the Trojan War, trade came to a standstill and poverty increased. There are few architectural remains from this period, and written language all but disappeared as people became isolated in separate villages. Little is known about this period.

By the mid-900s B.C., Greece began to prosper again. Town marketplaces, or agoras, became crowded. Women carried water in pitchers on their heads, shoppers argued noisily over prices, and poets recited verses aloud. This was the time when Homer lived and wrote. Greece was now made up of many independent communities, composed of villages and surrounding farmland. Called a **polis** in Greek (the root of the word "politics"), a city-state was governed by groups of powerful landowners. These nobles paid for armor, horses, and the army. This form of government by the nobility is known as an **aristocracy**.

As members of a polis, all citizens had rights as well as responsibilities. They had to obey the laws and take part in religious ceremonies. They were also expected to fight in the event of a war. Citizens **sponsored**, or paid for, athletic games, religious festivals, and drama contests.

By the 700s B.C., the Greeks developed a system of government called **democracy**, from the Greek words *demos* (people) and *kratos* (rule). Now all male citizens — not just nobles — were allowed to play an active role in decision making. The Greeks were proud of their system, as expressed by Aristotle (AR ihs taht l), one of their philosophers.

> **"T**his is the polis. It has come into being in order, simply, that life can go on; but now it exists so as to make that life a good life.**"**

What transformed these separate city-states into one people we call the Greeks? They all spoke Greek, with some variations. They also worshiped the same group of gods and goddesses. Most important, perhaps, they believed that the polis was the best way to live.

The Greeks needed many vases for carrying wine, water, and oil. Grain was shipped in jars, too. This detail of a vase is decorated with a painting of women filling water pots. Greeks painted many scenes from everyday life, and it is because of this practice that we know so much about them. **Arts:** *Find and describe the horizontal band on this vase called Greek Key.*

Events in Ancient Greece

1200 B.C.	1000 B.C.	800 B.C.	600 B.C.	400 B.C.	200 B.C.
c. 1200 B.C. Fall of Troy	950 B.C. Aristocracies in Greece	700 B.C. Democracy in Athens	490-480 B.C. Persian Invasions	c. 450 B.C. Athens's height of power	431-404 B.C. Peloponnesian Wars

Democracy in Ancient Greece

Focus *How did life differ in Athens and Sparta?*

The good life that Aristotle enjoyed was a direct result of the democratic system of government. Citizens could control much of what happened in their lives. The polis guaranteed their rights, and in turn, the citizens protected and maintained the polis.

Life in Athens

Aristotle was a citizen of Athens, perhaps the most famous city-state of ancient Greece. Democracy began here with the reforms of the statesman Solon. Between 594 B.C. and 560 B.C., Solon helped create a legal code for Athens that called for participation by citizens. Cleisthenes (KLYS thuh neez) and other statesmen reformed the Athenian government further to create a democracy.

By 450 B.C., Athens was at the height of its power. About 225,000 people lived there, making it a little smaller than present-day Miami, Florida, or Portland, Oregon. Because Athens was a great seafaring power, it became rich through trading. This wealth helped turn Athens into a center for the arts. Today, we can still see impressive public buildings such as temples and theaters. The Athenians must have been very proud of their city.

Not everybody experienced the good life. Not everyone was a citizen. Women were not given full citizenship. They could not vote, hold office, or own property. Like most other Greek cities, Athens also used the labor of enslaved people, who made up almost a quarter of the population. Often these people were captives from wars. They were of all races and came from different parts of the Mediterranean. In a way, we can say that their work enabled the citizens to experiment with government.

Those free males who were citizens could speak their minds at the Athenian Assembly, which met 40 times a year. A council of 500 citizens was selected to propose laws on which the entire Assembly would vote. Every citizen had a vote. Citizens could also serve on juries, just as American citizens do today.

Then & Now

Ancient Greeks lived in city-states, not nations. They paid taxes to the city and fought in its armies. People from different cities were considered "foreigners." Today we live in nations made up of many cities. How would citizenship of a city differ from that of a country?

Spartan Life

Life in Sparta was very different from that in Athens. Sparta lay inland on the peninsula of the Peloponnesus (peh luh puh NEE sus). It had conquered and enslaved the peoples around it by 600 B.C. To guard against possible slave rebellions, Spartan men were trained in the army from an early age. At age seven, boys were sent to camps where they learned to fight. They put up with many hardships so that they would be hardy soldiers. Today, we use the term **spartan** to mean "hard" or "severe."

A woman's position in Sparta, however, was better than in Athens. Women could train in athletics, and they could own property. By the 200s B.C., women owned two-fifths of Sparta's land.

The Agora

Beyond the haggling farmers, at the far end of the agora, stood the government center where citizens spent much of their time. **Citizenship:** *What functions do the buildings serve in your town's government center?*

The Acropolis started out as an ancient hilltop fortress but later it was turned into a holy place with many temples. The Parthenon, on top of the Acropolis, was built as a temple for the goddess Athena. Today, many of the buildings are in ruins, but the Acropolis is still a favorite place for tourists.

Tholos

Here the standard weights and measures were kept for use in the market. Coins were made here. Lawmakers also rested and ate here.

Meetinghouse

The Council of 500 met here to carry out the work on laws debated by the Assembly.

Archives

Laws and treaties enacted by the Council were stored here in papyrus scrolls.

If you had been a boy living in ancient Greece, would you have preferred to live in Athens or Sparta? Would you give the same answer if you had been a girl?

? ? ? ? ? ? ? ? ? ? ? ? ? ?

The Battle of Marathon was between the Greek army and the larger Persian army. **Map Skill:** *Trace the route from Marathon to Athens.*

Wars Abroad and At Home

Focus *What were some of the major causes of war in Greece?*

In the 400s B.C., Asia Minor was the heart of the Persian Empire, which ruled lands from India to Egypt. The Persians had conquered Greek colonies in Asia Minor and islands off its coast. By 500 B.C., the Persian Empire was larger and wealthier than Greece. The Greeks believed that the Persian king, Darius, was a **tyrant** — a ruler who governs by threat of force. Some of the Greek colonies rebelled against Darius' rule.

Determined to put an end to this rebellion, Darius invaded Greece in 490 B.C. On the way to Athens, Darius' ships landed at Marathon. The battle map below shows how the Greeks crushed Darius' troops. After the victory, a Greek soldier ran the 26 miles to Athens with the good news. This is the origin of today's marathon races.

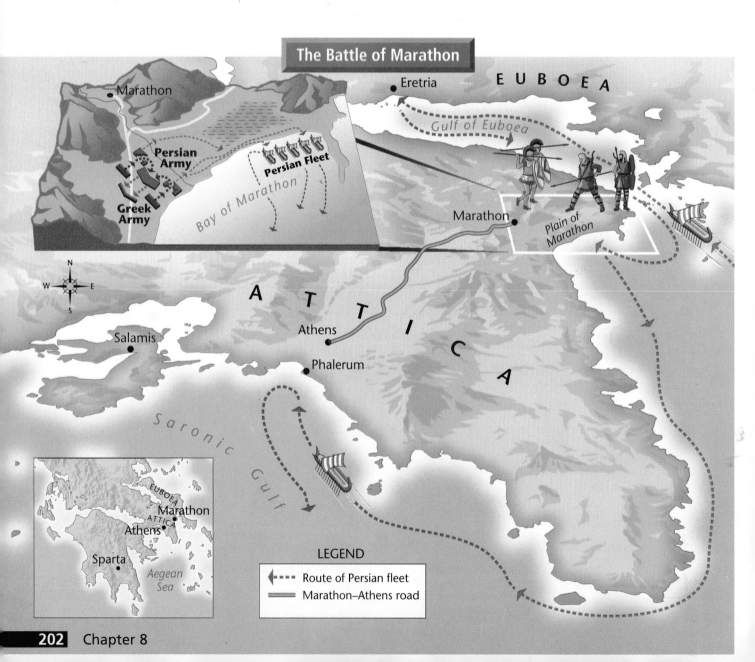

The Battle of Marathon

LEGEND

◄---- Route of Persian fleet
──── Marathon–Athens road

Ten years later, Darius' son, Xerxes (ZURK seez) also tried to conquer Greece. Uniting to fight a common enemy, Athenian and Spartan armies defeated the Persians at the sea battle of Salamis (SAL uh mihs).

Peloponnesian Wars

Having built up their armed forces to defeat the Persians, Athens and Sparta were the two most powerful city-states in Greece. Athens, whose strength was its navy, formed an alliance with other city-states. This soon developed into a small empire. But the unity that the Greeks had shown against the Persians could not last. Fearing the growing power of Athens, Sparta launched a series of attacks against the city.

By 431 B.C., war erupted between the two city-states. Sparta marched its army around Athens, destroying crops and property. The Athenians had built walls from the city to their harbor, Piraeus (Pih RAY uhs). They supplied themselves using ships. At the same time, they attacked Spartan supply lines.

By 404 B.C., the people of Athens were starving and exhausted. Much of the population had died. They finally surrendered to Sparta. The great age of Greek democracy was over.

The trireme (try REAM) was the Greek warship. Up to 120 feet in length, it had three tiers of oarsmen. A bronze battering ram on the bow was used to ram enemy ships and sink them. The trireme below is a model of an ancient one.

Lesson Review

600 B.C.	500 B.C.		400 B.C.
594 B.C. Reforms of Solon	**490 B.C.** Persian Invasion	**480 B.C.** Second Persian Invasion	**431–404 B.C.** Peloponnesian Wars

1 **Key Vocabulary:** Write a paragraph about Greek government using the following terms: **polis, aristocracy, sponsor, democracy, tyrant.**

2 **Focus:** What were Greek city-states, and how did they function?

3 **Focus:** How did life differ in Athens and Sparta?

4 **Focus:** What were some of the major causes of war in Greece?

5 **Critical Thinking: Interpret** Based on the definition of democracy you have learned, do you think Athens was a truly democratic city? Explain your answer.

6 **Geography: Science** How did the Greeks use their natural resources?

7 **Citizenship/Drama Activity:** Form small groups representing a number of different Greek city-states. Stage a meeting of the groups to debate whether or not the city-states should attempt to resist Xerxes' invasion of Greece in 480 B.C.

Participating

What Is Democracy?

Do your parents make the laws, or do they vote for people who make the laws? In a democracy, sometimes people vote directly, and sometimes they elect representatives. The important thing is that in a democracy, people who vote are part of the government. Pericles (PEHR uh kleez) in ancient Greece was one of the first firm believers in democracy.

Case Study

People Power in Athens

In the 460s B.C., Pericles became a very influential politician in Athens. He was responsible for building many of the city's great monuments, including the Parthenon, which pays tribute to Athena, goddess of wisdom, practical arts, and warfare, at left.

Pericles also believed that many people should take part in government. During his rule, each citizen had an equal vote in the Assembly. He said a citizen had to be born of Athenian parents, so only a minority of men were citizens. But as his speech below shows, he believed in democracy.

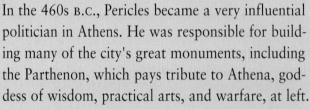

❝ *Our form of government is called a democracy because power is in the hands of the whole people, not of a few. . . . Everyone is equal before the law. Election to public office is made on the basis of ability, not on the basis of membership in a particular class. . . . And we pay special regard to those laws that are for the protection of the oppressed.* ❞

Take Action

The Greeks are famous for their myths about gods and mortals. One myth concerns Athens. The king who founded Athens had to choose a chief god for the city. A contest took place between Poseidon (poh SY den), god of the sea, and Athena. The king was to judge whose power was more valuable. Poseidon hurled a thunderbolt that hit a boulder and blasted a large hole in it. Then Athena made an olive tree grow out of the hole and offered it to the city.

Which power do you think would be more useful: the power to demolish something quickly if it's in your way, or the power to grow something that gives food, wood, and oil?

Decide the question by voting on it as a class. Try two different ways of voting: direct democracy and representative democracy.

1 Try direct democracy first. Write your vote, Poseidon or Athena, on a slip of paper. Collect the papers. Do not count the votes yet.

2 Now try representative democracy. Each group of four or five students elects a representative. Have the representatives write their votes on slips of paper.

3 Compare the results of the two votes. Were they the same?

4 Discuss the results of the elections and the differences between representative and direct democracy.

Tips for Participating

- Try not to interrupt another person when he or she is speaking. Instead, write down your thought on a piece of paper so that you will remember it when it is your turn to speak.
- Show that you have heard what other people are saying by repeating their main point using their words.

Research Activity

Create three pie charts to see who has voted in the United States for 1860, 1910, and 1990. Use an encyclopedia or almanac to find out what percentage of the population in 1860, 1910, and 1990 were women, Native American men, African American men, and white men. Divide up each pie chart accordingly. Then find out when each of these groups got the vote. Color the section of each pie chart that represents who the voters were at the time. How representative of the total population was the vote? How have the proportions changed?

Greek Culture

Main Idea The cultural accomplishments of Greek civilization continue to influence our society today.

Key Vocabulary

myth

shrine

oracle

tragedy

comedy

philosophy

Key Events

800 B.C. Age of Homer and Hesiod

776 B.C. First Olympic Games

461 B.C. Pericles takes power

A.D. 393 Last ancient Olympic Games

They came from all over Greece, traveling across mountains and plains to Olympia to honor the greatest of Greek gods, Zeus (ZOOS). Every four years, Greek city-states declared a truce and sent their finest athletes to compete in the Olympic Games. There were running races, javelin-throwing contests, and horse races, in which the horses had neither saddles nor stirrups. The pancratium was a combined boxing and wrestling match in which competitors often kicked and strangled each other! Thankfully, today's Olympic Games are not so violent.

Beginning in 776 B.C., these games were held regularly until A.D. 393. In the ancient world, they came to represent many Greek ideals. In particular, the games showed the spirit of *arete* (a RET ay), or striving for excellence. The first modern Olympics were held in 1896 in Athens. They were organized by a Frenchman, Baron Pierre de Courbertin (duh KOR behr tahn), who was inspired by the ancient Greeks.

Mythology and Religion

Focus *How did the ancient Greeks view their gods?*

Towering 9,570 feet, Mount Olympus reaches up into the skies above northern Greece. The ancient Greeks believed that the most powerful of their many gods and goddesses lived there, housed in a magnificent palace with many luxuries.

Chief of all the gods, Zeus ruled from Mount Olympus. He became the most powerful god when he dethroned his father, Cronos. Zeus was known to take many different forms.

How did the Greeks come to believe in these gods? For generations they had heard **myths,** or stories from the distant past that told about the beginning of the world and the birth of the gods and goddesses. These myths also explained the natural world. For example, thunder, lightning, and heavy rain were explained by myths as the work of Zeus, the all-powerful god of the sky and father of all people. Myths were passed down from generation to generation by word of mouth. It was not until around 800 B.C. that poets such as Homer and Hesiod began writing stories about the residents of Mount Olympus.

The Greeks believed their gods and goddesses to be very human in their behavior. They argued, fought, fell in love, and played tricks on each other. The myths tell the stories of these gods and goddesses, and discuss how they, like humans, were often driven in their actions by feelings of pride, anger, jealousy, or love.

The Greeks also believed that their gods and goddesses interfered in the lives of humans. Hoping that the gods would be kind to them and protect them, people offered prayers, hymns, and sacrifices to the gods. The Greeks often visited **shrines**, which were special sites where they believed the gods were housed. In some shrines, priests or priestesses delivered prophesies, called **oracles**. People paid a fee and were then able to ask what the future held for them. The photograph below shows the ruins of a shrine in Delphi (DEHL fy). Delphi was the home of perhaps the most famous oracle of the ancient world.

The Greeks thought that the gods particularly enjoyed fruit, flowers, milk, wine, and cooked meat. Many activities in daily life were done as a way of pleasing the gods. Athletes, singers, playwrights, and dancers often competed at festivals in order to honor the gods with their performances. The Olympic Games are a good example of this. Greek mythology continued to influence parts of the world for hundreds of years.

The painting from a pot shows a priestess reading a prophesy. She was separated from the temple priests by a curtain.

The picture below shows the ancient ruins of a shrine in Delphi.

The Legacy of Greek Culture

Focus | *What did the ancient Greeks add to our understanding of the world?*

The Greek culture played and plays an important role in our culture. Greek ideas in art, architecture, literature, drama, science, mathematics, and thought all underlie western culture.

Art and Architecture

In the mid–400s B.C., the Athenian ruler Pericles (PEHR ih kleez) decided to repair much of the damage done to his city during the wars against Persia. He wanted to honor the gods and show other city-states the growing power of Athens.

With the great artist Phidias (FIHD ee uhs) supervising, the Greeks set to work building several beautiful temples high atop the Acropolis (uh KRAH puh lis), a hill in the center of Athens. The most famous temple was the Parthenon (PAHR thuh nawn), dedicated to the goddess of the city, Athena. Built of white marble with rows of tall columns, the Parthenon is a prime example of ancient Greek architecture. Simple yet elegant, this style was to influence many generations of people to come, beginning with the Romans (see Chapter 9).

The Parthenon also provided some of the best examples of Greek sculpture, including a gold and ivory statue of Athena. Ancient Greek sculptors of the time studied the human body closely in order to make their works lifelike. They even painted their statues.

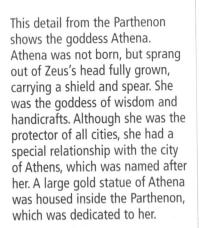

This detail from the Parthenon shows the goddess Athena. Athena was not born, but sprang out of Zeus's head fully grown, carrying a shield and spear. She was the goddess of wisdom and handicrafts. Although she was the protector of all cities, she had a special relationship with the city of Athens, which was named after her. A large gold statue of Athena was housed inside the Parthenon, which was dedicated to her.

Classical Architecture

Athens in Its Golden Age

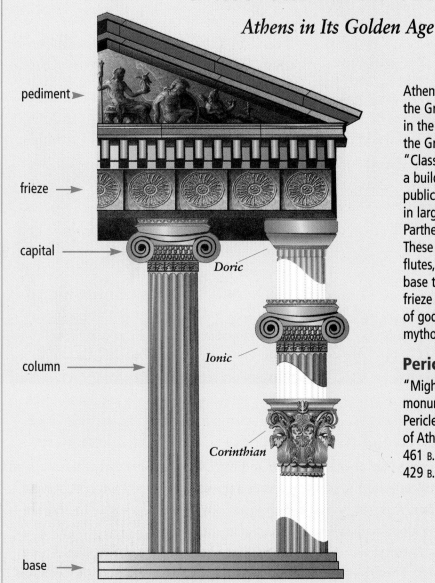

pediment ►

frieze →

capital →

Doric

column →

Ionic

Corinthian

base →

Athenian architecture was the envy of the Greek world. The style used in the city in the 400s B.C. became the standard for the Greek world and is known today as "Classical architecture." Every element of a building was a work of art. Temples and public buildings, in particular, were built in large numbers. In a temple such as the Parthenon, columns supported the roof. These were carved with grooves called flutes, which ran all the way from the base to the capital. The pediment and frieze displayed beautifully carved images of gods and goddesses taken from mythology.

Pericles

"Mighty indeed are the marks and monuments we have left." So said Pericles, the leader of Athens from 461 B.C. until 429 B.C.

Does this building look familiar? It is the New York Stock Exchange, in New York City. The architecture of Greece continues to influence us today.

This ancient theater once entertained large audiences. Often, such theaters were built in natural settings to heighten the drama. Painted statuettes, such as the one above, may have been handed out as souvenirs.

Poetry and Drama

Homer's epic poems, the *Iliad* and the *Odyssey*, were early influences on Greek culture and identity. Other ancient Greek poets wrote religious poetry, songs in praise of heroes, and love poems. Many of these were sung aloud with musical accompaniment.

Historians think that the earliest Greek plays began as dances and songs. These were performed every year at a festival honoring Dionysus (dy uh NY suhs), the god of wine and nature. Eventually, roles were created for actors who sang and danced these early plays, or dramas, from the Greek word for "action."

Some Greek plays were **tragedies**, serious stories involving men and women who met disastrous ends. The Greek writer Aristotle provides a good definition of tragedy: "A tragedy is the imitation of an action that is serious, with incidents arousing pity and terror." The tragic heroes and heroines were people with strong personalities. It was most often this very strength which was their downfall. They created situations which eventually turned against them and caused disaster. Sophocles (SAWF uh kleez), a famous playwright, wrote:

The Greek **comedies** were more lighthearted works, which often poked fun at aristocrats and gods alike. Politicians, generals, scientists, and poets were also common targets of comedies. In this way, ordinary citizens were allowed to laugh at the wealthier and more powerful figures in their society. Aristophanes (ar ih STAHF uh neez), one of the best-known Greek comedy writers, wrote about current affairs of the time. He especially enjoyed making fun of important figures: "Under every stone there lurks a politician!"

The actors and chorus performed the plays on a round stage set at the base of a hill. Above it rose curving rows of benches for the audience. This is known as an amphitheater (AM fuh thee uh tur). The actors wore masks that highlighted features of the characters they played. In comedy, the masks had laughing expressions; in tragedy, they seemed to weep. The oversized lips of the masks acted as megaphones to help the actors' voices carry to the back rows of the theater. Today, very few of the actual works of the Greek playwrights survive. But the ancient Greek ideas about comedy and tragedy — and many of their plots, too — survive today in movies and television, as well as the theater.

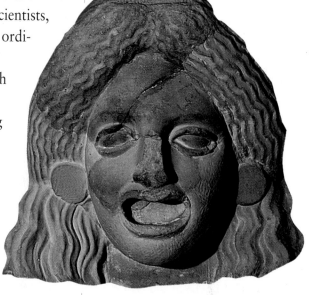

This marble sculpture from the first century B.C. shows the kind of masks the Greeks used in their theaters.

Science and Math

Greeks tried to understand or find laws that explained the natural world around them. Unlike most people of the time, who thought that sickness was caused and cured by supernatural forces, the physician Hippocrates (hih PAHK ruh teez) believed that sickness had natural causes. Hippocrates was the first to begin making careful records on illness and treatment and thus began the scientific practice of medicine. Pythagoras (pih THAG ur uhs), a mathematician, originated many theories which are still in use today.

Archimedes (ar kuh MEE deez) contributed greatly to the Greeks' understanding of physics and mathematics. The King of Syracuse once ordered a craftsman to make a golden crown for him. Suspecting that the man had mixed cheap metals with the gold, he asked Archimedes to test the crown for purity. Archimedes solved the problem when he stepped into his bath and saw the water level rise. He realized he could measure how much water ran over when the crown was placed in water, and compare it with the amount that ran over when one of pure gold was placed in water. Archimedes was so excited he jumped out of his bath and ran through the streets shouting, "Eureka!" (yoo REE ka) ("I found it!").

Curious Facts

Doctors today take an oath which was first written by the ancient Greek doctor Hippocrates:

"I will follow that method of treatment which, according to my ability and judgment, I consider for the benefit of my patients, and [not do] whatever is [harmful]."

Philosophy

Other Greek thinkers explored questions about human behavior and morals. This was known as **philosophy**, after the Greek words for the "love of wisdom." Many Greeks prided themselves on using their intellect to look at the world around them and their role in it.

Socrates (SAHK ruh teez), one of the most famous Greek philosophers, believed that

> " *The unexamined life is not worth living.* "

Socrates questioned everything: people's duty to the city-state, the value of religion, the need for laws. He had many debates.

Many of these philosophers formed schools and trained students to help answer important questions by thinking and reasoning. Plato (PLAY toe), for example, was a student of Socrates. He opened the Academy, one of the most famous of these schools.

Plato's books consider subjects such as the nature of love, courage, and goodness. Plato's book, *The Republic*, tells of Socrates' idea of philosopher-kings. Philosophers, he thought, would be most suited to govern because they understand such ideas as justice and goodness:

This painting by a French artist from the 1800s shows Socrates before he was executed. He had been convicted of causing the youth of Athens to lose faith in the gods of the city. Instead of leaving the city forever, Socrates chose to stand trial. He believed that death is just the beginning of another life for the soul. Here, he is holding a cup of hemlock, a deadly poison. His friends and students surround him in misery. **Art:** *Does Socrates seem afraid of his fate?*

Socrates
(469-399 B.C.)

"I am not a citizen of Athens, nor of Greece, but of the world."

Plato
(427-347 B.C.)

"No evil can happen to a good man either in life or after death."

Aristotle
(384-322 B.C.)

"All men, by nature, desire knowledge."

66 *There will be no end to the troubles of states, or indeed of humanity itself, till philosophers become kings in this world, or until those whom we now call kings and rulers become philosophers.* 99

Plato's student, Aristotle, studied at the Academy and wrote about art, physics, astronomy, weather, and biology, among many other things. In his book *Politics*, Aristotle discusses government. The work of these three philosophers influenced later thinkers for hundreds of years. It is still the basis of philosophy today. Greek culture has had a deep effect on the world.

Lesson Review

800 B.C.	400 B.C.	B.C.	A.D.	A.D. 400

800 B.C.	**776 B.C.**	**461 B.C.**	**A.D. 393**
Age of Homer and Hesiod	First Olympic Games	Pericles takes power in Athens	Last ancient Olympic Games

1 **Key Vocabulary:** Define the following terms: **myth, shrine, oracle, tragedy, comedy, philosophy.**

2 **Focus:** How did the ancient Greeks view their gods?

3 **Focus:** What did the ancient Greeks add to our understanding of the world?

4 **Critical Thinking: Conclude** The ancient Greeks lived in an unstable and dangerous time. How did they try to control the world around them?

5 **Theme: Growth and Change** How did drama develop from religious rites?

6 **Citizenship/Art Activity:** Design and draw a modern building that uses some elements of classical Greek architecture.

Greek Myth

ATALANTA'S RACE
A GREEK MYTH

❖

Retold by Shirley Climo
Illustrated by Alexander Koshkin

The ancient Greeks admired physical strength, beauty, and especially speed and athletic ability. So it was no surprise that when his long lost daughter showed up at his palace, King Iasus was happy to see her. Atalanta had grown into a beautiful young woman, skilled with the bow and incredibly fast on her feet.

King Iasus had once tried to get rid of Atalanta, his only child. Iasus had begged the gods of Mount Olympus for a son, an heir to his kingdom. Even though he was glad to have Atalanta back home again, King Iasus had a problem.

King Iasus once sent away his infant daughter, Atalanta.

King Iasus watched Atalanta with pride and pleasure, but his happiness was not complete. He yearned for a grandson to sit on Arcadia's throne.

"You should marry," he told Atalanta. "Is there no one you love?"

"Love!" she said. "I do not believe in it."

"Take care!" cried Iasus in alarm. "What if Aphrodite, the goddess of love, should hear you?"

Atalanta shrugged. "What that goddess overhears is no concern of mine."

When months had passed, and Atalanta had turned away one suitor after another, Iasus grew impatient. "With love or without it, I order you to wed!"

Atalanta smiled sweetly at her father and asked, "May I choose my husband in my own way?"

"Indeed!" Iasus agreed. "Choose whom and how you will."

"Then he who can outrun me in a race will win my hand," she declared, "but he who loses will lose his head."

Atalanta was pleased with her scheme. What man would risk his life so foolishly?

Atalanta picked a grassy valley where a curved track was laid out for the competition. Broad steps were cut into the hillside for the judges and the spectators to sit and watch the race. When the preparations were complete, King Iasus sent out messengers with a proclamation:

Years later, King Iasus was happy to see his long lost daughter. However, the King commanded his daughter Atalanta to marry.

The King's messengers proclaimed that if any man could win a race with Atalanta, he could marry her.

Many suitors and athletes came to the race.

Melanion wanted to race Atalanta to win her hand in marriage.

Be it known that any man of any nation who can outdistance Princess Atalanta of Arcadia in a race shall win her in marriage. The penalty for defeat is death.

Soon the Arcadian court swarmed with Greeks and Cypriots, Sicilians, Egyptians, and Ethiopians. Among the athletes were Olympic winners, confident of out-running a woman. Others, less famous, simply wanted to wed the beautiful princess.

The arrival of so many suitors dismayed Atalanta. Some were even too young to grow beards.

"Withdraw from the contest," she begged each one. "To do so is no dishonor."

A few listened. Those who did not lost their races and their lives.

Among the judges was a young Greek warrior named Melanion. He was hailed as a hero, and was an athlete in his own right. When Melanion first saw Atalanta, he thought she looked like any other mortal maiden. But when he saw the princess run, her hair streaming behind her like a cloud, beautiful as a goddess, he was determined to win her hand in marriage.

"No!" cried Atalanta when Melanion bid for the race. "A hero should not throw away his life."

"Give me the same chance you have given other men," Melanion insisted.

"If you must." Atalanta sighed. "Tomorrow, as soon as Apollo drives his sun chariot into the sky, we shall race."

Melanion slept badly that night. Strange images danced before him. Aphrodite, the goddess of love, appeared on a beam of moonlight and offered him three apples of purest gold. They were so bright they dimmed the stars above.

"With these apples you can win Atalanta's race," the goddess said, "and so teach that too-proud girl a lesson."

Melanion gazed at the golden apples. "How shall I use them?" he asked.

"That you must find out for yourself," Aphrodite answered, and vanished as suddenly as she had come.

To win the race, Melanion needed to know how to use the golden apples.

Meet the Author

Old stories and legends have provided the inspiration for some of Shirley Climo's other books. In *The Egyptian Cinderella, The Korean Cinderella,* and *The Irish Cinderlad,* the basic plot in each book is similar to Cinderella.

Additional Books to Read

The Children's Homer by Padraic Colum. Read the adventures of ancient heroes and heroines.

Umm El Madayan: An Islamic City Through the Ages by Abderrahman Ayoub, Jamila Binous, Abderrazak Grageub, Ali Mtimet, and Hedi Slim.

Response Activities

1. **Predict:** How can Melanion win the race if he uses the three golden apples from Aphrodite? Predict how he might use each apple during the race.

2. **Narrative: Conduct an Interview** Prepare a sports documentary called "You Were There." Imagine that you are a sportswriter who will interview Melanion and Atalanta before the race. Write down questions you will ask each of them.

3. **History: Make a Timeline** In 1900, women were allowed to participate in the Olympic track events for the first time. Make a timeline listing some of the women athletes who participated in the Olympics.

Using Specialized Dictionaries

In the Know

Where can you meet all the most important and influential people from ancient Greece? In the pages of a **specialized dictionary**. These are dictionaries that specialize in information about certain subjects. Use a specialized **biographical dictionary** to find out about famous people such as Homer, Aristotle, and Plato. Then pore over the pages of a specialized **geographical dictionary** to learn about Athens and Sparta. You'll find tips on where to get even more information, and you'll be an expert before you know it!

1 Here's How

Follow these steps to get the most out of specialized dictionaries:

- Decide what or who you want to find out about.
- Write two questions to focus your search. For example, if you are doing research on Aristotle, you might ask: What were Aristotle's most important accomplishments? In what period did he live?
- Decide which specialized dictionary will have the information you need. Look up your subject.
- Identify the main ideas of the entry.
- Find information that answers your focus questions.
- Take notes. Be sure to write down any other sources or subjects you could look up for further research.
- Record the source of the information to include in your report.

2 Think It Through

How is the information in a specialized dictionary different from the information in a dictionary of everyday language? How is it different from information in an encyclopedia?

3 Use It

1. Review this chapter, and choose an ancient Greek to learn more about. Look this person up in a biographical dictionary, like the one at the back of this book.

2. Write down the main ideas you've learned about this person from the entry.

3. Write down other subjects you could look up if you wanted to do more research on this person.

4. Go to the library and make a list of the different types of specialized dictionaries you find.

The Macedonian Empire

Main Idea Northern Greeks, or Macedonians, created an empire that took in many people of different cultures.

Alexander of Macedonia approached the chariot of the king of Gordium. A knot tied the chariot to the harness of an ancient king. A prophecy claimed that whoever could loosen the knot would go on to rule all of Asia. Heartened by his recent victories and dreaming of others, Alexander stepped forward and swiftly cut the knot.

Would the prophesy come true? Although this account is probably just a story, Alexander did become one of the greatest and most successful generals in history. He did rule almost all of Asia.

A Vast Empire

Focus *Who were Philip II and Alexander the Great, and what did they do?*

The Macedonians felt that they were the descendants of the heroes of Homer's poems. They were fierce fighters, trained through constant warfare with their neighbors.

It was Alexander's father, Philip II, who made Macedonia a powerful state. Philip II became king of Macedonia in 359 B.C. Building up a mighty army, he attacked the Greek city-states and crushed their combined forces at the Battle of Chaeronea (kehr uh NEE uh) in 338 B.C. But in 336 B.C., while beginning a new military campaign to take over Persia, Philip was murdered.

Alexander's Conquests

Alexander was barely 20 years old when his father died. He led the troops into Asia Minor in 334 B.C. in order to carry out his father's plans. He never saw his homeland again.

For the next 11 years, Alexander and his armies marched. A combined Macedonian-Greek force of 35,000, Alexander's army included spear and shield carriers, javelin throwers,

Key Vocabulary

- siege train
- Hellenistic

Key Events

359 B.C. Philip II becomes king of Macedonia

336 B.C. Alexander takes the throne

323 B.C. Death of Alexander

A detail from a work of art showing one of Alexander the Great's battles.

The Conquests of Alexander the Great, 334–323 B.C.

EUROPE

Black Sea

1 356 B.C. Birth of Alexander, ascends Macedonian throne at age 20.

3 334 B.C. Important victory at Battle of Granicus.

4 333 B.C. Defeats Persian King Darius III at Battle of Issus.

MACEDONIA

THRACE

Pella

Troy

Ancyra

2 335 B.C. Crushes rebellion in Thebes.

Cilician Gates

TAURUS MTS.

Tarsus

CYPRUS

Mediterranean Sea

5 332 B.C. Besieges Tyre and Gaza.

Tyre

LIBYAN DESERT

6 331 B.C. Founds Alexandria.

Alexandria Nile Delta

Gaza

LEGEND

- ▪▪▪▪ Alexander's empire
- ← Alexander's march
- ✕ Major battles
- ▪ Cities renamed Alexandria

km / mi 0 ——— 250

Siwa

Memphis

Nile River

7 Consults the oracle of Zeus Ammon.

AFRICA

The map illustrates Alexander's journey and conquests. **Map Skill:** *What were the names of the major battles, cities, and rivers in Alexander's campaigns? Where are these located on a modern map?*

Curious Facts

Alexander's conquests spread the Greek language to so many areas that, 100 years after his death, it was possible to travel from Italy to India, speak Greek, and be understood.

and archers. The army used portable towers and ramming devices to attack cities. This combination of equipment was called a **siege train**.

When Alexander reached India, in 326 B.C., his weary troops had fought enough. At the Jhelum River, they refused to continue. It was during the long journey home that Alexander died of a fever in Babylon in 323 B.C. He was only 32 years old.

The Spread of Greek Culture

Focus *How did Alexander's campaigns spread Greek culture?*

Although Alexander's empire began to unravel soon after his death, the changes he brought about lasted far longer. The Greek language spread, easing communication and expanding trade. The ideas of Greek philosophers, scientists, poets, and playwrights influenced people's thinking from Egypt to India. This new culture was called **Hellenistic** (hehl uh NIHS tihk) from the Greek word for Greece (Hellas).

Alexander built the great city of Alexandria in Egypt on the Nile Delta. This became a crossroads of trade and ideas in the Hellenistic world. The royal library there was a gathering place for scholars and is reported to have held half a million volumes.

The influence of Greece reached its peak in this Hellenistic Age

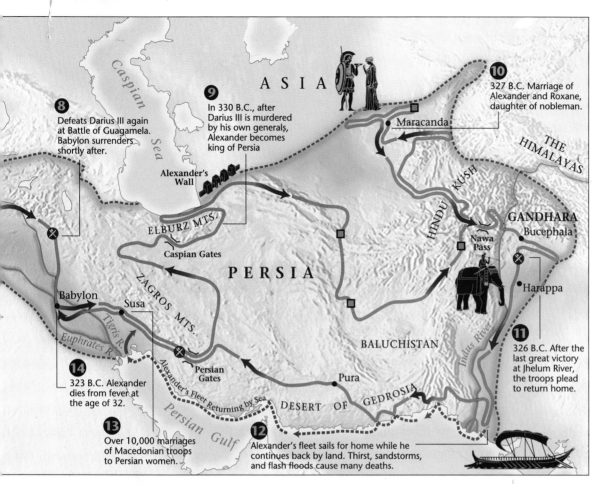

8 Defeats Darius III again at Battle of Guagamela. Babylon surrenders shortly after.

9 In 330 B.C., after Darius III is murdered by his own generals, Alexander becomes king of Persia

10 327 B.C. Marriage of Alexander and Roxane, daughter of nobleman.

Alexander's Wall

ELBURZ MTS.

Caspian Gates

PERSIA

THE HIMALAYAS

HINDU KUSH

GANDHARA
Bucephala

Nawa Pass

Maracanda

ASIA

Caspian Sea

ZAGROS MTS.

Babylon

Susa

Tigris R.

Euphrates R.

Persian Gates

14 323 B.C. Alexander dies from fever at the age of 32.

Harappa

Indus River

BALUCHISTAN

Pura

11 326 B.C. After the last great victory at Jhelum River, the troops plead to return home.

13 Over 10,000 marriages of Macedonian troops to Persian women.

Alexander's Fleet Returning by Sea

Persian Gulf

DESERT OF GEDROSIA

12 Alexander's fleet sails for home while he continues back by land. Thirst, sandstorms, and flash floods cause many deaths.

(323 B.C. to 27 B.C.), although the Greek city-states never regained their former glory. For many years, they remained under the influence of Macedonia. Then, in the first century B.C., the city-states fell to another growing empire, that of the Romans.

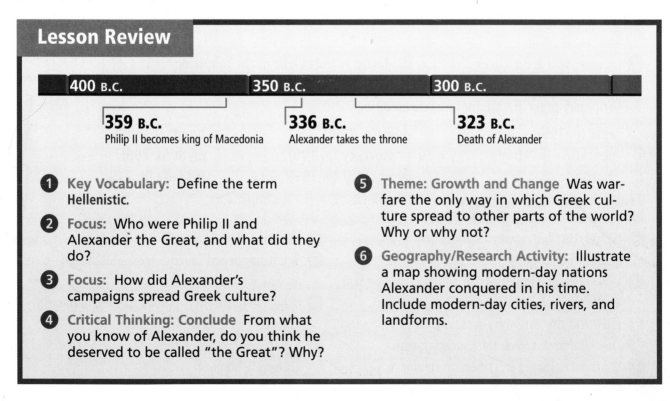

Lesson Review

400 B.C.	350 B.C.	300 B.C.

359 B.C.
Philip II becomes king of Macedonia

336 B.C.
Alexander takes the throne

323 B.C.
Death of Alexander

1 **Key Vocabulary:** Define the term Hellenistic.

2 **Focus:** Who were Philip II and Alexander the Great, and what did they do?

3 **Focus:** How did Alexander's campaigns spread Greek culture?

4 **Critical Thinking: Conclude** From what you know of Alexander, do you think he deserved to be called "the Great"? Why?

5 **Theme: Growth and Change** Was warfare the only way in which Greek culture spread to other parts of the world? Why or why not?

6 **Geography/Research Activity:** Illustrate a map showing modern-day nations Alexander conquered in his time. Include modern-day cities, rivers, and landforms.

Chapter Review

594 Reforms of Solon		**431-404** Peloponnesian Wars	

1000 B.C.   720 B.C.   440 B.C.   160 B.C.   A.D. 120   **A.D. 400**

776
First Olympic Games

800
Age of Homer
and Hesiod

323
Death of Alexander

461
Pericles takes power

393
Last ancient
Olympic Games

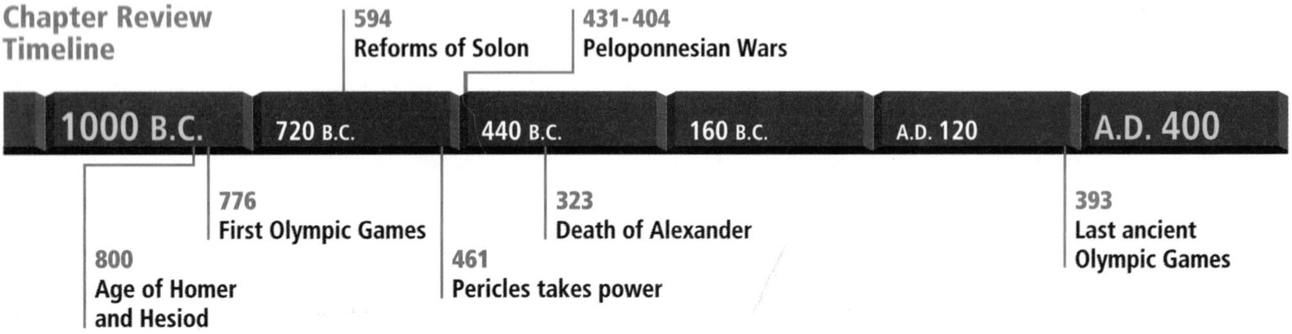

Summarizing the Main Idea

1 The ancient Greeks influenced the world in many areas. Copy the chart below and fill in the missing information to name the individuals and what they are remembered for.

Area of Influence	Greek Individual	Remembered for
Architecture		
Drama		
Medicine		

Vocabulary

2 Imagine you are a Greek drama critic. Using at least eight of the following terms, write a review of the latest play of Sophocles or Aristophanes. (You may make up the plot as you go along.)

epic (p. 195)   polis (p. 199)   tyrant (p. 202)

peninsula (p. 196)   aristocracy (p. 199)   myth (p. 206)

maritime (p. 197)   democracy (p. 199)   tragedy (p. 210)

Reviewing the Facts

3 Name four important features of the geography of Greece.

4 Who were the ancestors of the ancient Greeks, and what happened to them?

5 How did the early city-states develop?

6 Describe how Greek democracy began.

7 Who participated in Athenian democracy? Who didn't?

8 Describe Athens in 450 B.C.

9 What happened when Sparta and Athens went to war with each other?

10 What were the Acropolis and the Parthenon, and why were they important?

11 What were some of Alexander of Macedonia's accomplishments?

12 One specialized dictionary is the *Dictionary of World History*. It specializes in information about famous people, places, and subjects. First, decide what you want to research. Then write a question about what you want to write about. For example, if you are writing about ancient Athens you might ask: How did the Athenians earn a living? Then use the dictionary to find information that answers your question.

Geography Skills

13 How do you think the shape, climate and landscape of Greece influenced its role in the world?

14 If you were going to put a picture on a postcard to represent "Greece," what would you include in the photograph? Why?

Critical Thinking

15 **Comparing Then and Now** How is democracy, as practiced by the ancient Greeks, similar to democracy in the United States today? How is it different? Have these similarities and differences always been true about democracy in the United States?

16 **Predict** If ancient Greece, and its art, science and ideas, had not existed, what would the world today be like?

Writing: Citizenship and Economics

17 A citizen of Athens and a citizen of Sparta meet, and each tries to convince the other that their city and lifestyle is better. Write their conversation.

18 You are setting up your own stall to sell vegetables and fruits at the agora. Design some advertisements promoting your farm products.

Activities

History/Research Activity
Choose one of the ancient Greeks in the chart on the previous page, and do research to find out more about his or her accomplishments. Share your findings with the class.

Culture/Art Activity
Homer and Hesiod recited the ancient myths in their own words. Rewrite an ancient Greek myth in your own words. Some options include: write it in poetry; find music to accompany your version and recite or sing it to your class; illustrate it; act it out.

Internet Option

Check the **Internet Social Studies Center** for ideas on how to extend your theme project beyond your classroom.

THEME PROJECT CHECK-IN

Use the information in this chapter about ancient Greece to help you decide what kind of government you would like to choose. Ask yourself these questions:
• What form of government was developed in ancient Greece? How has it influenced modern governments?
• What were some of the important ideas developed by ancient Greeks?
• How were the ancient Greeks powerful outside their own borders?

CHAPTER 9 Ancient Rome and Byzantium

600 B.C.	400 B.C.	200 B.C.

The Roman Empire   27 B.C.

Find out how Augustus Caesar helped develop Rome. *Lesson 1, Page 229*

Water: Using Resources

Discover the technological wonder of the Roman aqueduct. *Lesson 2, Page 236*

The Household

What was life like for this young couple of Pompeii? *Lesson 2, Page 232*

The History of Ancient Rome

Main Idea Rome grows from a city-state into a world empire.

According to an ancient myth, two helpless baby boys were abandoned in a basket to drift down the Tiber River. They were the sons of the mighty Mars, god of war. Fearing that these twins, Romulus and Remus, would seize his kingdom one day, a jealous king had them placed in a basket and set afloat in the hope that they would drown. The myth tells us that a wolf found and rescued the two infants, an act that saved them from certain death. Later a shepherd brought them home and cared for them.

The myth continues. Romulus and Remus grew up and became bitter rivals, fighting over the cities they each began to build. After defeating his brother, Romulus went on to found the city of Rome. Mysteriously, one day, during a thunderstorm, a cloud lifted Romulus up from a mountaintop and carried him off into the sky above. Appearing later to an old friend, Romulus said that one day all nations would bow to Rome.

Key Vocabulary

republic
Senate
consul
patrician
plebeian

Key Events

509 B.C. Establishment of the Roman Republic

44 B.C. Assassination of Julius Caesar

27 B.C. Octavian becomes emperor

◀ The Colosseum in Rome was built to be an arena for public games.

B.C.|A.D.   A.D. **200**   A.D. **400**

Life and Teachings of Jesus

Judaea was a province of Rome. Find out why the birth of Jesus changed history. *Lesson 3, Page 241*

Faith represented in Art

After years of persecution Christianity was accepted by Rome. *Lesson 3, Page 244*

Christianity Today

Christianity is practiced today in many places across the world. *Lesson 4 Page 247*

This wall painting of an Etruscan woman decorates a tomb in Tarquinia. **Cultures:** *What can you learn about the fashions of the period?*

The Development of Rome

Focus *What were the origins of Rome?*

As Romulus predicted, Rome did grow into a mighty empire. This occurred over the course of hundreds of years of struggle. If you look at the map below you can see that Rome was well placed on the Italian peninsula. The Tiber River gave the Romans access inland. Many people carrying goods and materials of all kinds passed through Ostia, the Roman harbor, on their way to Africa and northern Europe. Protected from enemy attacks, yet enjoying easy access to the sea, Rome soon grew to become a world power.

Cultural Influences: Etruscans and Greeks

When Rome was first settled around 750 B.C., several different peoples lived on the Italian peninsula. In the northern area of Etruria (ih TRUR ee uh) were the Etruscans, who had come from settlements in the north of Italy. In Latium, in the center of the peninsula, people excelled at

Greek and Latin settlements began to dot the Italian peninsula. **Map Skills:** *What type of produce do you think would be grown on this rocky, dry land?*

Development of Rome, c. 700 B.C.

CORSICA

ITALY

ETRURIA

Tiber River

LATIUM

Rome

Ostia

ADRIATIC SEA

SARDINIA

Croton

Rhegium

SICILY

Megara Hyblaea

Syracuse

MEDITERRANEAN SEA

AFRICA

Legend
- Greek colonies
- Latin settlements

0   150 km.

0   100 mi.

The Tiber River and Tiberian Island as they look today in Rome. The Ponte Rotto Bridge is on the left and the Ponte Fabrico Bridge is in the distance.

agriculture and animal herding. Their language, Latin, eventually became the basis of the language spoken in Rome. From Greek colonies in the south came Greek culture, skills, and ideas, which would influence the Romans greatly.

Kings, Consuls, and Emperors

Focus *What were the major changes in government during the history of Rome?*

Originally, Rome was ruled by kings. In 509 B.C., the Romans overthrew their Etruscan king and established another form of government. It was called a **republic,** a nation in which power lay with the citizens.

The Roman Republic was not a true democracy. It was run by representatives elected by Roman noblemen. No one else had the right to vote. These representatives made up a ruling body called the **Senate** which was the highest decision-making body in the government. Every year, two **consuls** were elected by the senators to head the entire government and be responsible for its army.

Roman society had three distinct classes. At the top were the wealthy

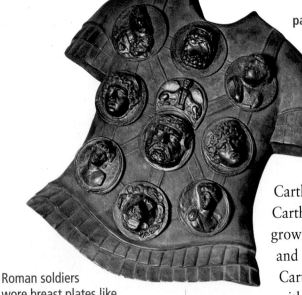

patricians (puh TRIH shuhns), who claimed that they could trace their roots back to the founding of Rome. The plebeians (plih BEE uhns) were the ordinary working citizens. They had the right to vote but could not hold public office. Enslaved Romans had no rights at all.

By the third century B.C., Rome had control over most of the Italian peninsula. The neighboring Carthaginians ruled North Africa and part of Spain. The Carthaginians were afraid that they would lose Sicily to the growing Roman Empire *(see map below)*. Tensions mounted, and eventually a series of wars broke out between Rome and Carthage. The first of these Punic (PYOO nik) Wars ended with the surrender of Carthage in 241 B.C. Almost 30 years later, the Carthaginian leader, Hannibal, led his huge army of 20,000 soldiers and over 6,000 cavalry against Rome. Hannibal surrendered to Rome in 202 B.C.

Rome continued to expand and spread its language, law, and culture into Spain, Gaul (now France), Greece, Macedonia, and Egypt. Despite fierce resistance, many peoples and kingdoms became part of the Roman Empire. By 146 B.C., the Romans controlled land all around the Mediterranean Sea, which they called *mare nostrum*, Latin for "our sea."

Roman soldiers wore breast plates like this one to protect them in battle. **Technology:** *What do soldiers wear for protection today?*

Rome continued to expand and share its language and culture in many lands surrounding the Mediterranean Sea. **Map Skill:** *Measure the distance from Carthage to Antioch, and from Byzantium to Alexandria. Which distance is larger?*

The Growth of the Roman Empire

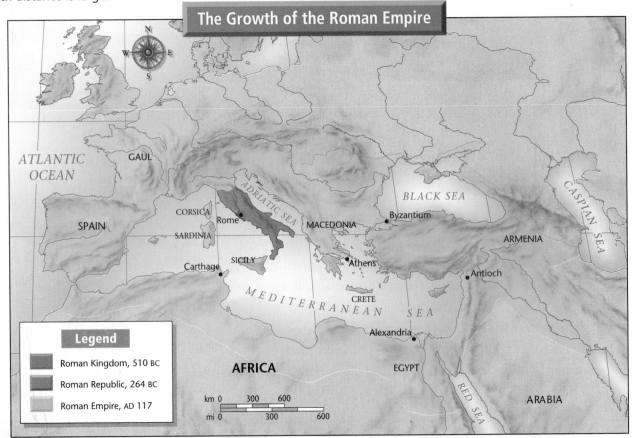

ATLANTIC OCEAN

GAUL

SPAIN

CORSICA

SARDINIA

Rome

ADRIATIC SEA

SICILY

Carthage

MACEDONIA

Byzantium

Athens

CRETE

MEDITERRANEAN SEA

Alexandria

BLACK SEA

CASPIAN SEA

ARMENIA

Antioch

AFRICA

EGYPT

RED SEA

ARABIA

Legend

Roman Kingdom, 510 BC
Roman Republic, 264 BC
Roman Empire, AD 117

km 0   300   600
mi 0   300   600

From Republic to Empire

Extending Roman control further, the famous general Julius Caesar (SEE zuhr) took power in Gaul *(see map on previous page)* and made himself its dictator. Caesar did not stop there; he continued on into modern-day England and Germany.

Caesar and Pompey, the consul of Rome, fought a fierce battle for control of the government. Pompey was murdered in Egypt, and his sons were defeated by Caesar in Spain. The Roman Republic collapsed; Caesar was appointed dictator for 10 years by the Roman Senate.

While popular with many Romans, Caesar angered the patricians with his total control of the Senate. Waiting for Caesar outside the senate house, several senators stabbed him to death on March 15, 44 B.C. Civil wars and unrest followed Caesar's murder. His great-nephew, Octavian, became Rome's dictator and was called Augustus, "respected," and Imperator, "emperor."

For almost 200 years, citizens of the Roman Empire enjoyed a time of peace and prosperity, which became known as the *Pax Romana,* or "Roman Peace." Architecture, law, philosophy, and a wealth of literature spread out from Rome, influencing Western civilization.

The Flemish artist Peter Paul Rubens painted this portrait of Julius Caesar, hundreds of years after the ruler's death.

Lesson Review

500 B.C.	250 B.C.	B.C.	A.D.

509 B.C.
Establishment of the
Roman Republic

44 B.C.
Assassination of
Julius Caesar

27 B.C.
Octavian becomes emperor

1 **Key Vocabulary:** Describe Roman government using republic, senate, consul, patrician, plebeian.

2 **Focus:** What were the origins of Rome?

3 **Focus:** What were the major changes in government during the history of Rome?

4 **Critical Thinking: Interpret** The Romans were determined never again to give up their freedom to a king. Why do you think they ended up with a dictator?

5 **Theme: Growth and Change** Name some possible ways that the Romans may have spread Roman culture to other people.

6 **Geography/Math Activity:** Measure the size of the Roman Empire (shown on the map left) in miles. Compute the distance from Rome to the various major cities on the map. Was Rome the center of the Roman Empire?

Human Systems

How Did Roads Link the Ancient Roman World?

There's an old saying: "All roads lead to Rome." By 100 A.D., the Romans had built more than 250,000 miles of road. This road network was one of the greatest achievements of Roman civilization.

The Romans built roads through many environments, from marshes to mountains. The original purpose of the roads was to allow Roman armies to move quickly. This helped the Roman government control its vast empire. But the roads affected much more than just armies.

These roads changed the geography of the Mediterranean world in many important ways. They improved trade and communication. News, ideas, and religious beliefs also traveled more quickly on the roads. People could travel to almost any city in the empire on a Roman road.

1 Rome

Roman Mail Coach
Roman roads produced one of the best message systems the world had ever seen. Romans in faraway provinces kept in touch with Rome via the Cursus Publicus, the Roman postal service. How was this a revolution in communication?

The Via Egnatia connected the main cities of ancient Macedonia, northeast of Greece. Why do you think the road has lasted until today, more than 2,000 years after first being constructed?

Science Connection

The high quality of Roman roads resulted from a technological breakthrough. Romans learned to mix lime and volcanic ash to make concrete, a remarkable new building material that was as hard as stone. How do concrete structures, like roads, bridges, or dams, affect the environment near where you live?

2 Southern Italy

The Appian Way
Roman leader Appius Claudius Caecus ordered construction of the first great Roman road, the Appian Way, in 312 B.C. By the end of the First Punic War, in 241 B.C., seven great roads connected Rome to other cities.

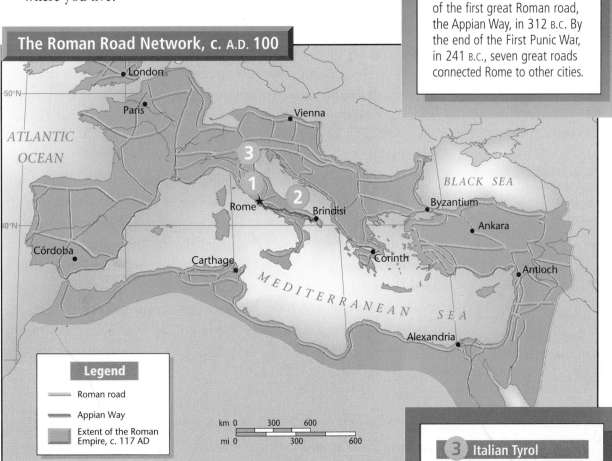

The Roman Road Network, c. A.D. 100

Legend
— Roman road
— Appian Way
▢ Extent of the Roman Empire, c. 117 AD

km 0   300   600
mi 0   300   600

After the Romans defeated Carthage in the Punic Wars, they extended their road system into North Africa. **Map Skill:** *Which city on the map is the farthest away from Rome?*

3 Italian Tyrol

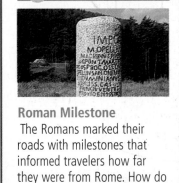

Roman Milestone
The Romans marked their roads with milestones that informed travelers how far they were from Rome. How do we mark distances today?

Research Activity

1 Find out how the Romans constructed their roads. Who was responsible for keeping the roads in good condition after they were built?

2 Write a report explaining your findings.

Roman Life

Main Idea The Romans developed a sophisticated civilization maintained by military power and discipline.

Key Vocabulary

atrium

paterfamilias

oratory

gladiator

aqueduct

This street in Pompeii was once busy with carts, animals, and people. High sidewalks kept people out of the muddy roads. The streets were laid out in a grid pattern. **Geography:** *Why might cities be designed in a grid pattern?*

A bove the town of Pompeii (pom PAY), a menacing black cloud grew. Hot ash and stone began to rain down everywhere. A bubbling river of lava flowed slowly from Mount Vesuvius (ve SUE vee us) into the town below. People ran, desperately trying to escape the destruction occurring all around them. As the lava burned its way through the town, houses were destroyed. Victims were overcome by poisonous fumes and suffocated by the same volcanic ash that hid the sun and filled the sky for the next three days.

On that day in A.D. 79, over 2,000 people lost their lives. When archaeologists began excavating Pompeii some 1,500 years later, they discovered a city long forgotten. The ashes had mixed with rain and formed molds of the bodies that lasted well after the victims themselves had turned to dust. These ashes had also sealed temples, theaters, and shops. Even the meals that the Pompeians were eating that day were preserved in ashes along with the pots in which they were cooked. From these remains, we get a glimpse of life in a Roman household in this era.

The Household

Focus *What was everyday life like in a Roman household?*

Moments before Mount Vesuvius erupted, a Pompeian household prepared for the main meal. Servants saw to it that the bread was baking, and the meat and fish were cooking. As usual, dinner would be served at 3:00 P.M. Guests would be arriving soon. They would be greeted at the door and led into the **atrium**, which was an entrance hall that opened out into a larger courtyard, called the peristyle. In this space, open to the sky, guests and family members would talk and children would play games nearby. The family's bedrooms, dining room, and kitchen were around the courtyards. The house was decorated with paintings, and the halls were lined with statues.

The weather was good that day, and the family considered whether to eat outdoors in the garden or perhaps under the grapevines. The family and their guests would eat in their customary style, leaning back on pillows and relaxing. The evening's entertainment, singers and a story-teller, would also arrive at any minute.

Bath and Heating System

Baths the size of swimming pools were heated from underneath by fire. The family and guests would spend long periods relaxing and washing.

Dining Room

Romans ate their meals around a central table. While they reclined on couches, they were waited upon by enslaved people. They ate with their hands and washed afterwards.

Atrium

The front door opened to the atrium, where guests were received. This led to a central, outdoor courtyard with trees and a fountain.

No one realized that the nearby volcano was about to erupt. All of these festive preparations were cut short with the eruption of Mount Vesuvius. The lava destroyed everything in its path, but the ash mixed with rainwater has left us with a perfect record of the times.

Roman Families

Large homes such as the one shown above often housed a married couple, their children, and a number of servants and slaves. The most powerful family member was the oldest male or **paterfamilias**. This "father of the family" made all the decisions and was obeyed by all. The care of the children belonged to his wife. Women were entitled to own property but could not vote.

Roman boys and girls from wealthy families attended school from an early age. Literature and **oratory,** the art of public speaking, were very important for boys. These subjects helped prepare them for life in the Senate. Girls, however, generally stopped going to school around the age

Roman Villa

Wealthy Romans lived in spacious homes called villas. The outside of these homes was very plain, and the high walls kept out the noise of passersby. The insides were decorated with murals and paintings. **Cultures:** *How do the walls of a Roman villa differ from the exterior of our homes today?*

of 12. They often learned to sing, dance, and play music at home. By age 14, a girl was considered fully grown and could marry someone chosen for her by her family.

Domestic Slavery

A Roman household included enslaved people as well as family members. These enslaved people did all of the cooking, cleaning, marketing, and other household chores. Depending on the nature of the master, the life of an enslaved person could be relatively easy or miserable. Sometimes enslaved people saved enough money to buy their freedom. Otherwise, an enslaved person could be set free in a master's will.

Life Outside the Home

Focus *In what ways was the forum the center of a Roman town?*

A vast crowd gathered in the Forum in Rome, the public square where government buildings, markets, and temples were located. Most Roman towns had a forum, but Rome's was the most impressive.

The Forum was both the center of Rome and the symbol of its

Curious Facts

Rome was crowded enough to have apartment blocks several floors high. In one written account of life at the time, an ox near the cattle market actually climbed to the third story of one of these buildings.

• Tell Me More •

Roman Forum

Civic Life in Rome

The photo above shows the ruins of the Forum as they can be seen today.

Roman coins usually had the image of an important person of the day. This one shows the image of Horace, a Latin poet.

The Forum was the center of Rome's government. The buildings in the Forum were designed to strike awe and respect into the hearts of Roman citizens. Lofty columns supported sweeping arches. In the buildings around the Forum were wall decorations, murals, and decorative architectural details. There were also many statues of Rome's leaders and gods in and around the area. In its great open spaces, people came to hear decisions made in the nearby Senate. They also came to buy goods in the market, and to worship at the temples.

power. This was where laws were made, goods were sold, and religious ceremonies were performed. Citizens voted on issues and heard decisions from the senate house in the Forum. Butchers, silversmiths, booksellers, florists, perfumers, and jewellers all had shops there. As you can see from the illustration below, the buildings in the Forum were impressive. Columns supported arches. Frescoes, murals, and architectural details decorated the buildings. There were also statues of Rome's leaders and gods all around the Forum.

The Forum was also holy ground. It housed the Temple of Castor, the horse tamer, and Pollux, the boxer, two symbols of Roman strength.

The Romans flocked to the Forum to enjoy sporting events, plays, and other types of entertainment. Julius Caesar himself staged spectacular gladiator games. **Gladiators** were usually slaves or condemned criminals who had been arrested and forced to fight each other with swords. They fought, often to the death, in huge Roman theaters.

The Colosseum in Rome is still an impressive sight today. It was built to be an arena for public gladiator fights. When it opened in A.D. 80 the Emperor Titus scheduled 100 days of events here. **National Heritage:** *Name some arenas we have for public events today.*

Combat in the Roman theaters appealed to the Romans' interest in military might. They cheered wildly as the gladiators fought. If clearly losing, a gladiator could appeal for mercy from the crowd. If the fighter deserved to be spared, spectators waved handkerchiefs and turned their thumbs up. The decision not to spare a gladiator was shown by thumbs turned against the chest.

Military Life

Combat and warfare were part of life in ancient Rome. The Empire was built by the victories of a large and well-trained army. Often, the sons of nobles became generals and went to war themselves.

The earliest Roman army was a copy of a Greek formation that consisted of eight or more lines of soldiers standing shoulder to shoulder on the battlefield. Eventually, these soldiers were organized into large units of 4,000 to 6,000 foot soldiers, called legions. Other soldiers on horseback supported these legions.

As they marched from place to place, soldiers carried their weapons, cooking gear, sleeping provisions, and tools. Each day they stopped and built a new camp protected by a wall of logs and a deep ditch. With their discipline and technological skills, they conquered a large part of the world, building forts and roads as they went.

Water: Using Resources

Focus | *What was the relationship between water and community in Roman life?*

One of the Romans' most remarkable technological accomplishments was their use of water. This was an important factor in the spread of Roman

Aqueduct in France

This aqueduct is in Nîmes, France.

Water channel

Above the top row of arches there is a channel built inside that carries water, very similar to the water pipes we use today.

Footpath

A footpath is below the water channel and allows people to use the aqueduct as a bridge.

culture.

Early in the history of Rome, architects learned to build tunnels and bridges for the transport of water. These structures were called **aqueducts**, from the Latin words *aqua,* which means "water" and *ducere,* which means "to lead."

Roman engineers had to ensure that the aqueduct was built at a constant downward slope. The slope had to be gradual enough that the water would not travel too quickly, but angled properly so that gravity would keep the water flowing. The aqueducts were built at ground level or even underground. Water that needed to flow across a valley or descend to lower land was channeled over a bridge. Through these aqueducts, millions of gallons of water flowed daily into Rome. Transporting water to places where it was needed, using it for public bathhouses, toilets, and private households enabled people to settle in once-empty areas of the expanding Roman Empire. In parts of the world that were Roman provinces, you can still see the remains of aqueducts.

Because the Romans could bring water to locations where it was needed, they were able to establish many public baths in the centers of both large cities and small towns. The baths were concrete and marble basins the size of swimming pools. Some had cold water; others were

Roman baths can still be seen today. The large photo above is in the town of Bath, England. The small inset photo shows the baths of Pompeii.

heated by fires burning underneath. The bathhouses were not simply places to wash. People came to talk, do business, and relax. The baths were for everyone — citizens, enslaved people, women, and children.

A World of Gods and Goddesses

Focus *What role did religion play in Roman society?*

The ancient Romans believed that gods and goddesses were involved in all aspects of their lives. For example, the goddess Ceres took care of the corn that grew in the fields. Janus, the two-headed god of doorways, and Vesta, a goddess who protected hearth and home, together guarded Roman houses against attack.

As their empire expanded, the Romans had increasing contact with other people. They often adopted gods and goddesses from these nations, especially from the Etruscans and Greeks. There were Roman versions of the Greek gods *(see the chart on the opposite page)* as well as of the gods of Asia Minor and Egypt. Jupiter, based on the Greek god Zeus, is one of the best-known examples of this influence.

The Pantheon in Rome was built by the emperor Hadrian to honor all the gods. It still stands today. This painting of its interior was created about 1750. **Arts:** *What architectural features make a building a masterpiece?*

Greek Name	Roman Name	Attributes
Zeus	Jupiter	Ruler of the gods
Athena	Minerva	Goddess of crafts, war & wisdom
Ares (AIR eez)	Mars	God of war
Artemis (AR tuh mihs)	Diana	Goddess of hunting & the moon
Poseidon (poh SYD n)	Neptune	God of the sea
Aphrodite (af ro DYE tee)	Venus	Goddess of love

Romans believed that offerings and prayers encouraged the gods to be friendly and helpful. Offerings included fruit, wine, and sweet cakes. Prayers were made at household altars, temples, or in other holy places.

The gods and goddesses thought to be most powerful were honored with temples built in the center of town. One of Rome's largest temples was called the Pantheon. Built by the Roman emperor Hadrian, this temple was dedicated to all the gods and still stands in Rome today.

The Temple of Jupiter stood on the Capitoline Hill, overlooking the Forum. One day, Julius Caesar was riding through the city when the wheel of his chariot buckled, nearly throwing the ruler onto the street. Taking this as a sign of the god's displeasure, Caesar decided to humble himself to avoid any further bad luck. He crawled up the steps of this temple on his knees before a crowd to show his respect for Jupiter and his gratitude for his battle victories.

Lesson Review

1 Key Vocabulary: Describe a tour around Rome using **atrium**, **gladiator**, and **aqueduct**.

2 Focus: What was everyday life like in a Roman household?

3 Focus: In what ways was the forum the center of a Roman town?

4 Focus: What was the relationship between water and community in Roman life?

5 Focus: What role did religion play in Roman society?

6 Critical Thinking: Why would the Romans have adapted their religion to the religions of the people they conquered?

7 Citizenship/Art Activity: Look at examples of mosaics, murals, or paintings depicting daily life in Rome. Create a mosaic about daily life today.

Finding Clues to Cause and Effect

Clues to the Past

The Colosseum, one of the architectural wonders of the world, was built in Rome in the first century A.D. Its archways and rounded shape were a Roman architectural invention, and remain a symbol of Roman architecture to this day. Also in the first century A.D., a colosseum was built in Nimes, France. Why do you think a Roman colosseum exists in France? Studying architecture is an important way to learn how one culture affected another.

① Here's How

- Compare two examples of architecture. For example, you can look at the photo of the Colosseum in Rome on page 235 and the photo to the right of the colosseum in France. What similarities do you notice?

- Think about the similarities between the two buildings. Recall what you know about each culture. For example, think about what you know about the Romans and their architecture.

- There are many reasons architecture from one culture might be found in another. Ask yourself what might have caused a Roman colosseum to have been built in France.

- Use reference sources to check your theories about these architectural clues to the past.

② Think It Through

Why is it important for archaeologists and historians to study architecture? How do art and artifacts help us know how one civilization influenced another?

③ Use It

1. Write down two similarities you see in the colosseums.

2. List possible reasons for these similarities.

3. Use an encyclopedia to see if you were right. Write a few sentences about what you learned.

Early Christianity

Main Idea Christianity began as a movement within Judaism and developed into a separate religion.

In 63 B.C., the Romans conquered Judaea (joo DEE uh), the ancient kingdom of Judah *(see Chapter 3)*. Once in charge they put their own king on the throne there. The Christian Bible tells us, about 60 years later, three wise men arrived at the Judaean village of Bethlehem. There they found the infant Jesus with his mother, Mary, and her husband, Joseph. Believing that this baby would one day be a great leader, they gave him their gifts of gold, frankincense, and myrrh. Angels sang and the wise men knelt out of respect and admiration for the newborn child.

Not everyone was happy about the news of this birth. Herod, the Roman-appointed king of Judaea, grew uneasy at the thought of this possible rival. He ordered that all male children two years old or younger be killed.

Joseph was warned in a dream that Herod would try to destroy the child, so he took Mary and their baby and fled to Egypt. They returned to Judaea only after the threat from Herod was gone.

Jesus inspired a new religion, Christianity. This religion shared many common ideas with the Jewish faith. It spread quickly to Rome and eventually far beyond.

Key Vocabulary

Gospel
disciple
parable
crucifixion
resurrection
persecution

Key Events

63 B.C. Romans conquer Judaea

C. A.D. 1 Rise of Christianity

A.D. 250–305 Persecution of Christians

A.D. 312 Constantine accepts Christianity

Bartolomeo Vivarini was a Venetian artist who painted this work called *Adoration of the Magi.* **Arts:** *Look at different artists' impressions of the same event.*

(at left) Frankincense and myrrh were considered valuable in Roman times.

Ancient Rome and Byzantium   **241**

The Teachings of Jesus

This mosaic of Jesus is in the Basilica de San Marco in Venice, Italy.

Focus Who was Jesus of Nazareth and what did he believe?

Most of what we know about the life of Jesus, including the story you just read, comes from the **Gospels**. Gospel means "good news" in Greek. The Gospels — written at least a half century after the life of Jesus by his followers — record his life, works, and teachings. These writings form part of the New Testament, which together with the Jewish Bible (which Christians call the Old Testament), form the Christian Bible.

The Carpenter from Nazareth

There is not much information about Jesus' childhood in the Gospels, other than he was born and brought up as a Jew. The Christian Bible does tell us that, at the age of 12, Jesus traveled to Jerusalem with Mary and Joseph to celebrate the holiday of Passover. At one point, Jesus disappeared. Frightened, Mary and Joseph searched everywhere for him, finally finding him in the Temple, the Jewish place of worship in Jerusalem. There he stood, discussing religion with a group of elders who were amazed by his wisdom. Later, when Mary scolded Jesus for running off by himself, he said that he was out doing the business of his Father.

These ruins in Capernaum *(see map right)* are the ruins of one of the oldest known synagogues. **Cultures:** *Look at the architectural details. How many classical architectural details can you identify?*

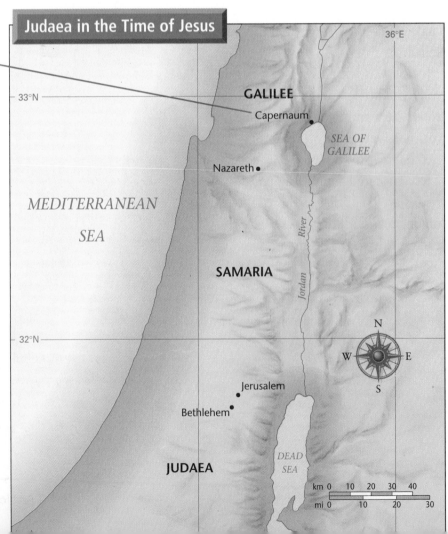

Judaea in the Time of Jesus

GALILEE

Capernaum

SEA OF GALILEE

Nazareth

MEDITERRANEAN SEA

SAMARIA

Jordan River

Jerusalem

Bethlehem

JUDAEA

DEAD SEA

36°E

33°N

32°N

N
W E
S

km 0   10   20   30   40
mi 0   10   20   30

Jesus considered God his Father and felt that he was helping his Father by teaching people about God.

As an adult, Jesus, together with his twelve **disciples** (followers who helped spread his ideas), traveled throughout the province known as Galilee. He taught people about his belief in the kingdom of God and forgiveness of their sins.

There are many stories in the Gospels that tell how Jesus performed miracles as a sign of the coming of the kingdom of God. One day, while speaking to a gathering of 5,000 hungry people, Jesus' disciples told him they had only five loaves of bread and two fishes, not enough to feed such a large crowd. Jesus took the loaves and fishes, blessed them, broke them, and told his disciples to give them to the crowd. After everyone ate, they collected what was left over and still filled 12 baskets.

Jesus, the Teacher

According to Jesus, all religious laws were meant to show how much God loved humankind. The basis of his teachings came from the Jewish belief in one God.

Jesus often told **parables**, or simple stories to share his ideas. He stressed the importance of forgiveness. The stories showed that God

The Jordan Valley, where Jesus lived and traveled, is ablaze with lush green foliage and spring flowers. **Geography:** *What makes the greenery and flowers grow so well in this area?*

would forgive even the worst sinner if he or she asked for forgiveness. Jesus taught people to love God and all people as well. These ideas became some of the guiding principles of Christianity.

Some people in Jerusalem were concerned that Jesus' teachings might threaten the law and order of the land. The Roman authorities worried that Jesus might be dangerous and were also troubled by his teachings.

The Romans arrested Jesus while he was in Jerusalem and, soon after, crucified him. **Crucifixion** was a Roman method of execution in which the victim was fastened onto a wooden cross and left to die. Jesus' death, and his words about his executioners (*see quote below*), became a sign of hope for all Christians.

> "**F**ather, forgive them, for they know not what they do."

Faith and Its Consequences

Focus *Why were the early Christians persecuted in Rome?*

Jesus' early followers believed he was the special messenger sent by God to rescue them from slavery and oppression. Indeed, the name "Christ" comes from the Greek word *christos*, or messiah which has come to mean "savior." Later on, Christians believed that Jesus was more than this: he was, they said, the son of God whose mission was to rescue the souls of all people after their death.

This portrait on glass of a family was sealed into the walls of the catacombs to mark the position of a family tomb. **Cultures:** *What do people use today to mark burial grounds?*

The Gospels recorded that, after his crucifixion, Jesus rose from the dead and appeared to his disciples. Jesus, the account continues, ate with his disciples, preached further to them, and then rose on a cloud to heaven. The Christian holiday of Easter is a celebration of this **resurrection**.

The teachings of Jesus were carried on by his disciples, one of whom was Saul. Like Jesus, Saul had been born a Jew and knew much about his religion. He was initially opposed to Jesus. The Christian Bible says that one day, Saul saw a bright light in the sky and heard a voice. Bewildered, Saul fell to the ground, asking, "Who are you?" The voice answered, "I am Jesus." Saul, who later changed his name to Paul, became one of Jesus' most faithful disciples.

It was Paul who took Jesus' message to Rome, where Christianity attracted many new believers. Rather than believing in many gods, Christians preached that there was only one. Instead of trying to please the gods so that they would be granted good fortune, Christians strove for God's love through their faith and behavior. Even the emperor was only one among God's many subjects, according to the Christians.

Soon, many Romans grew angry with the Christians for not respecting the authority of the emperor. Some even blamed natural disasters such as floods and earthquakes on the Christians, saying that they had angered the Roman gods by not believing in them. The Roman emperor was faced with rebellions and disorganization throughout the empire.

The dedicated followers of Jesus continued, sometimes in secret, to practice their faith. Many were killed for their beliefs. These people came to be seen as examples of bravery and faith for other Christians who had to face **persecution,** (the act of being harassed for differing beliefs in religion). Christians were most widely persecuted during the reign of Decius (DEE shuhs) (A.D. 250–251) and Diocletian (A.D. 303–305).

The conversion of St. Paul is shown in this painting by Lodovico Carracci (1555–1619). **Art:** *What does the expression on his face tell you about the artist's beliefs?*

The catacombs were the place where early Roman Christians buried their dead. This is the central gallery of the Catacomb of Priscilla, in Rome, Italy.

Constantine's Conversion

For the first three centuries of its existence, Christianity faced many obstacles. Then, a dramatic change occurred. In A.D. 312, as the Roman emperor Constantine was preparing for battle, he claimed that he saw a cross spread out against the sun. On it gleamed the words: "In this sign you will be the victor." When that day's battle turned out to be a success, Constantine believed that Jesus had been responsible. Converting to Christianity, Constantine ordered all persecution of Christians stopped.

Meanwhile, Rome's vast empire was becoming increasingly unstable. Local governments fell apart, and the central power of Rome was challenged. People were looking for new sources of comfort. Many found it in Christianity, which promised peace in heaven to people who believed in Jesus. More and more people began embracing this new religion which stressed the compassion of one supreme God.

Lesson Review

200 B.C.	B.C. A.D.	A.D. 200	A.D. 400

63 B.C.
Romans conquer Judaea

c. A.D. 1
Rise of Christianity

A.D. 250–305
Persecution of Christians

A.D. 312
Constantine accepts Christianity

1. **Key Vocabulary:** Describe the history of early Christianity using: **Gospel, disciple, crucifixion, resurrection** and **persecution.**

2. **Focus:** Who was Jesus of Nazareth and what did he believe?

3. **Focus:** Why were the early Christians persecuted in Rome?

4. **Critical Thinking: Interpret** Explain why Constantine's conversion was so important for the Christians.

5. **Theme: Growth and Change** How did the expansion of the Roman Empire affect Christianity?

6. **Citizenship/Research Activity** Research other ancient empires to find out how they accepted different religions within their boundaries. What policies would you set if you were an ancient ruler? Explain and defend your policies.

The Spread of Christianity

Main Idea While the Roman Empire declined, Christianity continued to spread.

Istanbul, Turkey, is a city that straddles two continents — Asia and Europe. An ancient city, it only received its modern name in 1930. For centuries before that, it was called Constantinople, named for the Roman emperor Constantine who rebuilt it and dedicated it in A.D. 330. Before that, for almost a thousand years, it was a Greek colony called Byzantium (bih ZAN tee uhm).

Byzantium and Rome had a profound effect on the way Christianity grew and spread throughout the world. As the Roman Empire fell apart, religion became the one unifying factor. The two great cities of Byzantium and Rome gave rise to two branches of Christianity. Their followers were the predecessors of all of today's Christians. A **predecessor** is a person who comes before another in time.

Key Vocabulary
predecessor
bishop
orthodox
denomination

Key Events
A.D. **330** Founding of Constantinople

A.D. **410** Rome destroyed by Visigoths

A.D. **476** End of Roman Empire

c. A.D. **600** Split of Roman and Orthodox Church

Originally built to be a church, the Hagia Sophia is today a mosque. From the interior picture *(left)* you can judge the size.

Ancient Rome and Byzantium   247

The Ruin of Rome

Focus *What factors contributed to the decline of the Roman Empire?*

In the fifty years between A.D. 235 and 285, some twenty emperors ruled Rome. The empire was becoming more difficult to govern as a whole. Many outlying provinces rebelled or were conquered by outsiders. Some leaders claimed to rule different areas of the empire.

It was with the armies who controlled small parts of the Roman Empire that the real power lay. They were loyal only to their commanders. The murder of many emperors resulted, as these commanders struggled for power.

Realizing that the Roman Empire had grown too large for one ruler, Diocletian divided it into two halves. He ruled the eastern half, called the Eastern Roman Empire, which included Thrace — in the modern day Balkan Peninsula — Egypt, and Asia. To govern Italy, Africa, Gaul, Spain, and Britain in the west, or Western Roman Empire, Diocletian chose an old friend. Diocletian also established a "four-man rule" by selecting one man to help each of the two Roman emperors. Generals

The routes of the barbarian invasions are shown on the map below. **Map Skills:** *What half of the Roman Empire was affected the most by these invasions?*

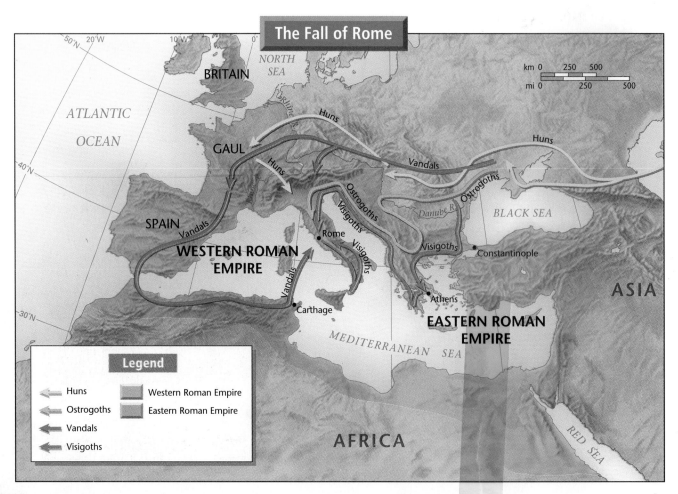

The Fall of Rome

Legend

Huns
Ostrogoths
Vandals
Visigoths

Western Roman Empire
Eastern Roman Empire

controlled the Germanic provinces. These reforms of Diocletian's were a first step toward increasing the independence of the eastern and western parts of the Roman Empire.

Problems Inside and Out

Rome's decline continued after the death of Diocletian. To support the army and bureaucracy, the government imposed heavy taxes. People all over the empire grew increasingly resentful of local authorities and the Roman government.

To make matters worse, people outside the empire, whom the Romans called "barbarians," kept attacking. The Visigoths, who came from the area of the Danube River, in Germany, captured and destroyed much of Rome in A.D. 410. The very last western Roman emperor, Romulus Augustus, was finally overthrown by the Germanic warlord Odoacer (oh doh AY sur) in A.D. 476. This was the official end of the Western Roman Empire.

This belt buckle is in the Historical Museum in Stockholm. It is an example of the equipment soldiers in ancient times would wear. **Science:** *What metal do you think this buckle was made out of? Would it be heavier or lighter than a buckle today?*

Byzantium: Head of All Other Churches

Focus *How did Byzantium continue the spread of Christianity?*

A new kind of ruler arose in Rome. He was the head of all the **bishops**, who were the leaders of the Christian Church in Rome. The head of the bishops was called the Pope, and he would have great religious and political power for centuries to come.

As the Roman Empire fell, Constantinople was reaching the height of its glory. It had a large empire in the east, also called Byzantium. In the fourth century, the Byzantine Emperor Julian tried to restore the ancient gods of the empire. After Julian died, the new emperor reversed this policy. Christianity became the official state religion.

Saint Sophia Cathedral of the Eastern Orthodox Church in the city of Kiev, Ukraine.

The kind of Christianity that developed in Byzantium won converts among people in the Balkans, Eastern Europe, and Russia. Eventually, this eastern form of Christianity became known as the Orthodox Church. **Orthodox** means "right believing" in Greek. This Church considered itself to be the closest to the original teachings of Christianity. Even today, members of the Eastern Orthodox Church recognize Constantinople

Christianity spread from the city of Constantinople. **Map Skill:** *How might early missionaries have traveled?*

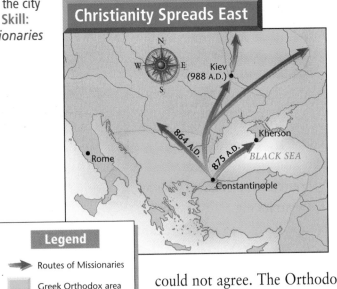

Christianity Spreads East

Kiev (988 A.D.)

864 A.D.

875 A.D.

Kherson

BLACK SEA

Rome

Constantinople

Legend

→ Routes of Missionaries

Greek Orthodox area

(now called Istanbul) as the center of their religion.

After the fourth century, Constantinople and Rome moved farther apart on ideas of Christianity. Rome claimed to be the seat of Christianity, but Constantinople referred to itself as the New Rome. It could boast that it was the home of the emperor and the imperial senate. By the 600s, the two religious powers could not agree. The Orthodox Church and the Roman Church officially split in 1054.

Modern Christianity

Focus *What do modern Christians have in common with one another?*

When people think of Christianity today, they might think of Christmas, the celebration of Jesus' birth. For many people, it's a joyful highlight of the year. Many Christians don't celebrate Christmas, however. Those who do, don't all celebrate it on the same day, or in the same way.

If you went to a Jewish home during the celebration of Passover, you would find unleavened bread, whether you were in Buenos Aires, Jerusalem, or Atlanta. If you were to ask Christians if there is some special food they have at Christmas, you'd get answers that range from peppermint candy canes to plum pudding. The different ways Christians celebrate Christmas — or don't celebrate it — show us something basic about the nearly two billion Christians in the world today: There are many different ways that people follow Jesus.

Jesus did not give his followers a detailed list of rules and commands. Instead, he put special emphasis on two great commandments in the Jewish tradition, "Love the Lord your God" and "Love your neighbor as yourself."

There is remarkable variety in how Christians express their faith — a simple Quaker meeting house in Maryland, a majestic Roman Catholic cathedral in Brazil, a Presbyterian congregation in Korea, a Russian Orthodox painting or icon in Moscow, an African American Baptist choir in Tennessee. There are hundreds of different **denominations**, or church groups, within Christianity. In the United States alone, there are 15 Christian denominations with more than two million members each.

On the surface, these denominations may seem very distinct in their forms of worship. Christians believe that outward worship is not the main part of what it means to be a Christian. For many Christians today, Jesus' teachings are not merely something to study or honor. They are meant to be part of one's daily living. Many Christians say they find faith in God's goodness when they focus on unselfish service to others. This service takes many forms — from religious ministries to working for political change.

What does a modern Christian look like? Jesus himself said you could identify his followers this way:

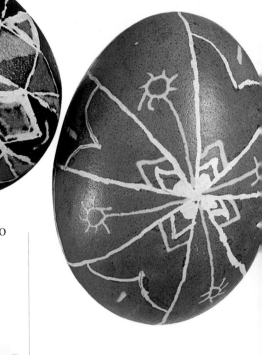

Easter eggs are often decorated by Christian children as a way to celebrate the holiday.

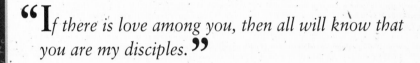

"**I**f there is love among you, then all will know that you are my disciples."

Many Christians say that to measure up to that description is the work of a lifetime.

Lesson Review

A.D. 300	A.D. 400	A.D. 500	A.D. 600
A.D. 330 Founding of Constantinople	**A.D. 410** Rome destroyed by Visigoths	**A.D. 476** End of Roman Empire	**c. A.D. 600** Roman Church and Orthodox Church split.

1 Key Vocabulary: Write a paragraph about Christianity using the words: **Bishop, Orthodox,** and **denominations.**

2 Focus: What factors contributed to the decline of the Roman Empire?

3 Focus: How did Byzantium continue the spread of Christianity?

4 Focus: What do modern Christians have in common with one another?

5 Critical Thinking: Cause and Effect How did Rome's dependence upon its army finally lead to its downfall?

6 Theme: Growth and Change In what ways did Byzantium preserve the values and beliefs of Rome long after the two cities had gone their separate ways?

7 Citizenship/Art Activity: Byzantine paintings and mosaics often depicted Christianity. Prepare a group project on several pieces of art that depict life today. Organize a bulletin board display of your examples, and write a group report explaining your choices.

Chapter Review

Chapter Review Timeline

A.D. 1
Rise of Christianity

600 B.C.	380 B.C.	160 B.C.	A.D. 60	A.D. 280	A.D. 500

509 B.C.
Establishment of Roman Republic

44 B.C.
Assassination of Julius Caesar

A.D. 312
Constantine accepts Christianity

A.D. 476
End of Roman Empire

C.A.D. 600
Roman Church and Orthodox Church split

Summarizing the Main Idea

1 Copy and complete the chart below, indicating each individual's accomplishments.

	Accomplishment
Romulus	
Julius Caesar	
Spartacus	
Jesus	

Vocabulary

2 Using at least nine of the following terms, write a short report of what your life would be like if you were attending school in ancient Rome.

republic (p. 227)

Senate (p. 227)

consul (p. 227)

patrician (p. 228)

plebeian (p. 228)

atrium (p. 232)

paterfamilias (p. 233)

gladiator (p. 235)

aqueduct (p. 237)

Reviewing the Facts

3 How did the mix of people living on the Italian peninsula influence the Romans?

4 Describe the changes in Roman government over the centuries.

5 How do we know as much as we do about daily life in ancient Rome?

6 Why was an army important to Rome?

7 What are some of the teachings of Jesus?

8 How did the Roman Empire deal with the early followers of Christianity?

9 What were some of the events that led to the fall of Rome?

Skill Review: Finding Clues to Cause and Effect

10 Compare the drawing of the Roman Forum on page 235 to the photograph of the remains of the Greek Parthenon on page 208. What similarities do you see? What differences? What clues can you find to the ways that Greek architecture influenced the buildings of Rome?

11 Compare Roman architecture to buildings in your own community. Can you find any Roman arches or columns? What kinds of buildings have those features? Why might that be true?

Geography Skills

12 Study the map of the Italian peninsula on page 226. What were some difficulties Rome's enemies would have reaching Rome?

13 Write a letter from a Roman soldier to his parents, describing the lands he is visiting.

Critical Thinking

14 **Compare Then and Now** How was the daily life in ancient Rome like our lives today? How was it different?

15 **Interpret** Why would the Romans at first be against Christianity?

16 **Predict** How would belief in Christianity spread throughout the world?

Writing: Citizenship and Economics

17 **Citizenship** Today the functions that were performed by Rome's Forum are divided between a city hall, mall, theater and sports arenas. Write a report of daily events in the Roman Forum.

18 **Economics** The aqueducts were the most remarkable technological accomplishment of the Romans. Write a proposal for an aqueduct to be built in your town.

Activities

Culture/Literature
Myths and parables are similar in that they each tell a story to make a point. Choose a myth or a parable and retell it in your own words. Then present it to the class either as an illustrated lecture, or in a dramatic performance.

Geography/Writing
Working in a group, write and deliver the evening news in ancient Rome (even though there were no TVs then!). Write your newscast for the day that Mt. Vesuvius erupted near Pompeii.

Internet Option

Check the **Internet Social Studies Center** for ideas on how to extend your theme project beyond your classroom.

THEME PROJECT CHECK-IN

Use the information in this chapter about ancient Rome to help you with your theme project. Think about these questions:
- What was the Roman system of government? Can you see examples of this system in modern governments?
- What inventions and technologies were developed by ancient Romans?

CHAPTER 10 Cultural Blending and Isolation

Chapter Preview: *People, Places, and Events*

| 500 | 700 | 900 |

Mecca **600s**

Why is this shrine considered Islam's holiest place? *Lesson 1, Page 256*

Islam Today

What are the "Five Pillars of Islam," the duties that all Muslims must fulfill? *Lesson 1, Page 258*

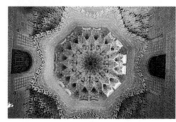

Spain's Alhambra Palace

Islamic culture spread throughout the world. *Lesson 2, Page 262*

254

The Rise of Islam

Main Idea In the 600s, the religion of Islam arose in the Arabian Peninsula; today it is one of the world's major religions.

Sometime around the year A.D. 579, a trading caravan was traveling through the desert of the Arabian Peninsula. The sun beat down on the men as they moved forward. When they finally reached an oasis, a fertile area surrounding a spring, a Christian monk who lived there invited the weary group to stop and share his food. They accepted the monk's offer and left their camels in the care of the youngest member of the group. The monk asked, "Is there not someone else in your party?" The nine-year-old boy who was tending the camels was called. According to Islamic teachings, the monk then revealed that the boy was to become a prophet. (**Prophets** are religious leaders. Their followers believe they proclaim the wishes of their god.) The boy was Muhammad Ibn Abd Allah (moo HAHM mihd ehb n AB du LAH), who was to become the prophet of the religion of Islam.

Key Vocabulary

prophet
revelation
Qur'an
Hijrah
mosque

Key Events

c. 570 Birth of Muhammad

622 Muhammad and his followers move to Medina

632 Death of Muhammad

◀ Hagia Sophia in Istanbul was once a Christian cathedral, and is now a Muslim mosque.

1100   1300   1500

Muslims in Africa   700s

How did Islam help to build and unite the kingdoms of West Africa? *Lesson 3, Page 269*

An Asian Power 600 – 1200s

Why did the culture of China influence Japan? *Lesson 4, Page 276*

The Korean Peninsula

Once controlled by China, Korean kingdoms were modeled after their neighbor. *Lesson 4, Page 277*

Prophet of Islam

Focus *How did Islam develop?*

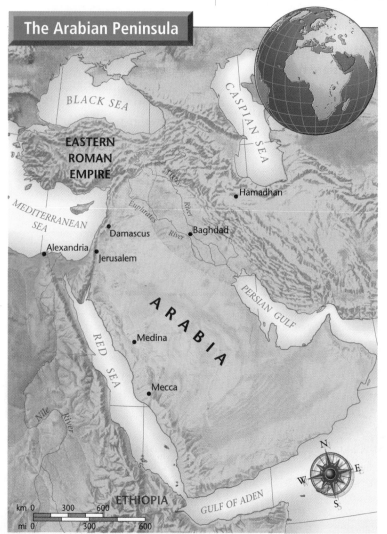

The Ka'bah *(above)* in Mecca is Islam's holiest shrine. Muslims come from all over the world to worship there. **Map Skill:** *Find the site of the Ka'bah on the map below.*

Muhammad was born about 570 in Mecca, a city in the western part of the Arabian Peninsula. Mecca was a bustling town on the trade route that linked southern Arabia with the Mediterranean Sea. People passed through with cargoes of spices and silk from the east. Mecca was also home to an ancient religious shrine called the Ka'bah (KA bah), a stone building. In its wall is a sacred black rock. Around the Ka'bah were 360 altars to different gods, many represented by idols or images of gods. The shrine attracted pilgrims from around the peninsula.

The people of Mecca were Arabs, and many were traders. They organized themselves into extended family groups called tribes, which were supposed to protect and support their members.

According to Muslim historians, Muhammad was successful as a trader. As he grew older he became concerned about what was happening in Mecca. Many merchants ignored their responsibilities to weaker members of their tribes. While the city appeared to be prospering, many individuals were not. Muhammad regularly went to a cave outside of the city to think about the problems around him.

One day when Muhammad was about 40, he was alone in the cave when a voice suddenly filled the silence. "Recite," the voice said, "Recite in the name of thy Lord."

Muhammad came to believe that he had been visited by the angel Gabriel and that what the angel said were **revelations,** or messages, from God. Trembling, he returned home to his wife, Khadijah (ka DEE jah), who reassured him. She was the first of millions of people to believe that Muhammad was a prophet. (Most of these details and other facts about Muhammad's life come from books called the *Sirah*.)

According to Islamic teachings, Muhammad received revelations from God for 23 years. These revelations were collected into a book known as the **Qur'an** (kur AHN), which in Arabic means "recitation." The Qur'an is the holy book of Islam. Muslims look to it for guidance in all aspects of their lives.

The Arabian Peninsula

BLACK SEA

CASPIAN SEA

EASTERN ROMAN EMPIRE

MEDITERRANEAN SEA

Tigris River

Euphrates River

Hamadhan

Damascus

Baghdad

Alexandria

Jerusalem

PERSIAN GULF

A R A B I A

RED SEA

Medina

Mecca

Nile River

ETHIOPIA

GULF OF ADEN

km 0   300   600
mi 0   300   600

Muhammad began preaching his revelations to the people of Mecca. He urged them to worship only one God, called *Allah* (ahl LAH) in Arabic, and not to worship idols. He promised rewards in heaven, but only for those who followed God and led a good life. (The word *Islam* means "to achieve peace through submission to God.") Muhammad taught that people who disobeyed God and his prophet would suffer. He also criticized the behavior of wealthy people of Mecca who did not take care of the less fortunate people around them.

The Qur'an is believed to be the actual word of God revealed to Muhammad. The book deals with issues such as the creation of the world and the role of the prophet. It also contains rules for preferred behavior for believers. The Qur'an helped spread the Arabic language throughout the Muslim world. **Language Arts:** *How are languages spread around the world today?*

Muhammad's message to the people of Mecca was not welcomed at first. They feared that Muhammad's teachings might end their profitable trade with the people who came to Mecca to sell goods and worship the idols at the Ka'bah. The Meccans began to persecute Muhammad and his followers, who were called Muslims.

In 622, the prophet escaped from the Meccans, who were plotting his death. He accepted an invitation to move to the nearby city of Medina. The move from Mecca to Medina by Muhammad and his followers is called the **Hijrah** (HIHJ ruh), or emigration. Muslims begin their calendar on the date the *Hijrah* occurred. The year A.D. 622 is the year 1 *A.H.* — the first year of the *Hijrah*.

In Medina, Muhammad founded and ruled over the first Muslim state. The Qur'an and the Sunnah, a record of Muhammad's words and deeds, laid out principles and laws for society. At this time, Muhammad also built a simple place of worship, called a **mosque** (MOSK).

While he was in Medina, Muhammad succeeded in winning over many of the tribes of the Arabian Peninsula to his religion. Other tribes, however, sided with the Meccans, whose forces continued to clash with the Medinans. The Meccans and the tribes that supported them, however, were unable to defeat the Medinans. Finally, a treaty was signed. In 630, the Muslims returned peacefully to Mecca. Muhammad went to the Ka'bah, where he destroyed all the idols, and dedicated it to the worship of the one God. He also forgave the Meccans who had persecuted the Muslims. Mecca became the center of the Islamic religion.

Muhammad died in 632. By then, many of the tribes in the Arabian Peninsula had become Muslims.

Islam Today

Focus | *Who are the Muslims, and what do they believe?*

All Muslims share a belief in one God and follow the teachings of Muhammad. They also believe that Muhammad was the last of a long line of prophets who revealed God's will to the world. These prophets include Abraham, Moses, and Jesus. (Muslims do not believe Jesus was the son of God, but they honor him as one of the most important prophets.)

The Five Pillars of Islam

All Muslims also share a belief in the "Five Pillars of Islam." These are considered the duties of all Muslims, both men and women. They are: *1) The Profession of Faith.* By proclaiming "there is no god but God, and Muhammad is the messenger of God," a Muslim accepts the Qur'an as

·Tell Me More·

Inside a Mosque

All mosques have certain features in common:

1 a courtyard, where the faithful gather to pray;

2 a minaret, or tower from which a *muezzin* (moo EZZ ihn), or crier, calls Muslims to prayer five times a day;

3 a prayer hall where people pray and listen to a sermon by the prayer leader.

4 a *mihrab* (MIHR eb), a niche that indicates the direction of Mecca.

Mosques are quiet, thoughtful places. People often use them to sit and read or simply meditate in peace.

4 **Mihrab**

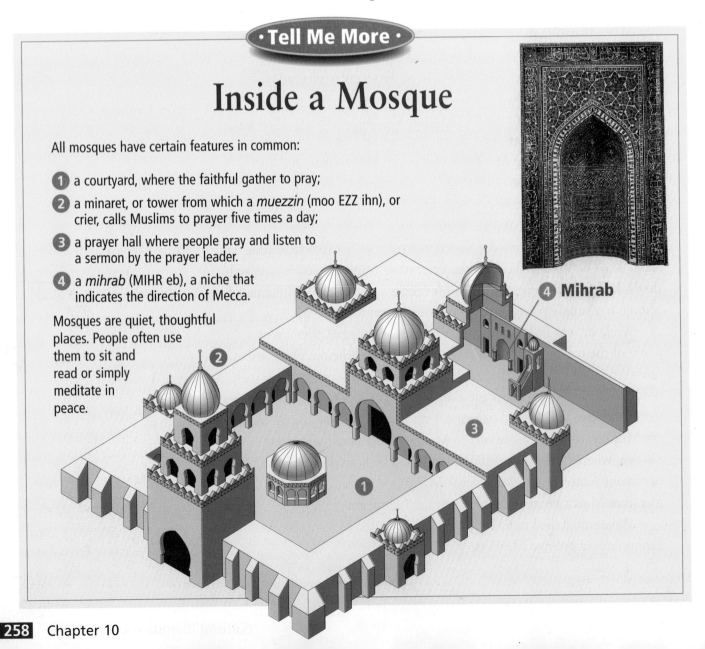

God's final message to mankind. *2) Daily Prayer.* Five times a day, Muslims stop whatever they are doing and pray while facing in the direction of Mecca. *3) Giving of Charity.* Muslims believe that they have a responsibility to help the poor. *4) Fasting.* During the holy month of Ramadan (ram uh DAHN), Muslims do not eat or drink between dawn and sunset. *5) Hajj,* or *Pilgrimage.* Once in their lives, Muslims who have the means must journey to Mecca to visit the Ka'bah.

The practices of Islam today are centuries old. For example, Muslims daily break the fast of the month of Ramadan just as their ancestors did. They often gather at the homes of friends for an evening of visiting and sharing food. Children are not required to fast, but they may if they wish to. The month closes with the Feast of Breaking the Fast, a major family event, with members sometimes traveling long distances to share festive foods.

Today, the majority of Muslims live in the Middle East, in Asian countries such as Indonesia, Pakistan, and India, and in African countries such as Nigeria. About four million Americans are Muslim. There are also many European Muslims, in countries like France, Italy, England, and Bosnia. Whatever a Muslim's race or nationality, Muslims consider themselves members of the worldwide community of believers.

During Ramadan in Egypt, children walk through the streets carrying lanterns and singing songs. **Cultures:** *In which holidays in the United States do children take an active part?*

Lesson Review

500	600	700

c. A.D. 570
Birth of Muhammad

622
Muhammad and his followers move from Mecca to Medina

632
Death of Muhammad

1 **Key Vocabulary:** Write a description of early Islam using these terms: **prophet, revelation, Qur'an, Hijrah, mosque.**

2 **Focus:** How did Islam develop?

3 **Focus:** Who are the Muslims, and what do they believe?

4 **Critical Thinking: Conclude** Why might it have been important for Muhammad to return to Mecca after the *Hijrah?*

5 **Theme: Growth and Change** How might daily life have changed for Arabs who chose to follow Muhammad's teachings after the founding of Islam?

6 **Geography/Art Activity:** Make a relief map of the Arabian Peninsula showing sites that were important to the spread of Islam.

The Spread of Islam

Main Idea The spread of Islam produced a large and diverse civilization.

Key Vocabulary

caliph

Shi'a

Sunni

mysticism

Key Events

632 Abu Bakr chosen as first caliph

661 Beginning of Umayyad dynasty

750 Abbassid caliphs take power

1258 Mongols invade Muslim empire

The fifth caliph of the Umayyad dynasty issued gold and silver coins for the Islamic empire in 696 and 698. The coin shown here includes a picture of the caliph, which is unusual since most Muslim leaders decorated coins with Arabic lettering. **Economics:** *How might the use of a single type of money have united the large Muslim empire?*

> "**O** *men, if you worship Muhammad, Muhammad is dead. If you worship God, God is alive.*"

These were the words that one of Muhammad's closest friends, Abu Bakr (AH boo BAH kuhr), offered Muslims after the prophet's death in 632. Muhammad had died without answering a very important question: Who would lead and guide the Muslims in his place? Abu Bakr reminded Muslims of the power of their faith.

Muslims knew that they could never replace Muhammad as a prophet, but they still needed a leader. So a group of Muhammad's earliest followers chose Abu Bakr to be **caliph** (KAH lihf), which means "successor" in Arabic. In his new role, he was considered the protector of the Islamic faith and the ruler of the lands that the Muslims controlled. Abu Bakr was the first of four leaders known as the Rightly Guided Caliphs. All of these men had known Muhammad, and later Muslims believed that they ruled the community as Muhammad would have done.

The Rightly Guided Caliphs created a Muslim state, which they ruled from 632 to 661. The kind of rule that they started became known as a caliphate, or a period of rule by a caliph. The caliphate system lasted for some 600 years and had a profound effect on the world.

Building an Empire

Focus *How did the early Muslims build an empire?*

Under the rule of the Rightly Guided Caliphs, Muslims moved to fulfill one of Muhammad's wishes: that Islam be carried to other peoples and areas beyond the Arabian Peninsula. Muslim armies fought many battles

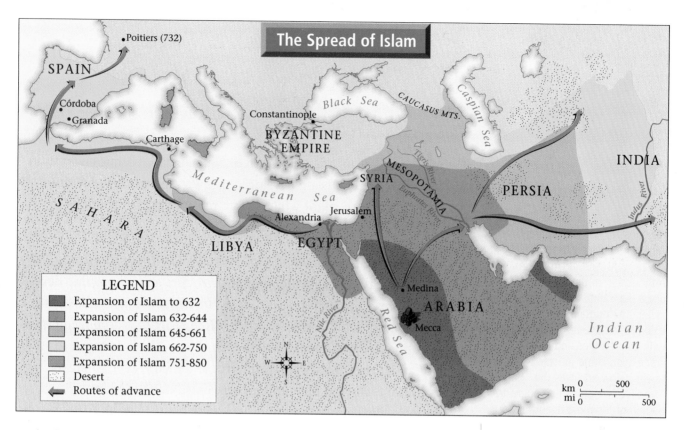

The Spread of Islam

LEGEND
Expansion of Islam to 632
Expansion of Islam 632-644
Expansion of Islam 645-661
Expansion of Islam 662-750
Expansion of Islam 751-850
Desert
Routes of advance

Poitiers (732)
SPAIN
Córdoba
Granada
Carthage
Black Sea
Constantinople
BYZANTINE EMPIRE
Mediterranean Sea
SAHARA
LIBYA
EGYPT
Alexandria
Jerusalem
SYRIA
MESOPOTAMIA
CAUCASUS MTS.
Caspian Sea
PERSIA
INDIA
Indus River
Tigris River
Euphrates River
Nile River
Red Sea
Medina
ARABIA
Mecca
Indian Ocean

km 0 500
mi 0 500

in the belief that they were strengthening Islam, removing its enemies, and bringing justice to other peoples. As you can see from the map above, Muslims took control of vast territories between 632 and 661.

In 661, a new dynasty called the Umayyads (oo MY ads) came to power. They added to the vast empire, which they ruled from the city of Damascus (in Syria today). Advancing east and west, their armies conquered all of North Africa and continued into Christian Spain. They pushed into France until Christian forces under a leader named Charles Martel turned them back in 732. By 850, Islam had followers — farmers, city dwellers, and people in villages — from Spain to India.

The Umayyad caliphs became very wealthy and powerful, but they also aroused much opposition. They had come to power in conflict with the fourth of the Rightly Guided Caliphs, Ali (AA lee), Muhammad's cousin and son-in-law. The first Umayyad ruler had put down Ali's supporters and had even caused the death of Ali's son, Hussayn (hoo SEHN). Ali's supporters became a distinct group of Muslims known as the Shi'a (SHEE uh). The majority of Muslims are called the Sunni (SOON ee).

In 750, the Umayyad dynasty was overthrown by a number of dissatisfied groups. A new dynasty, the Abbassids (AHB eh sihds), came to power and ruled the Muslims from the city of Baghdad, which today is in Iraq. Abbassid caliphs found it increasingly difficult to govern such a large empire. In Morocco, Iran, Syria, and elsewhere, local rulers seized power. In 1258, the Abbassids were overthrown by the invading Mongols from Central Asia. The Mongol victory brought to an end the period of caliph rule, which has since been called the Golden Age of Islam.

By 850, Islam had followers from Spain to India. **Map Skill:** *During which time period did the greatest expansion of Muslim-controlled territories occur?*

The Achievements of Islam

Focus *What were some of the notable achievements of Islamic civilization during its Golden Age?*

During the 600 years after the death of Muhammad, Islamic civilization reached great heights. Islam developed its own religious law, literature, art, and architecture, all of which made tremendous contributions to world culture and continue to be important today.

Scholarship and Art

During the Umayyad caliphate, Islamic mysticism and scholarship developed and spread through the Muslim world. **Mysticism**, also called Sufism (SOO fiz ehm) when it relates to Islam, is the belief that deep meditation can lead to a direct relationship with God. Many Muslims began to study the Qur'an intensely, devoting themselves at the same time to prayer. Other Muslims worked on a legal system based on the Qur'an.

In this same period, many mosques were built. Muslim artists began to use Arabic script for decoration. Many avoided using human figures in their religious art in order not to create idols. Complex and colorful designs were made from stone and tile — stars, circles, triangles, and spirals in interlocking patterns. Muslim artists also created beautiful leather-bound illustrated books and objects from glass, bronze, and ivory.

The Alhambra Palace

Built between 1238 and 1358 by Muslims in Granada, Spain, the Alhambra Palace is one of the jewels of Muslim architecture. Although from the outside it looks like a plain but strong fortress, inside are fountains, arches, and columns, all beautifully decorated with colored tiles and patterns of stone, wood, and plaster. The tower below encloses the "Hall of Two Sisters," which is thought to be one of the most beautiful parts of the palace. You can read about the palace's Court of the Lions on the next page.

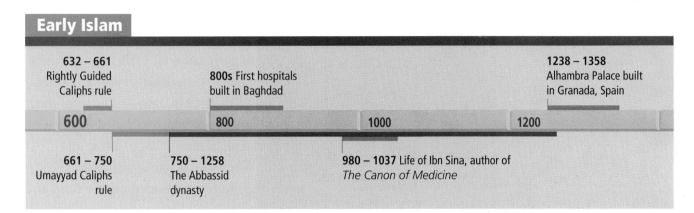

632 – 661 Rightly Guided Caliphs rule

800s First hospitals built in Baghdad

1238 – 1358 Alhambra Palace built in Granada, Spain

600   **800**   **1000**   **1200**

661 – 750 Umayyad Caliphs rule

750 – 1258 The Abbassid dynasty

980 – 1037 Life of Ibn Sina, author of *The Canon of Medicine*

Science, Mathematics, and Medicine

The Umayyads supported scientific work. Muslims needed to have some knowledge of astronomy, the study of the stars and planets, because the times of prayer and the direction of Mecca could be figured out only with such knowledge. Muslims set up astronomical observatories in their lands. Later Muslims prepared astronomical tables based on observations at Baghdad and Damascus. Many stars are still called by names of Arabic origin.

Muslims also made important contributions to mathematics. They introduced a number system from India to Southwest Asia and Europe. People stopped using Roman numerals and began using Arabic numbers, which you use every day. The Muslims also did important work in algebra and geometry. The word *algebra* comes from the Arabic language.

Medicine was another area in which Muslims made great advances. By the 800s, Baghdad had its first hospital, which was divided into wards, separate areas for the treatment of specific diseases. Soon after, records say, 34 hospitals were established throughout the Muslim world.

A Muslim physician, Ibn Sina (ihb uhn SEE nah), wrote *The Canon of Medicine*, one of the most famous books in the history of medicine. It gave some of the most complete descriptions of medical treatments ever written. The book was used in Europe as a medical reference for centuries.

Trade and the Spread of Knowledge

Islamic civilization played an important role in the spread of goods and knowledge from one part of the world to another. Muslim traders developed an extensive network of trade routes linking Africa, Asia, and Europe. Paper, spices, dyes, glass manufacturing, and technologies for making textiles came through or from Muslim lands from the 700s to the 1400s.

In addition, Muslims helped transmit the

The Muslim empire flourished over many centuries. **Timeline Skill:** *How many years went by between the start of the rule of the Rightly Guided Caliphs and the birth of Ibn Sina?*

Court of the Lions

One of the Alhambra's most beautiful courtyards is filled with columns. It is named after the 12 lion statues at the base of the central fountain. The photograph above looks out from beneath the columns facing toward the fountain. Find the fountain in the illustration on the previous page.

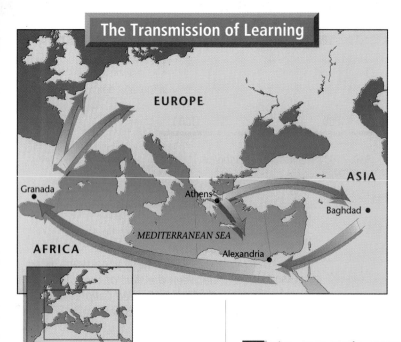

The Transmission of Learning

learning of early cultures. Under the Abbassid caliphs, scholars translated famous works of science and philosophy into Arabic from their original languages, which included Sanskrit (the early language of India), Greek, and Persian. When the Arabic copies reached Spain, they were retranslated into Spanish and Latin. European scholars could then study ancient thought as interpreted by Islamic thinkers.

An inscription on a building built in Spain under Muslim rule sums up some of the ideals of Islamic culture:

The map above shows how the learning of the ancient Greeks spread through Muslim-controlled territories. **Map Skill:** *In which areas did Muslim scholars first learn of Greek ideas?*

> "The world is supported by four things only: the learning of the wise, the justice of the great, the prayers of the righteous, and the valor of the brave."

These ideals have endured through the centuries and continue to shape our world today.

Lesson Review

600		700	1200

632
Abu Bakr chosen as first caliph

661
Beginning of Umayyad Dynasty

750
Abbassid caliphs take power

1258
Mongols invade Muslim empire

1. **Key Vocabulary:** Use the following words in a paragraph about the rise of Islam: caliph, Shi'a, Sunni, mysticism.

2. **Focus:** How did the early Muslims build an empire?

3. **Focus:** What were some of the notable achievements of Islamic civilization during its Golden Age?

4. **Critical Thinking: Conclude** Why is a large empire like the Umayyad's difficult to govern?

5. **Citizenship:** How was a caliph's role in governing the Muslim world different from Muhammad's role?

6. **Theme: Growth and Change/Art Activity:** Using library resources, write a short paragraph about why Islamic art developed as it did. Then design and draw a floral or geometric pattern that could be used to decorate a piece of Islamic pottery.

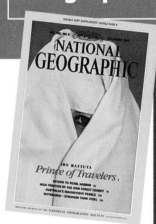

IBN BATTUTA
Prince of Travelers

by Thomas J. Abercrombie

Almost two centuries before Columbus, a young Moroccan named Ibn Battuta set off for Mecca; he returned home three decades later as one of history's great travelers. Driven by curiosity and sustained by the Qur'an, he journeyed to the far corners of the Islamic world — from North Africa, where caravans still dare the Sahara, to China and back.

Ibn Battuta (right) traveled for 29 years, through many regions of the world.

Painting by Burt Silverman

Little celebrated in the West save in scholarly footnotes, his achievements are familiar among Arabs. In 29 years of relentless roaming, Ibn Battuta crossed two continents, logging some 75,000 miles (tripling Marco Polo's travels) through 44 countries in today's atlas.

Ibn Battuta entered Mecca (above) with a caravan from Damascus 16 months after leaving the city of Tangier.

His memoirs brim with the flavor of his time, documenting a journey of hazard and hardship, opulence and adventure. It began in Morocco when he was only 21.

"I left Tangier, my birthplace, the 13th of June 1325 with the intention of making the Pilgrimage to [Mecca] . . . to leave all my friends both male and female, to abandon my home as birds abandon their nests."

In Delhi, Ibn Battuta met the storied Indian sultan Muhammad ibn Tughluq at his palace in Jahanpanah, in the Hall of a Thousand Pillars. The ruler was attended by his vizier, dozens of chamberlains, officials, and slaves — including the "keeper of the fly whisk," who stood behind him — all against the background of 200 soldiers in armor, 60 horses in royal harness, and 50 elephants in silk and gold.

Ibn Battuta greets Indian sultan Muhammad ibn Tughluq in his richly decorated palace.

Painting by Burt Silverman

Ibn Battuta's memoirs left only one clue to his appearance: As a recent portrait shows (above), he wore a beard.

Response Activities

1. **Conclude** What might have driven Ibn Battuta to travel for 29 years?

2. **Narrative: Write a Journal** Suppose you are Ibn Battuta in the court of Indian sultan Muhammad ibn Tughluq. Write a journal entry recording the days you spend with him.

3. **Geography: Draw a Map** Using research materials at your library, make a list of the regions of the world and kingdoms that Ibn Battuta visited. Then draw a world map with those regions and kingdoms marked.

Cultural Change in Africa

Main Idea The introduction of Islam to Africa brought political and cultural change to the region, and two powerful kingdoms with ties to Islam emerged.

The centuries following the introduction of Islam to Africa were times of change. Muslim traders moved throughout the Sahara region, bringing trade and wealth to kings and kingdoms. Kingdoms rose and fell, conquered and were conquered. One of the most important West African kingdoms, Mali (MAH lee), emerged in the 1200s. According to African tradition, Mali's first king, Sundiata (suhn dee AH tuh), overcame many difficulties to reach his position of power.

Looking at Sundiata as a young man, no one would have believed that his name meant "Hungering Lion." He was paralyzed and unable to walk. He was also totally alone. His father, once the king of the West African kingdom of Kangaba (kan GAH bah), was dead. A cruel neighboring ruler had murdered all 11 of Sundiata's brothers, claiming Kangaba as his own.

Sundiata was determined to live up to his name. He struggled to overcome his paralysis, first learning to stand and then to walk. Meanwhile, the neighboring king ruled Kangaba and taxed the people heavily while subjecting them to harsh laws.

One day in 1235, a brave warrior appeared with his own army behind him. It was Sundiata, who had returned to take back what was rightfully his. After a long battle, Sundiata and his people, the Mandinka, emerged victorious. To this day, West Africans tell stories celebrating the courage of the "Hungering Lion" who, against all odds, expanded Kangaba into the great empire of Mali.

Islam Helps Unite West Africa

Focus *What factors contributed to the growth of Mali and Songhai as empires?*

Mali had originally been a part of the empire of Ghana *(see Chapter 7)*. Sundiata led his army to a series of victories, taking control over much of Ghana's former territory and resources. The lands to the south supplied

valuable products such as gold. Mali also began to govern the trading centers of Gao (GOW) and Djenné (jen AY). Traders from across the Sahara brought salt from desert mines to exchange for gold. The kingdom grew rich by taxing traded goods.

Centuries before the Umayyad dynasty had conquered North Africa in the 700s, the valuable Saharan trade routes had come under Muslim control. A Muslim himself, Sundiata valued the bond he shared with fellow Muslim trading partners to the north. These religious links encouraged growth and prosperity.

A Powerful Muslim Emperor

Sundiata's grandnephew, Mansa Musa (MAHN sah MOO sah) ruled Mali from 1312 to 1337. (*Mansa* means "emperor.") One of the most famous African rulers of all time, he expanded the empire of Mali west to the Atlantic coast, north to the Sahara, and east beyond Gao and another major trading city, Timbuktu (tihm buhk TOO).

According to the Egyptian al-Umari (al uh MAR ee), who lived at the same time as Mansa Musa, Mali was "square in shape, being four months of travel in length and at least as much in breadth." Al-Umari may have exaggerated, but the kingdom was certainly extremely large.

To maintain order throughout his lands, Mansa Musa appointed representatives to oversee rulers in outlying regions. To keep peace with his

A *muezzin* calls the faithful to prayer at the Great Mosque in Djenné, Mali. The mosque is covered in mud plaster that must be repaired each year after Mali's rainy season. **Geography:** *What does the construction of the mosque tell you about the vegetation and terrain of Mali? What building materials are used?*

Biography

Ibn Battuta

Ibn Battuta is the best known of Muslim travelers. Born in Morocco, he visited many regions of the world during the course of his life: Africa, Persia, Syria, India, Indonesia, and China, to name just a few. He wrote detailed accounts of his adventures.

Ibn Battuta journeyed to Mali in 1352. Traveling with a camel caravan, he took the difficult route across the western Sahara. He spent months in Mali as a guest of the emperor. When he returned to Morocco, he reported to the king on the habits and customs of the people of Mali.

neighbors, he established relations with the Muslim rulers of Morocco and Egypt.

Mansa Musa was a devout Muslim. To express his faith, and to obey the requirements of his religion, he made a pilgrimage to the holy city of Mecca in 1324. *(See the story map below.)* Accompanying the emperor on one of the most famous trips in history was an enormous group that included family, friends, local rulers, and enslaved people, as well as hundreds of elephants and camels.

Returning to Mali, Mansa Musa brought with him an important Spanish architect to design new mosques for Timbuktu and Gao. Timbuktu was transformed into a center for Islamic study, as well as a center of commerce. During Mansa Musa's reign, the mosque of Sankore (san kor AY) in Timbuktu became a school for studying the Qur'an, Islamic history, and law. Eventually, the University of Sankore would develop from these beginnings.

According to al-Umari, Mansa Musa was "the most powerful, the richest, the most fortunate, the most feared by his enemies, and the most able to do good to those around him." By the time of his death in 1337, he had built Mali into a powerful empire.

Songhai Continues the Trading Tradition

Under Mansa Musa, the empire of Mali had included the lands along the Niger River of the Songhai (SONG hy) people. By the late 1300s, with Mali weakening after Mansa Musa's death, Songhai was resisting outside control. In the mid-1400s, the kingdom of Songhai separated from Mali, expanding upstream along the Niger River into Timbuktu. Djenné was added to the Songhai empire by the fierce ruler Sonni Ali (SOH nee AHL ee)

Mansa Musa's Journey to Mecca

In 1324, Mansa Musa, accompanied by hundreds of family members, friends, and enslaved people, left his home in Mali to make the *hajj*, a pilgrimage to the holy city of Mecca. The enormous group traveled about 3,500 miles across desert and grasslands, stopping at various cities along the way. Enslaved people carried food and water for the pilgrims. One hundred pack camels were each loaded with 300 pounds of gold. Mansa Musa's arrival in Cairo, the Egyptian capital, made a huge impression on the Egyptians. "This man spread upon Cairo the flood of his generosity: there was no person, officer of the court, or holder of any office . . . who did not receive a sum of gold from him," wrote al-Umari. Mansa Musa's pilgrimage caught the attention of the Muslim world. **Map Skill:** *Before arriving in Cairo, what cities did Mansa Musa visit?*

1 1324: Mansa Musa begins his pilgrimage from Timbuktu with thousands of family members, officials, chiefs, servants and slaves. Camels carry loads of gold and jewelry. ➤

Tlemce
Fez
TUA
Timbukt
Walata
MALI
Senegal River
Niger River
Djenné
G

→ Route of Mansa Musa

at the end of a seven-year **siege**, a battle in which a city is surrounded and blockaded in order to make it surrender. Sonni Ali maintained law and order by appointing officials to govern affairs in regions called **provinces**. He also created an army, and a navy that was based on the Niger River.

By the 1300s, many West African kings were Muslims. Sonni Ali was attached to the traditional African beliefs of the Songhai people. These beliefs had existed for many hundreds of years before Islam and were still present in Songhai. In 1493, only a year after Sonni Ali's death, Songhai was taken over by an army official named Askia Muhammad (AHSK ee ah moo HAHM ihd), who was a devout Muslim. After making his own pilgrimage to Mecca, Askia Muhammad returned with the authority to act as caliph of Islam in Songhai.

One of Askia Muhammad's greatest accomplishments was his system

This scroll from the 1400s is a souvenir of a pilgrim's journey to Mecca. The Ka'bah is shown in the middle of the picture.

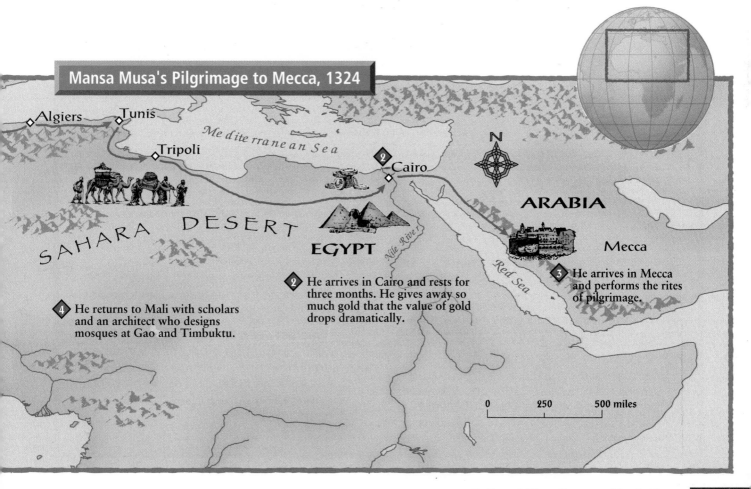

Mansa Musa's Pilgrimage to Mecca, 1324

Algiers
Tunis
Tripoli
Mediterranean Sea
Cairo
SAHARA DESERT
EGYPT
Nile River
ARABIA
Mecca
Red Sea
N

2 He arrives in Cairo and rests for three months. He gives away so much gold that the value of gold drops dramatically.

4 He returns to Mali with scholars and an architect who designs mosques at Gao and Timbuktu.

3 He arrives in Mecca and performs the rites of pilgrimage.

0   250   500 miles

of government. Regional administrators and government ministers controlled local areas. A system of taxation, and a permanent army, which included a fleet of war canoes, were established. Running smoothly under Askia Muhammad's government, Songhai prospered.

In 1528, Askia Muhammad was overthrown by his son and banished to an island in the Niger River where he died. The end of the Songhai empire followed in 1591, when it was invaded by the Moroccans. Still, long after its collapse, the Islamic empire of Songhai was seen as a model for the successful development of growing African states.

The Niger River flowed through Songhai. Both Sonni Ali and Askia Muhammad had navies that were based on the river. **Economics:** *What other ways might the residents of Songhai have used the river?*

Lesson Review

1200	1300	1400	1500	

1235
Sundiata begins building the empire of Mali

1324
Mansa Musa's pilgrimage to Mecca

1464
Sonni Ali comes to power in Songhai

1493
Askia Muhammad takes control of Songhai

① **Key Vocabulary:** Write a sentence about Songhai using the words **province** and **siege**.

② **Focus:** What factors contributed to the growth of Mali and Songhai as empires?

③ **Critical Thinking: Conclude** Mansa Musa's empire was depicted in many European maps from the late 1300s on. What does this tell us about the effect of Mansa Musa's pilgrimage?

④ **Theme: Growth and Change** How did ties to the larger Muslim world help the development of West African kingdoms?

⑤ **Citizenship/Writing Activity:** Write a dialogue between Sundiata and an author who is writing his biography. Sundiata should describe his struggles to become a leader of his people. The biographer should ask about Sundiata's achievements.

Cultural Change in East Asia

Main Idea As a political and cultural power in East Asia, China influenced its neighbors in the region.

Key Vocabulary

abacus

magnetic compass

Key Events

618 Beginning of the Tang dynasty

960 Beginning of the Song dynasty

Far to the east of the Muslim empire was a city humming with activity and culture, the capital of another great empire. It was the destination of Arab traders seeking silk and of the representatives of Muslim caliphates asking to meet with the powerful rulers who governed there. This city was Changan (CHAHN ahn), the capital of China during the Tang (TAHNG) dynasty (618–907).

Changan was a carefully planned city with tree-lined avenues, canals, grand palaces in landscaped parks, Buddhist and Taoist monasteries, and large, busy marketplaces. At its height, it was the largest city in the world, with about a million people living within its walls. Its residents included monks and nuns, government officials, poets, scholars, and many foreigners — Arabs, Tibetans, Turks, Persians, and Koreans, to name a few.

New ideas and styles flowed into China through these foreigners. Tang women wore foreign hairstyles; Central Asian music was the rage; and foreign acrobats performed for enthusiastic audiences. Ideas and styles also flowed out of China. Foreigners visiting Changan studied religion, arts, language, and forms of government, all of which were carried to other regions. Chinese culture shaped East Asia just as Islamic culture influenced the lands in the Muslim empire.

Artisans under the Tang dynasty were famous for the beautiful ceramics they created.

Cultural Blending and Isolation **273**

Empress Wu

As the wife of an ailing emperor, Empress Wu was the power behind her husband's throne for 23 years. She transformed China into a country run by educated officials, creating an atmosphere of peace. She spurred the country's military leaders on to conquer the Korean Peninsula.

In 690, several years after the the death of her husband, Empress Wu took the throne for herself. She ruled China for 15 years.

Cultural Splendor: The Tang and Song Dynasties

Focus *What were some of the main achievements of the Tang and Song dynasties?*

When the Han dynasty, which you read about in Chapter 5, fell in 220, the strong central government and the highly organized bureaucracy collapsed with it. China fell into disarray, splitting into three kingdoms. Later, the north was invaded by nomads and was governed for several centuries by non-Chinese rulers. It was a period of unrest and terror. In the south, six dynasties rose and fell. Despite the political turmoil, this was an important time — Buddhism was spreading across the region.

The Rise of the Tang Dynasty

China was not united again until 589, under the Sui (SWAY) dynasty. Sui rulers were only able to maintain their power for a little more than 30 years; military defeat and peasant revolts brought their collapse. A new powerful emperor, Tai Zong (ty ZUHN), soon controlled China. In the 300 years that followed — the period of the Tang dynasty — a strong government bureaucracy once more emerged, culture flowered, and the Chinese empire became one of the largest and most advanced of its day.

Tang emperors set up departments to run the affairs of this huge empire. Each department had its own responsibility: foreign affairs, education, transportation, the army, and so on. To find talented officials to staff these departments, the system of examinations first established during the Han dynasty was redeveloped and widely used. Young men hoping to become bureaucrats prepared for these exams by obtaining a serious education. Just as under the Han, the top scorers on the exams were selected for government jobs. Because a good education often brought success, great emphasis was placed on schooling during the Tang period.

The arts — poetry, pottery, painting — were also very important under the Tang emperors. Some of China's greatest poets lived and worked during this time. Many wrote about the beauty of nature. Poet Li Po (LEE poh) (701–762) captured this moment:

> **"G**ently I stir a white feather fan,
> With open shirt sitting in a green wood.
> I take off my cap and hang it on a jutting stone;
> A wind from the pine-trees trickles on my bare head.**"**

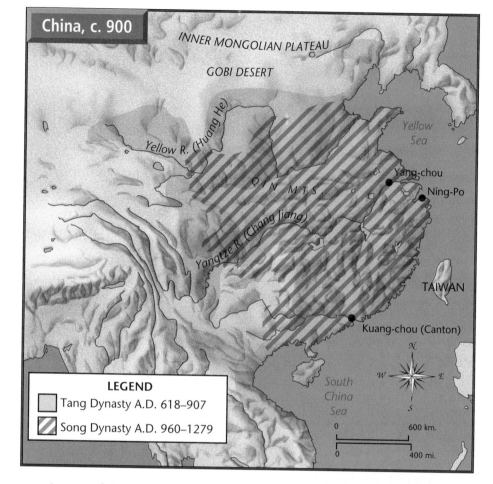

China, c. 900

INNER MONGOLIAN PLATEAU

GOBI DESERT

Yellow R. (Huang He)

Yellow Sea

Yang-chou

Ning-Po

QIN MTS.

Yangtze R. (Chang Jiang)

TAIWAN

Kuang-chou (Canton)

South China Sea

LEGEND
Tang Dynasty A.D. 618–907
Song Dynasty A.D. 960–1279

0   600 km.
0   400 mi.

Under the Tang and Song dynasties, China controlled large territories on the Asian continent. **Map Skill:** *Did the Song dynasty control more or less territory than the Tang dynasty?*

Artists of the time were known for their beautiful, colorfully glazed ceramics. Painting also flourished, influenced by Buddhism and Taoism.

The Song Dynasty

Even with all these successes, the Tang emperors had problems. Local rulers rejected their central authority. Rebellions in the provinces finally brought about the fall of the Tang in 907.

After a period of turmoil, the Song dynasty (960–1279) took control. This was a time of invention. One of the earliest calculators, called an **abacus**, was developed, as were gunpowder, movable type for printing, and the **magnetic compass**, an instrument that determines direction. Sturdy ships were built to carry Chinese goods throughout Asia. Paper money was introduced for the first time in history to support trade.

Under the Song dynasty, Confucianism grew again in popularity, now blending traditional beliefs with Buddhism and Taoism. Teaching that the role of educated people was to serve the state and try to maintain peace and order, Confucianism helped keep the government strong and stable. The Chinese population grew rapidly, exceeding 100 million people for the first time.

The Song dynasty is famed for its innovations in painting. Many subjects were considered worthy of art, but landscapes and scenes such as the one below were particular favorites.

China Influences Its Neighbors

Focus | *How did Chinese culture shape Japanese and Korean culture?*

As a political and cultural power in East Asia, China had great influence over its neighbors, especially Japan and Korea. In 108 B.C., the Chinese conquered parts of the Korean Peninsula and controlled territory there until A.D. 313. They carried Buddhism to the region. Japan, a group of islands separated from China by water, was not easily invaded by the Chinese. The Chinese did introduce Confucianism there, and it later spread across the island kingdom. Buddhism was brought to Japan from China and Korea. Both Korea and Japan developed unique cultures that borrowed heavily from China.

Japan

After Buddhism took hold in Japan in about 552, the Japanese began to look to China as a model. They worked to build a strong, centralized government. Soon, Chinese law codes were introduced as well.

The Japanese tried to re-create the Tang capital of Changan in their capitals of Nara (NAHR uh) and Heian (HAY ahn). They used Chinese architecture as their inspiration for developing these cities. Tang dynasty music and dances were adopted in the court of the Japanese emperor.

Japanese writing and literature also showed signs of China's influence. For example, the Japanese began writing their own language using the Chinese system of characters, though the two languages were completely different. Educated Japanese learned to compose Chinese poetry, and scholars wrote histories of Japan, modeled after similar records from China.

Although the Japanese eventually changed Chinese practices and customs to fit their own society, China played an important role in shaping Japanese culture.

Mount Fuji *(above)* was a favorite subject of Japanese painters for centuries. Chinese influence touched many aspects of Japanese and Korean culture. Map Skill: *Why was Korea easier for China to control than Japan?*

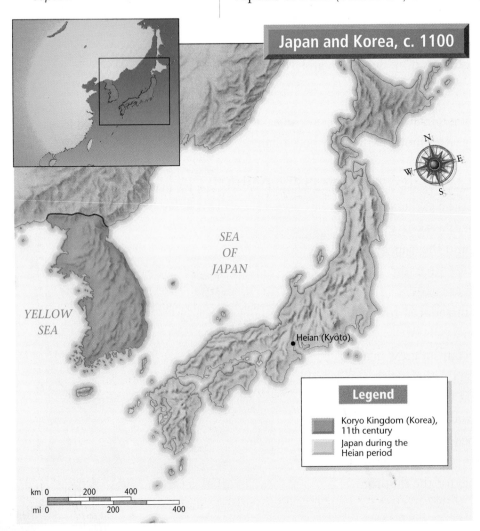

Japan and Korea, c. 1100

SEA
OF
JAPAN

YELLOW
SEA

Heian (Kyoto)

Legend

Koryo Kingdom (Korea), 11th century

Japan during the Heian period

km 0   200   400
mi 0   200   400

Korea

After 313, China no longer controlled territory on the Korean Peninsula, but Chinese influence continued for centuries. From the early 300s to the late 600s, the Korean Peninsula was divided into three kingdoms. Silla, one of these kingdoms, conquered the two others by 670 and modeled itself closely after Tang China.

Korean buildings, like the one shown here, were often styled after Chinese architecture.

Silla was divided into provinces, which were governed the way Chinese provinces were. Eventually, China's examination system for bureaucrats was adopted. Buildings in the Korean capital were built in the style of Chinese architecture. Chinese characters were adopted for writing the Korean language, although the Koreans later developed their own alphabet. A university was established for the study of Confucianism, and Korean monks traveled to China to study Buddhism. Just as in Japan, China's influence shaped Korean culture for centuries to come.

Lesson Review

| 600 | | 900 | |

618
Beginning of the Tang dynasty

960
Beginning of the Song dynasty

1 **Key Vocabulary:** Write a paragraph about Chinese inventions using the following terms: **abacus, magnetic compass.**

2 **Focus:** What were some of the main achievements of the Tang and Song dynasties?

3 **Focus:** How did Chinese culture shape Japanese and Korean culture?

4 **Critical Thinking: Cause and Effect** How might geography have affected the influence China had on Japan?

5 **Citizenship:** What political conditions might be necessary to support the kind of cultural flowering that occurred during the Tang and the Song dynasties?

6 **Geography/Writing Activity:** If you were traveling through Tang China, you might visit the capital city of Changan. Write a description of the streets, buildings, and events in the city.

Using Specialized Atlases

Wonders of the World

How can you grasp in your own hands the wonders of the world's cultures and religions? Grab a specialized atlas off the bookshelf. **Specialized atlases** are books of maps focused on particular topics. For example, historical atlases offer maps of places and events from the past. Religious atlases include maps that show the distribution of the world's religions. Specialized atlases may also include graphs, tables, and pictures that tell you more about places you're researching.

❶ Here's How

Follow these steps to get the most information from specialized atlases:

- Decide what subject you are trying to find out about. Do you think this information would appear in a specialized atlas? If so, decide what type of specialized atlas you should use.

- Use the atlas table of contents and index to look up the place you are interested in. Note the page numbers on which your map appears.

- Study the map and identify its main idea, or purpose. Note any details. If you are using a historical map, notice anything that differs from what you know about that country today.

- Look for any related information, such as graphs or tables, that may be helpful.

- Use a different specialized atlas to find another map of the same place. Compare the two to find similarities and differences. If you are using a historical map, compare it to a map from a modern atlas. What changes have occurred over time?

Here are just a few of the many types of specialized atlases you may find in your school or public library:

- Atlas of world wildlife
- Atlas of archaeology
- Climatic atlas
- Atlas of world history
- Atlas of astronomy
- Economic atlas
- Environmental atlas
- Atlas of Native Americans
- Atlas of the medieval world
- Astronomy atlas
- Atlas of early humans
- Atlas of World War II

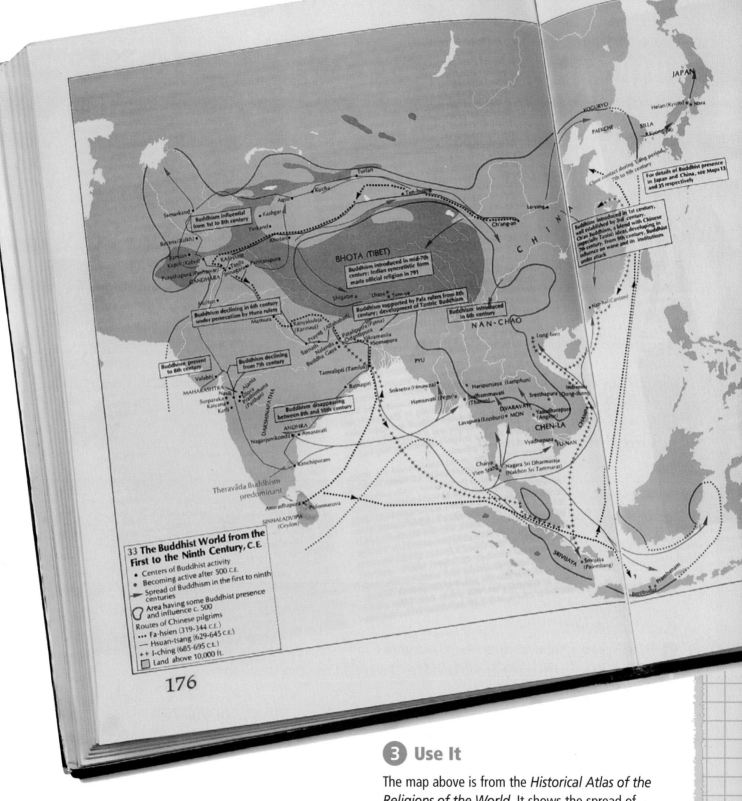

33 **The Buddhist World from the First to the Ninth Century, C.E.**

- Centers of Buddhist activity
- Becoming active after 500 C.E.
→ Spread of Buddhism in the first to ninth centuries
◯ Area having some Buddhist presence and influence c. 500

Routes of Chinese pilgrims
••• Fa-hsien (319-344 C.E.)
— Hsuan-tsang (629-645 C.E.)
++ I-ching (685-695 C.E.)
☐ Land above 10,000 ft.

Map labels:

JAPAN
Heian (Kyoto) • Nara
KOGURYO
PAEKCHE
SILLA
Kyongju

Close contact during T'ang period, 7th to 9th century

For details of Buddhist presence in Japan and China, see Maps 13 and 35 respectively

Turfan
Agsu • Kucha
Samarkand
Kashgar
Bactria (Balkh) • Yarkand
Bamian • Khotan
Kapisi (Kabul) • KASHMIR
Purushapura (Peshawar) Taxila
GANDHARA • Srinagar • Parihasapura

Tun-huang
Lo-yang
Ch'ang-an
CHINA

Buddhism influential from 1st to 8th century

Buddhism introduced in 1st century, well established by 3rd century; Chan Buddhism, a blend with Chinese (especially Taoist) ideas, developing in 7th century. From 9th century, Buddhist influence on wane and its institutions under attack

BHOTA (TIBET)
Buddhism introduced in mid-7th century; Indian syncretistic form made official religion in 791

Shigatse • Lhasa • Sam-ye

Buddhism declining in 6th century under persecution by Huna rulers
Multan • Mathura
Kanyakubja (Kannauj)
Prayag (Allahabad)
Pataliputra (Patna)
Sarnath Nalanda Vikramasila
Buddha Gaya • Odantapura • Somapura

Buddhism supported by Pala rulers from 8th century; development of Tantric Buddhism

Buddhism introduced in 6th century
NAN-CHAO
Nan-hai (Canton)

Long-bien

Buddhism present to 8th century
Valabhi
MAHARASHTRA
Nasik
Ajanta
Ellora
Surparaka • Prathisthana (Paithan)
Kalyana • Karli
DAKSHINAPATHA
ANDHRA
Nagarjunikonda • Amaravati

Buddhism declining from 7th century

Tamralipti (Tamluk)
Ratnagiri

Buddhism disappearing between 8th and 10th century

PYU
Sriksetra (Hmawza)
Hamsavati (Pegu)
Sudhammavati (Thaton)
Haripunjaya (Lamphun)
DVARAVATI
Lavapura (Lopburi) • MON
Sresthapura (Dong-duong)
Indrapura
Yasodharapura (Angkor)
CHEN-LA
Vyadhapura
FU-NAN
Chaiya
Vien Sralh
Nagara Sri Dharmaraja (Nakhon Sri Tammarat)

Kanchipuram

Theravāda Buddhism predominant

Anuradhapura • Polonnaruwa
SINHALADVIPA (Ceylon)

SRIVIJAYA
Srivijaya (Palembang)
Prambanam
Borobudur

176

2 Think It Through

Why is it helpful to look at a specialized atlas instead of a regular atlas when you're trying to get in-depth information about a subject?

3 Use It

The map above is from the *Historical Atlas of the Religions of the World*. It shows the spread of Buddhism in Asia. Compare it with a current map of Asia, which you can find in the back of this book.

1. Make a list of similarities and differences between the two maps.

2. What information is given on one map but not the other? What information is the same on both maps?

Chapter Review

| 500 | 700 | 900 | 1100 | 1300 | 1500 |

c. 570
Rise of Islam

960
Song dynasty begins in China

618
Tang dynasty
begins in China

622
Muhammad and his
followers move from
Mecca to Medina

1235
Sundiata begins
building the empire
of Mali

1324
Mansa Musa's
pilgrimage
to Mecca

Summarizing the Main Idea

1 Copy these two lists below and fill in more facts about how Islamic and
Chinese influence spread:

Islamic Influence	Chinese Influence
Muhammad and followers move to Medina	*Foreigners visit Changan*

Vocabulary

2 Divide these words into four or five categories and explain how they are
related. For example, one group could be "People." (You can create an
"Other" group if you want.)

prophet (p. 255)   Hijrah (p. 257)   Shi'a (p. 261)
revelation (p. 256)   mosque (p. 257)   Sunni (p. 261)
Qur'an (p. 256)   caliph (p. 260)   mysticism (p. 262)

Reviewing the Facts

3 Who was Muhammad, and what did he do?

4 What is the Hajj, and why is it important?

5 What do the Rightly Guided Caliphs, the
Umayyads, the Abbassids have in common?

6 List three achievements of the Islamic
Golden Age.

7 Describe Mansa Musa's empire.

8 How was the Tang government set up?

9 In what ways did Chinese culture influence
Japanese and Korean architecture, writing,
and education?

10 Look at the map on page 261. In what kind of atlas might this appear? According to this map, where did Islam begin and how did it spread?

11 The story map on pages 270–271 shows Mansa Musa's pilgrimage. What kind of atlas would show his pilgrimage? Where would you find a map showing these countries today?

Geography Skills

12 Look at the map on page 256. Plan the journey you might take if you lived in Alexandria and were going on a pilgrimage to Mecca. What route would you take?

13 The map on page 276 shows the location of Korea and Japan. Why might it have been difficult for any country other than China to have much influence over these two countries?

Critical Thinking

14 **Sequence** List three events in Muhammad's life in the order in which they happened.

15 **Problem Solving** You are an advisor during the rule of the Abbassid dynasty. What advice would you give to the caliph to help run this large empire?

16 **Conclude** Who do you think did the most for Islam: Sundiata, Mansa Musa, or Askia Muhammad? Explain your answer.

17 **Compare Then and Now** Which of the inventions of the Song dynasty are still important today?

Writing: Citizenship and History

18 **Citizenship** Write a paragraph that begins: "The achievement of the Umayyad dynasty that has the most influence on the world today is . . ." Explain the reason for your choice.

19 **History** Write a short personal narrative as if you were a Japanese or Korean scholar visiting China in the 700s. What would you do during your visit?

Activities

History/Math
Create a bar graph showing how long rule of the Rightly Guided Caliphs, the Umayyads, the Abbassids, the Tang, and the Song lasted. List 3 facts that your graph shows.

National Heritage/Arts
Places such as the Alhambra Palace in Spain and the Great Mosque in Mali have great significance for Muslims who live in those countries. Create a model or draw a picture of a place in the U.S. that has similar importance.

Internet Option

Check the **Internet Social Studies Center** for ideas on how to extend your theme project beyond your classroom.

THEME PROJECT CHECK-IN

To decide which ancient civilization you would like to choose, use the information about Islam and ancient Asia. Think about these questions:
• What important achievements were made by Islamic and ancient Asian peoples?
• How did the Islamic and ancient Asian empires grow?
• What role did these civilizations play internationally?

"Wisdom and knowledge shall be sought all over the world in order to promote the welfare of the empire."

Japanese Charter Oath

Contact and Interaction

❝ I think that people wanted to explore other areas of the world because they wanted to find other people, trade with others, and find treasures so they could be rich. ❞

Christina Lopez, Sixth Grade
South Bend, IN

When one culture comes into contact with another, several things can happen. In Europe, Christianity and Islam brought new learning and a longing to explore the world. Christianity sparked monumental works of art. Islam brought a new power to Asia. Meanwhile, the Aztecs united Mexico, and a new emperor tried to bring back old values to China. As cultures met, war, revolution, colonization, changes in government, trade, and — most important — the exchange of ideas resulted.

Theme Project

The Impact of Cultural Exchanges

Create a magazine titled "Cultural Exchanges" to show the contact and interaction between peoples:

- Make a chart of cultural exchanges with the following titles: "Ideas," "Products," and "Inventions."
- Draw or cut out illustrations of cultural exchanges.
- Write a diary entry from the point of view of an explorer who observes new cultural elements that he or she plans to share with people at home.
- List foods that come to you from cultural exchanges.

RESEARCH: Collect facts about the impact of a product or idea that was brought back to Europe from the Americas.

◀ The Duomo, Siena, Italy.

UNIT 4

WHEN & WHERE
ATLAS

As people began to move outward from their own societies and have more contact with other cultures, their interest in the larger world grew stronger. Some bold explorers ventured further to find out more about unknown parts of the world. The resulting interactions between peoples and cultures from different parts of the globe changed the world forever. More than just products and types of food were exchanged between the different areas shown on this map. Probably the most important result of the interactions was the exchange of ideas.

In this unit, you will learn how revolutions in ideas and religion transformed Europe. You will also read more about some of the world's great cultural centers, from Africa to the Americas.

Unit 4 Chapters

Chapter 11   Growth and Change in Europe
Chapter 12   Cultural Centers Around the World
Chapter 13   Toward Modern Times

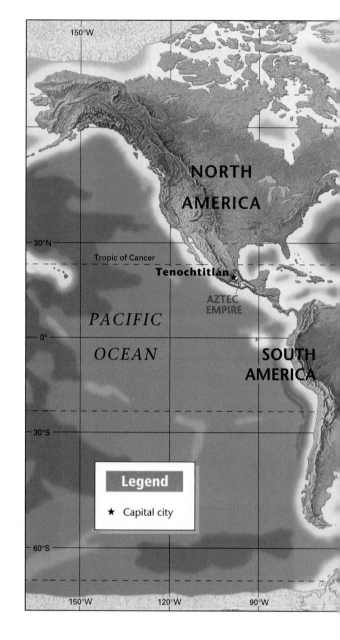

Unit Timeline

500	780	1060

Dante   1265–1321

This writer joined in the great rediscovery of ancient knowledge and culture. *Chapter 11, Lesson 3*

Mehmet II   1453

On May 29, 1453, he was at the gates of Constantinople. Why was he there? *Chapter 12, Lesson 2*

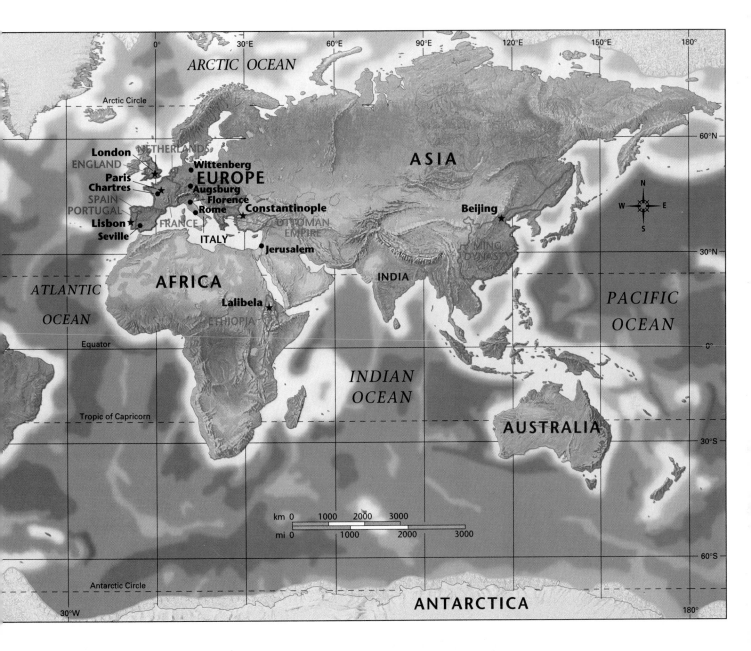

ARCTIC OCEAN

Arctic Circle

ASIA

London
ENGLAND   NETHERLANDS
Paris   ● Wittenberg
Chartres   EUROPE
SPAIN   ● Augsburg
PORTUGAL   ● Florence
Lisbon ★   ● Rome   Constantinople
Seville   FRANCE   OTTOMAN
            ITALY   EMPIRE
                         Jerusalem

Beijing ★
MING
DYNASTY

ATLANTIC
OCEAN

AFRICA

Lalibela ★
ETHIOPIA

INDIA

PACIFIC
OCEAN

Equator

INDIAN
OCEAN

Tropic of Capricorn

AUSTRALIA

km 0   1000 2000 3000
mi 0   1000 2000 3000

Antarctic Circle

ANTARCTICA

1340   1620   1900

Ming Tomb   1368–1644

This is the tomb of a man who was born a farmer and died an emperor. *Chapter 12, Lesson 3*

An Aztec Warrior   1420s

The Aztecs built a great civilization in Mexico. *Chapter 12, Lesson 4*

European Imperialism   1805

Why did this man want to carve up the world? *Chapter 13, Lesson 3*

Growth and Change in Europe

Chapter Preview: *People, Places, and Events*

800   960   1120

The Middle Ages   **800s**

This coin shows the profile of the emperor Charlemagne. Why is he famous? *Lesson 1, Page 288*

The Crusades   **1095–1300**

People fought over the city of Jerusalem for more than 200 years. Why? *Lesson 2, Page 296*

The Mongol Empire   **1200s**

Genghis Khan ruled the world's largest empire. Where was it located? *Lesson 2, Page 299*

Medieval Europe

Main Idea After the fall of the Roman Empire, western Europe broke into many small, self-governing groups.

The young boy struggles to steer the plow as the ox ahead of him pulls the heavy plow forward. At the sound of thunder, the boy looks skyward, puzzled. Then he sees them, charging over the hill: an army of men on horseback, suits of armor glinting in the sunlight, banners flying from raised lances. Enemy archers on foot let fly a volley of arrows as the boy runs back to the village, shouting a warning.

The villagers scurry for safety inside the thick, stone walls of their lord's castle. The boy darts across the drawbridge an instant before it is raised, leaving the enemy on the other side of the wide, water-filled moat. The siege is on!

Surprise attacks by enemy kingdoms and foreign invaders, like the one described above, caused people to build stone castles for protection. Castles were also the homes of the nobles, but living in one wasn't exactly comfortable. The stone walls and tiny windows made castles dark, damp, and drafty. Rodents and lice were a constant problem. Even so, for hundreds of years, castles were the best form of protection available from a world in disorder.

◀ Bodiam Castle, in England, was built in the 1380s.

Key Vocabulary

knight

chivalry

serf

guild

middle class

cathedral

monarchy

Key Events

A.D. **814** Death of Charlemagne

A.D. **1215** King John agrees to the Magna Carta

1280   1440   1600

Italian Renaissance   1400s

This military engine is only one of many inventions dreamed of by a great artist. *Lesson 3, Page 307*

Northern Renaissance

What was it like to live in Europe at this time? Paintings help us find out. *Lesson 3, Page 309*

The Reformation   1500s

What happened when the English King Henry VIII disagreed with the Pope? *Lesson 4, Page 317*

European Feudalism

Focus *What was feudalism and how did it organize life during the Middle Ages?*

After the final collapse of the Roman Empire in A.D. 476, many warring bands invaded western Europe. For most of the next 1,000 years, warfare, bloodshed, and fear filled the land. This period of history is called the Middle Ages, or the medieval (mee dee EE vuhl) era. It took place between the end of ancient times and the beginning of the modern world.

There was a brief period of order during the reign of the emperor Charlemagne (SHAHR luh mayn). This French king, who conquered much of western Europe, ruled from 768 to 814. He improved education, strengthened the government, and enforced the rule of law. He also supported the Christian Church. Charlemagne's empire did not survive his death. Between new invasions and internal rebellions, his heirs divided the empire into smaller, constantly squabbling kingdoms. The Christian Church remained the only stable institution of the time.

Soldiers and Their Code of Honor

As wars raged on among kingdoms, a new breed of warrior evolved: the knight. **Knights** were land-holding nobles who began training during childhood for a lifetime of duty to their lords.

A knight was part police officer, preserving the peace and bringing criminals to justice. He was also part soldier, ready at a moment's notice to defend his lord's castle or ride off to battle. A knight's most important weapon was his sword. The one shown below is from approximately 1100.

Knights lived by a strict code of honor called **chivalry** (SHIHV uhl ree). This code required them to be loyal and just, to protect the innocent, to show mercy to their enemies, and to live according to the values and teachings of the Christian Church.

This stained glass window from the Middle Ages shows the emperor Charlemagne on horseback. Medieval historians report that Charlemagne could read, but that he spent his entire adult life trying to master writing.

To prepare for knighthood, a seven - or eight-year - old boy went to live in a knight's household as a page (*see the illustration at right*). There the boy performed chores, trained in horsemanship and sword fighting, and was taught manners, music, and poetry. At 15 or 16, the page became a squire and accompanied the knight into battle. At 20, if judged worthy, the squire was tapped on the shoulders with a sword and "dubbed" a knight.

A New Way of Life Begins

The kings and lords of western Europe owned much land but had very little money. To pay their military officers, called vassals, rulers rewarded each vassal with a large tract of land, called a fief (feef). In return for their fiefs, vassals pledged eternal loyalty, fought for their ruler whenever required, and paid a yearly tax. This system is called feudalism.

Often a lord would divide a part of his land, or manor, into smaller units. (The manor meant both the house and the surrounding land. Locate the manor in the illustration below.) Because of unending wars and threats of invasions, poorer farmers moved onto these plots of land and accepted the lord's protection. In exchange, each farmer, called a **serf**, promised his labor, and that of his children, to the manor. Serfs became bound to the land by this pledge and could not move elsewhere without permission.

Serfs worked on their lord's land part of the time. The rest of the time, they worked on their own small plot of land. In times of poor harvests, invasions, or epidemics, many serfs died or went hungry. Even in good times, serfs had to give part of their own harvest to their lords.

Serf women worked alongside their husbands as equals, as seen in this painting from 1416. On the whole, however, feudal society granted few rights to women. Noblewomen could inherit a fief, but they were not permitted to rule over it. When a noble-woman's husband went off to war, she could rule in his place only until he returned.

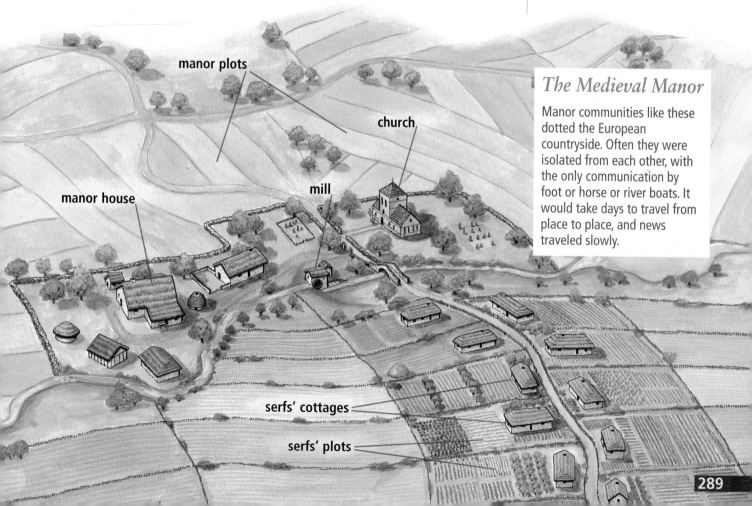

manor plots

church

mill

manor house

The Medieval Manor

Manor communities like these dotted the European countryside. Often they were isolated from each other, with the only communication by foot or horse or river boats. It would take days to travel from place to place, and news traveled slowly.

serfs' cottages

serfs' plots

The Economic Growth of Towns

Focus *How did life change as more people began to live in towns?*

By the mid-11th century, life was starting to improve for many people. Crop rotation began producing bigger harvests. To keep the soil fertile, people did not plant the same crops in the same field each year. Inventions such as the horseshoe and the harness allowed farmers to use horses as plow animals instead of the slower oxen. Two new energy-producing devices, the windmill and the water mill, helped farmers grind grain more easily. These devices also made it easier to power the large furnaces used to make iron tools.

These advances increased the food supply and decreased the time and effort it took to grow food. With new ideas and time-saving inventions, fewer farmers were needed. People began moving away from the countryside and into towns, which grew into thriving centers of trade.

Town Life

Some towns grew up around existing marketplaces. Others formed on the sites of abandoned towns. Freed serfs and poor farmers arrived, hoping to find new ways to earn a living. Towns offered new opportunities for women, who sometimes owned and ran their own businesses. Soon many merchants and craftspeople were competing, sometimes unfairly. So each craft and trade formed an association, called a **guild**. The guilds made sure prices and wages were fair, settled disputes, and set standards of quality.

The growth of towns in western Europe led to the rise of a **middle class**, people who ranked between nobles and serfs in society. They gained wealth and their position by work, rather than by being born rich.

Wealthy towns began to build (or rebuild) walls around the town and hire their own guards. They no longer needed kings and lords for protection. Some local rulers even allowed larger towns to govern themselves — as long as townspeople kept paying taxes, of course.

Merchants and craftspeople became important members of society during the Middle Ages. Some large guilds even negotiated with kings for more rights and protection for their towns. Wealthy merchants often used seals (*as shown above*) to identify their products. **Economics:** *This medieval illustration shows a street in a French town. Can you tell what each shop sells?*

A Typical Medieval Home

Many families in medieval times lived in wooden houses like this one. The roof was made of thatch, or plant stalks and leaves. The windows were small to keep out drafts. Family members slept on straw mats. Often, animals lived inside the house, too. Women swept ash and animal dung out of the house weekly.

Brick and plaster walls

Dirt floor

Family Dining

Women cooked meals in a fireplace that filled the house with smoke. Meals consisted of bread, porridge, bacon, vegetables, fruit, nuts, and sometimes other meat. When eating, the family sat on benches around a large table. Uneaten food was hung from the rafters to keep rats and mice from eating it. This jug is from the 1300s.

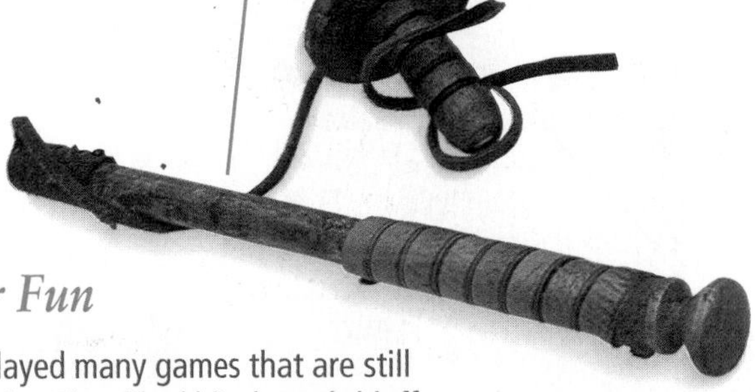

Fashion and Hygiene

Leather shoes like this one were common. The toes were often stuffed with straw to keep them pointy. When clothes were washed, they were soaked in lye, scrubbed, and hung up to dry. On average, people bathed less than once a month.

Just for Fun

Children played many games that are still popular today. They liked blind man's bluff, bowling, chess, checkers, and backgammon. This spinning top is carved from wood. The string is probably made from catgut, the dried intestines of an animal.

The Role of the Church

Focus *What role did the Christian Church play during the Middle Ages?*

"The Christian Church" doesn't refer to an individual building, but to all of organized Christianity. It includes everyone from the Pope, the Church's spiritual and political leader, to priests, who conduct religious services for communities. During the Middle Ages, the Church grew powerful in western Europe. It formed its own governing body, laws, courts, even a system of taxation. Worshippers paid the Church a part of their income, called a tithe. Sometimes a person couldn't start a business unless the Church approved it. And if the Church disapproved of a ruler, it could threaten him with excommunication — being cast out of the Church.

The Church built huge houses of worship called **cathedrals**. Their great size reflected the Church's power and influence. Buildings of this size also allowed an entire town to attend services at the same time. Cathedrals were monuments to God, and the workers who built them took great pride in every detail. Some cathedrals took hundreds of years and hundreds of people to complete.

Many people dedicated their lives in service to the Church. Women who did so became nuns. They spent their days in prayer, and often provided care for the sick and hungry. Men who were similarly devoted became monks. Monks sometimes spent their lives preserving ancient books and religious manuscripts. When the books became worn, the monks copied them by hand — a boring and time-consuming task. The photo at right shows a page from a medieval book.

During the Middle Ages, all Europeans were expected to be Christian. The Church made every effort to convert non-Christians, who were often hated and feared for their different beliefs and practices. The Jews were one such group. They were persecuted, expelled from western Europe, and sometimes even killed for their beliefs.

Governments Challenge the Church

Over time, rulers grew more powerful and began to form their own governments. A government headed by a king or queen is called a **monarchy** (MAHN uhr kee). In the later Middle Ages, monarchies began to challenge the authority of the Church. The Pope claimed that he had supreme authority over all Christian lands. The kings, especially in western

Chartres (SHAHR truh) Cathedral in France was built in the 1100s. The spires don't match because the one on the left burned down and was rebuilt in the 1500s.
Arts: *Describe three differences between the two spires.*

Europe, said that the Pope and other high-ranking Church officials interfered too much in matters of government.

In England, the monarch was also struggling for power with the nobles. In 1215, the English nobles forced King John to agree to the Magna Carta. This historic document limited the power of the king and gave certain rights to the nobles. You can read more about the Magna Carta in the Citizenship feature on pages 294–295.

These changing attitudes of rulers and nobles and the decline in the power of the Popes were signs that times were changing. The Middle Ages, a period that lasted for about 1,000 years, was coming to an end.

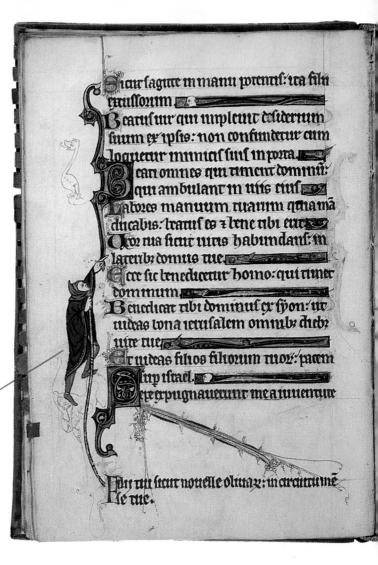

This page from a medieval manuscript shows how a clever copyist corrected a mistake. An illustration of a person, added to the margin, points to the place where a line of text was accidentally left out. The missing line is at the bottom of the page. **Technology:** *How are the printing methods of today more efficient for making similar changes?*

Lesson Review

800	1000	1200

A.D. 814
Death of Charlemagne

A.D. 1215
King John agrees to the Magna Carta

1 **Key Vocabulary:** Define the Middle Ages using knight, chivalry, serf, guild, middle class, cathedral, and monarchy.

2 **Focus:** What was feudalism and how did it organize life during the Middle Ages?

3 **Focus:** How did life change as more people began to live in towns?

4 **Focus:** What role did the Christian Church play during the Middle Ages?

5 **Critical Thinking: Interpret** Explain in your own words the structure of feudal society in western Europe during the Middle Ages.

6 **Theme: Contact and Interaction** What effect did the fall of the Roman Empire have on western Europe?

7 **Citizenship/Art Activity:** Draw or construct a model of a medieval castle. Label the three most important parts.

Resolving Conflicts

Can Rulers Do Whatever They Want?

Does the ruler of a country have to obey the law? What prevents rulers from doing whatever they want? The case study below shows that government usually involves negotiation.

Case Study

The Magna Carta

In 1215, England was at war in faraway lands. To pay for the war, King John asked the lords of England to give him money in taxes. The lords rebelled. They wrote out a new set of laws limiting the king's power. They said that people would pay taxes only if they had a voice in government. They also said that people could no longer be deprived of their property or sent to prison without a trial.

The lords said that they would support the king only if he met their demands. They were even prepared to send an army to fight the king's army. King John needed the lords' support and their tax money. He agreed to negotiate. The document that he signed was called the Magna Carta (MAG nuh KAR tuh), which in Latin means "great charter."

39. No freeman shall be seized, imprisoned, dispossessed, outlawed, or exiled, or in any way destroyed . . . except by the lawful judgment of his peers, or by the law of the land.

40. To none will we sell, to none will we deny, to none will we delay right or justice.

Magna Carta, 1215

Take Action

Like governments, people make agreements almost every day. These can be casual, such as an agreement to return a borrowed book later in the week. Or they can be formal, such as an agreement to deliver newspapers each day in return for a salary. These steps can help you to think about how to write a formal agreement.

1 You and a few friends have agreed to share responsibility for a pet dog. List the ways that the dog will need looking after (feeding, exercise, bathing, cleaning up after, and so on).

2 Decide how you will share the care. Who will do what, and on what schedule? What if one of you is sick or away? If disagreements arise among you, how will you settle them?

3 Suppose the dog owner wants you to walk the dog at midnight, or bathe and brush it every day. Suppose the dog chews a shoe. Who replaces the shoe? What are your rights and responsibilities as a dogsitter? List them.

4 Use this information to write up a contract. State clearly your rights and responsibilities. Sign and date the contract. Does it seem fair? Will it work? Share with the class your ideas for resolving any conflicts that might come up.

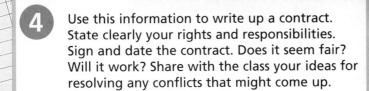

Tips for Resolving Conflicts

- Think about whether there is a difference between people's "demands" and their "wants."
- Focus on someone's "wants" when you are trying to work out a solution. This may mean helping them see how their "demands" aren't the only way to their "wants."

Research Activity

In 1689, the British Parliament wrote a Bill of Rights "declaring the rights and liberties" of the British people and limiting the powers of their rulers, William and Mary. "The suspending . . . or execution of laws by regal authority without consent of Parliament is illegal," read the first right. "Freedom of speech, and debates or proceedings in Parliament, ought not to be questioned in any court or place out of Parliament," read the ninth right. Find out more about these rights and compare them to rights presented in the United States Bill of Rights (Unit 1). Discuss their differences and similarities.

Cultures Affect Each Other

Main Idea Through the centuries, connections among Africa, Asia, and Europe increased.

Key Vocabulary

crusade

Eurasia

plague

Key Events

1096 The First Crusade begins

1340s–1350s The Black Death

The European mapmaker who made the map below in the Middle Ages placed Jerusalem at its center. Because of the city's religious importance, many Christians believed at the time that Jerusalem was the center of the world. Jerusalem was also of great importance to Jews and Muslims. Compare this map to the modern map on the next page. Look at the shape of the Mediterranean Sea in both. What other differences do you notice? The conflicts among different religious groups over Jerusalem set the stage for wars that lasted for almost two hundred years. Even today, conflicts over Jerusalem continue.

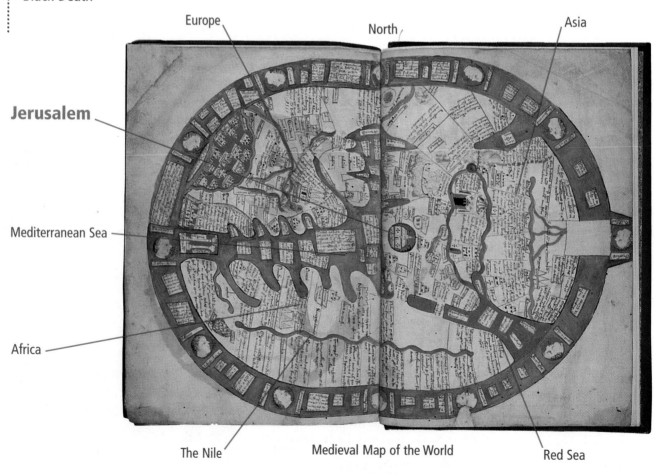

Europe   North   Asia

Jerusalem

Mediterranean Sea

Africa

The Nile   Medieval Map of the World   Red Sea

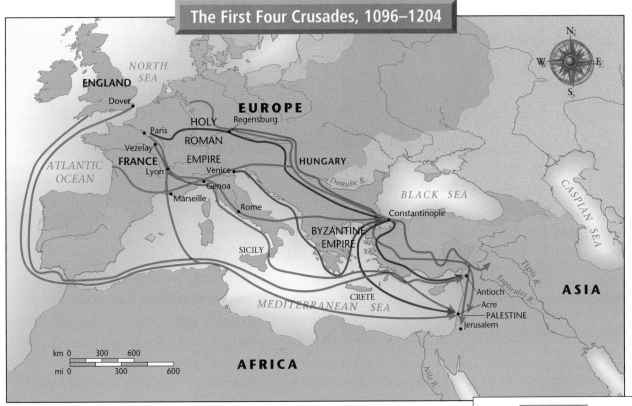

The First Four Crusades, 1096–1204

The Crusades

Focus *What were the Crusades and how did they affect the people of Europe and Asia?*

"God wills it!" cheered the crowd of French peasants and knights. They were responding to a speech by Pope Urban II in 1095. He had urged them to take back the city of Jerusalem for Christianity. By about the year 1000, Muslims had spread Islamic religion and culture throughout the area around Jerusalem. Sometimes they made it difficult for European Christians to make pilgrimages, or religious journeys, to the holy places there. The Pope wanted to make Jerusalem safe for Christians.

The Pope also had political motives for his speech: he wanted to reunite the Christian Church in Rome and the Orthodox Church in Constantinople. The two Churches had split 40 years earlier. When the emperor of Constantinople asked for help to fight the Muslims, the Pope saw his chance. He would send aid and promote unity at the same time.

The First Crusade

The first soldiers left France in 1096 and began a 3,000-mile journey to recapture Jerusalem. This was the first **crusade**, or religious war launched by European Christians. The map above traces the routes of the first four Crusades.

In their wish to serve God, the Crusaders fought fiercely against non-Christians. They fought battles on their way to Jerusalem and massacred

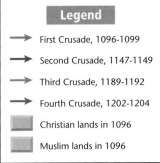

The map above compares the different routes of the first four Crusades. **Map Skill:** *Which route might have taken the most days to complete? Why?*

Illustrated above (*on the left*) is the Christian knight's uniform: armor, heavy pants, leather jacket, chain mail vest, and metal helmet. It was very uncomfortable to wear this outfit in the heat of the Middle East. By contrast, the Muslims (*at right*) were dressed for the climate. They wore light shirts, silk coats, short pants, chain mail, and leather hats. This illustration also shows weapons and shields carried by the opposing armies.

scores of innocent people. The Muslim historian Usamah Ibn Munqudh (OH saw mah ih buhn MUHN gawth) wrote: "All those who were well informed about the Franj [French] saw them as beasts superior in courage and fighting . . . but in nothing else." Although Muslim soldiers fought bravely, the Christian forces finally reached Jerusalem.

The walls of Jerusalem were old, and the Muslim defenders were not able to keep the Crusaders from breaking through. When the Muslims saw the Europeans near the city, they poisoned the wells. All who drank from them died. In the summer heat, the Crusaders suffered from thirst, but they did not give up. They fought a bloody battle that sickened everyone when it was over. This terrifying description of the slaughter of the Muslims was written by a European named Fulcher:

> " . . . *many were shot to death with arrows and cast down headlong from the roof [and] beheaded. If you had been there, your feet would have been stained up to the ankles with the blood of the slain. What more shall I tell? Not one of them was allowed to live. They did not spare the women and children.* "

In July 1099, Jerusalem fell to the Europeans. They held it only briefly before the Muslims took it back. Over the next 200 years, there were seven more main crusades. The Europeans briefly held the city several times during those years, but never permanently gained control of it.

Results of the Crusades

The Crusades left long-lasting impressions on both sides. The Muslims now saw Christians as uncivilized enemies. And when the Crusaders returned home, they carried with them a hatred for the non-Christian people of Europe.

But the Crusades also had positive effects. Europeans learned of the discoveries of Muslim scientists. The people of Asia and the Middle East found new markets for their spices, textiles, and jewelry — and "exotic" fruits like oranges! The contact also spread awareness of the customs and inventiveness of other cultures. But the Crusades hadn't prepared Europeans for contact with another culture from even farther east.

The Mongol Empire

Focus *Who were the Mongols and how did their empire help increase the flow of goods and ideas across Africa, Asia, and Europe?*

The Mongols were nomadic tribespeople who had been tending their herds on the plains of Asia since at least the 3rd century B.C. In A.D. 1206, Genghis Khan (JEHNG gihs KAHN) united these wandering tribes under his rule. Over the next twenty years, he led Mongol invasions throughout Europe and Asia. Because those two continents form one gigantic land mass, geographers sometimes refer to this region as **Eurasia**. The Mongols built the largest empire the world has ever known (*see map below*). Genghis, and then his sons and grandsons, ruled from the Pacific Ocean to Europe's Danube River.

The Mongols were fierce fighters and showed no mercy to the people they conquered. They attacked using great numbers of horsemen, but no infantry, or foot soldiers. This gave the Mongol armies an advantage. They had greater speed and mobility than the slow-moving infantry of their enemies. The Mongols are still regarded as the greatest horsemen in history. Mongol boys learned to ride horses when they were still babies. They began training as warriors just a few years later.

Reports of the Mongols' fierce reputation had reached Europe even before the Mongol armies arrived. The mere mention of the Mongols struck terror in the hearts of Europeans. After Genghis Khan's death in 1227, his son Ogdai (AHG dy) became ruler. In 1241, the Mongols

Curious Facts

Mongol warriors wore tightly woven silk undershirts as a kind of bulletproof vest. When hit by an enemy arrow, the shirt lessened the force of the arrow. The silk shirt also made pulling out the arrow easier.

This portrait shows the first Mongol leader, Genghis Khan. The growth of the Mongol Empire is shown in the map below.
Map Skill: *Why do you think the Mongols never conquered India?*

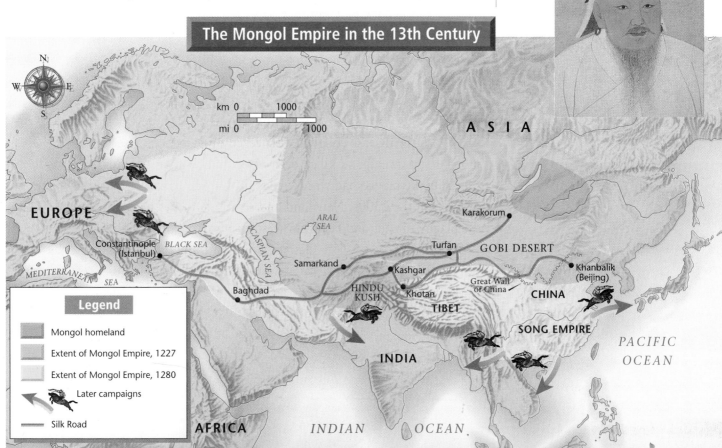

The Mongol Empire in the 13th Century

km 0 — 1000
mi 0 — 1000

ASIA

EUROPE

Karakorum

Constantinople (Istanbul) BLACK SEA

ARAL SEA

Turfan GOBI DESERT

MEDITERRANEAN SEA

Samarkand Kashgar

Khanbalik (Beijing)

Baghdad HINDU KUSH Khotan Great Wall of China CHINA

TIBET

Legend

Mongol homeland

Extent of Mongol Empire, 1227

Extent of Mongol Empire, 1280

Later campaigns

Silk Road

INDIA

SONG EMPIRE

PACIFIC OCEAN

AFRICA INDIAN OCEAN

In this Mongol battle scene, Genghis Khan's mother (in white) rides next to her 12-year-old son.

The photo below (magnified more than 50 times) shows a rat flea attached to a rat's fur. Caravans and ships spread the plague by carrying black rats covered with these fleas. Science: *Look up in a dictionary the words parasite and host. What is their relationship?*

planned to invade western Europe, but they were summoned home when Ogdai died later that year. They never returned to Europe.

Under the rule of Kublai Khan (KOO bly KAHN), grandson of Genghis Khan, the Mongol Empire became much more open to trade. The Silk Road and other Asian trade routes became busier than ever. (You can learn more about the Silk Road on pages 302–303.) Because much of Asia was now under the rule of a single people, ideas and goods from China made their way much more easily to Europe and Africa. In the 1270s, a young Italian traveler named Marco Polo went by caravan along the Silk Road with his father and uncle. Among his many experiences was meeting and then working for Kublai Khan. When he returned to Europe years later, Marco Polo published a famous description of his journeys.

After Kublai Khan's death in 1294, the Mongol Empire began crumbling. Family feuding and the difficulty of ruling so vast an empire led to the collapse of Mongol rule.

The Black Death

Focus *How did increased contact among people help spread the plague?*

In the late Middle Ages, a horrifying disease swept across Asia, North Africa, and Europe. The disease became known as the "Black Death" because of the dark blotches that appeared on the skin of its victims.

A disease that strikes over a large area is called a **plague**. The medieval plague struck in two ways. One form, called bubonic (boo BAHN ihk), was caused by rat fleas carrying the disease. People bitten by these fleas got sick in a week, and most died within 36 hours.

The other form, pneumonic (noo MAHN ihk), spread when somebody with the disease coughed or sneezed on somebody else. The pneumonic form spread and killed even more quickly than the bubonic.

Bubonic plague had struck Asia and Europe in earlier centuries, but never as in the 1300s. New land and sea trade routes helped to spread the plague further and faster. In western Europe alone, the Black Death claimed up to 25 million lives, roughly one-third of the population.

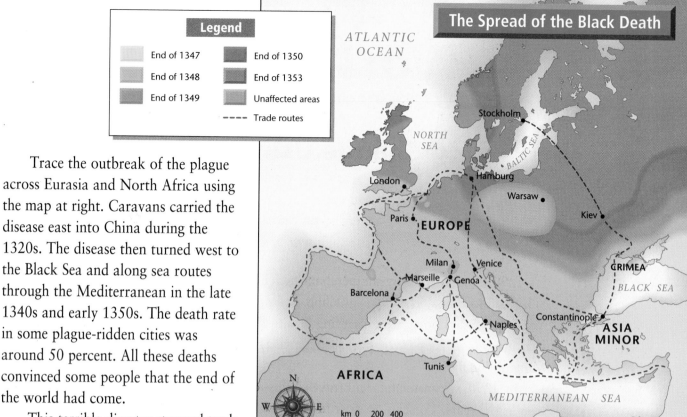

Legend

End of 1347
End of 1348
End of 1349
End of 1350
End of 1353
Unaffected areas
- - - - Trade routes

Trace the outbreak of the plague across Eurasia and North Africa using the map at right. Caravans carried the disease east into China during the 1320s. The disease then turned west to the Black Sea and along sea routes through the Mediterranean in the late 1340s and early 1350s. The death rate in some plague-ridden cities was around 50 percent. All these deaths convinced some people that the end of the world had come.

This terrible disaster stopped trade and resulted in a severe labor shortage. Oddly, this shortage helped many of Europe's poorest people. There were so few workers left that wages rose and workers gained a higher standard of living. These new economic conditions helped to end the serf labor system in Europe.

The plague spread from Asia to southern Europe and North Africa. **Map Skill:** *Why do you think some areas were unaffected?*

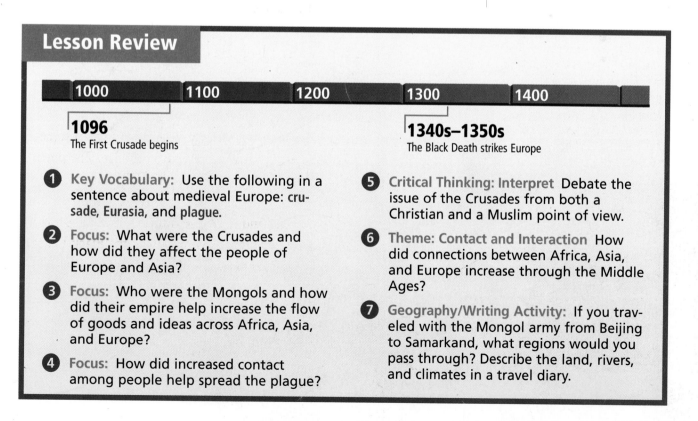

Lesson Review

| 1000 | 1100 | 1200 | 1300 | 1400 |

1096
The First Crusade begins

1340s–1350s
The Black Death strikes Europe

1. **Key Vocabulary:** Use the following in a sentence about medieval Europe: crusade, Eurasia, and plague.

2. **Focus:** What were the Crusades and how did they affect the people of Europe and Asia?

3. **Focus:** Who were the Mongols and how did their empire help increase the flow of goods and ideas across Africa, Asia, and Europe?

4. **Focus:** How did increased contact among people help spread the plague?

5. **Critical Thinking: Interpret** Debate the issue of the Crusades from both a Christian and a Muslim point of view.

6. **Theme: Contact and Interaction** How did connections between Africa, Asia, and Europe increase through the Middle Ages?

7. **Geography/Writing Activity:** If you traveled with the Mongol army from Beijing to Samarkand, what regions would you pass through? Describe the land, rivers, and climates in a travel diary.

Identifying Change Using Trade Maps

Trading Over Time

It's 1290. You are a European merchant traveling along the Silk Road to China. The trip is grueling, but you are not alone. You meet traders going west, carrying beautiful Chinese silk. You hear many languages as you pass through villages and cities of the Mongol Empire.

By 1290, silk merchants had traveled this road across Asia for over 1,500 years. You can see how trade changed during this time by comparing trade maps. The maps on these pages show trade routes between Europe and Asia in 200 B.C. and A.D. 1290. Study them to learn how trade developed and changed during this period.

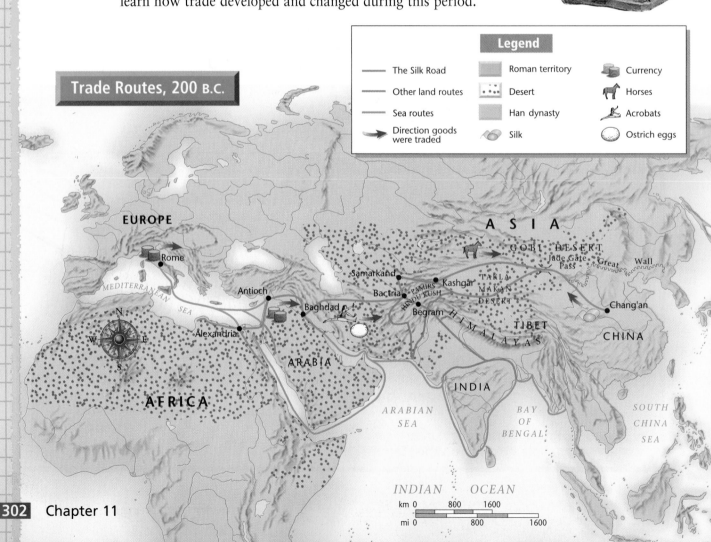

Trade Routes, 200 B.C.

Legend

— The Silk Road
— Other land routes
— Sea routes
→ Direction goods were traded

Roman territory
Desert
Han dynasty
Silk

Currency
Horses
Acrobats
Ostrich eggs

1 Here's How

- Study the legend to identify the different trade routes. What color stands for the Silk Road? What color stands for the sea routes? On each map, find all the routes.

- In the legends, look for symbols that represent trade products, such as silk and horses. Find the symbols on each map.

- Follow the direction of the arrows to see which way each product moved. For example, silk symbols have arrows pointing west.

- Compare the maps to see what changed over time. Which products and trade routes appear on both maps? Which appear only on the later map?

- Study the other information on the maps. Which trade centers appear on each map? Which empires appear on each map?

2 Think It Through

What factors do you think might cause trade routes and trade goods to change over time?

3 Use It

Study the maps and answer these questions:

1. What do the arrows stand for?

2. In which direction was each product traded?

3. List changes that occurred between 200 B.C. and A.D. 1290.

4. List possible physical, cultural, and technological reasons for these changes.

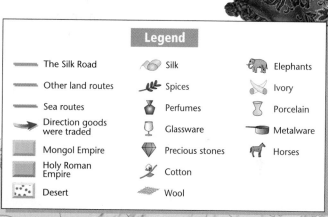

Legend

The Silk Road	Silk		Elephants
Other land routes	Spices		Ivory
Sea routes	Perfumes		Porcelain
Direction goods were traded	Glassware		Metalware
Mongol Empire	Precious stones		Horses
Holy Roman Empire	Cotton		
Desert	Wool		

Trade Routes, A.D. 1290

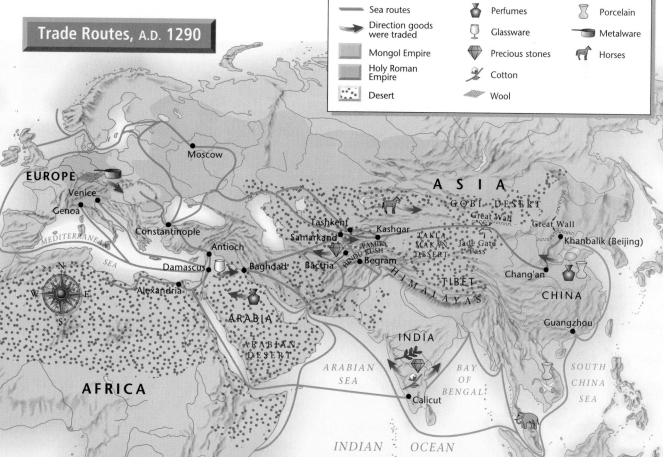

EUROPE · Venice · Genoa · Moscow · Constantinople · Antioch · Damascus · Alexandria · MEDITERRANEAN SEA · ARABIA · ARABIAN DESERT · AFRICA · Baghdad · Bactria · Tashkent · Samarkand · PAMIRS · HINDU KUSH · Begram · HIMALAYAS · TIBET · INDIA · Calicut · ARABIAN SEA · BAY OF BENGAL · ASIA · GOBI DESERT · Kashgar · TAKLA MAKAN DESERT · Jade Gate Pass · Great Wall · Khanbalik (Beijing) · Chang'an · CHINA · Guangzhou · SOUTH CHINA SEA · INDIAN OCEAN

km 0 800 1600
mi 0 800 1600

Growth and Change in Europe **303**

The Renaissance

Main Idea After the Middle Ages, a period of great achievements in the arts and learning occurred in Europe.

Key Vocabulary

Renaissance
patron
perspective

Key Events

1300s The Italian
Renaissance
begins

Modern restorers cleaned centuries of dirt and soot from the Sistine Chapel's ceiling. Above, you can see the ceiling before restoration. In the large photograph, from 1989, a worker cleans a small area. Today the restoration is complete.

The great artist lay flat on his back on a raised platform, high above the floor. Following a master plan, he painted one section at a time of the enormous blank surface. The artist was Michelangelo (my kuhl AN juh loh). The surface he was painting was the ceiling of the Sistine Chapel in Rome. The ceiling measured 132 feet long and 44 feet wide! It was so large, and the work so detailed, that it took Michelangelo four years to finish the painting. The biblical scenes he painted express the greatness of God and the beauty and importance of humans.

Michelangelo finished his masterpiece in 1512. This was an exciting time in the history of western Europe. The Middle Ages had ended, and a new era of creativity in the arts and sciences was in full bloom.

The Rise of City-States

Focus *How did life in city-states spark the beginnings of the Renaissance?*

During the Middle Ages, the writings of the Greeks and Romans were lost and forgotten in Europe. In Asia and North Africa, Muslim and Jewish scholars carefully preserved these ancient works. When the Crusades and trade increased the contact among Europe, Asia, and North Africa, these writings were rediscovered by Europeans. (*For a map of how the Muslims carried knowledge into Europe through Spain, see Chapter 10, page 264.*) This sparked a revival of interest in the cultures of ancient Greece and Rome. A period of history known as the "rebirth," or **Renaissance** (rehn ih SAHNS), began.

The Renaissance began in the 1300s in Northern Italy. Some Italians had become very wealthy from the growth of trade. Many became supporters of the arts. A wealthy person who gave an artist money, and sometimes a place to live and work, was called a **patron**.

Italy was not yet a unified country. It was made up of many independently ruled city-states. (You read about the city-states of ancient Greece in Chapter 8.) City-states began trying to outdo each other by building grander buildings, bridges, and outdoor sculptures. This competition, supported by patrons, produced some of the greatest artistic achievements of the Renaissance.

One of the biggest and most important Italian city-states was Florence (*shown below*). The Medici (MEHD uh chee), a family of wealthy bankers, ruled Florence and used their wealth to promote the arts. One of the major projects of the early 1400s was the completion of the Cathedral of Florence (*shown at right and below*).

Biography

Isabella d'Este

Isabella d'Este (DEHS tay) was a well-educated noble. As a patron of the city-state of Mantua, she supported local writers, poets, and painters. Isabella also exchanged ideas about art with other Italian artists, including Raphael.

The architect Brunelleschi (broo nuh LEHS kee) designed a Roman-style dome for the Cathedral of Florence. This was the first major dome built in Europe since ancient times. People feared the huge building might collapse, but it still stands today.

FIORENZA

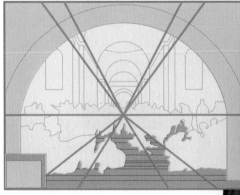

One of the best-known writers of the Renaissance was Dante (DAHN tay). Dante was from Florence and he wrote his most famous work, *The Divine Comedy*, in the Italian dialect spoken there. Because *The Divine Comedy* was one of the first works written in Italian, the Florentine dialect eventually became the standard form of the language.

The Blossoming of Arts and Learning

Focus *What characteristics did the works of the Renaissance thinkers and artists have in common?*

The Renaissance focused attention on the individual. European Christians began to believe that life was more than just a time in which to prepare for eternity. They believed it was an opportunity for personal achievement and fulfillment. Many scientists, inventors, and artists achieved greatness during this time, including Leonardo da Vinci (duh VIHN chee) — who was all three!

During the Renaissance, artists developed a new approach to painting. Even though works of art were still mainly religious, they now focused on the humanity of their subjects. Artists also began to use a technique called **perspective**. Perspective allows artists to create the illusion of distance and depth on a flat surface. The painting below is an example of this technique. Some people appear closer to us than others.

Writers also began acting on new ideas. In the Middle Ages, most books were about religion and were written in Latin by Church officials. During the Renaissance, an educated middle class, who could afford to buy books, arose throughout Europe. Writers began writing in the common languages of the people, such as English, Spanish, French, and, of course, Italian. They created popular literature that included comedies, drama, plays, tales of adventure, and poetry for these new readers.

Raphael's famous painting, *The School of Athens,* was completed in 1511. The diagram above shows the perspective lines. These lines, which come together at a distant point, helped Renaissance artists represent three-dimensional space.

Leonardo da Vinci

Master Painter, Scientist, and Inventor

Leonardo da Vinci (duh VIHN chee) (1452–1519) was an Italian Renaissance artist who devoted his life to study and learning. He was fascinated with finding out how things worked. His studies led to new ideas in science, architecture, painting, and sculpture.

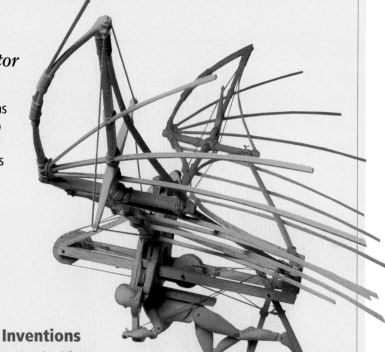

Inventions

During his lifetime, Leonardo filled thousands of notebook pages with ideas and sketches of inventions. Some would not be built for hundreds of years, including a type of helicopter, an alarm clock, and a flying machine (shown above).

Scientific Writings

To learn more about humans, Leonardo cut apart dead bodies. This drawing of a skull is from one of his notebooks. The left-handed artist wrote backwards from right to left! For what reasons might he have done this? Use a mirror to read his signature below.

Painting

The Mona Lisa is one of the most famous images in the history of art. Leonardo began the portrait in 1503. Today, it hangs in the Louvre (LOO vruh), a famous museum in Paris, France.

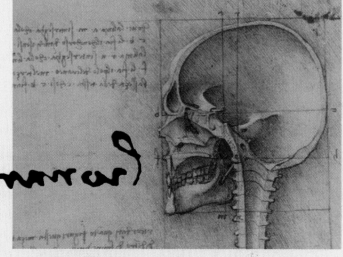

Pieter Brueghel (BROY gehl) (c.1525–1569) painted this scene called *The Peasant Dance*. **Cultures:** *Look at the clothing, actions, and buildings. What do these details tell you about life in northern Europe at this time?*

The Northern Renaissance

Focus *What special contributions were made by Renaissance artists and writers in northern Europe?*

The ideas of the Renaissance spread from Italy to other parts of Europe. In northern Europe, many artists and writers made important contributions of their own.

Some of the most famous painters came from Belgium, the Netherlands, and Luxembourg. They included Jan van Eyck (yahn van EYEK) and Rembrandt van Rijn (REHM brant vahn RYN). As shown by the examples on this and the next page, Northern Renaissance artists

The German artist Albrecht Dürer (DUR uhr) (1471–1528) created this famous watercolor of a hare in 1502. It is a good example of how Northern Renaissance artists captured the beauty and detail of nature.

painted nature, landscapes, and scenes from everyday life. They were also the first artists to paint with oil paints.

Northern Renaissance literature reached its height in the works of the English playwright William Shakespeare (1564–1616). Many of his plays, which include *Hamlet*, *Macbeth*, and *Romeo and Juliet*, are considered masterpieces. Shakespeare remains one of the world's most famous writers. Read more about him in the biography that begins on page 310.

Shakespeare wrote about human conflicts and emotions, and steered clear of the still-powerful Church. Other writers were not so cautious. Erasmus was a Dutch writer who criticized the Church for its excessive rituals and wealth, while remaining a faithful Church member. Sir Thomas More of England wrote *Utopia,* which criticized the political and religious problems of his society. More's book describes an ideal society, called Utopia, that is created through people's own efforts.

These writers were expressing ideas that were becoming more common throughout Europe. The achievements of the ancient Greeks and Romans inspired the Europeans of the Renaissance to develop new ideas of their own. But many of these new ideas, including the importance of the individual and the freedom to speak out, were bringing Europeans into conflict with the Church. This conflict was soon to boil over and cause further change across the continent.

The Dutch artist Judith Leyster (1609–1660) painted this self-portrait in 1630. Leyster was probably the only female member of the painters' guild in her town of Haarlem. Arts: *Why might that have been true?*

Lesson Review

1300   1400   1500

1300s
The Italian Renaissance begins

1 **Key Vocabulary:** Use **patron** and **perspective** in a sentence about the **Renaissance**.

2 **Focus:** How did life in city-states spark the beginnings of the Renaissance?

3 **Focus:** What characteristics did the works of the Renaissance thinkers and artists have in common?

4 **Focus:** What special contributions were made by Renaissance artists and writers in northern Europe?

5 **Critical Thinking: Decision Making** If you were a patron in Florence during the early Renaissance, what would you do to promote the arts?

6 **Theme: Contact and Interaction** How did increased contact among people contribute to the Renaissance?

7 **Citizenship/Language Arts Activity:** Select a short speech from one of Shakespeare's history plays. Read and explain it to the class.

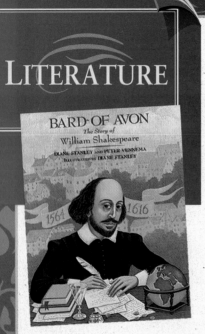

Biography

BARD OF AVON

The Story of William Shakespeare
by Diane Stanley and Peter Vennema
illustrated by Diane Stanley

From humble beginnings as the son of a glove maker in the little village of Stratford-upon-Avon, William Shakespeare rose to become the best writer of plays during his own age or any since. His plays were first performed at London's Globe Theater, and they were tremendously popular.

Shakespeare wrote, "All the world's a stage, and all the men and women merely players. . . ." He loved to use historical events and real kings and queens as a source of ideas for his plays. But at one point in his life, the world of plots and revolutions and powerful people got a little too close, a little too real for comfort.

In 1601, politics and danger entered Shakespeare's world. The events of that year seem to have touched him very deeply.

This is what happened: The Earl of Essex was one of Queen Elizabeth's great favorites. He was a dashing young nobleman who was fond of adventure and battle and was said to be the most popular man in England. But his life had taken strange turns, and that year he decided to mount a rebellion and overthrow the queen.

Essex's best friend was the Earl of Southampton, Shakespeare's old patron. He, too, was in on the plot.

Two days before the uprising was to take place, several of Essex's friends went to the Globe and offered forty shillings for a special performance of *Richard II* on the following day.

Richard II is one of Shakespeare's early plays. In it, an unfit king, Richard, is forced to give up his throne to a noble character, Bolingbroke,

shilling — *a coin used in England*

Shakespeare's *Richard II* is a play in which a king is forced to give up his throne.

who then becomes Henry IV. Essex hoped that the crowds watching the play would think of him as a sort of Bolingbroke and be inspired to join him on the following day. To add to the effect, Essex's friends clapped and cheered at all the right moments, hoping to stir the crowd.

The next day, when Essex rode through the streets of London to raise the revolution, the people just closed their doors. Essex and his friends were arrested, and most of them were put to death. Southampton was allowed to live, but he was imprisoned in the Tower of London.

Queen Elizabeth knew about the special performance of *Richard II*, and understood the reason for it. "*I* am Richard II, know ye not that!" she was heard to say. The actors were questioned under oath but not punished. Forty shillings seemed to be a strong enough reason for a troupe to put on an old play by special request. The queen was willing to believe that they hadn't done it for political reasons.

In Shakespeare's play *Macbeth*, three witches tell Macbeth that he will someday be king.

Macbeth

flaw — *a defect or shortcoming*

During these years, a profound change seems to have come over Shakespeare, and we see it in the plays he wrote. Perhaps he was frightened by his close brush with danger. He must have been horrified to think that the dashing Essex was dead, and his friend shut up in the Tower. It was also during this period that Shakespeare's father died. Now, instead of happy, romantic comedies, he began to create his great tragedies: *Hamlet*, *Othello*, *King Lear*, *Macbeth*, and *Anthony and Cleopatra*. In each of these stories, a great man is brought to destruction and death. His fall is caused partly by forces of evil and partly by some flaw in the hero. And both *Hamlet* and *Macbeth* are about plots to murder kings.

Even his few comedies written in these years became darker, as if he had come to think badly of mankind.

In 1603, Queen Elizabeth died. The new king, James I, was a man

who loved entertainment, and especially plays. His first week in London, he took over the patronage of Shakespeare's company. From then on, they were called the King's Men.

James I was also the king of Scotland. And for this Scottish king, Shakespeare turned to Scottish history to write *Macbeth*, one of his greatest plays. In it, he included many touches to please the king. There are witches and ghosts, bloody murders and mad scenes. But even with all the special effects, it is a dark and profound study of human nature.

Macbeth is a brave and loyal soldier until the witches tell him that he will someday be king. Ambition begins to burn in his heart, and he goes on to murder the king and everyone else who stands in the way of his goal. *Macbeth* is a chilling tale of a good man gone wrong, whose every step leads him closer and closer to his own destruction. It fascinated the playgoers of Shakespeare's time, and it fascinates us today.

Meet the Authors

Diane Stanley has illustrated all of the biographies that she and her husband, Peter Vennema, have written. Together they have told the stories of Queen Elizabeth I, Charles Dickens, Cleopatra, and Shaka, King of the Zulus.

Additional Books to Read

A Midsummer Night's Dream by William Shakespeare. This is one of Shakespeare's best-loved comedies.

The King's Fool by Dana Fradon. Read these fun facts about jesters.

Response Activities

1. **Interpret** What might Shakespeare have meant when he wrote, "All the world's a stage, and all the men and women merely players . . ."?

2. **Narrative: Write a Play Scene** Think about Shakespeare's reaction when he first learned that one of his plays was used in a plot against the queen. Write a scene from a play in which Shakespeare discusses the plot with a friend.

3. **History: Make a Timeline** From the story and your own research, create a timeline of major events in Shakespeare's life.

The Era of Reformation

Main Idea A new religious movement caused northern Europeans to break away from the Roman Catholic Church.

Key Vocabulary

heretic
Reformation

Key Events

1454 Gutenberg prints the Bible

1517 Martin Luther protests against the Church

A seventeen-year-old French girl had led her country's troops into battle against the English. She claimed that heavenly voices guided her to do so. In 1429, this teenager saved the town of Orléans (awr lay AHN), France, where the French and English had been fighting. Soon after, Joan of Arc (*shown in the statue below*) was captured and handed over to the English. The English then turned her over to the Inquisition, a court set up by the Church.

The Inquisition interrogated Joan for months and gave her a one-sided trial. In the end, they declared her to be a **heretic** and condemned her to death. A heretic is a person who holds and preaches beliefs that the Church considers wrong. Some people were executed for opposing the politics and power of the Church.

Joan of Arc, like many others considered to be heretics at the time, was put to death by burning. Events like her execution set the stage for the enormous shift in religious power that was soon to come in Europe.

Joan of Arc

This heroic statue of Joan of Arc was created by the French sculptor Emmanuel Fremiet (FRUH mee yay) in the 1870s. It is made of bronze and covered in gold. Copies of the statue stand in Paris, France, and Philadelphia, Pennsylvania. History: *Today Joan of Arc remains a symbol of French independence. Why might that be true?*

Martin Luther

Focus *What were the causes of the Reformation?*

During the 1300s and 1400s, critics attacked the Catholic Church for its wealth and increasing corruption. Monarchs were angry at the Church for interfering with political affairs of state. Throughout Europe, individuals and groups criticized the Church's teachings and activities. One of the most important and influential of these critics was Martin Luther.

A Challenge to the Church

One day, while returning from a visit to his parents' home, a young German law student named Martin Luther *(shown above right)* was caught in a thunderstorm. Dashing for safety, he was violently knocked to the ground — struck by a bolt of lightning! Luther took this as a sign from God. He gave up his study of the law and become a monk instead. Luther was very religious and well respected. He lectured on the Bible at the University of Wittenberg, where he also studied religion.

The more Luther studied, the more some of the Church's views troubled him. For instance, the Church taught that people could save their souls by doing good deeds. Luther came to believe that people could save their souls simply by having faith in God. Another thing that Luther opposed was the Church's practice of pardoning the sins of worshippers in exchange for money. This was called selling indulgences.

In 1517, Luther drew up a list of 95 theses, or questions to debate, on the selling of indulgences. He posted them on the Church door at Wittenberg, and sent copies to Church officials. It might have ended there, but for the invention of the printing press. (*Read the Tell Me More about the printing press on the next page.*) Copies of the 95 theses were handed out far and wide, and they were publicly discussed everywhere. In 1521, Luther was excommunicated for what was seen as an attack on the Church. Later he was declared an outlaw and a heretic by the Church. Fearing for his safety, Luther went into hiding.

Turn the woodcut portrait (*above left*) upside down to see what Martin Luther's opponents thought of him. The portrait of Luther above was painted by his friend Lucas Cranach in the 1500s. **Arts:** *How does an artist's opinion toward the subject affect the final work of art?*

· Tell Me More ·

The Printing Press

Gutenberg Uses Movable Type

In 1454, a German named Johannes Gutenberg (GOOT n burg) first used a new and faster method to print books. The first book he printed was the Bible. You will remember from Chapter 10 that the Chinese had invented a method for printing. But Gutenberg is thought to be the first European to use carved wooden blocks (like those shown below), called movable type. The printing press he designed to use this movable type was similar to the one shown at right.

The ability to print large numbers of books made communication faster and cheaper. Knowledge was now available to many more people than just educated Church officials. This invention helped spread both Renaissance attitudes and the new ideas of Martin Luther and other reformers.

This illustration from 1568 shows two men working on a printing press. They put ink on the type, placed paper on top, and then "pressed" the page under a screw-like device. In the background, two workers stand at containers used to store thousands of type blocks.

While in hiding, Luther translated the Bible from Latin into German, so that all Germans would be able to read it. Luther's ideas won over the peasants, the middle class, and many of the German princes who were tired of paying taxes to the Church. These ideas of ways to change the Catholic Church became known as the **Reformation**.

The individuals who followed the beliefs of Luther and other reformers were called Protestants, because they protested against the Church. There were still many who were devoted to the Church, and it wasn't long before the two sides were at war.

The Spread of Reform

Focus *What were the effects of the Reformation?*

Years of fighting between Catholics and Protestants in Germany finally ended with a compromise in 1555 called the Treaty of Augsburg. The treaty permitted German princes to decide which religion their lands would follow. The common people, however, still could not choose for themselves.

This marked the end of religious unity in Europe. The further a country was from Rome and the Pope, the more likely the country was to become Protestant. Protestantism was chosen by the rulers of northern Germany, Scandinavia, the Netherlands, England (*see the Biography at right*), and Scotland. The Catholic Church remained stronger in Spain, Italy, France, and southern Germany.

The Reformation had many positive effects on European society. To ensure that their followers could read the Bible, Protestants supported education. They also believed that values such as personal responsibility and hard work were especially important.

As a reaction to the spread of Protestantism, the Catholic Church launched a movement in the 1550s called the Counter Reformation. The Church stopped selling indulgences and founded teaching groups to spread Catholic ideas. The Church also published the Index, a list of books that Church officials were instructed to burn. And the Church revived the Inquisition to rid the Catholic countries of Protestant heretics.

At the beginning of the Middle Ages, the Church had been the single strongest force in Europe. By the end of the Reformation, the Church had been weakened and religious unity in Europe was shattered. These changes, together with the advances in learning made during the Renaissance, were signs that a new Europe was emerging.

King Henry VIII

King Henry VIII ruled England from 1509 to 1547. For most of his life, he was a devout Catholic. His dispute with the Church began when he asked the Pope to annul, or cancel, his marriage to Catherine of Aragon. Henry wanted to remarry because he had never had a son. The Pope refused his request. As a result, England broke away from the Catholic Church, and Henry VIII declared himself head of the Church of England.

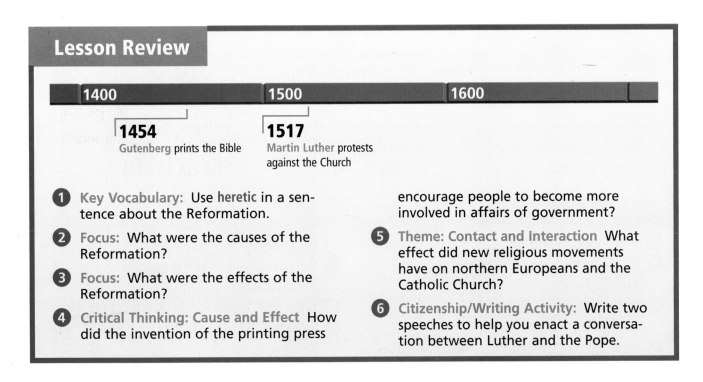

Lesson Review

```
1400                    1500                    1600
      1454                    1517
      Gutenberg prints        Martin Luther protests
      the Bible               against the Church
```

1 Key Vocabulary: Use **heretic** in a sentence about the Reformation.

2 Focus: What were the causes of the Reformation?

3 Focus: What were the effects of the Reformation?

4 Critical Thinking: Cause and Effect How did the invention of the printing press encourage people to become more involved in affairs of government?

5 Theme: Contact and Interaction What effect did new religious movements have on northern Europeans and the Catholic Church?

6 Citizenship/Writing Activity: Write two speeches to help you enact a conversation between Luther and the Pope.

Chapter Review

Chapter Review Timeline

800	960	1120	1280	1440	1600

1096
The First Crusade begins

1300s
The Italian Renaissance begins

814
Death of Charlemagne

1215
King John agrees to the Magna Carta

1454
Gutenberg prints the Bible

1517
Martin Luther protests against the Church

Summarizing the Main Idea

1 Copy and complete the chart. Choose a key person in each lesson and list his or her accomplishment.

	Key Person	Accomplishment
Lesson 1		
Lesson 2		
Lesson 3		
Lesson 4		

Vocabulary

2 Using at least seven of the terms below, write the biography of an imaginary western European man or woman.

knight (p. 288) cathedral (p. 292) plague (p. 300)
chivalry (p. 288) monarchy (p. 292) patron (p. 305)
guild (p. 290) crusade (p. 297) heretic (p. 314)

Reviewing the Facts

3 What was feudalism?

4 Why was the Church so powerful during the Middle Ages?

5 What were some of the reasons for the Crusades?

6 How did the Mongol Empire change under Kublai Khan?

7 What are some of the events that led to the Renaissance?

8 What was Martin Luther's impact on religion?

9 How did the Catholic Church respond to the Reformation?

Skill Review: Identifying Change Using Trade Maps

10 Find the trade map on page 186. Look at the legend. What products were carried on the trade routes across the Sahara? Find the symbols on the map. Where did each product originate? Study other information on the map. What were some of the major trading centers of the time?

Geography Skills

11 Look at the maps on pages 297 and 299, showing the Crusades and the Mongol Empire. Why do you think it was so difficult for Europeans to conquer Jerusalem and for the Mongols to maintain their empire?

Critical Thinking

12 **Interpret** Why do you think it was important for knights to have a code, such as chivalry, to obey?

13 **Conclude** Why was the serf system bound to end sooner or later?

14 **Predict** How do you think the Renaissance and the Reformation will continue to shape and change Europe?

Writing: Citizenship and Economics

15 During the Middle Ages, all Europeans were expected to be Christians. In the United States, freedom of religion is guaranteed to all. Write an essay explaining why freedom is better than forcing people to believe a certain way.

16 Imagine that you are the secretary of the guild of your choice during the Middle Ages. Write down the things that happen at a meeting of your guild.

Activities

History/Arts Activity
During the Renaissance, artists produced some of the most beautiful masterpieces of human history. Find out more about the artists mentioned in the chapter. Bring in art books from the library and analyze their works. Share your findings with the class.

Economics/Math Activity
Find out more about the growth of the middle class during the Middle Ages. Do outside research and draw charts and graphs that represent growth, increasing wealth, and how members of the middle class spent their time and money. Share your information with the class.

Internet Option

Check the **Internet Social Studies Center** for ideas on how to extend your theme project beyond your classroom.

THEME PROJECT CHECK-IN

Use the information in this chapter about the Middle Ages to begin your theme project. Think about these questions:

• What was the goal of the European Crusaders? What did they hope to bring to other lands?
• What did the Crusaders bring back to Europe from the countries where they traveled?
• What did the Mongol Empire exchange with Europe and Africa?
• What new ideas and things resulted from the Renaissance?

Cultural Centers Around the World

Chapter Preview: *People, Places, and Events*

1000   **1120**   **1240**

Christian Ethiopia   **1200s**

Ethiopia's churches fill visitors with awe. Find out why. *Lesson 1, Page 324*

The Ming Dynasty   **1400s**

The emperors of China lived in a huge palace. What did it look like? *Lesson 3, Page 334*

The Ming Dynasty   **1400s**

Ceramics tell amazing stories about life in China. Learn to read these stories. *Lesson 3, Page 337*

Christian Ethiopia

Main Idea Over the centuries, Ethiopia preserved an ancient form of Christianity.

Look at the window of this old Ethiopian building. It is carved in the shape of a Greek cross. How did a Greek cross come to Africa? There are buildings in Ethiopia with all kinds of windows. One building has an upper story with pointed Muslim arch-covered windows, and a lower one with windows in the shape of Christian crosses.

This mix of styles is not surprising in a land where trade routes crossed. Centuries ago, the rich markets of Ethiopia attracted merchants from all over the world. People from many religious and ethnic backgrounds traded goods — and ideas.

Ethiopia itself was mainly Christian in ancient times. Its population also included Muslims, Jews, and people who worshiped traditional local gods. From this rich cultural mix, Ethiopians created awe-inspiring monuments. They used architectural styles from various cultures, but their unique artistry made these monuments one of the world's treasures.

Key Vocabulary

- convert
- pilgrimage
- abdicate

Key Events

A.D. **1100s** The Zagwé dynasty begins

◄ The Imperial Palace, in Beijing, China, is a popular tourist attraction today.

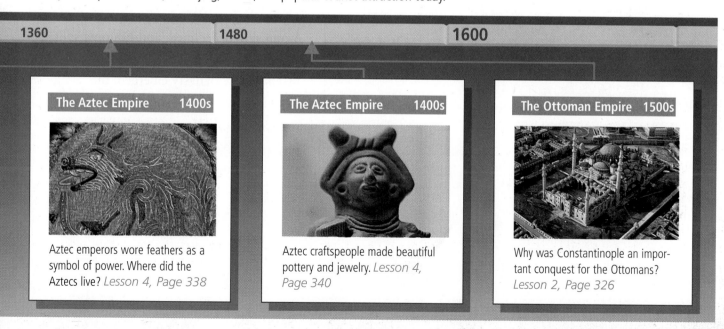

1360	1480	1600

The Aztec Empire 1400s

Aztec emperors wore feathers as a symbol of power. Where did the Aztecs live? *Lesson 4, Page 338*

The Aztec Empire 1400s

Aztec craftspeople made beautiful pottery and jewelry. *Lesson 4, Page 340*

The Ottoman Empire 1500s

Why was Constantinople an important conquest for the Ottomans? *Lesson 2, Page 326*

Early Christian Ethiopia

Focus *How did Ethiopia preserve its unique form of Christianity?*

Around 1000 B.C., people from Arabia crossed the Red Sea into Africa and settled in the northern part of what is now Ethiopia *(see map below)*. These early settlers of Ethiopia are known as Abyssinians (ab ih SIHN ee uhns). By the middle of the first century A.D., the Abyssinians had built a great kingdom governed from their capital at Axum (AHK soom).

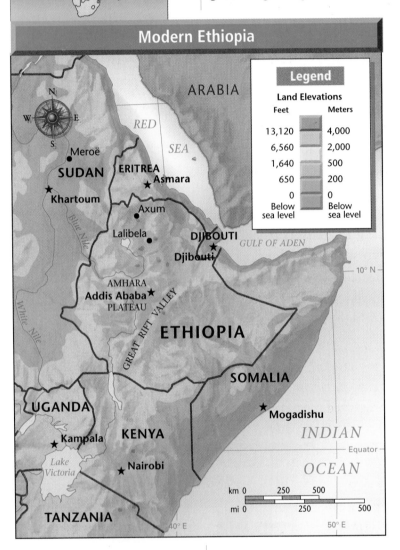

Modern Ethiopia

Legend
Land Elevations

Feet	Meters
13,120	4,000
6,560	2,000
1,640	500
650	200
0	0
Below sea level	Below sea level

Countries and boundaries exist today in Eastern Africa that did not exist at the time of the Zagwé dynasty. **Map Skill:** *What route might early people have followed as they migrated from Arabia to Ethiopia?*

Axum

The kingdom of Axum grew rich and powerful. Eventually, the Abyssinians conquered Meroë in ancient Nubia and gained control of the ivory trade in the Nile Valley. This linked Axum with the Christian lands of the Mediterranean.

One important ruler of Axum was King Ezana. In the A.D. 300s, Ezana became a Christian **convert**, someone who changes from one religion to another. Ezana made Christianity the official religion of his kingdom. The churches of Ethiopia had strong ties to Egypt, which was also Christian at this time. After the Islamic conquests of North Africa in the 600s and 700s, Egypt became a Muslim country. Axum was then cut off from Christian Europe.

The Zagwé Dynasty

Axum slowly declined, and Ethiopia split into separate kingdoms. Then, in the early 1100s, a new dynasty emerged: the Zagwé (zahg WAY). These leaders moved

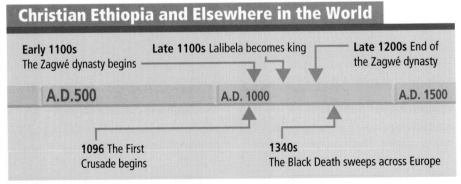

Christian Ethiopia and Elsewhere in the World

Early 1100s The Zagwé dynasty begins

Late 1100s Lalibela becomes king

Late 1200s End of the Zagwé dynasty

A.D.500   A.D. 1000   A.D. 1500

1096 The First Crusade begins

1340s The Black Death sweeps across Europe

their political center to the south of Axum. This mountainous area, called the Ethiopian highlands, isolated the Ethiopian Christians even further.

One of the Zagwé dynasty's greatest leaders was King Lalibela (lah lee BAY lah). He ruled during the late 1100s and early 1200s. This king created a powerful Christian state with its capital at Roha. The city was eventually renamed Lalibela, after the king.

King Lalibela decided to make his capital an important religious site. During his rule, the Ethiopians built 10 Christian churches. Each church was carved by hand from the solid volcanic rock of the highlands. Many Christians came to the kingdom on **pilgrimages,** journeys to religious sites. Over time, the city won the nickname "the New Jerusalem."

When workers finished the last church, King Lalibela decided to **abdicate,** or voluntarily give up, his throne. He devoted the rest of his life to prayer. Today, pilgrims from all over Ethiopia still travel great distances to worship in these churches. Pilgrims honor the king as a saint.

Later Ethiopia

In the centuries following the reign of King Lalibela, life in Ethiopia was similar to life under the feudal system in Europe described in Chapter 11. Farmers had to give a portion of their crops and livestock to the nobles who, in turn, paid taxes to the king. During this period, Ethiopia had no single capital. The king and his court were constantly on the move, visiting nobles and gathering taxes.

In 1306, the Ethiopians sent officials to European cities. Their trip brought Ethiopia to the attention of Christian Europe for the first time in centuries. Later, in the 1500s, Portuguese Christians visited Ethiopia and brought back news of its wonders to Europe. They described the churches with awe.

King Lalibela's churches are now almost a thousand years old. They are carefully being preserved and repaired. **National Heritage:** *What structures is your community working to preserve?*

The Church of Saint George stands on a high, stepped base that follows the outline of the building. The workers who carved the church had to be very careful because mistakes could not be corrected.

This historic wall painting shows an Ethiopian worker carving a church from the rock. The worker, sometimes said to be Lalibela himself, is using an axelike tool called an adz. **Technology:** *How is stone carved today?*

Cultural Contributions

Focus *What makes Ethiopia's Christian tradition so remarkable?*

The 10 churches of Lalibela form one of the world's great cultural sites. In constant use for almost 800 years, the churches represent the survival of a religious tradition in Ethiopia that dates back to the early centuries of Christianity.

The Church of Saint George

Unlike most other buildings, the Church of Saint George *(above)* was started at roof level. Workers first dug a 40-foot-deep trench out of the volcanic rock, leaving a solid block for the church *(see next page, top).* After they had carved the block into a cross shape, workers hollowed out the interior. They then sculpted arches, pillars, and aisles to form the inside. Finally, painters decorated the interior with colorful patterns.

A Continuing Religious Tradition

The Ethiopian Orthodox Church still preserves an ancient form of Christianity. Christmas, for example, is celebrated on January 7. The Ethiopian church follows a form of the calendar that dates back to Roman times. Like Jews and Muslims — and unlike other Christian groups — Ethiopian Christians do not eat pork. Ethiopian Christians also identify with stories from the Hebrew Bible. The rulers of the Zagwé dynasty traced their ancestry back to Moses, while later rulers claimed descent from the biblical figures Solomon and Sheba. Today, Christianity is no longer Ethiopia's official religion. Almost half of the people are Muslims. There is also a community of Ethiopian Jews. As in ancient times, these communities create a country of great diversity.

At left, a man stands near the edge of the trench that contains the Church of Saint George. Notice the Ethiopian highlands in the distance. In the aerial view above, the church's cross shape is clearly visible.

Lesson Review

A.D. 1100s
The Zagwé dynasty begins

1. **Key Vocabulary:** Write a paragraph about early Ethiopia using the following words: **convert, pilgrimage, abdicate.**

2. **Focus:** How did Ethiopia preserve its unique form of Christianity?

3. **Focus:** What makes Ethiopia's Christian tradition so remarkable?

4. **Critical Thinking: Interpret** Why might it have been important for Ethiopia's Christian rulers to develop trade with their Muslim neighbors?

5. **Theme: Contact and Interaction** How did Ethiopia's geographical position affect its culture?

6. **Geography/Writing Activity:** If you were a Portuguese explorer traveling through Ethiopia in the 1500s, what would you see? Describe your trip in a letter home.

The Ottoman Empire

Main Idea At its height, the Ottoman Empire ruled large parts of the Christian and Muslim world.

Before dawn on the morning of May 29, 1453, a large army stormed the massive walls of Constantinople. For six weeks, soldiers had tried to break into the city. Each time they attacked, they were forced back.

Mehmet II *(shown at right)* was the sultan, the Muslim ruler, of the attacking Ottoman forces. Once again his soldiers charged the defenses under a shower of arrows and stones. Suddenly, an enormous man named Hassan struggled to the top of the wall. He was followed by more and more soldiers. Soon the sultan's banners began appearing on the towers. The siege was over. The great Christian city, which had been the capital of the Byzantine Empire for more than 1,000 years, had fallen.

The ornate signature of a sultan is called a tugra. It was used to sign official documents. The tugra below belonged to the sultan Suleiman.

The Empire at Its Height

Focus *In what ways was Suleiman the Magnificent a remarkable ruler?*

Mehmet's victory added to one of the greatest empires the world has ever known. From its beginnings in what is now Turkey, the Ottoman Empire expanded across Asia, Africa, and Europe. When the Ottomans captured Constantinople, they made it their new capital. Over time, this ancient city once again became a world center of culture, politics, and religion.

Suleiman the Magnificent

During the reign of Suleiman (SOO lay mahn) from 1520 to 1566, the Ottoman Empire experienced a golden age of military and cultural achievement. The empire also grew to its greatest size. Suleiman extended

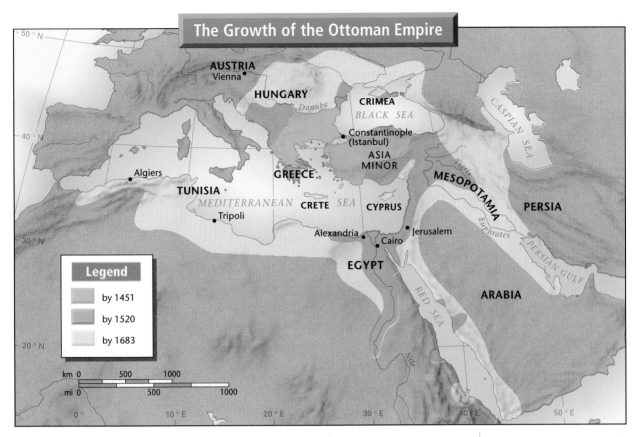

The Growth of the Ottoman Empire

Legend
- by 1451
- by 1520
- by 1683

km 0   500   1000
mi 0   500   1000

his rule to the North African coast and across the Middle East to the Persian Gulf *(see the map above)*. In central Europe, Suleiman's victories took him as far as the walls of Vienna, Austria. With each new conquest, Suleiman spread Islamic culture. Many people in eastern Europe became Muslim and adopted Eastern styles of art and dress.

Western Europeans, who both feared and admired Suleiman, called him "the Magnificent." To Muslims, Suleiman was known as "the Lawgiver." During his rule, the **Sharia** (shah REE ah), or Holy Law of Islam, governed every detail of daily life. The Sharia protected religious minorities, including Jews and Christians. Members of these religious groups were allowed to organize themselves into separate communities called **millets**. Ottoman society at this time was divided into two classes: the civilian and the military. Civilians worked to produce the wealth needed to support the military. In turn, the military defended the central

At the height of their power, the Ottomans controlled vast territories. **Map Skill:** *Locate areas where Ottoman armies may have met resistance from European armies.*

Curious Facts

The crescent moon was an important symbol of the Ottoman Empire. In the 1680s, the Ottomans tried again to conquer Vienna and failed. Soon after, according to legend, Viennese bakers began to bake crescent-shaped rolls of bread. People ate these rolls, which were the forerunners of today's croissants, as a symbol of their victory over the Ottomans.

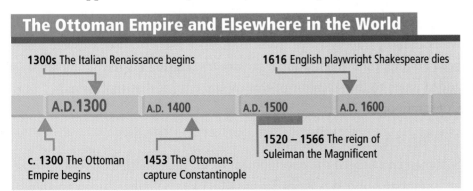

The Ottoman Empire and Elsewhere in the World

1300s The Italian Renaissance begins

1616 English playwright Shakespeare dies

A.D. **1300**   A.D. **1400**   A.D. **1500**   A.D. **1600**

c. 1300 The Ottoman Empire begins

1453 The Ottomans capture Constantinople

1520 – 1566 The reign of Suleiman the Magnificent

Koca Sinan

Koca Sinan was the royal architect during Suleiman's rule. He was born in 1489 to a Christian family in Turkey. He came to Constantinople as a soldier in 1512. Sinan worked in Persia and Egypt as a military engineer before becoming the royal architect. Over a period of 50 years, he designed hundreds of buildings, including the mosque at right.

government, which protected the people. In addition to his military and legal achievements, Suleiman was a supporter of the arts.

The Empire Declines

After the death of Suleiman, many factors led to the long, slow decline of the Ottoman Empire. *(Look at the map on page 26 to see how Ottoman territory shrank through the centuries.)* It faced increasing competition from old enemies. With silver and other goods from their colonies in the Americas, western European nations were able to increase their armies. The Ottomans also suffered from famine and the plague.

Finally, the nature of the government itself changed. During the height of the empire, high government positions had been awarded on the basis of merit. In later times, these positions were passed on from parent to child, regardless of ability. This practice gravely weakened the central government.

Over centuries, the Ottoman Empire continued to shrink and weaken. It officially ended in 1922. In 1930, Constantinople was renamed Istanbul.

Cultural Contributions

Focus *What are some examples of the arts and learning that flourished during the height of the Ottoman Empire?*

Today, Istanbul is the world's only major city located in two continents. It covers both sides of the Bosporus (BAHS pur uhs), a long channel of water that separates Europe from Asia. Since ancient times, this site had been an important international crossroads. During his reign, Suleiman added much to the splendor of this capital city, at that time called Constantinople.

The Suleimaniye Mosque

Suleiman encouraged the development of Ottoman architecture. His most important architect was Koca Sinan (KOH kah SY nihn). Sinan created

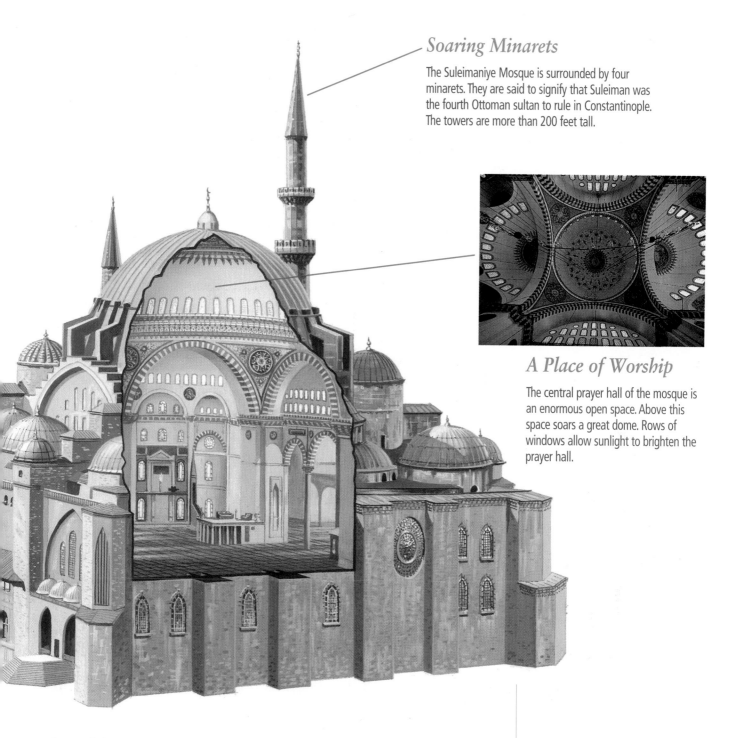

Soaring Minarets

The Suleimaniye Mosque is surrounded by four minarets. They are said to signify that Suleiman was the fourth Ottoman sultan to rule in Constantinople. The towers are more than 200 feet tall.

A Place of Worship

The central prayer hall of the mosque is an enormous open space. Above this space soars a great dome. Rows of windows allow sunlight to brighten the prayer hall.

beautiful monuments that have been admired for centuries. *(Read the biography on the previous page.)* Their soaring domes and immense interiors seem to express the confidence of the Ottoman Empire at its height.

One of Sinan's most magnificent buildings is the Suleimaniye (SOO lay mahn eye ah) Mosque, shown in the illustration above. This house of worship, completed in the 1550s, towers above Istanbul to this day. *(To review the architectural features that all mosques have in common, see Chapter 10, page 258.)* Thousands of workers labored for about seven years to build the great mosque. Suleiman himself was buried in a garden near the mosque after his death in 1566.

Religious and medical schools, a resting place for travelers, and a hospital were all part of the complex that surrounded the Suleimaniye Mosque.

Education

Throughout the Ottoman Empire, mosques were important centers of Muslim life. It was here that young boys attended school. They learned about Islam and recited passages from the Qur'an. If a boy was a very good student, he might be able to enter a *madrasa* (mah DRAHS uh). A madrasa is a formal school or college.

In the 1500s, Suleiman reorganized education throughout the Ottoman Empire. During his reign, there were eight madrasas. Many graduates from these schools became prayer leaders, teachers in the children's schools, or professors in the madrasas.

Within local communities, scholars who learned Islamic law formed respected groups called the Ulama (oo luh MAH). Some Muslim scholars who attended the madrasas became experts in the fields of astronomy, geography, and medicine. Their discoveries and inventions spread throughout the Ottoman Empire and to lands as far away as China. Many became famous throughout the world.

Lesson Review

1400		1500	

1453
Constantinople falls to the Ottomans

1520
The reign of Suleiman begins

1 **Key Vocabulary:** Write a description of Suleiman the Magnificent using the following words: sultan, Sharia, millet.

2 **Focus:** In what ways was Suleiman the Magnificent a remarkable ruler?

3 **Focus:** What are some examples of the arts and learning that flourished during the height of the Ottoman Empire?

4 **Critical Thinking: Generalize** What do you think were the advantages of the Ottoman system of education?

5 **Citizenship:** What signs exist in Eastern Europe today that the Ottomans once controlled the region?

6 **Geography/Art Activity:** Make a large map showing the expansion of the Ottoman Empire. Show each new territorial conquest by shading the area with a different color.

The Ming Dynasty

Main Idea The Ming dynasty was a culturally significant period in Chinese history.

Key Vocabulary

isolationism

kiln

porcelain

Key Events

1368 The Ming dynasty begins

1405 Voyages of Zheng He begin

For almost 600 years, these giant stone animals have guarded a quiet path in the Chinese countryside near the city of Nanjing. Farther along the path stand more statues of animals, generals, and officials. They announce that this is no ordinary country lane. It is a road that leads to the tomb of Zhu Yuanzhang (joo YOO ahn jang). Though he began life as a poor farmer, he died the first emperor of the Ming dynasty.

A Brilliant Dynasty

Focus *Why was the Ming dynasty a truly "bright" period for China?*

The Mongol Empire ruled China for almost 100 years. Kublai Khan was the last of these foreign rulers. When he died, the empire began to collapse. Rebellion spread across China. Zhu Yuanzhang, one of the leaders of the revolt against the Mongols, captured the capital city of Dadu (dah DOO). In 1368, taking the name of Hongwu, he declared himself emperor of China. Hongwu moved the capital to the south at Nanjing and set China on the path to one of its most shining eras.

These kneeling and standing animals are larger than lifesize. In some places, the road to Zhu Yuanzhang's tomb is wide enough to allow cars to drive between the statues.

This portrait of Emperor Yongle was painted more than 500 years ago. The wearing of yellow robes was a royal privilege. Because yellow was the color of the sun, it was a color reserved for the emperor. **Cultures:** *Why might the Chinese have made a connection between the sun and their emperor?*

The Move to Beijing

Hongwu's new dynasty was called the Ming, which means "bright" or "brilliant" in Chinese. It would be a bright period for China. After a century of Mongol domination, the Ming dynasty began to recover its own Chinese culture. When Hongwu died, his son Yongle (YOONG LUH) became emperor. Yongle reigned from 1403 to 1424. During this time he moved the capital back to Dadu, which he rebuilt and renamed Beijing (BAY jihng). Beijing remains the capital of China today.

Overseas Expeditions

During the Ming dynasty, the Chinese began to explore the world that surrounded them. Beginning in 1405, Emperor Yongle sent seven expeditions across the sea to distant lands. Under Admiral Zheng He (jung huh), huge ships sailed to India, Arabia, and Africa. Scholars believe that these voyages were intended to open up relations with the outer world. You can read more about them on the facing page.

Then, in 1433, the court stopped these expeditions. It also forbade further overseas travel. It was as if the Ming dynasty had gotten a glimpse of the outside world and found nothing it needed. Eventually China would come to practice **isolationism**, a national policy of not becoming involved — politically or economically — with other nations. The great empire reached out to the world, and then withdrew its hand.

End of the Dynasty

The Ming dynasty slipped into decline for many reasons. Beijing, the capital, was too far from China's new economic center, the Yangzi (YANG see) Valley, in the south. And it was too close to China's traditional enemies in the north. The splendor of Beijing also distracted emperors from affairs of state. In the same way that China cut itself off from foreign contact, the later emperors isolated themselves in the palace.

In 1644, Manchu invaders from the northeast crossed the Great Wall and entered Beijing. With that, the Ming dynasty came to an end. The new dynasty, the Qing (CHING), would rule the empire until the 1900s. It also would work to further isolate China from the rest of the world.

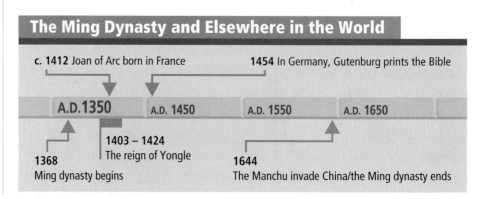

The Ming Dynasty and Elsewhere in the World

c. **1412** Joan of Arc born in France

1454 In Germany, Gutenburg prints the Bible

A.D.**1350** A.D. **1450** A.D. **1550** A.D. **1650**

1403 – 1424 The reign of Yongle

1368 Ming dynasty begins

1644 The Manchu invade China/the Ming dynasty ends

The Voyages of Zheng He

Zheng He's expeditions sometimes included more than 25,000 sailors and soldiers. His group of ships was called a treasure fleet. The fleet carried expensive Chinese goods, including silks and ceramics. These items were traded along the routes shown below.
Map Skill: *How long did the voyage take?*

LEGEND
→ Outward (1431–33)
┄→ Return (1433)
→ Ships sent on by Zheng He

PERSIA

Hormuz

Persian Gulf

Indus River

Red Sea

Jiddah

ARABIA

Aden

Nile River

AFRICA

Mogadishu

Malindi

0° Equator

60°E

Arabian Sea

Ganges River

INDIA

Calicut

Maldive Islands

INDIAN OCEAN

Bay of Bengal

Chittagong

90°E

Yangtze River

Nanjing

30°N

MING EMPIRE

Ayudah

PACIFIC OCEAN

South China Sea

PHILIPPINES

SUMATRA

BORNEO

Tuban

120°E

African Animals

Zheng He returned home with exotic animals from Africa, including zebras, leopards, and giraffes. They amazed people at court and were added to the Imperial Zoo.

The Treasure Fleet

The largest ships in Zheng He's fleet were giant junks, the traditional flat-bottomed ships of China. They had nine masts and were about 400 feet long. The illustration below compares a giant junk with the Santa María, one of Columbus's three ships. The Santa María was only 85 feet long.

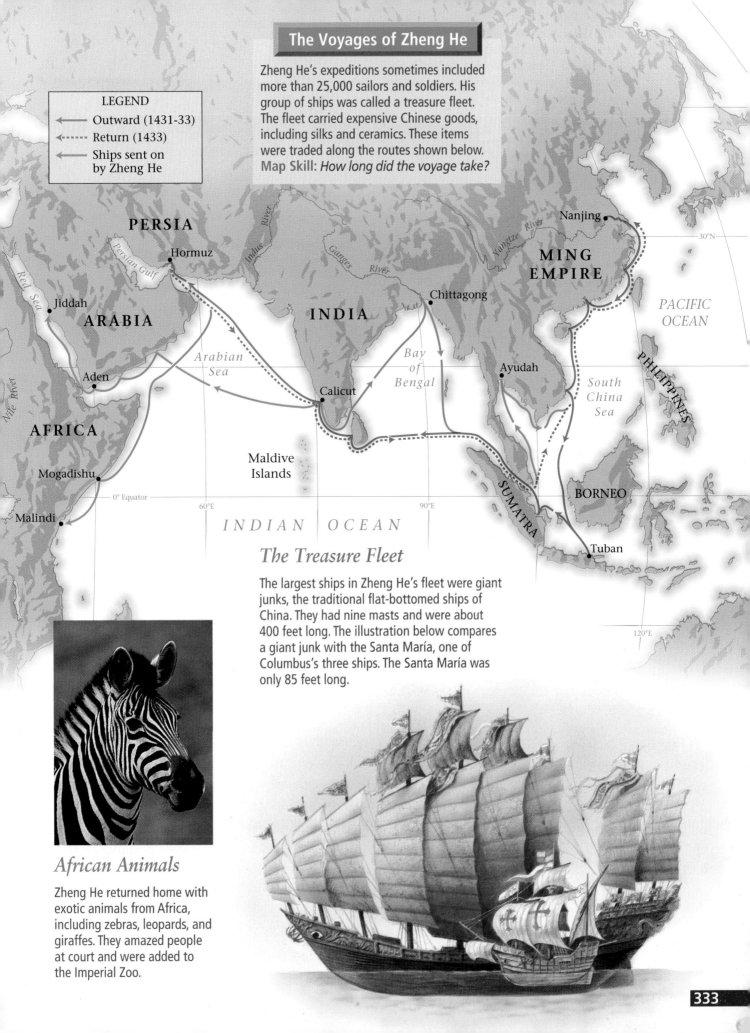

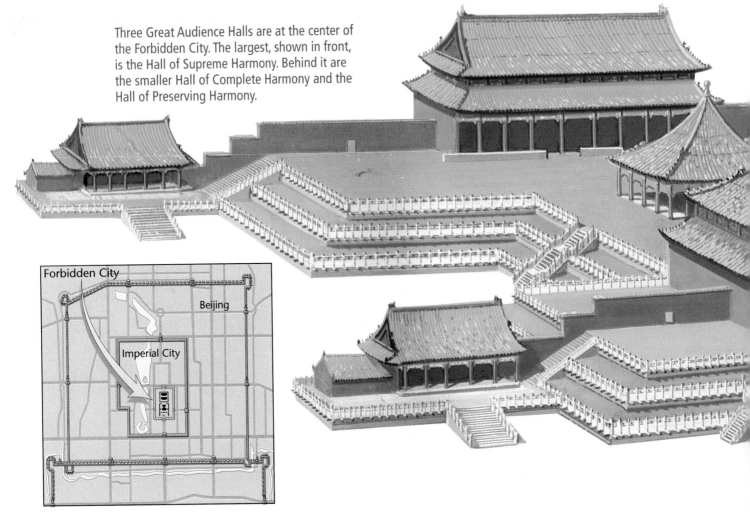

Three Great Audience Halls are at the center of the Forbidden City. The largest, shown in front, is the Hall of Supreme Harmony. Behind it are the smaller Hall of Complete Harmony and the Hall of Preserving Harmony.

Forbidden City

Beijing

Imperial City

The Ming capital consisted of three cities nested one inside the other. The outer city included houses and shops. Inside that was the Imperial City, which contained the Imperial Palace, also called the Forbidden City.

Ask Yourself

The emperor of China sat on a throne, surrounded by thousands of soldiers. Servants attended to his every need, and he almost never left the palace. Do you think it is important for leaders to be in touch with their people? Why?

? ? ? ? ? ? ? ? ? ? ? ? ? ?

Cultural Contributions

Focus *What were some cultural achievements of the Ming dynasty?*

The Ming period was a time of great advances. Chinese writers developed a new literary form — the novel. Scholars created vast encyclopedias. Master craftspeople produced exquisite furniture, rugs, and textiles. The Ming dynasty is perhaps most famous for the rebuilding of Beijing and for its ceramics, which are admired throughout the world.

The Forbidden City

The Ming emperor Yongle had the capital city rebuilt. Approximately one million workers labored for at least 10 years to complete the project. The new capital was actually three cities nested one inside the other, as shown in the map *(above left)*.

The outer city included houses, shops, and government buildings. Inside this was the walled Imperial City, which contained beautiful lakes and gardens. At the center of the Imperial City was the Imperial Palace. The palace, also called the Forbidden City, was protected by a high wall. It was off-limits to everyone except the emperor, his family, and his court. The design of these three cities symbolized the Chinese belief that the emperor was the center of the universe.

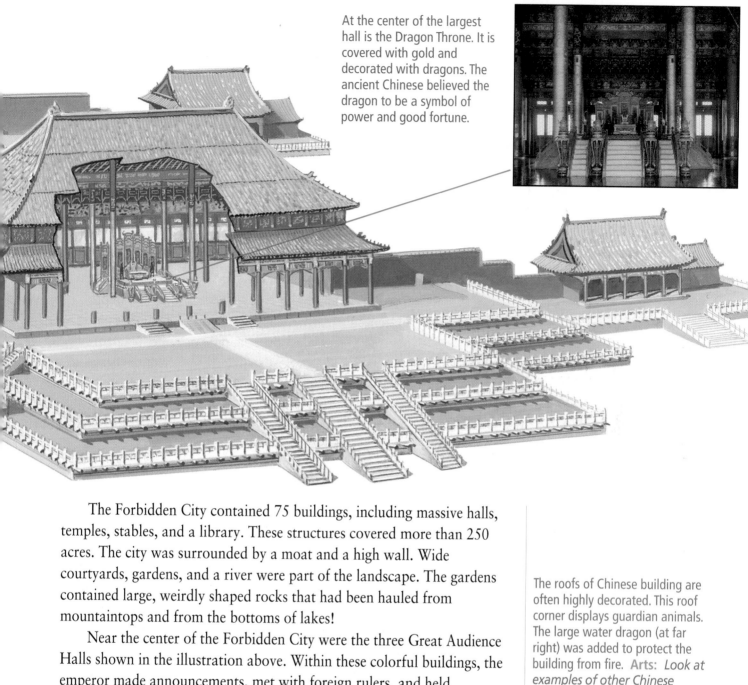

At the center of the largest hall is the Dragon Throne. It is covered with gold and decorated with dragons. The ancient Chinese believed the dragon to be a symbol of power and good fortune.

The Forbidden City contained 75 buildings, including massive halls, temples, stables, and a library. These structures covered more than 250 acres. The city was surrounded by a moat and a high wall. Wide courtyards, gardens, and a river were part of the landscape. The gardens contained large, weirdly shaped rocks that had been hauled from mountaintops and from the bottoms of lakes!

Near the center of the Forbidden City were the three Great Audience Halls shown in the illustration above. Within these colorful buildings, the emperor made announcements, met with foreign rulers, and held celebrations for the New Year and his birthday. The roofs of the palace buildings were covered with thousands of tiles. The large ovens that baked the tiles, called **kilns,** created a lot of smoke. To keep the emperor's air pure, a law was passed during the Ming dynasty requiring that the tiles be made at least one-and-a-half miles from Beijing. Many of the original buildings of the Forbidden City were destroyed over time because of war and fires.

The roofs of Chinese building are often highly decorated. This roof corner displays guardian animals. The large water dragon (at far right) was added to protect the building from fire. **Arts:** *Look at examples of other Chinese buildings. What kinds of decorations do you find?*

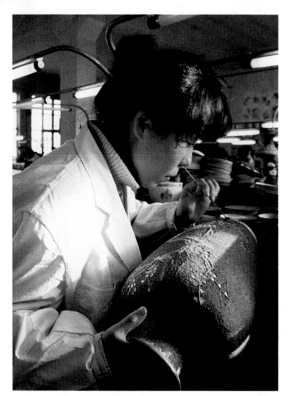

Today, Chinese craftspeople continue to make beautiful ceramics and other goods. In this photograph, a young Chinese woman adds hand touches to a machine-made vase. **Economics:** *Why do you think that most goods today are made by machine and not by hand?*

In the 1700s and 1800s, the Chinese restored the ornate palaces. Today, they are popular attractions for visitors from around the world.

Ming Ceramics

Hundreds of years before the Ming dynasty, the Chinese had invented a hard white kind of ceramic called **porcelain** (PAWR suh lihn). We call the plates, bowls, cups, and vases made from this material "china."

During the Ming dynasty, artisans created exceptionally beautiful ceramics. *(See the vase shown on the opposite page.)* The most famous style from this time is a blue pattern painted on a white background. The blue comes from cobalt, an ore mined in Iran, in western Asia. Cobalt was first shipped along trade routes to China when the country was under Mongol rule.

These same trade routes also helped to spread the beautiful finished vases. Artisans from other countries admired the Ming creations and began to make their own versions of the blue-and-white ceramics. Today, Ming ceramics are considered priceless works of art. They are collected by people and museums around the world.

The cultural center of Beijing (and much of China) remained a mystery to the outside world until the 1900s. Fine Chinese trade goods prompted foreigners to search for a shortcut to the country for centuries.

Lesson Review

1300		1400	

1368
The Ming dynasty begins

1405
Voyages of Zheng He begin

1 **Key Vocabulary:** Write a paragraph about Ming China using these words: isolationism, kiln, porcelain.

2 **Focus:** Why was the Ming dynasty a truly "bright" period for China?

3 **Focus:** What were some cultural achievements of the Ming dynasty?

4 **Critical Thinking: Cause and Effect** What do you think might have happened if the Chinese had continued their overseas voyages? How might world history have been affected?

5 **Theme: Contact and Interaction** How did other cultures influence the development of Ming ceramics?

6 **Citizenship/Writing Activity:** If you were the emperor of China, what would your day be like? Write a poem that tells about your life.

Learning Through Visual Evidence

Tales from Tabletops

The walls of the Forbidden City, built to protect the emperor and his court, kept the inhabitants hidden from public view. But the artifacts of the court that survived reveal much about how they lived. The pottery of the Ming dynasty, for example, tells tales of the life, culture, and beliefs of the time. Read the stories these objects of art have to tell.

1 Here's How

The next time you look at visual evidence, such as pottery or artwork, try to really look at it. It might have an amazing story to tell.

- Look at the whole object. Notice its shape and colors. What is it made of? How was it made? How was it used? Who was meant to enjoy it?

- Examine the designs. What designs do you see? Are there animals, people, or plants?

- Think about your observations and make decisions. What does the object tell you about the way of life of the people who created and used it? What was important to these people?

- Recall what you know and search for more clues. What do you already know about this time period? What else can you find out to add to the story?

2 Think It Through

If you chose visual evidence to tell about your culture and life, what would it be? What would it look like?

3 Use It

Examine this vase. What clues do you find about life and culture in its time? Record your findings in three columns labeled "What I know," "What I learned," and "What I still need to know."

The Aztec Empire

Key Vocabulary

- aviary
- mercenary
- alliance
- tribute
- chinampas

Key Events

1340s The Aztecs settle at Lake Texcoco

The shield at right, decorated with feathers, belonged to an Aztec emperor.

The Aztecs were a fierce warrior nation, but they also loved flowers and the colorful feathers of tropical birds. The beautiful shield shown here was decorated with feathers. Aztec emperors also wore robes made of feathers.

This art form was so important to the Aztecs that the emperor had a vast **aviary**, or birdhouse. In it he kept eagles and tropical birds, which supplied plumes for the master featherworkers who made his royal robes. The Aztecs' love of birds also had a religious side. One of their most important gods, Quetzalcóatl (keht sahl koh AHT l), was known as "the feathered serpent."

A Mesoamerican Empire

Focus *How did the Aztecs maintain their large empire?*

Long before the Aztecs rose to power, civilization had developed in what is now Mexico and parts of Central America (see Chapter 6). The Maya had built great cities in the tropical rain forests of the south. Further north, Teotihuacán had grown to be one of the largest cities in the world.

The Aztec Empire and Elsewhere in the World

1431 French hero Joan of Arc is executed		**1550s** In Europe, the Counter Reformation occurs	
A.D. 1300	A.D. 1400	A.D. 1500	A.D. 1600
1340s Aztecs settle at Texcoco	**1502** Aztec ruler Montezuma II comes to power	**1519** Spanish explorer Hernando Cortés arrives in Mexico	

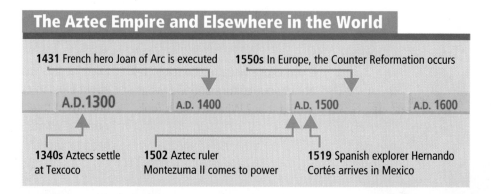

The Toltecs had also thrived in this region. By 1200, all these civilizations had shrunk or collapsed. This left an opening for a new power in Central America.

The Founding of a Great Cultural Center

Around 1200, numerous groups migrated into the Valley of Mexico. The largest of these groups called themselves the Mexica, after whom the modern nation of Mexico is named. They were a fierce people who came from the northwest. Today, these groups are known as the Aztecs.

The Aztecs forged a new, vibrant culture from elements of those that had gone before them. They admired the Toltecs and began to worship their god, Quetzalcóatl. At first the Aztecs became mercenaries for local city-states. A **mercenary** is a hired fighter. Then, in the 1340s, they moved to an island in the middle of Lake Texcoco. The island became their capital city of Tenochtitlán (teh nawch tee TLAHN).

Growth of an Imperial Culture

Eventually, the Aztecs formed an **alliance**, or union, with two other states in the region. From their protected island home, they continued to grow larger and more powerful. By the 1420s, the Aztecs had become the major power in the Valley of Mexico, as shown in the map below. The Aztec emperor had become the mightiest person in the land.

As the Aztec Empire grew, the imperial government created an economic system to support it. Groups of citizens were forced to pay a kind of tax called a **tribute**. It could be paid in crops, goods, or work.

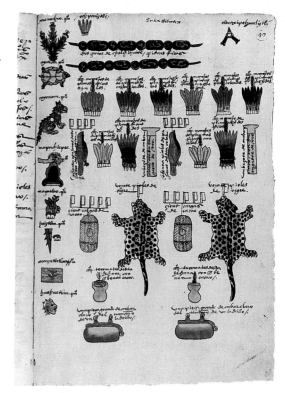

The page above was copied from an Aztec tribute roll, a kind of book with pages made of bark. It shows some of the varied goods that came into Tenochtitlán from the empire: jade beads, birds and feathers, animal skins, and pots of honey.

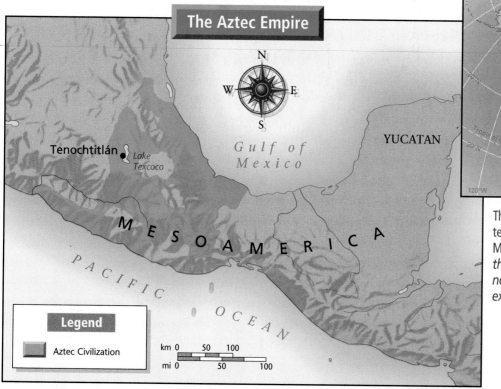

The Aztec Empire

YUCATAN

Gulf of Mexico

Tenochtitlán — Lake Texcoco

M E S O A M E R I C A

P A C I F I C   O C E A N

Legend

Aztec Civilization

km 0   50   100
mi 0   50   100

The Aztecs controlled a large territory in the region that today is Mexico. **Map Skill:** *Form some theories about why pockets of non-Aztec territory might have existed throughout the empire.*

For military protection, local rulers supplied the Aztec emperor with warriors to fight when needed. These warriors also met the empire's religious needs. To ensure that the sun would rise each day, the Aztec sun god was offered human blood. Wars against rival states provided a steady supply of prisoners. These prisoners were used as human sacrifices. Aztec warriors were highly respected, and the emperor rewarded success with land and other gifts.

Cultural Contributions

Focus | *What made the Aztec capital an extraordinary city?*

The Aztecs borrowed from earlier Mesoamerican cultures, but they also made contributions of their own. Artists carved gigantic stone figures of the gods. Craftspeople made beautiful jewelry and pottery. The Aztecs developed a writing system based on colorful hieroglyphs, similar to those of ancient Egypt. Throughout their empire, the Aztecs built great palaces and temples. The most magnificent were at the Aztec capital, the island city of Tenochtitlán.

This life-sized ceramic sculpture portrays an Aztec eagle warrior. Scholars believe that it was probably once covered with feathers.

The Great Temple

The group of buildings at the heart of Tenochtitlán is known as the Templo Mayor (TEM ploh my OHR), or Great Temple.

This double pyramid was dedicated to two Aztec gods. One was linked to rain and earth, the other to fire and warfare. The Aztecs sacrificed prisoners in front of these two structures.

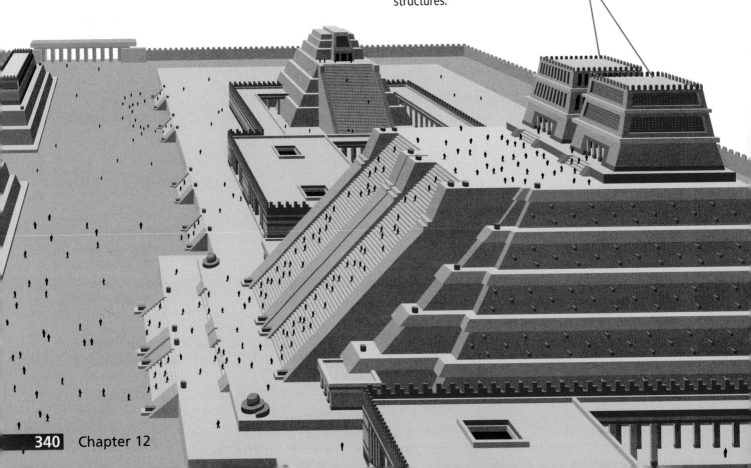

Tenochtitlán

At its height, the city of Tenochtitlán had an estimated population of at least 200,000. From this cultural and political center, the Aztecs governed an empire roughly half the size of California. Scholars think that the empire's total population may have been around six million people.

Tenochtitlán amazed Bernal Díaz (DEE ahs), who was one of the first Europeans to see it in the early 1500s. He wrote:

> **"W**ith such wonderful sights to gaze on we did not know what to say, or if this was real . . . . The lake was crowded with canoes. At intervals along the causeways there were many bridges, and before us was the great city . . . .**"**

The Aztecs expanded their island capital by draining the marshes of the lake. They constructed aqueducts to deliver water to the city. Long mounds of earth called causeways connected the city to the mainland. Amazingly, all this work was done without work animals or the wheel.

Tenochtitlán was a city bustling with people and activity. Priests, nobles, warriors, artisans, merchants, peasants, and enslaved people crowded the city. The ceremonial heart of the capital was a great stone-paved plaza, shown in the illustration below. Next to it, a huge temple topped with a double pyramid rose to the sky. On either side of the temple were the palaces of the emperor and his officials. It is no wonder that the first Europeans who saw this dazzling city on the lake thought they must be dreaming!

*This 16th-century Spanish map shows Lake Texcoco and the Aztec capital of Tenochtitlán. **Map Skill:** Find a map of modern-day Mexico City, which Tenochtitlán eventually became, and compare it with the one below.*

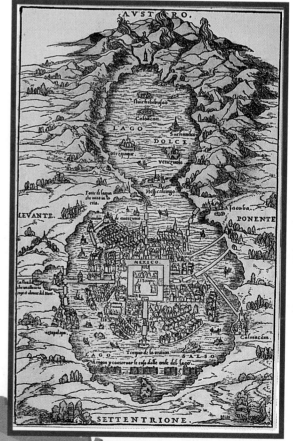

Palace Treasures

The Aztec palaces were filled with riches, including fine jewelry, armor, gold, silver, and gemstones.

A Mexican farmer in Xochimilco travels by boat to the local chinampas. This traditional method of farming has been used in Mexico for more than 500 years.

Trade and Agriculture

By 1500, Tenochtitlán was one of the largest cities in the world. As it expanded, it absorbed the rival island city of Tlatelolco (tlah teel OHL koh). This city then became the capital's marketplace. Each day, an estimated 25,000 people visited the marketplace. Goods such as food, animals, clothing, jewels, and medicine were sold there. Most products were exchanged through a barter, or trade, system. Aztecs bought items with cacao beans or feather quills filled with gold dust.

The market at Tlatelolco attracted farmers from the entire region. The lake was filled with canoes carrying fresh produce to support the city's large population. Much of this produce came from the nearby chinampas (chee NAHM pas). **Chinampas** are island fields created by digging up soil from the lake bottom. The soil is piled into mounds. Then tall plants and wooden stakes are placed along the edge of these mounds to hold the soil in place. As seen in the photograph at left, this method of farming is still used at Xochimilco (zoh chee MIHL koh), Mexico, today.

Change on the Horizon

The cultural centers of Christian Ethiopia, the Ottoman Empire, the Ming dynasty, and the Aztec Empire had much in common. They were all centers of government, trade, and religion. They also contained immense monuments that drew together large populations. Beginning in the 1400s and 1500s, these cultures would come into contact with the rest of the world. And in many cases, this contact would transform them forever.

Lesson Review

1300

1340s
Aztecs settle at Lake Texcoco

1 Key Vocabulary: Write a paragraph about the Aztecs, using the following: aviary, mercenary, alliance, tribute, chinampas.

2 Focus: How did the Aztecs maintain their large empire?

3 Focus: What made the Aztec capital an extraordinary city?

4 Critical Thinking: Conclude The Aztecs did not use money. They bartered for their goods. What are the advantages and disadvantages of each payment system?

5 Geography: What are the advantages and disadvantages of building a city on a marshy island in the middle of a lake?

6 Citizenship/Art and Research Activity: Draw a map of the Aztec capital at its height. Label the Great Temple, the marketplace, chinampas, and causeways.

People of all cultures are creative. The arts and crafts of a culture often reflect its beliefs and ideals. As the cultures of Europe, Africa, Asia and the Americas began to exchange their goods and their artwork, one culture would sometimes dominate another. Gradually, people have learned to respect and enjoy differences between cultures.

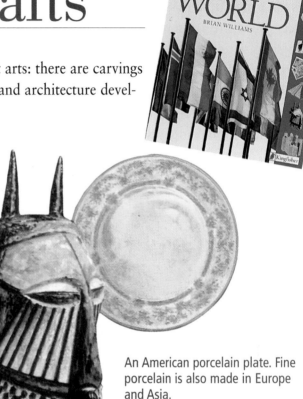

Arts and Crafts

The visual arts, painting and sculpture, are ancient arts: there are carvings and cave paintings over 15,000 years old. Pottery and architecture developed when people first became settled farmers, about 10,000 years ago. The performing arts include music, dance, theater, and motion pictures. The first three all have their origins in our prehistoric past; motion pictures (and radio and television) are 20th-century inventions. Literature began with storytelling; writing was only invented 5,000 years ago.

VISUAL ARTS
The visual arts include painting, sculpture, ceramics, and textiles. Traditional arts (carpets or masks, for example) may change little in style over the centuries. Painters

An American porcelain plate. Fine porcelain is also made in Europe and Asia.

A ceremonial mask made by the BaLuba of Central Africa.

and sculptors have constantly sought fresh ways to express their vision of the world.

THE PERFORMING ARTS
Dance was originally part of tribal ritual. It developed into drama — literature acted out with words and often accompanied by music. Western drama began in ancient Greece some 2,500 years ago. Eastern drama includes the Kabuki and Noh theater of Japan. The earliest written music is Indian, 3,000 years old. Ballet and opera developed in Europe during the 1400s and 1500s.

Kabuki actors in Japan, where these colorful melodramas have been performed since the 1600s.

Population

Culture embraces many aspects of human life: art, religion, customs, language, technology. Cultures are amazingly diverse, even though in the 20th century "world culture" (that is, western industrial culture) has touched almost every human group from the Amazon to the Arctic. Every year there are about 90 million extra people to share that culture. The human population grew slowly until the 1800s. Since then the rate of increase has quickened dramatically. However, population growth is not the same worldwide. In the more prosperous countries, birth rates roughly match the numbers of deaths, so that the populations stay stable or grow only slowly. In developing countries, birth rates far outstrip death rates, and consequently many of these countries have populations growing at two to three percent a year.

The earth's five billion people occupy only about 15 percent of the planet's land area. Vast areas of the earth are either too hot and dry, or too cold to support permanent human populations.

POPULATION DISTRIBUTION

This map shows human population density—which areas of the earth have the most people per square mile. Europe, South and East Asia, and the eastern United States are the most densely populated regions in the world.

(People per sq. mile)

- 800 and over
- 500-799
- 250-499
- 130-249
- below 130

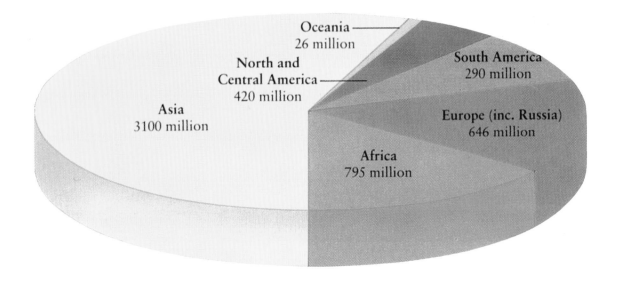

Oceania — 26 million

North and Central America — 420 million

Asia 3100 million

South America 290 million

Europe (inc. Russia) 646 million

Africa 795 million

ANNUAL RATES OF INCREASE	
World	1.7%
Africa	3.0%
South America	1.9%
Asia	1.8%
Oceania	1.4%
North America	1.2%
Europe	0.2%

The world's population is rising fastest in the so-called developing world, particularly in Africa. In Kenya the population doubles every 18 to 23 years. But in some Western countries (Sweden, for example) the population is actually falling.

POPULATION EXPLOSION

The growth of human population was slow until the 1700s. It doubled from the mid-1600s to 1850, and has more than quadrupled since then. In 1950 the earth's population was about 2.5 billion. In the year 2000 it will be over six billion.

POPULATION DISTRIBUTION

Of the seven continents, Asia has by far the most people. Nearly six out of ten people live in Asia. Between them China and India have nearly 40 percent of all the world's people.

Response Activities

1. **Generalize** Why might artists and craftspeople in all countries be excited to see the artwork of another culture?

2. **Descriptive: Tell About a Building** Imagine you're an architect who has visited Ming China, Christian Ethiopia, the Aztec Empire and the Ottoman Empire. Write a description of the building you are going to design to show elements of each of these cultures.

3. **Geography: Make a Map** Create a map that shows how one culture can influence another. Using the outline of a world map, create your own symbols to show cultural elements that move from one place to another. Show the direction of movement with arrows.

Chapter Review

Chapter Review Timeline

			1368 The Ming dynasty begins		
1000	1120	1240	1360	1480	**1600**

1100s
The Zagwé dynasty begins

1340s
Aztecs settle at Lake Texcoco

1405
Voyages of Zheng He begin

1453
Constantinople falls to the Ottomans

1520
The reign of Suleiman begins

Summarizing the Main Idea

1 Copy the chart below and fill in the missing information to compare four civilizations you studied in this chapter.

	Zagwé dynasty	Ottoman Empire	Ming dynasty	Aztec Empire
Capital City				
Influential Leader				
Cultural Achievement				
Religion				

Vocabulary

2 Suppose you were on a trip around the world in the 1400s to visit some of the major civilizations of the day. Use the following terms to tell the story of your journey.

convert (p. 322)
abdicate (p. 323)
sultan (p. 326)

Sharia (p. 327)
isolationism (p. 332)
porcelain (p. 336)

mercenary (p. 339)
alliance (p. 339)
tribute (p. 339)

Reviewing the Facts

3 How did Christian Ethiopia get cut off from European Christianity?

4 What is unique about the 10 churches of Lalibela?

5 Why did Europeans call Suleiman "the Magnificent"?

6 Why was the name of the Ming dynasty appropriate?

7 What was the Forbidden City? Describe it.

8 Who were the Aztecs and how did they come to power?

9 Describe life in the city of Tenochtitlán.

10 Find the Aztec shield on page 338. Notice its shape and colors. What is it made of? How might it have been made? What does it tell you about the Aztec way of life?

Geography Skills

11 Look at the map on p. 333, "Voyages of Zheng He." What parts of the world did China explore between 1431 and 1433? What parts did it miss?

12 Choose one of the four empires described in this chapter, and design a travel poster that would convince tourists to come visit the land of your choice.

Critical Thinking

13 **Compare** Compare the declines of the Ottoman Empire and the Ming dynasty.

14 **Generalize** What are some of the advantages of a policy of isolationism? What are some of the disadvantages?

15 In the chapter there were vivid descriptions of the churches of Ethiopia and the mosques of Koca Sinan. Use the description of the Suleimaniye Mosque on p. 329 as a model to write, from an architectural standpoint, a description of your place of worship, or other public building.

Writing: Citizenship and Geography

16 You are the captain of one of the ships of Zheng He's treasure fleet. Naturally you keep a log of your voyage. Write down the events of three days during the course of your voyage.

Activities

Citizenship/Research Activity
Choose two of the rulers mentioned in this chapter, and do research to find out more about their lives and achievements. Compare and contrast their lives in a presentation to the class.

Culture/Arts Activity
The Ming dynasty is still remembered for its ceramic vases. Using clay, and working from photographs of Ming artifacts, make and decorate a vase so that it resembles one from that era.

Internet Option

Check the **Internet Social Studies Center** for ideas on how to extend your theme project beyond your classroom.

THEME PROJECT CHECK-IN

Use the information in this chapter about cultural centers around the world to continue your project. Ask yourself these questions:
- What cultural exchanges took place in Ethiopia, the Ottoman Empire, the Ming dynasty, and the Aztec Empire?
- What cultural contributions were made by these cultures?
- What examples of art and learning from these cultures still exist today?

CHAPTER 13 Toward Modern Times

Chapter Preview: *People, Places, and Events*

1400	1500	1600

Age of Exploration   1400s

King Ferdinand's support of a young Italian explorer changed the world. *Lesson 1, Page 350*

Elizabethan Age   1500s

The reign of Elizabeth I was a high point in England's history. Find out why. *Lesson 1, Page 351*

Industrial Revolution   1700s

What happened when machines began to do work formerly done by people? *Lesson 2, Page 358*

European Exploration and Conquest

Main Idea European exploration led to changes around the world.

On September 8, 1522, a battered ship limped into the harbor at Seville, Spain. It had set sail three years earlier, with four other ships and a crew of about 250. Only 18 men remained. The others had been lost at sea, killed in battle, or had died of disease. Ferdinand Magellan, the expedition's commander, had been killed during one island stopover. Still, the survivors had done what they had set out to do: They were the first to **circumnavigate**, or sail completely around, the world.

Magellan's ambitious voyage was one of many journeys into regions unknown to Europeans. From information provided by explorers, Europeans' view of the rest of the world would change. The lives and civilizations of the people who lived in other lands would also change.

Key Vocabulary

circumnavigate

indigenous

Key Events

1492 Columbus arrives in North America

1519 Cortés meets Montezuma

1522 Magellan's crew returns from circling globe

◀ When European explorers returned home, they told tall tales about the strange sights they had seen.

| 1700 | 1800 | 1900 |

French Revolution   1789

Thousands of people were executed during the Reign of Terror. *Lesson 2, Page 362*

Napoleon Bonaparte   1799

This painting shows the French dictator Napoleon. Why is he famous? *Lesson 2, Page 363*

British Imperialism   1800s

It took 10 years to construct the Suez Canal. What were its benefits? *Lesson 3, Page 368*

The Age of Exploration

1497–1498
Vasco da Gama *Portuguese*
• established sea route around southern tip of Africa to India

1500
Pedro Cabral *Portuguese*
• claimed Brazil for Portugal

1513
Vasco Núñez de Balboa *Spanish*
• first European to see the Pacific Ocean

1513
Juan Ponce de León *Spanish*
• Discovered Florida while searching for the "Fountain of Youth"

1609–1611
Henry Hudson *English*
• Sailed up Hudson River and claimed region for the Netherlands

1673
Jacques Marquette and Louis Jolliet *French*
• explored Great Lakes and Mississippi River Valley

Focus *Why did European rulers finance voyages of exploration?*

Beginning in the 1400s, European kings and queens supplied the money for voyagers to explore the world. These rulers weren't just curious. They had economic and religious interests in mind as well.

The monarchs needed precious metals for coins. Europe's gold deposits had been used up, and its silver deposits were small. Many Europeans believed they would find treasure troves of gold and silver in faraway lands.

Spices were also valuable to the Europeans. Before refrigerators, meat spoiled easily. Large amounts of spices were used by the Europeans to hide the bad taste and to help preserve the meat. Spices were expensive and they grew far away — in distant Asia. Europeans were hoping to find faster and easier ways to get there and bring the spices back to Europe.

Finally, the Christian kings and queens of Europe wanted to spread their religion throughout the world. This was especially true of Portugal and Spain's Catholic rulers, who were ending Muslim rule of their lands.

Portugal, Spain, and England

Portugal, a small country on the western edge of Europe, was a nation of excellent sailors. They were experienced in navigating both the Mediterranean Sea and the Atlantic coast. Portugal's leader, Prince Henry (1394–1460), was even nicknamed "the Navigator." He believed, correctly, that reaching the southern tip of Africa would be a good way to sail to Asia. In Sagres, Portugal, Prince Henry set up a center for exploration, where Jews, Muslims, Italians, and later, West Africans gathered to share their knowledge.

Spain's rulers, Ferdinand and Isabella *(shown at left)*, were interested in exploration, too. In 1492, they financed a seaman named Christopher Columbus. He believed, incorrectly, that he could find a direct route to Asia by sailing west across the Atlantic. Columbus landed in the Americas instead. As a result of Columbus's error, Spain would become the most powerful nation of the time: By 1550, Spain ruled Mexico, Central America, most of South America, and what is now the southwestern United States.

In 1558 in England, Queen Elizabeth I came to power *(her portrait is on the next page)*. She, too, wanted to find a shortcut from Europe to Asia. During her reign, several English explorers searched for a water route through North America to Asia. They did not succeed. In the 1600s, Spain grew weaker, and England went on to set up colonies in the Americas, as well as in Africa and Asia.

This painting shows the marriage of Ferdinand and Isabella of Spain in 1469.

Sharing Ideas and Inventions

Contact with other cultures had brought many ideas and inventions to the Europeans. The Age of Exploration was made possible partly because Europeans were able to use the knowledge of others.

From the Arabs, Europeans learned to improve their wooden ships by adding triangular sails *(see below)*. To cross open oceans, European explorers used compasses made with magnetic needles. Such needles, in use in China about 400 years before, may have been brought to Europe over the Silk Road.

Another important source of "new" information was more than 1,000 years old! A copy of a set of books about geography by Ptolemy (TAHL uh mee) was brought to Italy in 1400. Ptolemy was a Greek who lived in Egypt in the A.D. 100s. These eight books summed up the ancient world's knowledge of geography. The Europeans now studied ancient texts.

Queen Elizabeth I of England (1533–1603) was the daughter of King Henry VIII. A very intelligent person, she learned Italian, French, Greek, and Latin. England's "Elizabethan Age," named for her, is known for its great writers and thinkers.

The Versatile Caravel

A new vessel called a "caravel" was well suited for exploration. The small ship could easily navigate shallow waters. The mix of square and triangular sails was designed to make use of shifting winds. The crew of about 20 men usually slept on deck.

What Happened to the Aztecs?

In 1519, the Spanish conqueror Hernando Cortés discovered the thriving Aztec Empire *(see Chapter 12)*. Within two years, he had destroyed it. How could Cortés and his few men defeat this mighty empire? For one thing, they had guns and horses, which the Aztecs had never seen before. In addition, the Aztecs had enemies who were willing to join Cortés in the battle against the Aztecs. Finally, Aztec warriors were weakened by disease. Epidemics swept through Mexico's population, which scholars estimate may have dropped more than 90 percent in just a hundred years.

The Spanish soldiers wore helmets like this one. In this 16th-century illustration, the Aztec ruler Montezuma *(on the right)* welcomes Hernando Cortés.

The Impact of Exploration

Focus *What were the results of European exploration in the Americas?*

Europeans were discovering many parts of the globe that had been unknown to them. Their arrival often led to great suffering for many **indigenous** (ihn DIH juh nuhs), or native, people they encountered.

The Effects of Exploration

Parts of the world that had been independent for centuries now came under the control of European nations. The Europeans, unknowingly, carried deadly germs with them to the Americas. The indigenous people had never been exposed to diseases such as smallpox and measles. Hundreds of thousands of them died *(read the Tell Me More, above)*.

Europeans also brought guns with them. They used these weapons to control the native people and force them to work. When the Native Americans got some of these guns, they often fought back.

The Europeans found gold and silver in the Americas, but they quickly realized the land itself was far more valuable. Europeans set up large farms, or plantations, to grow tobacco, sugar, and other cash crops. To work the land, they enslaved people from the western regions of Africa and brought them to the Americas on slave ships.

Missionaries and other Europeans converted many indigenous people to Christianity. Sometimes they used persuasion. Sometimes they combined the people's traditional beliefs with Christian ideas. Usually they used force to get the Native Americans to adopt Christian beliefs.

Some Europeans strongly opposed the mistreatment of the Native Americans. Bartolomé de las Casas, a Spanish missionary, demanded:

> **"T**ell me, by what right or justice do you keep these Indians in such cruel and horrible servitude? On what authority have you waged a detestable war against these people, who dwelt quietly and peacefully on their own land?**"**

The Europeans benefited from their conquests in many ways. Their countries grew wealthy, and the lives of individual Europeans improved. Maize (corn), potatoes, and chocolate brought back to Europe became popular food items. Sailors, who used to sleep on a ship's wooden deck, now strung up hammocks like those they had first seen used in the Americas. The world was changing quickly. Revolutions were soon to occur in the sciences, the workplace, and even the royal courts of Europe.

Ask Yourself

Explorers traveled the world to find treasure, to spread their religious views, and to discover better travel routes. They found foods, tools, styles of dress, and customs that they had never seen before. Many of these things were brought back to Europe to improve the lives of people there. What do we learn from other cultures today?

? ? ? ? ? ? ? ? ? ? ? ? ?

Lesson Review

1475	1500	1525

1492
Columbus arrives in North America

1519
Cortés meets Montezuma

1522
Magellan's crew returns from circling globe

1 Key Vocabulary: Use **circumnavigate** and **indigenous** to describe European exploration.

2 Focus: Why did European rulers finance voyages of exploration?

3 Focus: What were the results of European exploration in the Americas?

4 Critical Thinking: Predict How might the world be different today if the Age of

Exploration had never taken place?

5 Theme: Contact and Interaction How do you think Europeans reacted to items explorers brought home?

6 Geography/Writing Activity: Write a journal entry to describe the thoughts a sailor might have had as he voyaged across the ocean in search of a shortcut to Asia.

The World in Spatial Terms

What Did Captain Cook Learn About the Earth?

Nearly 250 years after Magellan led the first expedition to circle the globe, Europeans still knew little of the Pacific. By the late 1770s, however, most of the mysteries of "the Great South Sea" had been solved. This was largely due to the efforts of one man: British navigator and mapmaker James Cook.

Beginning in 1768, Cook led three long voyages to explore and chart the Pacific Ocean. The Royal Society of London, a British scientific organization, sponsored these voyages. Cook became the first European to reach and chart Australia's east coast and the islands of Hawaii. He also collected detailed information about the plants, animals, and people he found along the way. Cook's explorations literally put the southern Pacific on the map and led to the establishment of European colonies throughout the region.

1 Australia

Kangaroos
Cook and his crew gathered information about many plants and animals they had never seen before. When Cook first saw a kangaroo he nearly mistook it for a kind of dog. Do you know any other unusual animals that live in Australia?

This map shows "All places which Capt. Cook has visited and explored." The main area shows the earth as if viewed from over the South Pole. What continent is missing from the center of the map?

To calculate longitude, navigators needed an accurate clock. British clockmaker John Harrison developed just such a device, the chronometer, in 1759. Why do you think Cook described the one he took on his second voyage as "our never-failing guide"?

Science Connection

One of the greatest dangers faced by sailors in the 1700s was scurvy. This disease caused low energy, bleeding gums, loosened teeth, and death. Cook had heard that citrus fruits and vegetables could prevent it. To test the reports, he served his crew fresh fruits and vegetables. On three long voyages, not one member of Cook's crew died of scurvy. What other health problems can poor nutrition cause?

3 Hawaii

The "Sandwich" Islands
During his third voyage, Cook visited the Hawaiian Islands and claimed them for Britain. He called them the Sandwich Islands after Britain's naval minister, the Earl of Sandwich. What nation are the Hawaiian Islands a part of today?

Cook kept a daily "log" or journal in which he wrote observations about the voyage.

The Explorations of James Cook

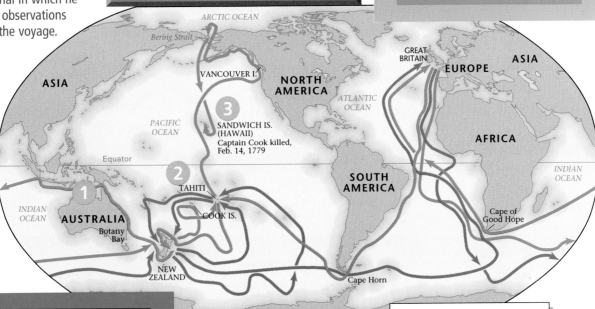

ARCTIC OCEAN

Bering Strait

VANCOUVER I.

NORTH AMERICA

ASIA

ATLANTIC OCEAN

GREAT BRITAIN

EUROPE

ASIA

PACIFIC OCEAN

3 SANDWICH IS. (HAWAII)
Captain Cook killed, Feb. 14, 1779

AFRICA

Equator

TAHITI

2

1

COOK IS.

SOUTH AMERICA

INDIAN OCEAN

INDIAN OCEAN

AUSTRALIA

Botany Bay

Cape of Good Hope

NEW ZEALAND

Cape Horn

ANTARCTICA

Legend

←	First Voyage 1768–1771
←	Second Voyage 1772–1775
←	Third Voyage 1776–1779

2 Tahiti

A Voyage for Astronomy
On his first voyage, Cook sailed to Tahiti to watch the planet Venus pass between the Earth and sun. By observing this event from different places, geographers were better able to calculate the Earth's distance from the sun.

In three voyages, Cook explored the South Pacific, but never saw Antarctica. He got within 75 miles of it but was forced back by the huge icebergs. **Map Skill:** *In which of his voyages did Cook sail east to reach the Pacific?*

Research Activity

1 Choose one place Cook explored and research it.
2 Find information about the plants and animals that live there. Which ones would have been new to Europeans?
3 Write a brief report and share your findings with the class.

The Age of Revolutions

Main Idea Scientific, industrial, and political revolutions changed daily life forever.

Key Vocabulary

scientific method

labor force

capitalism

constitutional
   monarchy

nationalism

Key Events

1600s Scientific
Revolution

1780s Introduction
of the steam
engine

1789 French
Revolution begins

1800s Spread of
Industrial
Revolution

1832 Britain's
Reform Act

"What time is it?" How many times have you heard, or asked, this question? Before the 1700s, most people in Europe never needed to know the answer. As farmers, their day began when the sun rose in the morning and ended when it set.

All this changed when people began working in factories. Suddenly, clock time became very important. People were paid to work a 14-hour day. To get to work on time, they had to wake up before sunrise. (One worker had the job of waking up the other workers by tapping on their windows.) Some people saved up their money to buy a watch, like the one shown here. The way people looked at time had changed. In fact, the whole world was changing around them.

This silver watch was made in 1724 by John Canter of Salisbury, England. **Economics:** *Do some research to find out how much the watch would have cost new and how that compared to people's weekly wages.*

The Scientific Revolution

Focus *How did the Scientific Revolution change the way people studied and learned?*

In the 1600s, scientific discoveries began to change the way people thought about the world. Not all discoveries were well received at first. Using a telescope, a new invention, the Italian astronomer Galileo Galilei (gal uh LEE oh gal uh LAY) found evidence that the Earth revolved around the sun. At the time, people believed that the Earth was the center of the universe. Galileo's discovery challenged the beliefs of the day. The Catholic Church forced Galileo to announce that he had changed his mind.

In spite of setbacks like these, scientists continued to make discoveries with far-reaching results. Advances in medicine, for instance, improved people's health. With more people living longer, the population rose. By the 1700s new inventions and discoveries began improving daily life for many Europeans. This period of rapid progress in the sciences is called the Scientific Revolution.

Leeuwenhoek and the Microscope

Antonie van Leeuwenhoek (LAY wuhn hook) (1632–1723) was a Dutch cloth dealer. He used a special instrument to inspect the quality of the cloth he sold. Leeuwenhoek never attended a university, but the improvements he made to the device shown below led to one of the most important instruments of modern science — the microscope.

In the 1670s, Leeuwenhoek thought of using his microscope to inspect something other than cloth. After examining marsh water, he wrote that a tiny drop of water contained "little animals." Today we know that those "little animals" are simple organisms known as bacteria. This discovery made Europeans realize there was another, unseen world under their very eyes.

The drawing at left shows an insect that Leeuwenhoek saw through his microscope. The central picture shows Leeuwenhoek in 1686.

The object to be studied was held in place on this screw.

In 1768, Joseph Wright painted *An Experiment on a Bird in the Air Pump.* The painting dramatizes an experiment with oxygen conducted by the French scientist Lavoisier (lah vwah ZYAY) *(shown in the red cloak).* Lavoisier is often considered the founder of modern chemistry because of his research on oxygen, which he named in 1777. **Arts:** *What is the mood of this painting?*

A New Way of Learning

The Scientific Revolution did more than produce new knowledge about the natural world. It also popularized a new way of doing research: identify a problem, gather evidence about the problem, propose an explanation for the evidence, and finally test the explanation. Known as the **scientific method**, this is how scientists still go about their work today.

Using reason as a way to state, observe, and solve problems would affect how people thought about other things as well.

The Industrial Revolution

Focus *How did the Industrial Revolution affect daily life in England?*

As science advanced, so did technology. Beginning in the 1750s, inventions such as the mechanical clock, power loom, and steam engine were introduced in England *(see the timeline below).* Work that had been done before by animals and humans was now done by machines.

Machines were grouped in large buildings called factories. Great amounts of goods could be produced cheaply and quickly in factories. By the end of the 1800s, machines had transformed the way people worked

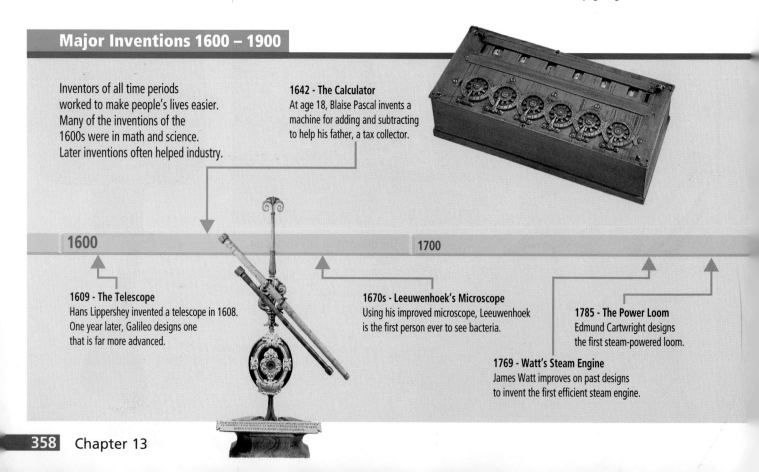

Major Inventions 1600 – 1900

Inventors of all time periods worked to make people's lives easier. Many of the inventions of the 1600s were in math and science. Later inventions often helped industry.

1642 - The Calculator
At age 18, Blaise Pascal invents a machine for adding and subtracting to help his father, a tax collector.

1600   1700

1609 - The Telescope
Hans Lippershey invented a telescope in 1608. One year later, Galileo designs one that is far more advanced.

1670s - Leeuwenhoek's Microscope
Using his improved microscope, Leeuwenhoek is the first person ever to see bacteria.

1785 - The Power Loom
Edmund Cartwright designs the first steam-powered loom.

1769 - Watt's Steam Engine
James Watt improves on past designs to invent the first efficient steam engine.

and lived in western Europe. This transformation is known as the Industrial Revolution.

The Machine Age

Artisans had once made goods with their own hands, but now a single factory could replace hundreds of workshops. In factories, each step in the making of a product was done by a different machine. Each machine did one part, over and over. Women, men, and even children tended the machine that did the work. The people available for work, called the **labor force**, did not need special training. Factory owners controlled the raw materials and the machines and made decisions about the organization of the work. The private ownership, by individuals or groups, of the equipment to produce the goods is called **capitalism**.

The British Textile Industry

The first factories in Great Britain made cloth, or textiles. They were built near streams to make use of water power. By the end of the 1700s, steam replaced streams, and the steam engine was used to run the machinery. Now factories could be built in or near cities. Over time fewer people made cloth by hand and more people worked in factories. As the chart on the next page shows, machines made cloth much faster than people did.

Cities grew as people moved from the countryside to find work in the factories. Cities became very crowded and dirty; diseases and crime spread. Factories changed the look, the smell, and the activities of cities.

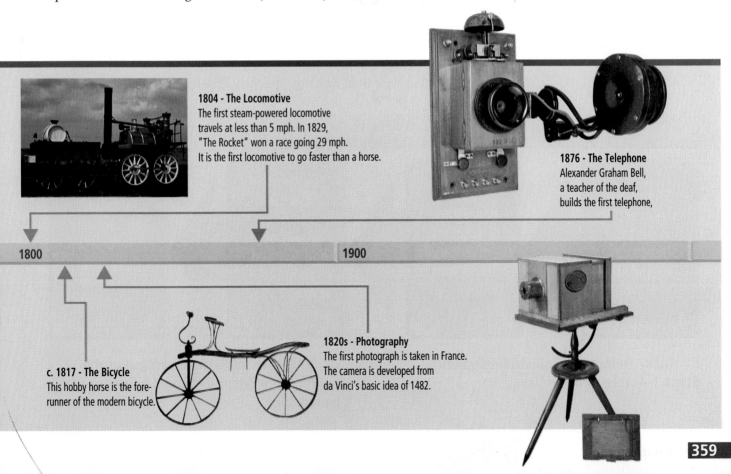

1804 - The Locomotive
The first steam-powered locomotive travels at less than 5 mph. In 1829, "The Rocket" won a race going 29 mph. It is the first locomotive to go faster than a horse.

1876 - The Telephone
Alexander Graham Bell, a teacher of the deaf, builds the first telephone,

1800   1900

c. 1817 - The Bicycle
This hobby horse is the fore-runner of the modern bicycle.

1820s - Photography
The first photograph is taken in France. The camera is developed from da Vinci's basic idea of 1482.

Before the Industrial Revolution, the common peppered moths of England were usually light gray or white, and dark-colored peppered moths were rare. After factories were built, their smokestacks covered nearby trees with soot. Birds now easily preyed on light moths; they could not see the dark ones. By 1898, dark peppered moths far outnumbered light ones in the industrial regions of England.

In 1854, the English writer Charles Dickens described one English cotton manufacturing town in his novel *Hard Times*. He wrote:

> "It was a town of red brick, or of brick that would have been red if the smoke and ash had allowed it... It was a town of machinery and tall chimneys, out of which interminable [unending] serpents of smoke trailed themselves forever and ever, and never got uncoiled. It had a black canal in it, and a river that ran purple with ill-smelling dye..."

Factory owners could hire and fire people at will. Because many married women had families to raise, they often were not given jobs. Young children, however, were desirable as workers. A seven-year-old spinner in a textile factory was asked how he could stick to a 15-hour-a-day schedule. He answered, "There were three overlookers; there was one head overlooker, and there was one man kept to grease the machines, and there was one kept on purpose to strap [beat the children]." Such mistreatment of young children in the early textile factories finally led to the passage of laws in the first half of the 1800s to protect them.

The Spread of Industrialization

The Industrial Revolution began in Great Britain and flourished there for a number of reasons. The country had rich natural resources, including the iron ore and coal needed to make and run machines. British society was stable, that is, it didn't change quickly. This encouraged businesses to

Clothmaking Before and After the Industrial Revolution

1 Sheep are *sheared*, or have their fleece cut, to provide raw wool.

2 The wool is *carded*, or combed, to disentangle fibers and remove dirt.

3 The combed fibers are *spun*, or drawn out and twisted, to make thread called *yarn*.

4 The threads of wool are *woven*, or interlaced at right angles, to create pieces of cloth.

BY HAND Before the Industrial Revolution, Steps 1-4 were done by hand.

BY MACHINE With the invention of the power loom, Steps 2-4 could be done by machine.

Children hired to work in the textile factories were often from poor families and were paid very low wages. They were also the only workers small enough to crawl under the machines when needed.

invest, or spend money in order to make more money. The government encouraged investment in business by not taxing British goods. These investors made money when demand for products increased in Great Britain and in its colonies. In a short time, the Industrial Revolution had spread throughout Europe and to the United States. More things for sale meant countries had to search for new sources of raw materials to make new goods. It also led to the search for new places to sell them.

Along with hardships, the Industrial Revolution brought progress. After epidemics of diseases like cholera (KAHL uhr uh) swept through overcrowded cities in the 1860s, governments built huge water and sewer systems. As countries became industrialized, they also began to build railways. The new railroads, along with new canals and highways, helped people, goods, and raw materials travel easily from place to place.

Changes in people's working lives made them wish for other changes as well. In addition to their new trade and business opportunities, people now wanted more political rights.

Political Revolutions

Focus *What were the goals and outcome of the French Revolution?*

During the 1600s and 1700s, some interesting ideas were beginning to spread. According to these ideas, all humans had the right to seek freedom, happiness, and knowledge. Society was described as a contract between those who govern and those who are governed. In the 1700s, these democratic ideas influenced the leaders of the American Revolution. Not long afterwards, the citizens of France began to think about these ideas. They, too, thought it was time for a new form of government.

Then & Now

What kinds of jobs do you do? Chores around the house, probably. Maybe you have a paper route. During the Industrial Revolution, kids your age had jobs, too. Only theirs were in factories and mines, and were often incredibly dangerous. If you get a job nowadays, you can be sure there are laws and regulations to protect you.

The French Revolution

In the 1770s, French society was divided into three classes: nobility, Church officials, and everybody else. This last group included the poor as well as the people in the middle class, or bourgeoisie (bur zhwah ZEE).

Because of unsuccessful investments and wars, by 1789 the French government was deeply in debt. The poor were increasingly resentful because of the heavy taxes they were forced to pay. As a result of a decline in the French textile industry, unemployment was high. Poor harvests had led to food shortages and starvation.

The French king, Louis XVI, called a meeting to address the country's problems. He met with representatives from each of the three classes. The representatives of the Church and the nobility found little to complain about. The poor and the bourgeoisie, however, voiced their anger. They demanded that France become a **constitutional monarchy**, in which a ruler's power is restricted by a written constitution and laws. They also announced that they were forming a National Assembly to help govern the country. The king agreed to some of their demands, but alarmed by the people's unrest, he gathered his troops near Paris.

The people of Paris, angered by the king's action, attacked the Bastille (ba STEEL). The city's prison and once a military fortress, the Bastille had become the symbol of the king's power. The people stormed and captured the fortress. It was July 14, 1789, and the French Revolution had begun. (Now known as Bastille Day, July 14 is celebrated as France's most important national holiday.) The storming of the Bastille inspired similar incidents throughout France. The uprising didn't last long, but when it was over, France had a new government.

A month later, the Assembly adopted the Declaration of the Rights of Man and of the Citizen. All people were declared free and equal; the nobility and the Church now had to pay taxes. In 1792, France became a republic. A republic is governed by a group of elected citizens, not by a monarch.

The revolution ended total rule by French kings and created a stronger middle class. It also awakened within citizens a feeling of **nationalism**, which is pride in and loyalty to one's country.

The Reign of Terror

King Louis XVI, found guilty of treason, was executed in 1793. But France was not yet calm. Some revolutionary leaders, not satisfied with the changes, became increasingly violent. People who opposed them became their targets. From September 1793 to July 1794, 17,000 people were executed. This period became known as the Reign of Terror.

During the Reign of Terror, the sound of carts taking people to the guillotine (GIHL oh teen) became common. This killing machine had a large sharp blade held between two posts. When a cord was cut, the blade fell and chopped off the victim's head.

Soon the leaders were struggling for power among themselves. In 1799, Napoleon Bonaparte, the French general and military hero, seized control of the government. The French Revolution was over. But France did not yet have a democracy. Instead, it had a dictator.

Reforms in Europe

The revolution in France had not worked out as planned, but people throughout Europe were inspired to ask for more political power. They were now workers in factories that produced goods; they were con-

The storming of the Bastille. Arts: *Can you tell the artist's point of view by looking at this painting? Was he for or against the Revolution?*

sumers who spent their wages in the markets. More and more, they were important to their countries' economies. Their demands could no longer be ignored. Power came slowly, but it came. Britain's Reform Act of 1832 gave manufacturers and middle-class professionals the right to vote. The rulers of Western Europe wanted more wealth and more power. They looked around and saw what other parts of the world had to offer.

Lesson Review

1600	1675	1750	1825	1900

1600s
Scientific Revolution

1780s
Introduction of the steam engine

1789
French Revolution begins

1800s
Spread of the Industrial Revolution

1832
Britain's Reform Act

1 **Key Vocabulary:** Describe the "Age of Revolutions" using **scientific method, capitalism, labor force, constitutional monarchy,** and **nationalism.**

2 **Focus:** How did the Scientific Revolution change the way people studied and learned?

3 **Focus:** How did the Industrial Revolution affect daily life in England?

4 **Focus:** What were the goals and outcome of the French Revolution?

5 **Critical Thinking: Compare Then and Now** Choose an environmental issue of today and compare it with a similar one from the Industrial Revolution.

6 **Theme: Contact and Interaction** How did the Industrial Revolution improve and worsen public health in different places?

7 **Citizenship/Writing Activity:** Create a short bibliography of books about the French Revolution. Ask teachers and librarians for suggestions.

The Building of European Empires

Main Idea European countries competed for control of the world.

It was the early 1800s. The French attempt at democracy had ended with the dictator Napoleon in power. England and other European countries were fighting to stop France from expanding. They were fighting each other, too.

Who would control the world's trade? Which would be the most powerful nation? Could Europe's appetite for riches ever be satisfied?

In 1805, James Gillray drew the cartoon below. According to him, Great Britain and France were carving up the world as if it were a big plum pudding.

William Pitt (1759–1806), prime minister of Great Britain, on the left, and Napoleon I (1769–1821), emperor of France, carve up the globe between them. Their countries occupied a small geographical region, yet when they made war, the world felt it. Economics: *Why did European wars have an impact on the world?*

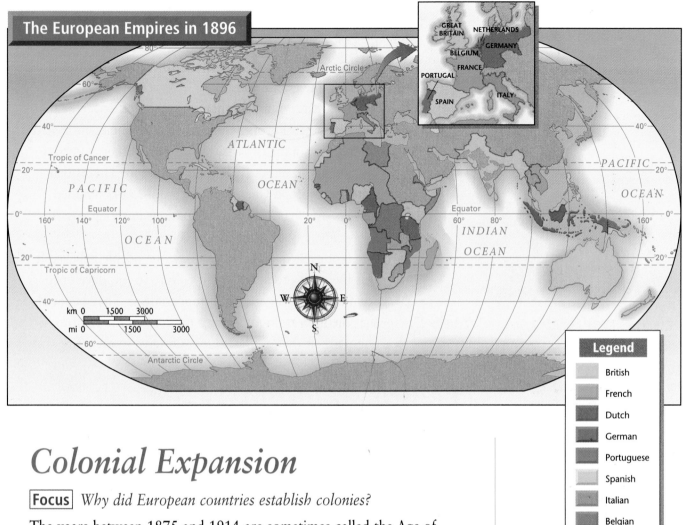

GREAT BRITAIN · NETHERLANDS
BELGIUM · GERMANY
FRANCE
PORTUGAL
SPAIN · ITALY

Arctic Circle

ATLANTIC OCEAN

PACIFIC OCEAN

Tropic of Cancer

PACIFIC OCEAN

Equator

Equator

INDIAN OCEAN

Tropic of Capricorn

km 0   1500   3000
mi 0   1500   3000

Antarctic Circle

Legend

British
French
Dutch
German
Portuguese
Spanish
Italian
Belgian

Colonial Expansion

Focus *Why did European countries establish colonies?*

The years between 1875 and 1914 are sometimes called the Age of Imperialism. When a country controls the affairs of one or more other countries by force, it is practicing **imperialism**. Imperialist countries are also called colonial powers, since they hold colonies. Just as Greece and Rome had done centuries earlier, by the end of the 1800s many nations of Europe had built large empires. As you can see in the cartoon to the left, the leaders of these nations were helping themselves to the portions of the world they wanted.

Europe Divides Up the World

How did the powers of Europe carve up the world? By the second half of the 19th century, France, Great Britain, Belgium, the German states, Portugal, Spain, and Italy had divided up most of Africa. Great Britain tightened its grip on India and the present-day countries of Myanmar (formerly Burma) and Malaysia. The Netherlands held on to the East Indies. France grabbed Indochina (Vietnam, Cambodia, and Laos). *(See the map above.)*

It was mostly economics that drove the European nations to build empires. They wanted mines and plantations that would supply raw

This map shows the portions of the world under the control of eight European nations near the end of the 1800s. **Map Skill:** *Which European countries had the largest empires at this time?*

materials for their growing factories. They wanted new places to sell the products their factories produced. They believed that for their economies to expand, their territories had to expand, too.

Competition among nations was another factor that contributed to European imperialism. If one country had colonies in southeast Asia, for instance, other countries became interested in colonizing there, too. The British statesman Joseph Chamberlain (1836–1914) summed matters up: "The day of small nations has long passed away. The day of Empires has come."

Not everyone agreed. While some people believed it was their duty to spread their culture to less developed countries, others condemned imperialism. They believed that the men and women of a nation had the right to choose their own representatives to govern them.

Europeans went to the colonies for a variety of reasons. Many hoped to advance their careers. Some were missionaries who wanted to spread Christianity. Others went in search of knowledge. These included naturalists like Maria Sybilla Merian (1647–1717). Her painting above was published in 1730.

The British in India

Focus *Why did Britain consider India "the jewel in the crown"?*

Most western European countries had empires, but — thanks to the valuable country of India — Great Britain's was the largest and wealthiest.

The British Empire

Great Britain is actually three countries — England, Wales, and Scotland — that share a single island. Wales and England came together in the 1500s, and Scotland joined them in 1707. Britain also controlled Ireland.

When Britain defeated France in the Seven Years' War (1756–1763), France gave up its colonies in India and North America, and Britain gained control. With no threatening French presence on the seas, Britain became active in the South Pacific and South Atlantic, along the coast of Africa, and in Asia. When Great Britain lost its 13 American colonies in 1783, it became more determined to conquer new territories and find new markets elsewhere.

By 1829 it was said that "the sun never set" on the British Empire. What does that mean? Because Great Britain's holdings were so vast, there was always sunlight in at least one part of the empire as the earth revolved. London was the center of international finance, and British goods dominated the world's markets.

The turmeric (TUR muhr ihk) root, *(below, top)*, the dried fruit of the cardamom (KAHR duh muhm) plant *(below, left)*, and the galangal (guh LANG guhl) root *(below, right)* are the kind of Indian spices that Europeans were looking for.

This period of Britain's great power is sometimes called the *Pax Britannica*, the Latin term for "British peace." During the Pax Britannica, Great Britain practiced imperialist policies without fear of challenge by other nations. The British Navy, the most powerful in the world, protected British interests around the globe. The Pax Britannica ended only when other nations reached Britain's level of industrial development.

The Jewel in the Crown

India was Great Britain's prize possession, "the jewel in the crown" *(see the map below)*. It was about the size of all of Europe, and it was rich in jewels, tea, cotton, and spices. The British East India Company was a large, successful company run by British businessmen. They had established trading posts in India in the 1600s, selling Indian spices, textiles, and other goods to Great Britain.

Until the early 1700s, the Mughal Empire ruled most of India. Following the death of the Mughal ruler in 1707, India fell into chaos. Rivalries among individual Indian rulers made it possible for a strong external power — Great Britain — to step in and take control.

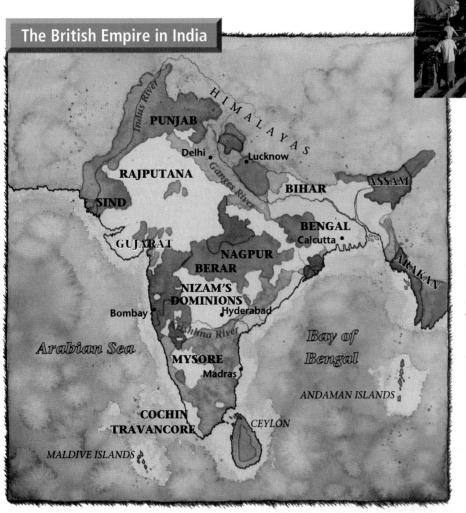

The British Empire in India

India was fragmented into many provinces and populated with many different kinds of peoples.

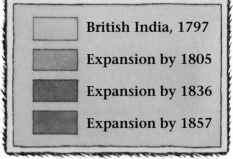

	British India, 1797
	Expansion by 1805
	Expansion by 1836
	Expansion by 1857

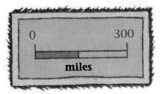

0   300
miles

This photograph shows Queen Victoria of England (1819–1901) (seated). She began her rule in 1837, while still a teenager. Forty years later she was given the additional title "Empress of India." Her long reign is known as England's Victorian Era.

The British East India Company built an army using Indian troops, called sepoys (SEE poyz). Worried about the growing power of the company, in 1773 the British government became directly involved in ruling India. It sent a series of **governors-general**, personal representatives from the king. These men set up the first Indian Civil Service, a bureaucracy staffed mostly by Indians.

The Indian Civil Service practically governed India. Most of the responsible positions in the service, however, were held by the British. The Indians resented this situation bitterly.

In 1857, a group of sepoys revolted. Hearing rumors that cartridges for new rifles had been smeared with pork and beef grease, the Indians refused to use them. (The Muslim religion forbids the eating of pork and the Hindus consider cows to be sacred.) Eighty-five sepoys were arrested and jailed. Other sepoys stormed the jail, released the prisoners, and set fire to their living quarters.

As Indian civilians joined in the fight against the British, the Sepoy Rebellion spread throughout northern and central India. The British were not able to put it down until the summer of 1858. Britain then closed the East India Company and took over control of the country. This marked the beginning of the British **raj**, or rule, over India.

Movement Toward Independence

Even after Britain restored peace in India in 1858, a gulf of suspicion and fear continued to separate the British from the Indians. British Queen Victoria created a new position, that of **viceroy**, to replace the governor-general as head of the Indian government. She also appointed a governor over each of the 11 provinces of British India. Her choices were always British citizens.

The Suez Canal connects the Mediterranean and Red seas. *(See the map in Chapter 17, page 458.)* The construction took 10 years to complete. After the canal opened in 1869, the British could travel to India in less than three weeks. Before, the trip around Africa to India took three months. **Geography:** *How do you think the Suez Canal changed relations between Britain and India?*

Hundreds of millions of Indians were now ruled by thousands of British officials. The British, living in suburbs completely separated from Indians, had social clubs and even railroad cars that were off-limits to Indians.

In 1876 Surendranath Banerjea (soo rayn dur NAHTH bayn ur JEE) helped found the Indian Association. A political organization, it brought together Hindus and Muslims. Indians now had a place to express their political views. Other organizations, such as the Indian National Congress, were also important in India's move toward independence. Largely through the work of Mohandas K. Gandhi (GAHN dee), India finally won its independence in 1947.

Entering the Modern World

During the Middle Ages, people's lives changed little. Despite frequent wars and famines, people lived nearly the same way for a thousand years.

Then things started to change. The Reformation changed the role of religion in people's lives. Revolutions occurred in the sciences, in the way people worked, and in the way they thought about government. By the time the 19th century had ended, exploration of the world had given way to imperialism. In the 20th century, empires collapsed and most colonized nations won independence.

Though the modern world is far different from the world of the past, some things have not changed greatly. In many places, people continue to work to solve problems that began centuries ago.

Biography

Gandhi

Some Indians began violent anti-British activities in the early 1900s. But it was the nonviolence and civil disobedience preached by Mohandas K. Gandhi (1869–1948) that finally drove the British out of India. Gandhi became head of the Indian National Congress, whose activities helped bring about India's independence.

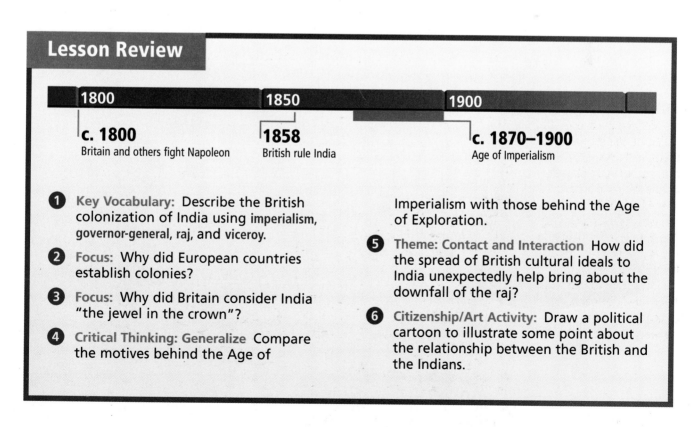

Lesson Review

1800	1850	1900

c. 1800
Britain and others fight Napoleon

1858
British rule India

c. 1870–1900
Age of Imperialism

❶ **Key Vocabulary:** Describe the British colonization of India using imperialism, governor-general, raj, and viceroy.

❷ **Focus:** Why did European countries establish colonies?

❸ **Focus:** Why did Britain consider India "the jewel in the crown"?

❹ **Critical Thinking: Generalize** Compare the motives behind the Age of

Imperialism with those behind the Age of Exploration.

❺ **Theme: Contact and Interaction** How did the spread of British cultural ideals to India unexpectedly help bring about the downfall of the raj?

❻ **Citizenship/Art Activity:** Draw a political cartoon to illustrate some point about the relationship between the British and the Indians.

Skills Workshop

Predicting Outcomes Using Maps

Look into the Future

In 1891, who could have guessed how much Africa would change under imperialism over the next twenty-three years? One way to predict the outcome of a changing situation is to look closely at existing **trends**. Studying maps that focus on the same subject area over time helps you see trends and make predictions about what might happen next.

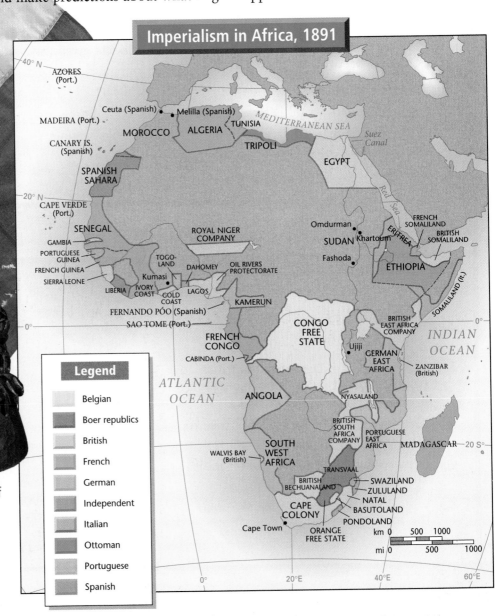

Imperialism in Africa, 1891

40° N

AZORES (Port.)

MADEIRA (Port.)

Ceuta (Spanish) • Melilla (Spanish)

MOROCCO   ALGERIA   TUNISIA   *MEDITERRANEAN SEA*   Suez Canal

CANARY IS. (Spanish)   TRIPOLI

SPANISH SAHARA   EGYPT

20° N

CAPE VERDE (Port.)

SENEGAL   ROYAL NIGER COMPANY   Omdurman   FRENCH SOMALILAND   BRITISH SOMALILAND

GAMBIA   SUDAN   Khartoum   ERITREA

PORTUGUESE GUINEA   TOGO-LAND   Fashoda   ETHIOPIA

FRENCH GUINEA   DAHOMEY   OIL RIVERS PROTECTORATE

SIERRA LEONE   Kumasi   SOMALILAND (It.)

LIBERIA   IVORY COAST   GOLD COAST   LAGOS   KAMERUN

FERNANDO PÓO (Spanish)   BRITISH EAST AFRICA COMPANY   INDIAN OCEAN

SAO TOME (Port.)   0°

0°   CONGO FREE STATE

FRENCH CONGO   Ujiji   GERMAN EAST AFRICA   ZANZIBAR (British)

CABINDA (Port.)

ATLANTIC OCEAN   ANGOLA   NYASALAND

BRITISH SOUTH AFRICA COMPANY   PORTUGUESE EAST AFRICA   MADAGASCAR — 20 S°

WALVIS BAY (British)   SOUTH WEST AFRICA

TRANSVAAL   SWAZILAND

BRITISH BECHUANALAND   ZULULAND   NATAL   BASUTOLAND

CAPE COLONY   PONDOLAND

Cape Town   ORANGE FREE STATE

km 0   500   1000
mi 0   500   1000

0°   20°E   40°E   60°E

Legend

- Belgian
- Boer republics
- British
- French
- German
- Independent
- Italian
- Ottoman
- Portuguese
- Spanish

This is an African statue of Queen Victoria.

1 Here's How

On these pages are maps of Africa in 1891 and 1914.

- Study both maps, note their titles, and read their legends. What is the main idea in these maps?

- Compare the maps. What do you notice that is the same on both? What has changed over time? What patterns do you notice? Identify the increases in European colonies on the 1914 map.

- Based on the trend shown in these maps, you can conclude that European empires expanded and strengthened between 1891 and 1914. You might then predict that this trend would continue in the years following 1914.

2 Think It Through

Suppose the main idea of these maps was to show areas of African independence. What if the trend were toward independence rather than imperialism? How would the maps look different?

3 Use It

1. What happened to Angola between 1891 and 1914? How might its borders change after 1914?

2. Based on these maps, what do you think might happen to Ethiopia and Liberia after 1914?

3. If you made a map of European imperialism in Africa after 1914, what European nations do you think would control the most African land?

4. Study maps of Africa from the 1920s and 1930s to prove or disprove your prediction.

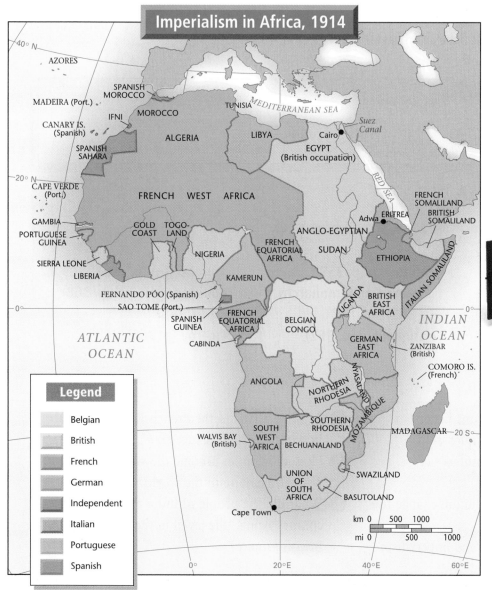

Imperialism in Africa, 1914

Legend
- Belgian
- British
- French
- German
- Independent
- Italian
- Portuguese
- Spanish

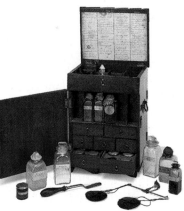

Until factors such as disease were brought under control, Europeans were unable to gain a foothold in African territory. This medicine chest contains quinine, which was very effective in treating malaria.

CHAPTER 13

Chapter Review

Chapter Review Timeline

1400 | 1500 | 1600 | 1700 | 1800 | 1900

- **1492** Columbus arrives in North America
- **1519** Cortés meets Montezuma
- **1780s** Introduction of steam engine
- **1789** The French Revolution begins
- **1800s** Spread of Industrial Revolution
- **1858** British rule India

Summarizing the Main Idea

1. Copy and complete the chart below, indicating a key person from each lesson and his or her accomplishment.

	Key Person	Accomplishment
Lesson 1		
Lesson 2		
Lesson 3		

Vocabulary

2. Using at least eight of the following terms, write a brief biography of an explorer, inventor or leader.

circumnavigate (p. 349)
indigenous (p. 352)
scientific method (p. 358)
labor force (p. 359)
capitalism (p. 359)
constitutional monarchy (p. 362)
nationalism (p. 362)
imperialism (p. 365)
governor-general (p. 368)
raj (p. 368)
viceroy (p. 368)

Reviewing the Facts

3. What were some of the reasons European royalty sponsored voyages of exploration?
4. What was Christopher Columbus's error, and how did it benefit Spain?
5. How did the Scientific Revolution change the world?
6. How were industrialization and imperialism connected?
7. In what ways did the French Revolution fail? In what ways did it succeed?
8. How did Britain become the wealthiest, most powerful empire in the world?
9. What did the people of India think of their country being "the jewel in the crown" of the British Empire?

10 Look at the two maps on pages 370–371. What happened to the Congo Free State? Predict what happened to Belgian colonies in the years following 1914. Study a map of Africa in the 1920s or 1930s to prove or disprove your prediction. Then look at a map of Africa today to find out what has happened to that part of Africa.

Geography Skills

11 Study the map on page 365, "European Empires." What problems might the countries of Europe face in controlling lands so far away?

12 Write two letters set at the time of the Industrial Revolution—one before a factory moves to your town, and one after. Describe the changes that have taken place.

Critical Thinking

13 **Conclude** Look at the map on page 365. Compare the sizes of the nations of Europe with the amount of land they controlled in their empires. How do you think they were able to control so much territory?

14 **Predict** Even though Galileo had to recant (or take back what he said), how do you think his discovery that the earth was not the center of the universe would affect the people of his day?

Writing: Citizenship and Economics

15 **Citizenship** Write a letter to Queen Victoria, or another ruler of the time, explaining your point of view on imperialism.

16 **Economics** Write out a conversation between a factory owner and one of the young children working in his factory.

Activities

History/Language Arts
Do research to find out more about one of the explorers, inventors, or political leaders mentioned in the chapter. Share your findings with the class in an illustrated lecture or dramatization.

Citizenship/Writing
Find out more about India's struggle for independence from Britain. Write a report describing Gandhi's role in the struggle. You may also compare it to the American War of Independence.

Internet Option

Check the **Internet Social Studies Center** for ideas on how to extend your theme project beyond your classroom.

THEME PROJECT CHECK-IN

Use the information about Europe in this chapter to finish your theme project.
- What would it have been like to explore a new land? What things might explorers have wanted to bring home with them?
- How did revolutions in science, industry, and politics affect European cultures?
- What cultural exchanges resulted from the growth of European empires?

5 Europe in the Modern Age

> "We are part of the community of Europe, and we must do our duty as such."

William Gladstone

· T H E M E ·

Separation and Union

❝ I think European people and countries learned they could accomplish more by working together instead of separately. ❞

Nakeisha Spears, Sixth Grade
Blountstown, FL

European nations led the world into two tragic world wars in the first half of the 20th century. Since then, they have learned that by working together, they can improve the lives of their people and ensure peace. The European Union is slowly weaving together a patchwork of nationalities, while other newly independent countries try to find their way alone. For all European countries, however, the quality of life is beginning to represent one of their most important concerns.

Theme Project

Guide to Separation and Union

Create a travel guide for a European country to illustrate how it has experienced separation and union.

- Construct a timeline that includes the major events in the country's history in the 20th century.
- Draw a diagram of the country's political system.
- Write an introduction about how this country has experienced separation and union.
- Draw a map that shows the major cities and geographic features.

RESEARCH: Collect facts on the major sites visited by tourists who come to this country.

◀ The Louvre Museum in Paris, France.

WHEN & WHERE
ATLAS

The map of Europe you see on these pages is very different from a map of this region in 1900. Two world wars swept the continent in the first half of the century. These wars killed millions of people, caused great destruction, and led to the end of some nations and the birth of new ones. The growth and death of communism also affected Europe in many important ways. In the aftermath of war and revolution, a new Europe has emerged — a Europe actively planning for its future.

In this unit, you will learn more about the geography of Europe. You will also read about the major historical events that affected the continent in the 20th century. Finally, you will learn more about the political, economic, and cultural life of Europe in detail by examining four European countries (shown in red).

Unit 5 Chapters

Chapter 14 Europe: An Overview
Chapter 15 Europe: Patterns of Living

GREENLAND

ICELAND

N
W ⊕ E
S

60°N

ATLANTIC

OCEAN

45°N

Legend

★ National capital

km 0 | 500 | 1000
mi 0 | 500 | 1000

30°N

45°W   30°W

Unit Timeline

| 1900 | 1920 | 1940 |

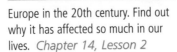

World War II   1939–1945

Europe in the 20th century. Find out why it has affected so much in our lives. *Chapter 14, Lesson 2*

Mikhail Gorbachev   1985

His reforms changed an entire political system. An empire collapsed. *Chapter 14, Lesson 2*

1960   **1980**   **2000**

The Berlin Wall   1989

When this wall came down, two halves of one country reunited.
Chapter 14, Lesson 2

The Streets of Prague

Now Eastern Europe is blossoming with freedom. *Chapter 15, Lesson 1*

Canals in Amsterdam

Old ways of life have been preserved thanks to people acting together.
Chapter 15, Lesson 3

Europe: An Overview

Chapter Preview: *People, Places, and Events*

1900	1920	1940

The Swiss Alps

Mountains form natural borders between many countries in Europe. *Lesson 1, Page 380*

European Trade

Rivers and canals provide convenient transportation. *Lesson 1, Page 381*

World War I   1914–1918

Find out why World War I was called the "Great War." *Lesson 2, Page 389*

The Geography of Europe

Main Idea Europe's geographical features and natural resources have helped the region thrive.

The choppy waters of the English Channel have challenged travelers and traders for centuries. Today, travel across the Channel — a narrow stretch of ocean that divides the British Isles from the rest of Europe — is faster and more convenient than ever before. This geographic barrier between Britain and France suddenly seemed to grow smaller when the Channel Tunnel, or "Chunnel," opened in 1994.

At Waterloo train station in London, England, a group of passengers steps aboard a train bound for France. Approximately one hour later, the train is speeding through a tunnel 146 feet beneath the floor of the English Channel. The train crosses beneath the Channel in about half an hour, arriving in Paris less than two hours later. The travelers have not seen a drop of ocean water the entire way.

◀ The Eiffel Tower, built in 1889, in Paris, France, was designed for the modern age.

1960	1980	2000

The Russian Revolution 1917

What happened after the Russian Revolution? *Lesson 2, Page 390*

World War II   1939–1945

This man predicted victory for Britain in World War II. What was the U.S. role? *Lesson 2, Page 392*

The Cold War   1945–1989

Removing pieces of the Berlin Wall — a highlight of 1989. *Lesson 2, Page 394*

Geography and Natural Boundaries

Ask Yourself

Europe is the second smallest continent, but it has one of the world's largest populations — more than 700 million people. That's an average of more than 180 people per square mile. Which geographical regions of Europe do you think have the greatest numbers of people?

? ? ? ? ? ? ? ? ? ? ? ?

This map shows the major geographic features of Europe, including mountains, rivers, and plains. **Map Skill:** *Find the Great European Plain. What rivers flow through it?*

Focus *What effects have Europe's main geographic features had on the region?*

Many geographic barriers in Europe separate one group of people from another. Mountain ranges, such as the Pyrenees and the Alps, extend across much of the continent, as you can see on the map below. The mountain ranges are one reason why Europe is divided into many different countries, each with its own language and culture.

Although the mountains divide one country from another, traders and explorers long ago discovered passes through the snow-covered peaks. In 218 B.C., the Carthaginian general, Hannibal *(see Chapter 9),* took an army of 40,000 men and a small troop of elephants across the Alps. They traveled through Spain, southern France, and Italy. Today, giant bulldozers have helped to build tunnels and elevated highways that allow a quick, safe journey through the mountains in most seasons. The high mountain roads still remain a challenge, however. The best sports cars in Europe are tested on these winding roads. Many roads are closed in severe winter weather and are prone to rock- and mudslides.

The Geography of Europe

Not all of Europe is mountainous. The map on the opposite page shows a vast flat area, called the Great European Plain, extending from the west coast of France to the Ural Mountains. This plain has some of the finest farmland in the world. It presents few barriers to travel. Since earliest times, the Great European Plain has made communication and travel within northern Europe relatively easy.

Europe's most important transportation advantage is its system of wide, navigable rivers, such as the Rhine and the Danube. You can trace some of the major European rivers on the map on the previous page. Barges and ships, loaded with coal, oil, automobiles, and other products, travel these rivers from one city or country to another. A system of canals connects one river with another, and the rivers connect the interior with the coast. Manufactured goods and resources can be shipped easily to other regions of the world. For example, toy dolls and canned hams can travel by ship from a city in the middle of Poland all the way to London.

Canals and rivers are vitally important to European trade. **Economics:** *Why is it easier and cheaper to transport goods by water instead of using a combination of water and land transport?*

How a Lock Works

To use a canal system, boats must travel through locks, since some rivers and canals lie at higher levels of elevation than others. The chart below shows how locks work when a ship moves to a lower water level. The same process works in reverse when a ship moves to a higher level. Water flows in and out of the locks by gravity. **Chart Skill:** *Under what circumstances are locks necessary?*

1 First, the gates open and the ship enters the lock from upstream. The gates shut behind the ship.

2 After the gates are shut, water is let out of the lock through openings called sluices (SLEW sez). Gradually the water lowers in the lock.

3 When the water level within the lock is the same as the water level downstream, the gates open and the ship passes into the lower channel.

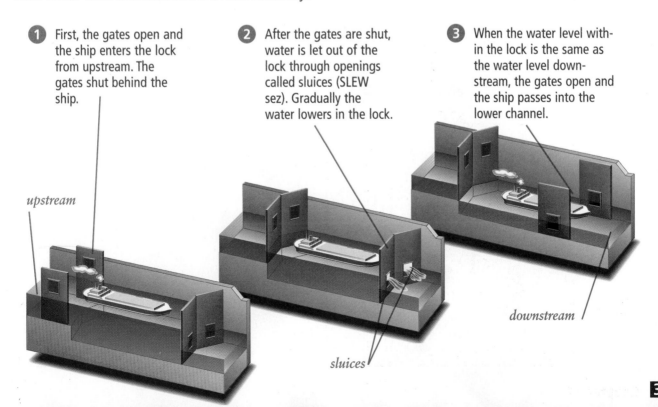

upstream

sluices

downstream

Many of the traditional foods of Europe are made from products unknown there 500 years ago. Tomatoes, corn, and potatoes all came from the Americas. Europeans combined these foods with regional ingredients to create such dishes as pizza (Italy) and fried potatoes (France).

European breads such as the English scone, the French baguette, and the German pretzel have become popular around the world.

Europe's Natural Resources and Products

Focus *How has Europe used its natural resources and geography to develop into a wealthy region?*

Although much of Europe lies as far north as Newfoundland, the climate is not bitterly cold. A branch of the **Gulf Stream**, a warm-water ocean current that starts in the western Caribbean Sea, warms the air. Moist winds off the Atlantic bring frequent rain. Most of western Europe has a **marine climate**, with relatively mild winters and cool summers. Farther away from the Gulf Stream, eastern European countries have a **continental climate**, with short, hot summers and long, cold winters. Most of the Great European Plain has a mild marine climate that allows a long growing season. Wheat fields, fruit orchards, and vineyards flourish in the rich soil.

Today, the population of Europe is so large that it consumes most of the food it produces. Originally, however, farmers in Europe had a surplus of food. Surplus food meant that some people could specialize in jobs other than farming. Specialization of labor *(see Chapter 3)* led to the development of cities, and the cities eventually became resources for industry. This growth is shown on the diagram on the next page.

Over the centuries, many unique cultures have developed within Europe's relatively small geographic boundaries. Like cultures all over the world, each grows or prepares certain agricultural and dairy products. Many of these products, such as Spanish olives, Italian pasta, Belgian chocolate, and Swiss cheese, are famous

The Growth of Cities Through Agriculture

1 Farming communities develop on rich, fertile plains.

2 Agricultural surplus supports growth of cities and their populations.

3 Growth of cities creates environment for development of industry.

4 Europeans trade their products and import more resources from abroad.

5 European interior also provides resources for industry. Pollution.

for their high quality and are exported around the world. Each country has its own style of cooking and preparing food, called its **cuisine** (kwih ZEEN). Regions can be defined by their cuisine, which usually makes good use of local produce.

Hidden deep under the soil of Europe are large deposits of minerals such as coal and iron ore. During the Industrial Revolution, these resources helped to make Europe a leading center of manufacturing and trade. Although Europe's mineral resources have brought wealth, they have also led to conflicts. Each country has wanted to have as many resources as possible. In the 20th century, disagreements about land and resources have caused two world wars. Today, however, the nations of Europe are discovering that they are more prosperous when they work together. They are learning ways to share their resources.

The chart above shows how cities developed in Europe. **Chart Skill:** *Think about how cities developed in the United States. Make a chart that shows their development.*

Lesson Review: Geography

1 **Key Vocabulary:** Write a paragraph for a travel advertisement for Europe using the following terms: **marine and continental climates, Gulf Stream, cuisine.**

2 **Focus:** What effects have Europe's main geographic features had on the region?

3 **Focus:** How has Europe used its natural resources and geography to develop into a wealthy region?

4 **Critical Thinking: Cause and Effect** What role has agriculture played in the development of cities and industry in Europe?

5 **Theme: Union and Separation** Give some geographic reasons for the variety of cultures within Europe.

6 **Geography/Research Activity:** Research Europe's extensive river and canal system and explain why it continues to be so heavily used today.

Understanding Seasons

Long Days, Short Nights

If you visited northern Norway in the summer, you would never see the sun set. In the middle of winter, it would be dark all the time. How can this be? When it's summer in Norway, why is it winter in New Zealand? These changes are caused by the tilt of the earth and the earth's rotation around the sun. Understanding the relationship of the earth and sun helps you understand more about seasons and climate.

Night and Day

Each day, the earth spins once around its axis, giving us night and day.

March

June

September

Around the Sun

Each year, the earth travels one full circle around the sun. This orbit, combined with the earth's tilt, is what causes different seasons. European temperatures are warmest in summer because this is when the Northern Hemisphere tilts toward the sun.

1 Here's How

Study the diagram below. It shows the earth's orbit around the sun. Find Europe in the Northern Hemisphere in each month.

- Notice that in December, the North Pole tilts away from the sun. In which direction does the South Pole tilt? What does this tell you about the seasons in the different hemispheres in December? In June?

- Notice that the North Pole is in darkness in December. Because of the earth's tilt, the closer to the North Pole you go in December, the shorter the days and the longer the nights become. What happens at the North Pole in June?

- To find out why it is cooler at the poles than anywhere else on earth — even in summer when there is 24 hours of daylight — study the diagram on the right. Because of the angle of the sun's rays, the coldest climates are near the poles. The warmest climates are near the equator.

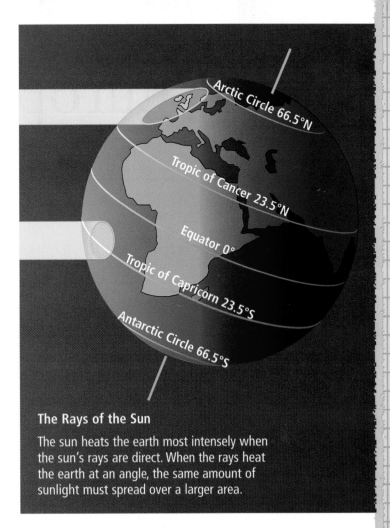

The Rays of the Sun

The sun heats the earth most intensely when the sun's rays are direct. When the rays heat the earth at an angle, the same amount of sunlight must spread over a larger area.

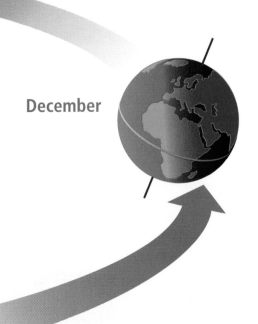

December

The Earth's Tilt

The earth is tilted as it revolves around the sun. Its tilt never changes. As well as causing different seasons, the tilt causes variations in the number of daylight hours from winter to summer. European temperatures are coldest in winter because this is when the Northern Hemisphere tilts away from the sun.

2 Think It Through

If the earth did not tilt, how would that change summers and winters at the poles?

3 Use It

1 In the diagram on the left, study the earth in June. Which hemisphere tilts toward the sun? Which tilts away from the sun? What season is it in each hemisphere in June?

2 When it is winter in Europe, in what continents is it summer?

3 Why are winters in Norway colder than winters in Spain?

4 In summer, why are there more hours of daylight per day in Norway than there are in Spain?

5 Compare a country in northern Europe with a country in southern Europe. Describe how they would be different in summer and winter.

Europe in the Modern Era

Main Idea War and tension divided Europe throughout most of the 20th century. Today, with many of these tensions gone, Europe hopes for peace and cooperation among nations.

Key Vocabulary

allies

communism

propaganda

anti-Semitism

Holocaust

Cold War

Key Events

1914–1918 World War I

1917 Russian Revolution

1939–1945 World War II

1961 Berlin Wall built

1989 Berlin Wall torn down

"You are free to go!" the government declared on the television's evening news. It was November 9, 1989, in East Berlin. The unthinkable was about to happen: The Berlin Wall began to come down.

The people of East Germany had been literally imprisoned in their own country. The symbol of their imprisonment was the Berlin Wall, built by the East German government beginning in 1961. The Wall cut the city of Berlin in two, separating Communist East Berlin from democratic West Berlin. Guarded by dogs and by soldiers with machine guns, the Wall cast a dark shadow on all who lived near it.

After the government's announcement, West Germans stood atop the Berlin Wall, celebrating. They shouted and sang as East Germans streamed past the border guards into West Berlin. Old friends and family members reunited joyfully. Many people shed tears.

This was a truly historic event, not just for the Germans but for people all over the world. The many years of tension between Communist and democratic countries were nearly over.

Hundreds of East and West Berliners gathered at the Berlin Wall in November of 1989 to celebrate the news that the Wall would soon come down. Their city would no longer be divided.

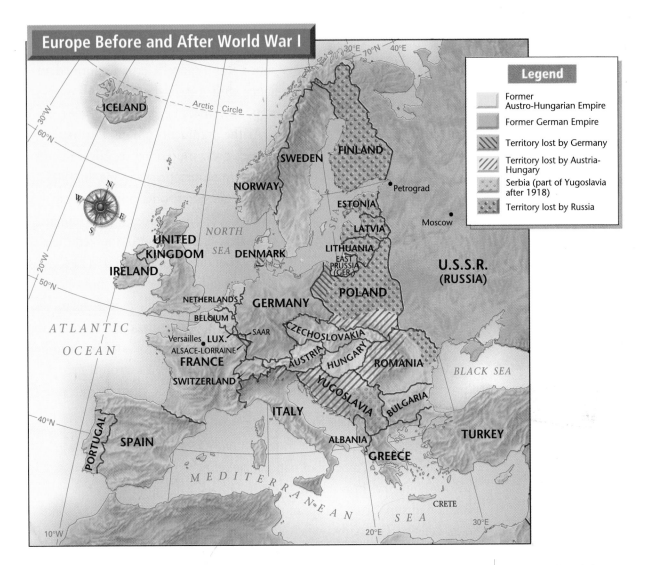

Europe Before and After World War I

Legend

- Former Austro-Hungarian Empire
- Former German Empire
- Territory lost by Germany
- Territory lost by Austria-Hungary
- Serbia (part of Yugoslavia after 1918)
- Territory lost by Russia

World War I

Focus *What caused the outbreak of World War I, and what was the result of the war?*

Conflicts existed among the major European powers long before the Berlin Wall was built. In the 19th century, the Industrial Revolution and prosperous trade with colonies brought great wealth to Europe. Many European nations, especially Great Britain, France, and Germany, became extremely powerful. Their power brought many disputes, however. The nations argued among themselves over ownership and control of certain territories and resources.

One particularly bitter argument arose between France and Germany. Both nations wanted to control a region in northeastern France called Alsace-Lorraine, a land rich in iron ore deposits.

Fearful of struggles like this one, European leaders formed close associations, called alliances, with other countries, agreeing to provide military support to one another if necessary. Countries that formed alliances

This map shows the many changes to the face of Europe after World War I. **Map Skill:** *What countries lost the most territory after World War I?*

This political cartoon shows how the alliance system worked. Each country says it will defend another in case of attack. The countries shown are (from left to right) Serbia, Austria-Hungary, Russia, Germany, France, and Britain. History: *Find Germany in the cartoon. Which country does Germany say it will defend?*

Curious Facts

The first funny cartoons were political cartoons. They began 300 years ago as detailed, exaggerated drawings that made fun of serious issues or important people. By the 19th century, political cartoons were a popular feature in newspapers and magazines.

were called **allies**. Great Britain formed an alliance with France. Germany formed an alliance with Austria-Hungary. All over Europe, countries began to take sides.

As the arguments among European countries grew more intense, governments spent more money on weapons. In 1905, Britain began work on a powerful new warship called the dreadnought. Germany and Austria-Hungary both doubled their military spending from 1910 to 1914.

Meanwhile, a nationalist movement was underway, fueling this race for weapons. Nationalism is a feeling of deep loyalty to one's nation. It is also the belief that people who share the same culture and language should have their own nation and be ruled by their own people, not by a foreign power. Some cultural groups in Europe, such as the Serbs, wanted their independence from foreign rule.

A War to End All Wars?

In this touchy situation, all it took was one event to spark all-out war. On June 28, 1914, a Serbian nationalist shot the future emperor of Austria-Hungary. In response, Austria-Hungary declared war on Serbia. Russia had supported Serbia in the past and therefore prepared to come to its defense. Germany, which had an alliance with Austria-Hungary, declared war on Russia. In a short while, all the European allies of these warring nations were involved. World War I had begun.

Most of World War I was fought in Europe. However, the war disrupted the lives of many people around the globe, especially in European colonies in India, Africa, and South America.

For most of the war, the German army faced the British and French in the fields of France and Belgium. Hundreds of thousands of men lost their lives there, in useless attempts to advance a few hundred yards at a time. This was the first war that used weapons of mass destruction such as machine guns and poison gas. The armies were deadlocked for three and one-half years, with neither side advancing.

The United States did not fight for most of World War I. However, in 1917, Germany announced that it would attack any ships bringing supplies to its enemies. When Germany attacked American supply ships and ocean liners on their way to Britain, the United States broke off relations with Germany and entered the war in 1917.

United States involvement was a turning point in the war. Germany, by now exhausted, was forced to negotiate peace. On November 11, 1918, at 11 A.M., World War I came to an end. A peace treaty, called the

ON HER THEIR LIVES DEPEND

WOMEN MUNITION WORKERS

Enrol at once

Treaty of Versailles (ver SIGH), was signed at the Palace of Versailles, France. The so-called "Great War" had cost the lives of more than eight million soldiers, including about 126,000 American soldiers. In Europe, an entire generation of young men was gone.

The Russian Revolution

"We want bread!" shouted the crowd outside the royal palace in Petrograd (St. Petersburg), Russia's capital, in March of 1917. The winter was bitterly cold, and many people starved. World War I demanded more and more weapons, food, and soldiers. Goods could not be produced fast enough to feed, clothe, and arm the troops. Many soldiers went hungry or had to fight without shoes in the freezing winter. Many Russians felt that their king, Czar Nicholas II, had failed them.

In the spring of 1917, organized groups of workers overthrew the czar and his government and established a weak temporary government. Then, on November 7, 1917, a crowd of people took over the Winter Palace, the czar's former home, and overthrew that government.

One of the leaders of this revolution was Vladimir Lenin. Lenin believed that the best path for Russia was a system called communism. He told the people that under **communism**, the people would own all the land and factories and run the government. He promised that he would give the people peace, land, and bread.

During World War I, soldiers had to live and fight in trenches, or deep ditches. These British soldiers *(above)* are climbing out of a trench in France.

On the home front, many women worked in weapons factories. Posters like this one urged women to "enroll at once" and support the war effort. **Art:** *Research other posters from World War I or World War II.*

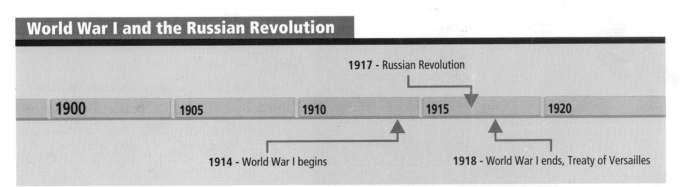

World War I and the Russian Revolution

1917 - Russian Revolution

| 1900 | 1905 | 1910 | 1915 | 1920 |

1914 - World War I begins

1918 - World War I ends, Treaty of Versailles

After World War II, the Soviet Union tried to improve its economy. The government celebrated the importance of work with posters like this one, which says "Let's all get to work, comrades." **Economics:** *Do you think that posters like this one can help improve a nation's economy?*

Hitler often spoke to his followers at huge rallies like this one, which took place in 1938.

Lenin and his political party, the Bolsheviks, took control of Russia. Then Lenin signed a peace treaty with Germany. Russia was out of World War I, but it faced a civil war. After nearly three years, Lenin and his forces defeated the czar's supporters. Lenin took over Russia's separate republics and formed the Union of Soviet Socialist Republics, or Soviet Union. Instead of letting the people govern, as promised, only Lenin and his supporters ruled.

World War II

[Focus] *What were the causes and results of World War II?*

In 1923, German factory workers pushed wheelbarrows full of money when they went home from work. The thousands of bills represented one week's pay. In a desperate effort to pay the country's debts, the government had printed too much money. Now all that money was practically worthless, and the German economy was in crisis.

Germany's economic problems were caused in part by the Treaty of Versailles. The treaty forced Germany to give up all the land it had occupied in World War I. It also forced Germany to pay large sums of money for war damages. As the German economy collapsed, some Germans grasped at desperate solutions.

The Rise of the Nazi Party

Many Germans thought that a new German political party, known as the National Socialist Party, was the answer to Germany's problems. The Nazi Party, as it was called, was headed by a man named Adolf Hitler.

Hitler told Germans to believe they were superior to people of other nationalities. To many Germans, shamed by their defeat in the last war and frustrated by a failing economy, the idea of German superiority was appealing. Hitler also led the Germans to believe they could blame someone for Germany's problems. He said that Germany's Jewish population was inferior and he accused Jews of destroying the German nation. These lies were a form of **propaganda**, which is slanted and exaggerated information organized to reflect a particular view or belief.

In the 1930s, Germany's economy collapsed. By 1933, Hitler became the leader of Germany. Again, Hitler blamed Germany's problems on the Jews. He seized their busi-

World War II Battles of Operation

Legend
- Allied countries
- Germany 1942-1945
- Other Axis countries and occupied areas
- Neutral countries
- ★ Major battle

ICELAND

NORWAY
SWEDEN
FINLAND
Leningrad

UNITED KINGDOM
IRELAND
DENMARK
Moscow
U.S.S.R.
Kursk July 1943
Stalingrad

NETHERLANDS
London
BELGIUM
Berlin
Warsaw
GERMANY
Battle of the Bulge December 1944
SLOVAKIA

ATLANTIC OCEAN

Invasion of Normandy June 6, 1944
Paris
SWITZERLAND
HUNGARY
Yalta
BLACK SEA

FRANCE
ITALY
YUGOSLAVIA
ROMANIA

Rhone Valley Invasion
Rome
Cassino November 1943
ALBANIA
BULGARIA
TURKEY

PORTUGAL
SPAIN
Anzio January 1944
Salerno September 1943
SICILY
GREECE
Invasion of Sicily July-August 1943
SYRIA
LEBANON
PALESTINE
TRANSJORDAN

Kasserine Pass February 1943
MOROCCO
TUNISIA
ALGERIA
LIBYA
El Alamein
EGYPT
Suez Canal

km 0 250 500
mi 0 250 500

This map shows the political positions of the European nations in World War II, and the locations of major battles in the second half of the war. **Map Skill:** *Compare this map with the map on page 387. What countries' borders are the same? What borders are different?*

The Nazis ordered all Jews to wear a gold Star of David with the word *Jude* (Jew) written on it. Few people survived the Nazi concentration camps. This woman and child were photographed a few months before the war's end at Auschwitz, one of the largest camps, where three million people died.

nesses and property, keeping their money for himself. He forced them to live in closed-off areas of the city called ghettos (GET ohz). Hitler and his followers spread hatred for Jews. This hatred is called **anti-Semitism**.

Europe at War Again

Hitler believed that Germany was entitled to win back by force the land it had lost at the end of World War I. He seized control of Austria and then part of Czechoslovakia in 1938. In 1939, Germany invaded Poland. Two days later, France and Britain declared war on Germany. By the spring of 1940, Germany had overrun Denmark, Norway, the Netherlands, Belgium, and Luxembourg. France fell to the Nazis soon afterward. For a time, Hitler and his allies had complete control over much of Europe.

During World War II, Hitler and his followers decided to get rid of all European Jews and other people they hated. They ordered millions of Jews, Gypsies, disabled

Many European cities were heavily bombed during World War II. Millions of people died and beautiful old buildings were destroyed. This is what the city of Nuremberg, Germany, looked like in 1945. **Arts:** *Research a town or city in Europe. What did it look like in 1900 and 1945? What does it look like today?*

people, political prisoners, and other groups from all over Europe to be taken to concentration camps in Germany and Eastern Europe. There, millions were deliberately killed. Others starved to death or died from disease. This massacre of Jews and others by the Nazis has come to be called the **Holocaust**.

The United States Enters the War

At first the United States tried to stay out of the European conflict. But Japan, an ally of Germany, grew more aggressive. Japan wanted scrap metal and oil from the United States to make into weapons. When the United States decided to stop shipping these goods to Japan, relations between the two countries became very tense. On a quiet, sunny December morning in 1941, Japanese warplanes began dropping bombs on Pearl Harbor, a United States military base in Hawaii. The base exploded into smoke and flames. After the bombing of Pearl Harbor, the United States entered the war.

Newspaper headlines proclaim the long-awaited news: Victory in Europe! **History:** *What was V-J day?*

World War II was fought primarily in two places — in Europe and in the Pacific. However, terrible battles were fought in the Soviet Union, East and Southeast Asia, Africa, and the Middle East. An estimated 15 to 20 million military personnel and 25 million civilians lost their lives.

After six horrible years, the

European conflict ended with the surrender of Germany in the spring of 1945. The war in the Pacific dragged on through the summer. Then, in early August, the United States dropped atomic bombs on two Japanese cities, Hiroshima and Nagasaki, killing thousands of people. Japan surrendered within a week.

The Cold War and the Fall of Communism

Focus *What was the Cold War, and what events led to the fall of communism?*

At the end of World War II, nations around the world agreed that such a war must never happen again. They discussed how to prevent a future world conflict. In 1945, 50 nations signed a charter establishing an organization called the United Nations. They hoped the United Nations would help to keep international peace and security.

New tensions began to develop. Germany was divided by the victors into four zones. The American, French, and British zones united into a democratic republic called West Germany. The fourth zone, East Germany, became a Communist republic with strong ties to the Soviet Union. The city of Berlin was divided between East and West Germany.

Meanwhile, the Soviet Communist government, led by the dictator Josef Stalin, claimed Poland, Hungary, and other Eastern European lands. These countries became joined with the Soviet Union in a forced economic and military union. The entire "Eastern Bloc" was an empire where the daily life of all people was determined by the government. Opposing political parties or disagreeing opinions were not permitted.

In 1946, Winston Churchill, former prime minister of Great Britain, described the situation in Europe. He said that an "iron curtain" had descended across the continent. This iron curtain shut off the Communist countries in the east from the freedoms of countries in Western Europe.

It soon became clear that the world's superpowers had organized

Biography

Winston Churchill

Winston Churchill was a distinguished British prime minister during World War II. As a child he was a poor student, but he later became an excellent soldier, writer, painter, and statesman. His brave deeds as a soldier helped him win his first political office. Churchill's speeches during World War II inspired all of Britain. He warned that war would bring them "blood, sweat, toil, and tears."

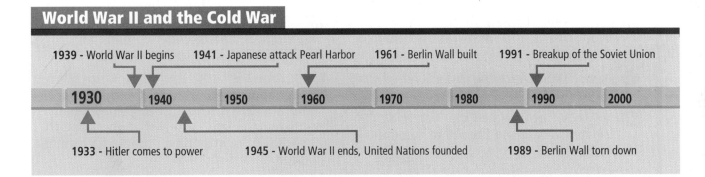

World War II and the Cold War

1939 - World War II begins   1941 - Japanese attack Pearl Harbor   1961 - Berlin Wall built   1991 - Breakup of the Soviet Union

1930   1940   1950   1960   1970   1980   1990   2000

1933 - Hitler comes to power   1945 - World War II ends, United Nations founded   1989 - Berlin Wall torn down

Mikhail Gorbachev

The son of farmers, Mikhail Gorbachev grew up in a country village and went to local schools. After studying law at Moscow State University, he went into politics. He was made head of the Communist Party in 1985. His name became well known in the West when he undertook a series of reforms that led to the eventual collapse of the Soviet Union in 1991.

into two enemy groups. One was composed of the democratic western countries, which formed an alliance called the North Atlantic Treaty Organization, or NATO. The Communist countries of Eastern Europe and the Soviet Union formed an alliance, known as the Warsaw Pact.

The two alliances were heavily armed with nuclear weapons. For the next 40 years, the threat of a nuclear war hung over the world. Since full-scale war never broke out, this period became known as the **Cold War**.

During the Cold War, the Western European countries slowly recovered from World War II. However, the Communist countries did not prosper. Their government-controlled economies gradually failed. People suffered from shortages of food and basic supplies. By the late 1980s, more and more people began to protest.

In 1985 Mikhail Gorbachev (meh KHYLE GAWR buh chawf) took power in the Soviet Union. He began reforms that led to the end of the Communist system. In 1989, the Communist governments of Poland and Czechoslovakia crumbled, the East German Communist government fell, and the Berlin Wall was torn down. By 1991, the Soviet Union's Communist government gave up its power. The iron curtain had been lifted.

Since the end of the Cold War, NATO's role in Europe has shifted. For example, in the late 1990s NATO played a key role in the conflicts in former Yugoslavia. Also, three nations of the former Warsaw Pact — Poland, Hungary, and the Czech Republic — joined NATO in March 1999. NATO's new role has caused people to wonder about its future.

Lesson Review

1900	1925	1950	1975	2000

1914–1918
World War I

1917
Russian Revolution

1939–1945
World War II

1961
Berlin Wall built

1989
Berlin Wall torn down

1 Key Vocabulary: Write a paragraph about World War II using these key vocabulary words: **propaganda, anti-Semitism, Holocaust**.

2 Focus: What caused the outbreak of World War I, and what was the result of the war?

3 Focus: What were the causes and results of World War II?

4 Focus: What was the Cold War, and what events led to the fall of communism?

5 Critical Thinking: Cause and Effect What do you think are the advantages of the end of the Cold War for Eastern European countries?

6 Theme: Union and Separation How did alliances lead to wider conflicts in Europe?

7 Citizenship/Writing Activity: Write a letter applying to a student exchange program with a school in eastern Germany. Explain in your letter what you hope to learn from attending school in a former communist country.

Number the Stars

A novel by Lois Lowry

The European country of Denmark was invaded and occupied by the Nazis on April 9, 1940. The Germans promised that the Danish government could remain, and the small country did not resist the invasion. However, throughout World War II, Danish citizens challenged Nazi control in many ways. When, in 1943, Danish Jews were forcibly deported to be executed in gas chambers, many Danes helped the Jews escape to freedom in Sweden. Some Danes also protected Jews in their homes. The following excerpt describes how one family in Copenhagen, Denmark's capital city, protected their daughter's friend Ellen from Nazi soldiers by pretending that Ellen was a member of their own family.

Historical Fiction

rationed— distributed in limited amounts because of wartime shortages

Annemarie eased the bedroom door open quietly, only a crack, and peeked out. Behind her, Ellen was sitting up, her eyes wide.

She could see Mama and Papa in their nightclothes, moving about. Mama held a lighted candle, but as Annemarie watched, she went to a lamp and switched it on. It was so long a time since they had dared to use the strictly rationed electricity after dark that the light in the room seemed startling to Annemarie, watching through the slightly opened bedroom door. She saw her mother look automatically to the blackout curtains, making certain that they were tightly drawn.

Papa opened the front door to the soldiers.

"This is the Johansen apartment?" A deep voice asked the question loudly, in the terribly accented Danish.

German troops marching in Denmark on April 9, 1940, the first day of German occupation.

"Our name is on the door, and I see you have a flashlight," Papa answered. "What do you want? Is something wrong?"

"I understand you are a friend of your neighbors the Rosens, Mrs. Johansen," the soldier said angrily.

"Sophy Rosen is my friend, that is true," Mama said quietly. "Please, could you speak more softly? My children are asleep."

"Then you will be so kind as to tell me where the Rosens are." He made no effort to lower his voice.

"I assume they are at home, sleeping. It is four in the morning, after all," Mama said.

Annemarie heard the soldier stalk across the living room toward the kitchen. From her hiding place in the narrow sliver of open doorway, she could see the heavy uniformed man, a holstered pistol at his waist, in the entrance to the kitchen, peering in toward the sink.

Another German voice said, "The Rosens' apartment is empty. We are wondering if they might be visiting their good friends the Johansens."

"Well," said Papa, moving slightly so that he was standing in front of Annemarie's bedroom door, and she could see nothing except the dark blur of his back, "as you see, you are mistaken. There is no one here but my family."

"You will not object if we look around." The voice was harsh, and it was not a question.

"It seems we have no choice," Papa replied.

"Please don't wake my children," Mama requested again. "There is no need to frighten little ones."

The heavy, booted feet moved across the floor again and into the other bedroom. A closet door opened and closed with a bang.

Annemarie eased her bedroom door closed silently. She stumbled through the darkness to the bed.

"Ellen," she whispered urgently, "take your necklace off!"

Ellen's hands flew to her neck. Desperately she began trying to unhook the tiny clasp. Outside the bedroom door, the harsh voices and heavy footsteps continued.

"I can't get it open!" Ellen said frantically. "I never take it off — I can't even remember how to open it!"

Annemarie heard a voice just outside the door. "What is here?"

"Shhh," her mother replied. "My daughters' bedroom. They are sound asleep."

"Hold still," Annemarie commanded. "This will hurt." She grabbed the little gold chain, yanked with all her strength, and broke it. As the door opened and light flooded into the bedroom, she crumpled it into her hand and closed her fingers tightly.

Terrified, both girls looked up at the three Nazi officers who entered the room.

One of the men aimed a flashlight around the bedroom. He went to the closet and looked inside. Then with a sweep of his gloved hand he pushed to the floor several coats and a bathrobe that hung from pegs on the wall.

There was nothing else in the room except a chest of drawers, the blue decorated trunk in the corner, and a heap of Kirsti's dolls piled in a small rocking chair. The flashlight beam touched each thing in turn. Angrily the officer turned toward the bed.

"Get up!" he ordered. "Come out here!"

Trembling, the two girls rose from the bed and followed him, brushing past the two remaining officers in the doorway, to the living room.

Annemarie looked around. These three uniformed men were different from the ones on the street corners. The street soldiers were often young,

German troops leaving Denmark after Germany's surrender in May 1945.

sometimes ill at ease, and Annemarie remembered how the Giraffe had, for a moment, let his harsh pose slip and had smiled at Kirsti.

But these men were older and their faces were set with anger.

Her parents were standing beside each other, their faces tense, but Kirsti was nowhere in sight. Thank goodness that Kirsti slept through almost everything. If they had wakened her, she would be wailing — or worse, she would be angry, and her fists would fly.

"Your names?" the officer barked.

"Annemarie Johansen. And this is my sister — "

"Quiet! Let her speak for herself. Your name?" He was glaring at Ellen.

Ellen swallowed. "Lise," she said, and cleared her throat. "Lise Johansen."

The officer stared at them grimly.

"Now," Mama said in a strong voice, "you have seen that we are not hiding anything. May my children go back to bed?"

The officer ignored her. Suddenly he grabbed a handful of Ellen's hair. Ellen winced.

He laughed scornfully. "You have a blond child sleeping in the other room. And you have this blond daughter —" He gestured toward Annemarie with his head. "Where did you get the dark-haired one?" He twisted the lock of Ellen's hair. "From a different father? From the milk-man?"

Papa stepped forward. "Don't speak to my wife in such a way. Let go of my daughter or I will report you for such treatment."

"Or maybe you got her someplace else?" the officer continued with a sneer. "From the Rosens?"

For a moment no one spoke. Then Annemarie, watching in panic, saw her father move swiftly to the small bookcase and take out a book. She saw that he was holding the family photograph album. Very quickly he searched through its pages, found what he was looking for, and tore out three pictures from three separate pages.

He handed them to the German officer, who released Ellen's hair.

"You will see each of my daughters, each with her name written on the photograph," Papa said.

Annemarie knew instantly which photographs he had chosen. The album had many snapshots — all the poorly focused pictures of school events and birthday parties. But it also contained a portrait, taken by a photographer, of each girl as a tiny infant. Mama had written, in her delicate handwriting, the name of each baby daughter across the bottom of those photographs.

She realized too, with an icy feeling, why Papa had torn them from the book. At the bottom of each page, below the photograph itself, was written the date. And the real Lise Johansen had been born twenty-one years earlier.

"Kirsten Elisabeth," the officer read, looking at Kirsti's baby picture. He let the photograph fall to the floor.

"Annemarie," he read next, glanced at her, and dropped the second photograph.

"Lise Margrete," he read finally, and stared at Ellen for a long, unwavering moment. In her mind, Annemarie pictured the photograph that he held: the baby, wide-eyed, propped against a pillow, her tiny hand holding a silver teething ring, her bare feet visible below the hem of an embroidered dress. The wispy curls. Dark.

unwavering — steady

The officer tore the photograph in half and dropped the pieces on the floor. Then he turned, the heels of his shiny boots grinding into the pictures, and left the apartment. Without a word, the other two officers followed. Papa stepped forward and closed the door behind him.

Annemarie relaxed the clenched fingers of her right hand, which still clutched Ellen's necklace. She looked down, and saw that she had imprinted the Star of David into her palm.

Meet the Author

Lois Lowry is the author of many popular children's books. Her interest in Danish wartime experiences grew in talking to a friend who was a child in Denmark during the Nazi occupation.

Additional Books to Read

Zlata's Diary: A Child's Life in Sarajevo by Zlata Filipovic. Read this moving account of life in a modern war zone.

The Hidden Children by Howard Greenfeld. This is the story of other Jewish children saved during World War II.

Response Activities

1. **Compare Literature and History** How does this story add to your understanding of life in Europe during World War II?

2. **Narrative: Write a Dialogue** Think about how the Johansen family and Ellen may have felt during the soldiers' invasion. Then write a dialogue relating what they say after the officers leave.

3. **History: Make a Timeline** Using your own research, make a timeline of the major events in Denmark during the German occupation of 1940–1945.

Participating

What Does It Mean to Be a Good Citizen?

Does being a good citizen mean always obeying the law? Does it mean standing up for a nation's principles or ideals, such as equal rights, justice, and freedom? Think about these questions as you read the case study below.

Case Study

Neighbors with Courage

It was a warm autumn day, but Ruth Ekman and her husband Ulf wore heavy winter overcoats. The Ekmans waited on a beach in Denmark with a large crowd of people, all strangely overdressed. At last the boats appeared. The Ekmans climbed aboard with the others. When the boats were full, they set out to sea.

The year was 1943. The German army had occupied Denmark three years before. The Nazis had ordered the arrest of Denmark's Jewish citizens.

During World War II, most Jews in Europe were sent to death camps. But Danish citizens would not accept such actions. Instead, they organized a fleet of boats and helped Denmark's Jews escape to Sweden. Because of their courage, nearly all of Denmark's Jews survived the war.

A mother and her daughter arrive in Sweden as war refugees from Denmark.

Take Action

Before the Danish Jews escaped to Sweden in World War II, the Nazis told the king of Denmark to order all Danish Jews to wear a yellow Star of David on their clothes. Instead, however, the king himself and many other Danes sewed yellow stars on their clothes. The Nazis' order was never carried out and they were unable to identify the Jews.

1 In small groups, list times when you have seen people discriminate against others. Was it based on their clothing? speech? What else?

2 From your list, pick one example of discrimination that you would like to stop. Think of four different ways you could protest the discrimination.

3 List pros and cons for each suggestion. Decide which strategy will be most effective.

4 Think of a name and slogan for your campaign. Create a poster and short speech to help unite supporters. Record your speech, if you can.

5 Present your work to the class. Are there any suggestions that you could put into practice now?

Tips for Participating

- Unpopular causes often do not get as much attention as popular ones. Try to find out more about both sides of an issue before making up your mind.
- When deciding how to treat people, try to put yourself in their shoes. How would you want to be treated if the situation were reversed?

Research Activity

Find out about people in your community who have volunteered to help others. Interview them to find out 1) how they got started in their work, 2) what their work involves, and 3) what makes them keep doing it.

CHAPTER 14

Chapter Review

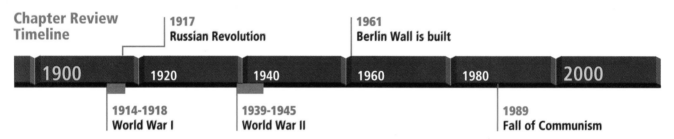

Chapter Review Timeline

1917
Russian Revolution

1961
Berlin Wall is built

1900   1920   1940   1960   1980   2000

1914-1918
World War I

1939-1945
World War II

1989
Fall of Communism

Summarizing the Main Idea

1 Copy and complete the chart below to compare different countries in Europe.

Country	Geography	Key Historical Event	Key Historical Figure
Great Britain			
Germany			
Russia			
France			

Vocabulary

2 Using at least eight of the following terms, write a short history of two countries in Europe since World War II.

Gulf Stream (p. 382)

continental climate (p. 382)

marine climate (p. 382)

cuisine (p. 383)

allies (p. 388)

communism (p. 389)

propaganda (p. 390)

anti-Semitism (p. 391)

Holocaust (p. 392)

Cold War (p. 394)

Reviewing the Facts

3 Give three examples of how people have overcome geographic barriers to travel and trade in Europe.

4 Why is the Gulf Stream important to Western Europe?

5 How did Europe's system of alliances lead it into World War I?

6 Describe the beginning of communism in Russia.

7 What were the causes of World War II?

8 How did Hitler come to power?

9 What was the Holocaust?

10 How did the Cold War begin?

11 Why did communism crumble?

Skill Review: Understanding Seasons

Look at the globe shown on page 385. Then look at the map of Europe on page 380, and answer the questions that follow.

12 You are planning a vacation to Spain. You want to go at a time of year when there will be lots of local fresh fruits and vegetables in the markets. When should you go?

13 Explain why there is colder weather at the North and South poles than there is near the equator, even at the same time of the year.

Geography Skills

14 Look at the map on page 380. How have Europe's mountains, plains, rivers, and canals affected the nations of the continent?

15 Trace the route that a shipload of olives might follow from Italy to Great Britain.

Critical Thinking

16 **Cause and Effect** How did the Treaty of Versailles at the end of World War I influence the events that led to World War II?

17 **Predict** What might happen in the former Soviet Union and Eastern Europe now that communism has fallen?

18 **Conclude** Why did people in 1918 refer to World War I as "The Great War," and not as "World War I"?

Writing: Citizenship and History

19 **Citizenship** Political slogans and speeches often contain propaganda. Write five political slogans that contain propaganda and explain how they could mislead people.

20 **History** You are a soldier living in a trench during World War II. Write a letter to the folks back home letting them know how you feel.

Activities

Geography/Research
Choose one of the countries mentioned in this chapter and find out more about the land, the climate, the economy, and the people. Share your findings with the class.

History/Music
World Wars I and II inspired many songs, such as "It's a Long Way to Tipperary" and "Over There." Find recordings of these war songs and others to share with the class.

Internet Option

Check the **Internet Social Studies Center** for ideas on how to extend your theme project beyond your classroom.

THEME PROJECT CHECK-IN

As you choose a European country for your theme project, use the following questions to help you:
- What geographic features of Europe influence separation and union?
- How did political and cultural conflicts cause separation in Europe?
- What different political systems have existed in Europe in the 20th century?

CHAPTER 15 Europe: Patterns of Living

Chapter Preview: *People, Places, and Events*

1900	1920	1940

The Velvet Revolution 1989

Find out why these people are cheering. *Lesson 1, Page 407*

Facing the Future

When is a battle tank not a battle tank? *Lesson 1, Page 410*

The European Union

Hopes are rising for a united Europe. *Lesson 2, Page 415*

The Czech and Slovak Republics

Main Idea After overthrowing their Communist government, the Czech and Slovak republics are becoming democratic, capitalist countries.

Key Vocabulary

planned economy

dissident

free-market economy

On a chilly New Year's Eve in 1992, crowds filled the narrow streets of the Eastern European city of Bratislava (brat ih SLAH vuh). People laughed and sang. Bands played traditional songs as couples danced in the streets. They had turned out to celebrate a new year and a new birth — that of the Slovak (SLOH vahk) Republic.

The Czech (CHECK) and Slovak Federative Republic was about to become two countries. The parting would take place without violence, but not without pain. Now many families and friends living near the border would be separated. Some people feared that the Slovak Republic — smaller and less developed than the Czech Republic — would suffer.

On this evening, though, the mood was joyful. Church bells rang and fireworks lit the sky. "The Slovaks have waited a thousand years for this night!" one woman exclaimed as the crowds cheered and danced.

Key Events

1918 Formation of Czechoslovakia

1968 Prague Spring

1989 Velvet Revolution

1993 Velvet Divorce

◄ Children play in the shadow of Europe's historical buildings.

| 1960 | 1980 | 2000 |

For Richer or Poorer

Why are these sheep blocking traffic on the streets of Paris? *Lesson 2, Page 417*

Planning a City

This European city is famous for its many canals. *Lesson 3, Page 421*

An Eye for Art

The queen's birthday is a good excuse for some fun in Amsterdam. *Lesson 3, Page 422*

The Final Days of Communism

Focus *What did the end of communism mean for Czechoslovakia?*

The Czech and Slovak people had lived together in Eastern Europe for many centuries. For much of that time, Czech and Slovak lands had been part of other, larger nations, most recently the Austro-Hungarian Empire. But in 1918, following its defeat in World War I, the Austro-Hungarian Empire collapsed.

Trials of a New Nation

Czech and Slovak leaders formed a new nation in 1918, called Czechoslovakia (chehk uh sluh VAH kee uh). Thirty years later and three years after the end of World War II, the young nation came under Communist control. The Communist leaders brought a new economy to Czechoslovakia, called a **planned economy**. In such a system, the government plans what products the country will make and sets the prices for products. It may also own farms and businesses. The Communists thought a planned economy would spread wealth equally among all citizens.

By the late 1960s, however, many Czechs and Slovaks had grown tired of Communist policies. They wanted the freedoms communism denied. People felt their lives were worse than before communism.

Early in 1968, a new Czech Communist leader, Alexander Dubček (DUBE check), took office. For many people, Dubček was a refreshing

When troops from the Soviet Union and other Communist countries invaded Czechoslovakia in 1968, many Czech citizens were outraged. In this photograph, a protester stands on top of a Soviet tank. Protesting did little good, and the Communists took firm control of the country. **Citizenship:** *Compare and contrast this photograph with the one on the next page. Which protest was more effective? Why?*

change. He offered elections to choose government officials and allowed greater freedom of expression. People began to call these spring months of reform the Prague Spring, after the capital city of Czechoslovakia.

Former Communist Countries

This map shows countries in Eastern Europe that were formerly Communist. **Map Skill:** *Trace the confrontation line between Communist Europe and free Europe.*

Legend

- Formerly a Communist country or region
- Formerly a republic of the Soviet Union
- Formerly East Germany

Meanwhile, other Communist leaders in the Soviet Union and Eastern Europe grew worried. The freedoms Dubček allowed seemed dangerous to these leaders. They worried that people in other Communist countries might also demand them. In August 1968, 600,000 troops with tanks, from the Soviet Union and other Communist nations, rolled into Czechoslovakia. Dubček was forced to resign. The brief Prague Spring came to a sudden end.

New Communist leaders clamped down hard against protesters. The government persecuted and imprisoned **dissidents**, people who disagreed with the government. The desire for change grew stronger among the people, however. Dissident political groups continued to demand freedom to express their ideas and freedom to choose their leaders.

The Velvet Revolution

When Mikhail Gorbachev came to power in the Soviet Union in 1985, almost 20 years later, he began many political and economic reforms. These signs of change encouraged dissidents in Czechoslovakia. More and more people began to speak out, demanding an end to communism.

In November 1989, Czechoslovakia filled with excitement as protesters took to the streets. Thousands of students took part in demonstrations and published newspapers disagreeing with the government. At a demonstration in Prague's central square, thousands of protesters jingled their key chains, filling the air with eerie music. Demonstrators gave flowers to the police as peace offerings.

In some country villages, local government officials cut the electricity so that people could not see these demonstrations on the television news. Still, news of the protests spread. The people had waited 20 years for this time. They were not going to give up now.

Many people attended demonstrations during Czechoslovakia's Velvet Revolution. This enthusiastic crowd is responding to a speech given by Alexander Dubček in November 1989.

Vaclav Havel

Vaclav Havel was born in Prague in 1936. As a young man he discovered he had a talent for writing plays. In 1963, his first play was performed on the stage. His criticism of the government landed him in prison, but public outcry forced officials to release him. In 1989, after the fall of communism, he was elected president of the new Czechoslovakia. He told the people: "This is the best chance in a lifetime that Europe may break out into a hotbed of peace."

In December 1989, under public pressure, the Communist government collapsed. The joyful population formed a new non-Communist government. The leaders gave the nation a new name — the Czech and Slovak Federative Republic. The new government made plans for the first free elections since 1946. "This is a success for all of us, both our nations," said Vaclav Havel (VAH tslav HAH vuhl), the new president. Almost 40 years of Communist rule were at an end.

In other Communist countries that had rebelled against their governments, there had been widespread violence, even loss of life. Czechoslovakia's upheaval was remarkable for its swiftness and little violence. Because the historic event took place so smoothly, people called it "The Velvet Revolution." Many people praised the important role of the student protesters in the Velvet Revolution. "We are just so grateful to the students for what they did to bring about this change," said one elderly woman.

The Velvet Divorce

In the new republic, Czechs outnumbered Slovaks 2 to 1. They also controlled more of the land and had closer ties to western business and industry. Czechs and Slovaks had a strained relationship even under Communist rule, but now their tensions increased. They disagreed about how quickly things should change. For example, most Czechs were eager to move quickly to a free-market economy. In a **free-market economy,** farms and factories are privately owned. The owners decide what to produce and what prices to charge. Slovaks wanted a free-market economy also, but they wanted to change at a slower pace.

The Slovaks feared that shifting to a free-market economy would mean greater hardships for them than for the Czechs. Some Slovaks also felt that the Czechs looked down on them. One said, "The Czechs . . . have always lorded over us. It is time to step out of Prague's shadow."

Czechoslovakia had negotiated a peaceful end to communism. Now its leaders negotiated the peaceful breakup of the nation. Some people

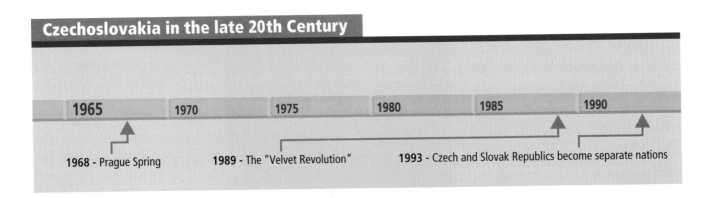

Czechoslovakia in the late 20th Century

1965	1970	1975	1980	1985	1990

1968 - Prague Spring   1989 - The "Velvet Revolution"   1993 - Czech and Slovak Republics become separate nations

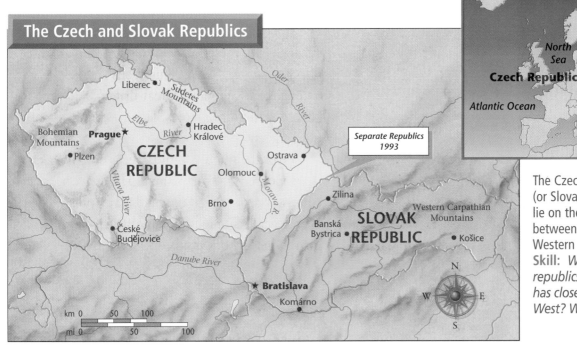

The Czech and Slovak Republics

Liberec
Sudetes Mountains
Bohemian Mountains
Prague ★
Elbe River
Hradec Králové
Plzeň
CZECH REPUBLIC
Oder River
Ostrava
Olomouc
Morava R.
Brno
Zilina
České Budějovice
Vltava River
Banská Bystrica
SLOVAK REPUBLIC
Western Carpathian Mountains
Košice
Danube River
★ Bratislava
Komárno

Separate Republics 1993

km 0 50 100
mi 0 50 100

North Sea
Czech Republic
Atlantic Ocean
Slovakia

The Czech and Slovak (or Slovakia) republics lie on the border between Eastern and Western Europe. **Map Skill:** *Which of the republics do you think has closer ties with the West? Why?*

called it "The Velvet Divorce." At the beginning of 1993, the two republics separated and agreed to a relationship of friendly trade and cooperation.

Facing the Future

Focus *How have the Czech and Slovak republics adapted to the new economic challenges they face?*

Every day the keepers of the castle in the Czech city of Cesky Krumlov (CHEHZ kee CRUM lawff) empty a barrel of apples into the dry moat around its walls. The apples are breakfast for two brown bears that live

in the moat. The ancient castle, a popular tourist spot, is one of 2,500 historic sites in the Czech and Slovak republics. Today, these beautiful castles, fortresses, and old towns attract tourists from all over the world. The travelers spend money in hotels, museums, shops, and restaurants, and boost the local economy.

The Czech and Slovak republics today are rebuilding their industries, which had not been modernized by the Communist leaders. Foreign companies are giving people jobs

The old stone gates of Prague attract both tourists and painters. **National Heritage:** *What historic landmarks attract tourists and painters to your community or state?*

and bringing much-needed cash into the country. Before 1990, there were no foreign companies in Czechoslovakia. Today, numerous countries, among them Germany, Great Britain, and the United States, have stores, factories, and gas stations there.

Over the centuries, the Czechs and Slovaks have endured great hardships. They have seen their countries divided and reunited many times. Their experience has taught them not to give up. As one man in his eighties put it:

During the Cold War, the Czechs and Slovaks made weapons for the Soviet Union. At the end of the Cold War, they were left with thousands of useless battle tanks. The Slovaks redesigned the tanks, turning them into fire engines (shown above). **Economics:** *Think of other ways that used or outdated machines might be recycled.*

" *Look, I was born in Austria-Hungary. I grew up in Czechoslovakia, suffered from Germans, spent 40 years in a colony of Russia — without ever leaving Prague! Now we're Czechs again, as we were for a thousand years. What's so bad about that?* "

Lesson Review

| 1900 | 1930 | 1960 | 1990 | |

1918
Formation of Czechoslovakia

1968
Prague Spring

1989
Velvet Revolution

1993
Velvet Divorce

1. **Key Vocabulary:** Describe changes in Czechoslovakia using: **free-market economy, planned economy, dissident.**

2. **Focus:** What did the end of communism mean for Czechoslovakia?

3. **Focus:** How have the Czech and Slovak republics adapted to the new economic challenges they face?

4. **Critical Thinking: Conclude** Do you think that the breakup of Czechoslovakia was good or bad for the Czech and Slovak people?

5. **Theme: Union and Separation** What factors led to the breakup of Czechoslovakia?

6. **Citizenship/Writing Activity:** You work for a newspaper in Czechoslovakia in December of 1989. Write an editorial about the liberation from communism that might appear in your newspaper.

A Tunnel Under the Sea

FROM THE PAGES OF
Boys' Life

By Mark Henricks

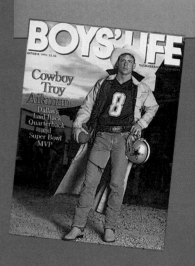

Britain and France have not always been the good neighbors they are today. Beginning with the Norman Invasion a thousand years ago, when French soldiers invaded Britain, the two countries have fought each other in a number of wars. During these conflicts, the English Channel was always there, providing a watery buffer zone between Europe and the British Isles. Today, that buffer zone is gone. In November 1994 a tunnel, called the "Chunnel," opened under the English Channel, connecting England with the continent of Europe. This amazing technical feat is an equally amazing political feat. Here's how it happened.

BRITAIN

FRANCE

This diagram shows the two main tunnels and service corridor. When tunnel diggers met in 1990, 10 miles from France and 14 miles from England, they were off by only 8 inches.

Making a Wild Idea Into Reality

When Frank Davidson was 12, he read about a wild idea. Someone wanted to build a tunnel under the sea. The tunnel would run beneath the English Channel, the body of water that separates England and France. People would be able to travel back and forth — without using a boat. The idea had come up before. Digging had even begun a couple of times. But it was a big job, and nobody got far.

Frank Davidson grew up and became a lawyer. He never forgot the wild idea. When it came up again in the 1950s, he helped draft an agreement between England and France to plan a tunnel. "The more we looked into the idea, the better it looked," says Frank, now 75 and a professor at the Massachusetts Institute of Technology. The project started, but stopped when British officials changed their mind. Years later, the two countries reached another agreement, and work began again. That was in 1986.

To build the world's longest underwater tunnel, tunnelers dug through solid rock, removing 10 million tons. They developed special digging machines, called moles. Each mole weighed 1,500 tons and was 300 yards long.

Three Tunnels in One

The Chunnel is actually three tunnels. Two have train tracks in them. They carry high-speed trains loaded with people, cars and freight. The

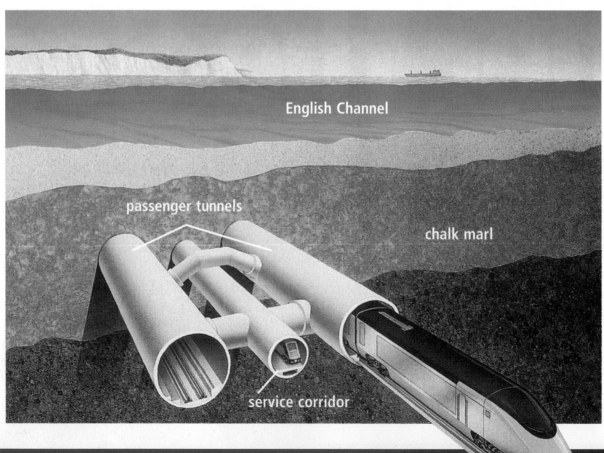

English Channel

passenger tunnels

chalk marl

service corridor

third tunnel is a service corridor with a road in it. Trucks use it to carry supplies and workers to keep the Chunnel in good shape.

Most passengers drive onto the train and stay in the comfort of their vehicles for the 35-minute ride. Others board train cars with bunks and dining rooms. At the far end of the tunnel, people drive off the train and go on their way.

What About Fire or Floods?

The Chunnel has no escape routes to the surface, except for the opening at either end. So what would happen in case of fire or flood?

First of all, the Chunnel is bored through a sturdy rock called "chalk marl." For good measure, the tunnels are lined with steel-reinforced concrete or cast iron. A roof collapse is extremely unlikely.

Fire is a bigger worry. If a fire starts on a train, automatic doors will slam shut to contain the blaze. Extinguishers will automatically snuff it with foam.

Having three separate tunnels is another safety feature. The three are connected with cross tunnels every quarter mile. In an emergency, conductors could stop trains and lead passengers to a different tunnel. From there, they could return to the surface.

Heat was a surprise problem. Engineers expected the Chunnel to be naturally cool. But they discovered the fast-moving trains would heat the air to a sizzling 130 degrees. At the last minute, they had to design one of the world's biggest air conditioners so passengers wouldn't roast.

No matter how well it's done, tunnel building is dangerous work. Eight English workers and two French workers died while building the Chunnel. That is a good safety record compared to other big projects. When the world's second-longest underwater tunnel was built in Japan, 30 workers died.

Bringing Europe Together

By making it easier to travel between the British Isles and the European continent, the Chunnel will bring European people together. That may help prevent wars which have cost millions of lives. And it may encourage millions of kids, like Frank Davidson, to dream of wild ideas.

Response Activities

1. **Predict** What do you think will be the advantages of the Chunnel for England and France? What will be the advantages for the rest of Europe?

2. **Informative: Write a News Story** Write a news story about the opening of the Chunnel as if you were a newspaper reporter in a European country. Include information that your readers would want to know.

3. **Technology: Design a Tunnel** Using the information in the selection, design your own imaginary tunnel. Decide on a location and purpose for your tunnel. Draw a diagram of your tunnel. Label your diagram.

LESSON 2

France and the European Union

Main Idea The European Union means a better life for most, but a harder life for some.

Key Vocabulary

- currency
- Common Market
- tariff
- European Union
- border control
- passport

Key Events

- **1958** Founding of Common Market
- **1986** Single European Act
- **1991** Maastricht Treaty proposed
- **1995** Seven nations end border controls

It is December 1992 on a busy street in the town of Bethune (beh TUNE) in northern France. A young farmer parks his pickup truck in the middle of the street and lowers the truck's tailgate. Hundreds of potatoes pour from the truck. Cars screech to a halt. Horns blare. Another truck stops and dumps more potatoes. Farmers on tractors spread tons of potatoes across the streets of the city, blocking traffic in every direction.

The farmers are angry about the new prices the government says they must charge for their potatoes and other produce. All across France in 1992, thousands of farmers took part in demonstrations like this one. They blocked railway tracks, threw tomatoes and eggs at government ministers, and dumped produce in town squares. They hoped that if they caused enough trouble, the government would listen to their views.

French farmers block a highway in 1992 to show their anger toward economic changes. The farmers feared that the changes would be bad for their jobs. **Citizenship:** *Do you think that these protests are a good way for the farmers to show their point of view? Why or why not?*

414 Chapter 15

Member Nations of the European Union 1995

Legend

Member nations of European Union

By the most recent count, 15 countries are members of the European Union. **Map Skill:** *Approximately what percentage of European countries are members of the European Union?*

The European Union

Focus *What is the European Union?*

While French farmers demonstrated in the streets, many countries in Europe were voting on an important proposal. The proposal would unite the countries in one large community, bringing them closer together than ever before. It would make travel and trade faster and more convenient between them. If the plan passed, the countries would use the same system of money, or **currency**, instead of using different money in each country.

Many people, like the farmers in France, were afraid of the plan. They thought it would take away their independence. Some were afraid they might lose their jobs. Other people were excited about the idea of a united Europe. They liked the idea of being able to live and work anywhere on the continent. They thought the proposal would be good for the economy of Europe.

The idea of uniting the countries of Europe in one community began long before 1992. During World War II, many European leaders desperately wanted to prevent such a horrible war from ever happening again. Winston Churchill, the prime minister of Great Britain, and other leaders suggested that the nations of Europe should form a union as a means of

Then & Now

Thirty years ago, supermarkets were almost unknown in France. The French bought their food at open air markets or at small shops. One shop was for bread, another for meat, and so on. Today, supermarkets are common in French cities, although many French still prefer the small specialty shops.

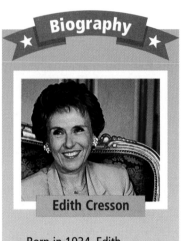

Biography

Edith Cresson

Born in 1934, Edith Cresson became the first woman prime minister of France in 1991. However, her outspoken manner was not popular. She spent only 321 days on the job. She declared, "I was appointed to be daring and vigorous."

preventing war. Churchill said, "We must build a kind of united states of Europe."

Plans for a united Europe developed in stages. In 1952, six nations — France, West Germany, Belgium, Luxembourg, the Netherlands, and Italy — organized their separate coal and steel industries into one industry. Six years later the same countries decided they wanted their economies to cooperate even more. They formed an organization called the European Economic Community, or **Common Market**. By 1986, the United Kingdom, Denmark, Ireland, Greece, Spain, and Portugal had all joined the Common Market. In 1995, Austria, Sweden, and Finland became members.

The Common Market made trade easier among member countries. It reduced **tariffs**, or fees charged on products brought into or out of a country. Tariffs make foreign products more expensive than local products. They discourage people from buying foreign goods.

The Common Market was very successful. Trade increased among member countries, whose economies are still growing. The countries decided to find other ways they could work together. They formed an organization called the **European Union**, to govern both economic and political cooperation in Europe. The European Union, or EU, has passed laws to clean up the environment. Through the EU, nations have shared information about scientific research and new technology. They have combined police forces to fight crime.

A Single Market

Focus *What is a single market, and what does it hope to achieve?*

Encouraged by their success, many member countries in Europe wanted an even stronger union. They wanted all of Europe to be a single market, with no trade barriers of any kind, as in the United States. People would be free to live, work, and trade anywhere within member countries. Goods could travel faster and more cheaply from one country to another.

So, the leaders of these countries passed the Single European Act in 1986. That act turned the Common Market overnight into the world's biggest economic power. The total value of all goods and services produced by the member nations was 6.7 trillion dollars.

During the 1980s and early 1990s, the member nations worked on a plan for even greater unity. They called it the Maastricht (MAHS trihkt) Treaty, after the town of Maastricht in the Netherlands, where it was signed by the European leaders. One aim of the Maastricht Treaty was to create a single currency for all of Europe.

Think of what it would be like if every state in the United States had a different currency. When you traveled from one state to another, you would have to change your money into the currency of that state before you could buy anything. That is what it is like in Europe, where each country uses different money. France uses francs, Germany uses marks, Spain uses pesetas, and so on. Each currency is worth a different amount.

For Europeans, the idea of a single currency was very new. Many people feared that a single currency would take away part of their national identity and an important part of their culture.

Some nations asked voters to decide on the treaty. Voters in Denmark at first turned it down while in France, the treaty barely passed. The leaders of the member countries were not discouraged. One official said, "When you look at what's been done in the past seven years, it's really a remarkable achievement." In 1993 the Maastricht Treaty was finally accepted.

In 1995, seven nations in Europe passed an important milestone. They agreed to end border controls with other members. Other nations considered taking this step. **Border controls** are customs checks, or border inspections. The controls are time consuming and expensive. For example, a truck can travel from London, England, to Italy in 36 hours, but border inspections can add 22 hours to the trip.

With border inspections gone, people within the seven nations can go from one country to another without ever having to show a passport. A **passport** is a government document that provides travelers with citizenship identification. It allows them to leave and reenter their country. Now people will carry Europassports, identifying them as citizens of a larger community.

A customs officer checks a truck at the French border. In 1995, border controls were lifted among seven EU countries. **Geography:** *What countries are on the borders of France?*

Forever French?

Focus *What problems does the European Union face today?*

Not all Europeans are happy about the changes brought by the European Union. Some people fear that a united Europe means giving up too much of their own culture. People in small countries like Denmark feel that their needs may be ignored by larger countries like Germany.

In France, economic change has meant that farmers no longer receive as much financial support from their government. That financial support in the past allowed farmers to set low prices. Now the farmers fear they

At this special shop in France, French and foreign items are for sale at the same price. The stars on the cap symbolize the 12 member nations of the European Union in 1992. **Economics:** *Why does the European Union want to sell local and foreign items at the same price?*

will not be able to compete successfully with other countries. "We don't protest to become richer, but to keep from losing it all," said one farmer who raises apples and pigs in central France.

People in France and other European countries also criticize the EU for ending border controls. They believe border controls help to keep a country safe. They also wonder how safety regulations and product standards can be supervised among so many countries.

Despite these concerns, most people agree that the European Union is here to stay. Today the EU represents more than 375 million people. It has created a prosperous new marketplace. There are now 15 members, and other countries are eager to join, among them former Communist nations. As one leader in the EU explained in 1992:

"When you consider that we're talking about 12 different countries with different traditions, cultures, and working practices — well, getting agreement across that range of divides is a great success."

Lesson Review

1950	1975	2000	

1958
Common Market founded

1986
Single European Act

1995
Seven members of EU end border controls

1 **Key Vocabulary:** Use the following words in a paragraph about France: currency, tariff, European Union, passport

2 **Focus:** What is the European Union?

3 **Focus:** What is a single market, and what does it hope to achieve?

4 **Focus:** What problems does the European Union face today?

5 **Critical Thinking: Decision Making** If you were a French citizen, voting on whether or not to have one European currency, how would you vote? Explain.

6 **Theme: Separation and Union** How have economic issues helped to unify European nations?

7 **Citizenship/Art Activity:** You are an artist hired by the European Union. Design a poster that persuades voters to adopt a single European currency.

The Netherlands: Quality of Life

Main Idea In the Netherlands, culture and economics have blended to produce a society concerned about the quality of life.

Marshall Plan
minimum wage
public housing
quality of life

I t is January 1945. A cold night falls over Amsterdam. People take shelter in their dark houses. Since the Germans have taken all food and gasoline away from the Netherlands, people have been hungry and cold. They search the freezing countryside, trading their last possessions for a few potatoes or even tulip bulbs to eat. They have cut down all the trees in the streets for firewood, and torn up ties from the railroad tracks. Three hundred years before, Amsterdam was a rich, powerful, and beautiful city. Now, many houses are empty — ghostly reminders of families that once lived there. Everything has been taken by desperate neighbors, even the wooden floors and staircases. During these last months of World War II, the people of Amsterdam die of hunger and walk in rags.

The winter of 1944–45 was known as the "hunger winter." Luxuries such as sugar were still hard to find in the Netherlands. When available, they sometimes were sold illegally at high prices. The women and girls in this picture are selling candy and cakes illegally on a side street in Amsterdam. **History:** *Find out what luxuries were hard to get in the United States during World War II.*

From Poverty to Prosperity

Focus *How did the Netherlands rebuild after World War II and what solutions did it find to help its people?*

When war finally ended in the Netherlands in May 1945, the country's roads, harbors, bridges, and rail lines were in ruins. The once-powerful banks were too poor to rebuild the country. The United States feared that so much poverty might lead Western Europeans towards communism, so it decided to rebuild their countries with the biggest aid program ever: the **Marshall Plan.** The Marshall Plan

North Sea

Amsterdam

Atlantic Ocean

was a U.S. program that loaned and gave money to Western European countries to buy machinery and build factories, allowing them to produce goods again. The Netherlands received more than a billion dollars. As recovery set in, people treasured every bite of food, and every little luxury. From the pieces of chocolate handed out by recovery workers to the new jobs created by the Marshall Plan, every sign seemed to point to good times again.

Rebuilding the Country

For a while after the war, many old divisions between rich and poor, Communists and capitalists, Catholics and Protestants, faded. Everybody had suffered together. This created an unusual feeling of unity among the Dutch. In 1950, the government organized a special committee to set economic goals for employers and employees. People were so eager to rebuild their country that between 1947 and 1957 an economic miracle took place. Wages — at first very low — doubled, and production rose to its prewar levels again. By the late 1950s, there was plenty of food and new housing. Some people were even buying refrigerators, cars, televisions, and washing machines.

As signs of prosperity returned, the Dutch turned their attention to the needs of the poor and elderly. Before the war, the state had begun programs to take care of the basic needs of its citizens. After the war, remembering horrible wartime poverty and hunger, the Dutch felt it was important for the state to revive and expand these programs. In 1947, when the Netherlands could barely afford it, it gave allowances for widows and orphans of soldiers killed in the war. By 1957, the country had promised health care, education, and housing to every citizen. Special government programs provided help for the unemployed and disabled. **Minimum wages** guaranteed workers a certain amount for each hour of work. Affordable **public housing**, paid for partly by the government, was built. All these programs cost money, of course, and resulted in high taxes. Still, as their wages increased, most Dutch were willing to give a lot.

The 1600s were the Golden Age in the Netherlands. Wealthy merchants stored their goods in tall, narrow buildings along canals. This painting from that period shows how ships could dock near the warehouses. **Economics:** *Why was it better to store goods along a canal than along a road?*

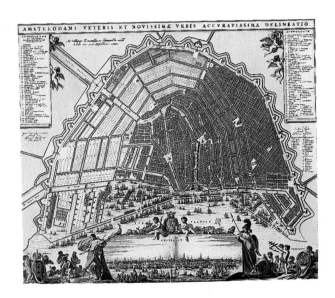

Transforming Amsterdam

Between 1945 and 1975, the population of the Netherlands increased by 50 percent, from 9 million people to 13.5 million. This made it the most densely populated of the world's old, industrial nations. Cities and roads became severely congested. Industrial sites covered the countryside. As wages kept on rising, people bought cars and built superhighways. More than half of the country's people were squeezed into one-eighth of the country's surface.

As the population grew, the historic old streets in the city of Amsterdam became a problem. They were too narrow for modern car and truck traffic. Amsterdam was founded about 800 years ago. It was built largely in the 1500s and 1600s, when it was Europe's biggest trading city. Back then, its harbors were full of ships bringing goods from all over the world. These goods were stored in hundreds of warehouses, waiting to be sold at a good price and shipped out again. Small canals crisscrossed the city, connecting the tall warehouses. The canals were just as important as roads. The city became a delicate pattern of small streets with narrow, tall houses, all linked together by thousands of bridges spanning the canals.

In the 1950s and 1960s, city planners began to draw up plans to destroy the old houses and canals. They wanted to build wide open roads and highways leading into and out of the city and connecting the city with big shopping malls and apartment blocks in the suburbs. Many growing businesses, public services, and universities left the city center and went to the suburbs. Long traffic jams stood between the city and the suburbs. However, when local governments decided to destroy old neighborhoods, they found that they were also destroying old ways of life.

The map (on the left) shows a city plan for Amsterdam in 1674. The photograph (on the right) is a view of Amsterdam from the air today. **Geography:** *Based on these images, in what ways has the city of Amsterdam changed? In what ways is it the same as it was hundreds of years ago?*

The western half of the Netherlands lies below sea level. The cities and farmlands in this area are protected from flooding by sand dunes and dikes. The people of the Netherlands have always had to work together to maintain the dunes and dikes. In what ways do people in your community work together to solve problems?

Quality of Life

Focus | *What problems did modern life bring to Amsterdam and how have the Dutch dealt with them?*

By the early 1960s, people in the Netherlands began to think more about the quality of their lives. The **quality of life** is more than the money people make. It includes the way they like to live everyday life. Most people in Amsterdam liked living in their small houses, on narrow little streets packed with small shops and cafés, bakeries, and flower stands. They liked knowing their neighbors and meeting their friends as they strolled through the city. The narrow roads, canals, and bridges might be too small for a modern city, but as far as the residents were concerned, they were just right. They created a friendliness and liveliness that the modern suburbs lacked. As more plans for modernization of the city center were proposed, people feared that their way of living would be sacrificed for economic growth. Resistance slowly started to take shape.

• Tell Me More •

What's So Great About Queen's Day?

The Netherlands has had a monarchy for almost 200 years, ever since Napoleon put his brother-in-law on the throne in 1806. Today the Netherlands is a democracy, and the monarch has little power. However, the Dutch are very fond of their Queen Beatrix *(shown above)* and her family. Ever since Queen Beatrix's grandmother's time, the Dutch have been celebrating the Queen's Birthday, called *Koninginnedag* (KOH ning in a dakh) in Dutch.

On *Koninginnedag* the streets in every Dutch town are filled with flags and other decorations. There are parties and parades everywhere. Bands play at town squares and people dance in the street. Vendors sell special cakes decorated with orange frosting, because the color orange represents the royal family. The holiday is like one gigantic birthday party attended by the whole country.

Amsterdam Fights Back

A loosely-organized group of young students called the "Provos" inspired resistance to the excesses of modernization. The students had not experienced the war. They had grown up in a new Netherlands, where the government had helped to create a better life for many people. The students could not understand why their government did not also care about creating a better environment. They thought it was wrong for a government to build highways and large buildings without consulting the people. The Provos and other groups felt that democracy should mean more than elections for parliament and city councils. They believed that a true democracy cared about how it protected and helped its citizens.

By the 1970s, the young Provos were no longer students. Some had become journalists, politicians, and professors. They still held their beliefs about democracy. Now there were enough of their followers on Amsterdam's city council to vote against new big construction. The council voted to restore the old houses there. It was a decisive victory.

Today, the Dutch continue to look for better ways to make their government more democratic and effective. At neighborhood councils and public meetings, people discuss and try out new proposals. In the Netherlands, democracy means not only that the majority rules, but that the majority protects and encourages the minority.

Curious Facts

The Netherlands is made up of 12 provinces. Two of those provinces are called Holland — North Holland and South Holland. The people who live in the Netherlands call themselves Netherlanders, but English speakers call them Dutch, a practice that began from a mistake. Early travelers thought the Netherlanders were German, and called them by the German word Deutsch (DOYTCH), meaning German.

Lesson Review

1 **Key Vocabulary:** Describe life in the Netherlands using these words: **public housing, minimum wage, quality of life.**

2 **Focus:** How did the Netherlands rebuild after World War II, and what solutions did it find to help its people?

3 **Focus:** What problems did modern life bring to Amsterdam and how have the Dutch dealt with them?

4 **Critical Thinking: Sequence** How did the streets of Amsterdam look at different times in history? Choose three dates: the 17th century, 1945, and the present. Describe the city at each of those times.

5 **Theme: Separation and Union** Why did the people of the Netherlands develop a sense of unity after World War II?

6 **Citizenship/Art Activity:** Think about the changes Amsterdam has gone through since World War II. In what ways has your city or town changed during the same time? Draw a plan showing what you think your city or town should look like 20 years from now.

Environment and Society

How Did the Dutch Create Their Environment?

An old saying goes, "God created the world, but the Dutch created Holland." More than half of the Netherlands now lies below sea level. The Dutch claimed this new land from the ocean. Without thousands of miles of dunes, dikes, and dams, the sea would flood the land twice daily.

The Dutch first built dikes around lakes and swamps in the 1200s. At that time, a dike was a simple wall of dirt or sand. Then, they pumped out the water. In the drained areas that remained, called *polders*, (POHL-duhrz) the Dutch built farms and cities. At first, they used windmills to run the pumps but later used steam and electric power.

The creation of this new environment has caused new problems. Most of the polders are below sea level and are vulnerable to flooding. The Dutch wage a continuous battle against the sea. They have built gigantic dams and are always exploring new technology to keep back the water.

1 Haringvliet Dam

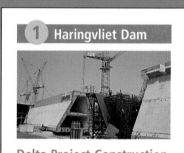

Delta Project Construction
A deadly storm struck the Netherlands in 1953. It killed 1,800 people and drove about 70,000 from their homes. The Dutch reacted with the Delta Project, a 30-year, five-billion dollar flood-control project.

Windmills are a common sight in Holland. Much of the Netherlands still relies on wind power and dikes made from earth and stone to control the water. Do you know of any windmills in the United States?

Art Connection

The first modern landscape paintings were done in the 15th century for the Count of Holland. Dutch art is famous for landscapes that show Holland's flat, canal crossed environment and vast, light-filled skies. Have you ever seen landscape paintings of your area?

Hundreds of miles of canals cross the Netherlands, controlling the flow of water to the sea. What else are canals used for?

The Netherlands, 1995

WEST FRISIAN ISLANDS

NORTH SEA

TEXEL ISLAND

Barrier Dam

IJsselmeer Zuider Zee

Vecht River

IJssel River

Amsterdam ★

Utrecht

NETHERLANDS

The Hague ●

Rotterdam ●

Lek River

Neder Rijn River

Waal River

Rhine River

GERMANY

Eindhoven ●

Maes River

BELGIUM

Meusse River

km 0   20   40
mi 0   20   40

Legend
- —— Dam
- ⊔⊔⊔⊔ Canal
- ▓ Fresh water
- ░ Area reclaimed since 1927

2 Amsterdam

Schiphol Airport
Amsterdam's airport is the only one in the world that was built on the site of a naval battle. Long after the 1573 clash between Dutch and Spanish ships, the Netherlands reclaimed the land from the sea. The airport is 13 feet below sea level.

The Zuider Zee (ZY dur ZEE) once covered the new land on the map. **Map Skill:** *How long is the Barrier Dam that closed it off?*

Research Activity

Although the Dutch have struggled with the sea, it has also helped them in many ways.

1 Research the ways the Dutch people have used the sea, like fishing, trade, and recreation.

2 Make a detailed list of all the ways the sea contributes to the Dutch way of life.

3 Explain your list to the class.

The Dutch can enjoy their passion for ice-skating when the canals freeze in the winter.

Using Almanacs

Information Please

If you looked up Czechoslovakia in an old encyclopedia, you wouldn't know that in 1989 the Czechoslovakian people overthrew the Communist government. If you read a book printed in 1991, you would still be out of date, because in 1993, Czechoslovakia split into two independent states — the Czech Republic and Slovakia.

To keep on top of the latest political events around the world, reach for an **almanac**. Almanacs are updated and published every year. They include statistics about weather, world populations, finances, and natural resources. They also have lists, graphs, tables, and timelines that help you compare the statistics and governments of different countries.

Czechoslovakia 1989

Slovakia 1993

Czech Republic 1993

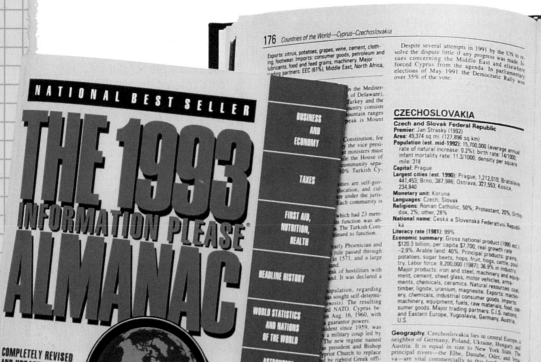

1 Here's How

Decide what sort of information you want to find in an almanac. Then follow these steps:

- Look up your subject in the table of contents or index. You may need to look up several subjects to find the exact information you need.

- Use the page references to find the location of the information.

- Study the statistics and graphs that appear on the pages you've turned to. Take notes of details you have learned.

- Decide if you have found all the facts you need. If not, look up a related subject.

2 Think It Through

How is information in an almanac different from information in an encyclopedia? In a newspaper?

3 Use It

Look at the almanac table of contents below. Write down what subject you might look under to answer the following questions:

1. How does the economy of the Czech Republic compare to the economy of Slovakia?

2. Were there any major earthquakes in Europe in the past year?

3. Who are Poland's representatives at the United Nations?

4. In the past year, what percentage of French people were out of work?

USING THIS ALMANAC

Information Please Almanac is divided topically into 55 major sections which cover the scope of the Almanac. Readers can quickly locate most of the facts they are seeking by turning directly to the appropriate section. For example, the TAXES section will contain the latest data on the Federal Income Tax. Information on Social Security and Medicare can be found in the SOCIAL SECURITY & AGING section. Current postage information can be located in the special POSTAGE section. In addition, the thumb tabs on the front and back covers permit fast access to the information you need.

To find a particular fact, date, or idea in the Comprehensive Index, one should begin by looking under the most specific word. For example, to find the population of Des Moines, one should start by looking for Des Moines. But that city is not listed separately. Therefore, the next step is to look under Iowa or Cities, U.S. Under Iowa, the designated page (761) gives the latest population for Des Moines. Under Cities, U.S., there is a sub-head, Population figures, with two alternatives: Largest (of which Des Moines is not one) and Largest by State (which refers back to Iowa).

For President George Washington, one should look under Washington, before checking President. Where general headings (such as Presidents, U.S.) are given, they refer to a section where the subject is treated at some length.

5

Capital and largest city (1992): Nicosia North (Lefkosa), 40,861; **Monetary unit:** Turkish lira; **Official language:** Turkish; **Religions:** Moslem, 99%; others 1%; **National name:** Kuzey Kibris Türk Cumhuriyeti (Turkish Republic of Northern Cyprus); **Literacy rate** (1991): 100%

Economic summary: Gross national product (1992): $585.5 million; per capita $3,343.40. Average rate of growth (1975–1992): 5.8%. Arable land (1992): 56.7%. Principal agricultural products: citrus, potatoes, tobacco, vegetables. Labor force (1992): 74,037; 25% in agriculture, 11.0% in industry. Major industrial products: concentrated citrus, hides, leathers, P.V.C. covered electric cables, footwear, clothing, cosmetics. Natural resources: gypsum, pyrite mine. Exports: dairy products, citrus, live animals, potatoes, readymade clothing, tobacco, carobs, hides and leathers. Imports: consumer goods, petroleum and lubricants, food, machinery and transport equipment, chemicals. Major trading partners: EC countries (mainly U.K. and Germany) and Turkey are the largest trading partners.

Geography. The Turkish Republic of Northern Cyprus covers the northern part of the island of Cyprus. North Cyprus consists of the coastal plains, the Besparmak (Five-Finger) Mountains the highest peak is Mount Selvili at 3,360 feet), and the interior plains.

Government. The Constitution envisages a Parliamentary democracy. The legislative power is exercised by an Assembly composed of 50 deputies elected for five years. The President is Head of State and represents the unity of the state. He appoints the Prime Minister from among the deputies.

Denktas dissolved parliament in October 1993 with a call for new elections in December, whose results led to the formation of a coalition government.

CZECH REPUBLIC

President: Vaclav Havel (1993)
Premier: Vaclav Klaus (1992)
Area: 30,464 sq mi. (78,902 sq km)
Population (est. mid-1994): 10,300,000 (average annual rate of natural increase: 0.0%); birth rate: 12/1000; infant mortality rate: 8.5/1000; density per square mile: 338.1
Capital and largest city (1993): Prague, 1,200,000. Other large cities (1991): Brno, 387,986; Ostrava, 327,553; Plzen, 173,129; Olomouc, 105,690. **Monetary unit:** Koruna; **Language:** Czech; **Religions:** Roman Catholic, major, other: Protestant, Orthodox; **Literacy rate:** 99%
Economic summary: Gross domestic product (1992 est.): $75.3 billion; Per capita $7,300; real growth rate, –5%; inflation 12.5%; unemployment, 3.1%. The Czech Republic has a developed but deteriorating industrialized economy—much of its plant equipment is among the oldest in Europe. Natural resources: hard coal, kaolin, clay, graphite. Industries: fuels, ferrous metallurgy, machinery and equipment, coal, motor vehicles, glass, armaments. Agriculture: diversified crops including grains, potatoes, sugar beets, hops, fruit, hogs, cattle and poultry; exporter of forest products. Labor force (1990): 5,389 million; industry, 37.9%; agriculture, 8.1%; construction, 8.8%; communications and other, 45.2%. Exports: $8.2 billion (f.o.b. 1992): manufactured goods, machinery and transport equipment, chemicals, fuels, minerals, and metals. Imports: $8.9 billion (f.o.b. 1992): machinery and transport equipment, fuels and lubricants, manufactured goods, raw materials, chemicals, agricultural products. Major trading partners.

1995 INFORMATION PLEASE ALMANAC

THE ULTIMATE BROWSER'S REFERENCE

COMPLETELY REVISED AND UPDATED
1994 CONGRESSIONAL &
GUBERNATORIAL ELECTION RESULTS
COMPLETE 1994 WORLD CUP SOCCER STATISTICS
SPECIAL YEAR-IN-PICTURES REVIEW

seek to achieve reunification of the island under one federated system of government.

History. Cyprus was the site of early Phoenician and Greek colonies. For centuries its rule passed through many hands. It fell to the Turks in 1571, and a large Turkish colony settled on the island.

In World War I, on the outbreak of hostilities with Turkey, Britain annexed the island. It was declared a

NORTHERN CYPRUS
Turkish Republic of Northern Cyprus
President: Rauf Denktas (1990)
Area: 1,295 sq mi. (3,355 sq km)
Population (est. 1991): Turkish Cypriots, 172,980; Greek Cypriots, 559; Maronites, 279 (1993), (average annual rate of natural increase: 1.3%); birth rate: 20.5/1,000; infant mortality rate: 13/1000; density per square km: 52.20

countries
es the Ju-
Germany

Havel was elected for a 5-year term as president in January 1993 by the 200-member parliament.

Chapter Review

Chapter Review Timeline

1900	1920	1940	1960	1980	2000

1918
Formation of Czechoslovakia

1939-1945
World War II

1958
Common Market founded

1968
Prague Spring

1989
Velvet Revolution

1991
Maastricht Treaty proposed

1993
Velvet Divorce

Summarizing the Main Idea

1 Copy the chart below and write a few phrases of information under each heading about each country or region.

	Region	Government	Economy	Quality of Life
Czech and Slovak Republics				
European Union				
The Netherlands				

Vocabulary

2 You are the leader of a formerly Communist country that now wants to join the European Union. Prepare a short speech, using at least eight of the following terms, explaining why your country should be allowed to join.

dissident (p. 407)

planned economy (p. 406)

free-market economy (p. 408)

currency (p. 415)

Common Market (p. 416)

tariffs (p. 416)

European Union (p. 416)

border controls (p. 417)

passport (p. 417)

Marshall Plan (p. 419)

minimum wage (p. 420)

public housing (p. 420)

quality of life (p. 424)

Reviewing the Facts

3 How does a planned economy work?

4 What was the Prague Spring? Why did it fail?

5 Why did the Czech and Slovak republics decide to separate in 1993?

6 What are the goals of the European Union?

7 Why did the Common Market reduce tariffs?

8 Why do some people oppose the changes proposed by the European Union?

9 How did the Marshall Plan help the Netherlands?

10 How did the government of the Netherlands help its citizens after World War II?

11 How have the people of Amsterdam improved the quality of life in their city?

Skill Review: Using Almanacs

12 List five recent world events that you could find information about in an almanac. Describe how to look up that information.

13 Describe where and how you would find information on the following subjects:

Current politics in France, the construction of the English Channel tunnel, the current population of the Netherlands, gold medal winners from Europe in the last Winter Olympics.

Geography Skills

14 Look at the map on page 415 that shows the member nations in the European Union. What problems do you think the countries of Eastern Europe might have in becoming part of the European Union?

15 If you lived beside an old canal in Amsterdam, what would you think if a big shopping center was planned for your neighborhood? Write a letter to your local newspaper explaining your opinion about the proposed project.

Critical Thinking

16 Conclude Why do you think free-market economies have been more successful at meeting people's needs than planned economies?

17 Compare Compare the demonstrations of the Czechoslovakian students, French farmers, and Dutch Provos. Which demonstrations were most effective? Why?

Writing: Citizenship and History

18 Citizenship In the Netherlands, voters feel it is important to protect and encourage everyone, including minorities. How are the rights of minorities protected in the United States? Write a list of reasons why the rights of the

minority are important.

19 History Songwriters often write songs about historical events. Write the words for a song about events in the Czech and Slovak republics, France, or the Netherlands.

Activities

History/Research
Find out more about one of the countries in the European Union. Find out what they gained and what they gave up to join, and what the people feel about their participation. Organize the information on a chart.

Citizenship/Writing
People in Amsterdam improved their quality of life. What is happening in your city, town or school that affects your quality of life? Write a letter to the people responsible and let them know how you feel.

Internet Option

Check the **Internet Social Studies Center** for ideas on how to extend your theme project beyond your classroom.

THEME PROJECT CHECK-IN

To complete your theme project, use the information in this chapter about Europe's individual nations. Ask yourself these questions:

• What major events in the country's history have influenced its separation and union?
• How has the country dealt with the challenges of separation and union?
• How does the country's political system cope with challenges?

Africa in the Modern Age

"I have always known that [my country's] greatest wealth is its people, finer and truer than the purest diamonds."

Nelson Mandela

· THEME ·

Independence and Interdependence

" *Independence is important to the countries of Africa because it means they get freedoms and opportunities they have not had for many years.* "

William Whisenant, Sixth Grade
Sweetwater, TX

Most of Africa's nations began the 20th century as colonies. They finish it proud and free. The struggle has been long and hard, and Africans are still working to build strong countries with rich traditions. They have found that with interdependence — working together — they can conquer the challenge of independence.

Theme Project

Guide to Independence and Interdependence

Choose an African country to show how it has experienced independence and interdependence.

- Construct a timeline that includes the major events in the country's history in the 20th century.
- Diagram the country's political system.
- Write an introduction about how this country has experienced independence and interdependence.
- Illustrate the geography, culture, and people of the country. Write captions for each.

RESEARCH: Collect facts on the major sites visited by tourists who come to this country.

◀ The city of Nairobi, Kenya.

6

WHEN & WHERE
ATLAS

At the beginning of the 20th century, much of Africa was still ruled by European countries. As the century progressed, nationalist movements led independence. With independence came new challenges. As the countries of Africa have struggled to move out from under the shadow of colonial rule, they have faced famine, economic turmoil, and conflict among ethnic groups. Rapid industrial development has also created tension between traditional and modern cultures.

In this unit you will learn more about the geography of Africa. You will also read about the history of Africa in the 20th century — a movement from a continent of colonies to a continent of proud, independent nations. Finally, four case studies will examine the culture, economy, sociology, and politics of four African nations (shown in red).

Unit 6 Chapters

Chapter 16 Africa: An
          Overview
Chapter 17 Africa: Patterns of
          Living

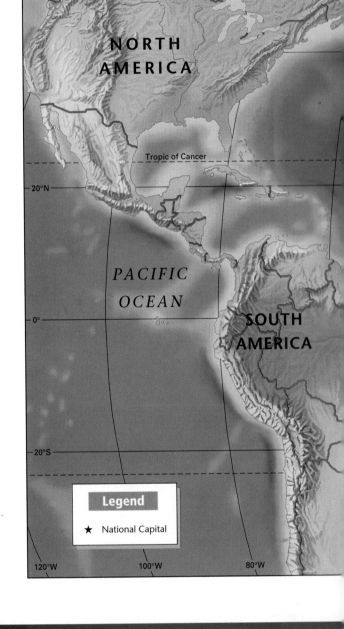

NORTH
AMERICA

Tropic of Cancer

20°N

PACIFIC
OCEAN

0°

SOUTH
AMERICA

20°S

Legend

★ National Capital

120°W   100°W   80°W

Unit Timeline

1850	1880	1910

The Sahel

The geography of Africa has a major effect on how people live. *Chapter 16, Lesson 1*

Highlands

Where are these cool, rainy areas found in Africa? *Chapter 16, Lesson 1*

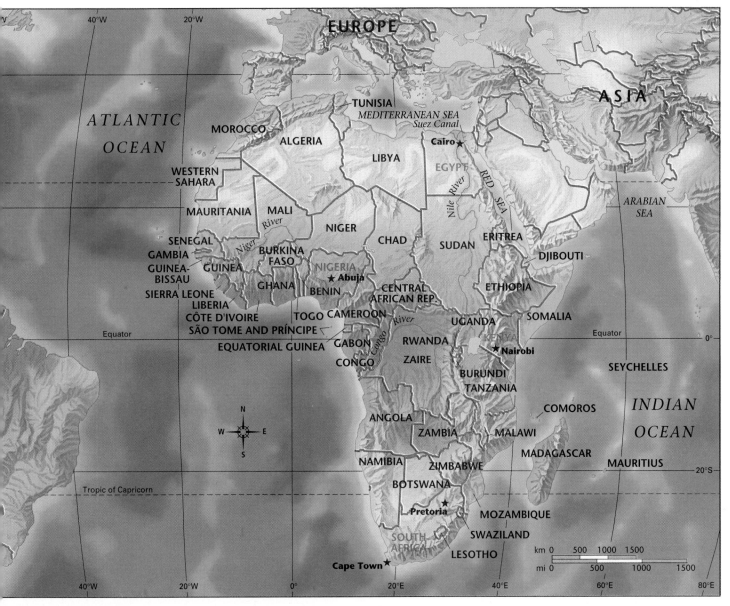

EUROPE

ASIA

ATLANTIC
OCEAN

TUNISIA
MEDITERRANEAN SEA
Suez Canal
MOROCCO
ALGERIA
Cairo ★
WESTERN
SAHARA
LIBYA
EGYPT
RED SEA
ARABIAN
SEA
MAURITANIA
MALI
River
NIGER
CHAD
SUDAN
ERITREA
DJIBOUTI
SENEGAL
Niger River
BURKINA
FASO
GAMBIA
GUINEA-
BISSAU
GUINEA
NIGERIA
★ Abuja
GHANA
BENIN
ETHIOPIA
SIERRA LEONE
LIBERIA
CÔTE D'IVOIRE
TOGO
CAMEROON
CENTRAL
AFRICAN REP.
SÃO TOME AND PRÍNCIPE
Congo River
UGANDA
SOMALIA
Equator
EQUATORIAL GUINEA
GABON
RWANDA
KENYA
★ Nairobi
Equator
0°
CONGO
ZAIRE
SEYCHELLES
BURUNDI
TANZANIA
N
W   E
S
COMOROS
INDIAN
OCEAN
ANGOLA
ZAMBIA
MALAWI
MADAGASCAR
MAURITIUS
20°S
NAMIBIA
ZIMBABWE
BOTSWANA
Pretoria ★
MOZAMBIQUE
SWAZILAND
SOUTH
AFRICA
LESOTHO
Cape Town ★
km 0   500   1000 1500
mi 0   500   1000   1500

40°W   20°W   0°   20°E   40°E   60°E   80°E

1940   1970   2000

Cairo, Egypt

Old and new exist side by side here.
Chapter 17, Lesson 1

The Hausa

These Muslim Africans are just one
of hundreds of ethnic groups in the
continent. *Chapter 17, Lesson 3*

Nelson Mandela   1994

MANDELA FOR PRESIDENT

He became the first black president
of South Africa in 1994. *Chapter
17, Lesson 4*

Africa: An Overview

Chapter Preview: *People, Places, and Events*

1900	1920	1940

Sahel

What do the Africans who live on the dry Sahel do to survive? *Lesson 1, Page 436*

Natural Resources

Mostly a rural continent, Africa is rich with natural resources. *Lesson 1, Page 436*

African Cities

Cities are growing rapidly, attracting Africans away from traditional village life. *Lesson 1, Page 439*

The Geography of Africa

Main Idea Africans have developed many different ways to use their continent's resources.

Key Vocabulary

subsistence farming
food crops
cash crops
drought
desertification
urbanization

The wind is hot, but it cools the women working under the African sun. A lifetime of farming has taught them to work efficiently. The musical sounds of the Kikuyu (ki KOO yoo) language fill the air as the women talk about their families, their farms, their village. The wind carries the sounds of their laughter as they plant young trees.

"Trees are miracles," says biologist Wangari Maathai (wahn GAH ree muh TY). The first Kenyan woman to earn the highest university degree, she started the Green Belt Movement in 1977. Since then, African women joining together in this movement have planted more than five million trees. The trees provide shade and firewood. More important, they enrich the soil and keep it from blowing away. Across the continent, Africans are making positive changes that will help improve their future.

◀ Victoria Falls stretches over a mile on the border of Zambia and Zimbabwe.

1960   1980   2000

Year of Freedom   1960

Find out how Africans regained independence at the end of colonialism. *Lesson 2, Page 445*

Independence Movements

What challenges do Africans face in building strong, independent nations? *Lesson 2, Page 446*

Education

Africans are educating themselves to participate in new democratic governments. *Lesson 2, Page 446*

Climate and Vegetation Regions

Focus *What are the major climate regions of Africa and what kinds of vegetation grow there?*

Africa is the world's second-largest continent, after Asia. Four times the size of the United States, it contains a marvelous variety of landscapes. From snow-capped mountains to deep valleys, from the world's largest desert to dense rain forests, Africa's geography is diverse. Africa has many different types of climate, too. The wetter climates are closer to the equator, and the drier ones are north and south of the equator. Identify the six climate regions on the map on the right. You will notice that the type of vegetation that can grow in each region depends on the amount of rain that falls there. Dense rain forests grow where there is year-round precipitation. The savanna is a grassy region with thick-trunked baobab (BAY oh bab) and graceful acacia (uh KAY shuh) trees. It has distinct wet and dry seasons. In the Sahel, a semiarid region between the savanna and the Sahara, vegetation is sparse. Few plants grow in Africa's deserts. In wetter coastal areas, there is heavier vegetation.

African women, like these in Kenya, have planted five million trees across the continent.

Abundant Natural Resources

Focus *How do Africans use their natural resources?*

Africa is mostly a rural continent, with little manufacturing. Over two-thirds of the more than 870 million Africans live far from cities. Throughout the continent, craftspeople use natural resources to make everyday items that people need. In village after village, furniture, tools, clothes, pottery, and other items are crafted by hand from local resources, such as wood, clay, and minerals.

Using the Land

Africa's land is perhaps the most-used natural resource. More than half the people in Africa farm their land for a living. Many Africans also live by herding. They raise cattle, goats, sheep, and many of the world's camels.

Most African farmers are subsistence farmers. **Subsistence farming** means that crops are grown only to feed a farmer's family. Such crops grown for eating, rather than to sell, are called **food crops**. Farmers from different ethnic groups may have different traditional ways of life, depending on where they live. But they all

Along the edges of the savanna and in the Sahel, herding (rather than farming) is a common way of life. **Geography:** *Why do you think most crops are hard to grow here?*

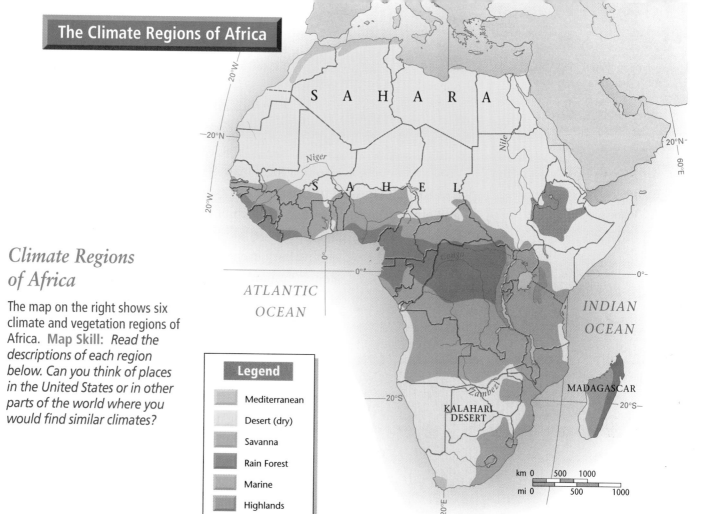

Climate Regions of Africa

The map on the right shows six climate and vegetation regions of Africa. **Map Skill:** *Read the descriptions of each region below. Can you think of places in the United States or in other parts of the world where you would find similar climates?*

Legend
- Mediterranean
- Desert (dry)
- Savanna
- Rain Forest
- Marine
- Highlands

Mediterranean

Mediterranean climates have two distinct seasons: hot, dry summers and mild, rainy winters.

Marine

Near the ocean, a moderate amount of rain falls throughout the year. Summers are warm and winters cool.

Highlands

More rain falls at higher altitudes and the weather is cooler than in lower regions.

Desert

The Sahara, the world's largest desert, is almost as big as the entire United States — 3.5 million square miles!

Rain Forest

Continuous rainfall and high temperatures create a tropical jungle.

Savanna

The savanna covers almost half of Africa. Elephants, lions, and other wild animals roam these areas.

A typical gold mine in South Africa is almost an underground city. Thousands of men work up to two miles under the surface. Find the following on the illustration:

1 main shaft
2 ventilation shaft
3 tunnels, or "cross cuts"
4 diesel trains

rely on Africa's land. One Nigerian woman has said, "We (Africans) are a continent of farmers."

More and more farmers in Africa are growing crops to sell, called **cash crops**. On larger farms and plantations, many cash crops such as cacao in Ghana and peanuts in Gambia are grown for export. Other cash crops are bought and sold at local markets.

Africa's land is a treasure chest of mineral wealth. Gold, copper, oil, and other minerals lie buried in much of the continent. The fishing waters, farmland, grazing lands, and minerals are important to the people for survival. An even greater resource in Africa is its human resource. Africa's people are working hard to understand and solve the problems of their environment.

Problems and Solutions

Hot sun, high temperatures, and dry winds are common in Africa. The harsh climate and poor soil can make farming and herding — the occupations of most Africans — very difficult, even in the best areas. Sometimes there is very little rain, and a **drought**, or extended dry period, occurs. During the 1960s and 1970s a drought in the Sahel went on for years. You can guess what terrible results this had.

The situation is made worse by **desertification**, or the expansion of deserts, in Africa. Deserts cover nearly half the continent and are growing every year. They are being expanded by people overusing the land, and by natural forces, such as shifting wind patterns.

Africans are rising to meet this challenge. The women you read about at the beginning of this lesson are one part of the solution. Special seeds that can survive droughts are another. In some places new methods of farming are being used. Experts estimate that, with modern farming methods, Africa could produce more than 100 times the amount of food it produces now!

Limits on the size of herds help protect the land from overgrazing. Farming and land preservation programs will help restore and preserve Africa's valuable land. Africans will continue to find new ways to use their natural resources to improve the quality of life.

African Cities

Focus *Why are the cities of Africa growing so rapidly?*

The two charts on the right show how quickly Africans are leaving the countryside and moving to the cities. In 1990, 70 percent of the African population lived in rural areas, and only 30 percent in cities. By 2020, just 30 years later, it is predicted that half of all Africans will live in the countryside and half in urban areas. **Urbanization**, or movement from rural to urban areas, is a sign of the dramatic changes taking place in Africa today.

Many people feel "pushed" out of rural areas. Exhausted land, desertification, and drought have made it impossible for them to continue to live by farming or herding. To many Africans, cities act as a magnet, pulling them toward a chance at a new and better life. The promise of modern medical care, schools, plumbing, and electricity attracts them. Often, men move to the cities for jobs while their wives and children stay in the villages. These men need to maintain close ties to their home villages. Many of the new city dwellers who are from the same village band together to help one another find shelter and food.

Despite changes in Africans' lives, two things remain the same: strong ties to family and a love of their rich African homeland. These ties bind the people of Africa together as they plant trees, farm the land, and build cities. Their dedication to each other and to Africa is serving them well during a difficult modern era.

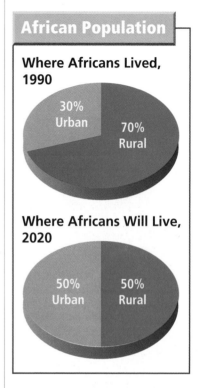

African Population

Where Africans Lived, 1990

30% Urban
70% Rural

Where Africans Will Live, 2020

50% Urban
50% Rural

Chart Skill: *What percent of Africa's population will move to the cities between 1990 and 2020?*

Lesson Review: Geography

1 **Key Vocabulary:** Describe Africa's geography using **subsistence farming, food crops, cash crops, drought, desertification, urbanization.**

2 **Focus:** What are the major climate regions of Africa and what kinds of vegetation grow there?

3 **Focus:** How do Africans use their natural resources?

4 **Focus:** Why are the cities of Africa growing so rapidly?

5 **Critical Thinking: Conclude** Make a list of the major resources of Africa. Then choose the one you think is the most important to Africa's future. Explain your conclusion.

6 **Theme: Independence and Interdependence** Explain how Africans who move to cities depend on each other and their home villages to survive.

7 **Geography/Research Activity:** Create a resource map of Africa. Conduct research to find out where Africa's major natural resources are located. Then make a map that uses symbols to show how these resources are distributed throughout the continent.

Testing Hypotheses Using Maps

Answers from Maps

You've been reading a lot about West Africa. Suppose you have a **hypothesis,** or educated guess, about a connection between land use and climate in that part of the continent. How can you use maps to test your hypothesis? How does knowing how to read maps help you form and test more hypotheses?

1 Here's How

- Look at the climate zone map of Africa on page 437. What does the map tell you about the climates in West Africa?

- You can use information about climate to form a hypothesis about land use. For example, in what climate areas would people farm? Raise animals?

- Now you can look at the land use map. See what the map tells about land use in West Africa.

- You have just tested a hypothesis. Did information from the land use map prove or disprove your hypothesis?

- You can also use the land use map to make some hypotheses about climate. For example, what kind of climate would there most likely be in an area that grew bananas? Use the climate map to test your hypothesis.

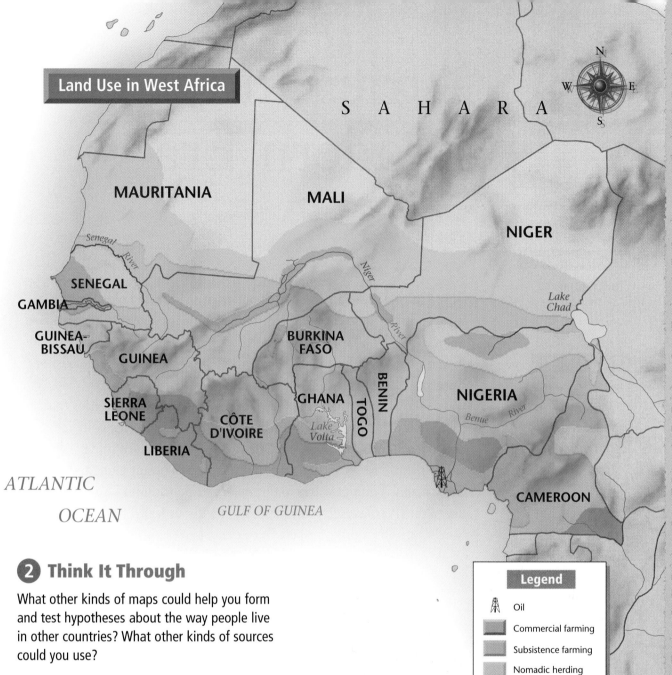

Land Use in West Africa

S A H A R A

MAURITANIA

MALI

NIGER

Senegal River

SENEGAL

Niger

Lake
Chad

GAMBIA

GUINEA-
BISSAU

GUINEA

BURKINA
FASO

BENIN

NIGERIA

River

SIERRA
LEONE

CÔTE
D'IVOIRE

GHANA

TOGO

Benue   River

Lake
Volta

LIBERIA

ATLANTIC

OCEAN

GULF OF GUINEA

CAMEROON

N
W   E
S

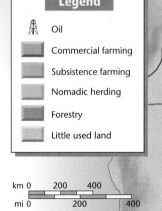

Legend

⚒ Oil

Commercial farming

Subsistence farming

Nomadic herding

Forestry

Little used land

km 0   200   400
mi 0   200   400

② Think It Through

What other kinds of maps could help you form
and test hypotheses about the way people live
in other countries? What other kinds of sources
could you use?

③ Use It

1. Use the land use map of West Africa to form
   two hypotheses about what the climate must
   be like in West Africa. Write down your
   hypotheses.

2. Test your hypotheses by checking what the
   climate map tells about West Africa.

3. Now use the climate map to form two
   hypotheses about land use in West Africa.
   Then use the land use map to test your
   hypotheses.

4. Write a short paragraph that tells about
   what you have learned.

Africa in the Modern Era

Main Idea Africans are working to overcome problems of the colonial past and build a better future.

Key Vocabulary

multiethnic

Key Events

1914 Only two countries remained independent

1945 World War II ends

1960 Year of Freedom

1993 Eritrea is the last African nation to regain independence

Carlos Miranda is excited about what the future holds for him, his wife, and their nine children. Not long ago, their country, Guinea-Bissau (gihn ee bih SOW), on the western coast of Africa, was not independent. It was a colony of Portugal, which is a country on the western coast of Europe.

Today, Guinea-Bissau stands independent and proud. Carlos fought to make it that way. "You ask what the difference between colonialism and independence means to me," he says, his voice full of pride. "Well, I will tell you. The difference is great. Now I go to bed at night and sleep comfortably. I do not worry about the secret police. And I do not tip my hat to the [Portuguese]. Now I speak . . . without fear. . . . That is all we fought for. The right to respect."

Life Under Colonial Rule

Focus *How were Africans affected by colonial rule?*

What if people from another country came — uninvited — into the community where you live? They wear strange clothes, practice a religion you've barely heard of, and don't even speak your language. Through interpreters, they tell you what to do. The strangers make your family move to a new place. They force you or your parents to work for them. This is what millions of people all across Africa lived with under European colonial rule.

Colonial Africa

As you read in Chapter 13, Europeans began to colonize Africa in the 1500s in order to expand their own power and wealth. They wanted natural resources, cheap labor, and good military locations. Through economic and military policies, they colonized almost all of the continent. By 1914, only two African countries remained independent.

How did colonial rule affect the peoples of Africa? Their lives were forever changed. Most Europeans thought that they and their cultures were superior to Africans and their cultures. They insisted that Africans learn European languages and accept European ways of life. One man expressed the pain that millions of Africans endured in these words: "There is no greater suffering for man than to feel his cultural foundations give way beneath his feet."

Rallies like this one show Africans supporting political freedom. **Citizenship:** *Have you ever taken part in a march or a rally for a special cause?*

Independent African Nations and Leaders

40°N

Strait of Gibraltar

MEDITERRANEAN SEA

MOROCCO 1956
TUNISIA 1956
ALGERIA 1962
LIBYA 1951
EGYPT 1922

WESTERN SAHARA (disputed)

CAPE VERDE 1975
MAURITANIA 1960
MALI 1960
NIGER 1960
CHAD 1960
SUDAN 1956
ERITREA 1993
DJIBOUTI 1977

SENEGAL 1960
GAMBIA 1965
GUINEA-BISSAU 1974
GUINEA 1958
BURKINA FASO 1960
BENIN
NIGERIA 1960
SOMALIA 1960

SIERRA LEONE 1961
COTE D'IVOIRE 1960
GHANA 1957
TOGO 1960
ETHIOPIA (independant for over 2000 years)

LIBERIA 1847
CAMEROON 1960
CENTRAL AFRICAN REPUBLIC 1960

EQUATORIAL GUINEA 1968
SAO TOME & PRINCIPE 1975
GABON 1960
CONGO 1960
ZAIRE 1960
RWANDA 1962
UGANDA 1962
KENYA 1963

RED SEA

INDIAN OCEAN

ATLANTIC OCEAN

BURUNDI 1962
TANZANIA 1961
SEYCHELLES 1976

ANGOLA 1975
ZAMBIA 1964
MALAWI 1964
COMOROS 1975

MOZAMBIQUE 1975
MADAGASCAR 1960

NAMIBIA 1990
ZIMBABWE 1980
MAURITIUS 1968

BOTSWANA 1966

Mozambique Channel

SWAZILAND 1968

SOUTH AFRICA 1910/1961
LESOTHO 1966

20°S

20°E

Legend

— National Boundary

---- Disputed Boundary

km 0 500 1000
mi 0 500 1000

Dates of African Independence

This map shows the year each African nation achieved independence. Below are three leaders who worked to free their countries from colonialism. Map Skill: *Match the leaders with the flags of their new nations. Then look at the map and find the date each leader's country became free.*

Zimbabwe

Ghana

Senegal

Leopold Senghor

(sahng GAWR)

The son of a small village trader, Senghor wrote poems while imprisoned in a Nazi concentration camp during World War II. He wanted to become a teacher and priest, but instead became a well-known poet and the first president of Senegal.

Kwame Nkrumah

(KWAH may uhn KROO muh)

A former teacher, Nkrumah worked hard to make Ghana independent. In 1950 the British put him in jail for being a nationalist. Ghanaians supported his election as their first African prime minister, but he was later overthrown in 1966.

Robert Mugabe

(mu GAH bee)

Mugabe grew up on a farm in Rhodesia (later named Zimbabwe). For 10 years the British kept him in jail, where he earned two college degrees. He went on to become the first president of Zimbabwe.

Regaining Independence

Focus *How did the peoples of Africa regain their independence?*

Africans suffered under colonial rule for hundreds of years. The two World Wars in this century (see Chapter 14) weakened European power. During World War II, talk of freedom led many in both Europe and Africa to view the idea of having colonies as wrong. Throughout Africa there was a growing sense of nationalism, or the belief that people should have and control their own nations.

The spirit of nationalism spread, and with it independence. In 1945, African leaders gathered in Europe at one of several special meetings held to discuss their common problems. They resolved to condemn colonialism and stand up for national freedom. Although they were from different countries, these African leaders agreed:

> **"W**e are determined to be free. We want education. We want the right to earn a decent living, the right to express our thoughts and emotions, to adopt and create forms of beauty . . . We will fight in every way we can for freedom.**"**

Tragically, many people did have to fight for that freedom. Carlos Miranda fought the Portuguese army in the hills of Guinea-Bissau. Africans in other countries, including Zaire, Angola, and Congo, also had to fight for their freedom. For some, the transition was more peaceful.

Once it began, the process of regaining independence happened quickly. Look at the map on the facing page to see the dates of independence for each nation. In 1960, the dramatic "Year of Freedom," you can see that 17 countries became independent *(see chart)*. In that year, Prime Minister Harold Macmillan of Great Britain said: "The most striking of all the impressions I have formed . . . is of the strength of this African national [awareness] . . . . The wind of change is blowing through this continent."

Across the continent, people celebrated their independence. Africans were optimistic about their future. They planned to build modern, democratic nations. In building new nations, they had two main strengths: their spirit of nationalism and their countries' vast natural resources. Still, they faced difficult challenges, many of which were a direct result of European colonial policies.

Ask Yourself

If you were an African, how would you explain your desire for independence?

? ? ? ? ? ? ? ? ? ? ? ? ?

Independence

Gained in 1960 from:

France
- BENIN
- BURKINA FASO
- CAMEROON
- CENTRAL AFRICAN REPUBLIC
- CHAD
- CONGO
- COTE D'IVOIRE
- GABON
- MADAGASCAR
- MALI
- MAURITANIA
- NIGER
- SENEGAL
- TOGO

Belgium
- ZAIRE

Britain
- NIGERIA

Italy
- SOMALIA

Chart Skill: *Why is 1960 called "the year of independence?"*

Building Nations

Focus | *What challenges do Africans face in building nations?*

Colonialism forever changed African economies and cultures. In the months leading up to independence, many Europeans left in a hurry, taking with them vital government records, technology, and knowledge. Often they left behind many problems for the new nations to solve.

Education is very important for new nations. Students learning to read today will be better prepared to govern their countries in the 21st century. Citizenship: *How does education support democracy?*

The Colonial Legacy

Some problems in building the new nations were the direct result of colonial policies. For example, the Europeans had established economies that favored one cash crop over many food crops. Independent Kenya, for example, was dependent on income from the coffee crop it sold. A bad year for coffee growing could mean disaster for Kenya.

Another problem was that Africans were not educated to participate as citizens of a democracy. During the colonial period, Europeans educated some Africans to serve as colonial officials and as workers. Most Africans, however, had little access to schooling.

Despite this past, the Africans pushed forward. Joseph Maitha (my EE thuh), a Kenyan economist, said, "We can't go on blaming the colonialists [forever] for all our problems." With this spirit, African nations made ambitious plans to build roads, railroads, airports, and new educational systems.

Multiethnic Nations

When many different ethnic groups live in the same country, it is called a **multiethnic** nation. All African nations are multiethnic. To build a unified nation, however, people need to communicate in one language and feel part of one nation. In Africa, ethnic ties are strong because they have existed for centuries. Many independent African nations are new. Sometimes conflicts have caused power struggles and even civil wars. Strong kinship and ethnic-group loyalties have also provided strength during the hard process of nation building.

Dictators and Democracies in Africa Today

When the new government of a country lacks the support of all its people, the country can become unstable and democracy can be threatened. This can provide an opportunity for a dictator to seize power.

Some African countries have had dictators. But democracy in many African nations now has a promising future. For example, Jerry Rawlings seized power in Ghana. Yet he later held elections. Kenya, with its constitution guaranteeing rights like freedom of speech and religion, has always been ruled by an elected president. South Africa became the newest African democracy in 1994.

Africa has changed rapidly in the past 100 years. Today, Africans face the challenges of building strong, independent nations. Diverse groups are learning to apply Kenyan President Jomo Kenyatta's idea of *Harambee* — "pulling together." Today's Africans are proud of their heritage. As Nigerian author Chinua Achebe (chee NOO ah ah CHAY bay) says:

> **"A**frican peoples did not hear of culture for the first time from Europeans;...their societies...frequently had a philosophy of great depth and value and beauty,...they had poetry, and, above all, they had dignity.**"**

Curious Facts

The African continent has more national boundaries than any other continent. It is home to more than 50 nations and over 2,000 different ethnic groups. At least 800 languages are spoken in Africa and hundreds of religions are practiced.

Lesson Review

1900   **1950**   **2000**

1914
Only two countries remained independent.

1945
World War II ends.

1960
Year of Freedom

1 **Key Vocabulary:** Use the word **multiethnic** in a paragraph describing Africa.

2 **Focus:** How were Africans affected by colonial rule?

3 **Focus:** How did the peoples of Africa regain their independence?

4 **Focus:** What challenges do Africans face in building nations?

5 **Critical Thinking: Comparing Then and Now** How do you think the Africans' experience under colonial rule might affect their dealings with Europe today?

6 **Theme: Independence and Interdependence** Why might many Africans feel more allegiance to their ethnic groups than to their countries?

7 **Citizenship/Research Activity:** Debate whether a colony in Africa should become an independent nation. One group should act as nationalist African leaders. A second group should take the role of European colonial officials.

South Africa's New National Anthem:

A Story in Words and Music

In 1994, Nelson Mandela, leader of a political party called the African National Congress, was elected president of South Africa. This was South Africa's very first one-person, one-vote election. Until 1994, white South Africans — less than 15% of the population — ruled the country. They made a system of laws called apartheid that gave special privileges only to white people.

Another thing that has changed since 1994 is the National Anthem of South Africa. A national anthem is supposed to make everyone feel good about his or her country. Because there have been such deep divisions between the peoples of South Africa, the new national anthem needed to reach out with something for everyone. It uses four different languages and two kinds of music.

The first verse of the song is written in the Xhosa (KOH sa) language, and the second verse is in the Sesotho (seh SOH thoh) language. These are African languages.

These words are part of a hymn. During the time of apartheid in South Africa, black people sang this as a protest song. The words and music of this hymn were composed in 1897 by a black South African, Enoch Sontonga. Here is what the words of this part of the song say in English:

1
Lord, bless Africa
May her spirit rise high up
Hear thou our prayers
Lord bless us, your family.

2
Lord, bless Africa
May her spirit rise high up
Hear thou our prayers
Lord bless us, South Africa, South Africa.

The third verse of the song is written in a language called Afrikaans. Afrikaans is the traditional language of the white Dutch settlers who colonized South Africa in the 1600s. These words are from the old national anthem of South Africa. The music for the rest of the song is also from the old national anthem. The music was composed by a white South African, Reverend M.L. de Villiers in 1921. Here is what the words of this part of the song say in English:

3 *Ringing out from our blue heavens, from deep seas breaking round*
Over everlasting mountains where echoing crags resound.

The fourth verse of the song is written in English. English is a more "neutral language." People of all races in South Africa can use it and understand it. The words in this part of the song are new, like the new united government and the new country where all citizens have equal rights. These final words emphasize the idea of unity, one nation for everyone:

4 *Sound the call to come together, and united we shall stand.*
Let us live and strive for freedom in South Africa our Land.

National Anthem of South Africa

1 *Nkosi Sikelel' iAfrika*
Maluphakanyisw' uphondo lwayo
Yizwa imithandazo yethu.
Nkosi sikelela
Thina lusapho lwayo.

2 *Morena boloko setjhaba sa heso*
O fedise dintwa le matshwenyeho.
O se boloke, o se boloke.
Setjhaba sa heso, setjhaba sa.
South Afrika, South Afrika.

3 *Uit die blou van onse hemel, uit die diepte van ons see,*
Oor ons ewige gebergtes waar die kranse antwoord gee.

4 *Sound the call to come together and united we shall stand,*
Let us live and strive for freedom in South Africa our Land.

Response Activities

1. **Compare** Think about patriotic songs you know about America and how they make you feel. Does this song remind you of any of them? What do the words tell you about South Africans' feelings about their country?

2. **Descriptive:** Write about different music you could use to write a new anthem for the United States. How would the music you choose express your feelings about our country?

3. **Cultures: Choose Languages** If you wanted to write a song about America, with verses in different languages, which languages would you choose? In what parts of the country do you think these verses would be most popular?

Journey to Jo'burg
A SOUTH AFRICAN STORY
Beverley Naidoo

Fiction

Journey to Jo'burg

A SOUTH AFRICAN STORY

by Beverley Naidoo

Getting to Johannesburg has been an adventure for thirteen-year-old Naledi and her little brother Tiro — an adventure with a serious purpose. Their baby sister is so ill that she may die, and they have come 300 miles to get their mother and take her back home. They have reached the big city safely, but where is the rich home where their mother works?

At the time of this story, the laws of South Africa gave special privileges to white people. And for two young black children from the country, Jo'burg could be a dangerous place.

windscreen — *British term for windshield*

As they turned toward the road, there was a bus with the word "PARKTOWN" in big letters on the front. It was slowing down a little way up the road and the doors were opening. Through the front windscreen they could see the driver was black.

"Come on, Tiro!" called Naledi, pulling him by the arm. They were just about to jump aboard, when someone shouted at them in English, "What's wrong with you? Are you stupid?"

Startled, they looked up at the angry face of the bus driver and then at the bus again. White faces stared at them from inside as the bus moved off.

Naledi and Tiro stood on the side of the road, shaken, holding hands tightly, when a voice behind them said, "Don't let it bother you. That's what they're like. You'd better come out of the road."

A young woman put out her hand to bring them onto the pavement.

"You must be strangers here if you don't

know about the buses. This stop has a white sign, but we have to wait by the black one over there."

She pointed to a small black metal signpost.

"You must also look at the front of the bus for the small notice saying 'Non-whites only.'"

"I'm sorry. We forgot to look," Naledi explained.

"It's not you who should be sorry!" said the young woman forcefully. "They should be sorry, those stupid people! Why shouldn't we use any bus? When our buses are full, their buses are half empty. Don't you be sorry!"

The children looked at each other. This person was different from their mother. Mma never spoke out like that.

The young woman asked where they were going. Naledi took out the letter, and when the young woman looked at the address, she exclaimed, "But this is near where my mother works. I'm on my way to visit her today, so I can show you the place."

"Thank you, Mma." The children smiled. Lucky again.

"By the way, I'm Grace Mbatha. Now who are you both, and where are you from? You speak Tswana the way my mother does. Maybe you live near my mother's people."

So, once again, the children began their story.

Luckily the bus wasn't full when it arrived. Grace had warned them that in the rush hour you were almost squeezed to death. As the bus trundled along, stopping and starting with the traffic, there was a chance to stare out the windows. Tiro thought the cyclists were very brave, riding in between all the cars. Naledi kept trying to see the tops of the tall buildings, twisting her neck around until it began to hurt!

The bus now heaved its way up a steep hill and soon they were leaving the city buildings, seeing the sky again, as well as trees, grass lawns and flowers on either side of the road. Behind the trees were big houses, such as they had never seen before. Grace smiled at the way the children were staring, amazed.

"Don't you know the people in this place have a lot of money? My mother looks after two children in a very big house, and there is another person just to cook, and another person to look after the garden."

Mma — *Mother, in the Tswana language. Also used by children when speaking to a woman*

Naledi and Tiro listened with interest. Mma never liked to talk much to them about her work when she was at home, although once they had overheard Mma talking to Nono about the child whom she looked after. Mma had said, "The little girl is very rude. She thinks I belong to her mother. You should hear how she can shout at me."

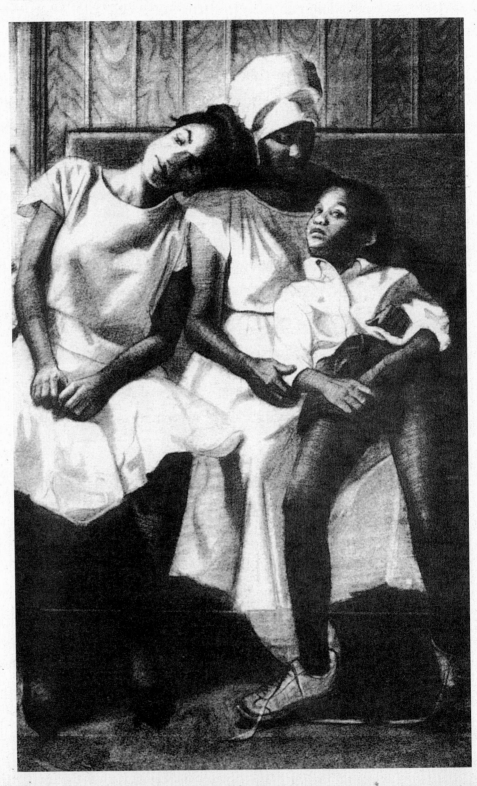

Naledi wanted to ask Grace to tell them some more, but she was still a little shy, and soon they had reached their stop.

They stepped off the bus onto a wide pavement along a street lined with great leafy trees.

"That's the road where your mother works at number twenty-five. My mma works at number seventeen in the next road down there. Can you manage now?"

The children nodded, and then Grace added, "If you need somewhere to stay tonight, you can come back with me to Soweto. I'm going at six o'clock, O.K.?"

Tiro and Naledi thanked Grace, although they were a little puzzled about needing somewhere to stay. After all, they would be with their mother now and they would be going home with her as quickly as possible, back to Dineo.

As they turned to go down the road, they suddenly felt very excited — and anxious too. So much had been happening that they hadn't been thinking all along of their little sister.

Please let her be all right now pounded in Naledi's brain.

Half walking, half running, they made for number 25.

Meet the Author

Beverley Naidoo was born in South Africa in 1943, and lived there until she moved to England in 1965. Her experiences in South Africa led her to write *Journey to Jo'burg*. She also wrote *Chain of Fire*, another novel set in South Africa.

Additional Books to Read

Shaka, King of the Zulus by Diane Stanley and Peter Vennema. Read about a remarkable leader of 18th-century Africa.

Desmond Tutu by David Winner. Learn about a modern religious leader devoted to freedom.

Response Activities

1. **Predict** How will life change for black South African young people now that apartheid has ended?

2. **Write a Story: Narrative** Write your own story about feeling left out or being forbidden to do something that other kids were allowed to do.

3. **History: Research** Find a book about South Africa under apartheid and make a list of rules and restrictions that black people had to follow.

Chapter Review

Chapter Review Timeline

| 1900 | 1920 | 1940 | 1960 | 1980 | 2000 |

1914
Only two countries in Africa remain independent

1945
World War II ends

1960
Year of Freedom—
17 countries regain independence

1993
Eritrea is the last African country to regain independence

Summarizing the Main Idea

1 Copy the chart below, and write a few sentences describing the aspect of Africa listed.

Climate	Colonial rule
Food	Independence
Crafts	Democracy
Mineral resources	

Vocabulary

2 You are an African diplomat at the United Nations. Using six of the following terms, deliver a speech describing two or three of your major concerns to the General Assembly.

subsistence farming (p. 436)   drought (p. 438)   multiethnic (p. 446)

food crops (p. 436)   desertification (p. 438)

cash crops (p. 438)   urbanization (p. 439)

Reviewing the Facts

3 Name three of the most impressive features of Africa's geography and climate.

4 How do the majority of the people of Africa make their living?

5 What is the difference between food crops and cash crops?

6 What is desertification, and what is causing it?

7 What are the people of Africa doing to fight desertification?

8 Why are many Africans moving to the cities?

9 How does past colonial rule continue to affect Africa today?

10 How has Africa's ethnic diversity affected the development of new nations?

11 Make a hypothesis about the differences in ways of life between Africans who live in cities and Africans who live in rural areas. Test your hypothesis in the following way:

1. Find maps that show population growth in African cities.

2. Pick two cities with fast population growth.

3. Research information about ways of life in those cities and in rural areas in the same countries.

4. To test your hypothesis, compare it with your researched information.

Geography Skills

12 Look at the climate map on page 437, "Climate Regions of Africa." Compare it to the political map on page 444, "Independent African Nations." Choose one climate region, and name the nations that fall within it. How do you think this climate affects these nations?

13 Pick one climate region described on p. 437. Make a chart listing the pros and cons of living in such a climate.

Critical Thinking

14 **Cause and Effect** Africa's deserts are expanding, reducing precious farmland. If this continues, how will it affect Africans? If it is stopped, how will that affect the future?

15 **Compare** Africa and the United States are both multiethnic societies. How are they similar, and how are they different? What can we learn from each other?

Writing: Citizenship and Culture

16 **Citizenship** In Africa, the Green Belt Movement is trying to save the land. In the United States, many environmental groups are working to protect land or animals here. Write a letter to one of them asking for information on something that interests you.

17 **Culture** Write a paragraph explaining how you think a nation is affected by having a variety of cultures existing within it.

Activities

Economics/Science
Farming methods have improved a lot in recent years. Find out how various technologies in Africa are making it possible for African farmers to produce more food, even under difficult conditions. Report your findings to the class.

History/Research
On page 444, three leaders of African independence are described. Choose one of the other 46 African nations that regained independence and find out who its first leader was. Write a short biography of this leader.

Internet Option

Check the **Internet Social Studies Center** for ideas on how to extend your theme project beyond your classroom.

THEME PROJECT CHECK-IN

As you choose an African country for your theme project, use the information in this chapter and these questions to help you.
- What African geographic features influence independence and interdependence?
- How did political and cultural conflicts bring independence and interdependence in Africa?
- What different political systems have existed in Africa in the 20th century?

CHAPTER 17

Africa: Patterns of Living

Chapter Preview: *People, Places, and Events*

1860	1888	1916

Anwar el-Sadat   1918–1981

How did this Egyptian leader help build up his country? *Lesson 1, Page 459*

Nairobi, Kenya

Ride the "Lunatic Express" to Kenya's capital. *Lesson 2, Page 464*

On Safari!

Join tourists as they search for giraffes, lions, and elephants. *Lesson 2, Page 466*

Egypt: A Strong Cultural Identity

Main Idea Egyptian culture has been influenced by many groups of people, both ancient and modern, but it remains strong and independent.

Key Vocabulary

dialect

nationalize

fellahin

Egyptian workers looked on as the gigantic stone heads of Pharaoh Ramesses II and his queen, Nefertari, were lifted to the sky. More than three thousand years before, the pharaoh had ordered laborers to build two magnificent temples at Abu Simbel (ah boo SIHM buhl), on the banks of the Nile. He had giant stone statues of himself and his wife carved to guard the temple entrance. Now modern workers undid the task of their ancient counterparts, cutting the statues into a thousand blocks, each weighing about 30 tons. Why? Rising waters caused by the building of the Aswan High Dam were threatening to flood the temples. Giant cranes lifted the blocks to higher ground, where they were reassembled. Today, Ramesses II and Nefertari still look out across the mighty river, reminding Egyptians how their ancient heritage has blended with modern ways.

Key Events

1869 Suez Canal opened

1922 Egypt gains independence from Great Britain

1956 Egypt nationalizes Suez Canal

◄ **Many different buildings can be seen in Cairo, the capital of Egypt.**

1944	1972	2000	

A Mosaic of Cultures

Nigeria is a nation of many peoples and cultures. Learn about their traditions. *Lesson 3, Page 472*

Life Under Apartheid

From the 1940s to the 1990s, racial groups were separated by South African law. *Lesson 4, Page 480*

Nelson Mandela

The South African president works to rebuild and reunify his country. *Lesson 4, Page 482*

Egypt as a Crossroads

Focus *Why has Egypt been called a crossroads?*

"It looked as though the funnels of ships steamed right through the desert," said a boat's captain, recalling his trip through Egypt's Suez Canal. It also must have looked like a parade of nations — ships flying flags from Liberia, Norway, Greece, and other countries. People, goods, and ideas from around the world were passing through Egypt that day.

Opened in 1869, the Suez Canal is the busiest international waterway in the world today. By connecting the Mediterranean and Red seas, the Canal has helped make Egypt a crossroads of the world. For centuries, deserts to the east, west, and south and a broad sea to the north discouraged foreign visitors and invading armies. The Nile's cataracts in the south also limited outside contact from that direction. This isolation allowed the ancient Egyptians to build their great civilization, as you read in Chapter 4.

Egypt's central location eventually became more important than these obstacles, which were overcome. Located where the continents of Africa and Asia touch, and bridging the two seas, Egypt became a natural meeting place of peoples and cultures.

For thousands of years, people have traveled to and through Egypt. Some have come to conquer, others to trade. All have left their mark. Standing on a street corner in Cairo (KY roh), the capital, you can see the influence of many cultures. The skyline is outlined by modern skyscrapers, buildings influenced by European and American architecture. They share the sky with minarets, the thin towers of mosques. These are signs of the Islamic culture introduced to Egypt by the Muslims more than 1,000 years ago. You can also see Roman structures, left from the time when Egypt was a province of the Roman Empire.

The people of Cairo also reflect the many cultures that have touched them and their ancestors. Most speak the city's unique dialect of the

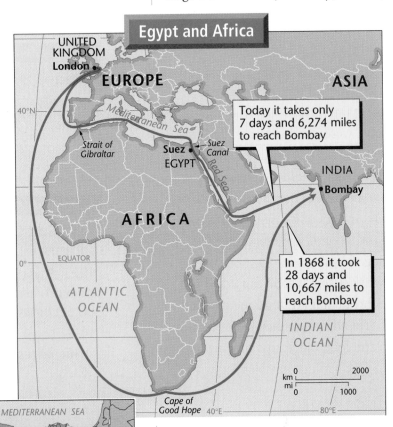

Egypt and Africa

Today it takes only 7 days and 6,274 miles to reach Bombay

In 1868 it took 28 days and 10,667 miles to reach Bombay

These maps show why the Suez Canal is the busiest waterway in the world. **Map Skill:** *How many days can today's travelers save when going from London to Bombay compared to those who traveled the same route in 1868?*

Arabic language. A **dialect** is a variation of a language spoken in a region or by a particular group of people. You can also hear business people speaking in French, a language used here since Napoleon's invasion nearly 200 years ago. You also hear the sounds of English, a holdover from British control of Egypt. Modern Egyptians are descendants of the ancient Egyptians, as well as of Nubians, Persians, Greeks, Romans, Arabs, Turks, French, and British, to name a few.

A Strong National Identity

Despite constant contact with other peoples, Egyptian culture is strong. Egyptian identity was challenged, however, after the British took control of Egypt in 1882, largely to control the Suez Canal. (The Canal offered the British a shorter route to India, as you can see on the map, opposite.) Egypt gained independence in 1922, but British troops remained. Egyptians had little control over their own government. Many feared losing their national identity. In 1952, army officers revolted and seized power.

One of the officers who led the fight to break ties from Great Britain was Gamal Abdel Nasser (NAS ur). Nasser would lead Egypt as prime minister and president until his death in 1970. His reforms provided free education, increased the standards of health care, and improved agriculture. Nasser's emphasis on nationalism restored Egyptians' pride in their culture, their heritage, and their nation.

In a bold move that shocked the world, Nasser **nationalized** the Suez Canal in 1956. In other words, he took the Canal away from its private owners and put it under the control of the government. Britain and France, who relied on the Canal for transporting oil, attacked Egypt. With support from the United States and the Soviet Union, Egypt stood firm. Today, the Suez Canal remains under complete Egyptian control.

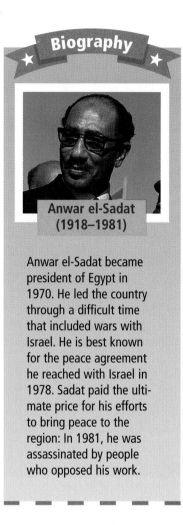

Biography

Anwar el-Sadat (1918–1981)

Anwar el-Sadat became president of Egypt in 1970. He led the country through a difficult time that included wars with Israel. He is best known for the peace agreement he reached with Israel in 1978. Sadat paid the ultimate price for his efforts to bring peace to the region: In 1981, he was assassinated by people who opposed his work.

A U.S. battleship steams through the Suez Canal. Every day, ships from all over the world use the waterway.

Life in Egypt Today

Focus *What do Egyptians who live in cities have in common with those who live in rural areas?*

Wearing long shirts called galabias (juh LAH bee uhz), loose pants, and turbans, farmers at a village market argue over the price of farm animals. In a nearby city, friends discuss which movie they would like to see. Both scenes are common in Egypt today. They reflect a culture in which old and new ways of life exist together.

Nearly all Egyptians, however, have ties to the beautiful Nile River. Called "the Mother of Egypt," the river gives life to the desert and supports the 99 percent of Egyptians who live along its banks. About half of them live in cities. The other half live in rural areas.

Living Off the Land

Egyptian peasants, called **fellahin** (fehl uh HEEN), farm the land along the Nile as they have for thousands of years. Many follow traditional ways, using water wheels to draw water from the river. The water irrigates small plots where grain, fruits, and vegetables grow. Near the plots, the houses of the fellahin — small mud homes with thatched roofs — stand in small villages. Cotton, for which Egypt is well known, grows in larger fields.

Life in Cairo

Egypt's city dwellers, especially the people of Cairo, lead very different lives from those of the fellahin. In contrast to the rural villages, Cairo is a crowded, sprawling, busy city, a mixture of old and new. Modern buildings line ancient streets.

Cairo dominates Egypt as few other cities in the world dominate a country. Besides being the nation's capital, it is an economic, religious, educational, and cultural center. It is the largest city in Africa, with a rapidly growing population in the mid-1990s of 10 million people.

Growth has challenged Cairo as it has other African cities. Traffic jams, housing shortages, inadequate public transportation, and overburdened water, electrical, and sewage systems are big problems. In recent years, the government has made dramatic improvements. Yet these improvements draw even more people to the city from the countryside, where it is sometimes difficult to make a living.

An Egyptian merchant sells many of his goods at a Cairo bazaar, or market.

Cairo is a mixture of ancient and modern buildings. **Culture:** *Identify the mosque in the photo.*

Preserving Egyptian Identity

All Egyptians share a strong pride in their country and their culture. They are linked by the Nile. They are also tied by religion: Most Egyptians (about 90 percent) are Muslims.

Since the late 1960s, Egypt has been undergoing an Islamic revival. Egyptian Muslims have become concerned with living lives that are closer to the ideals of Islam, which you read about in Chapter 10. This revival is part of a larger movement throughout the region and the world. Because Egypt is one of the Islamic nations most open to Western culture, the revival has special significance there. In Egypt, many want to see religion play a bigger role in government, as it does in other Arab countries. These Egyptians want their country, as a whole, to embrace Islam more fully. Other Egyptians disagree. They are pleased to weave new ideas and elements of foreign cultures into the fabric of Egyptian life.

This struggle to determine Egypt's future will probably continue through your lifetime. It is a struggle about what it means to be an Egyptian, about how to maintain a distinct identity in a nation that is a cultural crossroads. Like many countries in Africa, Egypt is a nation in which Muslim, African, and European influences have blended.

A Muslim family from Cairo stands in front of a mural depicting scenes from the hajj, the Muslim pilgrimage to Mecca.

Lesson Review

1800	1900	2000

1869
Suez Canal opens

1922
Egypt gains independence from Great Britain

1956
Egypt nationalizes Suez Canal

1 Key Vocabulary: Write a paragraph about Egypt, using **nationalize** and **fellahin**.

2 Focus: Why has Egypt been called a crossroads?

3 Focus: What do Egyptians who live in cities have in common with those who live in rural areas?

4 Critical Thinking: Conclude Why may some groups have had more impact on Egyptian culture than others?

5 Geography: What geographic features make a region a crossroads?

6 Theme: Independence and Interdependence/Art Activity Create a collage showing one form of Egyptian dependence on Africa or the rest of the world.

THINK LIKE A
GEOGRAPHER

Environment and Society

How Has the Aswan Dam Affected its Environment?

For thousands of years Egyptians were at the mercy of the Nile. Low floods meant dry fields and famine. High floods swept away crops, soil, and houses. A series of canals and dams helped store water for year-round irrigation, but could not control the summer flooding.

Egypt's President Gamal Abdel Nasser dreamed of a dam that would control the Nile's floods and provide water to raise food for Egypt's growing population. Egypt began building the Aswan High Dam in 1960 and completed it ten years later. The dam has done more than prevent destructive floods. It stores water for droughts, has added more than 1 million new acres to Egypt's farmland, and generates much of Egypt's electricity.

Altering Egypt's environment has had unwelcome side effects as well. The dam has blocked rich soil from reaching farmlands downstream. It has also turned the water in the Nile saltier, destroyed the sardine industry, and increased the danger of a disease-carrying parasite.

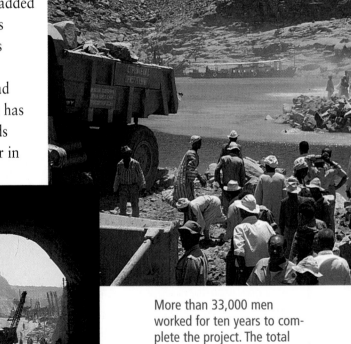

The Aswan High Dam is a monument of engineering. Its massive structure is about 2.38 miles long and 364 feet high. The dam is 17 times larger than the Great Pyramid at Giza. Do you know of any large dam projects in countries other than Egypt?

More than 33,000 men worked for ten years to complete the project. The total cost was over a billion dollars. The Soviet Union helped Egypt pay for the enormously expensive project.

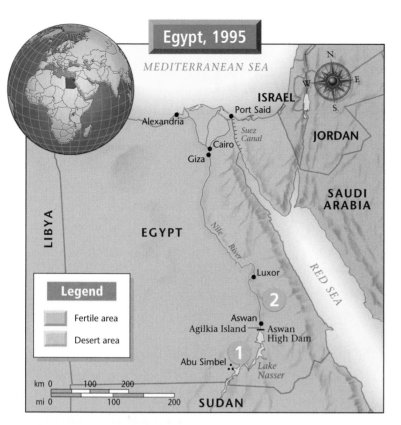

Egypt, 1995

MEDITERRANEAN SEA

ISRAEL
Port Said
Alexandria
Suez Canal
JORDAN
Cairo
Giza
SAUDI ARABIA
LIBYA
EGYPT
Nile River
RED SEA
Luxor
2
Aswan
Agilkia Island — Aswan High Dam
1
Abu Simbel
Lake Nasser
SUDAN

Legend
Fertile area
Desert area

km 0   100   200
mi 0   100   200

100 million tons of sediment that once washed downstream each year is now trapped behind the Aswan High Dam. **Map Skill:** *What is the distance from the Aswan High Dam to the mouth of the Nile River?*

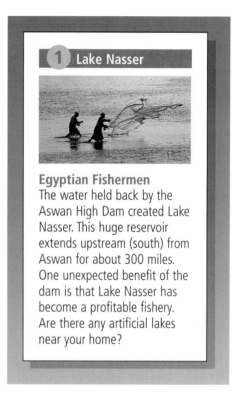

1 Lake Nasser

Egyptian Fishermen
The water held back by the Aswan High Dam created Lake Nasser. This huge reservoir extends upstream (south) from Aswan for about 300 miles. One unexpected benefit of the dam is that Lake Nasser has become a profitable fishery. Are there any artificial lakes near your home?

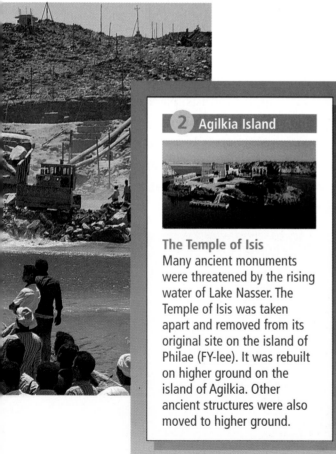

2 Agilkia Island

The Temple of Isis
Many ancient monuments were threatened by the rising water of Lake Nasser. The Temple of Isis was taken apart and removed from its original site on the island of Philae (FY-lee). It was rebuilt on higher ground on the island of Agilkia. Other ancient structures were also moved to higher ground.

Science Connection

Before the Aswan High Dam, the Nile's annual flooding cleansed the river by flushing waste into the sea. Now water often stands year-round in canals and ditches. This water has become the breeding ground for a microscopic worm that bores its way through the skin. The result is an incurable disease that has sickened many Egyptian farmers. Do you know of any other insects that breed in stagnant water?

Research Activity

Large dam projects often cause dramatic changes in their environments.

1 Research another major dam project. What impact did the dam have on the environment in which it was built? What were the benefits? Were there any unexpected problems?

2 Share your findings with the class in a short oral presentation.

Kenya: An Economic Journey

Key Vocabulary

preserve

tourism

commercial agriculture

gross domestic product (GDP)

informal economy

population density

Main Idea People in many professions and from all walks of life contribute to Kenya's strong economy.

A ll aboard the Lunatic Express! That's the nickname of the railway the British built across Kenya a century ago, when Kenya was a British colony. They built it to connect another colony in Uganda, Kenya's neighbor, to the coast. Many Kenyans thought the railway was a foolish, or lunatic, idea. Still, the railroad runs today and is an important means of transport for the region. It follows the original tracks inland from the port city of Mombasa (mahm BAS uh).

Waiting to board the train are several people. Two women of Indian descent are discussing the hotel they run for tourists. Next to them, several men in business suits are talking about the day's news in the Kikuyu (kih KOO yoo) language. The men work in Nairobi (ny ROH bee), the capital. These people have one thing in common: They participate in Kenya's economy. A trip on the Lunatic Express reveals just how remarkable the Kenyan economy truly is.

The Lunatic Express travels across Kenya. Economics: *How do trains help a nation's economy?*

Departure for Nairobi

After leaving Mombasa, the train heads for Kenya's modern capital, Nairobi *(above)*.

Focus *What roles do exports, tourism, and agriculture play in Kenya's economy?*

The busy port city of Mombasa, where the train line begins, lies partly on an island in the Indian Ocean, and partly on the mainland. A raised roadway, or bridge, connects the two parts of the city. Mombasa is beautiful and ancient. Settled more than 1,000 years ago by Arab traders, it soon became an important port where ivory, gold, and timber were traded. Sailing ships carried these goods to Europe and other places around the world.

Looking around today, you can see that Mombasa is still an important port. The rumbling diesel engines of modern freighters have replaced the graceful sails of the old ships, but exports continue to pour out of Mombasa. Ships carry goods from countries such as Uganda, Burundi, and Rwanda, which do not have access to an ocean, as well as from Kenya.

Coffee and tea are some of Kenya's key exports. Above, a Kenyan woman harvests coffee beans.

Freighters Filled with Coffee and Tea

Exports are important to Kenya. In the early 1990s, they brought in about $1 billion a year. Half of Kenya's exports are agricultural products, chiefly coffee and tea. Their sale on the international market is the largest single source of income for the Kenyan economy. If a captain of a ship docked in Mombasa would allow you to explore the hold of his vessel, there's a good chance you would find it filled with coffee or tea. A large cargo ship can easily carry well over 10,000 tons of coffee!

The huge ships docked at Mombasa also bring goods into the country. Kenya, like other countries, imports goods it cannot make itself or can buy more cheaply abroad. Kenya's major trading partners include the United States, Great Britain, and Japan.

Coffee beans after roasting

Africa: Patterns of Living **465**

Elephants, Leopards, Zebras, and Tourists

Beyond the docks lie beautiful beaches. Tourists from around the world flock to Kenya and stay in fancy hotels. But most don't come for the beaches. Hop on board the train, and you'll soon see what so many tourists hope to see.

As the train leaves Mombasa, it chugs northwest. Work began on this railway in 1895. To lay the rails, the British brought more than 30,000 workers from India. As they worked inland, the railroad builders had their first deadly encounter with Kenya's wildlife. By the time the railway was finished, at least 30 men had been killed by lions.

Today, Kenya's wildlife is considered not a threat, but its chief tourist attraction. As the train picks up speed, you cross Tsavo (SAH voh) National Park, Kenya's largest wildlife **preserve** (a place where wild animals are protected). After the export of coffee and tea, **tourism**, the selling of services to tourists, brings more money into Kenya than any other economic activity. About 50,000 Kenyans make their living from the tourist trade. Many of the Asians descended from the workers who built the railroad run hotels and restaurants and make arrangements for safaris — trips to see wildlife *(see map)*.

· **Tell Me More** ·

On Safari!

A group of all-terrain vehicles creep quietly across the Kenyan plain and then come to a standstill. Heads emerge through the car roofs, and binoculars scan the horizon. Suddenly there is an excited cry: "Zebras! Over there! And look! There's a lion stalking one of them!" This is a Kenyan safari, and these tourists are getting what they came for: close encounters with animals in their natural habitats. By the end of the day, the travelers will likely see elephants, giraffes, rhinoceroses, ostriches, and many other creatures.

About one million people from all over the world come to Kenya every year, armed with cameras and camcorders. The nation has established more than 25 national parks and wildlife preserves across the country in order to protect its rare animals.

Tourism does have some drawbacks. Many Kenyans recognize the need to protect the wildlife on which tourism depends. Others feel that the needs of the animals have been put before the needs of the people, especially farmers. Wildlife preserves take up much-needed farmland, and animals sometimes wander off preserves and destroy crops.

Farming the Land

As the train continues toward its destination, you enter farm country. Field after field of crops rushes in and out of view. Cash crops, including coffee, tea, cashews, and sisal (SY suhl) — which is used to make fiber for rope — grow in the fields of plantations. These huge farms can stretch over 5,000 acres. The farmers who work these plantations are engaged in **commercial agriculture,** in which crops are grown to be sold for income.

Many of Kenya's farmers engage in subsistence agriculture, in which crops are grown for the farmer's own use. Kenyan subsistence farmers have small farm plots called *shambas,* usually only a few acres in size.

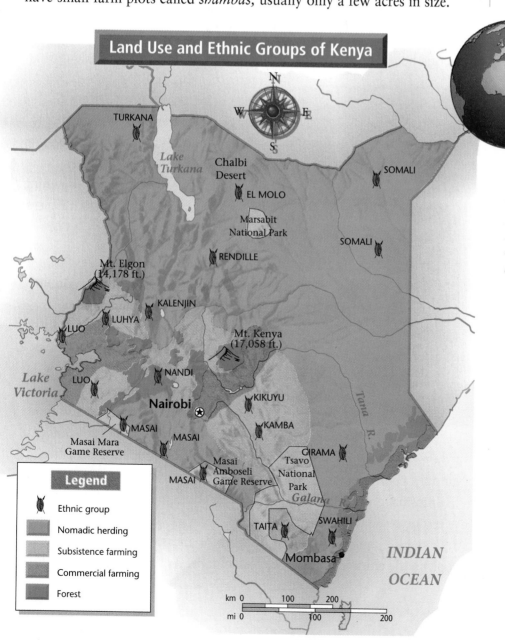

Land Use and Ethnic Groups of Kenya

TURKANA

Lake Turkana

Chalbi Desert

EL MOLO

SOMALI

Marsabit National Park

SOMALI

Mt. Elgon (14,178 ft.)

RENDILLE

KALENJIN

LUHYA

Mt. Kenya (17,058 ft.)

LUO

NANDI

Lake Victoria

LUO

Nairobi

KIKUYU

MASAI

KAMBA

MASAI

Masai Mara Game Reserve

GIRAMA

Masai Amboseli Game Reserve

Tsavo National Park

MASAI

Tana R.

Galana R.

TAITA

SWAHILI

Mombasa

INDIAN OCEAN

Legend

Ethnic group
Nomadic herding
Subsistence farming
Commercial farming
Forest

km 0   100   200
mi 0   100   200

In the 1990s, one-third of Kenya's total economic output was agricultural. **Map Skill:** *Locate Mombasa and Nairobi. How many different land uses can you find in the area between the two cities?*

Often, their fields produce barely enough food to feed their families. Corn is the major food crop, along with cassava, beans, and wheat.

Like every other African economy, Kenya's economy is chiefly agricultural. In the 1990s, one-third of the country's total economic output was connected to agriculture. Three out of four Kenyans make their living from agriculture. All Kenyans, whatever their job, contribute to the nation's **gross domestic product (GDP)**, which is the total value of all the goods and services produced in a country during a single year. In 2000, Kenya's GDP was equivalent to over $10 billion (in U.S. dollars). As the train approaches Nairobi, you'll see a part of the Kenyan economy that is growing in importance.

Arrival in the Capital

Focus *How do the informal economy and organized industry contribute to the Kenyan economy?*

In 1899, the workers building the train line reached a flat area that had a watering hole. They set up camp in this area known as *Enkare Nairobi*

Nairobi, a city of more than one million people, attracts tourists from all over the world.
Geography: *In what ways does it look like cities in the United States?*

— a term meaning "cold water" in the language of the Masai people. Kenya's capital, Nairobi, grew out of this tent city.

Today, Nairobi is home to more than one million people. With skyscrapers, luxury hotels, and trendy shops, this booming city attracts tourists and business travelers from all over the world.

The Informal Economy

On the outskirts of Nairobi, an informal economy thrives. In an **informal economy,** people without steady jobs come up with creative ways to earn a living. They clean homes, carry goods for people, and sell everything from souvenirs to bus tickets. Metal crafters, clothing makers, and food vendors set up shop in small stalls under the hot sun. Most of the people involved in the informal economy live in Nairobi's poorest areas.

Informal economies exist nearly everywhere in the world, but they are certain to be found in Africa's growing cities. Rapid urbanization in Africa, which you read about in Chapter 16, means that there are more people in the cities than there are formal jobs. As the cities grow, so do the poor areas and the informal economies that thrive in them.

Nairobi is becoming more and more crowded. It has a **population density** of more than 4,000 people per square mile. That means if the residents were distributed evenly throughout the city, more than 4,000 people would live on each square mile of land. Nairobi is expanding so quickly that the city cannot keep up with the need for schooling, housing, health care, and jobs. Kenya's population is growing at one of the highest rates in the world. Developing an economy that can meet the needs of this expanding population is one of the main challenges Kenya faces.

Nairobi's Industry

As the train pulls into the station at Nairobi, another important part of the Kenyan economy becomes visible: factories and industry. Together with Mombasa, Nairobi is the industrial center of Kenya — the most industrialized country in eastern Africa. Kenya's factories turn out a wide variety of goods, including cement, textiles, chemicals, and transport equipment. Oil refining and agricultural processing are other important industries. Many consumer products, including footwear, leather goods, clothing, soap, and various plastic items, are also manufactured in Kenya. Industry provides Kenyans with jobs, income, and products to buy.

For many travelers, Nairobi is the last stop, although the railroad tracks continue northwest. From Mombasa's busy port to the bustling city of Nairobi, your railroad journey across Kenya has revealed a diverse economy. You have seen everything from cargo ships to coffee plantations, from cheetahs to cement factories. Kenyans making a living as farmers, safari operators, factory workers, craftspeople, and at dozens of other jobs all contribute to its economy.

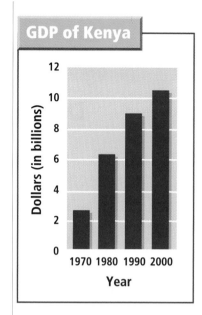

GDP of Kenya

In the 1990s, one-third of Kenya's total economic output was agricultural. **Chart Skill:** *What does the chart tell about Kenya's economy?*

Lesson Review

1. **Key Vocabulary:** Write a paragraph about Kenya's economy, using the following terms: **tourism, commercial agriculture, informal economy,** and **gross domestic product.**

2. **Focus:** What roles do exports, tourism, and agriculture play in Kenya's economy?

3. **Focus:** How do the informal economy and organized industry contribute to the Kenyan economy?

4. **Critical Thinking: Conclude** Why are informal economies more common in urban areas than in rural ones?

5. **Geography:** Make a chart with two columns, headed "Rural" and "Urban." Under each heading, list the sections of Kenya's economy that are based in each area.

6. **Citizenship/Writing Activity:** Write a paragraph about your community, explaining the industries, businesses, and services that are part of the economy. Describe how people earn their living.

Drawing Inferences Using Maps

People Patterns

A journey across South Africa might begin in Cape Town, a major coastal city. As you head inland, city streets give way to villages and farmland. Continue across sparsely populated grazing lands and past towering mountains. You'll travel through the world's richest gold fields as you approach industrial Johannesburg, which bustles with people.

What causes these changes in population density? You can make **inferences,** or assumptions, about this and other questions by comparing a population map with another type of map.

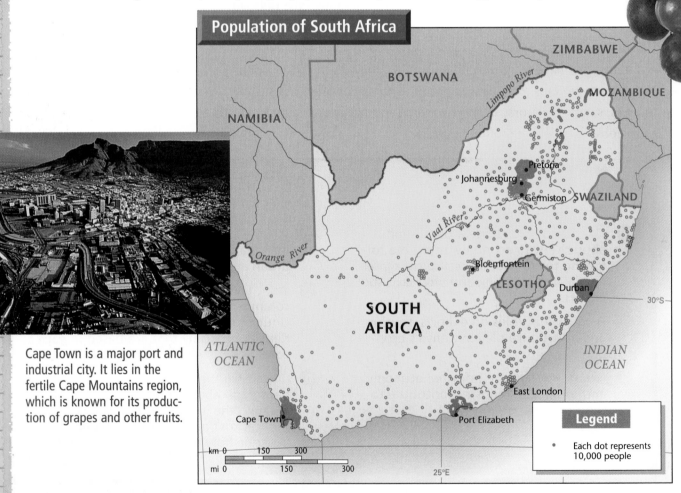

Population of South Africa

ZIMBABWE
BOTSWANA
MOZAMBIQUE
NAMIBIA
Limpopo River
Pretoria
Johannesburg
Germiston SWAZILAND
Vaal River
Bloemfontein
Orange River
LESOTHO Durban
SOUTH AFRICA
30°S
ATLANTIC OCEAN
INDIAN OCEAN
East London
Cape Town
Port Elizabeth

Legend
• Each dot represents 10,000 people

km 0 150 300
mi 0 150 300
25°E

Cape Town is a major port and industrial city. It lies in the fertile Cape Mountains region, which is known for its production of grapes and other fruits.

① Here's How

- Study the population distribution map on the left. What does each dot represent? Look for clusters, or patterns, of dots. Which areas are most densely populated? Which are least densely populated?

- Now study the map of economic resources below. The symbols and colors represent economic activities. Find examples of each symbol on the map. Then notice where each economic activity takes place.

- Now compare the patterns on the two maps. Notice where most South Africans live. Then notice where most economic activities take place. Are these areas the same? Can you think of reasons for these patterns? What other connections between population and economic activity do you see?

② Think It Through

What other kinds of maps might help explain where people live? What could you learn about population from a climate map? An elevation map?

③ Use It

Answer these questions about South Africa's population patterns.

1. Why do you think so few people live in the grazing lands?

2. Why might so many South Africans live near Johannesburg and Cape Town?

3. What areas of South Africa have the least dense population? Why do you think this is so?

4. How would you explain the population pattern along the coastline?

Above is the Big Hole diamond mine. South Africa is one of the world's chief diamond mining countries.

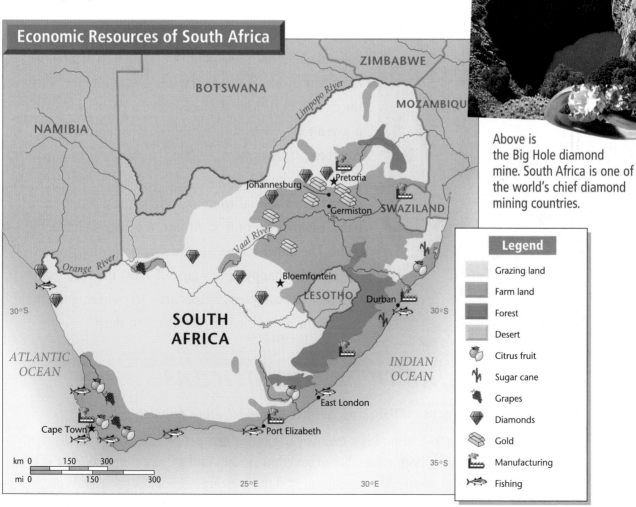

Economic Resources of South Africa

ZIMBABWE
BOTSWANA
Limpopo River
MOZAMBIQUE
NAMIBIA
Pretoria
Johannesburg
Germiston
SWAZILAND
Vaal River
Orange River
Bloemfontein
LESOTHO
Durban
30°S
SOUTH AFRICA
ATLANTIC OCEAN
INDIAN OCEAN
East London
Cape Town
Port Elizabeth
35°S
25°E
30°E
30°S

km 0   150   300
mi 0   150   300

Legend

	Grazing land
	Farm land
	Forest
	Desert
	Citrus fruit
	Sugar cane
	Grapes
	Diamonds
	Gold
	Manufacturing
	Fishing

Nigeria: A Mosaic of Cultures

Key Vocabulary
mosaic

compound

Main Idea Nigeria has one of the most varied populations in Africa, with many ethnic groups forming one nation.

There is great happiness this day in a small Nigerian town. Another child has joined the Yoruba (YOR eh buh) people of western Africa. Today an eight-day-old baby will be named and blessed. The ceremony begins.

A tiny amount of alligator pepper, a hot spice, is placed in the baby's mouth, making him cry. His mother comforts him as she and the other adults gathered in the courtyard pray that the child will have a fruitful life and children of his own. Sweet honey, a symbol of happiness, is also given to the baby, with a prayer that the child will be happy. Since water quenches fire, water is given to the baby as a symbol of triumph over evil. Another prayer is made — that the child will triumph. Kola nut, palm oil, salt, and other symbolic items are taken from a special white container and given to the baby, each with a prayer. At last, it is time to name the child. The father names his son *Ibidunni,* which means "born into a happy family circle." Now the Naming Ceremony is complete. Smiles are everywhere, and laughter fills the air as the baby drifts off to sleep.

One out of every seven Africans lives in Nigeria. Nigeria is a single nation made up of many different cultures.

One in Seven Africans

Focus *What characteristics define Nigeria's population?*

Little Ibidunni is a member of the Yoruba people. He is also a Nigerian. Being both a member of an ethnic group and a citizen of a country is typical on the African continent. Ethnic groups date back thousands of years, but the boundaries of countries are just decades old. As a Yoruba, Ibidunni will grow up learning the traditions of a complex culture that has thrived in western Africa for centuries. As a Nigerian, he will grow up as part of the largest and most diverse population in all of Africa.

About one out of every seven Africans lives in Nigeria. With about 93.5 million people, the country has the largest population in Africa by far. It has the tenth largest population in the world. When you think of these numbers, keep little Ibidunni in mind, and remember that the numbers refer to real people, individuals who have joys, sorrows, and interests, just as you do.

About one-third of the individuals who make up the Nigerian population live in urban areas. More than one million people are crowded into Lagos (LAY gos), Nigeria's former capital and largest city. More than a million more live in Ibadan (ee BAHD n). Several other cities are each home to more than a quarter of a million people. The other two-thirds of Nigerians live in rural areas.

The day Ibidunni was born to the Yoruba people, thousands of other children were born into other ethnic groups all across Nigeria. Like a

The map below shows the different cultures who live in Nigeria. **Map Skill:** *Which groups of people are involved with commercial farming?*

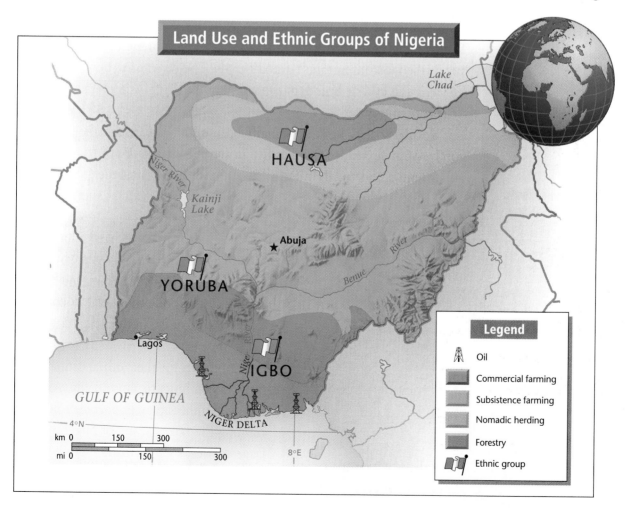

Land Use and Ethnic Groups of Nigeria

Lake Chad

HAUSA

Niger River

Kainji Lake

★ Abuja

Benue River

YORUBA

Lagos

Niger River

IGBO

GULF OF GUINEA

NIGER DELTA

4°N

km 0   150   300
mi 0   150   300

8°E

Legend

- Oil
- Commercial farming
- Subsistence farming
- Nomadic herding
- Forestry
- Ethnic group

Africa: Patterns of Living   **473**

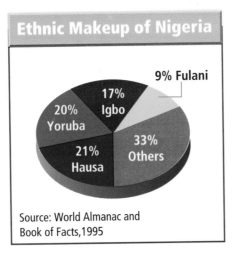

Ethnic Makeup of Nigeria

9% Fulani
17% Igbo
20% Yoruba
21% Hausa
33% Others

Source: World Almanac and Book of Facts, 1995

This chart shows the major ethnic groups living in Nigeria. **Chart Skill:** *Which ethnic group is the largest? Which group identified on the chart is the smallest?*

mosaic, a picture made of many small pieces of stone or tile, Nigeria is a single nation made up of many different peoples, each with their own culture. Two hundred fifty ethnic groups are represented in Nigeria: the Yoruba, the Hausa (HOW suh), the Igbo (EE boh), the Nupe (NOO pay), the Tiv (teev), the Efik (EH fihk), and many, many more. Each has its own language, history, customs, traditions, and values.

Three Nigerian Ethnic Groups

Focus *What are Nigeria's three largest ethnic groups, and how do they express their values and traditions?*

The three largest ethnic groups in Nigeria — the Yoruba, the Hausa, and the Igbo — make up nearly 60 percent of the population. As you read the following sections about each culture, try to imagine life among these different peoples who share Nigerian citizenship.

The Yoruba: Commitment to Family

The Naming Ceremony you read about at the beginning of this lesson is one of the most important Yoruba rituals. The ceremony shows how the Yoruba, like other ethnic groups, have a tradition of valuing family and close community ties.

Yoruba society has traditionally been organized around the extended family. Many extended families live in **compounds,** a series of rooms laid out around a courtyard. In the main courtyard, people gather to eat meals, discuss the day's events, listen to music, and watch dances. Ceremonies are often held there, too.

Many school children in Nigeria wear school uniforms, as these Yoruba girls do.

The Yoruba people have a long urban tradition, having lived in towns for centuries. Near the compound the family grows food crops such as corn, manioc, and yams. In the fields farther away are cash crops, such as cacao and palms (grown for their oil). Yoruba farmers commute to those fields. All family members play important roles in running the farm. Many of Nigeria's largest cities, such as Ibadan, grew from such Yoruba communities.

Many Yoruba women work as craftspeople, making clothing and other products people need for their families. Others are artists, whose artwork, including wood carving and metal sculpture, is highly respected. The women sell their crafts and art, along with extra vegetables from their farm plot, at local markets. The money a woman makes pays for her family's food and her children's education. Her work for her children will be repaid.

One elderly Yoruba widow explains: "My children pay for my food and light and washing. I've done as much for them: I brought them up since they were small, and married the senior ones to good wives. They can't leave me to suffer now."

The Hausa: Muslim Tradition

The windows in the clay house are small slits, well above eye level. Cleverly designed, they let in light and air while protecting the privacy of the people inside. A male visitor arrives and is greeted by the owner of the house in the cool, dim interior of the meeting room. "A smiling face dispels unhappiness," the host says, quoting a traditional proverb. Although the host welcomes his guest warmly, the visitor is not allowed into the rest of the house. This is a Muslim home, and in the inner rooms live the women of the family. (According to Muslim tradition, men

The Hausa are the largest Nigerian ethnic group and live mostly in northern Nigeria. Many in this group are Muslim.

visiting a home stay separate from women to whom they are not related.) In another part of the house lies a beautiful courtyard. This home is similar to many in the Middle East.

Yet this is Nigeria. There are more Muslims in Nigeria than in any Middle Eastern country. The Hausa, the single largest Nigerian ethnic group, are mostly Muslim. The Hausa live primarily in northern Nigeria, where mosques can be seen in many cities. The Hausa follow customs similar to those of other Muslim cultures, which you read about in Chapter 10.

The Igbo: Respecting Achievement

Among the Igbo, the third largest Nigerian ethnic group, the traditional way for a man to become a village leader is by earning a series of titles. This lengthy process begins when he is a child and continues into adulthood. For each title, he makes a payment and goes through a complex ritual. Each title gives the man privileges. The higher the title, the more

The third largest Nigerian ethnic group are the Igbo. The Igbo were very prominent in helping win Nigerian independence in 1960.

say the man has in village meetings.

Status is based on achievement. The Igbo admire a successful farmer, for example, or a popular public speaker. When the British colonized Nigeria, many Igbo were quick to find new ways to achieve. They attended schools opened by Christian missionaries. Many converted to Christianity. They became government clerks, army officers, teachers, and leaders in other professions in every part of Nigeria. Igbo were instrumental in helping win Nigerian independence in 1960.

Many other Nigerians resented the Igbo because of their success. There were violent attacks on the Igbo, especially in northern Nigeria. Many Igbo refugees streamed back to their hometowns. In 1967, the Igbo tried to declare their part of the country independent, but they lost the bloody civil war that resulted.

Conflict and Cooperation

> "**N**igeria is not a nation. It is a mere geographical expression."
>
> Chief Obafemi Awolowo

This Nigerian was referring to the many different cultures and languages that exist in Nigeria. Each ethnic group is like its own nation. Religious differences also divide Nigeria. About 50 percent of Nigerians are Muslim, and about 40 percent are Christian. Building a nation with such a diverse population is extremely difficult, but it is not impossible.

During the many decades they have been united by common boundaries and a common government, Nigerians have struggled to cooperate. People from different ethnic and religious groups normally live and work together peacefully in cities, schools, businesses, and government offices. Many people can speak several languages, while English is the official language of government and education.

As the country with the largest population on the continent, Nigeria is an important African leader. Its attempts at promoting harmony among its people are watched and studied in many other African countries that face similar challenges.

Lesson Review

1. **Key Vocabulary:** Write a description of Yoruba life, using the words **compound** and **mosaic**.

2. **Focus:** What characteristics define Nigeria's population?

3. **Focus:** What are Nigeria's three largest ethnic groups, and how do they express their values and traditions?

4. **Critical Thinking: Conclude** How might the existence of so many different ethnic groups in Nigeria affect the Nigerian government?

5. **Theme: Independence and Interdependence/Writing Activity:** What factors tie all Nigerians together, and what qualities keep ethnic groups distinct from one another?

6. **Geography/Art Activity:** Select a Nigerian ethnic group not discussed in this chapter. Find out more about the traditions and values of the group. Draw a map of Nigeria, showing the areas where they live.

South Africa: Building a New Nation

Main Idea After years of government-sponsored racial separation, South Africa is attempting to forge a unified nation.

Key Vocabulary

- veldt
- Afrikaner
- apartheid
- Bantustans
- township
- boycott

Key Events

- **1910** Union of South Africa established
- **1948** Apartheid policies established
- **1960** Sharpeville Massacre
- **1989** de Klerk works to end apartheid
- **1994** First free election for all South Africans

For many years in South Africa, people were classified according to their heritage. "Whites" were people of European ancestry. "Blacks" were native Africans. "Asians" were people from India or other places in Asia. "Coloureds" were people of mixed ancestry. The law required that blacks, Asians, and coloureds live in separate areas from whites. A black South African named Mark Mathabane remembers seeing what he calls the "white world" for the first time:

> **"I** glued my eyes to the window [of the bus], anticipating my first look at the white world. . . . The red-brick building stood on a vast tract of land with . . . athletic fields, merry-go-rounds, an Olympic-sized swimming pool, tennis courts, and rows of brightly leafed trees. . . . Not even the best of [black] schools in . . . the whole of South Africa . . . came close. **"**

A History of Separateness

Focus *How did a varied population develop in South Africa?*

How did children like Mark Mathabane come to live in an environment so different from other children's? Understanding the origins of South Africa's peoples is key to understanding the country's painful history of racial separation.

About three-fourths of the current population are descendants of South Africa's original inhabitants, the Khoisan-speaking (KOY san) people and the Bantu-speaking people. The Khoisan-speakers lived in the southern and western parts of South Africa. The Bantu-speaking people settled in the eastern part of South Africa, having migrated from the north in the centuries before 1500. For hundreds of years, these peoples were isolated at the southern tip of the African continent. There they developed their own unique cultures.

Then, in 1652, Dutch traders set up a fort near the Cape of Good Hope. They restocked Dutch ships on the journey around Africa to the East Indies. Eventually the fort grew into Cape Town. At first, most settlers lived in Cape Town. Some soon moved outside to raise cattle on the grassy prairie, known as the **veldt** (VEHLT), the Dutch word for "field."

As more and more Dutch settlers claimed the veldt for themselves, they clashed with the Khoisan-speakers. Settlers killed Khoisan-speakers and took away their land and cattle. The loss of their lands forced many to work for the Dutch. Diseases brought by the European settlers killed large numbers of Khoisan-speakers. Because the settlers needed replacement laborers, they brought enslaved people from the East Indies and other parts of Africa. By 1800, the Khoisan-speakers had almost died out.

In their place was a new population known as the coloureds. Some were descended from Dutch and Khoisan-speaking parents. Others were descendants of a Khoisan-speaking parent and an enslaved parent.

In 1806, Great Britain gained control of the colony. The British freed the enslaved people in the region and tried to limit the amount of land settlers could control. Some settlers, unused to such government regulation, would not accept these changes. Starting in 1835, they began moving north and east, seeking independence. This migration was called the Great Trek. As the settlers moved inland, they fought with Bantu-speaking peoples. Although kingdoms like the Zulu had large and disciplined armies, still, they were no match for the better armed settlers.

In the late 1800s, diamonds and gold were discovered in South Africa. Whites seeking to make their fortunes arrived in large numbers. In addition, the British brought people from India to work on sugar plantations along the coast.

By the 1860s, the British and the descendants of the Dutch, who called themselves **Afrikaners** (ahf rih KAH ners), controlled most of South Africa. In 1910, the Afrikaner and British colonies were combined as the Union of South Africa.

South Africa is located at the southern tip of the African continent. **Map Skill:** *Why was Cape Town a good location for a city?*

Early settlers raised cattle on the grassy prairie, known as the veldt, near Cape Town.

Decades of Injustice

Focus *What kinds of discrimination did black South Africans face under apartheid?*

Life in the new Union of South Africa was harsh for blacks, who made up the majority of the population. The new government passed laws that discriminated against all who were not white. Blacks, for example, had only a limited right to vote, which was later taken away.

As time went on, Afrikaners established a political party. In 1948, this party gained control of the government. An Afrikaner named Daniel F. Malan became prime minister. Malan and his fellow Afrikaners wanted a society in which there was no racial mixing at all.

He set up a system called **apartheid** (uh PAHRT hyt), or "apartness." It made racial separation the official policy in South Africa. The small white minority held all the political and economic power. Although black South Africans did the labor, the wealth of South Africa's farms and its diamond and gold mines went into the hands of the white minority.

Life Under Apartheid

Under apartheid, a person's skin color determined how he or she was treated. Blacks fared the worst. Apartheid laws limited the training blacks received at school, and barred them from entering post offices, libraries, restaurants, parks, and other public areas set aside for whites. The apartheid laws regulated what kinds of work people were allowed to do and made sure that blacks were paid far less than whites for doing the same kind of job. Apartheid regulations even determined whom people were allowed to marry.

Under apartheid, blacks moving within their own country were required to carry passports for identification.

During a peaceful demonstration in the township of Sharpeville, police fired into a crowd of black protesters, killing 69 people.

Apartheid also determined where people lived. Blacks and other nonwhites were forced to move away from areas set aside "for whites only." Many black South Africans were already living on crowded reserves. The new laws declared these reserves **Bantustans** or "homelands," as if these places were where black South Africans had originally lived. Each group of blacks was assigned to its own Bantustan.

The apartheid policy also set up a series of "pass laws." All black South Africans had to carry identification papers. They had to show these papers to any police officer who demanded to see them. The passes controlled blacks' travel from the poor rural Bantustans to **townships,** black-only residential settlements near white cities. Passes also allowed blacks to go to jobs in white areas.

Asians and coloureds faced fewer limitations under apartheid. Still, even they had no hope of achieving equality with whites.

Signs such as this one, for a "white only" private beach, were common under apartheid.

The Struggle for Justice

Focus *How did black South Africans respond to apartheid?*

Black South Africans did not meekly accept these unjust policies. When they protested, however, the government responded with force. On March 21, 1960, a peaceful demonstration in the township of Sharpeville turned tragic. Police fired into a crowd of black protesters, killing 69 people. The Sharpeville Massacre was the beginning of a new era of increased violence in South Africa's racial struggle.

Ask Yourself

How do you think you would feel if you were a young black person living under apartheid in South Africa? How would you feel if you were a young white person living there?

?????????????

A man named Nelson Mandela led the struggle against apartheid. He became a leader of the African National Congress (ANC), a political organization that worked to help South African blacks gain equal rights. After Sharpeville, the government outlawed the ANC. Operating in secret, the ANC changed its longtime policy of nonviolent protest against apartheid. It began armed attacks against government property. As its leader, Mandela was charged with high treason and sentenced to life in prison. High treason means an intention to overthrow a government.

The situation in South Africa drew attention from around the world. People began to speak out against apartheid. Many countries — including the United States — joined a boycott of South Africa. In a **boycott,** people refuse to do business with a company, group, or country.

As the boycott weakened the South African economy, its leaders began to consider changes in apartheid. In 1989, the government of F. W. de Klerk began the process of ending apartheid. In February 1990, after 27 years in prison, Mandela was freed, and the government promised elections in which all South Africans could take part.

In April 1994, when 93-year-old Miriam Mqomboti voted for the first time, she said: "I never thought it could happen here. I thought I would never be able to vote." The following month joyous crowds welcomed Mandela as South Africa's first black president.

After Apartheid

Focus | *What steps did Nelson Mandela take to unify South Africa?*

Mandela's rise to power was not the end of the struggle in South Africa. "We have not taken the final step of our journey, but the first step on a longer and even more difficult road," he said after becoming president. The new government faced many challenges.

Apartheid had left the majority of blacks poor and uneducated. It had driven millions from their homes. It also built up enormous mistrust between blacks and whites. The wounds of apartheid would take time to heal, but Mandela had faith they would.

Nelson Mandela served as South Africa's first black president, from 1994 to 1999.

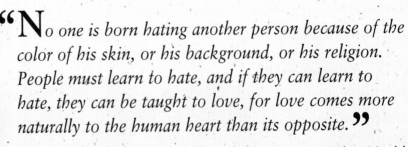

"**N**o one is born hating another person because of the color of his skin, or his background, or his religion. People must learn to hate, and if they can learn to hate, they can be taught to love, for love comes more naturally to the human heart than its opposite."

Nelson Mandela

By giving blacks hope and embracing whites as "South Africans just like ourselves," Mandela led his country through an orderly change to rule by the black majority. Whites who had once been his jailers served him loyally. Within its first year, the new government started a school meal program and a free health clinic for the poor. It also began to buy back land from white farmers and return it to the blacks from whom it had been taken.

Change in South Africa has not been easy. People are still working to develop a strong education system for all children after apartheid. Crime rates are high, and unemployment is at about 30 percent. Despite these constant challenges, Mandela's legacy of democracy continues. In 1999, Mandela retired, and Thabo Mbeki (TAH boh mm BEHG ee) of the ANC was elected president of South Africa. Mbeki has worked closely with Mandela for years, playing a central role in many aspects of South Africa's government. As president, he is committed to maintaining a strong democracy and to facing the challenges in South Africa. These challenges may be difficult, but, through democracy, South Africans are determined to overcome them.

South African President Mbeki *(right)* and South African Foreign Minister Nkosazana C. Dlamini-Zuma *(left)* at a United Nations news conference in September, 1999.

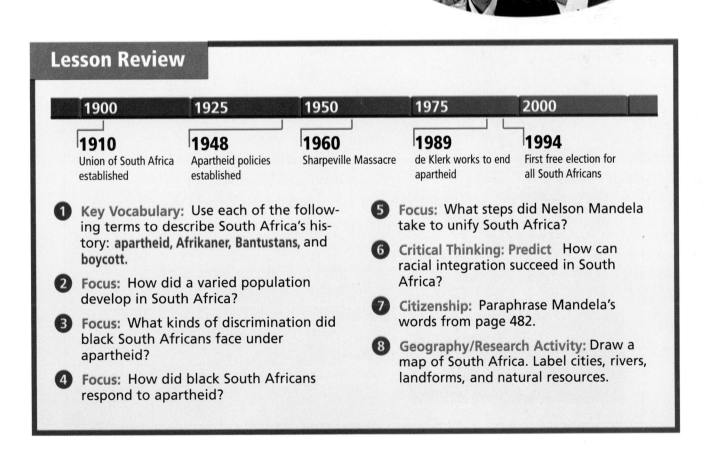

Lesson Review

1900	1925	1950	1975	2000

1910	**1948**	**1960**	**1989**	**1994**
Union of South Africa established	Apartheid policies established	Sharpeville Massacre	de Klerk works to end apartheid	First free election for all South Africans

1 **Key Vocabulary:** Use each of the following terms to describe South Africa's history: **apartheid, Afrikaner, Bantustans,** and **boycott.**

2 **Focus:** How did a varied population develop in South Africa?

3 **Focus:** What kinds of discrimination did black South Africans face under apartheid?

4 **Focus:** How did black South Africans respond to apartheid?

5 **Focus:** What steps did Nelson Mandela take to unify South Africa?

6 **Critical Thinking: Predict** How can racial integration succeed in South Africa?

7 **Citizenship:** Paraphrase Mandela's words from page 482.

8 **Geography/Research Activity:** Draw a map of South Africa. Label cities, rivers, landforms, and natural resources.

★ CITIZENSHIP ★

Resolving Conflicts

Can You Make Peace?

Have you ever forgiven someone for something hurtful that they did? Did someone ever forgive you for something you did? Forgiving takes place between people, but it is also something that is done by governments. The case study below shows how this happened in South Africa.

Case Study

Looking to the Future and the Past

In 1994, Nelson Mandela became South Africa's first black president. Just four years earlier, he had been released from prison. He had been jailed for 27 years because of his efforts to stop the country's apartheid policies. At the time of his release, black people were not allowed to vote in South African national elections.

When Mandela became president, he said that what was most important was South Africa's future. He called for a pardon, or amnesty, for those who had committed political crimes in the past. The country had fought a civil war for many years. President Mandela believed that forgiveness would help the country to heal its wounds.

He also believed that it was important for the truth about the past to be told. So his government said that only people who admitted what they had done would be pardoned.

Take Action

Does an apology undo what happened in the past? If not, what does it do? Why might you want to forgive someone who had hurt you? Why might you hesitate to apologize? If one of your friends, in an angry moment, called another friend a hurtful name, what would you do? If these friends stopped talking to each other, how would you advise them to handle the situation? These steps can help you to think about how to handle conflict between people.

 1 Divide into pairs or groups of three.

2 Have each person propose a way of handling the conflict between the two friends above.

3 Together, identify how each method does or does not address the problem.

4 Make a list of what you gain when you forgive someone. Make a list of what you give up.

5 Present your lists to the class. As a group, discuss the pros and cons of different ways of handling a conflict between people.

Tips for Resolving Conflicts

- Think about what you want the outcome of the conversation to be. What would need to happen in order to be friends again?
- Choose a private time and place to talk. Having other friends around may make talking openly more difficult.
- Think about how you could let the other person know how you feel, without blaming. Use I felt instead of You did.
- Listen to the other person's side of the story.

Research Activity

The United States government apologized to Japanese Americans who were forced to leave their homes in World War II, and paid them money for their lost property. Research this case or other cases in which a government has apologized. (For example, the German government apologized for its role in World War II.) Write a paragraph explaining why the decision was made to apologize.

Chapter Review

Chapter Review Timeline

1850	1880	1910	1940	1970	2000

1910
Union of South Africa established

1956
Egypt nationalizes Suez Canal

1869
Suez Canal opened

1922
Egypt gains independence from Great Britain

1948
Apartheid policies established in South Africa

1994
Nelson Mandela elected president of South Africa

Summarizing the Main Idea

1 Copy the chart below and fill in the missing information to compare Egypt, Kenya, Nigeria, and South Africa.

	Nigeria	Egypt	Kenya	South Africa
Ethnic groups				
Natural resources				
Industry				

Vocabulary

2 Using at least eight of these words, write a conversation between four people, one from each of the four countries discussed in this chapter.

dialect (p. 459)

nationalize (p. 459)

fellahin (p. 460)

preserve (p. 466)

tourism (p. 466)

gross domestic product (p. 468)

population density (p. 469)

compound (p. 474)

mosaic (p. 474)

veldt (p. 479)

Afrikaners (p. 479)

apartheid (p. 480)

Bantustans (p. 481)

townships (p. 481)

boycott (p. 482)

Reviewing the Facts

3 What are some of the ways Egyptians preserve their national identity?

4 Why is the Nile River so important to life in Egypt?

5 What is the Lunatic Express? What role does it play in Kenya's economy?

6 Why did an informal economy develop in Nairobi?

7 Describe Yoruba family life.

8 How do Igbo men and women become more influential in their villages?

9 What happened to the Khoisan-speaking people after the arrival of Dutch settlers?

Skill Review: Drawing Inferences Using Maps

10 Look at the map of Nigeria on page 473. Which ethnic group lives closest to the Niger Delta? How do they use the land? Why might they use the land that way?

11 Copy the outline of the map of Kenya on page 467 and shade in the areas where farming occurs. In a different color, shade the areas which get the most rain on your map. Where are these two areas the same? Where are they different? How might Kenyans water their crops in places where there is less rain?

Geography Skills

12 Look at the small map of Egypt on page 458. How did the location of Cairo contribute to its varied architecture?

13 Based on the description given in the lesson, draw a map of Kenya and show what you think is the path of the Lunatic Express.

Critical Thinking

14 **Problem Solving** How might groups in Egypt that want Islam to have more influence over the government and those who disagree compromise on this issue?

15 **Compare Then and Now** How were black South Africans treated years ago? How are they treated now?

Writing: Citizenship and Culture

16 **Citizenship** You are a South African government official elected in 1994. Write a speech in which you try to convince all South Africans to work together to create the best future for their country.

17 **Cultures** Write a few paragraphs explaining how Nigeria's Yoruba, Hausa, and Igbo people are alike and how they are different.

Activities

History/Research Activity
Research the origin of the Suez Canal or Tsavo National Park. Use at least two sources. Write a report about what you find out.

Economics/Math Activity
Create a chart or graph comparing the current gross domestic products of Egypt, Nigeria, and South Africa to Kenya's GDP. Which one has the highest? The lowest?

Internet Option

Check the **Internet Social Studies Center** for ideas on how to extend your theme project beyond your classroom.

THEME PROJECT CHECK-IN

To complete your theme project, use the information in this chapter about Africa's individual nations. Ask yourself these questions:
- What major events in the country's history have influenced its independence and interdependence?
- How has the country dealt with the challenges of independence and interdependence?

Asia and Australia in the Modern Age

"*We will surely get to our destination if we join hands.*"

Aung San Suu Kyi

· THEME ·

Challenges and Opportunities

66 *Both Asia and Australia are using agricultural improvements, like new ways of farming, fertilizers, and better seeds, to meet some of the challenges they face.* **99**

Adla Britton, Sixth Grade
Bismarck, ND

Asia and Australia are the homes of civilizations thousands of years old. The 20th century has been a time of great change for both continents. Economic powers have been born. Military machines have risen and fallen. Millions of young people have come to the forefront of a "Cultural Revolution." In the 20th century, the population of China alone has grown tremendously. The challenge now is to care for all these people. The opportunity is what they will provide to the world.

Theme Project

Guide to Challenges and Opportunities

Create a travel guide for Australia or an Asian country to show how it has met challenges and opportunities.

- Construct a timeline that includes the major events in the country's history in the 20th century.
- Diagram the country's political system.
- Draw a map of the country that includes its major cities and geographic features.
- Illustrate the geography, culture, and people of the country. Write captions for each.

RESEARCH: Collect facts on the major sites visited by tourists who come to this country.

◀ A Chinese junk in the harbor of Hong Kong.

WHEN & WHERE
ATLAS

 Large parts of Asia were controlled by European nations at the beginning of the 20th century. Australia was still a dominion of Great Britain. After a century of wars, revolutions, and independence movements, dozens of newly independent countries emerged. Today increasing economic and cultural ties are binding Asian nations and Australia closer together.

In this unit you will learn more about the geography of Asia and Australia. You will also read about how events have transformed these continents in the 20th century. Finally, through profiles of five Asian countries and Australia (shown in red), you will learn about the economic, political, and cultural forces that govern these continents today.

Unit 7 Chapters

NORTH AMERICA

ATLANTIC OCEAN

SOUTH AMERICA

Arctic Circle

Equator

60°W

30°W

0°

Legend

★ National capital

Unit Timeline

1900	1920	1940

Tien Shan, China

Find out where other mountain ranges are located in Asia. *Chapter 18, Lesson 1*

Japanese Bullet Trains

Will Japan leave its traditional ways of life behind? *Chapter 19, Lesson 1*

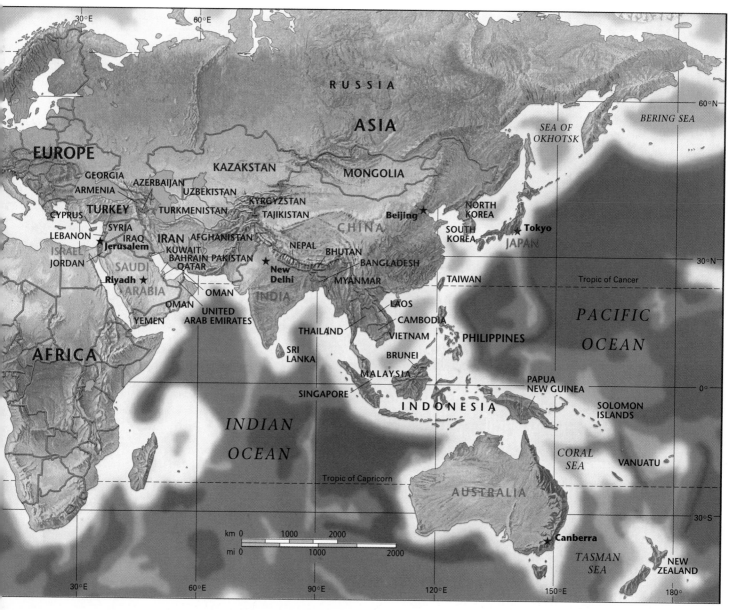

1960   1980   2000

Ganges River

This river is an important part of the daily life of the people of India. *Chapter 20, Lesson 1*

The Great Mosque in Mecca

All Muslims try to visit this place. What does Saudi Arabia do for its visitors? *Chapter 20, Lesson 2*

A Greenhouse in Israel

In Israel's dry climate they have to water plants "with a teaspoon." *Chapter 20, Lesson 3*

CHAPTER 18
Asia and Australia: An Overview

Chapter Preview: *People, Places, and Events*

1900	1920	1940

Rice Fields

Would it be easy to farm this land? *Lesson 1, Page 495*

Fishing the Li River

Why does this man have birds on his boat? *Lesson 1, Page 497*

Wallaby Crossing

Unusual animals are only some of Australia's many resources. *Lesson 1, Page 499*

Geography of Asia and Australia

Main Idea Asia and Australia contain a wide variety of geographic regions and valuable natural resources.

The longest railroad in the world stretches 5,778 miles (9,310 kilometers) from Moscow to Vladivostok. It takes eight days to ride the rails all the way across Asia, the world's largest continent. Australia is the world's smallest continent, but to travel across it by train, from Perth to Sydney, would still take three and one half days.

These two regions contain some spectacular landforms. Asia contains the world's lowest point, the Dead Sea, which lies between Israel and Jordan. The surface of this saltwater lake is not constant, but averages 1,312 feet (400 meters), almost a quarter mile, below sea level. Asia also contains the world's highest point. Mount Everest, at 29,035 feet (8,850 meters), is about five and a half miles above sea level. Australia, however, is the world's flattest continent. These geographic extremes have produced an area rich in diversity of people, places, and resources.

◀ In Rangoon, Myanmar, this eight-sided pagoda rises into the night sky.

1960   1980   2000

World at War   1941–1945

Where are these planes going? *Lesson 2, Page 505*

Diverse People

Many people together make up one culture. *Lesson 2, Page 504*

Modern-day Skyline

Where could this city be? *Lesson 2, Page 508*

493

Asia: Regions and Resources

[Focus] *What are the various geographic regions and what resources are found in Asia?*

Look at the sheer size of Asia on the map below. Asia is so large that its boundaries are four large bodies of water — the Arctic Ocean in the north, the Indian Ocean in the south, the Pacific Ocean in the east and the Mediterranean Sea in the west. Asia's size leads to diversity as well. It has very cold regions to the north in Siberia that record average temperatures below zero, and very warm tropical regions in the south that often have cyclones and monsoons.

The six diverse regions of Asia are shown on the map. **Map Skill:** *Which region has the largest land mass in Asia?*

1 A view of the Himalayas from Pokara, Nepal, in South Asia.

2 The tombs at Petra are in the hills of Jordan, in Southwest Asia.

3 The Pamir Mountains are found in Central Asia.

The Regions of Asia

EUROPE

BLACK SEA
GEORGIA
ARMENIA AZERBAIJAN
TURKEY
CYPRUS
LEBANON SYRIA
ISRAEL IRAQ
JORDAN
KUWAIT
BAHRAIN
SAUDI QATAR
ARABIA UNITED
ARAB
EMIRATES OMAN
AFRICA
YEMEN

CASPIAN SEA

KAZAKHSTAN
UZBEKISTAN KYRGYZSTAN
TURKMENISTAN TAJIKISTAN
AFGHANISTAN
IRAN
PAKISTAN
NEPAL BHUTAN
BANGLADESH
INDIA

SRI LANKA

MALDIVES

INDIAN OCEAN

Legend
- North Asia
- Central Asia
- East Asia
- Southwest Asia
- South Asia
- Southeast Asia

km 0 500 1000
mi 0 500 1000

60°E 75°E 90°E

This continent includes not only places in the eastern region of Asia — places like China, Russia, and Japan — but it also includes India and what is often called the Middle East. Study this map, and compare it with the maps on pages 698-701. How many countries are there? How many mountain ranges can you find? Which mountain range is the longest? How many deserts? Where do the major rivers flow? Estimate the miles to travel from Jerusalem to Hong Kong. Identify the major Asian regions.

Asia's resources are enormous. Land and water resources have supported centuries of farming, fishing, and trade throughout the region. The varied land offers minerals ranging from oil in Southwest Asia to bauxite in Southeast Asia.

4 These reindeer are from Siberia in North Asia.

5 This mountain range in Tien Shan, China is in East Asia.

6 In Southeast Asia you will find many rice fields in Bali, Indonesia.

This woman is tending a rice farm in central Kyushu, Japan.

Resources from the Land

Three-fifths of the people in Asia work the soil. Some are subsistence farmers, producing only enough to meet their own needs. Others own small farms that produce enough to sell on the open market. Still others work on large estates or plantations, like the rubber plantations of Southeast Asia. Grains of all types, but particularly rice, are grown throughout the region. Rice is a major ingredient of the diets of most of the people of the East and South of Asia.

Water Resources

Fishing is a major industry throughout Asia. From the tropical Mekong River to cold Lake Baikal, the deepest lake in the world, Asia's bodies of water teem with fish. Small boats and commercial fleets fish the waters of the Indian and Pacific oceans. In East Asia, fish are raised in village ponds for the local market.

The larger bodies of water have for centuries allowed for trade among and within the various Asian countries. These same waters have brought explorers from other parts of the globe. The Dutch, French, British, Portuguese, and Spanish all arrived in search of spices to preserve and flavor foods of Europe. All stayed to colonize.

Minerals and Mining

Many Asian nations are rich in the mineral ores needed for industrial products, and Southwest Asia possesses the oil to keep machines running. Large deposits of bauxite in Asia provide aluminum for everything from airplane parts to soft-drink cans. Iron, steel, tin, gold, and silver can all be found in Asia. For centuries Asian craftsmen have created gorgeous objects in silver and, especially, gold.

People

The people of Asia are themselves the continent's most valuable resource. Their sheer numbers, their varied cultures, and their vast labor potential all add to the riches of the land.

Australia: Regions and Resources

Focus | *What resources can be found in Australia's various regions?*

Australia is the only country in the world that is also a continent. About the size of the United States without Alaska, the country is a plateau made up of three regions — the Eastern Highlands, the Central Lowlands, and the Western Plateau — and an island called Tasmania. It is also the flattest and driest of the continents and can be described as a land of great plains. In addition to natural resources, each region of Australia possesses its own stunning — and unique — natural beauty.

This fisherman is using cormorants to help him fish on the Li River in China. The cormorants dive into the water and bring the fish to the surface.

An aerial view of the Great Barrier Reef and the Low Isles in Queensland, Australia.

Kata Tjuta in Central Australia has very little rainfall each year.

The deep red land of Bungle National Park in Western Australia.

Australia is a dry continent surrounded by water. Map Skill: *What eastern landform spans Australia from north to south?*

Regions of Australia

Most of the fertile land in Australia is found along the eastern coast of the country. The bulk of the population (80 percent) lives in the area that curves from Adelaide to Brisbane. *(See the map on page 535.)* Along the coast to the north lies the Great Barrier Reef. For millions of years, small marine animals lived and died here, and their bodies hardened and piled up, forming a coral mass — a **reef** — that rose above the surface of the aqua sea. Joining with small islands in the area, these deposits gradually formed the reef. This geological formation draws countless visitors each year, and fuels Australia's tourist industry.

As you move west, away from the coastal cities, you pass through steep-sided mountains and narrow valleys into the Central Lowlands. It is a region where no rain falls for years on end, while other years bring serious floods. Few of the mountains in this region are higher than 1,000 feet.

The Western Plateau covers more than half of the continent. It is interrupted by occasional solitary mountains of deep red sandstone, weathered by water and wind. Here you will find Uluru, known also as Ayers Rock, one of Australia's outstanding landmarks, rising straight up from the flat plain.

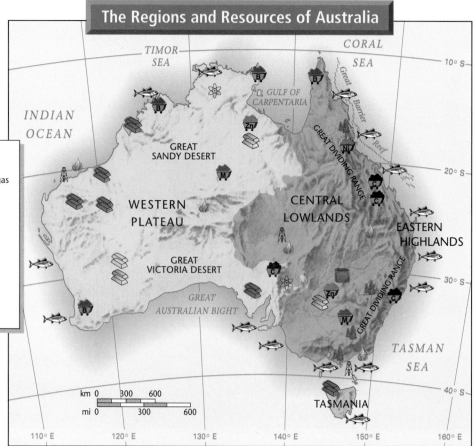

The Regions and Resources of Australia

Legend

Iron ore	Natural gas
Coal	Oil
Gold	Copper
Bauxite	Uranium
Nickel	Other minerals
Zinc	Fish
Silver	Timber

Resources of Australia

Like Asia, much of Australia's land is devoted to agriculture. Unlike Asia, agriculture in Australia is made up mainly of raising cattle and sheep on the vast stretches of the interior plains.

Tropical lands near the north coast in Queensland yield sugar cane and tropical fruit. Tuna fishing is good along the coast of South Australia. Tuna accounts for more than one tenth of Australia's total fish yield.

The land is also rich in minerals — bauxite, lead, coal, copper, iron ore. Australia is one of the world's leading iron ore and nickel exporters. On the west coast, cities like Perth have grown to be industrial centers, bringing to Australia the challenges of protecting the environment.

With a population of about 18 million, Australia averages only six people per square mile — compared to about 315 in China and 730 in India. In Chapter 19, you'll learn more about the people who live in present-day Australia.

The continents of Asia and Australia have a wealth of resources, and they both have enormous human potential. The next lesson tells how these continents have been transformed in the last 50 years.

Investigating the coral reefs off Heron Island in Australia *(top)* and a woman scuba diving among crinoids of reef coral.

Lesson Review: Geography

1 **Key Vocabulary:** Discuss what a reef is.

2 **Focus:** What are the various geographic regions and what resources are found in Asia?

3 **Focus:** What resources can be found in Australia's various regions?

4 **Critical Thinking: Comparing** Choose two regions of Asia and compare and contrast them.

5 **Citizenship:** Compare population per square mile in your community to that found in Australia and in Asia.

6 **Geography/Art Activity:** Plan a voyage along the coast of Asia for yourself and a group of friends. Draw a map of the continent and its countries on butcher paper. Mark from east to west all the places you will visit.

Physical Systems

How Does the Ring of Fire Affect People's Lives?

Just thinking about earthquakes and volcanic eruptions makes many people feel nervous — and for good reason. Over the centuries, these dramatic geological events have destroyed cities and killed thousands of people. These earthquakes and volcanic eruptions are natural physical processes that shape the Earth's surface.

Today most of the world's active volcanoes and a large percentage of its earthquakes are concentrated in a belt surrounding the Pacific Ocean. This belt is known as the Ring of Fire. Earthquakes and volcanoes not only shape the geography of this part of the world but also affect the lives of the people who live there.

Science Connection

According to the theory of plate tectonics, the Earth's crust is divided into sections of rock called plates. These plates move slowly over a layer of partly melted rock. Earthquakes and volcanoes may begin in areas where plates collide, spread apart, or slide past one another. What areas in the United States have earthquakes or volcanoes?

Two plates are moving toward each other. The heavier one begins to slide below the other.

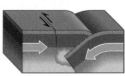

Pressure and heat build below the plate boundary. Cracks form in the plate above it.

Melted rock moves to the surface and forms volcanoes. Release of pressure between plates causes earthquakes.

1 Kobe, Japan

Ruins of a Home
The earthquake that hit Kobe in January 1995 killed more than 5,000 people. Scientists study earthquakes to look for ways to protect against them.

The Ring of Fire

ASIA

JAPAN

1

2

AUSTRALIA

3

NEW ZEALAND

PACIFIC OCEAN

NORTH AMERICA

SOUTH AMERICA

Legend

= Plate boundary

= Earthquake and volcano zone

The Ring of Fire curls around the Pacific from New Zealand all the way to the tip of South America. **Map Skill:** *How many continents are affected by the Ring of Fire?*

Volcanoes like the one above are common around the Ring of Fire.

2 Indonesia

The Remains of Krakatoa
The explosion on the island of Krakatoa in August 1883 was heard 3,000 miles away. Huge waves washed away whole villages. Volcanic ash plunged nearby islands into darkness for several days.

3 New Zealand

Energy from the Earth
Despite their destructive power, volcanoes can be useful. In New Zealand people generate electricity using the underground steam found in volcanic regions. This is called geothermal energy.

Research Activity

There are many stories of earthquakes and volcanoes along the Ring of Fire.

1 Research one of the earthquakes or volcanic eruptions that occurred along the western rim of the Ring of Fire.

2 Find out how it affected the area where it occurred and the people who lived there.

3 Present your findings to the class.

Asia and Australia in the Modern Era

Main Idea The peoples of Asia and Australia have experienced enormous changes since World War II.

Tea drinking is an age-old art in Japan, and the ancient city of Uji (oo jee) has been famous for its tea for centuries. The aroma of roasting tea leaves has filled the countryside for many generations. Yet only a few miles away, the air is filled with factory smoke and car exhaust. Ancient and modern times clash even in the air Asians breathe.

Tea drinking has an actual ceremony in Japan. Tea is also enjoyed in India, Sri Lanka, China, Indonesia, Bangladesh, and Taiwan. All of these countries export tea. While tea is the focus of a social ritual, it also provides jobs and economic prosperity. Ways of life that are thousands of years old are still present in modern Asia and Australia.

Japanese women picking tea on a farm in Uji *(above)*, while a bullet train leads into the city of Tokyo *(right)*. New and old cultures coexist in Japan.

Modern Asia and Australia

Focus *What forces have shaped modern Asia and Australia?*

Both Asia and Australia have undergone major political and social changes in the 20th century. In the last hundred years, traditional ways of life with deep roots have been questioned and in some cases uprooted, in others strengthened.

Asia is the birthplace of several major religions and philosophies: Judaism, Christianity, and Islam were all born in Southwest Asia. Taoism and Confucianism come from China, and Shintoism from Japan. Buddhism and Hinduism began in South Asia, with Hinduism spreading throughout the Indian subcontinent. These belief systems have shaped how people lived and how countries were formed and governed. When the European powers colonized Asia and Australia, they often tried to impose their own ideas of how societies should be run. However, in the

The map below shows the areas where Asians practice religions. **Map Skill:** *Identify the religion that is practiced over the largest area and the religion that is practiced over the smallest area.*

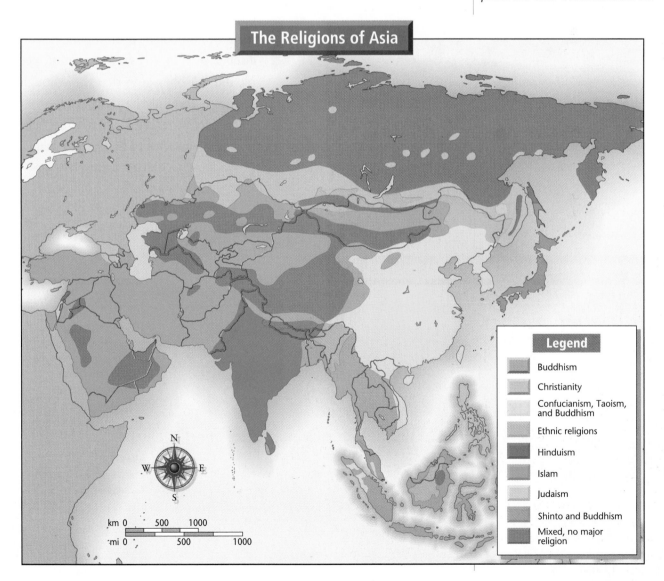

The Religions of Asia

Legend

- Buddhism
- Christianity
- Confucianism, Taoism, and Buddhism
- Ethnic religions
- Hinduism
- Islam
- Judaism
- Shinto and Buddhism
- Mixed, no major religion

20th century, two movements have reshaped the political framework: nationalism, which is the desire for independence from outside rulers, and communism, a system in which the state or the people as a whole own resources and means of production.

Nationalism

At the beginning of the 20th century, many Asian nations were colonies of European countries. In some nations **guerrilla bands**, groups of citizens who are not part of a formal army but use the countryside to fight their enemies, attacked colonial powers. Many of these bands later aligned themselves with the Communist party.

This political poster shows the diversity of the Chinese people and glorifies the idea of working together.

In India, Mohandas Gandhi (mah HAHN duhs GAHN dee) rejected violence in his efforts to rid the country of its British rulers. He believed independence could be gained by practicing a form of nonviolent protest called **civil disobedience**. In this way to protest, people did not obey laws that they thought were unfair; they stopped working, and — certainly hardest of all — stood strong holding on to their beliefs even when violence rose up during their protests. His followers allowed themselves to be beaten, dragged off to jail, and worse, without raising a hand to defend themselves or fight back.

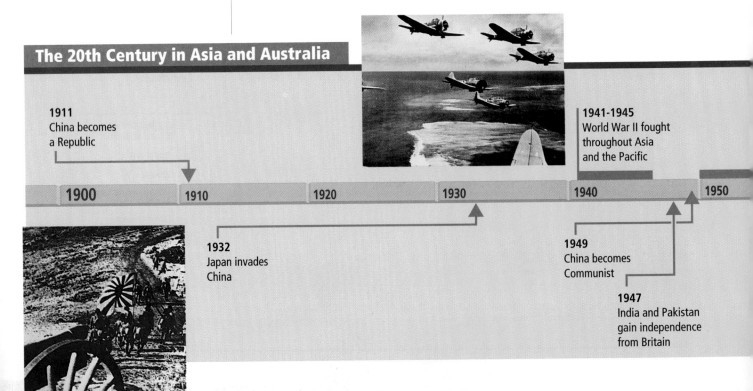

The 20th Century in Asia and Australia

1911
China becomes a Republic

1941-1945
World War II fought throughout Asia and the Pacific

1900   1910   1920   1930   1940   1950

1932
Japan invades China

1949
China becomes Communist

1947
India and Pakistan gain independence from Britain

In Southwest Asia, Kemal Atatürk, the founder of modern Turkey, combined nationalism with efforts to modernize his country. He had transportation and communication networks and factories built, as well as having electricity installed to update workplaces and homes.

Japan, which had never been conquered by Western powers, combined its own nationalism with its military force in efforts to expand its territory. By 1932, Japan had gained control of Manchuria. In the early 1940s, Japanese forces had invaded China and were pushing into Southeast Asia. Only their defeat in World War II made the Japanese abandon conquered lands. World War II was fought throughout the Pacific.

World War II weakened the colonial powers. After the war, some nationalist groups in Southeast Asia fought to gain their independence, while others gained theirs without a battle. Independence did not mean an end to war. In Southwest Asia, age-old conflicts among countries and the creation of new countries launched decades of fighting. Terrible fighting between people of different religions followed independence in South Asia when it was split into India and Pakistan. Another cause of conflict was the growth of Communist movements.

Communism

In 1927, sixteen years after China became a republic, the country was caught in a bitter struggle between Nationalists, led by Chiang Kai-shek (JYAHNG KY SHEK), and the Communists. In 1934 the well-equipped Nationalist army drove the Communists north. For the next year, the Communists, led by Mao Zedong (MOW DZUH DOONG), continued to flee north, fighting the Nationalists as they went. Of the 100,000

Biography

Aung San Suu Kyi

Aung San Suu Kyi *(awng sahn su chee)*, a woman from Myanmar, (formerly Burma), was released from imprisonment in July of 1995. She is the daughter of the General Aung San who was the nation's independence leader and founder of the Burmese army. During her imprisonment she was awarded the Nobel Peace Prize in 1991 for her work toward democracy, a cause she plans to continue.

1950-1953
US troops fight in the Korean War

1980-1988
Iran - Iraq War

1960   1970   1980   1990

1964-1973
US involvement in the Vietnam War

1990
Persian Gulf War "Desert Storm"

A North Korean general arrives for the 1953 peace talks that ended the Korean War. **History:** *Create a scrapbook on other conflicts the United Nations has helped or attempted to resolve.*

people who began the Long March (as it became known), not many survived. The records are not clear and the number of survivors recorded differs from as few as 8,000 up to 20,000. By 1949, Mao and his forces had driven the Nationalists out of mainland China and proclaimed the People's Republic of China. *(See Chapter 19.)*

The Soviet Union, which then included much of Central Asia and all of North Asia, was also a Communist nation. The United States and other democratic nations were concerned when China also became a Communist nation. To many, it seemed only a matter of time before the rest of Asia would also be in Communist hands. These fears seemed to come true in 1950 when Communist North Korea invaded South Korea, an act which began the Korean War.

The Korean War lasted until 1953. At first the forces of the United Nations, with a great deal of help from the United States, pushed the Communists back into North Korea. Then China sent troops to help the North Koreans. The war seesawed, with neither side gaining a clear victory. It ended with a continuation of Korea's division between the North and the South.

In Southeast Asia, nationalism and Communism led to a long and deadly civil war. During World War II, under the leadership of Ho Chi Minh, the Vietnamese Communists joined the Nationalists to fight the Japanese. After the war, France tried to take back its control of Vietnam but was soundly defeated in 1954. Then Communist North Vietnam tried to bring South Vietnam under its control. Once again, fearing the spread of Communism, the United States stepped in. The Vietnam War lasted until 1975. The conflict caused terrible destruction in Southeast Asia, and social upheaval in the United States, where many citizens protested American involvement.

Forces Shaping Australia: Geography and History

Geographically, Australia has always stood alone. In prehistoric times, the land connections, or "bridges," between Asia and Australia vanished beneath the sea. The native people of Australia were isolated. Europeans did not land on the continent until the 1700s, and even then they were not sure exactly where they were, whether the land was a new continent or part of Asia.

Early European — particularly English — settlements were isolated, far from the home country, in territory mapped only sketchily. By the beginning years of the 20th century, white Australians, largely of British descent, occupied the continent. *(See Chapter 19.)* Under these geographic and historic conditions, many Australians viewed themselves as an isolated Western outpost, far from their country of origin.

West Java in Indonesia has farmlands that stretch for miles and look like a patchwork quilt from the sky. **Geography:** *What part of the United States has farmland similar to this?*

Asia: Economic Growth

Focus | *What form of economic growth is taking place in Asia?*

In many parts of Asia and Australia, large numbers of people still work the land, and farm life has changed little in centuries. Modern-day Asians find the old and familiar ways changing, and with amazing speed. Here are some examples.

Economy in the Countryside

The island of Java in Indonesia has some of the most fertile farmland in the world. Java's population is a sign of the land's productivity, having soared from 28 million in 1900 to about 110 million today. Farmland on Java forms a patchwork of greens and browns that you can see for miles. Misty blue peaks of volcanoes loom in the distance. The volcanoes sometimes erupt and rain ash down upon the land. The combination of fertile volcanic soil,

If your family had a chance to move to Asia, where would you choose to live? Think about the different regions and climates.

? ? ? ? ? ? ? ? ? ? ? ? ? ?

A view of the Singapore skyline, the Singapore River, and the city's financial district. **Geography:** *How does the use of the land differ in the city from the countryside?*

good rains, and hot sun allows farmers to grow two or more crops of rice each year.

A plentiful labor force makes it possible to tend the fields without using costly machinery. Water buffalo help with the labor by pulling plows. Most farmers use the same tools that have been used by their ancestors for centuries. Their workday lasts from sunrise to sunset. This age-old picture can be found — with variation of detail depending on geography — throughout present-day Asia.

The Economy in the Cities

In Jakarta, the capital of Indonesia, people dine at fancy restaurants, and shop in large new malls for the latest styles in clothing and the newest electronic equipment. Bangkok, Thailand, echoes to the sound of dozens of building projects. Traffic roars through its streets, and neon signs light up the night. Jakarta and Bangkok are examples of the economic boom that is transforming East and Southeast Asia.

During the past 30 years, Asian countries have been growing faster than all other nations. In 1965, their exports made up 10 percent of the world total, about the same as developing countries in other regions. By 1990, these Asian nations had doubled their exports.

Japan already shares a high rank with the United States and Germany as being among the world's most industrial nations. In Malaysia,

the population living in poverty dropped from 37 percent in 1960 to less than five percent in 1990.

Many Asian countries experienced prosperity as a result of governments keeping taxes low and encouraging people to invest their money. Prosperity helped to create a middle class in eastern Asia. This class was swept by **consumerism** — when more goods are consumed, the economy will benefit, and profits can remain high. (Consumerism isn't the same as **materialism**, the idea that the more goods you buy, the happier you will be.)

To further encourage Asia's economic boom, some countries also took part in **joint ventures**, efforts in which different countries share the costs of running a business. Also, people from foreign countries invested billions of dollars in Asian companies. For example, between 1990 and 1996, 41 percent of Thailand's GDP came from investments.

In the late 1990s, the economic boom in Asia turned to bust. Foreign investors lost confidence in Asia's prosperous economies and withdrew funds. The value of currencies such as the Thai baht and the Indonesian rupiah dropped, while unemployment increased. Despite these struggles, Asians are working to regain economic strength as they enter the 21st century.

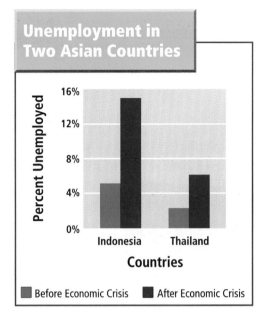

The Asian economic crisis has dramatically increased unemployment. **Chart Skill:** *Which country has faced higher unemployment since the economic crisis?*

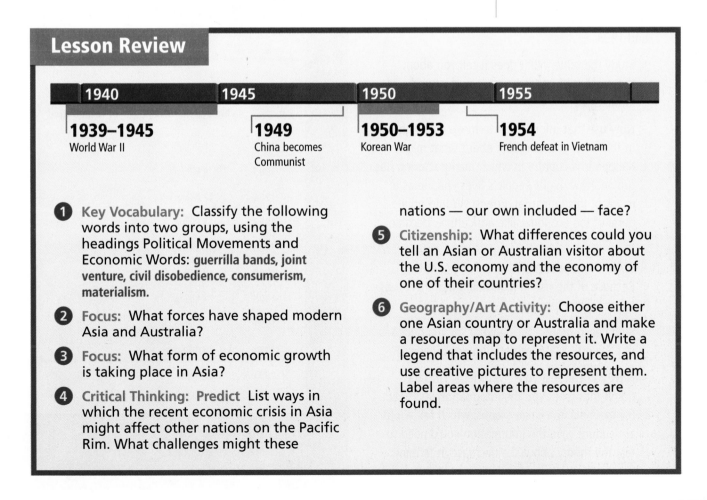

Lesson Review

1940	1945	1950	1955

1939–1945
World War II

1949
China becomes Communist

1950–1953
Korean War

1954
French defeat in Vietnam

❶ **Key Vocabulary:** Classify the following words into two groups, using the headings Political Movements and Economic Words: **guerrilla bands, joint venture, civil disobedience, consumerism, materialism.**

❷ **Focus:** What forces have shaped modern Asia and Australia?

❸ **Focus:** What form of economic growth is taking place in Asia?

❹ **Critical Thinking: Predict** List ways in which the recent economic crisis in Asia might affect other nations on the Pacific Rim. What challenges might these

nations — our own included — face?

❺ **Citizenship:** What differences could you tell an Asian or Australian visitor about the U.S. economy and the economy of one of their countries?

❻ **Geography/Art Activity:** Choose either one Asian country or Australia and make a resources map to represent it. Write a legend that includes the resources, and use creative pictures to represent them. Label areas where the resources are found.

Skills Workshop

Testing Hypotheses Using Graphs and Tables

What's In a Graph?

Suppose you are looking at a graph that shows a rise in people's income in Malaysia. You could make the educated guess, or **hypothesis,** that the Malaysian economy is growing. How can you find out if your hypothesis is right? You can use other graphs and tables to test your hypothesis.

1 Here's How

The graphs and table on these pages show how the nation of Malaysia has changed between 1984 and 1993.

- Study the table. What does it tell you about the number of goods being manufactured in Malaysia?

- Now use that information to make a hypothesis. In this case, you can think about what might happen in a country in which manufacturing has grown. How might people's lives change as a result of this industrial growth? Would other parts of the economy, like agriculture, become less important?

- Write down your hypothesis. For example: Because of the rise in manufacturing, there was a decrease in farming.

- Study each graph. Decide what the main idea is of each one. What information does it show?

- Now you can test your hypothesis. Find the graph that gives you the information you need. For example, the circle graphs, which tell about agriculture, give the information you'd need to test the theory about the decrease in farming.

A Growing Malaysia, 1984-1993

	Manufactured Goods in Malaysian Dollars	Percentage of Total Output
1984	6 Billion	18
1985	9 Billion	19
1986	12 Billion	20
1987	13 Billion	22
1988	16 Billion	24
1989	18 Billion	25
1990	21 Billion	27
1991	25 Billion	29
1992	28 Billion	29
1993	30 Billion	30

② Think It Through

What other ways could you test your hypothesis? What other sources of information could you use?

③ Use It

1. Choose one of the graphs. Think about the information you see there.

2. Use the information in that graph to form a hypothesis of your own about life in Malaysia.

3. Use the other graphs or the table to test your hypothesis.

4. Write a few sentences that tell about what you've learned.

Kuala Lumpur, above, and on the opposite page, is the capital city of Malaysia. On the right is shown a traditional Malaysian farmhouse.

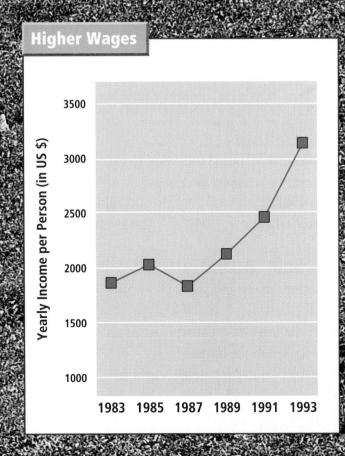

Where Are the Jobs?

The Malaysian Work Force

1985

- 35%
- 33%
- 16%
- 16%

1993

- 21%
- 45%
- 23%
- 11%

■ Manufacturing   ■ Government
■ Agriculture   ■ Other

Higher Wages

Yearly Income per Person (in US $)

Year	
3500	
3000	
2500	
2000	
1500	
1000	

1983 1985 1987 1989 1991 1993

Chapter Review

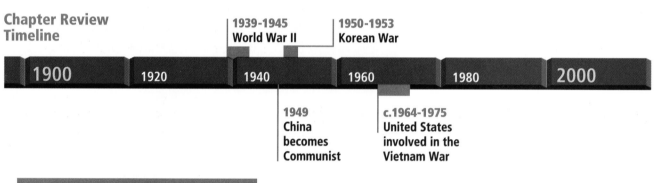

Chapter Review Timeline

| 1900 | 1920 | 1940 | 1960 | 1980 | 2000 |

1939-1945 World War II
1950-1953 Korean War
1949 China becomes Communist
c.1964-1975 United States involved in the Vietnam War

Summarizing the Main Idea

1 Copy the chart below, and fill in the missing information with a statement or two to compare the continents of Asia and Australia.

	Asia	Australia
Geography		
Resources		
Agriculture		
Population		

Vocabulary

2 Using at least three of the following terms, write a description of how one Asian country's economy developed.

reef (p. 498)
civil disobedience (p. 504)

guerrilla bands (p. 504)
joint venture (p. 509)

consumerism (p. 509)
materialism (p. 509)

Reviewing the Facts

3 Describe three major geographical features of Asia.

4 What are the three different types of Asian farms described in the chapter?

5 How do Asia's water resources benefit its people?

6 What are two features that make Australia geographically unique?

7 What is the Great Barrier Reef?

8 Give two examples of the effects of nationalist movements in Asia.

9 Describe some of the ways Asians achieved their independence.

10 How did the United States respond to the influence of communism in Asia?

11 How has the rise of consumerism influenced the economic growth of Asia?

12 What might the pie chart on page 511 tell you about the kind of career you might plan for yourself in Malaysia?

13 Which charts could show you a possible relationship between rising wages and an increase in manufacturing?

14 How could using charts like these help Malaysians prepare for the future?

Geography Skills

15 Study the map of Asia on pages 494–495. Why might the continent be divided into the regions shown there?

16 If you visited Australia and picked up five postcards displaying the natural beauty of the land, describe the pictures you would select.

Critical Thinking

17 **Generalize** Why are human resources necessary to the wealth of Asia?

18 **Interpret** Why do you think the United States opposed communist expansion in Asia?

Writing: Citizenship and Economics

19 **Citizenship** Write a letter to the editor supporting or criticizing Mohandas Gandhi's strategy of civil disobedience.

20 **Economics** Write a story about two friends, one a farmer from Java, still living as his ancestors did hundreds of years ago, and another who lives in the modern city of Jakarta.

Activities

History/Research Activity
Do research to find out more about one of the armed conflicts discussed in this chapter: The Japanese invasion of Manchuria, the struggle between Chiang Kai-shek and Mao Zedong in China, the Korean War and the Vietnam War. Share your findings with the class.

Economics/Math Activity
Choose a country in Asia, and look for magazine articles about its economic development. Display your findings in a graph and share it with the class.

Internet Option

Check the **Internet Social Studies Center** for ideas on how to extend your theme project beyond your classroom.

THEME PROJECT CHECK-IN

As you begin your theme project, use the information in this chapter about Asia and Australia to help you. Think about these questions:

• What geographic features have brought challenges and opportunities to these continents?
• What economic, political, and cultural factors have brought challenges and opportunities?
• How have these continents met the challenges and opportunities of the 20th century?

CHAPTER 19

East Asia and Australia: Patterns of Living

Japan's High-Tech Workplace

How is the role of Japanese women in Japan's high-tech economy changing? *Lesson 1, Page 518*

Japanese Schools

How are Japanese students taught to contribute to a rapidly growing economy? *Lesson 1, Page 518*

Chairman Mao Zedong

How did the dramatic reforms made by Communist leader Mao Zedong affect China? *Lesson 2, Page 526*

Japan: Formula for Economic Growth

Main Idea Modern Japan achieves rapid economic growth by combining traditional attitudes and modern methods.

Key Vocabulary
work ethic
literacy rate

Key Events
1945 Japan defeated in World War II
1947 Japan adopts Peace Constitution

In stores from Austria to Australia, the one thing shoppers can always find are electronic products made in Japan. The Japanese have made a specialty of producing such high-tech goods as computers, televisions, and camcorders. Nowadays, the influence of Japanese technology is felt around the world. This exchange of ideas was not always the case. For a hundred years following Europeans' arrival in the 1540s, a brisk trade developed. When the Japanese ruler expelled all foreigners except the Chinese and Dutch, most of the world lost contact with Japan for almost 200 years. Now, this balance between outside and inside influences, between modern technology and age-old tradition, has given Japan one of the largest economies in the world.

◀ The Sydney Opera House is a modern landmark of Sydney, Australia's largest city.

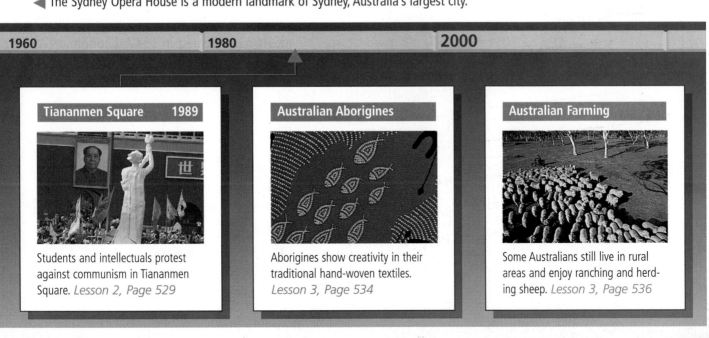

1960   1980   2000

Tiananmen Square   1989

Students and intellectuals protest against communism in Tiananmen Square. *Lesson 2, Page 529*

Australian Aborigines

Aborigines show creativity in their traditional hand-woven textiles. *Lesson 3, Page 534*

Australian Farming

Some Australians still live in rural areas and enjoy ranching and herding sheep. *Lesson 3, Page 536*

Traditional Values/New Economy

Focus *What traditional attitudes help the Japanese build their modern economy?*

For centuries, the Japanese were somewhat isolated, or removed, from the rest of the world. The 4,000 islands that make up Japan stretch for nearly 2,000 miles off the coast of Asia. Many of these islands are actually the tops of underwater volcanoes that are now mostly inactive. Most of the country's 125 million people live along the coast of Honshu (HAHN SHOO), the largest island, where land is relatively flat. The Japanese have always made use of the sea and have developed skills as fishermen and boat builders. They lack resources like coal, oil, and iron ore. Over the past one hundred years, however, Japan sometimes tried to take these resources from other countries by aggression, or force. Japan's involvement in World War II is an example.

The map shows some industries of Japan. **Map Skill:** *Why do you think the industries shown have developed in Japan?*

Industries of Japan

Legend
- ★ National capital
- Cars
- Shipbuilding
- Opticals
- Electronics
- Fishing

SEA OF JAPAN

HOKKAIDŌ

Sapporo

HONSHŪ

Niigata

Tokyo
Yokohama

Kyōto
Kōbe
Ōsaka Nagoya

Hiroshima

Kitakyūshū

Fukuoka

SHIKOKU

KYŪSHŪ

km 0 100 200
mi 0   100   200

World War II led to great destruction in Japan. Over two million Japanese died in the war. Millions more were left without homes or jobs. Farm production was cut in half, threatening mass starvation. At the end of the war, Japanese leaders signed documents promising Japan's commitment to peace. Then, helped by the United States and its military forces that remained in Japan, the country began rebuilding. The new Japanese Constitution, based partly on democratic ideals, was created in 1947. Economic changes came into force. Factories and businesses that had been destroyed by bombs were modernized as they were rebuilt.

Japan's Postwar Economy

Today Japan is one of the world's major economic powers. It competes with the United States and Europe in many industries. Japan's major exports include ships and automobiles, iron and steel products, electronic products, ceramics, and textiles.

Much of Japan's success after the war was achieved by government efforts to build an economy for peace rather than to rebuild its military. However, the character of the Japanese worker is equally important to Japan's fast economic growth.

The Company Spirit

To build a new economy, modern Japanese have applied their traditional work ethic. A **work ethic** is a system of beliefs and ideals about how work should be performed. In Japan this means being loyal to the group, honoring the wisdom of elders, doing one's part for the good of all, and respecting and caring for the family.

Typical Japanese workers usually work more hours than Americans with similar jobs. Wages are high, but so are prices. A large population and a shortage of land make living conditions cramped, even for middle-class families. Cities are crowded, but Japan's public transportation system is very efficient. Subway workers push the maximum number of people into subway trains at rush hour.

Most workers feel loyal to their employer and proud to be part of

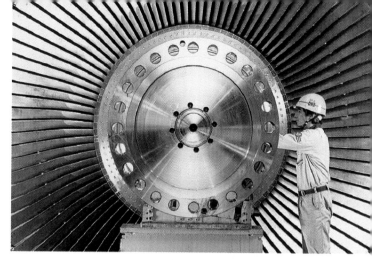

In the photo above, a Japanese worker inspects a large turbine engine.

• Tell Me More •

Fast as a Speeding Bullet

The shinkansen (SHEEN KAN SEN) whooshes into Tokyo Station. Foreigners have nicknamed Japanese trains like this "bullet trains" because of their shape and high speed. Silently, the bullet train comes to a smooth stop.

Ordinary trains are pulled by a locomotive. Bullet trains, using high-speed rail technology, have wheels that are individually powered. This distributes their weight evenly and allows them to reach a maximum speed of over 140 miles per hour.

An average trip on a bullet train from Tokyo to Osaka takes under three hours.

Japan is now developing a new train that may travel up to 300 miles per hour and has no wheels at all! Instead, it floats above the tracks, propelled down the rails by magnetic pulses.

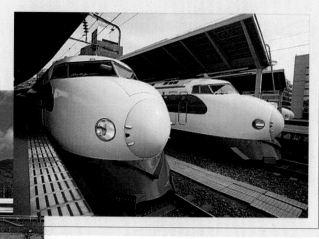

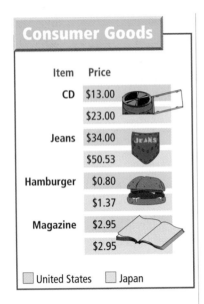

Consumer Goods

Item	Price
CD	$13.00
	$23.00
Jeans	$34.00
	$50.53
Hamburger	$0.80
	$1.37
Magazine	$2.95
	$2.95

☐ United States ☐ Japan

Chart Skill: *Which product has the greatest price difference between the United States and Japan?*

Cultures: *What role does the family play in educating Japanese children?*

the group. They wear the company uniform and attend social events run by the company. Many workers stay at the same company for most of their lives. Their company spirit and traditional values contribute to rapid economic growth for Japan.

Home and School

Focus *What role do women and children play in the Japanese economy?*

Traditionally most Japanese women did not participate in Japan's economy. They did not work outside the home. After World War II, this slowly changed. By the 1960s, many young single women had jobs. They often quit work when they married and cared full-time for their families. Today, more and more Japanese mothers go back to work when their children start school. Although many Japanese women of working age have college degrees, few of them hold top positions.

Japanese women are usually in charge of managing the household money and raising the children. A mother's daily schedule is busy. She provides meals — from breakfast before dawn to her husband's dinner at 10 o'clock at night. She does the laundry, housework, and daily shopping. She chooses schools for the children, talks with their teachers, and helps with homework. If her son or daughter becomes ill, she may sit in her child's class at school and take notes!

Japanese students will not get good jobs after completing school unless they earned good grades. From the time students start school, there is great pressure to work hard. The Japanese school year is longer than the one in the U.S., and students go to school five and a half days a week. In addition to studying math, science, writing, social studies, art, and music, students study English. In the evening, many young Japanese go to a special school to be tutored in difficult subjects.

From an early age, students are taught to work in groups and to respect others. This helps them to live in such a crowded country. Japanese teachers believe it is the student's job — with a parent's help, if necessary — to learn what the teacher teaches. In the classroom, students also learn to help each other.

Competition for entry into the universities is stiff. High-school students have a period of testing they call "exam torture." Their test scores are used to decide their future. If they do poorly, they can't go to college or get a good job. Some Japanese teachers criticize this system. Still it remains a strong tradition, and parents want their children to succeed.

Japan's emphasis on improving students' education has contributed to one of the highest literacy rates in the world, 99.9 percent. The **literacy rate** of a country is the percentage of its people who are able to read and write.

In the late 1990s, Japan experienced an economic downturn, the most severe since the end of World War II. This downturn has led to unemployment across much of Japan. However, education remains important as the Japanese work to rebuild their economy in the 21st century.

Japanese children work hard in school. **Technology:** *How might education affect technology?*

Lesson Review

1940	1950
1945	**1947**
Japan defeated in World War II	**Japan** adopts Peace Constitution

1. **Key Vocabulary:** Describe Japan's economy using the term **work ethic.**

2. **Focus:** What traditional attitudes help the Japanese build their modern economy?

3. **Focus:** What role do women and children play in the Japanese economy?

4. **Critical Thinking: Predict** How might the Japanese attitude towards education help Japan regain economic strength?

5. **Theme: Challenges and Opportunities** What challenges and opportunities did the end of World War II bring to Japan?

6. **Citizenship/Writing Activity:** Write a letter to Japanese students describing the differences between your school and theirs.

Interpreting Cartograms

How Do You Measure It?

We can measure countries in many ways. On a standard world map, Japan is small. Standard maps show a country's physical size, or land area. How can a map show Japan's economic size? A **cartogram** is a map that changes the size of a country to show some other value, such as gross national product (GNP). GNP is the total value of all goods and services produced by a country in a single year. It tells a lot about the strength and size of a nation's economy. So a small country with a big economy, like Japan, appears large on a GNP cartogram.

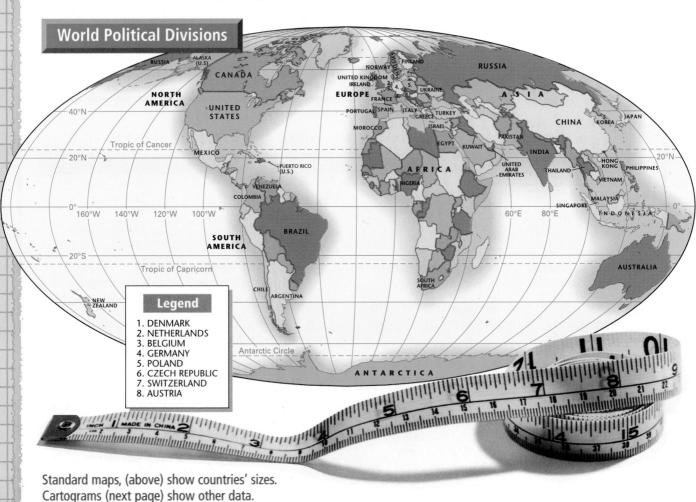

World Political Divisions

Legend

1. DENMARK
2. NETHERLANDS
3. BELGIUM
4. GERMANY
5. POLAND
6. CZECH REPUBLIC
7. SWITZERLAND
8. AUSTRIA

Standard maps, (above) show countries' sizes.
Cartograms (next page) show other data.

1 Here's How

- Read the legend of the cartogram to find out what value it measures. On this cartogram, country size reflects the size of its gross national product.

- Study the legend. How is economic size measured in this cartogram? Find out what value each color represents. What colors represent the largest economies? The smallest?

- Compare sizes of various countries on the cartogram. Which countries are largest? Which are smallest? What does this tell you about their economies?

- Compare the cartogram and the world map. What differences do you see in country size and shape? What do these changes in size and shape tell you about these countries?

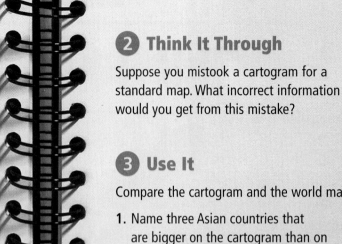

2 Think It Through

Suppose you mistook a cartogram for a standard map. What incorrect information would you get from this mistake?

3 Use It

Compare the cartogram and the world map.

1. Name three Asian countries that are bigger on the cartogram than on the world map.

2. Name three Asian countries that are smaller on the cartogram than on the world map.

3. What countries have economies equal to or larger than Japan's?

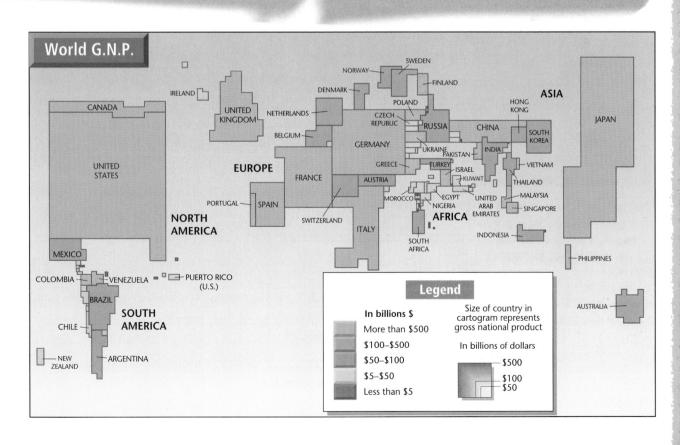

World G.N.P.

ASIA
JAPAN
SWEDEN
NORWAY
FINLAND
IRELAND
DENMARK
HONG KONG
UNITED KINGDOM
NETHERLANDS
POLAND
CZECH REPUBLIC
RUSSIA
CHINA
SOUTH KOREA
CANADA
BELGIUM
GERMANY
UKRAINE
PAKISTAN
INDIA
VIETNAM
UNITED STATES
EUROPE
GREECE
TURKEY
ISRAEL
KUWAIT
THAILAND
FRANCE
AUSTRIA
MALAYSIA
PORTUGAL
SPAIN
MOROCCO
EGYPT
UNITED ARAB EMIRATES
SINGAPORE
NORTH AMERICA
SWITZERLAND
NIGERIA
AFRICA
ITALY
INDONESIA
MEXICO
SOUTH AFRICA
PHILIPPINES
COLOMBIA
VENEZUELA
PUERTO RICO (U.S.)
BRAZIL
SOUTH AMERICA
AUSTRALIA
CHILE
NEW ZEALAND
ARGENTINA

Legend

In billions $
- More than $500
- $100–$500
- $50–$100
- $5–$50
- Less than $5

Size of country in cartogram represents gross national product

In billions of dollars
- $500
- $100
- $50

A DELL YEARLING BOOK

0-440-47465-5 • U.S. $3.50
CAN. $4.50

Courage and spirit made Sadako a heroine to children in Japan.

Historical Fiction

Sadako and the Thousand Paper Cranes

by Eleanor Coerr
illustrated by Ronald Himler

America entered the fighting in World War II after the Japanese launched a surprise attack at Pearl Harbor, Hawaii, on December 7, 1941. After four years and millions of deaths, World War II had ended in Europe, but not in the Pacific region. The Japanese army vowed to keep on fighting to the last man, and it looked as if Allied forces would have to attack the islands of Japan.

American military leaders believed that an invasion of Japan might take years, and would certainly cost millions of additional lives. In order to end the war, U.S. President Truman ordered the use of a terrible new weapon, the atomic bomb. The target was the Japanese city of Hiroshima, and the date was August 6, 1945.

Sadako Sasaki was a very little girl when the bomb exploded. She was not close enough to be hurt right away, and she grew up so straight and strong that it looked as if she would be fine. More than anything, she loved to run, and she won many races.

But one day Sadako began to get weak, so weak that her parents took her to the hospital for tests. Her parents, her brother Masahiro, her best friend Chizuko — everyone was afraid that she had leukemia, a blood disease they called "the atom bomb disease."

leukemia (loo KEE mee ah) — *a disease of the blood cells.*

The next morning Sadako woke up slowly. She listened for the familiar sounds of her mother making breakfast, but there were only the new and different sounds of a hospital. Sadako sighed. She had hoped that yesterday was just a bad dream. It was even more real when Nurse Yasunaga came in to give her a shot.

"Getting shots is part of being in the hospital," the plump nurse said briskly. "You'll get used to it."

That afternoon Chizuko was Sadako's first visitor. She smiled mysteriously as she held something behind her back. "Shut your eyes," she said. While Sadako squinted her eyes tightly shut, Chizuko put some pieces of paper and scissors on the bed. "Now you can look," she said.

"What is it?" Sadako asked, staring at the paper.

Chizuko was pleased with herself. "I've figured out a way for you to get well," she said proudly. "Watch!" She cut a piece of gold paper into a large square. In a short time she had folded it over and over into a beautiful crane.

crane — a large, wading bird that lives on fish.

Sadako was puzzled. "But how can that paper bird make me well?"

"Don't you remember that old story about the crane?" Chizuko asked. "It's supposed to live for a thousand years. If a person folds one thousand paper cranes, the gods will grant her wish and make her healthy again." She handed the crane to Sadako. "Here's your first one."

Sadako's eyes filled with tears. How kind of Chizuko to bring a good luck charm! Especially when her friend didn't really believe in such things. Sadako took the golden crane and made a wish. The funniest little feeling came over her when she touched the bird. It must be a good omen.

"Thank you, Chizuko chan," she whispered. "I'll never part with it."

When she began to work with the paper, Sadako discovered that folding a crane wasn't as easy as it looked. With Chizuko's help she learned how to do the difficult parts. After making ten birds, Sadako lined them up on the table beside the golden crane. Some were a bit lopsided, but it was a beginning.

chan (CHAHN) — a Japanese word friends call each other or older relatives use when talking to children.

"Now I have only nine-hundred and ninety to make," Sadako said. With the golden crane nearby she felt safe and lucky. Why, in a few weeks she would be able to finish the thousand. Then she would be strong enough to go home.

That evening Masahiro brought Sadako's homework from school. When he saw the cranes, he said, "There isn't enough room on that small table to show off your birds. I'll hang them from the ceiling for you."

Sadako was smiling all over. "Do you promise to hang every crane I make?"

Masahiro promised.

"That's fine!" Sadako said, her eyes twinkling with mischief. "Then you'll hang the whole thousand?"

"A thousand!" her brother groaned. "You're joking!"

Sadako told him the story of the cranes.

Masahiro ran a hand through his straight black hair. "You tricked me!" he said with a grin. "But I'll do it anyhow." He borrowed some thread and tacks from Nurse Yasunaga and hung the first ten cranes. The golden crane stayed in its place of honor on the table.

After supper Mrs. Sasaki brought Mitsue and Eiji to the hospital. Everyone was surprised to see the birds. They reminded Mrs. Sasaki of a famous old poem:

Out of colored paper, cranes
come flying into
our house.

Mitsue and Eiji liked the golden crane best. But Mrs. Sasaki chose the tiniest one made of fancy green paper with pink parasols on it. "This is my choice," she said, "because small ones are the most difficult to make."

After visiting hours it was lonely in the hospital room. So lonely that Sadako folded more cranes to keep up her courage. Eleven . . . I wish I'd get better.

Twelve . . . I wish I'd get better.

Meet the Author

Eleanor Coerr is an American, but she lived in Japan, Thailand, and Taiwan for a total of nine years. She has written books set in each of these countries. *Meiko and the Fifth Treasure* is a recent book of hers that is also set in Japan shortly after World War II.

Additional Books to Read

Grandfather's Journey by Allen Say. Grandfather remembers life in two cultures.

Journey Home by Yoshiko Uchida. Read about life during World War II for a Japanese-American family.

Response Activities

1. **Identify Main Idea:** What do the cranes in this story represent?

2. **Narrative: Write a Story** Write your own ending to the story.

3. **History: Learn About World War II** Do research on the end of World War II in Japan. How did the dropping of the bomb at Hiroshima affect the Japanese? Which parts of Japan were affected most?

China: A Series of Sweeping Changes

Main Idea China has undergone enormous political changes since 1949.

Each morning, after a breakfast of rice gruel (a thin, watery cereal made from boiled rice), Zheng Tian Ren (JUHNG TEE YEHN REHN) jumps on his bicycle and pedals the three miles to his job in a bookstore. Like most Chinese bookstores and other businesses, it is owned by the government. On the way, he passes the open market where porcelain is sold. For a thousand years, his city, Jingdezhen (JIHNG DUH JUHN), has been famous for its dishes, delicate jars, small figures, and other objects made of a thin earthenware, beautifully decorated and glazed.

Zheng works hard, but he is eager to work even harder at lunch time. At noon he bicycles up the street to a six-table restaurant. A few months ago, he and his brother opened this eating place near the porcelain museum. The two brothers run the restaurant during the lunch hour and after work. They don't mind the long hours. The business belongs to them and the restaurant is usually packed. Small businesses like Zheng's are a sign of the enormous changes taking place in China today.

China's New Spirit

Focus *What changes did Mao Zedong and his Communist Party bring to China?*

In 1949, after a long civil war, China became a communist nation. It named itself the People's Republic of China. (You can read about this in Chapter 18.) Mao Zedong, revolutionary leader and head of the Communist Party, led this large nation. His goals included (1) reducing foreign influence on China, (2) dividing up large, privately owned tracts of land and distributing them evenly among all citizens, and (3) building a new government based on communism.

In 1958, he launched the **Great Leap Forward**. This program

established large communes. **Communes** are places where people live and work as a group, sharing all responsibilities. Land for the communes was nationalized. This means that land that belonged to families was taken by the government in order to build the communes.

Approximately 25,000 communes were formed. More than 500 million workers lived on them. The workers ate in large dining halls and lived together in army-style buildings. All children went to daycare centers while all the adults worked. Even the elderly were assigned jobs.

The communes were much too large to be practical. The directors of these huge operations often knew little about farming. Still, people whose families had struggled for centuries under rich landowners were hopeful. They thought they were better off than ever before. Loyalty to Mao Zedong was high — but not high enough for Chairman Mao. He wanted to strengthen his position.

In 1966, Mao called for a **Cultural Revolution** to bring back the communist spirit. He felt that some citizens did not live up to communist ideals or had been influenced by foreigners. He gathered together bands of young people and named them the Red Guard. Their job was to take action against these Chinese "enemies to communism." The Red Guard stormed the country. Teachers, scientists, writers, artists, and others were terrorized. Universities were forced to close. Anybody with foreign contacts was questioned. The Red Guard rounded up officials who disagreed with them and forced these people

Mao Zedong's reforms improved living conditions for the poorest Chinese peasants, but also brought political oppression. His "little red book" inspired a generation of Chinese young people.

Chart Skill: *Approximately what fraction of the world's population lives in China?*

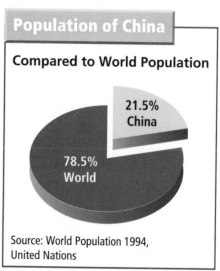

Population of China

Compared to World Population

21.5% China

78.5% World

Source: World Population 1994, United Nations

to make public confessions — even if they had done nothing wrong. Thousands were imprisoned and tortured, or they simply disappeared. The exact number killed may never be known.

It took years for the fear and pain of the so-called Cultural Revolution to fade from China, and deep scars still remain. The movement was so brutal that many lost faith in Mao. The leader's weakened power eventually led China's premier, Zhou Enlai (JOH EN LIE), to take more control over the state.

On the Brink of the 21st Century

Focus *How have Deng Xiaoping's reforms reshaped China?*

Both Mao and Zhou died in 1976. One of the next leaders, Deng Xiaoping (DUHNG SHEE OW PING), believed that China's strength depended on improving living and economic conditions. His efforts transformed the country. Today, China is growing very fast. Some experts believe it will have the world's largest economy by the year 2010.

A Series of Reforms

Deng invited countries in the West to share science and technology with China. He encouraged foreign companies to invest in China through programs in which Chinese and non-Chinese worked together. Instead of factories and farms run by the government, Deng proposed a "responsibility system." Under this plan, each factory and farm set its own rules and goals. The result was that production grew sharply, and incomes tripled. Family farms were allowed to sell their products on the open market instead of giving them to the people through the Communist system of distribution. Many small businesses were started, like the restaurant owned by Zheng Tian Ren and his brother.

China's leaders recognized that a strong nation needs literate people. To make the language easier to read, written characters were simplified *(see Tell Me More)*. These changes have helped raise the literacy rate in China from 20 percent in 1949 to 80 percent today.

China still has serious problems. Only the best students can continue school past the sixth grade, and only the very top attend universities. The government still keeps tight control of its citizens. For example, people cannot leave the country without permission. Poverty is widespread. Millions live without running water, electricity, and indoor plumbing — cooking over fires and drawing water from wells. At the same time, industrial pollution poisons the environment. Today China remains under the control of the Communist Party.

Resistance and Reaction

The power of Communist control was made clear in 1989. In April a few hundred students gathered in Tiananmen (TI AN UHN MUHN) Square in Beijing, where Mao had announced the birth of the People's Republic 40 years earlier. (Tiananmen Square is right in front of the Forbidden City, which you examined in Chapter 12. Compare the photo on the right with the illustration on page 504.) These demonstrators called for democracy and an end to government corruption. Through April and May of 1989, the protest grew. Dissidents (people who oppose the government) in other cities added their voices, chanting,

Chinese students protesting in 1989 in Tiananmen Square.
Economics: *Why do you think people growing up in China would want democracy and the opportunity to build their own businesses?*

> "**L**ong *live democracy! Long live freedom! Down with corruption! Down with bureaucracy!*"

• Tell Me More •

The World's Most Spoken Language

Chinese is spoken by more people — over a billion — than any other language on earth. So when Chinese changes, the language of one in every five people in the world changes!

In 1977, Chinese leaders decided to simplify written Chinese characters so that more people could read them. Unfortunately, the changes caused confusion, and words on signs all over Beijing ended up misspelled. In a project called "Let the spring wind drive away wrong characters," 500,000 school children carried their dictionaries around the city looking for mistakes. Within only a few weeks, they corrected over 40,000 wrong characters on signs!

Foreign journalists reported from Tiananmen Square as the crowd swelled to the tens of thousands. Ignoring world opinion, Deng Xiaoping called in the army. On the night of June 3 and the morning of June 4, television viewers around the world watched in horror as troops and tanks rumbled into the square. No one knows how many were killed. A massive roundup of Chinese students, teachers, and thinkers followed.

Hong Kong: Promises to Keep

Located off the southeast coast of China, the island of Hong Kong came under British rule in 1841. As a British colony, Hong Kong was often called the banking capital of the world. Its airport and harbor were among the busiest in the world.

Today, Hong Kong is no longer a British colony. It is a free region under China's communist state. As of July 1, 1997, when Britain returned Hong Kong to China, the Chinese government agreed to recognize Hong Kong's freedom for the next fifty years. Its 6.8 million residents enjoy a higher standard of living than people in the rest of China.

Recently, Hong Kong residents have been concerned that their freedoms will be limited. Some people worry that the strength of the economy is weakening. It remains unclear how China will continue to manage this special region.

Hong Kong is a busy center of international trade. The city is so crowded that passenger jets must land just beyond skyscrapers.

Lesson Review

1950	1960	1970	1980	1990
1949 China becomes communist	**1958** Great Leap Forward	**1966** Cultural Revolution	**1989** Protests in Tiananmen Square	**1997** Hong Kong returned to China

1. **Key Vocabulary:** Write a paragraph using the terms: Great Leap Forward, communes, Cultural Revolution.

2. **Focus:** What changes did Mao Zedong and his Communist Party bring to China?

3. **Focus:** How have Deng Xiaoping's reforms reshaped China?

4. **Critical Thinking: Predict** What might the Chinese government learn from the people of Hong Kong?

5. **Theme: Challenges and Opportunities** Explain why Chinese efforts to build small businesses like the Zheng brothers' restaurant are so important.

6. **Citizenship/Arts Activity:** Create a short play or draw a picture that expresses your reaction to the events that took place in Tiananmen Square on June 3 and 4, 1989.

PANDAS IN PERIL

China is home to many unique animals. Few are as well known as the giant panda. Even though the Chinese government is officially in favor of keeping the pandas safe, in the past it has not done enough to keep people from killing pandas or ruining their habitat and food supply. Can earth's most populated nation afford to save this gentle creature? Can it afford not to?

The giant panda races against time. If it wins, it lives. If not, it dies. Are humans doing enough to save this lovable animal?

Eat. Sleep. Wander through the forest when you're bored. What a great life the giant panda has.

No school, no chores, not even many enemies. Great, huh?

Wrong. The giant panda is in big trouble.

Just Plain Cute

With Mickey Mouse ears, black-and-white coats and cuddly-looking bodies, giant pandas appear sweet and comical. Most people find them just plain cute.

They are shy, gentle creatures that generally avoid encounters with each other and with humans.

But encounters with civilization are getting harder to avoid. The giant panda is one of earth's most endangered species. Only about 1,000 pandas survive in the wild, in the remote bamboo forests of China.

What's the Problem?

The panda's plight is confusing. The animals have few natural predators (mainly the leopard). People all over the world seem to love them. And the Chinese government considers the panda a national treasure.

So why is the species on the brink of extinction?

In 1980 George Schaller, a world-famous wildlife biologist, began researching that question. He became the first Westerner ever invited by China to study the panda in its native habitat. For four years he tracked pandas through the forest.

What he found was disturbing. Pandas were in trouble.

Hunters stalked pandas for their valuable hides, killing many each year. Many other pandas died at the hands of careless hunters who actually were after other species.

Not only that, but the pandas were losing their homes. Humans cut down the trees, then plowed the soil in their quest for wood and land.

Deep in the bamboo forests, pandas should have plenty of food — and be safe from unfriendly human visitors.

PANDA FACTS

•Scientists disagree about how to classify the giant panda. Some believe it should be grouped with bears. Others say it is more closely related to raccoons. Panda researcher George Schaller says, "The panda is a panda" and should be given its own classification.

•The panda's black-and-white coat helps it avoid encounters with other pandas. The black patches around the eyes make its stare appear fiercer and more threatening to opponents. To show it has no aggressive intentions, a panda will hide its face or cover its eyes with its paws.

•An adult panda may reach six feet in length and weigh 220 pounds, but size can vary greatly.

•At birth, a panda is smaller than a rat.

•Bamboo, a plant, is the panda's principal diet. This is odd because pandas are classified as "carnivores," or meat eaters. Carnivores are the group of animals that have teeth like those of a dog or wolf.

•The animals eat as much as 33 pounds of bamboo leaves and stems or up to 90 pounds of juicy young shoots every day. A panda requires more than 12 hours a day to eat that much.

•The panda produces a variety of sounds, including honking, moaning, clacking of teeth and smacking of lips. It also emits a high-pitched bleating sound.

•Pandas may live as long as 30 years in captivity. Animals in the wild tend to have shorter life spans.

A new policy will let some pandas stay in their native refuges in China and others visit American zoos.

The animals were forced to retreat farther up in the mountains until there was nowhere else to go.

A Brighter Future — Maybe

The Chinese government and international conservation groups are working to ensure the panda's survival.

Because of their efforts, the panda has become an international symbol of conservation.

But no one knows whether the results will be triumph or tragedy. Here's how humans are trying to save the panda:

Tougher laws:

Killing pandas is illegal in China, but until 1987 the penalty was not severe — only two years or less in prison. Now people who kill pandas or try to sell the animals' fur face life in prison, sometimes even death.

New, safer homes:

Many new panda reserves have been created, and there are plans to designate almost all of the animal's range as protected zones. Tree-cutting will be restricted or banned. People living in reserves will move elsewhere when possible.

More panda pathways:

New forests are being planted to link panda regions. This will provide food and cover for the animals as they travel between their territories.

It will not be easy, but there is still hope that one of the planet's most adorable creatures can be saved.

Larry Rice

THE OTHER PANDA

When you think about pandas, you probably picture the cute, black-and-white bear-like giant panda.

But there's another panda species: the red, or lesser, panda. Nocturnal and mild-mannered, the much smaller, raccoon-like animal is at home in the high-altitude bamboo forests of southeast Asia.

No one knows exactly how many red pandas are in the wild. But their numbers are surely dwindling.

PANDA WATCHING

Up to 100 pandas live in zoos in China. Fifteen to twenty live in other zoos.

A plan in the works might allow more pandas to come to the United States for extended visits.

Response Activities

1. **Predict** What do you think will happen to the panda population? Why?

2. **Narrative: Write a Story** Write a story as if you were one of the last pandas to survive in your natural habitat.

3. **History: Learn about Endangered Animals** Research animals that have already become extinct. What do they have in common? Then research other currently endangered animals and make a list of ways to save them.

The World Comes to Australia

Main Idea Australia is becoming a multicultural society.

Have you ever heard of the land "down under"? English speakers have used this term in a joking way to describe Australia, because it is in the Southern Hemisphere, far from other continents where English is spoken. People who have never traveled to this interesting continent sometimes accept a traditional stereotype of Australians. A **stereotype** is a general idea about a place or people that exaggerates some of their aspects and ignores others.

If you haven't seen Australia, you might expect to find modern-day cowboys swaggering through a dusty, rough land that looks a lot like America's Old West. Or you might think only about its unusual wildlife: odd-looking animals with fascinating names like wallaby (WAHL uh bee), koala, wombat, kangaroo, platypus (PLAT ih puhs), quokka (KWAHK uh), Tasmanian devil. This image, however, is only partly true. If you visit Australia you will discover a land far more varied and interesting than the stereotypes.

A Variety of People

Focus *What kinds of people make up the population of present-day Australia?*

Australia has a **multicultural** population, that is, one made up of many cultures. Each culture has its own customs, beliefs, arts, and history. Present-day Australians take pride in both their past and present, and in all the cultures that make up their country.

The First Inhabitants

The **aborigines** (ab uh RIHJ uh neez), the original inhabitants of Australia, arrived there over 40,000 years ago.

An aboriginal tour guide and his partner work on a backcountry road in the Northern Territory.

They came from Asia, probably across land bridges, small islands that have long since vanished beneath the ocean. (Compare the migrations with that of the Native Americans you studied in Chapter 6. Groups of Native Americans crossed from Asia to Alaska over a land bridge located in what is now the Bering Strait.)

Aborigines have one of the world's oldest surviving cultures. As hunter-gatherers, they moved with the seasons in search of food. They respected both the land and Australia's indigenous, or native, wildlife. When the Europeans arrived, there were more than 600 different tribes of aborigines living on the continent. At least 200 different languages were spoken there. Now, there are fewer than 206,000 aborigines, making up about one percent of the Australian population.

European settlers changed the land of the aborigines. For centuries, the indigenous peoples were treated as second-class citizens by the settlers. Most groups died out; some of their children moved to the cities or abandoned their old ways.

Those aborigines who haven't abandoned the old ways carry on an unusual artistic tradition. One form of expression is painting on pieces of bark small enough to carry from place to place. Another is sand painting for religious ceremonies. There is also an impressive oral tradition — stories passed by word of mouth from one generation to the next. These

Curious Facts

The city of Perth on the southwest coast of Australia is closer to Singapore in Southeast Asia than it is to Brisbane, a city on Australia's east coast.

Like the United States, Australia is divided into states. **Map Skill:** *Which state borders do you think were created by natural features?*

Sophie Parbury, age 7, lives in the Australian Outback. She is so far from school that she learns through two-way radio lessons and receives her tests and other teaching materials in the mail. Her teachers are stationed at broadcasting centers in various parts of the country.

stories include creation myths, as well as stories about the aborigines' arrival on the continent, early life, the relationships among the tribes, the arrival of the first Europeans, and the effects of the modern world on their land.

European Settlement

Europeans arrived in Australia in the late 1700s, when Britain claimed control over the continent. Among them were explorers, traders, settlers, and a large number of criminals from the British Isles. During that time in Great Britain, poor economic conditions and harsh laws created a huge criminal class. Many of these people were "transported" to prison colonies in Australia. (There was even a colony for child criminals!) Living conditions were horrible in places like Botany Bay, New South Wales, and Van Diemen's (VAN DEE mehnz) Land. The city of Sydney was first settled by convicts.

For anyone who went to Australia, life was hard. As you learned in Chapter 18, Australia is huge, and some parts of the continent — the deserts and vast stretches of dry, treeless plain, for example — are uninviting. Outside of the coastal settlements, distances are so great that the land seemed to swallow people up. This is the region called the Australian Outback. This vast area of arid and semiarid land stretches westward from the lush, tropical coast of Queensland to cover almost one-quarter of the continent. The ranchers and **graziers** (people who raise sheep) who lived in the interior were independent and self-sufficient.

A Changing Culture

In the years since the first Europeans arrived, millions of settlers have immigrated to Australia. To some Americans who went there, Australia

Australian graziers raise sheep for wool and meat. Instead of rounding up his sheep on horseback, the Australian in the photo travels by motorcycle.

offered a new frontier to explore, long after America's "Wild West" had been settled. After World War II, the Australian government encouraged people from southern and western Europe whose homes had been destroyed to resettle there. Many other immigrants were drawn by economic possibilities. Most were attracted to Australian cities, which are as modern as American cities. The arts are thriving in places like Sydney, whose futuristic-looking opera house has become a symbol for Australian progress.

A Multicultural Society

At present, different groups in Australia are coming to value, preserve, and share each other's cultures. In recent years, Australians have made important efforts to preserve the aborigines' land and way of life.

Australia is also taking steps toward welcoming people from other nations. Until 1973, the government held to a policy that kept out non-white immigrants. Today the country accepts more than 100,000 new immigrants from all parts of the world each year. Now, 33 percent are Asian. Like the aborigines, who arrived in Australia from Asia centuries ago, they hope to make Australia their descendants' home for many centuries to come.

Modern-day aborigines have preserved traditional forms of art, including beautiful woven textiles and bark painting, shown in the photo above. **Arts:** *Do some research and find other native peoples' art.*

Lesson Review

1. **Key Vocabulary:** Use each of the following words in sentences that tell you what they mean: **stereotypes, aborigines, graziers.**

2. **Focus:** What kinds of people make up the population of present-day Australia?

3. **Critical Thinking: Cause and Effect** What are the reasons that modern Australia has a multicultural society?

4. **Theme: Challenges and Opportunities** What challenges do the aborigines still face? What challenges do you think new immigrants to Australia face?

5. **Geography/Science Activity:** Australia is the only country in the world that is also a continent. Create (with markers on clear plastic) maps of the United States and Australia, using the same scale. Lay the maps on top of each other. Compare the size of the United States with that of Australia.

★ CITIZENSHIP ★

Participating

Why Should People Vote?

When the United States was founded, most people who lived here were not allowed to vote in elections. Groups such as African American men, women, and Native Americans won the right to vote after major political battles. Now, every citizen aged 18 or older has the right to vote. Yet many people don't vote. In Presidential races, barely half of those who are eligible to vote actually do so. In other elections, even fewer go to the polls. Why do many citizens not bother to vote? The case study below shows how another country treats this issue.

Case Study

Penalties for Nonvoters in Australia

It is election day in Australia. If you were an Australian citizen 18 years or older you would almost certainly vote today. In fact, Australians of voting age are required to vote in all local, state, and national elections. If eligible citizens do not vote, they can be fined up to 50 Australian dollars.

The government makes it easy to vote. They hold elections on Saturdays, when many people are home from work. They open polls in schools, churches, and town halls. People who are sick or away from home can send in ballots by mail. As a result, nearly all eligible voters participate in Australian elections.

Take Action

What are the advantages of requiring all eligible voters to vote? Are there any disadvantages? Debate the following proposition: Americans should be required to vote in all elections. Each eligible person who fails to vote should be subject to a $20 fine.

1 Divide into three groups. Group 1 is in favor of enforced voting; Group 2 is against enforced voting; Group 3 judges the debate.

2 Groups 1 and 2 prepare their arguments based on the advantages and disadvantages of enforced voting.

3 Hold a debate on enforced voting. Each side should have a chance to present its argument without interruption.

Tips for Participating

• Try to use the words "and more," and the words "but less." This shows that you do not necessarily disagree with everything, but have something to add.

• Focus on what it is that you and the other person actually disagree about.

• Criticizing the other side's point of view is less effective than proposing a way to change their plan so it will work better.

Research Activity

Find out more about which groups of people in the United States could and could not vote when the country was founded. How did African American men win the right to vote? How did women win the right to vote? How did Native Americans win the right to vote? How did 18-year-olds win the right to vote?

4 Group 3: Decide which side's arguments are most persuasive. Each judge should explain the reasons for his or her vote. Votes should be based on the persuasiveness of the arguments, not on personal opinions.

Chapter Review

CHAPTER 19

Chapter Review Timeline

1945
End of World War II

| 1900 | 1920 | 1940 | 1960 | 1980 | 2000 |

1946
Japan adopts Peace Constitution

1949
China becomes Communist

1966
Cultural Revolution

1989
Dissidents protest in Tiananmen Square

1997
Return of Hong Kong to China

Summarizing the Main Idea

1 Copy the chart below and write a sentence or two in each block to compare the three countries discussed in the chapter.

	Japan	China	Australia
Government			
Economy			
Culture			

Vocabulary

2 Using at least eight of the terms below, compare the history of Japan, China, and Australia after World War II.

work ethic (p. 517)
literacy rate (p. 519)
Great Leap Forward (p. 526)

communes (p. 527)
Cultural Revolution (p. 527)
stereotype (p. 534)

multicultural (p. 534)
aborigines (p. 534)
graziers (p. 536)

Reviewing the Facts

3 What were the effects of World War II on Japan?

4 How did Japan rebuild its economy?

5 What is the role of women in Japan?

6 What was China's Great Leap Forward?

7 What did Mao Zedong hope to accomplish by the Cultural Revolution? What happened instead?

8 List three steps Deng Xiaoping took to reform China after Mao's death.

9 What happened in Tiananmen Square on June 3, 1989?

10 How is Hong Kong different from the rest of China?

11 Who are Australia's aborigines?

Skill Review: Interpreting Cartograms

12 Using the maps on pages 520–521, list Japan, China, and Australia in order of physical size. Then list them in order of economic size. Pick three more countries in Asia and three in Europe, and compare.

Geography Skills

13 Study the map of Japan on page 516. Japan is made up of about 4,000 islands. What effect do you think this has on Japanese society?

14 Imagine that you are the Royal Planner of Prisons for Great Britain, sent to Australia in the late 1700s to survey the continent as a possible site for future prisons. What would you say in your report?

Critical Thinking

15 **Compare** What are some of the differences between your school experience and going to school in Japan? What are some similarities?

16 **Predict** What do you think will happen to Hong Kong over the next 100 years?

17 **Cause and Effect** What effect do you think Australia's immigration policy will have on the country in the future?

Writing: Citizenship and Economics

18 **Citizenship** The right to protest government actions is an important part of belonging to a free, democratic society. Write an editorial article expressing your opinion about the events in Tiananmen Square.

19 **Economics** You are in charge of the advertising campaign to attract passengers to the new magnetic trains in Japan. Write a television, radio, or newspaper ad promoting the new train and comparing it to bullet trains.

Activities

Geography/Science
Do research on one of the animals of Australia (wallaby, koala, wombat, etc.). Share your findings with the class.

Culture/Spelling
In the spirit of China's effort to simplify its language, make five rules to simplify the English language (for instance, no more silent letters like the "k" in "knife"). Share your rules with the class, and decide if they can actually be used.

Internet Option

Check the **Internet Social Studies Center** for ideas on how to extend your theme project beyond your classroom.

THEME PROJECT CHECK-IN

As you continue to work on your theme project, use the information in this chapter about some of the nations in East Asia and Australia. These questions will help you:

• What major events in this nation's history have caused challenges or opportunities?
• How has the country dealt with its challenges and opportunities?
• How does a nation's political system affect its challenges and opportunities?

East Asia and Australia: Patterns of Living **541**

South and Southwest Asia: Patterns of Living

Chapter Preview: *People, Places, and Events*

1900	1920	1940

Bombay, India

How does modern India blend tradition and diverse cultures? *Lesson 1, Page 544*

India's Textile Industry

How are industry and education changing in modern India? *Lesson 1, Page 547*

Oil Refinery

What effect has the discovery of oil had on Saudi Arabia? *Lesson 2, Page 552*

lack of unity continued to cause problems, however. At the time of partition, bloody riots between Hindus and Muslims erupted. As many as a million people lost their lives. Since then, violence has broken out repeatedly. Mohandas Gandhi (moh HAHN duhs GAHN dee), whom you read about in Chapter 13, taught peace and tolerance. Unfortunately, he was killed by an assassin during one outbreak of violence in 1948. An **assassin** is a murderer who kills a public figure, usually for political reasons. Several decades later, assassins killed Nehru's daughter, Prime Minister Indira Gandhi. Her son Rajiv, who became the next prime minister, was also killed a few years later.

Because India has undergone so many changes, Indians usually feel more loyal to their own region than to the country as a whole. India's constitution recognizes 18 different languages. This adds to the sense of separateness among people from different regions of the country. India is also the home of hundreds of different dialects. A dialect is a version of a language shared by people who live in the same region and distinct from that spoken in other regions. Many Indians speak two or more languages and understand many dialects because they need to communicate with people from other regions of their country. The most common languages are Hindi and English. Spoken by millions in the north, Hindi is the country's official language, while English, introduced by the British, is an "associate official language." As in many countries that once were colonies, the colonial language continues to be used in big business, international trade, diplomacy, and higher education.

Along with diverse regions and languages, India has citizens who practice many religions. The vast majority of people — about 80 percent — are Hindus. But Muslims make up a large minority. And there are other religions, too, including Christianity, Jainism (JEYE nihz uhm), and Sikhism (SEEK ihz uhm).

Biography

Mother Teresa

Mother Teresa, a Roman Catholic nun from Eastern Europe, was sent to India to teach school. She started many programs for people living in poverty. She was respected around the world for helping orphans, the sick, the poor, and the elderly. In 1979 she received the Nobel Peace Prize. "We can do no great things," she wrote, "only small things with great love."

The Ganges is India's chief river and is considered sacred by many Hindus.

Problems and Progress

Focus | *How is India dealing with its problems?*

With just over a billion people, India is the second most populous country in the world. Its population is growing so rapidly that it may soon surpass China as the world's most populous country. The size of India's land is fixed — and already overcrowded. Poverty is a major problem both in rural and urban areas. Many tiny farms can barely support the families that depend on them. Cities are crammed to bursting. In Mumbai (formerly Bombay), for instance, many people live in huts or on the street.

Progress in the Villages and Cities

About three-fourths of India's people live in rural areas. There they raise crops such as wheat, millet, lentils, and rice — usually just enough to feed their families.

The Patels and their children live in a small village in a region called Rayalseema (ry uhl SEE mah) in the southern part of India. Their two-room house is made of mud thatched with grass. At sunrise, the mother and two older daughters prepare breakfast — flat millet cakes — over a small wood-burning stove. The father and his three older sons, hoes in hand, walk to their two-acre farm to work.

Household chores require many hours: collecting wood in a nearby forest, bringing water from the neighborhood well, washing clothes, caring for the three younger children. After a supper of rice and vegetables, the family watches a television set shared by the whole village for an hour before going to bed.

It is nearly impossible to grow large quantities of crops with small farms, uncertain weather, and all labor performed by hand. For a long

Indian women and men are active participants in the growing economy. **Technology:** *How do you think the new computer software industry is changing India's economy?*

Major industrial goods are exported around the world from many parts of India. **Map Skill:** *Which locations do you think would be best for exporting textiles, iron, and steel?*

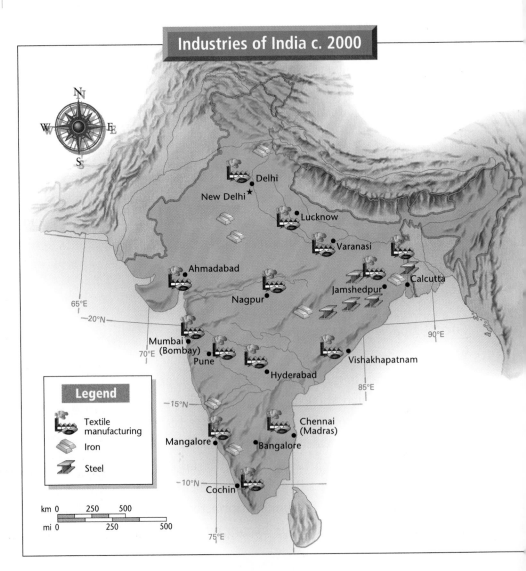

Industries of India c. 2000

Delhi
New Delhi ★
Lucknow
Varanasi
Ahmadabad
Calcutta
Jamshedpur
Nagpur
65°E
—20°N
90°E
Mumbai (Bombay)
70°E
Pune
Hyderabad
Vishakhapatnam
85°E
—15°N
Chennai (Madras)
Mangalore
Bangalore
—10°N
Cochin

Legend

Textile manufacturing
Iron
Steel

km 0   250   500
mi 0   250   500
75°E

time, India had to import food to prevent famine.

Since the 1980s, however, India has been able to feed itself. How was this accomplished? Combining the use of special seeds, fertilizer, irrigation, and machinery, some Indian farmers successfully transformed their farming methods. In one region of northwest India, for example, farmers doubled production in less than ten years. This dramatic change in agriculture is known as the Green Revolution. Even with this improvement, however, India's farms can barely keep up with the country's expanding population.

Modernization has not been limited to village life, but applies to India's cities as well. Advances in industry and education have occurred quickly. India has become one of the top 20 industrialized countries in the world.

Progress in India's educational system has been just as dramatic. More than twice as many Indians can read and write now as in 1947. This means that about half of the population is literate.

These and other signs of progress make India a model for other nations in the region. The challenges of its large and diverse population are being met as the country works toward continued economic growth.

Education in India has changed in many ways since 1947. Some students in Indian cities now have the opportunity to learn to use computers.

Lesson Review: Geography

1 **Key Vocabulary:** Describe political events in India, using **partition, assassin.**

2 **Focus:** What makes India's population so varied?

3 **Focus:** How is India dealing with its problems?

4 **Critical Thinking: Conclude** Using the Patel family as an example, identify some of the obstacles villagers face in improving their living conditions.

5 **Theme: Challenges and Opportunities** What are some of the reasons Indians might feel that unity is a challenging goal to attain?

6 **Citizenship/Writing Activity:** Research the accomplishments of Mother Teresa in India. Write her a letter as if you were one of the judges awarding the Nobel Peace Prize. Explain why her efforts are worthy of such a distinguished award.

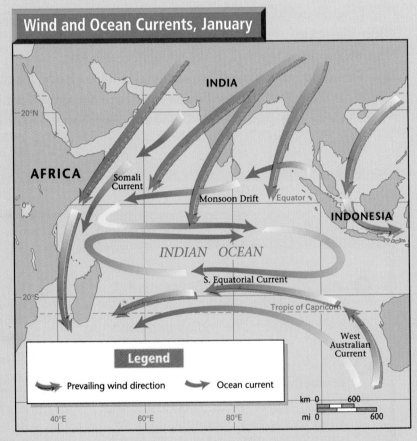

Skills Workshop

Reading Wind and Ocean Current Maps

Blowing Hot and Cold

Long ago, Arab traders used the movement of the wind and ocean, or **currents**, to help them sail. They planned trips to make use of the powerful onward motion of these currents. Sailing in the same direction as a current is much easier than sailing against it. You'll find out more about prevailing winds — which blow mostly in a certain direction — and the direction of ocean currents by studying wind and ocean current maps.

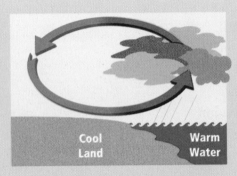

Cool Land

Warm Water

In Southwest Asia, the prevailing winds follow a monsoon pattern. From October to April, the monsoon wind blows from the cool land toward the warm ocean. Because the wind blows from the land, the land receives little or no rain in winter. Fields become dry and parched, as in the photo below. The monsoon wind causes the ocean currents to flow away from India during the winter season.

Wind and Ocean Currents, January

20°N

INDIA

AFRICA

Somali Current

Monsoon Drift   Equator

0°

INDONESIA

INDIAN OCEAN

S. Equatorial Current

20°S

Tropic of Capricorn

West Australian Current

Legend

Prevailing wind direction

Ocean current

km 0   600

mi 0   600

40°E   60°E   80°E

① Here's How

The maps on these pages show seasonal changes in wind and ocean currents in the Indian Ocean.

- Study the map legends. What do the arrows stand for? What color stands for wind direction? What color stands for ocean currents?

- Find the wind and ocean currents on both maps.

- Compare the wind arrows on both maps. How do the winds change in different seasons?

- Compare the ocean current arrows on both maps. Do they point toward or away from India?

- Draw conclusions about how wind and ocean currents would affect sailing in the Indian Ocean. How would they affect farming in India?

② Think It Through

Why does the monsoon wind blow from cool areas to hot areas? Can you picture how this happens? Here is a hint: Hot air rises.

③ Use It

Decide whether to do each activity below in January or July. Explain each answer.

1. sail from East Africa to India

2. sail from northern to southern India

3. plant rice in India

4. travel in India when there is good weather

5. sail from Africa to Indonesia

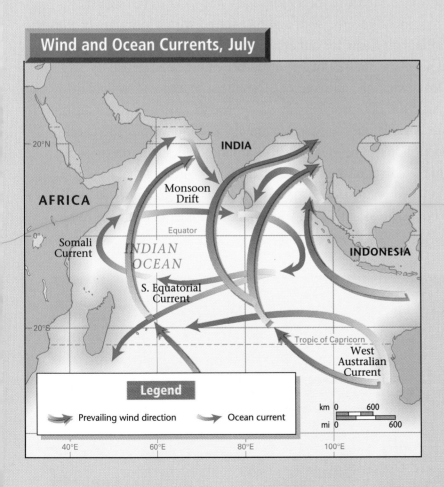

Wind and Ocean Currents, July

INDIA

AFRICA

Monsoon Drift

Equator

Somali Current

INDIAN OCEAN

S. Equatorial Current

INDONESIA

20°S

Tropic of Capricorn

West Australian Current

Legend

Prevailing wind direction   Ocean current

km 0   600
mi 0   600

40°E   60°E   80°E   100°E

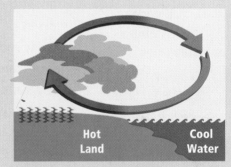

Hot Land   Cool Water

From May to September, the land heats up and the wind direction shifts. The monsoon wind now blows from the cool ocean toward the hot land. It brings with it life-giving rain, which showers down on everything below it. In summer, the monsoon wind causes the ocean currents to flow toward India.

South and Southwest Asia: Patterns of Living   **549**

Saudi Arabia: Wealth Amid Tradition

Key Vocabulary

- bedouin
- geologist
- petrodollars
- desalinization

Key Events

1932 Kingdom of Saudi Arabia established

1938 Oil discovered in Saudi Arabia

Main Idea Saudi Arabia uses its oil wealth to modernize while maintaining strong religious and cultural traditions.

Omar Miller is ready to make his once-in-a-lifetime pilgrimage to Mecca to fulfill one of his religious duties as a Muslim. *(See Chapter 10.)* It's a long trip to Saudi Arabia from his home in Indianapolis, Indiana, but far easier than it was for his grandparents. He remembers their stories about their trip to Mecca in the 1930s. They had trekked through the desert on foot in 120-degree heat, and had stayed with a local family who made room in their home for hundreds of pilgrims each year.

When his plane lands, Omar is amazed by how different Saudi Arabia is from what he had pictured. The huge modern air terminal in Jeddah, which 100,000 people a day pass through, is shaped like a gigantic open-air tent. He rides to Mecca in an air-conditioned bus and checks into a modern hotel. When Omar walks around the Ka'bah, the ancient structure in the center of the city, he enters a new building that holds about 730,000 worshippers at a time, with escalators that move 15,000 people an hour. Air conditioning, sound, and sprinkler systems are run by computers.

Tents offer refreshments and shelter from the heat to the many pilgrims who come to Saudi Arabia. This center for worship has been modernized to welcome more than one million Muslims each year.

The Saudis have built one of the most modern cities on earth to meet their ancient religious obligation to provide food and water for Muslim pilgrims. Why do the Saudis go to such expense? How can they afford such hospitality? The answers lie in the ancient traditions and modern wealth that have shaped the nation of Saudi Arabia.

The Kingdom That Runs on Oil

Focus *Why is oil important in Saudi Arabia?*

Saudi Arabia is mostly dry, but has a varied landscape. Desert plants and animals thrive on scarce water in some places, and oases bloom in others. In some parts of the country, years go by without rain. The largest continuous sand desert in the world is in the southeast of Saudi Arabia. Its Arabic name, *Rub'al-Khali* (roob ahl KHAH lee), means "empty quarter" because few people could live there. Since the discovery of oil, however, Saudi Arabia has become one of the world's richest nations. With this wealth, the Saudis have developed modern agriculture, industries, and cities. They also have built elaborate facilities to receive Muslim pilgrims who pour into Mecca from many parts of the world.

Muslim pilgrims from around the world still gather at Mecca. As part of their pilgrimage, they walk around the large black structure called the *Ka'bah*.

An Arab worker oversees oil production at a refinery in Saudi Arabia. Saudi Arabia exports more oil than any other nation. **Economics:** *How has the discovery of oil changed the Saudis' economy?*

The Birth of Saudi Arabia

Saudi Arabia's history is long and complex. As a modern nation, it has been shaped both by its strong religious and cultural traditions and by its wealth. One of the stereotypes Westerners often have about modern life in Saudi Arabia is that most Arabs are bedouin (BEHD uh win). The word **bedouin** comes from the Arabic for "the people who appear." It refers to ancient tribes of nomads who sometimes had to cross through the desert sand and wind with their camels and would seem to appear suddenly. Now, as most nomads have settled down, few people still live in the traditional bedouin manner.

Beginning in the 1800s, England and France attempted to extend their control over the Arabian Peninsula and its resources. The Saudis managed to keep the country from becoming a colony. Their most powerful leader was Abdul Aziz Ibn Saud (AHB dool ah ZEZ IHB uhn sah OOD). He captured the Muslim holy cities of Mecca and Medina after World War I. Defeating the leaders of other families, he united the local Arab tribes. In 1932, he established the Kingdom of Saudi Arabia, with himself as its first king.

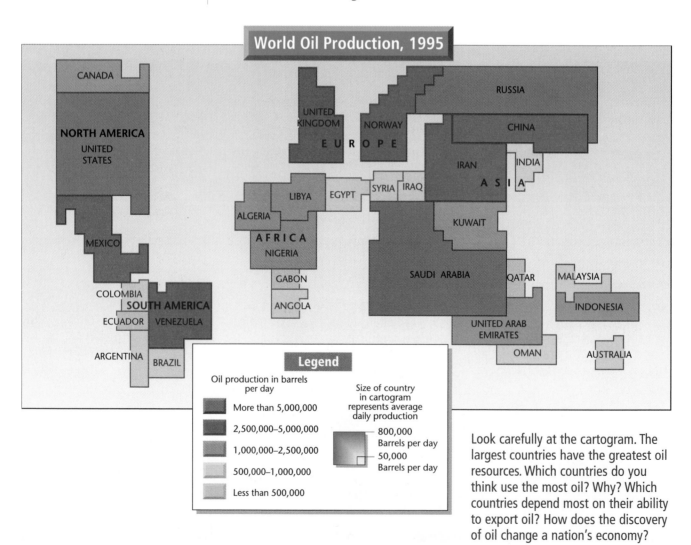

World Oil Production, 1995

Legend

Oil production in barrels per day

More than 5,000,000

2,500,000–5,000,000

1,000,000–2,500,000

500,000–1,000,000

Less than 500,000

Size of country in cartogram represents average daily production

800,000 Barrels per day
50,000 Barrels per day

Look carefully at the cartogram. The largest countries have the greatest oil resources. Which countries do you think use the most oil? Why? Which countries depend most on their ability to export oil? How does the discovery of oil change a nation's economy?

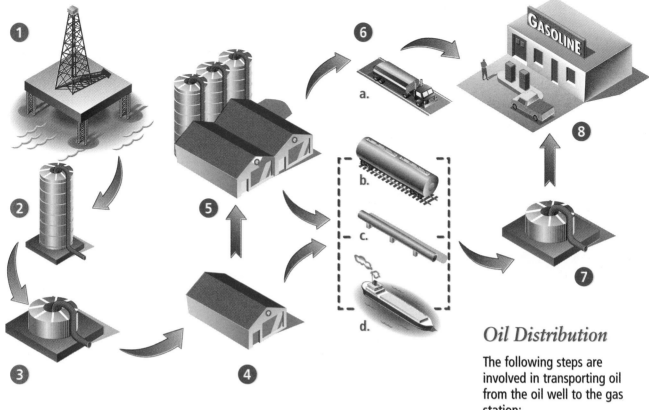

The nation founded by Ibn Saud was unified in having one people, the Arabs; one language, Arabic; and one religion, Islam. Unity is also maintained by the very powerful Saudi king: his country has no constitution, no legislature, and no political parties.

Oil Resources

Saudi Arabia was changed forever in 1938. That year, an American geologist found oil there in enormous quantities. A **geologist** is a scientist who studies the structure of the earth. The king gave permission to American oil companies to pump the oil. Within 20 years, Saudi oil production rose to a million barrels a day. The country proved to have the largest oil reserves on earth — about 25 percent of the world's supply. Saudi Arabia exports more oil than any other nation. Oil exports have brought in billions of **petrodollars** — foreign currency earned by selling oil.

Saudi Arabia's wealth is shared by a very small population. Population density is only about 21 persons per square mile. In order to have enough workers to process its oil, Saudi Arabia must hire thousands of people from other countries. Of the country's total population of about 17 million, over one third are foreign residents. Many are Muslims from the Middle East and South Asia, but many Americans work there, too. In fact, Saudi Arabia has one of the largest American populations outside of the United States, numbering about 50,000.

Oil Distribution

The following steps are involved in transporting oil from the oil well to the gas station:

1 Oil well

2 Oil/gas separator

3 Storage tank

4 Pump station

5 Petroleum refinery

6 Transportation vehicles:

   a. Truck

   b. Railroad

   c. Pipeline

   d. Tanker

7 Storage tank

8 Gas station

Spending the Wealth

How do the Saudis use their oil income?

Until oil was discovered there, Saudi Arabia was mostly undeveloped. The Saudis soon embarked on a major program of modernization. They constructed almost 100,000 miles of highway and more than two dozen airports. They built hundreds of schools, including seven universities. For Saudi citizens, who pay no taxes, both education and health care are free.

Because they are proud of being the homeland of Islam, the Saudis have taken special care to improve conditions for pilgrims. Each year, as many as two million Muslims from outside the country visit Mecca. They travel on special jets, and are welcomed by guides and interpreters.

The Saudis are working hard to expand their economy to become less dependent on income from oil. They must prepare for the day when the vast resources of oil finally run out. Growing industries include chemicals, gold mining, construction materials, and food processing. New irrigation systems benefit Saudi farmers. The government also assists farmers through its program of **desalinization** — removing the salt from seawater. Saudi Arabia is the world's largest producer of desalinized water.

Like many nations in this region of the world, the discovery of oil has transformed not only Saudi Arabia's economy, but the lives of the people living there. Yet Saudi Arabia has managed to modernize its economy while maintaining both religious and cultural traditions.

World Muslim Population

Percentage of World Muslim Population by Location

- 0.5%
- 17%
- 15%
- 42%
- 10%
- 14%
- 1.5%

- United States
- Africa
- Arab Nations
- Other Nations
- Saudi Arabia
- Southeast Asia
- Central Asia

Muslims from all over the world go to Saudi Arabia for religious pilgrimage. **Chart Skill:** *In what region do most Muslims live? What percentage lives there?*

Lesson Review

1900	1950

1932
Kingdom of Saudi Arabia established

1938
Oil discovered in Saudi Arabia

1. **Key Vocabulary:** Define these key terms: bedouin, geologist, petrodollars, and desalinization.

2. **Focus:** Why is oil important in Saudi Arabia?

3. **Focus:** How do the Saudis use their oil income?

4. **Critical Thinking: Problem Solving** What should the Saudi government do to prepare for the day when the oil supply runs out?

5. **Theme: Challenges and Opportunities** Compare and contrast Saudi Arabia's and India's challenges in preserving traditions in an increasingly modernized nation.

6. **Geography/Research:** Locate oil reserves in the United States on a map. Make a chart comparing amounts of oil in Saudi Arabia and the three American states with the largest oil reserves.

Israel: Changing the Environment

Main Idea Located in an arid region, Israel has developed new technologies to deal with a lack of water.

The woman stood rooted to the ground in shock. She watched the young soldier climb down from his jeep and walk up to the ticket booth in front of the movie theater. She was a stranger in Israel, having arrived just a few days earlier from her native Poland. The year was 1949, and four years had passed since the end of World War II. The woman, Rivka Waxman, was shopping in downtown Haifa (HEYE fuh) when she saw the soldier and her heart began to pound. She managed to call out, "Chaim?" The young man turned. The two stared at each other for several seconds before they rushed together for an embrace. Mother and son had not seen each other for eight years. Each was sure that the other had been killed.

The Waxmans were just two of the thousands of Jews who took refuge in Israel after the horrors of the Holocaust. What they found there was mostly arid land and Arab residents who were not happy with the newcomers' arrival. Israelis have worked hard to build their country into a modern state. In doing so, they have faced some difficult environmental as well as security problems. Their solutions to environmental challenges are one of the 20th century's great success stories. The Israelis are credited with having "made the desert bloom."

Key Vocabulary

sovereignty
kibbutz
drip irrigation
aquifer

Key Events

1948 State of
Israel established

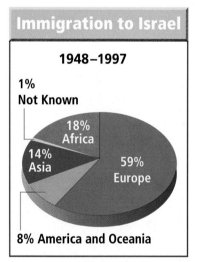

Immigration to Israel

1948–1997

1% **Not Known**

18% Africa

14% Asia

59% Europe

8% America and Oceania

Chart Skill: *What percentage of immigration to Israel has come from Asia and Africa?*

Many Jewish immigrants from Europe settled in Israel after World War II.

555

Building a New Nation

Focus *How has Israel developed since its founding?*

Israel is one of the world's smallest countries. Most of its people live in a narrow strip of land along the coast of the Mediterranean Sea. Jerusalem, Tel Aviv, and Haifa are the major cities.

The majority of Israelis are Jewish. Beginning in the 1890s, people in a movement called Zionism (ZEYE uh nihz uhm) urged Jews to relocate in the homeland of their ancestors, called Canaan several thousand years ago. You can read about early Jewish nationhood in Chapters 3 and 9.

The trickle of immigrants that started in the 1890s grew to a flood during and after World War II. By 1948, about 600,000 Jews had settled in the region then called Palestine. That year, the United Nations recognized the modern state of Israel, which now has a population of over five million.

Sources of Tension

Israel is surrounded by Muslim Arab neighbors. Until recently, many of them resented the idea of a Jewish state in their midst. Over a period of 30 years, there were many armed conflicts and three major wars. A major reason for these conflicts was that Muslim Palestinians lived on the land that the Jewish settlers came to. With the creation of the Jewish state, many of them fled their homes. Most ended up in refugee camps in Arab nations that surround Israel. In a 1967 war with its neighbors, Israel captured the lands where some of these Palestinians lived. Most Palestinians in these lands and in Israel have resented Israeli rule, and conflicts have erupted.

One of the most hopeful developments of the recent past was a peace treaty between Israel and Egypt, signed in 1979. In 1994, a peace treaty was signed with Jordan. The Israelis and the Palestinians began working out the details of an agreement to give **sovereignty** (SAW ver en tee), or self-rule, to the Palestinians. Peace talks stalled in the fall of 2000 and tensions rose again. Palestinians and Israelis clashed over the future of a Palestinian state, with people from both sides dying in the struggle.

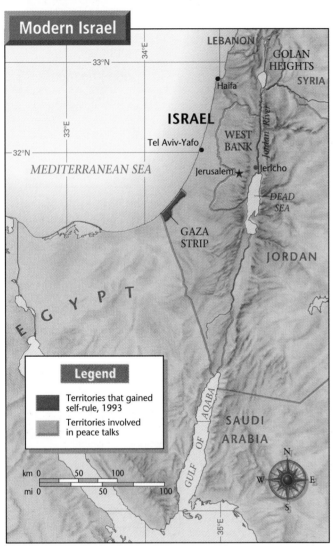

Modern Israel

LEBANON

GOLAN HEIGHTS

SYRIA

33°N

34°E

Haifa

ISRAEL

33°E

Tel Aviv-Yafo

WEST BANK

Jordan River

32°N

MEDITERRANEAN SEA

Jerusalem ★ Jericho

DEAD SEA

GAZA STRIP

JORDAN

E G Y P T

Legend

■ Territories that gained self-rule, 1993

■ Territories involved in peace talks

GULF OF AQABA

SAUDI ARABIA

N W E S

35°E

km 0   50   100
mi 0   50   100

Map Skill: *Compare this map with the one of ancient Canaan on page 80.*

Transforming the Land

Focus *How have Israelis used their limited natural resources to make the land productive?*

Israel has a hot climate and few natural resources. Over half of the land — the Negev (NEHG ehv) — is a desert, and rainfall is sparse elsewhere, too. But hard work and modern technology have made much of the country productive.

Thriving Agriculture

In the early 1900s, when the area was poor and underpopulated, most Jewish settlers worked as farmers. They developed cooperative settlements to make their tasks easier. In the best-known type of collective farm, the **kibbutz** (kih BUTS), everyone shared the labor and received needed goods and services in return. Over the years, farmers increased their acreage and their yields. Today Israel grows almost everything it needs to feed its people. It also exports agricultural products, especially citrus fruits. Israel provides Europe with fruits and vegetables in the winter.

The biggest problem for Israeli farmers is getting enough water. They have become experts in diverting and storing water, in the use of hothouses, and in irrigation. In a special form, **drip irrigation**, plastic tubes carry water (and fertilizer, if necessary) directly to each plant. Israelis joke that this is "feeding the plant with a teaspoon." Their drip irrigation systems are often controlled by computers that rely on automatic sensors to tell when the ground is getting too dry.

In Israel, both men and women serve in the military.

Tomatoes are grown under small "tents," keeping them moist and protected in the desert.

Ecological Problems and Solutions

Over the past 50 years, Israel has invested about $30 billion in water-management systems. It is already one of the most water-efficient countries in the world, taking dirty drinking water and waste water and recycling it back for use in farms and industry.

In the 1950s, however, one of the most important land and water management projects was the draining of Lake Hula, in northern Israel near the Sea of Galilee. The entire lake area was cleared of swamps and mosquitoes. When the project was finished, farmers had created about 15,000 acres of the richest farmland in Israel. Unfortunately, this project left behind an ecological problem that could only be solved by refilling the lake.

In 1993, bulldozers returned to Lake Hula, this time to scoop it out, not fill it in. The reflooding is creating a wetland wildlife park that will include a lake, islands, and marshes that support native animals. The birds have already returned.

One of the main sources of fresh water used for irrigation is ground water. Ground water is water stored deep in the soil, between rocks,

· Tell Me More ·

Life on a Kibbutz

A kibbutz may be the size of a small village, but in many ways it is more like a large family. Everything on the kibbutz is owned by everyone. Working without pay, each person is provided with free housing, clothing, and food.

At some kibbutzim (the plural of kibbutz), the children live at a special "children's house," and spend only weekends with their parents. The children work, too, in their gardens or taking care of the farm animals.

Young people from all over the world go to Israel to work on kibbutzim. Since 1989, African American teens have joined in a special program. Many of the students are from poor, inner-city neighborhoods. They are expected to work just like the other members of the kibbutz, spending a six-hour shift each day in the fields or a factory. One American teen said that no one had ever expected her to work so hard before. For the first time in her life, she realized how much she was able to accomplish.

sand, roots, and other objects. Water moves down into the earth until it reaches a layer of rock or soil that it is unable to penetrate. The water accumulates on top of this layer, forming an aquifer. An **aquifer** is a saturated area of rock, like a big sponge, that gradually fills up with water.

In recent years, Israel has pumped some rivers and aquifers to the point where almost all the water is used up. While shortage of water is one of Israel's most urgent environmental problems, researchers are trying to solve another problem. Pesticides have contaminated some of Israel's water sources, making water unsafe for drinking. Salt water also sometimes seeps into the fresh water supply. With the help of new technologies, Israeli scientists and researchers are working to solve this and other environmental problems.

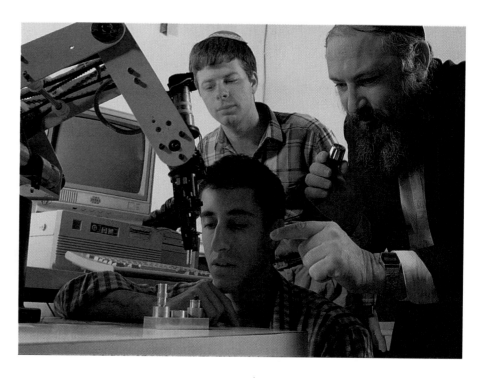
Israeli researchers continue to develop new technologies.

Lesson Review

1940   1950

1948
State of Israel established

1. **Vocabulary:** Use the following in a paragraph about Israel: **sovereignty, kibbutz,** and **drip irrigation.**

2. **Focus:** How has Israel developed since its founding?

3. **Focus:** How have Israelis used their limited natural resources to make the land productive?

4. **Critical Thinking: Decision Making** List factors that create tension in Israeli society. Decide which is the most important to resolve and explain why.

5. **Theme: Challenges and Opportunities** What challenges do Israel and Saudi Arabia share? How are their opportunities different?

6. **Citizenship/Writing Activity:** Make a list of the pros and cons of living on a kibbutz. Write a paragraph explaining why you would or wouldn't like to work on one.

CHAPTER

Chapter Review

1932
Kingdom of Saudi Arabia established

| 1900 | 1920 | 1940 | 2000 |

1924
**Sauds
take Mecca**

1938
**Oil discovered
in Saudi Arabia**

Summarizing the Main Idea

1 Copy the chart below and write a sentence or two in each block to compare the three countries discussed in the chapter.

	India	Saudi Arabia	Israel
Culture			
Religion			
Economy			

Vocabulary

2 Use at least eight of the terms below to write a brief historical or feature article about Asia.

partition (p. 544)
assassin (p. 545)
bedouin (p. 552)
geologist (p. 553)

petrodollars (p. 553)
desalinization (p. 554)
sovereignty (p. 556)

kibbutz (p. 557)
drip irrigation (p. 557)
aquifer (p. 559)

Reviewing the Facts

3 Why didn't India achieve peace after it gained independence from Britain?

4 What are some of the problems India is facing because of overpopulation? How are the Indians solving them?

5 Briefly describe the origin of Saudi Arabia.

6 What difference has oil made to the people of Saudi Arabia?

7 How are the Saudis preparing themselves for when their oil runs out?

8 Why have thousands of Jews immigrated to Israel?

9 Why is Israel in conflict with its Arab neighbors?

10 How have the Israelis made the deserts bloom?

Skill Review: Reading Wind and Ocean Current Maps

11 Choose two places on the maps on pages 548-549. Plan the best trade route between these two places based on the information on wind and ocean currents. Decide which way you would sail in January, and which way you would sail in July.

Geography Skills

12 Look at the map of India on page 544. Why do you think that Pakistan, where most of the Muslims live, is located where it is? (For a hint, look at the map on page 503, The Religions of Asia).

13 Write a brochure advertising a trip to India, Saudi Arabia, or Israel. Focusing on the land, write a short description of what people can expect to see there.

Critical Thinking

14 **Problem Solving** Israel has not focused on solving its water shortage problems by desalinization, like its neighbor Saudi Arabia. Why do you think they haven't used this method?

15 **Compare** Compare the kibbutzim with the agricultural communes in China described in the previous chapter. How are they similar? How are they different?

Writing: Citizenship and Culture

16 **Citizenship** India, Saudi Arabia, and Israel have all made tremendous strides in improving the quality of their citizens' lives. What do you think the United States, or your local city or town, could do to improve the quality of its citizens' lives? Write a letter to the editor of your local newspaper describing what should be done.

17 **Culture** If you were chosen to spend a summer on a kibbutz, you might keep a journal of your experiences. Write three journal entries — one from the day you first arrive, one from the middle of your stay, and one from the day you leave.

Activities

Art/Research
Do research to find out more about a traditional art form in India, Saudi Arabia, or Israel. Share your findings with the class in an oral presentation with pictures.

Geography/Science
Interview an expert (either a local farmer or an expert at a local college or university) or do research about irrigation and agriculture. Give a report to your class on the latest techniques.

Internet Option

Check the **Internet Social Studies Center** for ideas on how to extend your theme project beyond your classroom.

THEME PROJECT CHECK-IN

To complete your theme project, use the information in this chapter about some of South and Southwest Asia's nations. Consider these questions:
• What new technologies has the country developed to meet its challenges?
• What natural resources does the country have? How have these helped the country?
• What environmental challenges has the country faced? How has it met them?

Central and South America in the Modern Age

"Peace is a never-ending process . . . It cannot ignore our differences or overlook our common interests. It requires us to work and live together."

Oscar Arias Sánchez

· THEME ·

Union and Individuality

❝ *Many groups of people moved to Central and South America, so the culture there is really a mix of many different cultures.* ❞

Danielle Derrick, Sixth Grade
Salem, OR

Central and South America have Native American roots going back thousands of years. The arrival of European explorers and settlers in the 1500s set off a process of cultural exchange and blending. When Europeans began to bring enslaved Africans to the Americas, yet another culture was added to this process. Over the centuries, the nations of Central and South America have built strong new identities, drawing on both the original cultures of native peoples and those of peoples who came or were brought there later.

Theme Project

Guide to Union and Individuality

Create a guide for a Central or South American country to show how it has experienced union and individuality.

- Construct a timeline that includes the major events in the country's history in the 20th century.
- Diagram the country's political system.
- Write about how the country's recent history reflects the theme of union and individuality.
- Draw a map of the country that includes its major cities and geographic features.

RESEARCH: Collect facts on the major sites visited by tourists who come to this country.

◄ Cerro Santa Lucía, Santiago, Chile.

UNIT 8

WHEN & WHERE
ATLAS

The heritage of Central and South America includes the cultures of native peoples, Europeans, and Africans. You can see this blend in the food, clothing, language, and religion of people in Central and South America today. Foreigners have shaped the history of many parts of this region. The 20th century has been a turbulent one for many of the nations of this area. They are a growing economic and political force today.

In this unit you will learn more about the geography of Central and South America. You will also read about events that shaped this area in the 20th century. Finally, you will find profiles of four countries (shown in red) to learn more about the economy, culture, and politics of this part of the world.

Unit 8 Chapters

Chapter 21   Central and South America: An Overview

Chapter 22   Central and South America: Patterns of Living

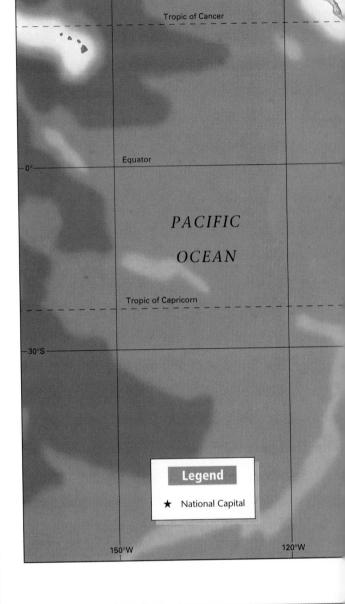

Tropic of Cancer

Equator

Tropic of Capricorn

PACIFIC

OCEAN

30°N · 150°W · 120°W

0°

30°S

150°W · 120°W

Legend

★   National Capital

Unit Timeline

1500	1600	1700

Amazon River

This river is enormous. How big and how wide is it? *Chapter 21, Lesson 1*

Argentinian Protesters 1980s

These people demonstrated for democracy in their country. *Chapter 22, Lesson 1*

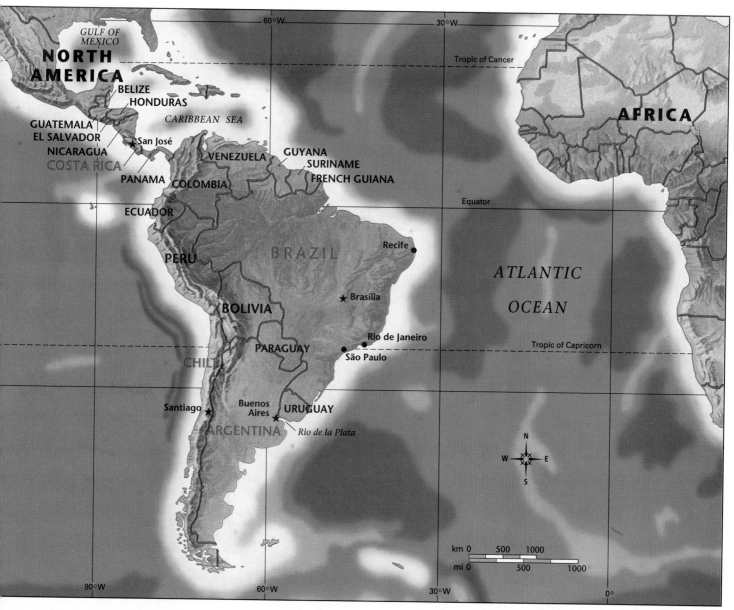

GULF OF
MEXICO

NORTH
AMERICA

BELIZE
HONDURAS

CARIBBEAN SEA

GUATEMALA
EL SALVADOR
NICARAGUA   San José
COSTA RICA

PANAMA

VENEZUELA   GUYANA
                   SURINAME
COLOMBIA   FRENCH GUIANA

ECUADOR

PERU   BRAZIL   Recife

BOLIVIA   Brasília

PARAGUAY

CHILE   Rio de Janeiro
                   São Paulo

Santiago   Buenos   URUGUAY
           Aires
ARGENTINA   Rio de la Plata

AFRICA

Tropic of Cancer

Equator

ATLANTIC
OCEAN

Tropic of Capricorn

N
W   E
S

km 0   500   1000
mi 0   500   1000

90°W   60°W   30°W

60°W   30°W   0°

1800   1900   2000

A Chilean Mine

What natural resource can be found here? *Chapter 22, Lesson 2*

Carnival in Brazil

Three very different cultures are represented in this parade. *Chapter 22, Lesson 3*

Costa Rican Rain Forests

These forests contain thousands of types of life forms. *Chapter 22, Lesson 4*

Central and South America: An Overview

Chapter Preview: *People, Places, and Events*

1500	1600	1700

Simón Bolívar   **1813**

This young Venezuelan led the war for independence from Spain. *Lesson 2, Page 574*

The Andes

These majestic mountains form the backbone of South America. *Lesson 1, Page 568*

The Amazon River

Find out why the Amazon was called "the river sea." *Lesson 1, Page 569*

The Geography of Central and South America

Main Idea Central and South America are lands of variety and extremes that hold a wealth of resources.

When European sailors caught their first glimpse of the coast of South America, they were astounded by what they saw. Amerigo Vespucci, an explorer, wrote home: "The land in those parts is very fertile and pleasing, abounding in numerous hills and mountains, boundless valleys and mighty rivers, watered by refreshing springs, and . . . impenetrable forests full of every sort of wild animal."

These words described the continent well. As Europeans moved inland they learned what native peoples had known for centuries: Central and South America offer an incredible variety of animal and plant life, of climate and landforms.

Key Vocabulary

- tributary
- rain forest
- gaucho
- pampas

Key Places

- Amazon River
- Paraná-Paraguay River system

◀ Hanging high above a Costa Rican oak and bamboo forest, an ecologist measures tree growth.

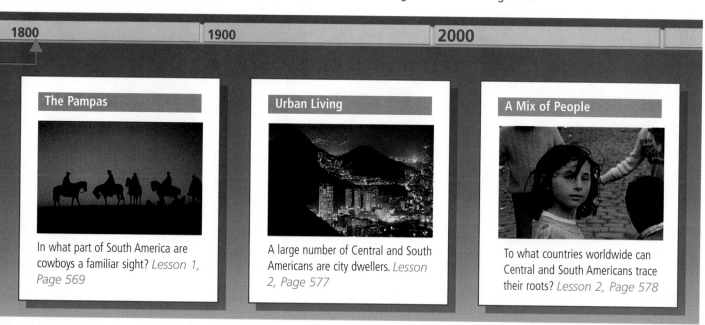

1800	1900	2000

The Pampas

In what part of South America are cowboys a familiar sight? *Lesson 1, Page 569*

Urban Living

A large number of Central and South Americans are city dwellers. *Lesson 2, Page 577*

A Mix of People

To what countries worldwide can Central and South Americans trace their roots? *Lesson 2, Page 578*

The Land and Its Wealth

Focus *What are the main physical features and resources of Central and South America?*

To talk about the geography of Central and South America, you need words like *longest, largest,* and *driest*. These regions contain the world's longest mountain range, largest rain forest, and one of the driest deserts. They are lands of variety and extremes, as the map below shows.

A chain of majestic mountains called the Andes (AN deez) forms the backbone of South America, running over 5,000 miles along its western edge. The Andes are part of the Ring of Fire, a great circle of volcanoes and earthquake zones around the Pacific Ocean. The same forces that shake California also cause earthquakes in Central and South America.

South America is so rich in mineral treasures that the streets of one early settlement — Potosí (poh toh SEE) — were paved with silver. Located in what is now Bolivia, Potosí's mines yielded huge amounts of

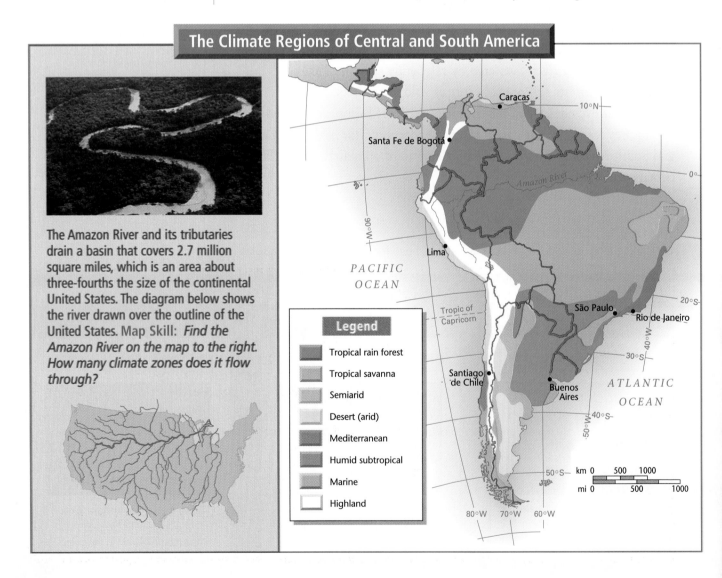

The Climate Regions of Central and South America

The Amazon River and its tributaries drain a basin that covers 2.7 million square miles, which is an area about three-fourths the size of the continental United States. The diagram below shows the river drawn over the outline of the United States. Map Skill: *Find the Amazon River on the map to the right. How many climate zones does it flow through?*

Legend
- Tropical rain forest
- Tropical savanna
- Semiarid
- Desert (arid)
- Mediterranean
- Humid subtropical
- Marine
- Highland

Caracas
Santa Fe de Bogotá
Amazon River
Lima
PACIFIC OCEAN
Tropic of Capricorn
São Paulo
Rio de Janeiro
Santiago de Chile
Buenos Aires
ATLANTIC OCEAN

10°N
0°
20°S
30°S
40°S
50°S

80°W   70°W   60°W

km 0   500   1000
mi 0   500   1000

silver. Today, silver, copper, and tin are mined in Chile and Bolivia.

Flowing across northeastern South America is a river so enormous that European explorers called it "the river sea." The Amazon River and its **tributaries**, streams that flow into a major river, carry more water than any other system in the world. This basin is three-fourths the size of the United States. Compare their sizes on the chart on the opposite page.

If you paddled a canoe up the Amazon, you'd hear monkeys shrieking, millions of insects chirping, and rain splattering on leaves. A dense, tropical region — the Amazon **rain forest** — lines the river banks. The heat and humidity typical of regions near the equator, as well as at least 120 inches of rain per year, produced this tropical forest. Central America has its own smaller forests. Much of the earth's oxygen is produced by rain forest plants and trees. Forest resources include ingredients for medicines, nuts, cocoa, rubber, rare woods, and gold.

Farther south, the Paraná-Paraguay River system forms an important means of communication and transportation for inland areas of Argentina, Paraguay, Bolivia, and Brazil. Traveling by boat along these waterways, you would be surrounded by rolling plains. If you went ashore, you might meet a Spanish-speaking cowboy, called a **gaucho**, tending a herd of cattle. Gauchos have long been important people on the **pampas**, or plains, of Argentina. The rich soil of this region produces wheat, corn, soybeans, and beef products that are in demand worldwide.

Most of Central America is densely populated. But in South America, 9 out of 10 people live in coastal regions. Mountains, rain forests, and deserts have made inland settlement difficult. In some regions, the rugged geography has separated people from one another. In others, it has brought them together through the sharing of resources and fertile land.

Like South America itself, the territory of Argentina contains a wide variety of terrain, from the rugged peaks of the Andes *(top)* to the rolling pampas *(bottom)*. Geography: *How might the life of a gaucho be different from the life of someone living in the mountains?*

Lesson Review: Geography

1 Key Vocabulary: Describe Central and South America using the following terms: **tributary, rain forest, gaucho, pampas.**

2 Focus: What are the main physical features and resources of Central and South America?

3 Critical Thinking: Interpret Which regions of South America do you think had the fewest people living in them for the longest periods of history? Why?

4 Theme: Union and Individuality Which physical features of Central and South America made communication difficult between peoples and nations? Which made it easy?

5 Geography/Art Activity: Make a map by tracing the outline of Central and South America on a piece of paper. Locate and label the countries and their capitals. Pick a country and mark the location of some of the natural resources that can be found there.

Central and South America: An Overview   **569**

THINK LIKE A
GEOGRAPHER

Environment and Society

Why Was Building the Panama Canal Difficult?

The Spanish explorer Vasco Nuñez de Balboa crossed the narrow Isthmus of Panama in 1513. He saw a huge ocean that Europeans had not known was there — the Pacific Ocean. At that time, the only way to sail from the Atlantic Ocean to the Pacific was to go around the tip of South America.

Many people wanted a canal across Panama to connect the two oceans. But the geography of Panama presented serious obstacles. Rugged hills and huge swamps filled with disease-carrying mosquitoes would make construction difficult.

In the early 1900s, the United States was eager to try. Some doubted whether the geographical problems could be overcome. When the canal opened in 1914, many people viewed it as nothing short of an engineering miracle.

1 Gatun Lake

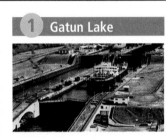

The Gatun Locks
Parts of the Panama Canal are higher than sea level. Locks raise and lower water levels for ships moving through. (See chart on page 381.) What is the highest level of the canal?

Building the Panama Canal took about ten years and required more than 43,000 workers. Roughly 5,600 workers died from disease or accidents. These workers are standing by giant concrete mixers near the Miraflores Locks.

② The Gaillard Cut

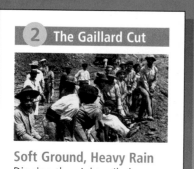

Soft Ground, Heavy Rain
Digging the eight-mile-long cut between Contractor's and Gold hills was the most difficult job of the project. Soft earth from the hills often slid down to fill the holes that workers had just dug.

Mathematics Connection

Ships sailing from New York to San Francisco around the southern tip of South America had to travel a distance of roughly 13,000 miles. The Panama Canal shortened this trip to around 5,200 miles. About how many miles did the Panama Canal cut from the sea voyage from New York to San Francisco?

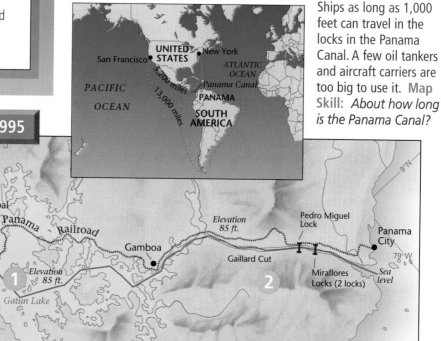

Ships as long as 1,000 feet can travel in the locks in the Panama Canal. A few oil tankers and aircraft carriers are too big to use it. **Map Skill:** *About how long is the Panama Canal?*

The Panama Canal, 1995

PACIFIC OCEAN
80°W

Colón
Cristobal
Panama · Railroad
Sea level
Gatun Locks (3 locks)
Gatun Dam
① Elevation 85 ft.
Gatun Lake

Gamboa

Elevation 85 ft.
Gaillard Cut ②

Pedro Miguel Lock
Panama City
79°W
Miraflores Locks (2 locks)
Sea level

ATLANTIC OCEAN

9°N

Legend
⊢⊣ Lock
— Ship route
⌣ Dam
⊢⊢⊢ Railroad

km 0   5   10
mi 0   5   10

About 12,000 ships pass through the canal each year. Cargo ships like this one on Gatun Lake haul about 168 million tons of cargo.

Research Activity

Many of the people who worked on the Panama Canal decided to settle in Panama.

① Research how these new residents affected the nation of Panama. What new cultural ideas did they bring?
② Prepare a brief oral report. Share your findings with the rest of the class.

Relating Climate and Elevation

Climate Ups and Downs

You're hiking up a mountain in Ecuador. You began in lush tropical rain forest but now that you've climbed higher, you're hiking over snow and ice. You're still near the equator, but it's as cold as Alaska. Why?

You know that latitude affects climate. The farther north or south you are from the equator, the cooler the climate. Did you know that elevation also affects climate? The temperature drops about 3°F every 1,000 feet of elevation, and as the air gets colder it also gets drier. This is why, in the Andes, in just two days you can hike from a tropical climate up to a climate that's like the North Pole.

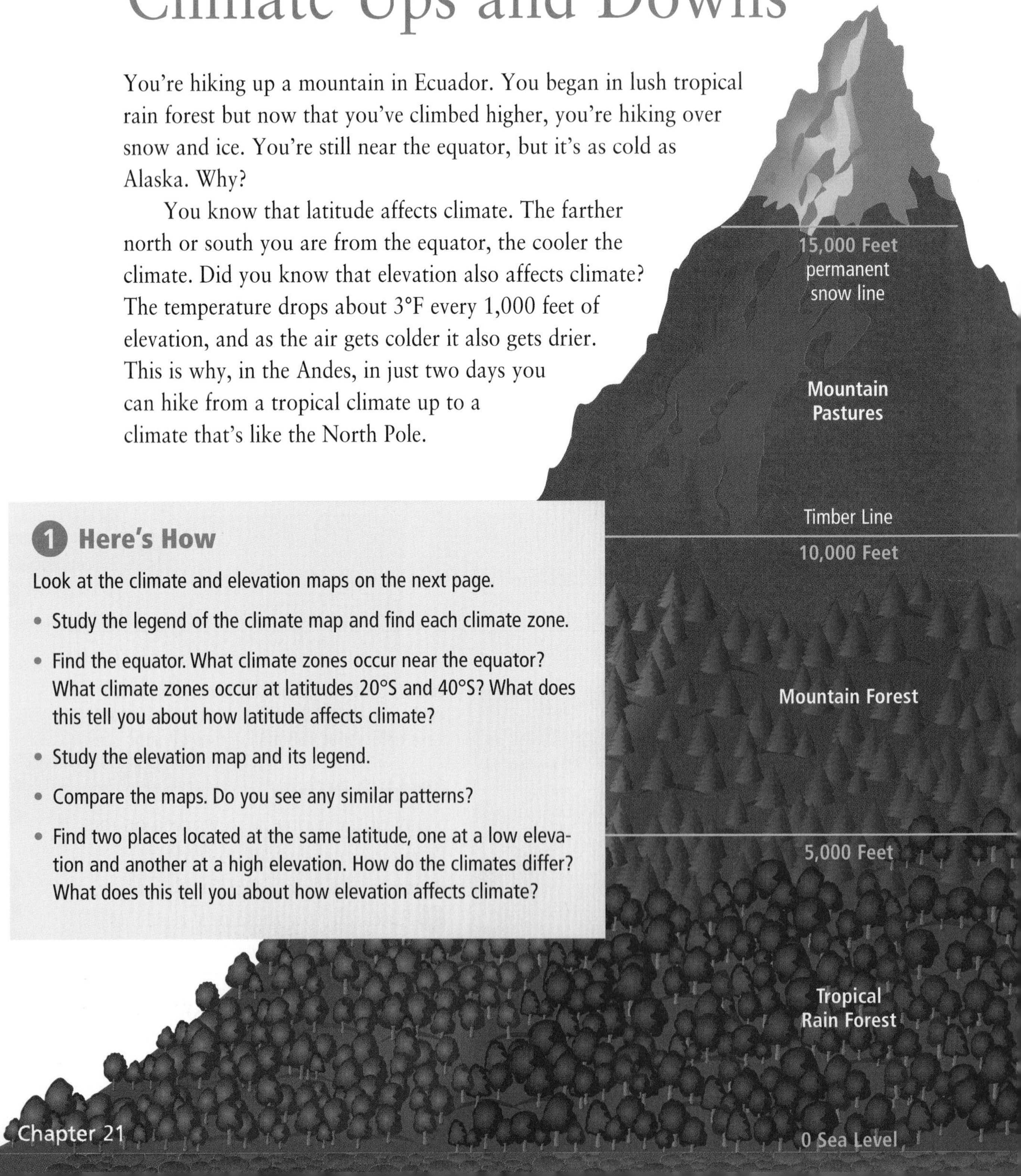

15,000 Feet
permanent
snow line

**Mountain
Pastures**

Timber Line

10,000 Feet

Mountain Forest

1 Here's How

Look at the climate and elevation maps on the next page.

- Study the legend of the climate map and find each climate zone.

- Find the equator. What climate zones occur near the equator? What climate zones occur at latitudes 20°S and 40°S? What does this tell you about how latitude affects climate?

- Study the elevation map and its legend.

- Compare the maps. Do you see any similar patterns?

- Find two places located at the same latitude, one at a low elevation and another at a high elevation. How do the climates differ? What does this tell you about how elevation affects climate?

5,000 Feet

**Tropical
Rain Forest**

0 Sea Level

The Andes: Elevations

Caracas ★
Pico Bolívar
(16,427 ft.) ▲
VENEZUELA

Santa Fe
de Bogotá ★
COLOMBIA

Quito ★
Equator 0°
ECUADOR
Guayaquil ●
Mt. Chimborazo
(20,702 ft.) ▲
Iquitos ●

B R A Z I L

P E R U
Mt. Huascarán
(22,133 ft.) ▲

Lima ★
Cuzco ●
BOLIVIA

PACIFIC
Illimani
(20,741 ft.) ▲

OCEAN
Tropic of Capricorn

Lullaillaco
(22,110 ft.) ▲
Tucumán ●

Aconcagua
(22,834 ft.) ▲
ARGENTINA
Santiago ★

Legend

Land Elevations

Feet		Meters
13,120		4,000
6,560		2,000
1,640		500
650		200
0		0
Below sea level		Below sea level

▲ Mountain peak
★ National capital

The Andes: Climate

Caracas ★
Pico Bolívar
(16,427 ft.) ▲
VENEZUELA

Santa Fe
de Bogotá ★
COLOMBIA

Quito ★
Equator 0°
ECUADOR
Guayaquil ●
Mt. Chimborazo
(20,702 ft.) ▲
Iquitos ●

B R A Z I L

P E R U
Mt. Huascarán
(22,133 ft.) ▲

Lima ★
Cuzco ●

PACIFIC
Illimani
(20,741 ft.) ▲

OCEAN
Tropic of Capricorn

Lullaillaco
(22,110 ft.) ▲
Tucumán ●

ARGENTINA
Aconcagua
(22,834 ft.) ▲
Santiago ★

Legend

- Tropical rain forest
- Tropical savanna
- Semiarid
- Desert (arid)
- Mediterranean
- Humid subtropical
- Marine
- Highland

② Think It Through

Suppose you were on the top of a mountain at the equator. What would the temperature be like?

③ Use It

Find the following pairs of places on the maps above. For each pair of places, decide which has the coolest climate. Explain each answer.

1. Aconcagua and Santiago, Chile

2. Quito and Guayaquil, Ecuador

3. Caracas and Pico Bolívar, Venezuela

4. Lima and Mt. Huascarán, Peru

Central and South America in the Modern Era

Key Vocabulary

dictatorship

plantation

hacienda

mestizo

Key Events

1538 First enslaved Africans brought to Brazil

1813 Bolívar's war for independence from Spain begins

1888 Last enslaved Africans freed in South America

Main Idea Settlement of Central and South America by Europeans brought a mingling of peoples that helped determine the course of history in the region.

Fighting words spilled out of the young man's mouth. He vowed to free his homeland, Venezuela, from Spanish control:

> **"I** *swear before you, I swear before the God of my forefathers, that my arm shall not rest nor my soul be at peace, until I have broken the shackles that bind us to Spain.* **"**

The young man, Simón Bolívar (boh LEE vahr), was a 22-year-old Creole, a South American-born descendant of the original Spanish settlers of Venezuela. The men who ruled South America were usually born in Spain. They believed that Creoles were inferior, and they would not permit them to run the government.

Bolívar resented Spanish rule. By 1813, he had gathered a group of soldiers and had begun fighting for independence from Spain. After nine years, he drove the Spanish out of Venezuela. They also won victories on other parts of the continent.

José de San Martín (deh sahn mahr TEEN), another leader in the fight for independence, waged a struggle in areas that are today Argentina, Chile, and Peru. By 1826, most of the region was free from Spanish rule.

South Americans honored Simón Bolívar for his role in the war for independence from Spain. The city of Lima, Peru, presented him with this jewel-decorated sword.

Rule by Dictators

Focus *What factors made it easier for military leaders to take control of Central and South American countries?*

Ask Yourself

What freedoms do you have as a resident of the United States that you might not have if you lived in a country controlled by a dictator?

? ? ? ? ? ? ? ? ? ? ? ? ? ? ?

After independence, the military leaders who helped Bolívar and others free South America wanted positions of power in the new governments. Many seized control of the regions where they lived. The people gave them the name *caudillo* (caw DEE yo), which means "chief" in Spanish. These "chiefs" named themselves "Restorer of the Laws" and "Protector," titles that made them sound like kind rulers. In reality, many were *caciques* (ka SEE kez), or dictators — leaders who held total power. Many maintained peace by destroying the people who opposed them. They imprisoned their enemies, took away their lands, exiled or even killed them.

Cacique rule had some benefits. Caciques improved living conditions by building roads, railroads, and schools. Their aim, however, was usually to increase their own power and popularity.

These **dictatorships** — governments run by a dictator — were widespread in Central and South America. In time, the cacique legacy made it possible for dicators to use their armies to limit free speech and prevent elections. Three such governments are described below.

Recent decades have seen the downfall of many dictatorships. Some dictators — like the Somoza family in Nicaragua — were overthrown. Others — such as the generals who ruled Argentina — were forced to resign in disgrace. The 1990s ushered in new hope for democracy in Central and South America. By 1991, all the countries in the region had elected leaders, most of them from outside the military.

Chart Skill: *Do some research on one more Central or South American country and create a chart similar to this one.*

South American Dictatorships

	Somoza Family	Juan Domingo Perón	Augusto Pinochet Ugarte
Country	Nicaragua	Argentina	Chile
Date of rule	1934-1979	1946-1955, 1973-1974	1973-1990
Points of interest	• Anastasio Somoza and his two sons ruled through this dictatorship • Controlled industry and farmlands • Family wealth estimated to be $500 million • Critics were jailed, tortured, or assassinated	• Juan Perón and his wife Eva ruled this dictatorship • Argentina's factory workers, peasants, and poor supported this rule • Worked to improve the lives of Argentina's poor • Irresponsible economic policies brought Argentina's economy to ruin	• A military dictatorship run by General Augusto Pinochet • Abolished freedom of speech • Resorted to kidnapping, torture, or murder to silence critics • Inflation devastated the economy of Chile

Rigoberta Menchú

Rigoberta Menchú has crusaded around the world for the rights of indigenous people in Guatemala, her native country. Several members of her family were brutally murdered by the Guatemalan army. Menchú leads a campaign, writing and lecturing about human rights abuses against the Maya in Guatemala. She also raises money to assist Guatemalan refugees. In 1992, she received the Nobel Peace Prize for her work.

Control of the Land

Focus *Who has owned and controlled the land in Central and South America since the European conquest?*

For centuries, whether a person in Central or South America was rich or poor, well-fed or starving, depended on who controlled the land. In the Inca Empire, which endured for several hundred years in what is now Peru, the land was owned jointly. Everyone shared in the annual crop, and food was distributed carefully to make sure no one went hungry. When the Spanish and Portuguese arrived in the early 1500s, Europeans took control of the lands native peoples had traditionally farmed.

The Spanish and Portuguese set up two main types of agricultural operations: plantations and haciendas (ah see EN dahs). **Plantations** were large farms that used the labor of enslaved people brought from Africa to grow crops for export. **Haciendas** were estates that grew food and other crops used mainly to feed Spanish soldiers, laborers, and their animals. On haciendas, native people provided their labor in return for small plots of land on which they could grow their own food.

The poorest land in hard-to-reach areas was left for small groups of independent native farmers to produce food for themselves. The members of these communities owned land jointly and used simple tools like hoes to tend their crops. They were forced to pay heavy tribute, or high taxes, to the authorities.

In the early decades of the 1800s, Europeans and Americans became increasingly interested in the resources and products of Central and South America. They wanted wheat and meat from Argentina, coffee and sugar from Brazil, and bananas from Honduras.

As a result, foreign businesses bought Central and South American plantations and became the new landowners. For example, by the 1890s, two American fruit companies controlled large portions of Honduras. These companies housed workers in barracks and sometimes paid their salary with vouchers, or certificates, that could only buy goods at stores the companies owned. These businesses were interested in growing large numbers of bananas for export.

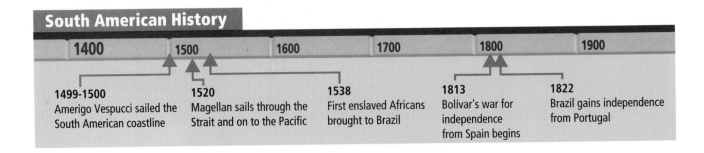

South American History

1400	1500	1600	1700	1800	1900

1499-1500 Amerigo Vespucci sailed the South American coastline

1520 Magellan sails through the Strait and on to the Pacific

1538 First enslaved Africans brought to Brazil

1813 Bolívar's war for independence from Spain begins

1822 Brazil gains independence from Portugal

An old photograph of workers on a South American plantation loading bananas for market.

In the second half of the 20th century, many countries took important steps to develop their own industries in order to become equal partners in the world economy. Those foreign companies that still own plantations try to pay their workers fair wages. Good working conditions, schools, and hospitals are much more common.

Moving to the Cities

Life in the countryside is often difficult. Seventy percent of rural Central Americans are seasonal migrant workers, such as coffee-bean pickers, who must travel to distant plantations to earn wages.

When poor farmers who can no longer make a living from the land leave the countryside, they often go to the city in search of jobs. Many settle on the edge of urban areas. Urbanization is a fact of life in Central and South America. In 1994, for example, 86 percent of all Argentinians lived in urban areas. Sixty-two percent of Nicaraguans were city dwellers.

The downtown areas of Central and South American cities are like those in the United States. Communications technology has increased the ability of city dwellers to buy and sell their products all over the region and the world.

Poor farmers who move to the city often end up in unplanned urban areas like this one in Brazil's Rio de Janeiro. **Economics:** *How could cities better plan for newcomers from rural areas?*

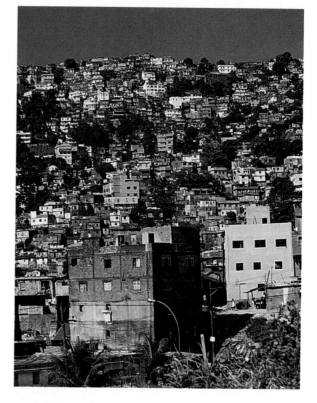

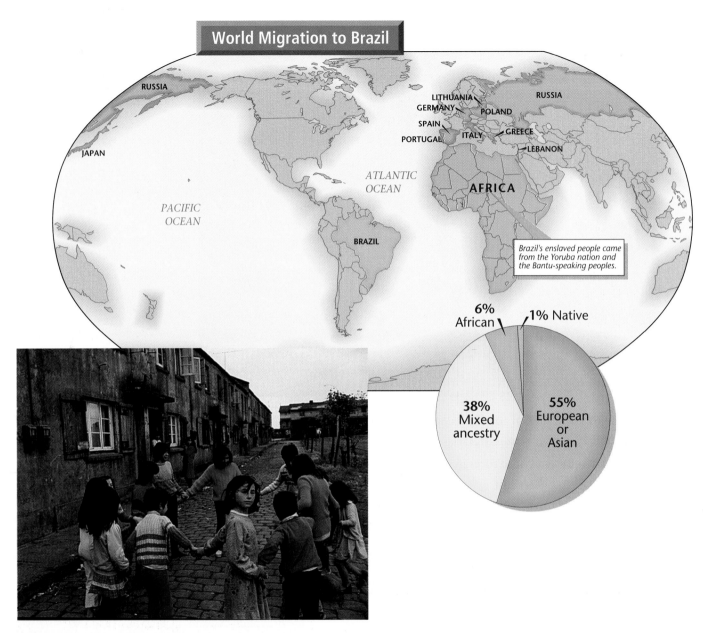

RUSSIA

JAPAN

PACIFIC
OCEAN

ATLANTIC
OCEAN

BRAZIL

LITHUANIA
GERMANY
SPAIN
PORTUGAL
ITALY
GREECE
LEBANON
POLAND
RUSSIA

AFRICA

Brazil's enslaved people came
from the Yoruba nation and
the Bantu-speaking peoples.

6%
African

1% Native

38%
Mixed
ancestry

55%
European
or
Asian

The map above shows the major ethnic groups represented in Brazil and the countries of their origin. Compare it to the pie chart showing the percentages of these groups in Brazil in 1980. **Map Skill:** *What does the map tell you that the chart cannot?*

A Mix of Peoples

Focus *Who are the ancestors of most Central and South Americans today?*

Central and South America have a rich culture. The region's music, dance, art, and literature are enjoyed worldwide. While the people of this continent can trace their roots to every corner of the earth, there is a common thread uniting them. At least 89 percent consider themselves Roman Catholic, and most speak Spanish or Portuguese.

Three Cultural Traditions

Many people in the region are descendants of three groups: native peoples, Africans, and Europeans. Many have a mixed ancestry. For example, 70 percent of all Panamanians are **mestizo** (mixed European and native heritage). Today, countries like Guatemala, Ecuador, and Peru have large native populations, while Brazil, Colombia, and Nicaragua have a high proportion of African descendants. People of European descent dominate the populations of Costa Rica and Argentina.

This mix of peoples is a result of the region's history. Soon after their arrival in the 1500s, European soldiers enslaved the native people. Many died from diseases Europeans brought to the region, as well as from harsh working conditions on plantations and in mines.

Europeans searched for replacement laborers. In 1538, the Portuguese brought the first enslaved Africans to Brazil. Over the next three centuries, about 3.6 million Africans followed. Spain brought at least 1.5 million more. The slave trade continued until the mid-1800s. By 1888, the last of these millions of people were freed.

While the Spanish and Portuguese brought more Africans, they barred other Europeans, letting in only their own citizens. After countries won their independence, immigration policies loosened. In the late 1800s and early 1900s, over 8 million European immigrants arrived, mostly Italians, Spaniards, and Portuguese. They settled mainly in Argentina and Brazil. After World War II, Germans and Japanese flowed to South America. All these people brought their own traditions to the region, while at the same time blending into Central and South American culture.

Curious Facts

In the Andes of Peru, you can ride the highest railroad in the world. It travels from Huancayo to Lima and climbs to an altitude of 15,885 feet. This high altitude is reached on one of the bridges over a pass in the mountains.

Lesson Review

1500	1700	1900

1538
First enslaved Africans brought to Brazil

1813
Bolívar's war for independence from Spain begins

1888
Last enslaved Africans freed in South America

1 Key Vocabulary: Use the following in a paragraph about Central and South America: **dictatorship, plantation, hacienda.**

2 Focus: What factors made it easier for military leaders to take control of Central and South American countries?

3 Focus: Who has owned and controlled the land in Central and South America since the European conquest?

4 Focus: Who are the ancestors of most Central and South Americans today?

5 Critical Thinking: Conclude How is the mix of people in Central and South America different from the mix of people in North America and Europe?

6 Theme: Union and Individuality How are cultures enriched by coming into contact with other cultures?

7 Citizenship/Research Activity: Look for newspaper and magazine articles about one country in Central or South America today. Keep a file of these articles. Write a short report about current events in the country you have chosen.

Soccer's Positions

In soccer, it used to be that defenders defended, forwards attacked, midfielders ran like crazy to do both, and everyone pitied the poor goalkeeper, who might not see much action. Today, soccer is a more free-flowing game in which defenders often go on attack and vice versa.

True, modern soccer teams still have

SWEEPER

The *sweeper* is an extra defender with no specific opponent to guard. He marks (guards) defenders who come near the goal and "sweeps" away stray balls.

STOPPER

The *stopper* has the difficult job of marking the opponents' most dangerous player, usually the striker.

GOALKEEPER

Goalkeepers wear shirts different in color from their teammates' shirts. Good goalkeepers have quick reflexes and outstanding catching and punting skills. They must be able to "shake off" goals scored against them and not get upset.

FULLBACKS

Fullbacks are positioned near the sidelines to mark the other team's wingers.

5 SKILLS EVERY SOCCER PLAYER SHOULD HAVE

SHOOTING

► **SCORING GOALS IS** a tough task. Good finishing (shooting) requires a wide variety of skills, the ability to decide in a split second which technique to select, and composure. For maximum power, lean forward and drive through the ball so that you land on your kicking foot. Tip: Don't be shy. Remember, 100 percent of all shots not taken don't go in!

► **ADVANCING THE** ball with your feet takes lots of practice! Tip: Learn how to dribble without looking at the ball, while developing your ability to change speed and direction.

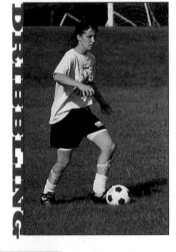

DRIBBLING

◄ **TO STRIKE THE** ball with your forehead, you must keep your eyes open and your mouth closed and attack the ball aggressively. Tip: "Throw" your eyes at the ball.

HEADING

▲ **THE BASIC PUSH** pass uses the inside of the foot to allow for maximum accuracy. Tip: Lock your ankle so your foot remains perpendicular to the direction in which the ball is aimed.

PASSING

different positions with different demands, but the better teams feature well-rounded players. To excel as a defender, you need good ball skills. Even if you're a forward, you'd better help out on "d" (defense) when you're needed.

MIDFIELDERS

Midfielders usually come in groups of four or five and play between their own defenders and forwards. They must be all-around players whose passing helps the offense and whose defense keeps the pressure off their own back line.

WINGERS

Wingers are forwards who play near the sidelines. Their biggest responsibility is setting up teammates for scoring opportunities.

STRIKERS

Strikers, who are forwards, are usually a team's scorers. That's their chief job.

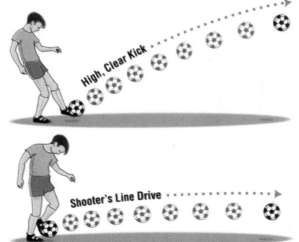

WHAT DIFFERENCE does it make how you stand when you kick the ball? Leaning back when you kick the ball causes it to lift high because your foot has gotten under it. Standing over the ball when you kick it makes it go in a low, straight line.

High, Clear Kick

Shooter's Line Drive

◄ GETTING THE ball from an opponent by using the feet (tackling) requires controlled aggression. Tip: Lean forward to achieve a low center of gravity and better balance.

Response Activity

1. Narrative: Write a Pep Talk
Pretend you are a soccer coach. What would you say to your defensive and offensive players before the game? Write a few sentences directed to each in the form of a pre-game pep talk.

Chapter Review

Chapter Review Timeline

1500	1600	1700	1800	1900	2000

1538
First enslaved Africans brought to Brazil

1813
Bolívar's war for independence from Spain begins

1888
Last enslaved Africans freed in South America

Summarizing the Main Idea

1 Describe how Central and South America's vast resources led to the region's current mix of nationalities.

Vocabulary

2 Using at least three of the following terms, write a message to a South American dictator demanding more freedom.

rain forest (p. 569)   **dictator (p. 575)**   **hacienda (p. 576)**

gaucho (p. 569)   **plantation (p. 576)**   **mestizo (p. 578)**

pampas (p. 569)

Reviewing the Facts

3 What are some of the extreme features of Central and South American geography?

4 Why are the rain forests important to both South America and the world?

5 Name eight products that Central and South America export to the rest of the world.

6 What were the pros and cons of cacique rule?

7 What were some of the differences between the ways the Inca and the Europeans managed the land they controlled?

8 What were the differences between a plantation and a hacienda?

9 Why did Europeans begin bringing enslaved Africans to Central and South America?

10 Who were the ancestors of the people who live in Central and South America today?

11 Look at the map on page 573. How many countries does the Andes mountain range pass through? How do you think these countries were affected by such an imposing presence?

12 In two journal entries describe the weather of a summer day near the top of the Andes and one at the bottom of the Andes.

Geography Skills

13 Re-read the description written by the early European explorer on page 567. Continue his description of the geography of South America as he continues inland.

14 How far (in miles) is South America from each of the world's other six continents?

Critical Thinking

15 **Generalize** Describe what it would be like to live in a rain forest.

16 **Predict** What might Simón Bolívar think about South America's trend toward democracy today?

Writing: Citizenship and Economics

17 **Citizenship** Write a speech for an imaginary cacique, describing all the wonderful things he's done for his people — and then write a response that a person opposing him might give.

18 **Economics** Write a story about a family that decides to move from the countryside in Central or South America to the city.

Activities

History/Research Activity
Do research on a Central or South American dictator. Find out how and when he was removed from office, and what kind of government replaced him. Share your findings with your class.

Culture/Art Activity
Find a recording of music from Central or South America. Read about its origins — chances are it was strongly influenced by other cultures from around the globe. Share it with the class, and describe its origins.

Internet Option

Check the **Internet Social Studies Center** for ideas on how to extend your theme project beyond your classroom.

THEME PROJECT CHECK-IN

As you begin your theme project, use the information in this chapter about Central and South America to help you choose a country. Think about these questions:
• What geographic features have affected the union and individuality of this area?
• What forms of government have existed throughout Central and South America?
• What industries have thrived in this region? How have they affected the union and individuality of nations?

Central and South America: Patterns of Living

Chapter Preview: *People, Places, and Events*

1900	1920	1940

The Heart of Argentina

Find out how life in Argentina's capital reflects the ups and downs of politics. *Lesson 1, Page 586*

Stand Up for Democracy!

How did Argentines show their support for the new freedoms? *Lesson 1, Page 588*

Smelt Down

Why is this man from Chile dressed like this? What is he doing? *Lesson 2, Page 597*

Argentina: The Search for Stability

Main Idea The ups and downs of Argentina's politics shape events in Buenos Aires.

Graceful palm trees bow and sway over bright flower gardens in a large open square in the heart of Argentina's chief city, Buenos Aires (BWEH nohs AI rehs). On this beautiful square, called the Plaza de Mayo, many key events in the nation's history have unfolded.

For nearly two hundred years, Argentines have rallied on the plaza to bring political change. Argentina's movement for independence from Spain began there in 1810. Thousands poured into the square in 1945, calling for the release from prison of Colonel Juan Perón (peh ROHN), opening the way for him to rule the country. Since then, Argentines have assembled to demand democracy in their nation. Whenever an issue is important to the people of Argentina, it finds its way to the Plaza de Mayo. The story of Buenos Aires shows the type of political issues common to countries in Central and South America.

◀ The National Congress in Buenos Aires, Argentina.

Key Vocabulary

estuary

inflation

Key Events

1976–1983 Military controls Argentina's government

1977 Plaza de Mayo demonstrations for "the disappeared" begin

1983 Raúl Alfonsín elected president

| 1960 | 1980 | 2000 |

Celebration Brazilian-Style

What does Rio de Janeiro's Carnival tell us about Brazil? *Lesson 3, Page 600*

Frogs Galore

Thousands of frogs (and other creatures) live in the rain forests of Costa Rica. *Lesson 4, Page 607*

Plant a Tree

How have Costa Ricans worked together to save damaged rain forests? *Lesson 4, Page 610*

The Heart of Argentina

Focus *Why is Buenos Aires an important city?*

If the Plaza de Mayo is the heart of Buenos Aires, then Buenos Aires is the heart of Argentina. Eleven million people, one-third of the country's population, live in this city. It is the nation's capital, where the government is headquartered.

Buenos Aires sits on the banks of the Río de la Plata, as you can see from the map on this page. The Río de la Plata is an **estuary**, a broad inlet of an ocean, in this case the South Atlantic. The city's location helped make it a major port. Inland from the city, the pampas stretch for miles. Ranchers from the pampas send cattle, sheep, wheat, and corn to the port to be shipped around the world.

By the early 1900s, Buenos Aires had become the richest city in South America, thanks to port trade. Residents rebuilt the city to display their wealth by laying out broad new avenues. They built mansions, theaters, and government buildings.

Argentina's wealth drew immigrants who hoped to earn their fortunes. Between 1880 and 1930, 2.5 million people arrived from countries like Italy, Spain, France, and Germany. Their numbers also included Irish shepherds, Jewish craftsmen from Russia, and Arab shopkeepers. The immigrants' different backgrounds have blended to create a special culture. It is a culture where people are as likely to drink English tea as mate (MAH teh), a South American herb tea.

Buenos Aires has faced hard times in recent decades. Yet the city's energy survives. A famous writer described the city's magic:

> **"T**o me it is a fairy tale that Buenos Aires was founded. It seems as eternal as water and air.**"**

Residents of Buenos Aires say that 9th of July Avenue *(below right)* is the widest street in the world. The grand Colón Opera House *(below)* occupies a whole block of the street. *Arts: Argentines spent millions on their theater. Why is it so important to them?*

Hopes for Democracy

Focus *What was the "dirty war"?*

Every Thursday since 1977, a group of women has gathered in the Plaza de Mayo. They grasp pictures of men, women, and children. The women are the Mothers of the Plaza de Mayo. They are trying to learn the fate of their loved ones who disappeared during years of military rule (1976–1983). Their protest is a product of military rule and reflects the nation's hopes for democracy.

The problems that led to military rule stretched back to the 1940s. In the 1960s, the military tried to crush the followers of Juan Perón, the Argentine president described on page 575. (Perón left office in 1955, but his supporters were a large, powerful group.) Strikes brought the country to a standstill. Unrest grew. Urban guerrillas, small groups of fighters organized against the government, robbed banks and murdered their political enemies.

At the same time, **inflation**, a sharp increase in the price of goods and services, hit Argentina's people hard. (Because of rising prices, people needed more money to buy the same amount of food and other products. Salaries, however, did not increase as fast as inflation.) The nation fell into debt. The government was unable to solve these problems.

Finally in 1976, the armed forces took over. Military officers headed branches of the government and many businesses. They believed that they could restore order and the nation's economic health. They planned to hold down wages and cut government benefits for the needy.

To ensure the success of their programs, military leaders fought a "dirty war." They targeted guerrillas and people who spoke out against military rule. "Death squads" in unmarked cars prowled the streets of Buenos Aires and picked up people they suspected. Students, lawyers, reporters, and innocent bystanders disappeared. The military questioned and tortured suspects. Some were jailed, then released. Others were killed. Between 10,000 and 30,000 people vanished. In Spanish, they are called *los desaparecidos* (lohs deh sah pah reh SEE dohs), "the disappeared."

Using these tactics, military leaders crushed the urban guerrillas. Yet they could not quiet all opposition,

A policeman stands in front of posters made by families of "the disappeared." The posters give the names of loved ones and the dates they vanished. **Citizenship:** *How are these posters a form of protest?*

especially when their economic programs failed. By the early 1980s, inflation soared again. Protestors filled the Plaza de Mayo, calling for free elections.

Military leaders tried to rally support by getting the nation to support a war against Great Britain. They were fighting to gain control of the Malvinas, or Falkland Islands, off Argentina's coast, which the British had governed since 1833. The war failed miserably. The leaders who planned the Malvinas invasion resigned in disgrace. Free elections were held, and Raúl Alfonsín (rah OOL ahl fohn SEEN) was elected president in 1983.

The Taste of Freedom

Focus | *What changes have taken place in Buenos Aires that show signs of renewal?*

In Buenos Aires today, rows of abandoned factories and run-down buildings line the streets. They are leftovers from decades of failed economic policies. Yet there is another side to the city. New hotels and fashionable shops are springing up. New telephone cable is being laid to provide businesses with up-to-date communications. Such projects show that economic well-being is returning.

The road to recovery has not been easy. Alfonsín tried to restore the confidence of the people by bringing top military officers to trial for crimes of the "dirty war." Over two hundred were charged.

The president's action angered the military. Officers staged a revolt against his government in 1987. Citizens flooded the Plaza de Mayo to show their support for democracy. The military revolt failed, but Alfonsín had to stop the trials.

Alfonsín had trouble taming inflation. By 1989, the annual rate of inflation was over 1,000 percent. Streets were empty because people could not afford gas for cars. Bread prices could double in a week. In the past, such conditions could have led to a military takeover. Instead, Argentines elected a new president, Carlos Menem, in 1989, hoping he would solve their problems. Democracy in Argentina continued.

Menem sold off government-owned businesses like the national airline. He laid off

In the 1980s, the spirit of freedom brought Argentines into the streets to demonstrate for democracy. One protester's sign reads, "Yes to democracy!"

Political rallies are now common in Argentina. People show their support openly for issues that affect their lives.

workers and cut the government's budget. He ended state control of wages and prices. People grumbled, but inflation fell. Businesses grew.

Menem also moved to end the threat of further military takeovers. He pardoned officers convicted of crimes during the dirty war. This won the goodwill of military leaders. He also reduced the size of the army. In the late 1990s, Argentina suffered in a world-wide economic downturn. Still, the country's commitment to democracy continued.

Argentina was not the only country in Central and South America with a changed government. Power has shifted from the military to freely elected leaders in many nations. Democracy has spread throughout the region.

Ask Yourself

How do you tell if a country is "free"? What is necessary?

? ? ? ? ? ? ? ? ? ? ? ? ?

Lesson Review

1970	1975	1980

1976–1983
The military controls Argentina's government

1977
Mothers of "the disappeared" begin demonstrating

1983
Raúl Alfonsín elected president

1 Key Vocabulary: Define the following terms: **estuary, inflation.**

2 Focus: Why is Buenos Aires an important city?

3 Focus: What was the "dirty war"?

4 Focus: What changes have taken place in Buenos Aires that show signs of renewal?

5 Critical Thinking: Conclude Why did inflation lead to unrest among Argentines?

6 Theme: Union and Individuality Why might the Mothers of the Plaza de Mayo have banded together to protest? Would they have been more or less successful if they had worked individually?

7 Citizenship/Art Activity: Create posters or banners that demonstrators in the Plaza de Mayo might have carried to protest military rule.

ON THE PAMPAS
María Cristina Brusca

Autobiography

estancia — *a South American cattle ranch*

ON THE PAMPAS

by María Cristina Brusca

It's not going to be an ordinary summer for María. She had visited her grandparents' cattle ranch before, but this summer she's going without her parents and brother. And this summer, she's going to learn what it takes to be a gaucho, a South American cowboy. This is a true story.

I grew up in Argentina, in South America. I lived with my family in the big city of Buenos Aires, but we spent our summers in the country, at my grandparents' *estancia*. One summer my parents and brother stayed in the city, so I went without them. My grandmother met me at the station in Buenos Aires, and we had breakfast as we rode through miles and miles of the flattest land in the world — the pampas. All around us, as far as we could see, were fences, windmills, and millions of cattle grazing.

Our station, San Enrique, was at the end of the line, where the train tracks stopped. My grandfather was there to meet us in his pickup truck and take us the five miles to the *estancia*.

The ranch was called La Carlota, and the gates were made of iron bars from a fort that had been on that very spot a hundred years before. As we drove up to the gates, we were greeted by a cloud of dust and thundering hooves — it was my cousin Susanita, on her horse.

Susanita lived at the *estancia* all year round. She knew everything about horses, cows, and all the other animals that live on the pampas. Even though she was three years younger than me, she had her own horse, La Baya. Susanita was so tiny, she had to shimmy up La Baya's leg to get on her back. But she rode so well that the gauchos called her La Gauchita — "The Little Gaucho." I didn't have a horse of my own, but old Salguero, the ranch foreman, brought me Pampita, a sweet-tempered mare, to ride. She wasn't very fast, but she certainly was my friend.

Susanita and I did everything together that summer. She was the one who showed me how to take care of the horses. We would brush their coats, trim their hooves, and braid their manes and tails.

Susanita was always ready for an adventure, no matter how scary. She used to swim in the creek holding onto La Baya's mane. At first I was afraid to follow her, but when she finally convinced me, it was fun.

I wanted to learn all the things a gaucho has to know. I wanted to ride out on the pampas every day, as Salguero did, and to wear a belt like his, with silver coins from all over the world and a buckle with my initials on it. Salguero said I'd have to begin at the beginning, and he spent

hours showing Susanita and me how to use the lasso.

It was going to take me a while for me to become a gaucho. The first time I lassoed a calf, it dragged me halfway across the corral. But Salguero told me that even he had been dragged plenty of times, so I kept trying, until I got pretty good at it.

Whenever the gauchos were working with the cattle, Susanita was there, and before long I was too. Sometimes the herd had to be rounded up and moved from one pasture to another. I loved galloping behind hundreds of cattle, yelling to make them run. I never got to yell like that in the city!

Meet the Author

This book is autobiographical. María Cristina Brusca grew up in Argentina, and she loved visiting her grandparents' ranch in the summers. She lives in the United States now, but her brother still manages her mother's ranch in Argentina.

Additional Books to Read

Carnavalia! African-Brazilian Folklore and Crafts by Liza Papi. Learn about folklore, costumes, and dances.

Tintin's Travel Diaries: Peru and the Andean Countries by Chantal Deltenre and Martine Noblet. Read about adventure in the Andes.

Response Activities

1. **Comparing Then and Now** Gauchos have worked on the pampas for centuries. How might the life of the ranch hands be the same today as it was 100 years ago? How might it be different?

2. **Narrative: Write a Dialogue** Think about what Salguero the ranch foreman might tell the girl who is the narrator about a gaucho's life on the pampas. Then write a dialogue between Salguero and the narrator.

3. **Geography: Draw a Map** Make an illustrated map of Argentina by tracing the outline of the country and marking the location of the pampas. Then add pictures of gauchos, cattle, lassos, saddles, and other people and objects that are part of everyday life on an Argentine ranch.

Chile: The Story of Copper

Main Idea Chile's reliance on a single export, copper, limited its economic growth for many years, but recently it has begun to develop other industries.

Like all kids, Dan and Sue needed a little extra spending money. Dan decided he would mow his neighbors' lawns — for a small fee, of course. Sue also went into the mowing business. Since she liked dogs, however, she offered her services as a paid dog walker as well. Suddenly, a drought hit. Lawns turned brown and stopped growing. Dan was out of business, but Sue still had change in her pocket. Why? Because she had branched out. She had several ways to earn money.

Dan and Sue aren't real, but their economic problems are. Chile, like many other countries in Central and South America, is a country that for many years depended on the sale of a single product. That product is copper. When demand for the metal decreased and buyers and profits were not plentiful, Chile faced economic hardships. In this lesson, you'll read how Chile solved these problems by branching out.

The Atacama Desert *(left)* is one of the driest places in the world, but its copper mines draw many people to work there. Copper *(below)* is plentiful in this region.

595

At Chile's Chuquicamata mine, huge trucks with wheels taller than a man carry copper ore out of the pit. **Technology/Economics:** *Why do you think equipment manufacturers developed such large trucks?*

Curious Facts

The world's largest underground copper mine is located near Chile's capital, Santiago. It contains 994 miles of tunnels. If you laid these tunnels end to end, they would stretch from New York City to Memphis, Tennessee.

From Mine to Market

Focus *How is copper mined and manufactured?*

The Atacama Desert in northern Chile is one of the driest places on the earth. In parts of this desert, no rainfall has ever been recorded. The land seems barren and lifeless. Still, the wealth hidden under its surface has drawn thousands of people to this arid spot.

A vast pit — two miles long, half a mile wide, and half a mile deep — has been dug into the desert. This is the Chuquicamata (choo kih kah MAH tah) copper mine. It is the largest of the many Chilean mines where copper ore is dug from the earth. (Ore is a metal mixed with other minerals and rock.) The raw ore contains just a tiny amount of pure copper, so huge amounts of rock must be dug and processed.

As you see from the pictures above, Chuquicamata is an **open-pit mine**. A series of steep terraces have been carved into the pit's walls from top to bottom. Across these terraces roar huge trucks, with wheels about twelve feet high. Each truck picks up tons of raw ore that have been blasted from the sides of the pit and takes it for processing.

Underground mines, with shafts and tunnels, are another way to extract copper from the earth. Underground mining is far more expensive than open-pit mining, but when there is a large amount of copper in the ore, underground mining becomes worthwhile.

However the ore is taken from the ground, it is processed by crushing and mixing it with water to make a paste. The paste is stirred into a foam with more water, chemicals, and air. Many unwanted materials sink out as mud, while the copper remains in the foam and is skimmed off.

This copper substance is now between 30 and 40 percent pure. It is heated, or smelted, in a series of ovens. The heating removes iron, sulfur, and other metals. What remains is called blister copper. It is about 99 percent pure.

Both copper ore and processed copper are taken to Chile's ports and loaded on ships for sale abroad. There, they will be further processed and turned into countless copper products. Among the biggest customers for Chile's copper are Germany, Finland, South Korea, and Japan.

Depending on Copper

Focus *What are the problems with an economy that depends on a single product?*

Copper became an important export for Chile soon after the nation won independence from Spain in 1818. By the 1950s, copper represented more than 50 percent of all of Chile's exports. In the following decade, that figure reached 80 percent. Taxes on the export of copper made up one-fifth of the government's income.

Hard Times

There are problems and dangers when a nation's economy relies too heavily on the export of one product. Demand for that product may drop if substitutes for it are discovered. New sources for the product might be found. In such cases, prices for the product drop, sometimes sharply. In the case of copper, prices could fall by 500 percent in a year.

The effect of such a price drop can ripple out through the whole nation. Producers of the product may lay off workers or cut wages. They may also stop buying machinery or supplies for their businesses. Companies that make the machinery or supplies for the producers may also have to lay off workers and cut wages. There are fewer workers in the nation with less money to spend. They buy less, reducing income for still other businesses, and on and on.

Meanwhile, because less of the product is exported, the government's income from taxes on exports falls. Money for highways and schools may be cut. If the nation does not produce enough food or basic consumer goods, it may do without or borrow money to buy those things from other countries. As a result, the nation goes into debt, owing money to foreign governments or investors.

This is what happened in Chile. In 1971, the government thought it

The map shows the areas where copper is mined in Chile.
Map Skill: *What port might the copper be shipped from?*

could solve some of its economic problems. It took over, or nationalized, the copper companies. Now the state would run the companies and make the profits. It took over banks, large farms, and other businesses as well. The government also froze prices and tried to raise wages.

The new measures did not work. Prices continued to rise. Other nations cut their investments in Chile. Unemployment and unrest swelled. Finally, military leaders seized power in 1973.

Branching Out

A military government ruled Chile for almost seventeen years. Its leaders aimed at reducing government control of the economy. Price controls ended. Tariffs, or taxes on imported goods, were slashed. Many businesses went back into private hands, although the large copper mines remained under government ownership. The government also welcomed foreign investors.

After some sharp ups and downs, the economy began to recover. When a democratically elected government came into power in 1990, it continued most of these economic policies.

Under these policies, Chile's economy **diversified**. This meant that it drew income from a variety of products, instead of relying on only a few products for its income. Back in 1973 for example, Chile exported 412 different products. By 1988, it was exporting 1,343 products. Because Chile is in the Southern Hemisphere, Chile's summer is winter in the

Fresh Chilean fruit represents one of the ways Chile has diversified its economy. The fruit is shipped by sea to North America.

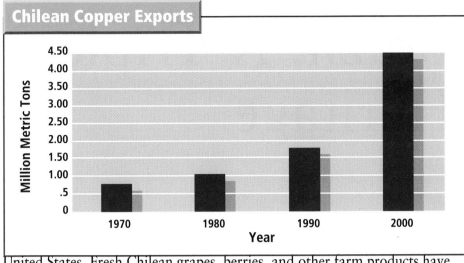

Chilean Copper Exports

Million Metric Tons

4.50
4.00
3.50
3.00
2.50
2.00
1.50
1.00
.5
0

1970   1980   1990   2000

Year

The graph shows the metric tons of copper exported over the last 30 years from Chile. **Chart Skill:** *Do you think the amount will increase or decrease in the next 20 years?*

United States. Fresh Chilean grapes, berries, and other farm products have found a growing market in North America.

In addition to selling more types of products, Chile is selling them to more countries. In 1971, it exported goods to 58 countries. By 1988, that number had grown to 112. Today, the United States is the leading buyer of Chilean products, followed by Japan. In addition, Chile is making an effort to increase trade with its Central and South American neighbors. For example, Argentina and Brazil are major trading partners.

With all these changes, copper still remains important to Chile. In 1999, copper exports made up about 40 percent of the total value of all Chile's exports.

In the late 1990s, Chile's economy was affected by a recession that hit countries around the world. A drought also hurt crops and decreased the amount of water-generated electricity. The economy began to recover in 2000. Higher copper prices helped in that recovery, but Chile continues to to develop other industries to diversify its economy.

Lesson Review

1 **Key Vocabulary:** Write a paragraph about Chile's economy using the following terms: **open-pit mine, underground mine, diversify.**

2 **Focus:** How is copper mined and manufactured?

3 **Focus:** What are the problems with an economy that depends on a single product?

4 **Critical Thinking: Classify** Make a chart of the advantages and disadvantages of

a national government controlling a major industry or industries in a country.

5 **Geography:** How do the land and the rivers in South America provide support to each other in the production and export of grapes and fruit?

6 **Citizenship/Writing Activity:** You work for the government of Chile. Write a letter to a foreign company explaining the advantages of doing business in Chile.

Brazil: A Triple Heritage

Main Idea In Brazil, different cultures and traditions have blended to create a culture that is new and uniquely Brazilian.

Every year, thousands of people dressed in masks and costumes parade down the avenues of the Brazilian city of Rio de Janeiro (REE oh dah zhuh NAIR oh) — a riot of music, dance, and color that is part of a nonstop party called Carnival. It is an example of the way the three cultural traditions in Brazil — the native, the African, and the European — blend to give the country a unique flavor. Brazil is like many Central and South American countries where many cultures merge into one.

The Portuguese, who were mostly Roman Catholic, brought Carnival to Brazil from Europe in the 1500s. It was a last outburst of high spirits before the solemn religious season known as Lent. Brazilians who are descendants of enslaved Africans gave Carnival its music, the samba.

Neighborhood groups called "samba schools" take part in Carnival's huge parades. They march and dance to the beat of African-style drums, rattles, and bells. Each school has a theme for its performance. Often these themes honor the traditions of the nation's native peoples. A school might create a float illustrating legends from the Amazon region.

Even kids join Carnival's glittery celebration. Here a Brazilian girl marches in costume with a "samba school." She is part of the huge parade that weaves through Rio on Carnival's last two nights.

Native Peoples in Brazil

Focus *How do the traditions and practices of native peoples influence modern-day Brazil?*

Today, scientists travel deep into the Amazon jungles of Brazil. Some are seeking *pagés* (pazh EHS), the healers of native peoples. Scientists hope to learn about jungle plants and insects that can be used as medicines. Other researchers, anthropologists, are trying to understand and help preserve the native peoples' unique traditions and languages. They are concerned that this way of life will disappear, along with the Amazon rain forests.

Before Europeans reached the Americas, between 2.5 and 4 million native people lived in what is now Brazil. They belonged to some 880 groups. When the Portuguese arrived in the early 1500s, they tried to enslave these peoples, forcing them to work on sugar plantations. Many native people lost their lives fighting slavery. If enslaved, many native people died on the plantations because of disease or terrible working conditions.

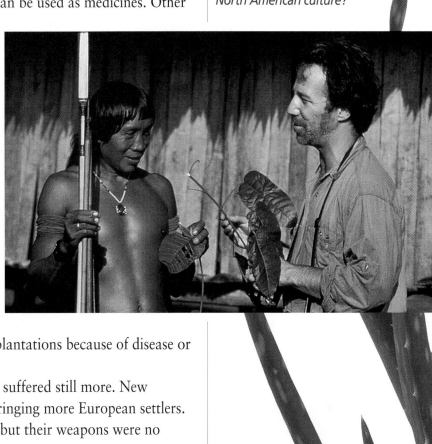

Scientists study plants with native people. The plants are used to make medicines. **Cultures:** *How have Native South Americans contributed to North American culture?*

As Brazil developed, the native people suffered still more. New farmlands, mines, and railroads opened, bringing more European settlers. Native peoples tried to defend their lands, but their weapons were no match for the settlers'.

Today, only about 200,000 indigenous people live in Brazil. Almost 700 tribal groups have vanished. Some now live on **reservations,** land set aside by the government for their use. Others live deep in the Amazon jungle. But the forest is being cleared. Loggers, gold prospectors, and other jungle workers have brought disease to the native peoples. For many indigenous peoples, it is a struggle to keep their age-old traditions alive.

The influence of these native peoples on Brazil lives on, however. Their medicines may help cure others. At least 20,000 words from native languages have become part of modern Brazilian Portuguese. The native people taught the Portuguese how to use canoes and sleep in hammocks, which are still widely used. Native foods like corn, manioc, tapioca, and cashews still are part of the Brazilian diet. Another native crop, tobacco, is a major Brazilian export.

Africans in Brazil

Focus *What traditions and practices did Africans bring to Brazil?*

Brazil

The Brazilian state of Bahia. **Map Skill:** *What part of the country is it in?*

Cowboys of African descent ride in a rodeo in Bahia.

On a street corner in the Brazilian city of Salvador, a musician is playing a one-string instrument called a *berimbau* (beh rih BOW). In front of him, two men practice an art form from Africa.

This is *capoeira* (kah poh AIR ah). In Africa, it had been a form of foot-fighting, a martial art like kung fu. Enslaved Africans brought the technique to Brazil. Portuguese slave owners, however, did not want the Africans fighting and made the practice illegal. The Africans then disguised the foot-fighting as dancing. This tradition has stayed alive to the present.

The first enslaved Africans arrived in Brazil in 1538. Between 3.5 and 5 million people were brought from Africa over the next 350 years. Early on they worked on the sugar plantations of northeast Brazil. Later, they worked in the country's gold mines and on its coffee plantations.

Enslaved Africans lived in poor conditions. Work was unending, and food, clothing, and shelter were poor. Some Africans bought or earned their freedom. Others ran away. Still others fought slavery. In the early 1800s, nine rebellions in less than 30 years shook Bahia (buh EE ah), the Brazilian state with the largest African population. *(See map at left.)* Resistance to slavery did not end until slavery was

outlawed in 1888. Eight hundred thousand blacks won freedom that year.

Today, the African influence is present everywhere in Brazil. Perhaps 45 percent of Brazil's people have some African ancestors. African words and speech patterns can be found in the Portuguese language as it is spoken in Brazil. The religious practices that helped Africans survive slavery have lasted into modern times. Feijoada (fay ZHWAH dah), the Brazilian national dish that combines black beans, rice, meats, green vegetables, and manioc flour, was first cooked by enslaved Africans.

Still, blacks and people of mixed African and European ancestry often do not have as many opportunities as whites. Black Brazilians earn less than white Brazilians on average. Sometimes they are kept from renting apartments in "white" buildings or from joining private clubs.

Some Brazilians are struggling against racism by trying to make their fellow citizens aware of what blacks have accomplished. One of the things they point to with pride is the story of Palmares (pahl MAR ehs).

The Republic of Palmares

In the 1600s, Africans fleeing slavery settled in ten villages along Brazil's northeast coast. The largest village was known as the Republic of Palmares. For more than 50 years, some 20,000 people lived in this area, which is about the size of Rhode Island. Warriors from Palmares raided nearby plantations to free other enslaved Africans.

Under their leader, Zumbi, the Africans turned back attack after attack by the Portuguese. Finally, in 1694 the Portuguese captured Palmares. They killed some of the inhabitants and sent others back into slavery. Zumbi and a band of warriors escaped and fought on for 18 more months. In the end, Zumbi was caught and killed.

Zumbi is a folk hero to many Brazilians. People in this march wear shirts to honor him. **Citizenship:** *What part of his story makes Brazilians remember him as heroic?*

The story of Palmares was passed down the generations by enslaved Africans and their descendants. Recently, archaeologists have found evidence at the site of Palmares to support the stories.

Black Brazilians are taking new pride as the story of Palmares becomes more widely known. Restaurants, dance companies, and even city neighborhoods have adopted Zumbi's name.

Pelé

Brazil's king of soccer is Edson Arantes do Nascimento — better known as Pelé (PAY lay). Born in 1940, he learned to play soccer barefoot in the slums of a city in the state of São Paulo. By age 15, Pelé was playing for one of the nation's top teams. He led Brazil to three World Cup championships before retiring.

Europeans and Other Immigrants in Brazil

Focus *What traditions and practices did the Portuguese and other immigrants bring with them to Brazil?*

Families happily munch on German sausages as a brass band belts out German music. The buildings that overlook these festivities could be straight from the German city of Munich (MYOO nihk). This is the Brazilian city of Blumenau (BLOO men aw). Every year, nearly a million visitors descend on Blumenau to take part in the city's Oktoberfest. The celebration is the nation's second largest after Carnival. It is a reminder that European immigrants played a large part in the creation of Brazil.

The Portuguese were the first European immigrants, and Portugal ruled Brazil from the 1500s until 1822. Portuguese remains the language of Brazil today, although it has been influenced by the languages of native people and Africans. The religion that the Portuguese brought, Roman Catholicism, remains the most widely practiced in the country today.

As slavery drew to an end in the late 1800s, the Brazilian government looked for a new supply of workers. It encouraged immigration from Europe. Between 1884 and 1973, five million people arrived. The largest number of newcomers came from Italy. Other immigrants came from Portugal, Spain, Germany, Russia, Poland, Lithuania, and Greece.

After the end of the U.S. Civil War, about 20,000 southerners immigrated to Brazil. In the early 1900s, some 700,000 people arrived from what are today Syria and Lebanon. Immigration from Japan began in 1908. Today, more Japanese live in Brazil than in any other nation except for Japan.

Soccer was introduced in Brazil in 1894 by a Brazilian of English descent. The game is so popular that it could be considered part of Brazil's national heritage.
National Heritage: *What sports are part of the U.S. national heritage?*

These varied immigrants have brought skills, customs, ideas, and outlooks that have helped build and change Brazilian society.

How Cultures Blend in Brazil

Focus *How is the practice of religion in Brazil an example of cultural blending?*

The blending of cultures is especially evident in Brazil's religious practices. Ninety percent of Brazilians describe themselves as Roman Catholic. Yet up to a third at times practice forms of worship that can be traced back to Africa.

Ritual, which includes chanting, dancing, and bringing offerings, is an important part of *candomblé* (kah DO bleh) and *umbanda* (uhm BAN dah), forms of Afro-Brazilian worship. These practices have been influenced by Christianity. Under slavery, Africans were baptized as Catholics but were taught little about the faith. So they combined their beliefs with what they knew about Christianity.

Blending of traditions is typical of Central and South America, where cultures meet and mingle with each other in many different ways.

The work of master sculptor Aleijadinho as it is seen in front of a church in Brazil.

Lesson Review

1 Key Vocabulary: Use the following word in a paragraph: **reservation.**

2 Focus: How do the traditions and practices of native peoples influence modern-day Brazil?

3 Focus: What traditions and practices did Africans bring to Brazil?

4 Focus: What traditions and practices did the Portuguese and other immigrants bring with them to Brazil?

5 Focus: How is the practice of religion in Brazil an example of cultural blending?

6 Critical Thinking: Conclude Why might the Portuguese have felt threatened by Zumbi and his warriors?

7 Citizenship: How does cultural blending occur in the United States?

8 Theme: Union and Individuality/ Music Activity Listen to some records of Brazilian music. What cultures might have influenced this music?

Costa Rica: Saving the Rain Forests

Main Idea The rain forest is of immense value to people and the planet.

Costa Rica's Corcovada National Park is mosquito heaven. Thousands buzz everywhere. Corcovada is a lush jungle dripping with something the pesky insects need — water. The region gets up to 20 feet of rain a year. This rain forest is teeming with other life too: 500 kinds of trees, 367 species of birds, 117 kinds of reptiles, and 10,000 types of insects. All this in just 100,000 acres (about the size of Denver, Colorado). The park is a national treasure.

To some people, Corcovada holds another kind of treasure: gold. In the 1980s, miners rushed into the park. They cut down trees to make clearings to grow food in. They hunted the park's rare animals. Faced with the destruction of the park, the Costa Rican government sent in the National Guard to force the miners out. Unfortunately, Corcovada is typical of many rain forests in Central and South America and around the world. How can we balance the human desire to use their resources with the need to preserve the forests?

A Priceless Resource

Focus *Why are rain forests important to humans and to our planet?*

Tropical forests are rich in **biodiversity**: They contain large varieties of life forms. Costa Rica makes up only three ten-thousandths of the earth's land surface. (That means that if the land on earth were divided into ten thousand pieces, Costa Rica would take up three pieces.)

Costa Rica

NICARAGUA

Lake Nicaragua

CARIBBEAN SEA

COSTA RICA

Puerto Limón

Liberia

Alajuela San José

Puntarenas   Cartago   Turrialba

10°N

86°W

PACIFIC OCEAN

PANAMA

8°N

84°W

km 0   50   100
mi 0   50   100

Legend

- National park
- Ranching
- Rain forest
- Other tropical forests
- Commercial farming

Yet it contains 5 percent of all the plant and animal species known to exist. (If all the species on the earth were divided into 10,000 groups, 500 groups would live in Costa Rica.)

Rain forests also serve as "lungs" for the planet. The trees absorb carbon dioxide from the atmosphere. In ever-growing amounts, carbon dioxide is produced by cars, by factories, and by burning of fuels like coal and oil. The forests "recycle" the carbon dioxide and produce oxygen, which we need to breathe. The fewer trees there are, the more carbon dioxide that builds up in the earth's atmosphere. Some scientists believe such buildups can cause the world's climates to grow warmer.

In the forests, incredible patterns of life have developed. Moss, ferns, orchids, and vines grow upon trees. Hummingbirds build nests on spider webs. Frogs live far above the floor of the forest and raise their young in pools of water trapped in different types of plants. Dead logs provide food for mushrooms and moss, insects, and other trees.

Scientists are only beginning to understand the complex life of the forests. In Costa Rica, a program to make a list of all of the country's different life forms is under way. Despite large numbers of people working on the project, just 65,000 species of insects out of an estimated 225,000 species have been found and identified.

Understanding what the tropical forests contain and how they work may produce important benefits. For example, about a quarter of all medicines in use today come from plants. However, scientists have so far only studied about 1 percent of all tropical plants for use as medicines.

Scientists are seeking out the medicine men of native peoples in Brazil in order to learn more about plants used for medicines. Researchers are also learning native healing methods in Costa Rica.

These are some of the interesting species of animals found in the rain forest.

1 Red-eyed tree frog hanging on to a branch.

2 A spider on a web found in a Costa Rican rain forest.

3 A female three-toed sloth.

4 Colubridae tree snake in the rain forests of South America.

Pressures on the Forest

Focus *How does human activity threaten the Costa Rican rain forest?*

What happened in Corcovada National Park has happened in different ways to other rain forests across Costa Rica and around the globe. It is estimated that half the world's rain forests have already been destroyed. An area of rain forest the size of a football field is burned up, chopped down, or bulldozed each second. Some 130 different species of rain-forest plants and animals around the world become extinct each day.

Why is this happening? Because pressure to use the forests and their resources is great.

In Costa Rica, people who can't find jobs often turn to the forests to find ways to survive. In order not to starve, they cut down and burn the jungle to clear ground for planting crops. Because of the heavy rainfall, **erosion**, the washing away of soil, becomes a problem after a few years. Nutrients in the soil are also used up quickly. Farmers must then clear more forest to plant new fields.

Another pressure on the rain forests has come from the development of industries such as cattle ranching. In the 1960s, many acres of forests were turned into pastureland. Erosion became a major problem again.

How the Rain Forest Grows

1. **Forest Floor.** Trees shade the forest floor from the sun. It is dark and nearly always wet, with rain falling every day. The ground is covered with decaying dead plant and animal materials. The soil is shallow.

2. **Shrub Layer.** Smaller plants grow here. They are home to mammals, amphibians, and reptiles.

3. **Understory.** Trees up to about 50 feet tall make up this level. Exotic birds live here, as do many insects and mammals like sloths.

4. **Upper Canopy.** The densest layer of vegetation is 65 to 100 feet above the ground. Trees are exposed to full sunlight. Flowers and seeds are produced here. Flying squirrels, monkeys, tree frogs, and other animals make their homes here. Some never come down to ground.

5. **Emergent Trees.** Some trees, called emergents, tower above the others. They stand alone, not having to compete for sunlight as the trees in the crowded canopy do.

The photo shows how dense the vegetation is deep in the rain forest. It is easy to get lost in such a lush and full area.

Large-scale agriculture can also damage the forests. Raising bananas is big business in Costa Rica. On the banana plantations, the rich variety of forest plants is destroyed and replaced with a single crop. Fertilizers and insecticides pollute the soil and the streams, often killing wildlife.

Furniture makers and consumers around the world love items made of slow-growing rain forest woods like mahogany. To get to this popular wood, logging companies cut down other forest trees. They take the mahogany, leaving the other trees to rot on the delicate forest floor.

Because of all these activities, more and more of the rain forest was destroyed. In 1950, forests covered 72 percent of Costa Rica. By 1985, that figure dropped to 26 percent. The forests were in danger of disappearing.

How the Rain Forest Dies

1 **Slash-and-Burn Agriculture.** When farmers need to clear jungles to grow food for their families, they cut and burn the trees. Smoke from the fires pollutes the air.

2 **Logging.** Loggers cut down trees, sometimes leaving the ones they do not want to rot on the delicate forest floor.

3 **Erosion.** Without tree roots to hold topsoil in place, erosion quickly becomes a problem. Plants and trees cannot grow without the nutrients of the soil.

4 **Endangered Species.** Rare plants and animals die out when their forest homes are destroyed. Valuable plants that provide ingredients for medicines are lost.

5 **Oxygen.** Rain forests convert carbon dioxide into oxygen. When large numbers of trees are cut down, less oxygen is produced.

Costa Ricans plant seedlings of rain forest trees. The government has encouraged reforestation. **Science:** *Why is reforestation only a partial solution to the destruction of the rain forests?*

Saving the Forest

Focus *What steps has Costa Rica taken to protect its forests?*

In response to the vanishing rain forests, Costa Rica created **reserves**, areas of protected land where hunting and logging are not allowed. Scientists can study in these protected forests. Tourism is encouraged in the hopes that tourists will become active in saving the environment.

The lands that Costa Rica has set aside protect plants and wildlife. They also provide jobs for people nearby. Some become assistants to scientists, caretakers, or guides. The reserves also become schools for local people. They learn better ways to manage their cattle, fight fires, and preserve plants and wildlife.

Today, Costa Rica has a large network of protected lands, including national parks, reserves, and wildlife refuges. About 27 percent of Costa Rica is protected in parks and reserves. No other country comes close to protecting that much of its land. The government is also encouraging **reforestation**, the planting of trees in areas that have been cleared. Reforestation helps restore some but not all plant life.

As Costa Rica has shown, the destruction of the rain forest can be slowed when people get involved in preserving it. It is a model for other countries in Central and South America.

Lesson Review

1. **Key Vocabulary:** Describe the rain forest using the following: **biodiversity, erosion, reserve, reforestation.**

2. **Focus:** Why are rain forests important to humans and to our planet?

3. **Focus:** How does human activity threaten the Costa Rican rain forest?

4. **Focus:** What steps has Costa Rica taken to protect its forests?

5. **Critical Thinking: Interpret** Why do other nations care about Costa Rica's rain forests?

6. **Theme: Union and Individuality** Why do people from different walks of life need to work together if they want to preserve the rain forest?

7. **Citizenship/Drama Activity:** Form small groups in which some students play the roles of farmers, Costa Rican ecologists, and government officials. Explain to a group of visiting tourists how you worked together to save the rain forest near your homes.

Investigating Topics in the Media

Digging Deeper

Suppose you heard a report about rain forests on a television news program last night. The reporter made some interesting points, and you'd like to learn more about what she described. How could you use the media to investigate this subject?

❶ Here's How

- **Newspapers.** Look for the latest articles and editorials about the rain forest. Your library has indexes for some newspapers. These will help you identify articles in past papers. Look up "rain forest" and see what you can find.

- **Magazines.** You've learned how to use the Readers' Guide to locate magazine articles about a particular subject. (See the Skills Workshop on page 169.) Magazine articles may go into greater depth than a radio or television news report.

- **Radio and Television.** Keep an eye out for special radio and television programs devoted entirely to one subject. You might find special programs just about the rain forest, for example.

- **Books.** If you want to find out even more, go to the school or local library and find books on your topic.

❷ Think It Through

How can news programs help you keep up with what is going on in the world? Why is it important to investigate topics in depth?

❸ Use It

Choose a story in the news tonight.

1. Make a brief summary of what you learned from the program.

2. Find other media sources on your topic. Go to the library, for example, and find a magazine article and a book about the same subject.

3. Describe what you learned from your in-depth investigation.

★ CITIZENSHIP ★

Resolving Conflicts

How Do You Plan Ahead?

People wearing glasses or contact lenses can be nearsighted or farsighted. These words can also refer to a different kind of vision. "Nearsighted" people make decisions based on what looks best in the immediate future. "Farsighted" people base decisions on what looks best in the long run, perhaps decades into the future. The case study below shows how nearsighted and farsighted ways of seeing can put people in conflict.

Case Study

Rich in Forests, Short on Cash

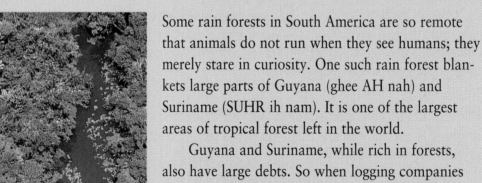

Some rain forests in South America are so remote that animals do not run when they see humans; they merely stare in curiosity. One such rain forest blankets large parts of Guyana (ghee AH nah) and Suriname (SUHR ih nam). It is one of the largest areas of tropical forest left in the world.

Guyana and Suriname, while rich in forests, also have large debts. So when logging companies offered millions of dollars to cut down the trees for wood, government leaders saw a quick way to pay their bills. In the long run, however, the deal looked bad to environmentalists. Logging would cause land erosion, and loose soil would clog rivers. Animals and plants would disappear. How could the government earn money without losing its forests?

Take Action

You are the mayor of a town that has a beautiful park, which includes a large playground, gardens, benches, and two playing fields. Last week, the children of your town wrote you a letter. "We would like to have half of the park black-topped," they wrote. "We want a safe place to rollerblade, practice skateboarding, and play basketball and street hockey."

The green park has been the pride of your community for a long time. You are hesitant to pave it, but you know the children need a safe place to play, too. What should you do?

1 Write down a list of the people who use the park. For each of these users, what are the short-term advantages and disadvantages of paving the park? Write them down.

2 For each of these users, list the long-term advantages of paving the park. Write down the disadvantages, too.

3 Study your lists. Which advantages and/or disadvantages seem most important to you? Make your decision. Then decide what you should do. Write down your reasons.

4 Write and present a three-minute speech for the local TV six o'clock news. Show your community how carefully and thoughtfully you have tried to weigh short- and long-term views. Videotape your speech, if you can.

Tips for Resolving Conflicts

- Try to stay open to other people's needs and arguments while you are figuring out your own position.
- Show the people who disagree with you that you have carefully and thoughtfully weighed the alternatives.
- Think of several possible solutions before you pick one, or offer a few solutions for others to pick for themselves.

Research Activity

Find out about the national park or state park nearest your community. How did this land become a protected area? Who uses the land and for what purposes? Are there any conflicts over the land or how it should be used? Write a short report on the different points of view people have about that park, about other public land, or your state's environmental laws.

Chapter Review

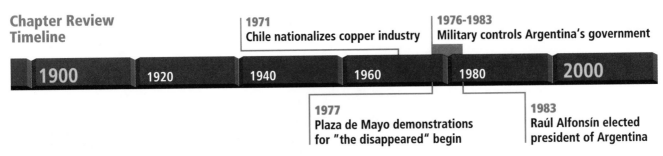

Chapter Review Timeline

| 1900 | 1920 | 1940 | 1960 | 1980 | 2000 |

1971 Chile nationalizes copper industry

1976-1983 Military controls Argentina's government

1977 Plaza de Mayo demonstrations for "the disappeared" begin

1983 Raúl Alfonsín elected president of Argentina

Summarizing the Main Idea

❶ Write a few sentences describing the relationship between politics and the economy for each of the countries discussed in the chapter.

Country	
Argentina	
Chile	
Brazil	
Costa Rica	

Vocabulary

❷ Write a short conversation between a Central or South American politician and a citizen, using at least five of the following terms.

estuary (p. 586)   diversify (p. 598)   erosion (p. 608)

inflation (p. 587)   reservation (p. 601)   reserve (p. 610)

open-pit mine (p. 596) biodiversity (p. 606)   reforestation (p. 610)

underground mine (p. 596)

Reviewing the Facts

❸ What factors made Buenos Aires the richest city in South America in the early 1900s?

❹ Who were "the disappeared"?

❺ Why did Argentina's military leaders declare war against Great Britain?

❻ Why is it a bad idea for a country to depend on mainly one product for export? How did Chile learn this lesson?

❼ How did Brazil get such a diverse population?

❽ Why is the biodiversity of the rain forests so important to the planet?

❾ What are some of the ways the people of Costa Rica have used and abused the rain forests?

Investigating Topics in the Media

10 What is one very recent news source that is not listed under Here's How?

11 Why is keeping a journal a good way to keep track of an event over a period of weeks?

12 How might coverage of a news topic in a book and its coverage in a magazine be different?

Geography Skills

13 Compare the maps of the four countries reviewed in this chapter (p. 586, 597, 602, and 606). How do you think their long coast-lines affected their development?

14 Using the information about the rain forest on page 608 (How the Rain Forest Grows) and 609 (How the Rain Forest Dies), along with the rest of the information in Lesson 4, create a newspaper ad about the rain forests.

Critical Thinking

15 **Decision Making** President Carlos Menem had some tough decisions to make as president of Argentina. The chapter lists six steps he took (sold government-owned businesses, laid off workers, cut the government budget, ended wage and price controls, pardoned military officers, reduced the size of the army). Weigh the pros and cons of each step.

16 **Compare** Compare life for the native people of Brazil before and after the arrival of the Europeans.

Writing: Citizenship and Culture

17 **Citizenship** In this chapter we read about people who stood up for what they believed in—in Argentina, the relatives of the disappeared; in Costa Rica, people who wanted to save the rain forests. Choose a current issue that concerns you, and write a plan of action about what you can do to make a difference.

18 **Culture** In the lesson on Brazil, we read about the influence of different cultures on the people who live there. Write about how the different cultures of the United States affect you.

Activities

Economics
In Chile, copper is one of many products exported. Find out what products the United States exports, how much money each earns, and to which countries we sell them. Present your findings to the class in a graph or chart.

Culture/Music
In Brazil, Africans introduced the samba and a style of dancing based on foot-fighting. Choose your favorite kind of music and find out what cultures influenced it. Present your findings to the class.

Internet Option

Check the **Internet Social Studies Center** for ideas on how to extend your theme project beyond your classroom.

THEME PROJECT CHECK-IN

To complete your theme project, use the information in this chapter about some Central and South American nations. Ask yourself these questions:
- What political, economic, and cultural events have influenced the country?
- What kind of political system does the country have?
- What other nations has this country interacted with?

North America and the Caribbean in the Modern Age

"Lift up your eyes
Upon this day breaking for you.
Give birth again
To the dream."

Maya Angelou

· THEME ·

Movement and Transformation

"North America and the Caribbean have been affected by the different people who came here. In the U.S., there are many nationalities, languages, and customs."

Ryan Craig, Sixth Grade
Phoenixville, PA

Native American, Spanish, African, French, British, Chinese — the list of cultures that mix in North America and the Caribbean seems endless. The meeting and blending of their traditions has not been without conflict. As different groups struggle to adjust to a new nation and to one another, suspicion and tension have sometimes resulted. Nevertheless, the diversity of the population has enriched the region and transformed it into an economic and political powerhouse.

Theme Project

Guide to Movement and Transformation

Create a travel guide for a North American or Caribbean country to show movement and transformation in it.

- Construct a timeline that includes the major events in the country's history in the 20th century.
- Diagram the country's political system.
- Draw a map of the country that includes its major cities and geographic features.
- Illustrate the geography, culture, and people of the country. Write captions for these pictures.

RESEARCH: Collect facts on the major sites visited by tourists who come to this country.

◀ The city of Miami, Florida.

WHEN & WHERE ATLAS

The histories of North America and the Caribbean are largely histories of immigration. Waves of immigrants brought their cultures and heritages with them. The resulting diversity is a striking feature of North American and Caribbean society. The short distance between North America and the Caribbean, which you can see on this map, has led to growing ties between the two areas.

In this unit you will learn about the geography of these two places. You will also read about some of the events that influenced them during the 20th century. Finally, through profiles of five nations, you will learn about the cultural, economic, and political forces that give North America and the Caribbean their unique identities.

Unit 9 Chapters

ASIA

Legend

★   National capitals

160°E

Unit Timeline

1450	1560	1670

Haitian Art

Haitian art is bold and bright. What are its influences? *Chapter 24, Lesson 1*

Santo Domingo   c. 1542

The Spanish presence in the Dominican Republic was strong. *Chapter 24, Lesson 1*

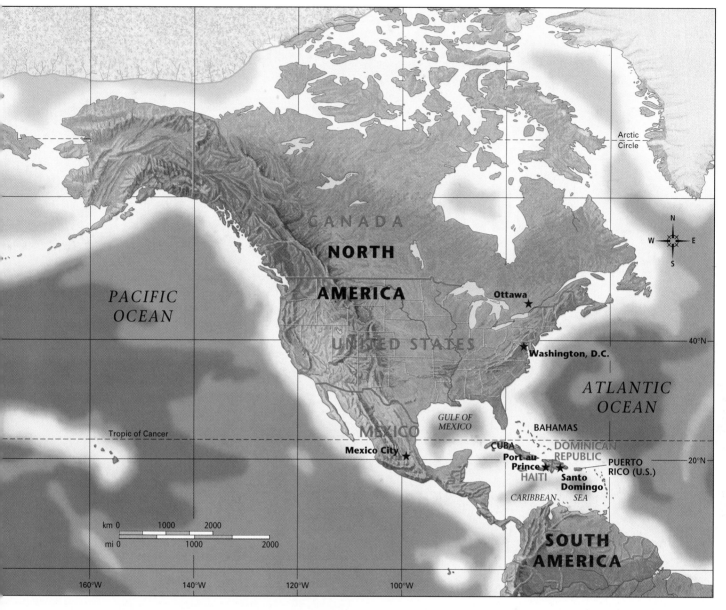

Arctic Circle

CANADA

NORTH

AMERICA

PACIFIC OCEAN

UNITED STATES

Ottawa ★

40°N

Washington, D.C.

ATLANTIC OCEAN

MEXICO

GULF OF MEXICO

BAHAMAS

CUBA

DOMINICAN REPUBLIC

Port-au-Prince ★

PUERTO RICO (U.S.)

Mexico City ★

HAITI

Santo Domingo

20°N

Tropic of Cancer

CARIBBEAN   SEA

km 0   1000   2000

mi 0   1000   2000

SOUTH AMERICA

160°W   140°W   120°W   100°W

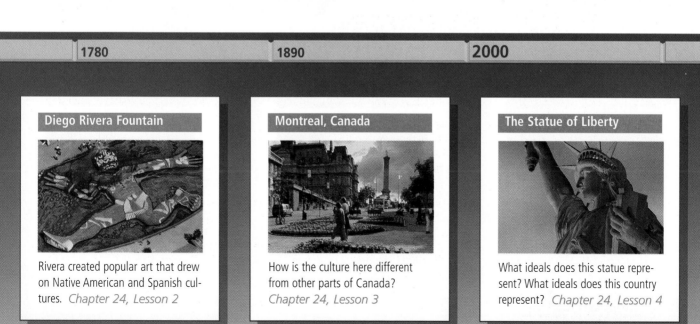

1780   1890   2000

Diego Rivera Fountain

Rivera created popular art that drew on Native American and Spanish cultures. *Chapter 24, Lesson 2*

Montreal, Canada

How is the culture here different from other parts of Canada? *Chapter 24, Lesson 3*

The Statue of Liberty

What ideals does this statue represent? What ideals does this country represent? *Chapter 24, Lesson 4*

North America and the Caribbean: An Overview

San Juan National Forest

North America's landforms include mountains, flat plains and barren deserts. *Lesson 1, Page 622*

Fishing in the Caribbean

The clear, blue water of the Caribbean Sea attracts more than fish. *Lesson 1, Page 624.*

Natural Disasters

Find out how a hurricane is formed. *Lesson 1, Page 625*

The Geography of North America and the Caribbean

Main Idea North America and the Caribbean are composed of different regions and people, and are linked by a shared dependence on resources.

Every morning, from Hudson Bay to the Gulf of Mexico, fishers set out in boats to harvest the sea. For thousands of years, North Americans and Caribbean islanders have used their magnificent coastlines for fishing and trading, for safe protection against enemies, and for sports and recreation. From Alaska to Aruba, the people of this continent are "all in the same boat" in many ways. They share unique lands and resources.

North America is the third-largest continent in area. Only Asia and Africa cover larger areas. Within this vast area, there are dramatically different regions with diverse climates, varying landscapes, and abundant natural resources.

◀ A satellite view of North America and the Caribbean, taken at night.

1960　　　　1980　　　　2000

July 4th in Boston, Mass.

Why do we celebrate July 4th? *Lesson 2, Page 627*

Mexico City, Mexico

A new trade agreement includes this city in a free trade zone. *Lesson 2, Page 630*

Toronto, Canada

This city began as a small fur-trading post. *Lesson 2, Page 630*

Landforms and Resources

Focus | *What kinds of landforms, climates, and resources characterize North America and the Caribbean?*

North America includes Canada, Greenland, the United States, Mexico, Central America, and the islands of the Caribbean Sea. Three of the nations of North America — Canada, the United States, and Mexico — have among them a variety of landforms, from flat coastal plains, to wind-swept deserts, to high, jagged mountain peaks. All three nations stretch from the Atlantic Ocean to the Pacific Ocean. The interiors of Canada and the United States consist mostly of rolling plains, while Mexico's interior is high plateau. All three countries have mountains, including the Rocky Mountain chain which extends from Mexico, through the United States and Canada, all the way north to the Arctic.

Running through the Rockies is the **Continental Divide**. This ridge divides the continent's water systems. All rivers that run from the Divide flow either west toward the Pacific or east toward the Atlantic. North America has great river systems, such as the Saint Lawrence, Mississippi, and Columbia rivers, and the Rio Grande. There are also many large lakes, like Lake Chapala in Mexico, and Lake Superior, shared by the United States and Canada.

The climate of North America ranges from polar to tropical, with many climates in between. Some polar areas in parts of Alaska and northern Canada are covered year-round with ice and snow and never have summer temperatures above freezing (32°F).

Areas in the central United States and Canada have long, cold winters and short summers of mild, warm days, allowing a variety of plant

St. John *(below)*, one of the U.S. Virgin Islands in the Caribbean Sea, has a year-round tropical climate. Badlands National Park *(bottom)*, located in southwestern South Dakota, is a region of barren ravines, cliffs, and low hills.

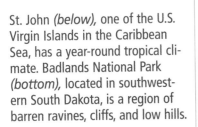

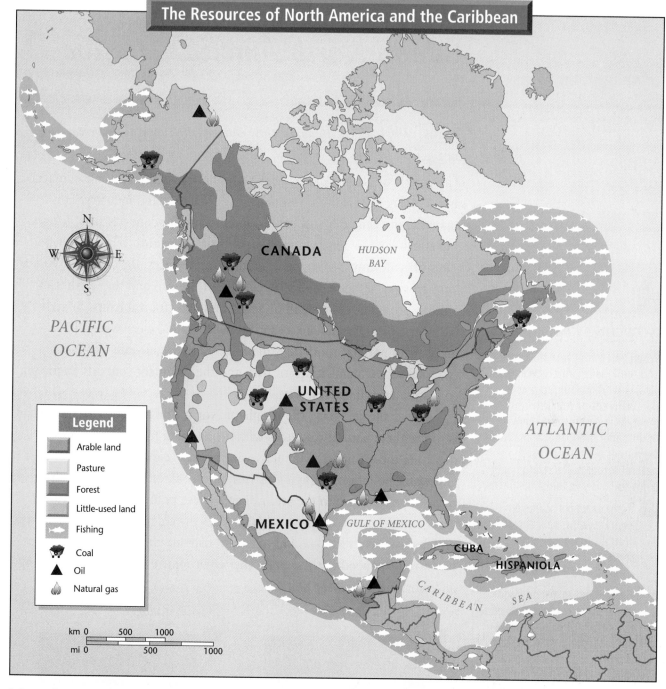

Legend

Arable land
Pasture
Forest
Little-used land
Fishing
Coal
Oil
Natural gas

PACIFIC OCEAN

CANADA

HUDSON BAY

UNITED STATES

ATLANTIC OCEAN

MEXICO

GULF OF MEXICO

CUBA

HISPANIOLA

CARIBBEAN SEA

km 0   500   1000
mi 0   500   1000

life to flourish. Many coastal areas in eastern and western North America have mild, moist winters and hot summers, promoting the growth of various fruits and other crops.

In the dry, desert, and semi-arid areas of Mexico and the United States, there is usually less than 20 inches of annual rainfall. Daily summer temperatures are over 100°F. A number of plants and animals have adapted to the high temperatures and scarcity of water.

The landscapes of the Caribbean islands contain sandy beaches, coral lagoons, grassy plains, mountains, and volcanoes. Located close to the equator, these islands have a humid climate with heavy rainfall and average temperatures of 80°F. Some mountains in Haiti have heights over 6,000 feet. The year-round warm climate creates lush, green landscapes.

North America, the third largest continent in area, is rich with natural resources. **Map Skill:** *Looking at the resources of Canada, the United States, and Mexico, what do you think the most successful industries are for each nation?*

North America and the Caribbean   **623**

Life in North America and the Caribbean

Focus *What effects do landforms, climate, and natural resources have on the way people live in North America and the Caribbean?*

The people of North America have adapted to living in diverse climates and to using their natural resources in agriculture and industry. For example, the United States and Canada have abundant pastures, forests, and **arable** land — fertile land that is fit for agriculture. Their rivers and lakes provide ample fresh water, and in some places, the climate favors a long growing season. The warm climate of Mexico and the Caribbean nations promotes the growth of vegetables and tropical fruits. In addition, their pleasant climate, beautiful beaches, and clear waters have made them popular tourist destinations. The coastal waters of North America supply many kinds of fish, and the continent contains major oil, coal, and natural gas reserves.

The challenge facing the people of North America and the Caribbean is to use these natural resources without harming the environment or depleting the resources. Manufacturing and car exhaust can lead to air and water pollution. Many industries burn coal, oil, and gas, which releases pollutants into the atmosphere. These pollutants are carried by wind and deposited on the earth's surfaces in rain and snow. **Acid rain,** as polluted rain is called, can kill trees and fish and damage soil. Many people have responded to these and other environmental threats by recycling and working to prevent pollution.

The Four Steps in Recycling Paper

When you throw your milk cartons and drink boxes into recycling bins, you are helping to preserve the resources of your environment. Milk cartons and many other paper products are made from trees — a highly used natural resource. Recycling paper helps to conserve forest resources.

1 Paper products are taken from recycling bins and brought to a local recycling center where they are crushed into small bundles.

2 These bundles are dumped into a large container called a pulper, which is like a washing machine for the paper. Water and chemicals in the pulper remove ink from the paper, turning it into a mushy, wet material called pulp.

3 The pulp is then passed through screens that sift out unwanted items like foil and plastic. The clean pulp is mixed with clean water until it becomes a thick, white substance.

4 This thick substance is spread into a thin layer and then heated, dried, and smoothed onto rollers. The paper is now ready to be made into new products like tissues or writing paper.

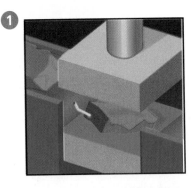

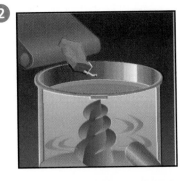

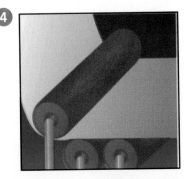

How Natural Disasters Affect People

Some of the greatest threats to the people of these regions come from nature. In Mexico there are many active volcanoes which erupt, covering the ground with black ash. The 20th century's most deadly volcanic eruption, on the Caribbean island of Martinique in 1902, killed 28,000 people. Earthquakes are common in North America: a 1985 earthquake in Mexico City destroyed hundreds of buildings, killing about 7,000 people.

Hurricanes travel through the Caribbean each year, sometimes hitting the islands, Mexico, or the United States. **Hurricanes** are whirling storms that form above the ocean with wind speeds over 75 miles per hour *(see below)*. Other weather disasters include blizzards and floods. Blizzards may kill livestock in open areas, and floods may wash away homes and businesses, drowning people and animals. Sometimes flood

A volcanic eruption sends burning lava down the mountainside, destroying everything in its path.

• Tell Me More •

What makes a hurricane?

Wind, heat, and moisture are necessary to form a hurricane.

1 Winds meet over the surface of the water.

2 Moisture comes from the ocean.

3 The ocean also provides heat. The water temperature must be at least 80° F.

4 The heat causes the winds to rise, bringing the moisture with them. The wind, heat, and moisture are twisted together by the earth's rotation to form a column-shaped hurricane.

Non-hurricane winds often break into the rising moisture and stop the hurricane from forming. These winds in the upper atmosphere can help by carrying away rising air.

pre-existing winds

pre-existing winds

pre-existing winds

warm water

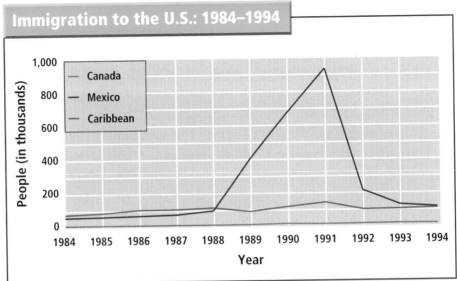

Immigration to the U.S.: 1984–1994

This chart shows immigration to the United States between 1984 and 1994. **Chart Skill:** *Which country or region had the greatest increase in immigration to the United States?*

Upon arriving in New York from the Dominican Republic, Maria Miguelena Barbuena went to work sewing dresses in a factory. Today, she owns a restaurant called Las Tres Marias *(above)* with her four daughters.

waters do not recede in time for farmers to plant crops. Many governments have relief measures to help citizens recover from natural disasters.

People on the Move

Millions of people travel from the mainland of North America to the Caribbean each year. Many are tourists leaving the snowy, cold winter behind to sun, swim, fish, and play sports at Caribbean resorts. Trade also sends business people to the Caribbean and Mexico.

Many people travel from the Caribbean to the mainland of North America for economic reasons. Some settle, get jobs, and later send for family members to join them. Others return to their native land with new skills and experience. Maria Miguelena Barbuena (bar BWAY na) left the Dominican Republic when she was 12 years old and eventually opened up a restaurant. "I dreamt of this, and I got it," said Barbuena.

Lesson Review: Geography

1 **Key Vocabulary:** Use each of these terms in a sentence: **Continental Divide, arable, acid rain, and hurricane.**

2 **Focus:** What kinds of landforms, climates, and resources characterize North America and the Caribbean?

3 **Focus:** What effects do landforms, climate, and natural resources have on the way people live in North America and the Caribbean?

4 **Critical Thinking: Classify** Identify two places in North America that are located in different climate zones. Describe what you think would be the benefits and drawbacks of living in each place.

5 **Geography** How do the people of North America and the Caribbean depend on each other in terms of sharing natural resources?

6 **Theme: Movement and Transformation/ Writing Activity:** Write a letter to a penpal in the Caribbean, inviting him or her to visit you. In your letter, explain how the climate and activities of your region differ from those in the islands.

North America and the Caribbean in the Modern Era

Main Idea Countries in North America and the Caribbean became independent nations and now try to forge strong trade links.

O n the morning of April 19, 1775, shots rang out at the bridge leading into the town of Concord, Massachusetts. A group of local farmers fired on troops from Great Britain. At the time, Massachusetts was a British colony. The Battle of Concord marked the start of the American Revolution. In 1776, the 13 American colonies declared their independence from Great Britain. In 1783, a new nation was born: the United States of America.

When the American poet Ralph Waldo Emerson wrote about the Battle of Concord, he referred to "the shot heard round the world." Emerson's words reflect the influence the American Revolution had on many other colonies throughout North America and the Caribbean. Inspired by Americans, who fought for and achieved their independence, the people of many other colonies would soon fight for their independence.

Independence in the Modern Age

Focus *What events and leaders were important in independence movements in Haiti and Mexico?*

European exploration led to the colonization of many North American and Caribbean areas. Later, these regions became independent nations, like Haiti and Mexico.

Key Vocabulary

megalopolis
NAFTA

Key Events

1776 American Revolution

1804 Haiti gains independence

1821 Mexico gains independence

1867 Canada gains independence

1992 NAFTA is signed

Haiti

Columbus claimed the island of Hispaniola for Spain in 1492. The Spanish colonized the island, and in 1697 gave France the western portion of the island, present-day Haiti. French citizens gradually built plantations there and established a system of slavery. Enslaved Africans were brought to help grow sugar cane, coffee, and cotton.

In 1791, a rebellion began in Haiti, led by Toussaint L'Ouverture (too SAN loo vehr TOOR) and Jean-Jacques Dessalines (zhahn zhahk day sa LEEN). In 1803, the rebellion ended when the enslaved Africans finally drove out the French. Jean-Jacques Dessalines became governor-general and declared Haiti an independent nation in 1804.

Mexico

The Spanish arrived in Mexico in 1519, and within a few years defeated the Aztec people. Gradually, the population of Mexico came to be made up of three distinct groups: people of Spanish descent, Native Americans, and people of mixed Spanish and Native American descent. The people of Spanish descent generally owned the land and ran the government, while the other two groups worked in the fields and mines.

By the early 1800s, word of other nations' revolutions had reached Mexico. As Mexican resentment of the colonial system increased, the idea of independence from Spain grew more appealing. On September 16, 1810, a priest named Miguel Hidalgo y Costilla (mee GEHL ee DAHL go ee kohs TEE yah) delivered a sermon in the village church of Dolores, Mexico. He urged his followers to take up arms against their Spanish oppressors. The date of Hidalgo's famous speech is celebrated today as

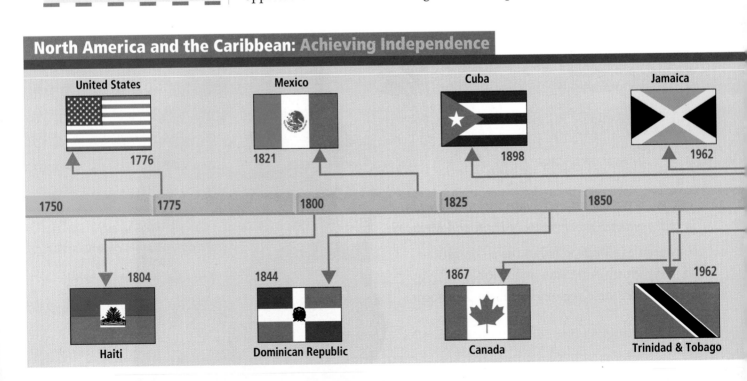

North America and the Caribbean: Achieving Independence

United States — 1776
Mexico — 1821
Cuba — 1898
Jamaica — 1962

1750   1775   1800   1825   1850

Haiti — 1804
Dominican Republic — 1844
Canada — 1867
Trinidad & Tobago — 1962

Mexico's Independence Day.

Father Hidalgo led a revolt that captured land from the Spanish and gave it to the poor. Hidalgo was successful at first, but in 1811 the Spanish defeated, captured, and executed Hidalgo. The fight for independence continued, however, led by another village priest, Father José María Morelos y Pavón (hoh SEH mah REE ah moh REH lohs ee pah VOHN). With an army he had organized and trained, Father Morelos gained control of most of southern Mexico until, in 1815, he too was captured and executed.

In 1820, a revolt in Spain created a new government that called for more political power and new taxes. The Spanish in Mexico did not want to be controlled by this new government. Soon they favored independence from Spain. In 1821, Mexico became an independent nation.

The country underwent years of unrest and a frequent turnover of governments. In 1929, Mexican President Plutarco Elías Calles formed the Partido Nacional Revolucionario (National Revolutionary Party). The PNR stood for the economic and social goals of the Mexican Revolution. The PNR, now called PRI, remained in power until Vincente Fox Quesada of the National Action Party was elected president in 2000. It was the first peaceful democratic transfer of power in Mexico's history.

Displayed in the Government Palace in Guadalajara, Mexico, this mural shows the first leader of the Mexican Independence Movement, Father Hidalgo y Costilla.

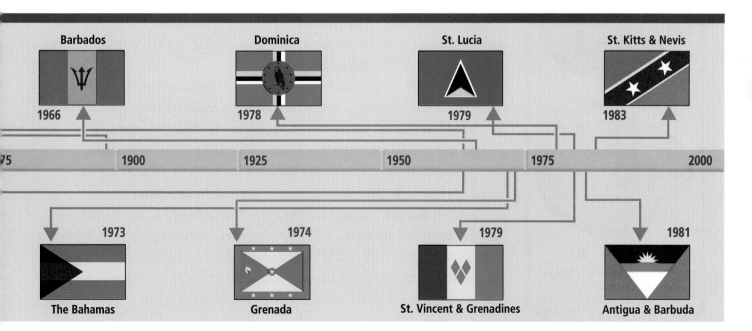

Barbados 1966

Dominica 1978

St. Lucia 1979

St. Kitts & Nevis 1983

75   1900   1925   1950   1975   2000

1973 The Bahamas

1974 Grenada

1979 St. Vincent & Grenadines

1981 Antigua & Barbuda

Economic Growth and Partnerships

Focus *How have changing economies and the enactment of NAFTA helped the economic growth of North America?*

When the North American nations gained their independence, their economies were based on agriculture, mining, and fishing. During the late 1700s and 1800s, most North Americans lived on farms. Today, more than 75 percent of North Americans live in urban areas. They earn their living in manufacturing and service industries, such as education, government, law, finance, real estate, and trade.

Toronto, in the Canadian province of Ontario, is a good example of a city that has experienced this rapid urban growth. It began as a small fur-trading post. Over the years, the city's industries and population grew. Today, it is the capital of Ontario and the largest city in Canada.

In some North American areas, several large cities located near each other grew so much that they began to blend. As the major cities and the areas surrounding them continued to attract people and industries, they started to grow together. Finally the metropolitan areas and the towns between them formed one large urban area, called a **megalopolis**. In the United States, for example, the area that includes Boston, New York City, Philadelphia, Washington, D.C., and Baltimore is a megalopolis sometimes referred to as "Boswash."

NAFTA

On December 17, 1992, the presidents of Canada, the United States, and Mexico signed the North American Free Trade Agreement, or **NAFTA**. The goal of the treaty was to create a "free trade zone," with 370 million consumers in a $6.6 trillion market.

A free trade zone would allow goods and services to be traded freely between the North American nations. Existing trade barriers, such as tariffs, would be eliminated. For example, before NAFTA, Mexicans who bought cars manufactured in the United States had to pay a special tariff — 20 percent of the car's price. This extra tax made it difficult for many people to buy U.S. cars. Instead, they often bought cars from other nations that did not charge an import tax. Under NAFTA, the import tax will be eliminated by the year 2004. Then Mexican consumers will be able to pay less for U.S.-made cars, and the U.S. car manufacturers will be able to sell more cars in Mexico. Supporters of NAFTA believe the free trade zone will benefit consumers and business in all three countries.

This chart shows the varying reactions to NAFTA in 1993. **Chart Skill:** *Did businesses or the general public react more favorably to NAFTA? Why might that be?*

Reactions to NAFTA, 1993

"Based on what you now believe regarding NAFTA's possible future effect on US business and trade, do you support the agreement?"

General Businesses*

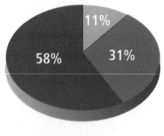

58% 31% 11%

General Public**

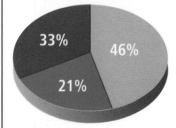

33% 46% 21%

■ Don't know   ■ No   ■ Yes

* 1,529 senior executives, managers and small business owners
** 1,529 registered voters

A New Need for Cooperation

On September 11, 2001, terrorists hijacked passenger airplanes and flew them into the World Trade Center in New York City and the Pentagon outside Washington, D.C. Thousands of people, including hundreds of rescue workers, were killed.

Because of the events of September 11, President George W. Bush declared a war on terrorism. Nations around the world joined the United States in fighting that war. As part of the effort, American and British planes bombed Afghanistan, attacking terrorist bases there.

In addition to fears of more terrorist attacks, people were unsure about the future of the economy. The American economy had stayed strong through the 1990s, even as the economies of other nations weakened. In the first years of the 21st century, however, the American economy began to slow down. The attacks made people worry about an even greater economic decline.

But the attacks and the war against terrorism also created a new spirit of cooperation for many people. Led by the United States, nations around the world combined forces to fight terrorists. At home, Americans showed a renewed patriotism and determination to keep their nation, and its economy, strong and successful.

President George W. Bush, shown here at the site of the World Trade Center, led an international coalition in a war against terrorism.

Lesson Review: Geography

1 Key Vocabulary: Write a sentence about the North American economy using **megalopolis** and **NAFTA.**

2 Focus: What events and leaders were important in independence movements in Haiti and Mexico?

3 Focus: How have changing economies and the enactment of NAFTA helped the economic growth of North America?

4 Critical Thinking: Predict What might have happened to Haiti and Mexico if the American and French Revolutions had not taken place?

5 Theme: Movement and Transformation What economic challenges confront the people of North America and the Caribbean?

6 Citizenship/Research Activity: Find out how Americans reacted to the attacks of September 11, 2001, and to the war on terrorism that followed.

WILD TIMES AT THE WHITE HOUSE

1860s Tad, youngest of Abraham Lincoln's three sons, received a pretend military commission from the Secretary of War. Taking his "job" seriously, Tad wore a Union Army uniform and once bombarded the Cabinet Room door with a toy cannon. Once he broke up a meeting to plead for the life of a turkey planned for Christmas dinner.

1870s Until 1878 children in Washington, D. C., celebrated Easter by rolling dyed eggs on the Capitol grounds. Then Congress passed a law banning the practice. So Lucy Hayes, wife of President Rutherford Hayes, invited the children to hold their egg roll on the White House lawn. It's been held there most years since then.

1880s Irvin and Abram Garfield were 11 and 9 when their father, James Garfield, became President. Although the Garfields lived only a few months in the White House, the boys still had time to stage pillow fights in the East Room. They raced about on the polished floors aboard large-wheeled tricycles called velocipedes.

1890s An assortment of family members joined Benjamin Harrison at the White House. One was grandson Benjamin "Baby" McKee. Baby McKee often rode around the grounds in a goat cart. Once the goat, called His Whiskers, raced out onto Pennsylvania Avenue dragging Baby McKee with it. Chasing after both ran the frock-coated, top-hatted President.

National Geographic

World

COOL Cats!

1900s The lively family of Theodore Roosevelt turned the White House into a playhouse. The younger ones rollerskated through hallways and threw spitballs at presidential portraits. Quentin, the youngest, loved animals. Once he borrowed a selection of snakes from a pet shop. Racing home to show his father, he burst in on an important meeting and dropped the snakes on his father's desk. The meeting ended quickly.

When Archie got the measles, his brother Quentin decided a visit from the family pony would cure him. So he smuggled the animal onto the elevator and into Archie's upstairs bedroom.

1960s When his family arrived at the White House, John Kennedy, Jr., was just 2 months old. Soon he discovered that the President's huge desk in the Oval Office made a perfect fort. "John-John" would crawl around his father's feet and hide behind a panel that opened and closed his fort. The doorman of the White House had to shoo him away so his dad could work.

1970s Amy Carter was 10 when her dad, Jimmy Carter, became President. One Friday Amy had a puzzling homework question about the industrial revolution. Her mother, not understanding the question either, asked an aide to call the Department of Labor for help. On Sunday a truck delivered piles of computer printouts. A Labor Department computer team thought the question came from the President and worked all weekend on it.

Response Activity

History: Write a Biography
History isn't all about adults. Sixteen-year-old Sybil Ludington was a hero in the American Revolutionary War. Write about other young people who made history.

Skills Workshop

Making Maps

Island Hopping

If you are traveling through the Caribbean islands, you'll want to remember interesting facts about each island you visit. Taking photographs and keeping a journal are two ways to record information about a place. Sketching and filling in maps is another great way to capture important details about a place.

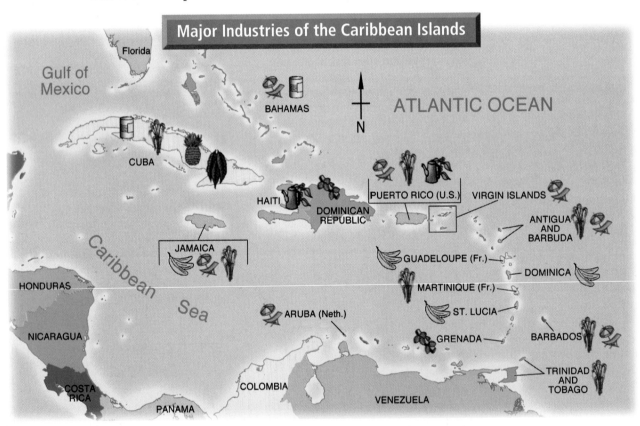

Major Industries of the Caribbean Islands

 Tourism

 Food Processing

 Sugar Cane

 Cacao

 Coffee

 Bananas

 Tobacco

 Pineapple

This map shows the Caribbean islands. Each island has a small picture, or icon, showing its major industry. Haiti has a coffee pot and coffee plants to show that coffee is its major product. What icons do you see on other islands? What do the icons tell you?

① Here's How

• Sketch a map of the world on a large piece of paper. Do not trace the map from a book. Use your memory of continents and oceans to fill in the map. As you sketch, ask yourself questions. What shape is this continent? What shape is this ocean? How big is this continent compared to others? Have I put things in the right places? If necessary, study the world map in an atlas. Don't worry if your map is not perfect.

• Look at the chart to the right. It gives information about ten large islands. Locate each island and write its name on your map. Use an atlas if you need help.

• Decide what symbols or colors you will use to stand for the data in the chart, and create a map key.

• Think of other information you want to find about these islands. You might look for other products, interesting animals, or favorite sports. Use an encyclopedia or almanac to find this information.

• Add the new information to your map. For each island, draw an icon that represents the information you have added.

② Think It Through

How is the chart different from the map? Which method of giving facts would you use in a report? Why?

Island Products

Island	Products	
Greenland	Fish	Metal Ores
Borneo	Rice	Pumpkins
Madagascar	Coffee	Vanilla
Sumatra	Rubber	Tobacco
Honshu	Rice	Tea
Great Britain	Coal	Oil
Sri Lanka	Tea	Coconuts
Hawaii	Sugar cane	Coffee
Newfoundland	Fish	Iron
South Island (New Zealand)	Wool	Apples

③ Use It

1. Using the chart and your map, name the islands located in a) the Atlantic Ocean, b) the Pacific Ocean, c) the Indian Ocean.

2. Looking at the information you have put on your map, decide which of these islands might be most interesting for you to visit. What features make them appealing to you?

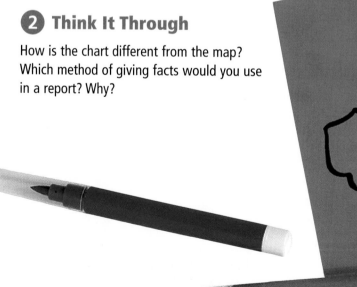

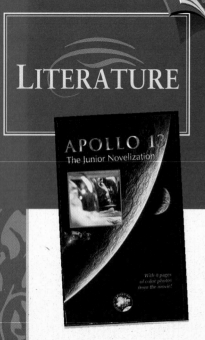

Narrative nonfiction

APOLLO 13

The Junior Novelization

adapted by Dina Anastasio from a motion picture written by William Broyles Junior & Al Reinert and John Sayles

Based on the book Lost Moon by Jim Lovell and Jeffrey Kluger.

The Apollo 13 astronauts would be using the very latest technology to travel to the moon. Why would they choose to name their command module and their lunar landing craft after the voyage of an ancient Greek and a goddess of ancient Egypt?

Perhaps there was something about heading off to set foot on the moon that made them think of the whole history of the world. Humanity had taken many steps through the ages —steps into the unknown, steps toward a better understanding of our planet and the universe.

The steps of Jim Lovell and Fred Haise onto the moon would be that kind of adventure. But first, they had to get there. And to do that, all three of the travelers—and their craft—had to be ready.

Lunar module — *the portion of the spacecraft that would descend to the moon*

Command module — *the portion of the spacecraft that would return to Earth*

The wait was almost over. No more watching. No more second best. The crew of Apollo 13 was going to the moon.

In November of 1969, Alan Shepard had developed an ear infection, and Jim Lovell was chosen to replace him as commander of the mission. Fred Haise would be the lunar module pilot. And Ken Mattingly would be in charge of the command module. Now, just nine days before lift-off, the three astronauts were preparing to cast their own shadows across the golden circle.

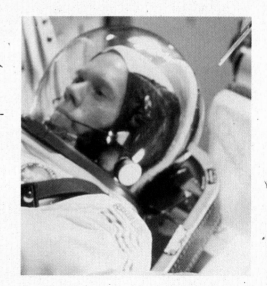

In the movie, Bill Paxton, Kevin Bacon, and Tom Hanks *(left to right)* played astronauts Fred Haise, Jack Swigert, and Jim Lovell.

Inside the command-module simulator, the crew concentrated on the control panel in front of them. The command module simulator was exactly like the command module that would take them to the moon. In it, they could practice every possible maneuver, preparing themselves for any event. Then, when it was time to go inside the actual spacecraft, they would be ready. . . for anything. Right now, they were practicing docking the command module to the lunar excursion module, or LEM for short. Nose to nose. Docking was a way of connecting the two vehicles so that the astronauts could move from one into the other.

The astronauts had decided on the name Odyssey for their command module. It would be a long voyage, and the word "odyssey" meant just that. The command module would be their home until it was time to land on the moon. Then, while Ken stayed in the command module, Jim and Fred would enter the LEM and pilot it down to the moon's surface.

They had decided to call their lunar module Aquarius, after the Egyptian goddess who was thought to have brought life and knowledge to the Nile valley in Egypt. In the same way, the astronauts hoped, Aquarius would bring life to the moon, and knowledge to the people on Earth.

Ken took over the simulator's controls and went to work. Right now, this was his ship. He would have to pilot it while the others were performing their scientific experiments on the moon. He watched the blip that represented the LEM shake on the screen in front of him. The trick was to line up that blip between the crosshairs of the screen. If he could catch it right on the cross, the maneuver would be perfect.

"Houston, we're at one hundred feet and closing," Fred reported over his radio. Fred's job was to read the measurements on the panel in front of him and communicate them to the other astronauts and to Mission Control.

"You're looking good," Mission Control answered.

"Seventy-five feet and closing," Fred announced. "Coming up on docking, Houston."

The Houston controllers turned off their mikes. "Let's blow the aft thrusters on him," one of them suggested.

The other controller nodded in agreement.

It was a test, a simulated test to see the astronauts' response to an emergency situation. If it didn't work, it would be all right . . . this time. But if it didn't work later, when they were in space, it could be a disaster. Better to correct any problems now.

With a flip of a switch, the controller turned off the aft thrusters, the engines on the command module's rear.

Suddenly, the LEM seemed to veer to the right.

"Whoa! I lost something!" Ken announced. "I can't translate left."

"We're losing altitude, Houston," Fred said.

"Barber poles on two isolation valves," Jim suggested. "Try recycling the valves."

"There isn't time for that!" Ken insisted.

"Let me recycle the valves!" Jim said.

"No! I got it. I got it."

"Ten feet." Fred was watching the controls carefully. The lunar module was closing into the center of the crosshairs.

"Ten feet," Ken announced. The LEM was lining up perfectly. He could feel the command module simulator respond to his every touch, as if it were part of his body.

Ken hit a button and listened as the machine simulated a solid THUNK.

"We have capture, Houston," Ken shouted.

"Beautiful maneuver, Odyssey," the controller answered. "You guys are quick."

But Ken didn't think it was perfect. This was one of the most important maneuvers of the flight, and it had to be exactly right. During launch, the LEM rode behind the command module. Once they were in space, the LEM had to be repositioned so that it was nose to nose with the command module and accessible to the astronauts.

If Ken didn't line his ship up exactly, instead of docking with the LEM, the command module's probe could puncture the lunar module's thin foil skin, making it unuseable for a moon landing.

Ken shook his head and sat back in his couch. "I want to do it again," he said, as the others left the simulator. "My rate of turn seems too slow. Listen guys, I want to work it again."

Fred and Jim were used to it. Nothing was ever good enough for Ken. Sometimes it was annoying, but it was also why Ken was one of the best pilots in the program.

Meet the Author

Dina Anastasio wrote this book, but this is a special kind of book: a novelization — a novel based on a movie. This novelization follows the story told by the movie, Apollo 13; and the movie writers based their movie script on a book written by the astronaut, Jim Lovell.

Additional Books to Read

Roll of Thunder, Hear My Cry by Mildred D. Taylor. This book tells the quiet triumphs of an African American family

Portrait of a Farm Family by Raymond Bial. Read about life on a modern farm in the United States

Response Activities

1. **Predict** Ken expected only the very best from anything he did. Why did this make him the best pilot in the program in Jim and Fred's eyes?

2. **Narrative: Write a Dialogue** The astronauts of the Apollo 13 crew took time to decide the names of their command module and their Lunar Excursion Module (LEM). Write a few sentences that could have been part of their discussion.

3. **History: Make a Timeline** From the story and your own research, create a timeline of the Apollo 13 mission.

CHAPTER 23

Chapter Review

Chapter Review Timeline

	1821 Mexico becomes independent				
1750	1800	1850	1900	1950	**2000**

1776 American Revolution
1804 Haiti becomes independent
1867 Canada becomes independent
1992 NAFTA is signed

Summarizing the Main Idea

1. Copy the chart below and fill in the missing information to compare North America to the Caribbean.

	North America	Caribbean
Industry		
Culture		
Climate		
Agriculture		
Landscape		

Vocabulary

2. Create a rebus with each of the following words. Write a paragraph about North America and the Caribbean, but when you use one of the vocabulary words, draw a small picture to represent it instead of writing the word itself. For example, for NAFTA you could show a handshake or a document dated December 17, 1992.

Continental Divide (p. 622)   acid rain (p. 624)   megalopolis (p. 630)
arable (p. 624)   hurricane (p. 625)   NAFTA (p. 630)

Reviewing the Facts

3. What are the landforms, climates, and resources of North America?

4. Why must countries be careful in the way they use their natural resources?

5. Why do people travel within North America and the Caribbean?

6. Describe the changes in the North American economy since the late 1800s.

7. What are the possible benefits of NAFTA? Possible problems?

Skill Review: Making Maps

8 Look at the map on page 623. Write a description of the shapes of Cuba and Hispaniola. Using only your description, try to draw these two places. Compare your map to the one in the book: How accurate is it?

9 Draw an outline of North America and the Caribbean. Draw in your state and an icon for your hometown. Then add three other icons for cities mentioned in this chapter. Use an atlas if you need help finding these places.

Geography Skills

10 Look at the map on page 623. What resources are more likely to be found on the coasts? Which ones are common in the interiors of countries?

11 Using the timeline on pages 628–629, create a map of independence. Create a legend and use three colors or shadings — one for places that achieved independence in the 1700s, another for the 1800s, and a different one for the 1900s.

Critical Thinking

12 **Problem Solving** What solutions can you think of to reduce the amount of acid rain in North America?

13 **Sequence** Create a timeline of the Mexican fight for independence.

14 **Cause and Effect** How might the growth of industry in a city affect its population?

Writing: Citizenship and Economics

15 **Citizenship** Write a short story about a family who lives in an extreme climate in North America or the Caribbean, such as a polar or desert region. How does the environment affect their daily life?

16 **Economics** Suppose you were a supporter or opponent of NAFTA trying to gain public support for your opinion. Design a brochure giving reasons for or against NAFTA.

Activities

Geography/Science Activity
Find out more about a type of natural disaster that strikes North America or the Caribbean. Find examples of this disaster occurring and compare the amounts of damage done to different areas.

Cultures/Arts Activity
In what ways is the spirit of independence that existed during the American Revolution shown in the arts of the United States?

Internet Option

Check the
Internet Social Studies Center
for ideas on how to extend your theme project beyond your classroom.

THEME PROJECT CHECK-IN

To begin your theme project, use the information in this chapter about North America and the Caribbean. Ask yourself these questions:
• What geographic features have caused movement and transformation in this area?
• How have economics affected and been affected by movement and transformation in this area?

North America and the Caribbean: Patterns of Living

Haiti

Haitian art is known for being vibrant and colorful. *Lesson 1, Page 645*

Dominican Republic

One of the oldest churches in the Americas is in the Dominican Republic. *Lesson 1, Page 646*

Emiliano Zapata

Who was this Mexican hero, and what was he famous for? *Lesson 2, Page 651*

Hispaniola: One Island, Two Nations

LESSON 1

Key Vocabulary
Creole
yucca

Main Idea Haiti and the Dominican Republic share cultural influences common to other parts of the Caribbean.

Jacques and Juan both live on the Caribbean island of Hispaniola (his puhn YOH lah), which is divided into two nations — Haiti on the west and the Dominican Republic on the east. Jacques lives in the northern city of Fort Liberté (lee behr TAY) and speaks Haitian **Creole,** a dialect of French. Juan lives in the northern city of Dajabón (dah ha BOHN) and speaks Spanish. Although the two boys live only a few miles from each other, each lives in a different country with a different culture. Despite their different cultures, the two Caribbean peoples are connected by their common island.

◄ A statue by Picasso in Chicago, Illinois.

1960	1980	2000	

City of Montreal	**Statue of Liberty**	**Rosa Parks** 1955
Name the province in Canada where Montreal is located. *Lesson 3, Page 656*	It was a gift from the French to the American people. *Lesson 4, Page 660*	Rosa Parks played an important role in the civil rights movement. *Lesson 4, Page 663*

ATLANTIC OCEAN

CUBA

TORTUGA I.

Windward Passage

Cap Haïtien

20°N

Santiago

DOMINICAN • San Francisco de Macorís

ÎLE DE LA GONÂVE HAITI CORDILLERA CENTRAL REPUBLIC

Port-au-Prince

Santo Domingo

Mona Passage

MASSIF DE LA HOTTE

18°N

Cayes

CARIBBEAN SEA

74°W 72°W

km 0 50 100
mi 0 50 100

Haiti and the Dominican Republic are located on the island of Hispaniola. **Map Skill:** *How many miles is it between the two capitals?*

Hispaniola — The Island of Two Cultures

Focus *How are Haiti and the Dominican Republic different?*

The Caribbean island of Hispaniola is located between the islands of Cuba and Puerto Rico. Beautiful seas surround the 400-mile-long island, which is warmed by tropical breezes. Mountains and rivers stretch across both Haiti and the Dominican Republic.

Haiti

The country of Haiti is as rugged as it is beautiful. The Arawak people who first lived there gave the land its name, which means "land of mountains" or "high ground." Today, most Haitians farm the valleys between the steep mountains or live along the coast.

Most Haitians are descended from Africans. Their enslaved ancestors were brought to Haiti by the French, who once controlled Haiti as a colony. French is the official language that is used in schools and government, but most Haitians speak Haitian Creole. This unique language is a mixture of French and African languages with a little bit of Spanish and English.

French and African cultural traditions are also strong in Haitian religious life. The official religion is Roman Catholicism, but many Haitians practice vodou, which originated in Haiti. Vodou, a West African word meaning "spirit," combines traditional African religions with some Christian elements. For centuries, this religion helped Haitians keep their cultural identity and African heritage alive while enslaved by the French.

The conch shell was a symbol of Haitian independence. It may have been used as a horn instrument to rally the troops. **History:** *Can you name some symbols of the American Revolution?*

Haitian Culture

"They are African," is how one man described the people of Haiti. Descended from Africans forced to Haiti as enslaved persons, Haitians proudly display their roots in African-style clothing, artwork, and food. Their religion and their music also echo with the sounds of Africa.

Haitian Art

The art of Haiti is a rainbow of different styles and techniques. Some of the art of Haiti is world famous for its bold design and bright colors. "The artists here have very different styles," says one of them, "but we all share the same African cultural roots. . . We are all Haitians."

Haitian Music

Haitian bands use special musical instruments called vaccines (vak SANH), *below,* and a grage (GRAZH), *above.*

The Dominican Republic

The people of the Dominican Republic share the island of Hispaniola with their Haitian neighbors, but their culture is very different. A short trip from Port-au-Prince, Haiti, to Santo Domingo, the Dominican capital, would bring you to a place that looks and sounds very different. The Spanish legacy among Dominicans is as strong as the African legacy among Haitians. The Spanish of Dominicans has a definite Caribbean sound. Another legacy from Spain is Roman Catholicism, the religion of most Dominicans. The architecture, food, and art of Dominicans also have a distinctive Spanish style.

This Spanish legacy stretches far back into history. Santo Domingo is the oldest permanent European city in the Americas. Spanish settlers, led by Bartholomew Columbus, a brother of Christopher Columbus, founded the city just four years after the famous explorer came to the Western Hemisphere. Spanish influence has affected the land ever since.

When the Spanish arrived, the present-day Dominican Republic was occupied by the Taino (TY noh) people, a Native American group. Their

Curious Facts

There are more Dominican baseball players on U.S. major- and minor-league teams than from any other Caribbean nation.

legacy remains today in the heritage of Dominicans. Three-fourths of the people have a mixture of Spanish, other European, African, and Native American ancestry. Some Taino traditions continue in the Dominican culture of today. For example, the Taino used the **yucca** (YUHK uh), a plant similar to the potato, for food and as a source of fiber for making rope, baskets, and even soap. Today, Dominicans still use the yucca in cooking and as a material for their handicrafts.

Although Haitians and Dominicans share the island of Hispaniola, relations between the two peoples have not been friendly. After the independence of Haiti in 1804, Dominicans suffered under Haitian rule. Tensions continued until they reached a breaking point in 1844. In that year, Juan Pablo Duarte (DWAHR tay) led the Dominicans in a successful war of independence. The conflict led to strained relations that still continue today between the two countries.

· Tell Me More ·

Dominican Culture

Most people of the Dominican Republic are of mixed race, but their culture is definitely Spanish. Dominican buildings, music, and art reflect Spanish styles. No one has celebrated this legacy more than Joaquín Balaguer (hwah KEEN bah lah GAIR). A poet and author of many books on Dominican history, Balaguer has also been president of the country seven times.

Architecture

The Cathedral of Santo Domingo (shown above) was the first cathedral built in the Americas. It was completed about 30 years after Christopher Columbus's first voyage.

Music

Dominican bands use different musical instruments such as the guiro (GWEE ro), *bottom,* and marimba (ma REEM bah), *top.*

The Caribbean Diaspora

The word *diaspora* (dy AS pur uh) means a scattering of people away from their homeland. The peoples of Hispaniola have experienced dramatic diasporas. Nearly one-fourth of Haitians live outside of Haiti, in cities in North America, Europe, and Africa. Many Dominicans live abroad, too, including a large population that lives, all or some of the time, in New York City.

What has caused these diasporas? A major reason is economic hardship. Haiti is the poorest country in the Western Hemisphere. More than half of the population is unemployed. The Dominican Republic, although better off than Haiti, is also poor. Another reason for the diasporas is political hardship. In the past, both Haiti and the Dominican Republic have suffered under harsh political rule. Many people fled their countries to escape persecution.

The people who have left have not forgotten the island. Those who live abroad send money back home to help their families. They return to Hispaniola as often as they can to visit family and friends. Many of them return home permanently, bringing with them valuable skills and knowledge. One Dominican in New York put it simply: "Everyone is depending on me."

Every year the West Indian Carnival takes place in Brooklyn, New York. People dress up in colorful costumes and parade through the streets.

Lesson Review

1. **Key Vocabulary:** In your own words, describe the terms **Creole** and **yucca**.

2. **Focus:** How are Haiti and the Dominican Republic different?

3. **Critical Thinking: Problem Solving** How might Haiti and the Dominican Republic work together? How would you try to ease the tensions between the two countries?

4. **Theme: Movement and Transformation** How would life be different for a Hispaniolan family now living in the United States?

5. **Geography/Research Activity:** Research the climate and vegetation of Hispaniola and create an illustrated map of the island.

North America and the Caribbean: Patterns of Living   **647**

Mexico: Blending Cultures and Economics

Main Idea Economics in Mexico today reflect influences of past Spanish and Native American cultures.

Walk through the city of Guanajuato (gwa nah HWA toh), nestled in the mountains about 170 miles northwest of Mexico City. You will see a blending of commerce and culture. Guanajuato, the provincial state capital, is famous for its centuries-old gold and silver mines, some of which were worked through the 1980s. The mines helped people and the city thrive in the past. Today, Mexico still relies on its mineral wealth.

Two Cultures, One Economy

Focus *How did Native American and Spanish cultures blend to create a Mexican economy?*

Mining and farming were economic activities already practiced by Aztecs and other Native Americans in Mexico when the Spanish arrived. The Aztecs were excellent farmers who used fertilizers and irrigation to grow corn and beans. Some were merchants who traveled outside the Aztec Empire to exchange goods with traders from other places. In the Aztec marketplace, skilled craftsworkers traded pottery and woven goods for cacao beans and jewels brought in by outside visitors.

Under Spanish rule, silver and gold mining and farming were major activities. The Spanish grew wheat and sugar cane on large ranches. They built sugar mills and shipyards. They traded cotton, silk, and other goods to Spain in exchange for Spanish products.

In Mexico, celery is being harvested for export to the United States and other countries.

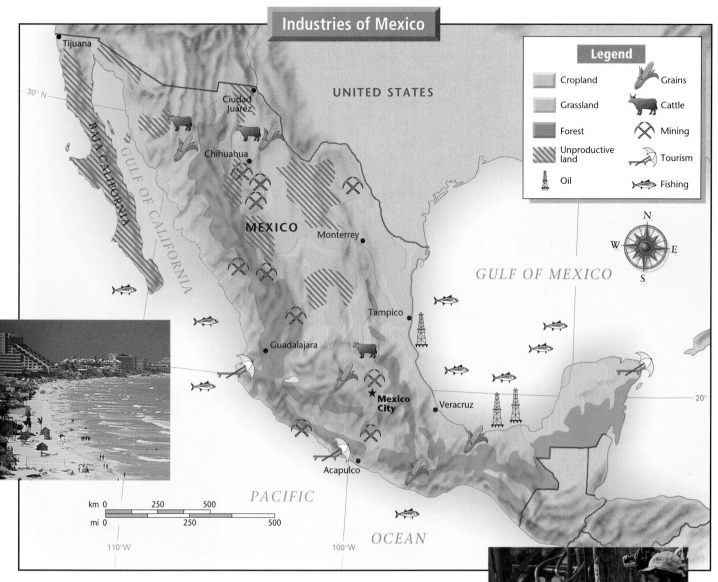

Industries of Mexico

Legend

- Cropland
- Grassland
- Forest
- Unproductive land
- Oil
- Grains
- Cattle
- Mining
- Tourism
- Fishing

UNITED STATES

Tijuana

30° N

Ciudad Juárez

Chihuahua

BAJA CALIFORNIA

GULF OF CALIFORNIA

MEXICO

Monterrey

GULF OF MEXICO

Tampico

Guadalajara

Mexico City

Veracruz

20°

Acapulco

PACIFIC

OCEAN

km 0   250   500
mi 0   250   500

110°W   100°W

Economic Activity Today

Modern Mexico's economy is based mainly on petroleum, natural gas, and tourism. Mexico is one of the world's leading exporters of oil and petroleum products. Other main industries include steel manufacturing and textiles.

Tourism is one of the most important industries in Mexico. Vacationers from all over the world come to Mexico to enjoy the scenery and weather and visit ancient sites. They also buy silver jewelry, woven blankets and mats, painted pottery, and handcrafted art items. Much of the artwork in Mexico is influenced by Aztec and other native cultures of the region.

Even the food they eat reminds Mexicans of their history. For centuries, Aztec and other North American groups ate maize (corn), chilis, and cocoa. The Spanish introduced beef and other foods to Mexico. Today, these ingredients combine to create a world-famous national cuisine. Mexican culture travels around the world.

Mexico is one of the world's leading exporters of oil and petroleum products. Tourism is also an important part of Mexico's economy. **Map Skill:** *On which coast are most of the oil fields? Which cities are popular tourist attractions?*

Skilled craftsworkers weave a variety of fabrics creating blankets and clothing. Many of the designs on the woven blankets and clothes are influenced by the art of Native American cultures.

Rural and Urban Life in Mexico

Focus *How do people make a living in the rural and urban areas of Mexico?*

Mexico contains a mix of rural and urban areas. The rural regions include beautiful open spaces, dense forests, and rugged mountains. They are dotted by many farms, ranches, and small villages. The majority of Mexicans, however, live in cities. Many of these urban areas have grown from small communities. Others have grown up along the border between Mexico and the United States, where people cross back and forth between the two countries every day.

Rural Life

Many Mexicans live in the countryside, or *campo*, and are called **campesinos**. Some campesinos are farmers. They farm small plots, raising corn (the staple food of Mexico), beans, potatoes, tomatoes, cotton, and other crops. A **staple food** is a basic food that almost all people consume. Other campesinos raise livestock such as cattle for beef and dairy products. Sheep, pigs, and chickens are also found on farms.

Large families are considered a blessing by campesinos, both for the joy they provide and the extra hands to do the work. All family members pitch in, tending the plants and animals and doing household chores. Boys are expected to help farm and tend livestock. Girls perform household tasks and help with selling the produce.

Villages are centers of campesino life. Many Mexican villages were former Spanish settlements. In most of them a Roman Catholic church is the main structure. Other villages have remained truly Native American villages, where life has not changed much since before the arrival of the

Spanish. Whether of Spanish or Native American origin, almost every Mexican village has a local marketplace where campesinos meet once a week to bargain, barter, buy, and socialize.

Most villagers are poor, and their small farms often cannot support their large families. As a result, many campesinos are forced to leave their land and their villages and migrate to cities to find work and a better life.

Urban Life

The majority of Mexicans live in cities. About 50 Mexican cities have a population of more than 100,000 people, and some are larger than 500,000. Many of these cities are concentrated on the "waist of Mexico." This is a band that stretches from Guadalajara (gwah dahl a HAH rah) in the west, across Mexico City in the center, to Veracruz in the east. Find the region and these cities on the map on page 649.

Esteban Mendez Gonzalez is a typical campesino who left a farm to move to the city: "We came because we thought it would be heaven here. But it's not, is it?" More than 30 percent of the work force is unemployed, and many people live in poverty. Campesinos who move to the city, like Gonzalez, live as street merchants or do poorly paying jobs. Millions of them live in shantytowns in and near large cities. These places are called "lost cities."

For many people, the cities of Mexico are places of wealth and beauty. There is a growing middle class and a small group of very rich Mexican citizens. They enjoy all the good things cities have to offer: modern homes, shopping centers, theaters, good roads, hospitals, and schools. But the wealthy also share city problems. One of the worst problems is air pollution in Mexico City, caused by too many vehicles. Each year

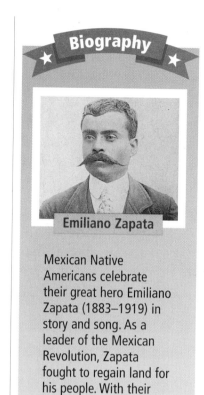

Biography

Emiliano Zapata

Mexican Native Americans celebrate their great hero Emiliano Zapata (1883–1919) in story and song. As a leader of the Mexican Revolution, Zapata fought to regain land for his people. With their battle cry, "Land and liberty!" Zapata's peasant army seized land and distributed it among Mexico's poor.

Diego Rivera (1886–1957) was a Mexican artist who portrayed the mixed history and culture of the Mexican people. He believed that art belonged to the people and created many works in public places. He also painted many murals for public buildings. Rivera was deeply influenced by both Native American and Spanish artists. This fountain he designed is outside Mexico City's waterworks.

A Blending of Cultures in Mexico

The Plaza of the Three Cultures

Mexico City is one of the largest cities in human history — home to 22 million people. The Plaza of the Three Cultures (Plaza de las Tres Culturas) is a famous landmark in Mexico City visited by millions of tourists each year. Here visitors can see at a glance evidence of Aztec culture, Spanish culture, and the modern mixture. A plaque at the site contains the following inscription:

"On the 13th day of August, 1521, defended by the heroic Cuauhtémoc (kwow TEH mohk) (Montezuma's successor), Tlatelolco fell under the power of Hernán Cortés. It was neither a triumph nor a defeat. It was the painful birth of the mixed race that is the Mexico of today."

1 Spanish

The Spanish contribution to Mexican culture is called to mind by the ruins of a Roman Catholic church. This church was built in 1609 — about 80 years after the Spanish conquered Tenochtitlán and began to build Mexico City.

2 Aztec

The Aztec legacy of Mexico is symbolized by the ruins of Aztec temples. These magnificent structures were centers of Aztec religious life. The Spanish destroyed them and used the rubble for building.

3 Modern Fusion

Towering over the old Spanish and Aztec ruins are new buildings built by the Mexican government.

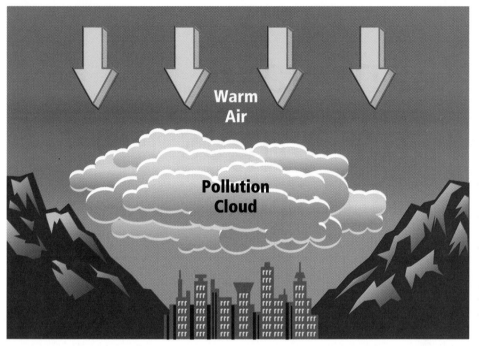

The illustration shows how the air in Mexico City becomes polluted. The pollution problem in Mexico City is made worse by geography. The mountains surrounding the city prevent winds from carrying away the polluted air. Other cities that are surrounded by mountains have similar air pollution problems.

many people are hospitalized due to pollution-related illnesses. Mexico City's government is addressing this problem by requiring stickers on each automobile, indicating which day of the week that vehicle is prohibited from being on the roadways.

NAFTA

The North American Free Trade Agreement (NAFTA) eliminated almost all trade barriers between Mexico and the United States and Canada. Signed into law in 1993, NAFTA was designed to help the economy of all three countries. It provides jobs for Mexicans in companies that manufacture goods for export to the United States and Canada.

Cities in Mexico do face social and economic challenges. The people of Mexico, campesinos and city dwellers alike, have a strong culture on which to build a brighter future.

Lesson Review

1. **Key Vocabulary:** Write about Mexican life using the word campesinos.

2. **Focus:** How did Native American and Spanish cultures blend to create a Mexican economy?

3. **Focus:** How do people make a living in the rural and urban areas of Mexico?

4. **Critical Thinking: Compare** How is the day in the life of a campesino different from and similar to your own?

5. **Geography/Economics:** How are Mexico's natural resources important to its future well-being?

6. **Citizenship/Writing Activity:** Suppose you are the mayor of a large city in Mexico. List three actions you will take to improve the lives of the people who live in the "lost cities."

Canada: Challenges to Unity

Main Idea Canadians have maintained a society made up of diverse groups of people.

The border between Canada and the United States is unlike any other international boundary. It is the longest undefended international border in the world. The border stretches 3,900 miles across the entire width of the North American continent. There are no armies, few guards, and fewer fences separating these two traditional friends.

Nations Within a Nation

Focus *How did the British and French control Canada's colonial past?*

Although Canada is the second-largest country in the world, its name is a Huron word meaning "a small village." Today, the major Native American groups, including the Inuit (IHN yoo iht), make up just two percent of the population. These peoples originally had the land to themselves. This quickly changed when the Europeans set their sights on the riches of the Western Hemisphere.

The British and French in Canada

Explorer Jacques Cartier (cart YAY) claimed eastern Canada for France in 1534. Over the next 200 years, the French explored Canada and established many settlements, including Québec (kwih BECK) (1608) and Montreal (mahn tree AWL) (1642). They prized the region for its rich coastal fishing and as a source of furs. Seeking greater wealth and power, the French tried to control more of North America. Confident in their claim, they called the land "New France."

This did not sit well with the British. They, too, claimed much of present-day Canada for themselves. John Cabot, an Italian sailing for the British, had actually landed in Canada before the French. He claimed the land for England in 1497. The British continually expanded their presence in North America through exploration and settlement. In 1670, they established the Hudson's Bay Company, which competed with the French in the valuable fur-trading business.

Soon, the French and the British were poised for war. Conflicting claims to the fur trade, territory, and fishing rights, and a history of conflict, finally drove the two countries to fight several wars. The final conflict, the Seven Years' War, was won by the British in 1763. The two countries signed the Treaty of Paris, in which all of France's Canadian land was handed over to the British.

When the treaty was signed, the 70,000 French-speaking people in Québec came under British control. Because of their large numbers and pride, the French-speaking people kept their culture alive. The French influence in Québec has lasted to this day.

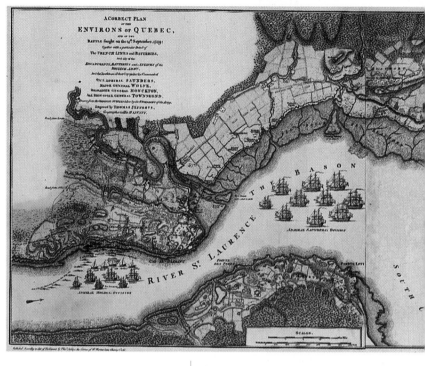

This map was published in 1759. It shows British ships sailing in the St. Lawrence River. The ships are carrying soldiers to do battle with the French in Québec. **Map Skill:** *Compare the map above with a present-day map. How are the maps different? How are they alike?*

A Mosaic of Peoples

Focus *What groups make up the Canadian population?*

Some people compare the population of Canada to a mosaic, a single picture made up of many small tiles. The largest pieces in the Canadian mosaic of over 28 million people are French and British. Today, the British legacy continues. Queen Elizabeth II of Great Britain is the queen of Canada, though Canada became an independent nation on July 1, 1867.

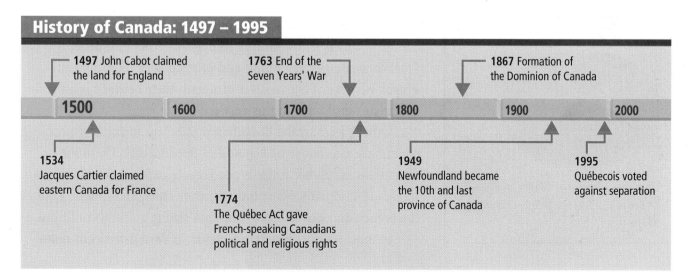

History of Canada: 1497 – 1995

1497 John Cabot claimed the land for England

1763 End of the Seven Years' War

1867 Formation of the Dominion of Canada

1500   1600   1700   1800   1900   2000

1534 Jacques Cartier claimed eastern Canada for France

1774 The Québec Act gave French-speaking Canadians political and religious rights

1949 Newfoundland became the 10th and last province of Canada

1995 Québecois voted against separation

Montreal attracts thousands of tourists from around the world. This section of the city is called Jacques Cartier.

Canada is now a member of the British Commonwealth of Nations. The commonwealth is made up of more than 40 independent nations that have lived under British law and government in the past.

Ethnic Groups in Canada

Today, Québec is unique in Canada. Most of its people are descended from the original French settlers. They are called French Canadians or Québecois (kay beh KWAH). Canada has two official languages, English and French. In Québec, however, many outdoor signs are written in French, and most children attend French schools. "Bonjour" (bahn JOOR) — good day or hello — is the common greeting. The art, architecture, and food of the region have a distinct French style. In religion, too, the legacy is French. Many Canadians are Protestant, like their British ancestors. Most Québecois are Roman Catholic, like the French.

Québec is powerful in Canada, largely because it is home to one-fourth of the population. Although it is a province, its parliament refers to itself as a National Assembly. Québec even celebrates its own national holiday. Throughout Canadian history, there have been strong movements within Québec to become independent. This movement, called **separatism,** is the desire for a people to separate themselves socially, culturally, and politically from the rest of a country. Why is the separatist feeling so strong in Québec? Québecois are fiercely proud and protective of their distinct French heritage. Their wish to maintain their heritage is an issue Canadians deal with to this very day.

Other pieces of the Canadian mosaic are formed by people commonly referred to as Canada's "third force." These are Canadians of neither English nor French ancestry. They include Italians, Ukrainians, West Indians, Pakistanis, and others. Like the French and British, they maintain strong cultural traditions.

In much of northwestern Canada, Native Americans make

This pie chart shows the different ethnic groups in Canada. **Chart Skill:** *Which ethnic group represents 20% of the population?*

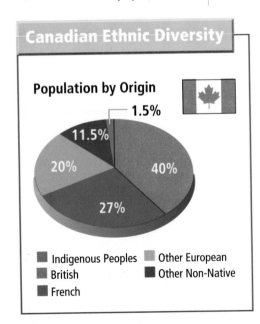

Canadian Ethnic Diversity

Population by Origin

1.5%
11.5%
20%
40%
27%

- Indigenous Peoples
- British
- French
- Other European
- Other Non-Native

up the majority of the population. As in the United States, they were pushed off their land and forced to live on reservations. This has led many Native American groups to support their own separatist movements. The Inuit, for example, have fought for and won political control over a huge tract of northern Canada, called Nunavut ("our land").

Most Canadians were born in Canada but have kept alive the ways of life of their immigrant ancestors. Recently, many immigrants have come across the Pacific from China and Japan. Today in coastal Vancouver, there are numerous Chinese residents. The combining of several individual cultures is called multiculturalism. Multiculturalism is encouraged by the Canadian government. Canada declared itself a multicultural society in 1971 with these words:

> "Cultural variety is the very essence of Canadian identity, and every ethnic group has the right to preserve and develop its own culture and values within a Canadian context."

At times, the Canadian mosaic has threatened to break apart into individual tiles. Separatist movements, especially in Québec, are an ongoing threat to national unity. In 1995, Québec voted narrowly to stay in Canada. The mosaic can serve as a model for separation and unity: David Lam, a Chinese immigrant who became a government official, said, "I believe in multiculturalism because it adds to our strength."

Ask Yourself

Suppose you are a French Canadian citizen living in Québec.

Would you vote to separate from the rest of Canada? Why or why not?

? ? ? ? ? ? ? ? ? ? ? ? ? ?

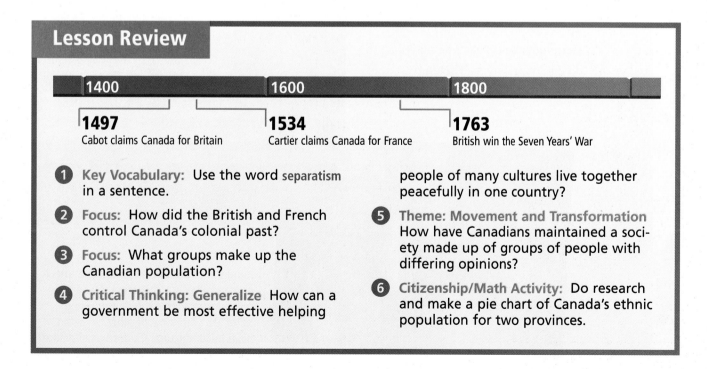

Lesson Review

1400	1600	1800

1497
Cabot claims Canada for Britain

1534
Cartier claims Canada for France

1763
British win the Seven Years' War

1. **Key Vocabulary:** Use the word separatism in a sentence.

2. **Focus:** How did the British and French control Canada's colonial past?

3. **Focus:** What groups make up the Canadian population?

4. **Critical Thinking: Generalize** How can a government be most effective helping

people of many cultures live together peacefully in one country?

5. **Theme: Movement and Transformation** How have Canadians maintained a society made up of groups of people with differing opinions?

6. **Citizenship/Math Activity:** Do research and make a pie chart of Canada's ethnic population for two provinces.

Human Systems

How Did Immigrants Affect Vancouver?

Vancouver once seemed like a remote place at the end of Canada. It was far away from the large cities in eastern Canada, not in the center of things, like Toronto, Montreal or Québec. But — thanks largely to immigration from Hong Kong — Vancouver has acquired a new image as the gateway between North America and Asia.

Migration from Hong Kong to Vancouver started in the mid 1980s. In 1984, Great Britain agreed to turn the colony of Hong Kong over to the People's Republic of China in 1997. Many residents of Hong Kong began to think of settling elsewhere.

Because of incentives offered by the Canadian government, many people leaving Hong Kong chose to live in Vancouver. They have brought about a startling transformation of the city.

Immigrants from Hong Kong have affected Vancouver's architecture. Many new buildings resemble the ones in Hong Kong. Do you know of other cities that have buildings with Chinese architecture?

Math Connection

Vancouver had a population of about 1.8 million people in 1995. About 200,000 people of Chinese descent lived there. About what percentage of the people of Vancouver had ancestors from China?

① Vancouver

Chinese Neighborhood
Bilingual signs are now a common sight, as are Chinese language newspapers. Whole neighborhoods have become largely Chinese in the space of a few years.

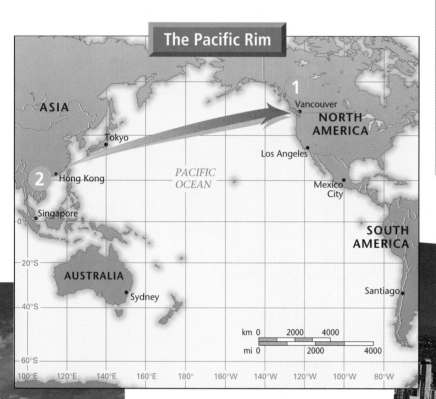

The Pacific Rim

Vancouver is linked more closely to Hong Kong than to other Pacific Rim cities.
Map Skill: *How far apart are Vancouver and Hong Kong?*

Chinese immigration has affected the way people in Vancouver think about their city. Today, increasing numbers of Vancouver residents perceive their city as part of the eastern edge of the Pacific Rim.

Research Activity

① Research what impact immigrants from Hong Kong have had on the economy of Vancouver.

② Look for magazine and newspaper articles that show how the economy of Vancouver improved.

③ Write a brief report. Share your findings with the rest of the class.

② Hong Kong

Commuting by Air
Some Chinese immigrants return to Hong Kong for work, while keeping their residences in Vancouver. They are known as "astronauts," because they spend so much time in the air. Do you know of people that travel long distances to work?

LESSON 4

Key Vocabulary

discrimination

civil rights

Key Events

1865 Slavery outlawed

1920 Women win the right to vote

1924 Native Americans given citizenship

1954 Segregation declared unconstitutional

1990 Americans with Disabilities Act

The Statue of Liberty.

The United States: Strength in Diversity

Main Idea Diversity in the United States can exist because Americans strive to uphold the Constitution's ideals of liberty and justice for all.

The more than 280 million people of the United States have roots in more than 150 different countries and practice more than 50 religions. Many speak a language other than English at home. The food, music, and art of nearly every world culture are available across the land.

The United States is also the world's most powerful nation. It stands among the leading democracies and has the largest economy in the world. How has such a diverse nation managed to stay together, let alone become so successful? The answer is found in the U.S. political system, based on the Constitution. This document guarantees every U.S. citizen freedom and equality under the law.

From Many, One Nation

Focus *Why is the United States a diverse nation?*

You have probably heard the United States referred to as "a nation of immigrants," and it is true. This immigrant history has helped make the United States the diverse nation it is.

Since about 1600, when European colonization began, more than 60 million people have immigrated from all over the world to the present-day United States. The first group of immigrants has come to be called "the old migration."

The Old Migration

During colonial times (1607–1776), about 60 percent of immigrants were English. Others from the British Isles included Scottish, Irish, and Welsh peoples. People came in fewer numbers from other countries in northwestern Europe, but still they came from France, Germany, and Sweden. Most were searching for better lives for themselves. Some sought religious freedom. All of them left their mark on Colonial America.

One group of immigrants did not come to America by choice. Enslaved Africans were forced to come. By 1808, when importing slaves became illegal, about 700,000 Africans had been brought to America against their will. Individuals suffered terribly, but as a group they managed to persevere and contribute greatly to the nation.

Between 1820 and 1870, another wave of immigrants arrived on American shores. Many of these seven million people were Irish, most of whom came to escape famine in their land. Another large group were German. They left poverty and political unrest in their native land. During this period, immigrants came from China too. Chinese immigrants did much of the work on the Transcontinental Railroad, which linked a young United States together in 1869.

The New Migration

Between the 1880s and 1920s, "the new migration" of immigrants came to the United States. You can see how large their numbers were from the chart on page 662. What distinguished these "new" immigrants from the "old" immigrants were their countries of origin. These new travelers came chiefly from countries in southern and eastern Europe. The population of the United States swelled with Polish, Italian, Austrian, Hungarian, Czech, Slovak, and other peoples. Like earlier immigrants, most came to escape the poverty of their homelands. More than two million Jews came to the United States during this time to escape religious persecution.

Chinese, Japanese, and Filipino people immigrated across the Pacific from Asia. Some immigrants traveled from Mexico for economic opportunity and to escape political unrest there.

(Bottom left) A large number of immigrants came to America between the 1880s and 1920s from southern and eastern Europe. Most of them went to Ellis Island, a reception center for immigrants in New York.
(Bottom right) Many Asian immigrants came from Japan, Korea, China, Vietnam, and the Philippines.

The graph shows the number of immigrants who came yearly to the United States. **Chart Skill:** *What years show the lowest number of immigrants? The highest?*

Modern Migration

The United States continues to attract immigrants. In recent years, many newcomers to the United States have come from Asia, including Vietnam, the Philippines, Korea, and China. Many more have come from Latin America. The desire to come to the United States is so strong that hundreds of thousands of people enter the United States each year from Mexico, Central America, and the Caribbean islands.

"We are the ones who built America," said one immigrant. From building railroads to writing books, from serving in the armed forces to leading the government, immigrants — Americans — have built a great country. Unfortunately, these diverse peoples have also had to struggle to uphold their rights.

Upholding Our Rights

Focus *How does the Constitution provide civil rights for all U.S. citizens?*

Despite their countless contributions, immigrants and their descendants have all faced discrimination. **Discrimination** is the unfair treatment of people based on their membership in a certain group. Discrimination is a tragic fact of human history: virtually all groups have had to fight it. Native Americans were forced onto reservations. Mexican Americans have been denied housing. Women have been denied jobs. Jews have been denied an education.

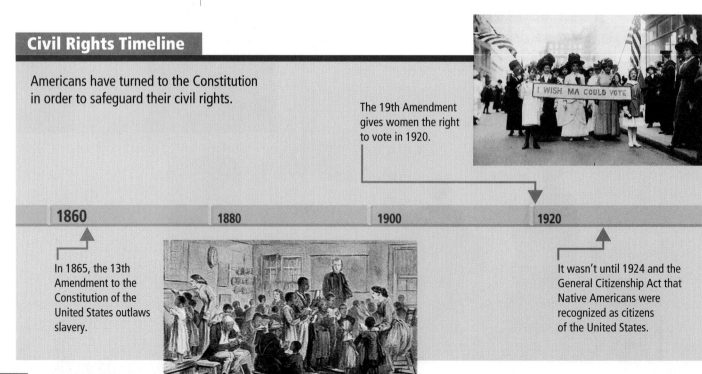

Civil Rights Timeline

Americans have turned to the Constitution in order to safeguard their civil rights.

The 19th Amendment gives women the right to vote in 1920.

I WISH MA COULD VOTE

1860   1880   1900   1920

In 1865, the 13th Amendment to the Constitution of the United States outlaws slavery.

It wasn't until 1924 and the General Citizenship Act that Native Americans were recognized as citizens of the United States.

African Americans have faced discrimination. Forced to come here through slavery, they were still treated as second-class citizens for a hundred years after becoming free in 1865. Even after the Civil War, segregation laws forced African Americans to attend separate schools and use separate public facilities. The civil rights movement of the 1950s and 1960s assured African Americans the rights they were guaranteed under the Constitution.

A 1954 Supreme Court case gained much attention for the civil rights movement. **Civil rights** are rights guaranteed to citizens by the Constitution and the laws of the nation. The story is simple: Seven-year-old Linda Brown, an African American in Topeka, Kansas, was forced to attend a school far away from her home. The school in her neighborhood was reserved for white students. Linda's father challenged this segregation law in court. He argued that it was unfair to make children attend separate schools just because of the color of their skin.

The Supreme Court agreed. The Court decided that Linda had been denied "the equal protection of the laws" guaranteed by the 14th Amendment to the Constitution. That decision, *Brown v. Board of Education,* stands as a turning point in America. It inspired millions of citizens — Hispanic Americans, women, Asian Americans, and others — to work for civil rights.

The first words of the Constitution are "We the people of the United States." You now know how diverse "we the people" are. You have learned that American citizens have fought for their rights. The Constitution, with its promises of "equal protection of the laws,"

Rosa Parks

Rosa Parks was born in 1913 in Alabama. She is an African American who was arrested in 1955 for refusing to give up her seat on a bus to a white passenger. This began a bus boycott in Montgomery, Alabama, which helped begin the modern civil rights movement in the United States.

With the passing of the Civil Rights Law of 1964, Congress outlaws segregation in all public places.

In 1990, the Americans with Disabilities Act is signed into law.

1940	1960	1980	2000

In 1954, the U.S. Supreme Court rules that segregation in public schools is unconstitutional.

In 1974, Congress passes the Indian Self-Determination and Education Assistance Act.

"justice," and "the blessings of liberty" provides a framework for achieving these rights.

On the 200th anniversary of the Constitution, author Roger Wilkins described his personal feelings about the historic document.

> "I viewed the Constitution as a Promise, a basket . . . of things I'd heard about. [They] added up in my young mind, to promises of freedom and equality and justice to all of us 'We the people,' in a country great enough to dream up those promises in the first place."

The earth seems to be getting smaller. High-speed communication systems and advances in transportation have made it easy for diverse peoples to communicate around the world.

Looking Toward the Future

As the world enters a new millennium, a span of one thousand years, it seems to appear smaller every day through advances in transportation and communication. This brings the diverse peoples of the earth into closer contact. How can diversity and freedom successfully combine in the United States and throughout the world in the future? How can people like you make a difference?

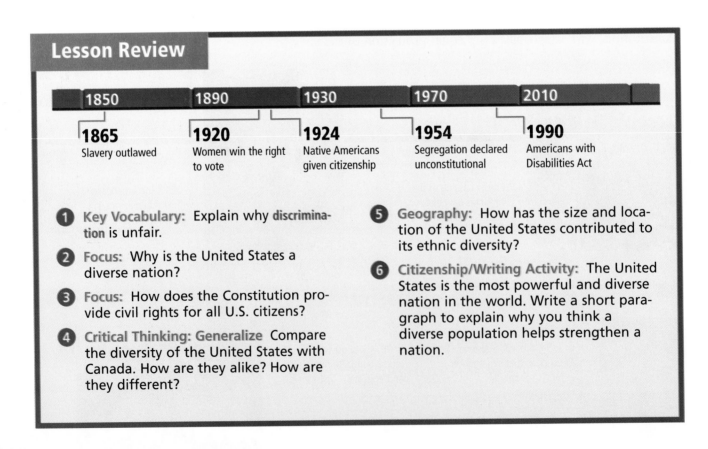

Lesson Review

1850	1890	1930	1970	2010

1865
Slavery outlawed

1920
Women win the right to vote

1924
Native Americans given citizenship

1954
Segregation declared unconstitutional

1990
Americans with Disabilities Act

❶ **Key Vocabulary:** Explain why **discrimination** is unfair.

❷ **Focus:** Why is the United States a diverse nation?

❸ **Focus:** How does the Constitution provide civil rights for all U.S. citizens?

❹ **Critical Thinking: Generalize** Compare the diversity of the United States with Canada. How are they alike? How are they different?

❺ **Geography:** How has the size and location of the United States contributed to its ethnic diversity?

❻ **Citizenship/Writing Activity:** The United States is the most powerful and diverse nation in the world. Write a short paragraph to explain why you think a diverse population helps strengthen a nation.

Gathering Information Using Questionnaires

You Asked for It

Name one subject that all people know a lot about. Themselves, of course! Now name one way you can get people to give you information about their favorite subject. It's easy — use a **questionnaire**. A questionnaire can help you find out interesting and valuable facts and opinions. Once you've gathered your information, you can summarize it in a report, or you can simplify the results using a graph or table. Before you begin, choose carefully the people you will survey and the questions you will ask.

1 Here's How

- Decide what information you want to collect, and from whom.

- Write down the questions you will ask. It's important to ask questions that have simple answers.

- The simplest questions ask for a "yes" or "no" answer. ("Were your parents born in the United States?")

- Other questions ask for one-word answers. ("Where was your mother born?")

- For opinions, ask people to answer using number ratings. ("How important is basketball to you?" 1=not important, 2 = fairly important, 3 = extremely important) If you don't use numbers, it will be difficult to organize the answers.

- Distribute the questionnaire, and tell people when to return it.

- Sort the answers to each question into categories.

- Draw conclusions and make comparisons based on the information.

2 Think It Through

How does an interview differ from a questionnaire? When do you think a questionnaire might be more useful than an interview?

3 Use It

1. Prepare a questionnaire that you can use to interview people about their heritage.

2. Conduct the interviews.

3. Create a chart showing the results of your questionnaire.

★ CITIZENSHIP ★

Making Decisions

What Are You Proud Of?

Do you ever wonder why "The Star-Spangled Banner" is sung before a baseball game? Are fireworks displays just fun, or are there other reasons why we have them each Fourth of July? Every country has patriotic traditions like these. Think about why countries adopt pledges of allegiance and national anthems as you read the case study below.

Case Study

The Story of the Pledge of Allegiance

Francis Bellamy probably never imagined that his words would still be famous after more than a century. In 1892, he wrote an article on patriotism for a young-people's magazine, *The Youth's Companion*. The article featured a pledge for schoolchildren. It became known as "The Pledge of Allegiance." In 1942, the United States government officially recognized the Pledge. In 1954, President Dwight D.

Eisenhower asked Congress to add the words, *under God*. Now we say: "I pledge allegiance to the flag of the United States of America and to the Republic for which it stands, one Nation under God, indivisible, with liberty and justice for all."

In Texas, people also say a state pledge: "Honor the Texas Flag: I pledge allegiance to thee, Texas, one and indivisible." Many states sing songs to honor their flags. In Alaska, people

sing to "the eight stars of gold on a field of blue," "the brilliant stars in the northern sky," and "the simple flag of a last frontier."

Take Action

Flags, pledges, and anthems are symbols and expressions of feelings for a nation or state and what it stands for. The United States anthem and Pledge of Allegiance speak of liberty, loyalty, and unity.

Suppose you and your classmates wanted a new pledge of allegiance or anthem for your class or school. What beliefs would you like to celebrate in your pledge or anthem? Here are some steps to take:

1 Divide into small groups to decide and list what beliefs might go into a pledge or anthem.

2 Decide what words or images could represent those beliefs.

3 Choose the beliefs, words, and images you want to include in the pledge or anthem. Write your new versions.

4 Share your pledge or anthem with the class. Is it similar to other groups' pledges and anthems? How do you explain the similarities and differences?

Tips for Making Decisions

- Different people have different styles of doing things. People who are faster or louder may or may not be smarter. People who are quiet may have much to contribute. Make an effort to include everyone in a group.
- Different cultures have different styles. For example, arguing may be considered rude in one culture but acceptable in another. Even small things, like looking people in the eye, differ from culture to culture.
- Use clear, plain language to express yourself.

Research Activity

Another place where people from different states show their pride is on their license plates! What is the story behind your state license plate? Does it have a motto or picture, or both? Find out about your state license plate, and find some other license plates, too. (Can you find plates from all 50 states?) Pick out some you like. Then design a license plate for your community, school, or state. Decide on a motto and picture. Share your finished design with the class and explain your choices.

Chapter Review

CHAPTER 24

Chapter Review Timeline

1450	**1560**	**1670**	**1780**	**1890**	**2000**

1534 Cartier claims Canada for France

1497 Cabot claims Canada for Britain

1867 Canada becomes independent

1920 U.S. women win the right to vote

1990 Americans with Disabilities Act

Summarizing the Main Idea

1 Copy the chart below and complete it to describe the history of independence of each country.

Country	Colony of	Independence	Challenges
Haiti			
Dominican Republic			
Mexico	Spain	1821	poverty, pollution
Canada			

Vocabulary

2 Using at least three of these words, write a letter to the editor of a newspaper or magazine describing an issue that you think is important.

Creole (p. 643)　　　　staple food (p. 650)　　　　discrimination (p. 662)

campesinos (p. 650)　　separatism (p. 656)　　　　civil rights (p. 663)

Reviewing the Facts

3 What are the differences between Haiti and the Dominican Republic?

4 What is the "Caribbean Diaspora"?

5 Why are people from Mexico's countryside moving to the cities?

6 Why did the French and the British fight over Canada?

7 How is Québec unique among the many provinces of Canada?

8 List the cultures that contribute to Canada's multiculturalism.

9 Describe the differences between the old and new migration of peoples to the United States.

10 Who is Linda Brown, and what happened to her in 1954?

11 Why is it a good idea to use a numbers rating for opinion questions on a questionnaire?

12 If you were to create a questionnaire to send to Native Americans in the Dominican Republic, Canada, and the United States, what would your questions be? What information would you want to find out?

Geography Skills

13 Copy an outline of a map of the world on a piece of paper. Shade in the areas where you would find the cultures you have learned.

14 Look at the map on page 649. What are Mexico's natural boundaries? Are they the same as Mexico's political boundaries?

Critical Thinking

15 **Conclude** Would you rather visit Haiti or the Dominican Republic? Explain your choice.

16 **Interpret** How does farming in Mexico demonstrate both a Native American and a Spanish influence?

17 **Problem Solving** How might the students in a school in Québec show pride in both a French heritage and a Canadian nationality?

18 **Compare Then and Now** Why did immigrants come to the United States in the 1600s? In the 1800s? Now? Are the reasons the same, or are they different?

Writing: Citizenship and Cultures

19 **Citizenship** Write a personal narrative describing what it is like to go to a foreign country. If you have never been in another country, pick a place in this book and explain why you would like to visit there.

20 **Cultures** Suppose you are a Dominican who has moved to New York City. Write a letter to relatives in the Dominican Republic. Describe what you miss most, and then tell them about an exciting new experience you had.

Activities

Citizenship/Music Activity
"We Shall Overcome" was a famous song popular during the civil rights movement. Find a copy of the words. Does this song still have meaning for people today?

Cultures/Research Activity
Find out more about Nunavut, the land the Inuit have won political control over in Canada. Write a short report describing what its boundaries are and what is happening there today.

Internet Option

Check the **Internet Social Studies Center** for ideas on how to extend your theme project beyond your classroom.

THEME PROJECT CHECK-IN

Use the information in this chapter about some of the individual nations of North America and the Caribbean to complete your theme project. Consider these questions:
• What important events have caused movement and transformation in this country?
• What geographic features have affected movement and transformation there?
• What political, economic, and cultural factors have affected this country?

Reference Databank

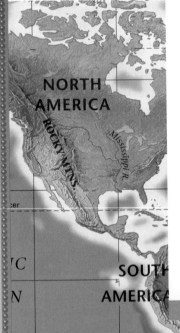

Handbook for Learners

As you look through this book, you'll notice that it is filled with maps, graphs, paintings, photographs, and diagrams. These images bear out an old Chinese proverb that says, "One picture is worth more than ten thousand words." One map can show us the route Marco Polo took from Italy to China. One graph impresses us with how the world's population has skyrocketed in the last 150 years. Maps, graphs, timelines, photographs, and diagrams expand our understanding of other times, places, and people.

Contents

Reviewing Map and Globe Skills

Reading Maps

The world is a very large place. At its widest, along the equator, the earth is almost 25,000 miles around. What if you wanted to find the location of one small part of the world, such as the Central American nation of Costa Rica? To see where Costa Rica is in relation to the world's large landmasses, you can look at a world map. If you want to take a closer look at Costa Rica, use a map that enlarges this area. The inset map of Costa Rica on the next page tells us about the land and its uses.

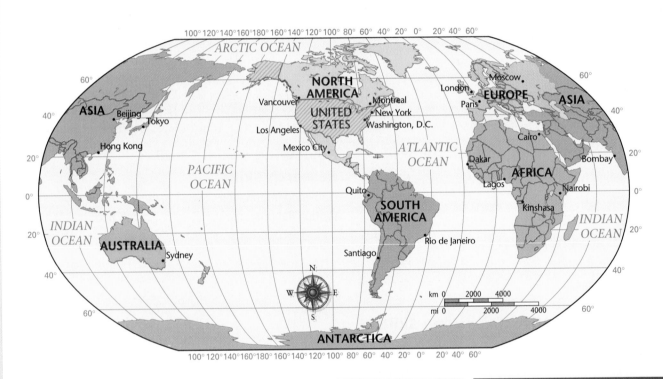

Use It

Look at the world map. Choose a city, such as Cairo or Vancouver. Describe where it is in relation to the United States, South America, Europe, and Asia.

Going Further

Make a map of your state that includes a compass rose, a scale, and an inset map that provides a closer look at your town. Add a locator map locating your state in the United States.

The world map to the left was drawn with the help of satellites, which you can see around the illustration of the globe at right. The United States has developed the Global Positioning System. It allows us to determine the position of a place or country using signals from satellites. A map made with the help of satellites gives us an extremely accurate view of an area's shape and size.

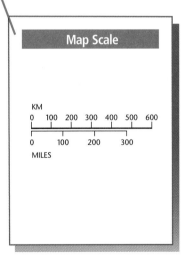

Costa Rica

NICARAGUA

Lake Nicaragua

CARIBBEAN SEA

COSTA RICA

Liberia

Alajuela San José Puerto Limón
Puntarenas Cartago Turrialba
10°N
86°W

PACIFIC OCEAN

PANAMA

8°N

84°W   82°W

Legend

National park
Ranching
Rain forest
Other tropical forests
Commercial farming

North America

Atlantic Ocean

Costa Rica   South America

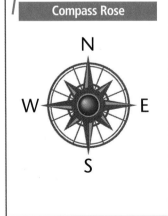

Compass Rose

N

W   E

S

A **compass rose** is a direction finder. The tips of the compass rose point to the four cardinal directions — north, south, east, and west. Some compass roses also identify intermediate directions.

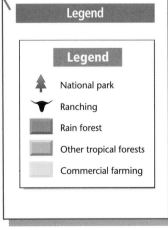

Legend

Legend

National park
Ranching
Rain forest
Other tropical forests
Commercial farming

A **legend** identifies and explains the symbols on the map. Symbols used can include small pictures, lines, dots, circles, and numbers. Color can also be used to distinguish land and water, for example.

Map Scale

KM
0   100 200 300 400 500 600

0   100   200   300
MILES

A **map scale** tells you how much real distance on the earth is represented by the distances shown on the map. The maps in this book show scale with two lines — one for miles and one for kilometers.

Dividing Up the Globe

A map is a flat picture of an area that is not really flat. Because the earth is round, you can get a better idea of the size and location of land and water areas by looking at a globe. A globe shows that the earth is shaped like a ball, or sphere. In studying the earth, geographers divide its sphere into halves, or **hemispheres**. They also use latitude and longitude. Lines of latitude and longitude, which make an imaginary grid around the earth, allow us to pinpoint the exact location of any place. This grid can be seen on the map at right.

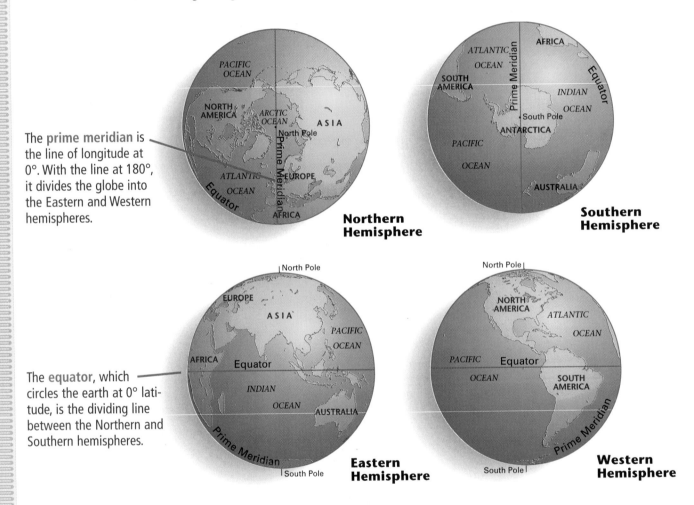

The **prime meridian** is the line of longitude at 0°. With the line at 180°, it divides the globe into the Eastern and Western hemispheres.

Northern Hemisphere

Southern Hemisphere

The **equator**, which circles the earth at 0° latitude, is the dividing line between the Northern and Southern hemispheres.

Eastern Hemisphere

Western Hemisphere

Use It

Continents can be in more than one hemisphere. Asia, for instance, is in the Northern Hemisphere and the Eastern Hemisphere. How many hemispheres is Antarctica in?

Going Further

What are the exact coordinates of your city or town? Use an atlas to find the latitude and longitude in degrees and minutes.

World Political Divisions

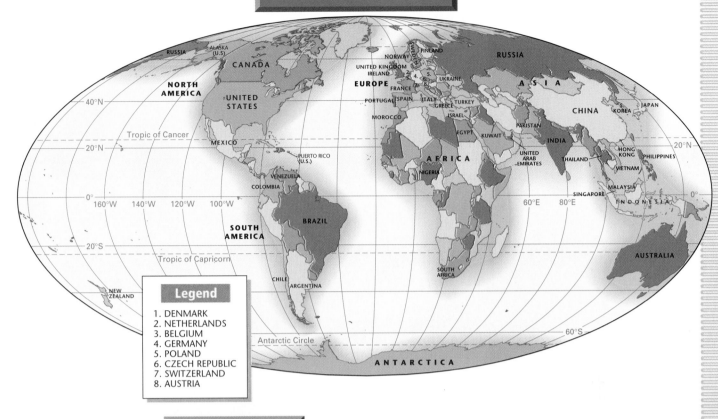

Legend

1. DENMARK
2. NETHERLANDS
3. BELGIUM
4. GERMANY
5. POLAND
6. CZECH REPUBLIC
7. SWITZERLAND
8. AUSTRIA

The Netherlands

Key

— National boundary

— Provincial boundary

⊛ National capital

• City

Mapmakers use the 360 **degrees** in a sphere to create a "global address" system with latitude and longitude. You will find these numbers along the edges of many maps. To give the exact location of a place, you need to use its **coordinates** of latitude and longitude. Each degree is divided into 60 **minutes**, written with the sign '. The line of latitude halfway between 50'N and 51'N is 50'30"N. Most of the time we use only degrees to identify a location. However, when you are trying to locate places using a map of a small area like The Netherlands, including minutes can be useful.

Maps of the Land

Do you want to see where it is sunny? Where gold is mined? Special purpose maps can show this kind of information and more. Special purpose maps illustrate specific information. The maps on these pages are special purpose maps that show physical information about parts of the earth.

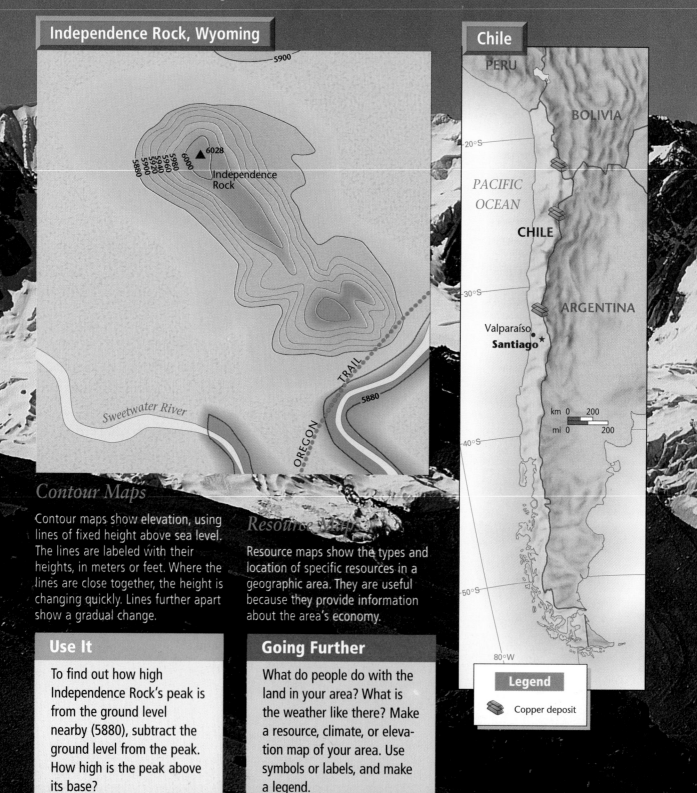

Independence Rock, Wyoming

5900

6028
Independence Rock

5980
5960
5940
5920
5900
5880

6000

Sweetwater River

OREGON TRAIL

5880

Chile

PERU

BOLIVIA

20°S

PACIFIC OCEAN

CHILE

30°S

ARGENTINA

Valparaíso
Santiago ★

40°S

km 0   200
mi 0   200

50°S

80°W

Legend

Copper deposit

Contour Maps

Contour maps show elevation, using lines of fixed height above sea level. The lines are labeled with their heights, in meters or feet. Where the lines are close together, the height is changing quickly. Lines further apart show a gradual change.

Resource Maps

Resource maps show the types and location of specific resources in a geographic area. They are useful because they provide information about the area's economy.

Use It

To find out how high Independence Rock's peak is from the ground level nearby (5880), subtract the ground level from the peak. How high is the peak above its base?

Going Further

What do people do with the land in your area? What is the weather like there? Make a resource, climate, or elevation map of your area. Use symbols or labels, and make a legend.

The Andes: Elevations

Legend

Land Elevations

Feet	Meters
13,120	4,000
6,560	2,000
1,640	500
650	200
0	0
Below sea level	Below sea level

▲ Mountain peak

★ National capital

Elevation Maps

Elevation maps show the height of mountains, plains, and any other landforms in an area. They often show the elevation of very high points with numbers. Elevation maps are color-coded to represent a range of feet or meters above or below sea level. An elevation of "0" means that the land is at sea level.

The Andes: Climate

Legend

- Tropical rain forest
- Tropical savanna
- Semiarid
- Desert (arid)
- Mediterranean
- Humid subtropical
- Marine
- Highland

Climate Maps

Climate maps tell you about the average weather in a place, such as average temperature or hours of sunshine. By providing this data, a climate map gives us clues about the kinds of crops that can be grown and the uses people can make of the land.

Maps About People

Special purpose maps can also help you learn about people and their ways of life around the world. Maps can show how people live in a particular part of the world, what crops they raise, and what languages they speak.

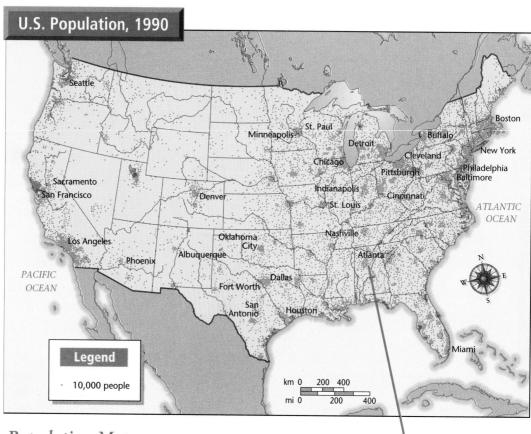

U.S. Population, 1990

Legend

· 10,000 people

Population Maps

Population maps show you how many people live in an area. These maps may use color or dots to represent the number of people living in an area. On this map, one dot represents 10,000 people.

Clusters of dots indicate areas with dense populations. By examining the color or dot distribution patterns, you can see which areas are most densely populated.

Use It

What can you learn from the population map of the United States? Compare two areas and describe why they might have smaller or larger populations.

Going Further

List five maps you could make to show human activity in your state. What would you show on a culture map? A population map? An economic map? Make a key for each map you would like to draw.

Economic Maps

Economic maps tell you about an area's economy — how people earn a living, what industries there are, how much money families have.

Culture Maps

Culture maps give information about the ways people live. On this map you can learn about the cultures that immigrants to America brought with them when they settled in the Dakota Territory.

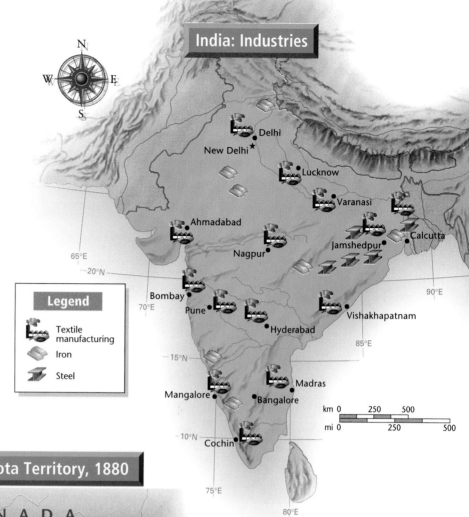

India: Industries

Delhi
New Delhi ★
Lucknow
Varanasi
Ahmadabad
Nagpur
Jamshedpur
Calcutta
Bombay
Pune
Hyderabad
Vishakhapatnam
Mangalore
Bangalore
Madras
Cochin

65°E
20°N
70°E
15°N
10°N
75°E
80°E
85°E
90°E

Legend

Textile manufacturing

Iron

Steel

km 0   250   500
mi 0   250   500

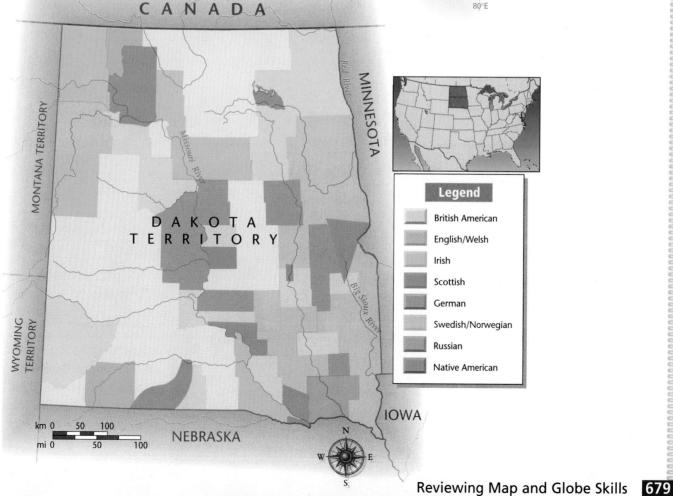

Immigration to the Dakota Territory, 1880

CANADA

MONTANA TERRITORY

Missouri River

Red River

MINNESOTA

DAKOTA TERRITORY

WYOMING TERRITORY

Big Sioux River

IOWA

NEBRASKA

km 0   50   100
mi 0   50   100

Legend

British American

English/Welsh

Irish

Scottish

German

Swedish/Norwegian

Russian

Native American

Historical Maps

To understand the world you live in today, you are learning about the world as it was in the past. Maps are a key that can open many doors to the history of our world. Some of these maps were drawn long ago. By studying them we can better understand how people saw the world in another time. Modern mapmakers can also show us the past by creating maps that show a place at a certain date in history or that show change over time.

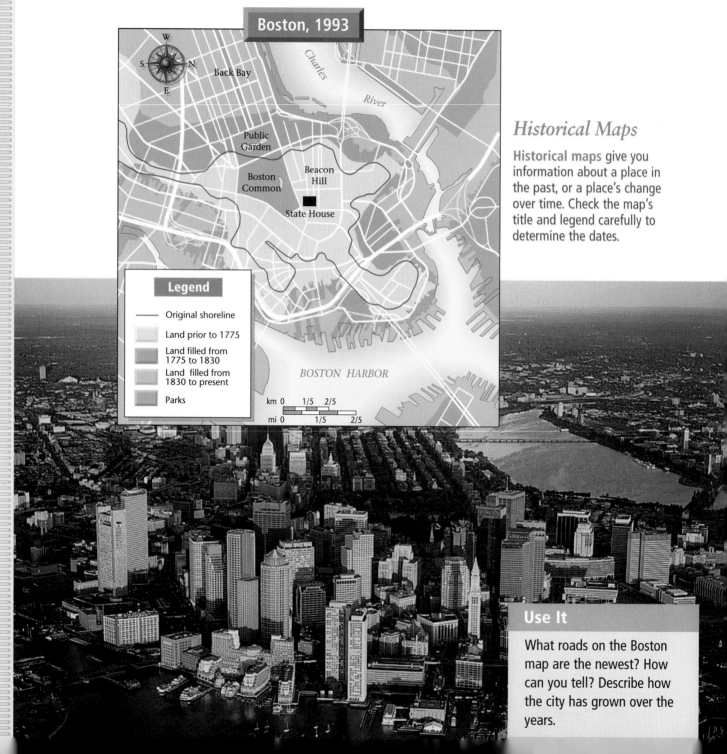

Boston, 1993

Back Bay

Charles River

Public Garden

Boston Common

Beacon Hill

State House

Legend

—— Original shoreline

Land prior to 1775

Land filled from 1775 to 1830

Land filled from 1830 to present

Parks

BOSTON HARBOR

km 0   1/5   2/5
mi 0   1/5   2/5

Historical Maps

Historical maps give you information about a place in the past, or a place's change over time. Check the map's title and legend carefully to determine the dates.

Use It

What roads on the Boston map are the newest? How can you tell? Describe how the city has grown over the years.

Story Maps

How did the cattle ranchers get their stock to the railroads in the 1800s? While you could find the answer to this question in books and encyclopedias, you can also find it on some maps. A story map shows you how something happened and where.

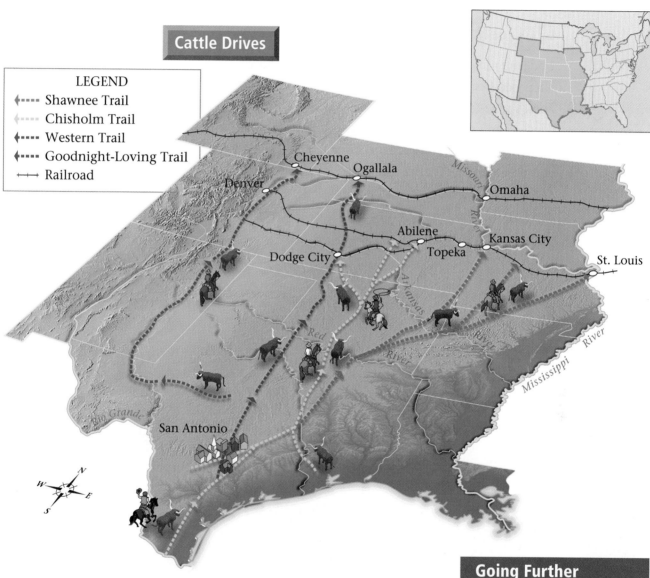

Cattle Drives

LEGEND
- ◄---- Shawnee Trail
- ◄---- Chisholm Trail
- ◄---- Western Trail
- ◄---- Goodnight-Loving Trail
- ┼──┼ Railroad

Cheyenne
Ogallala
Denver
Omaha
Abilene
Kansas City
Dodge City
Topeka
St. Louis
Missouri River
Arkansas
Red River
Mississippi River
Rio Grande
San Antonio

Story Maps

Story maps tell their story as a sequence of events. Some have numbered captions that provide the details of the narrative. Pictures of people, places, or events help you follow the story.

Going Further

Look in the newspaper and create a story map for one of the articles on the front page. Read through the article first, making notes of the important people and places in the story. Then prepare a map, adding pictures and numbered captions.

Reviewing Visual Learning Skills

Organizing Information

Understanding time — what happened when and what happened first — is an important skill for this book's time-travel trip around the world. Clocks and time zones are not the only ways to "tell time." Calendars can tell you the time of year, and timelines can tell you when events occurred and in what order.

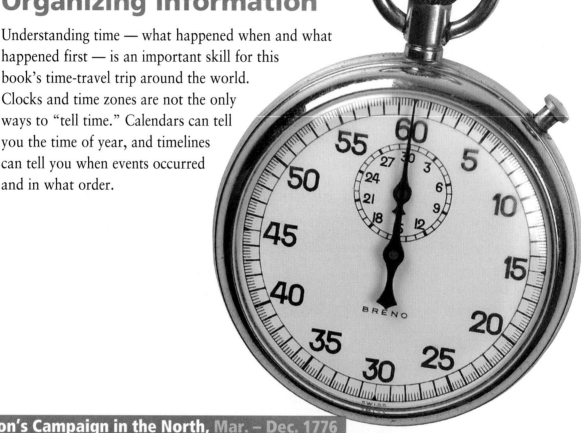

Washington's Campaign in the North, Mar. – Dec. 1776

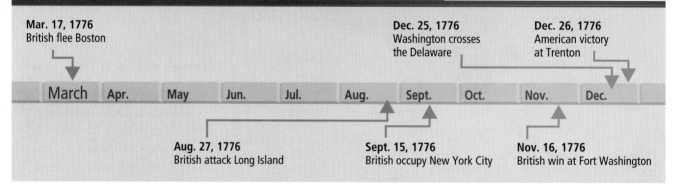

Mar. 17, 1776
British flee Boston

Dec. 25, 1776
Washington crosses
the Delaware

Dec. 26, 1776
American victory
at Trenton

March | Apr. | May | Jun. | Jul. | Aug. | Sept. | Oct. | Nov. | Dec.

Aug. 27, 1776
British attack Long Island

Sept. 15, 1776
British occupy New York City

Nov. 16, 1776
British win at Fort Washington

Timelines Timelines like the one shown above put important events in chronological order along a vertical or horizontal line. *Chronological order* is the order in which the events happened, from earliest to most recent.

The span of years that is covered in a timeline is divided into equal parts. This timeline is divided into month intervals.

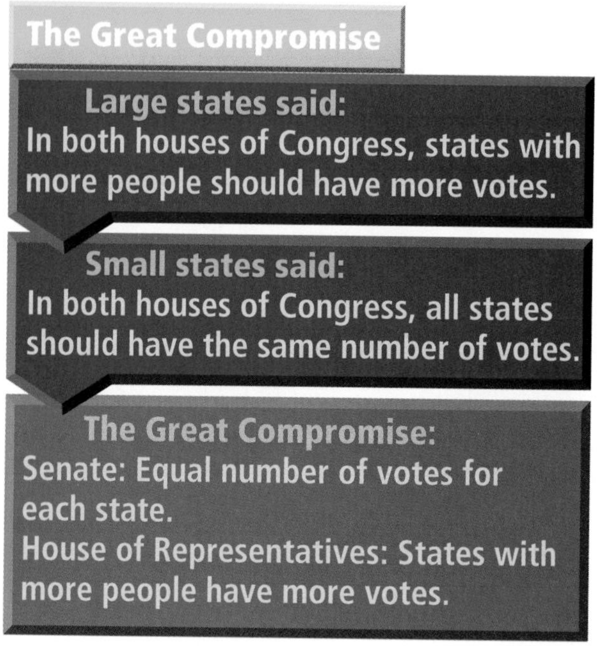

The Great Compromise

Large states said:
In both houses of Congress, states with more people should have more votes.

Small states said:
In both houses of Congress, all states should have the same number of votes.

The Great Compromise:
Senate: Equal number of votes for each state.
House of Representatives: States with more people have more votes.

Cause-and-Effect Charts

A cause-and-effect chart shows the relationships between one event or factor — the cause — and what results from it — the effect. Arrows help you link cause and effect. Here the causes — the desires of the different states — led to the effect, the formation of the Senate and the House of Representatives.

OLYMPIC COMMITTEE • approves the sports to be included • selects the host cities • meets annually and before the games

EXECUTIVE BOARD OF THE OLYMPIC COMMITTEE
• handles the committee's business between meetings • elected by the committee

ORGANIZING COMMITTEE OF THE HOST CITY
• helps to plan the games
• decides the sports to be included

INTERNATIONAL GOVERNING BODY OF EACH OLYMPIC SPORT • helps to plan the games • conducts games and appoints judges and referees

Organizational Charts

An organizational chart shows you the relationship among the people who work at many levels of an organization. Who has power? Who reports to whom? This chart on the International Olympic Committee, the governing body of the Olympic Games, also gives you information about people's duties.

Use It

If you were part of a Host City Organizing Committee for the Olympics to whom would you report? If you were on the Executive Board, to whom would you report?

Going Further

Create an organizational chart of your school's administration.

Graphs

One way to make sense of some statistics is to show them visually so that they are easy to read and understand. The best way to do this is with graphs. Graphs are a special way of picturing data. They allow us to make comparisons and to see change over time.

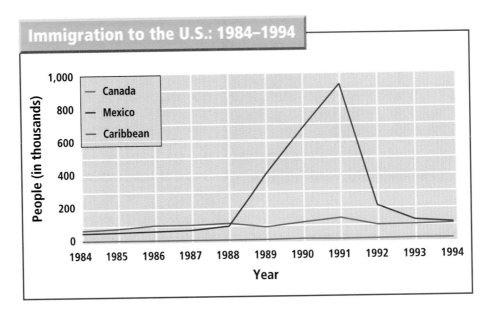

Immigration to the U.S.: 1984–1994

People (in thousands)

Legend:
— Canada
— Mexico
— Caribbean

Year

Line Graphs

Line graphs show change over time, using points that are connected by a line. Multiple line graphs show changes in different sets of numbers over the same period of time. By studying the direction of the lines, you can see trends, or directions, and make predictions.

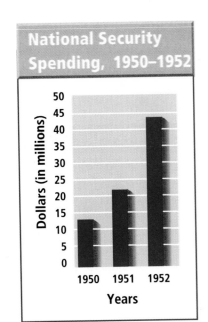

National Security Spending, 1950–1952

Dollars (in millions)

Years

Bar Graphs

A **bar graph** uses bars of different heights or lengths to help you compare data. Bar graphs might compare data for one year or allow you to compare across years.

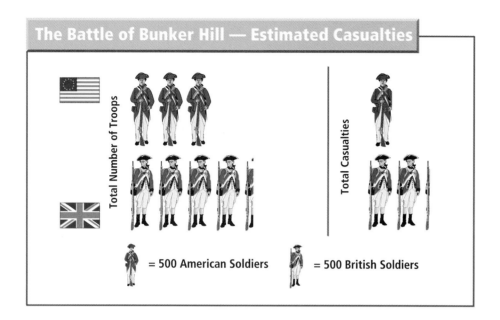

The Battle of Bunker Hill — Estimated Casualties

Total Number of Troops

Total Casualties

 = 500 American Soldiers   = 500 British Soldiers

Picture Graphs

A picture graph uses pictures to represent information. On the picture graph above, each figure represents 500 American or British soldiers.

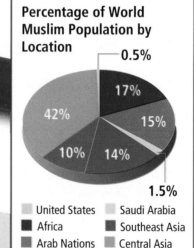

World Muslim Population

Percentage of World Muslim Population by Location

0.5%
17%
15%
42%
10% 14%
1.5%

United States   Saudi Arabia
Africa   Southeast Asia
Arab Nations   Central Asia
Other Nations

Circle Graphs

A circle graph divides data into parts of a whole. Why do you think these graphs are sometimes called pie graphs? You can compare the "pieces" of the pie and see how they compare to the whole. On this circle graph you can compare the Muslim populations in various locations in the world.

Use It

On the picture graph, you can see the number of American and British soldiers. Which side had the most soldiers? Which had the most casualties?

Going Further

Do some research, maybe on the number of people per cars in your community, or the number of people per house. Make a picture graph showing your results.

Illustrations and Diagrams

There are other ways that pictures can show information. Sometimes we need to show the process of change, not just the result. One good way to do this is to make a diagram. The arrows in a **flow chart** show which way the action is going. **Diagrams** are drawings that can show how the parts of something are arranged, or how the parts are related. A diagram can also show changes that have been made to these parts. Another way to get information is to compare kinds of **illustrations**, like photographs or paintings.

Formation of an Oxbow Lake

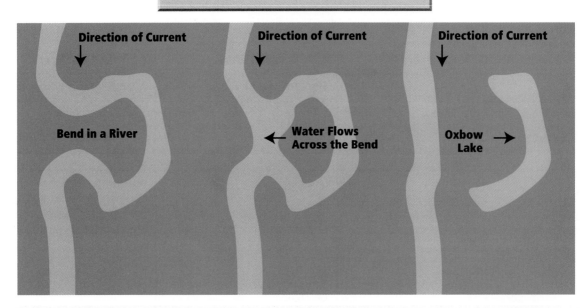

Direction of Current

Direction of Current

Direction of Current

Bend in a River

Water Flows Across the Bend

Oxbow Lake

Flow Charts

Flow charts are diagrams with arrows to show the direction of the process from stage to stage. In this flow chart, you see the stages a river goes through in the formation of an oxbow lake.

Use It

Make a flow chart of how to turn a page in a book. How does putting arrows in make it clearer?

Going Further

Create a cutaway diagram of a building you know. This might be your home, school, local library, or recreational center. Make sure you give your diagram a title, label rooms or areas, and provide a key if necessary.

Illustrations

When you look at the *photograph* and the *diagram* of the tepee, you can see the differences and similarities among the different kinds of illustrations. You can use those differences and similarities to see change over time and make comparisons.

Cutaway Diagrams

Cutaway diagrams are drawings that "cut off" the outside of something to show an inside view. Cutaway diagrams can help you understand how something is built or how it works.

The red line indicates the line where the tepee has been "cut away" so that we can see the inside.

Reviewing Social Studies Research Skills

Gathering Information

Part of your social studies journey is a trip through history. You need to know what's happened in the past to understand the present and prepare for the future. There's a lot to learn about this world that we live in! Who lived when? What did they do and think? Where can you get information? Research skills can help you find answers to some of your questions. There are many sources. You can look in books, use the computer, and talk with people who have firsthand knowledge of a place, event, or time. You could conduct a survey, interview someone, or write a letter to request information.

Have you ever taken a trip on a jet plane?
√yes
no
Where did you go?
to another country
√to another state
How long did you stay?
√less than 1 week
1-2 weeks
more than 2 weeks

Interviews

Interviews help you find out as much as you can about one person's experience.

Surveys

A survey is useful when you want to get information and opinions from a large number of people.

Use It

Make a survey card you would use to ask people about an event in recent history, like the landing on the moon or the fall of the Berlin Wall.

Going Further

Find a primary source or historical document and write a secondary text about it. Remember that you can find other information on the source from other places.

When you're doing research, you will come across primary and secondary sources. These can be used for different things. A primary source can help you understand the events or situation of the time. You can use a secondary source to get another point of view on the situation.

We the People of the United States, in Order to form a more perfect Union, establish Justice, insure domestic Tranquility, provide for the common defense, promote the general Welfare, and secure the Blessings of Liberty to ourselves and our Posterity, do ordain and establish this Constitution for the United States of America.

Primary Sources

A primary source is a firsthand account, based on the personal experiences of the writer, or a historical document, like the Constitution of the United States. Here we have the famous preamble to the Constitution.

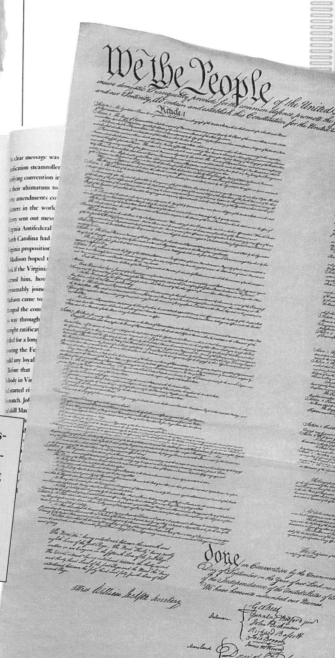

"The Sacred Fire of Liberty"

"Liberty. In the form of the Goddess of Youth giving Support to the Bald Eagle."
Print and Photographs Division

An emotional outburst followed the first announcement of the completed Constitution. This allegorical engraving, depicting the Goddess of Youth in the form of a young woman, symbolized the feeling that America was about to launch a great venture among the nations of the world.

Jefferson and John Adams read the trans-Atlantic mails and their American newspapers with unusual interest with the coming of winter in 1787. They exchanged letters with comments on the proposed Constitution and found themselves in agreement. "What think you of a Declaration of Rights?" Adams asked. "Should not such a Thing have preceeded the Model?" Jefferson agreed, and his republican instincts forced him to say that the president created by the Constitution "seems a bad edition of a Polish king." Jefferson was equally frank in writing Madison his first impressions, listing first the constitutional features he liked (separation of powers, the taxing power in Congress), and then moving to "what I do not like. First the omission of a bill of rights." To another Virginian, Jefferson suggested that the necessary nine states ought to ratify the Constitution while the last four held out for amendments. Silently, Madison must have wished Jefferson had not been so indefatigable a penman.

"Jefferson and John Adams read the trans-Atlantic mails and their American newspapers with unusual interest with the coming of winter in 1787. They exchanged letters with comments on the proposed Constitution and found themselves in agreement."

Secondary Sources

A secondary source is an account written by someone who was not present at the events described, or an article or text about the primary source. This is from a book about the Constitution.

Writing Reports

One of the best places to find information on any subject is a library. There you'll find resources of all kinds, including books, encyclopedias, atlases, films and videos, newspapers, and magazines. More than one of these sources may be helpful to you in your research.

To find resources that would help you write a report on governments, for example, begin with the catalogue. Today, library catalogues come in many forms. Some list books and other sources on cards. Others put their collections in books or on a computer.

The library catalogue lists books by subject, author, and title. When giving you information about a book or other material, the catalogue will also give you a call number. Libraries arrange their material on shelves in numerical order. The call number helps you to find the sources you are looking for.

The catalogue also identifies materials that are in media other than books. For example, videos are usually labeled "Video" before the call number. Videos and other media may not be on open shelves in the library. You may have to ask a librarian to get these materials for you.

This is an example of a card in the card catalogue. The books are listed by author, subject, and title, with publishing information and their locations in the library system.

```
                Clowns.

jY       Sobol, Harriet Langsam.
             Clowns / by Harriet Langsam So-
         bol ; photographs by Patricia Agre.
         - New York : Coward, McCann & Geoghegan,
         c1982.

             SUMMARY: Follows the activities
         of clowns as they dance, juggle, skate,
         put on costumes and makeup, look silly
         or sad, and exercise their special magic.
             ISBN 0-698-20558-8 : $9.95
```

Use It

How many different kinds of media are there? Make a list of them and write down what kind of information you can get from each one.

Writing a good report requires organization. You need to take careful notes about what you read. You need to make a good outline before writing. And you need to write in a clear and interesting way.

He made the builders start the main stairway to th...

He moved the front door to the north side of the building and turned the old entrance area into the Blue Room. (p. 64)

 **1** To organize your research, make a list of the questions you want your report to answer. Then write each question at the top of the notecard.

 **2** Write down the information you find to answer each question. Carefully note the title, author, and pages of the books you use.

The White House in the Ear...

I. John and Abigail Adams were t... occupants of the White House.
A. The White House was... they moved in in Nov...
B. There was no laundr... were hung up to dry.
C. There was a shortage... house was very cold.

II. Thomas Jefferson changed the Whit... it more livable.
A. He had the main stai... floor built.
B. He moved the front door to...

 **3** When you have the information you need, organize your notecards into groups by topic. Then you can begin an outline like this one. Use Roman numerals for the main ideas. Use capital letters for the supporting details.

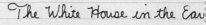
Going Further

Choose a topic for a report. Make a list of the questions you would like answered. Arrange your questions into groups, and prepare an outline that shows what the main idea of your report will be.

4 Use your outline to write the report. A good report includes an introduction, the main body of the report, and a conclusion. In the introduction, tell the reader the main ideas of your report. Present details about each idea in the body of the report. Summarize those ideas in the conclusion.

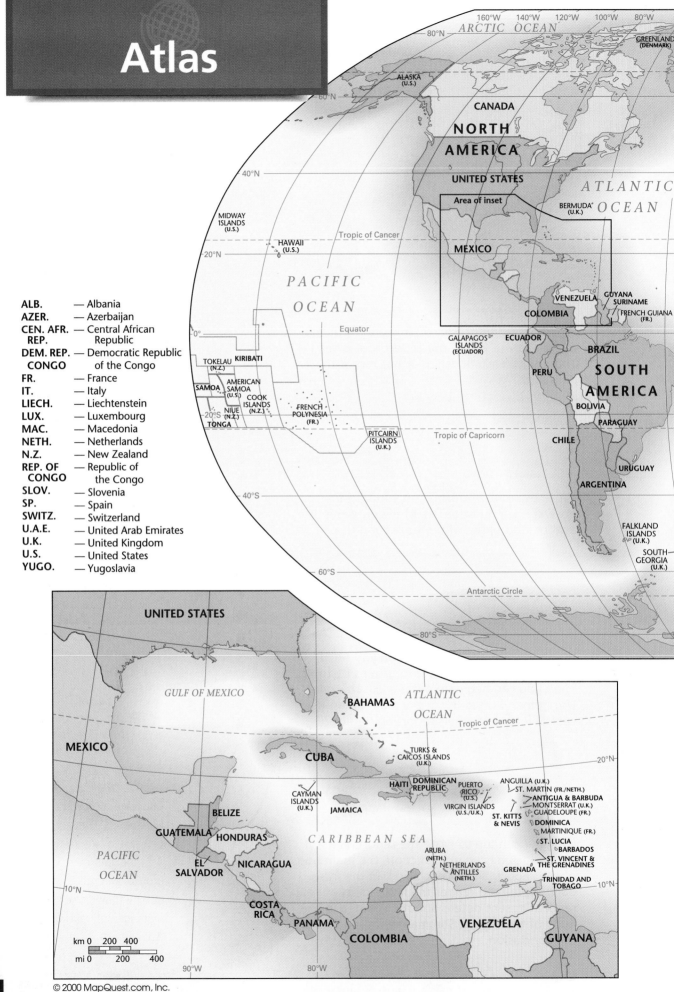

Atlas

ALB. — Albania
AZER. — Azerbaijan
CEN. AFR. REP. — Central African Republic
DEM. REP. CONGO — Democratic Republic of the Congo
FR. — France
IT. — Italy
LIECH. — Liechtenstein
LUX. — Luxembourg
MAC. — Macedonia
NETH. — Netherlands
N.Z. — New Zealand
REP. OF CONGO — Republic of the Congo
SLOV. — Slovenia
SP. — Spain
SWITZ. — Switzerland
U.A.E. — United Arab Emirates
U.K. — United Kingdom
U.S. — United States
YUGO. — Yugoslavia

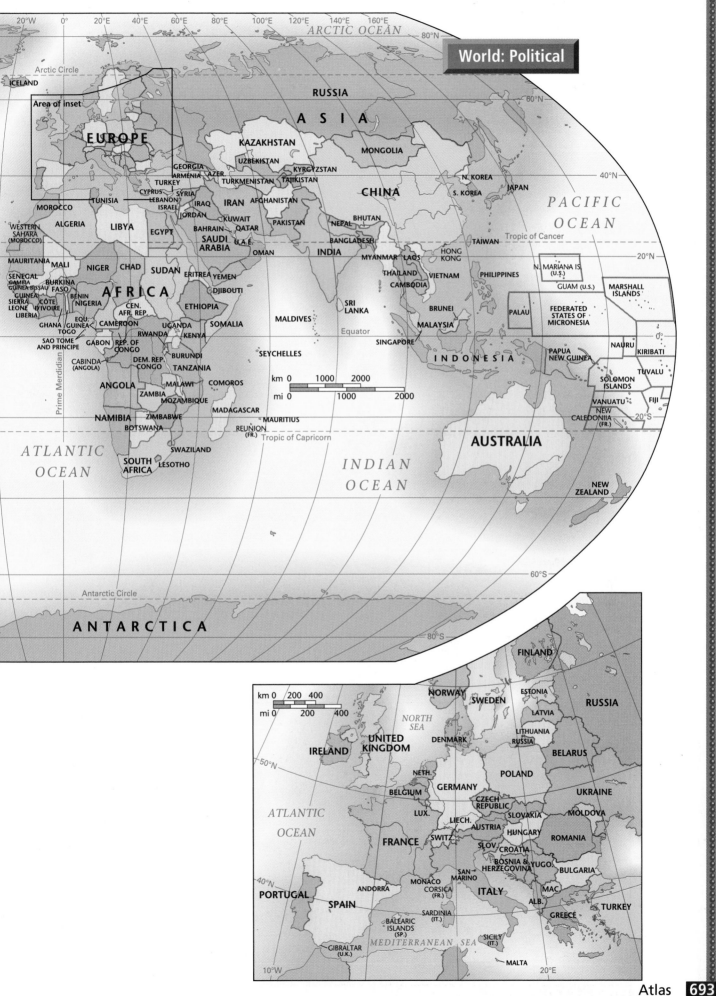

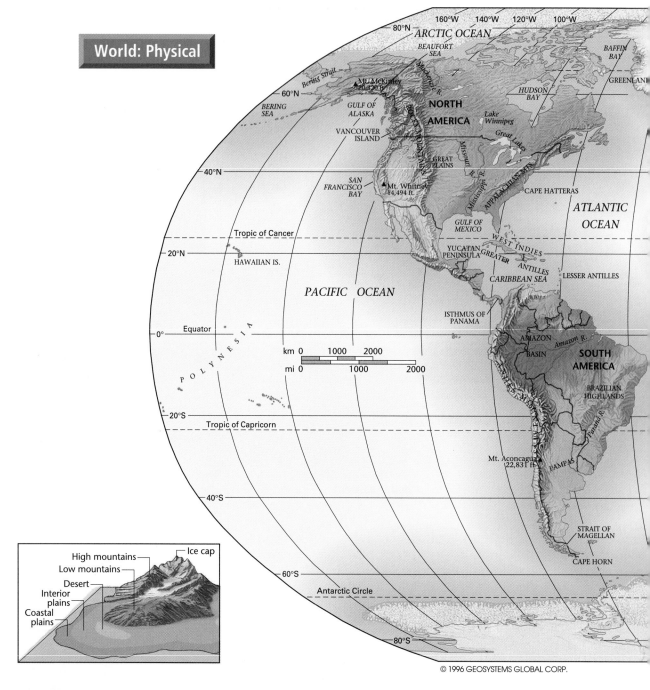

World: Physical

160°W 140°W 120°W 100°W
80°N
ARCTIC OCEAN
BEAUFORT
SEA
BAFFIN
BAY
60°N
Bering Strait
Mackenzie R.
GREENLAN
HUDSON
BAY
BERING
SEA
Mt. McKinley
20,320 ft.
GULF OF
ALASKA
NORTH
AMERICA
Lake
Winnipeg
VANCOUVER
ISLAND
ROCKY MOUNTAINS
Great Lakes
40°N
Missouri R.
GREAT
PLAINS
SAN
FRANCISCO
BAY
Mt. Whitney
14,494 ft.
APPALACHIAN MTS.
Mississippi R.
CAPE HATTERAS
ATLANTIC
OCEAN
Tropic of Cancer
20°N
GULF OF
MEXICO
WEST INDIES
HAWAIIAN IS.
YUCATAN
PENINSULA
GREATER
ANTILLES
LESSER ANTILLES
CARIBBEAN SEA
PACIFIC   OCEAN
ISTHMUS OF
PANAMA
AMAZON
Amazon R.
Equator
0°
BASIN
SOUTH
AMERICA
P O L Y N E S I A
km 0   1000   2000
BRAZILIAN
HIGHLANDS
mi 0   1000   2000
20°S
ANDES MTS.
Paraná R.
Tropic of Capricorn
PAMPAS
Mt. Aconcagua
22,831 ft.
40°S
STRAIT OF
MAGELLAN
60°S
CAPE HORN

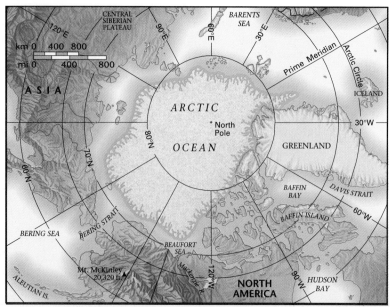

High mountains
Low mountains
Ice cap
Desert
Interior
plains
Coastal
plains

Antarctic Circle
80°S

© 1996 GEOSYSTEMS GLOBAL CORP.

CENTRAL
SIBERIAN
PLATEAU
120°E
90°E
60°E
BARENTS
SEA
30°E
km 0   400 800
30°E
mi 0   400   800
Prime Meridian
Arctic Circle
ASIA
ICELAND
ARCTIC
North
Pole
30°W
80°N
OCEAN
GREENLAND
70°N
60°N
BAFFIN
BAY
DAVIS STRAIT
BERING SEA
BERING STRAIT
BAFFIN ISLAND
60°W
BEAUFORT
SEA
Mackenzie R.
Mt. McKinley
20,320 ft.
120°W
90°W
HUDSON
BAY
ALEUTIAN IS.
NORTH
AMERICA

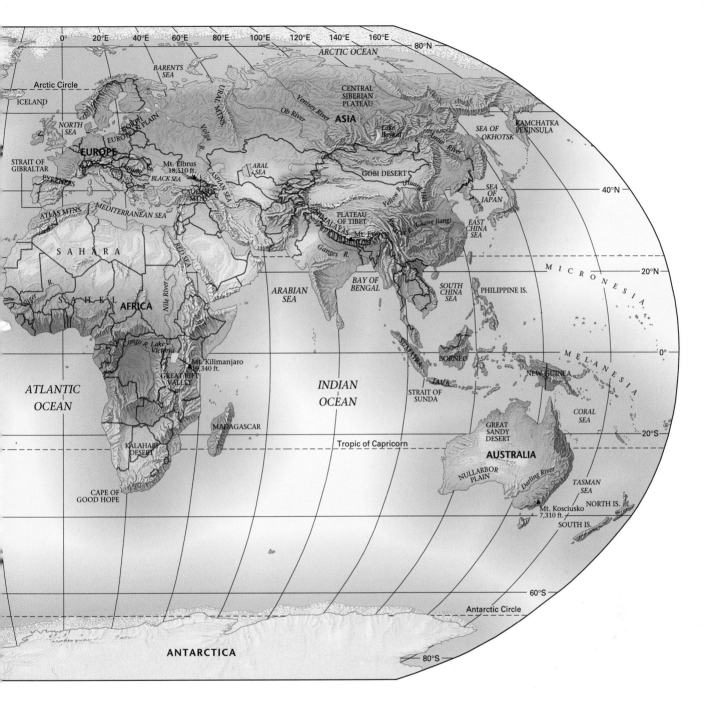

0° 20°E 40°E 60°E 80°E 100°E 120°E 140°E 160°E 80°N

ARCTIC OCEAN

Arctic Circle

ICELAND

NORTH SEA

BARENTS SEA

URAL MTNS.

CENTRAL SIBERIAN PLATEAU

Ob River

Yenisey River

Lake Baykal

Amur River

SEA OF OKHOTSK

KAMCHATKA PENINSULA

EUROPE

NORTH EUROPEAN PLAIN

Volga R.

Danube

Mt. Elbrus 18,510 ft.

BLACK SEA

CAUCASUS MTNS.

STRAIT OF GIBRALTAR

PYRENEES

ATLAS MTNS.

MEDITERRANEAN SEA

CASPIAN SEA

ARAL SEA

ASIA

GOBI DESERT

Yellow R. (Huang He)

SEA OF JAPAN

40°N

PLATEAU OF TIBET

HIMALAYAS

Mt. Everest

Yangtze R. (Chang Jiang)

EAST CHINA SEA

S A H A R A

Niger R.

Nile River

RED SEA

Ganges R.

ARABIAN SEA

BAY OF BENGAL

SOUTH CHINA SEA

PHILIPPINE IS.

M I C R O N E S I A

20°N

S A H E L

AFRICA

Congo R.

Lake Victoria

Mt. Kilimanjaro 19,340 ft.

GREAT RIFT VALLEY

SUMATRA

BORNEO

JAVA

NEW GUINEA

M E L A N E S I A

0°

ATLANTIC OCEAN

INDIAN OCEAN

STRAIT OF SUNDA

MADAGASCAR

GREAT SANDY DESERT

CORAL SEA

20°S

Tropic of Capricorn

KALAHARI DESERT

AUSTRALIA

NULLARBOR PLAIN

Darling River

TASMAN SEA

NORTH IS.

CAPE OF GOOD HOPE

Mt. Kosciusko 7,310 ft.

SOUTH IS.

60°S

Antarctic Circle

ANTARCTICA

80°S

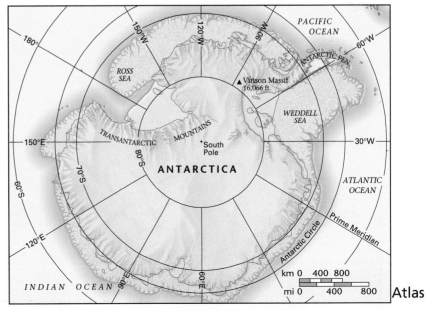

180°

150°W

120°W

90°W

60°W

PACIFIC OCEAN

ROSS SEA

ANTARCTIC PEN.

Vinson Massif 16,066 ft.

WEDDELL SEA

150°E

TRANSANTARCTIC MOUNTAINS

80°S

South Pole

ANTARCTICA

30°W

120°E

70°S

90°E

60°E

ATLANTIC OCEAN

Antarctic Circle

Prime Meridian

INDIAN OCEAN

km 0   400 800

mi 0   400   800

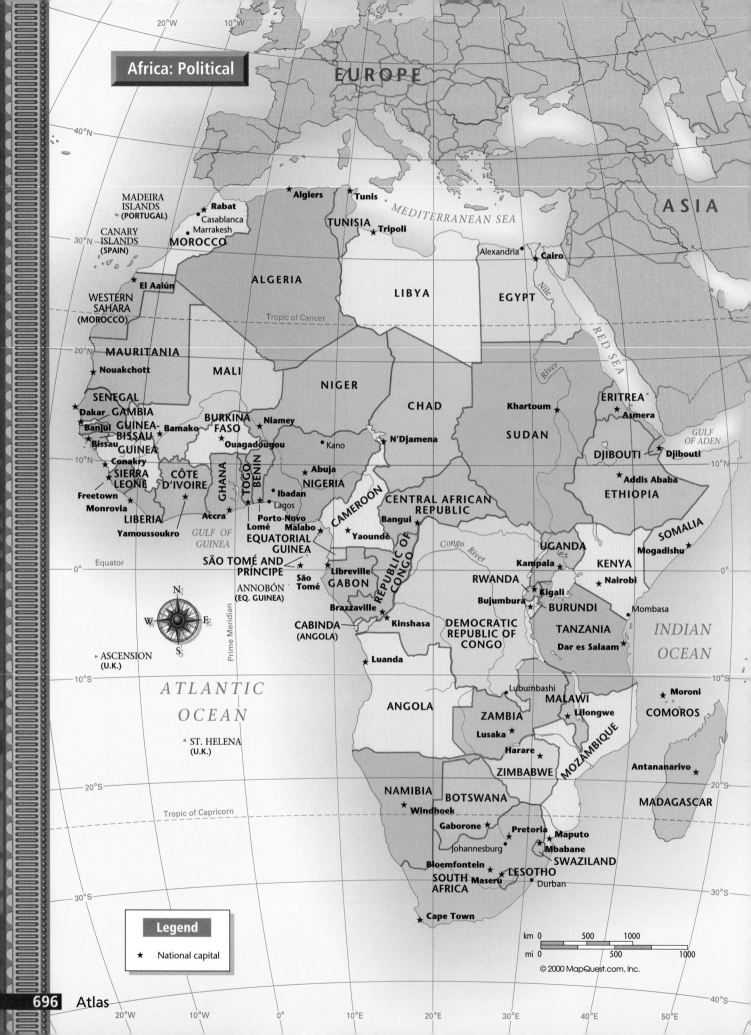

Africa: Political

EUROPE

ASIA

MEDITERRANEAN SEA

MADEIRA ISLANDS (PORTUGAL)

• Rabat
Casablanca
• Marrakesh
MOROCCO

CANARY ISLANDS (SPAIN)

★ Algiers
★ Tunis
TUNISIA
★ Tripoli

★ El Aaiún

WESTERN SAHARA (MOROCCO)

ALGERIA

LIBYA

EGYPT

Alexandria
★ Cairo

Nile River

RED SEA

GULF OF ADEN

Tropic of Cancer

MAURITANIA

★ Nouakchott

MALI

NIGER

CHAD

Khartoum ★

SUDAN

ERITREA
Asmera ★

DJIBOUTI
★ Djibouti

SENEGAL
Dakar ★ GAMBIA
Banjul ★ GUINEA-BISSAU
Bissau ★
GUINEA
Conakry ★
SIERRA LEONE
Freetown ★
Monrovia ★
LIBERIA

Bamako ★ BURKINA FASO
★ Niamey
Ouagadougou ★
• Kano
★ N'Djamena

CÔTE D'IVOIRE
GHANA
TOGO
BENIN
★ Abuja
NIGERIA
• Ibadan
• Lagos
Accra ★
Lomé ★ Porto-Novo
Malabo ★
EQUATORIAL GUINEA
Yamoussoukro

CAMEROON
Yaoundé ★
★ Bangui
CENTRAL AFRICAN REPUBLIC

Addis Ababa ★
ETHIOPIA

SOMALIA
Mogadishu ★

SÃO TOMÉ AND PRÍNCIPE

São Tomé ★
Libreville ★
GABON

REPUBLIC OF CONGO

Congo River

UGANDA
Kampala ★

KENYA
★ Nairobi

Equator

ANNOBÓN (EQ. GUINEA)

Brazzaville ★
CABINDA (ANGOLA)

★ Kinshasa

DEMOCRATIC REPUBLIC OF CONGO

RWANDA
★ Kigali
Bujumbura ★
BURUNDI

Mombasa •

TANZANIA
Dar es Salaam ★

INDIAN OCEAN

★ Luanda

ASCENSION (U.K.)

N
W   E
S

Prime Meridian

ATLANTIC OCEAN

ANGOLA

Lubumbashi •

MALAWI
Lilongwe ★

ZAMBIA
Lusaka ★

Moroni ★
COMOROS

★ ST. HELENA (U.K.)

Harare ★
ZIMBABWE

MOZAMBIQUE

Antananarivo ★

MADAGASCAR

Tropic of Capricorn

NAMIBIA
Windhoek ★

BOTSWANA

Gaborone ★
Johannesburg •
Pretoria ★ Maputo ★
Mbabane ★
SWAZILAND

Bloemfontein •
SOUTH AFRICA
Maseru ★ Lesotho ★
Durban •

★ Cape Town

Legend

★ National capital

km 0   500   1000
mi 0   500   1000

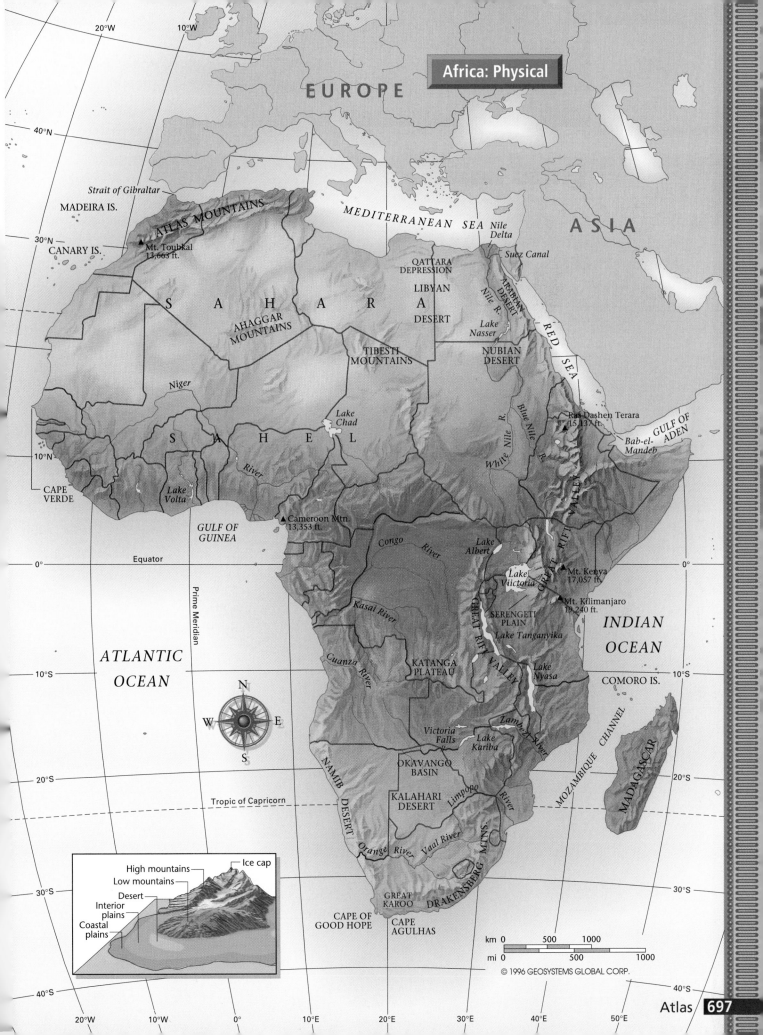

Africa: Physical

EUROPE

ASIA

MEDITERRANEAN SEA

Strait of Gibraltar

MADEIRA IS.

ATLAS MOUNTAINS

Mt. Toubkal
13,663 ft.

CANARY IS.

S A H A R A

AHAGGAR
MOUNTAINS

QATTARA
DEPRESSION

LIBYAN
DESERT

Nile
Delta

Suez Canal

ARABIAN DESERT

Nile R.

RED SEA

TIBESTI
MOUNTAINS

Lake
Nasser

NUBIAN
DESERT

Niger

Lake
Chad

S   A   H   E   L

CAPE
VERDE

River

Lake
Volta

GULF OF
GUINEA

Cameroon Mtn.
13,353 ft.

Equator

Prime Meridian

White Nile R.

Blue Nile R.

Ras Dashen Terara
15,157 ft.

GULF OF
ADEN

Bab-el-
Mandeb

GREAT RIFT VALLEY

Congo   River

Lake
Albert

Lake
Victoria

Mt. Kenya
17,057 ft.

Mt. Kilimanjaro
19,340 ft.

Kasai River

SERENGETI
PLAIN

Lake Tanganyika

INDIAN
OCEAN

ATLANTIC
OCEAN

Cuanza River

KATANGA
PLATEAU

GREAT RIFT VALLEY

Lake
Nyasa

COMORO IS.

N
W   E
S

Zambezi River

Victoria
Falls

Lake
Kariba

MOZAMBIQUE CHANNEL

MADAGASCAR

NAMIB DESERT

OKAVANGO
BASIN

KALAHARI
DESERT

Limpopo

River

Tropic of Capricorn

Orange   River

Vaal River

DRAKENSBERG MTNS.

GREAT
KAROO

CAPE OF
GOOD HOPE

CAPE
AGULHAS

Ice cap
High mountains
Low mountains
Desert
Interior
plains
Coastal
plains

km 0   500   1000
mi 0   500   1000

© 1996 GEOSYSTEMS GLOBAL CORP.

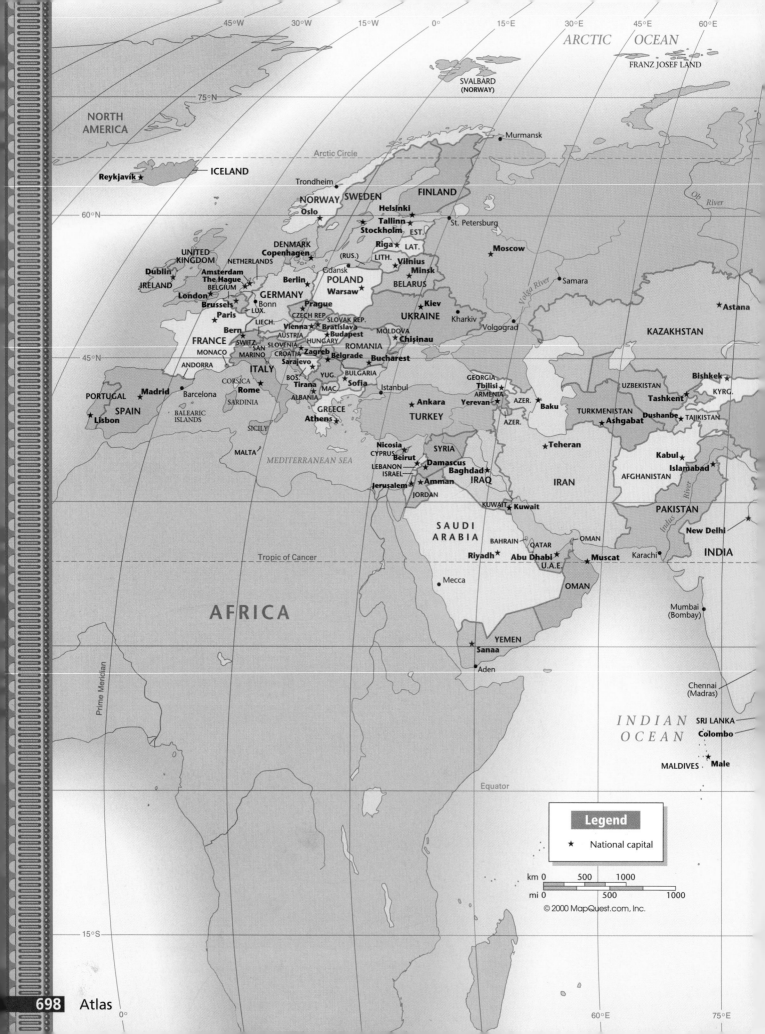

ARCTIC OCEAN

FRANZ JOSEF LAND

45°W   30°W   15°W   0°   15°E   30°E   45°E   60°E

SVALBARD
(NORWAY)

75°N

NORTH
AMERICA

Arctic Circle

• Murmansk

Ob River

Reykjavík ★   ICELAND

Trondheim •

60°N

NORWAY   SWEDEN   FINLAND
Oslo •   Helsinki •
★ Tallinn
Stockholm ★   EST.   • St. Petersburg   • Moscow
DENMARK   Riga ★   LAT.
Copenhagen •   Vilnius   LITH.   Samara •
(RUS.)   Minsk ★
UNITED
KINGDOM   NETHERLANDS   Gdansk   BELARUS   Volga River
Dublin   Amsterdam ★   Berlin •   POLAND
The Hague ★   GERMANY   Warsaw ★   Kiev ★   • Astana
IRELAND   BELGIUM   Bonn •   Prague ★   UKRAINE
London ★   Brussels ★   LUX.   CZECH REP.   Kharkiv •   KAZAKHSTAN
Paris ★   Vienna ★★ Bratislava   SLOVAK REP.   Volgograd •
Bern ★   AUSTRIA   Budapest ★   MOLDOVA
FRANCE   SWITZ.   SLOVENIA ★   HUNGARY   ROMANIA   ★ Chişinau   Bishkek ★
45°N   MONACO   SAN   CROATIA   Zagreb ★   Belgrade ★   Bucharest ★   UZBEKISTAN   KYRG.
ANDORRA   MARINO   Sarajevo ★   YUG.   GEORGIA   Tashkent ★
ITALY   BOS.   Sofia ★   BULGARIA   Tbilisi ★   TURKMENISTAN   Dushanbe ★
PORTUGAL   Madrid ★   Rome ★   Tirana ★   MAC.   Istanbul •   ARMENIA   AZER. ★ Baku   Ashgabat ★   TAJIKISTAN
SPAIN   Barcelona •   SARDINIA   ALBANIA   Athens ★   GREECE   Ankara ★   Yerevan ★   AZER.
Lisbon ★   BALEARIC   TURKEY   • Teheran   Kabul ★   Islamabad ★
ISLANDS   SICILY   Nicosia ★   SYRIA   AFGHANISTAN   PAKISTAN
MALTA   MEDITERRANEAN SEA   CYPRUS   Beirut ★   Damascus ★   New Delhi ★
LEBANON   Baghdad ★   IRAN   Indus River
ISRAEL   IRAQ
Jerusalem ★   ★ Amman   KUWAIT ★ Kuwait   INDIA
JORDAN
Tropic of Cancer   SAUDI   BAHRAIN   QATAR   OMAN   Karachi •
ARABIA   Riyadh ★   Abu Dhabi ★   Muscat ★
• Mecca   U.A.E.   OMAN   Mumbai
(Bombay) •

AFRICA   Chennai
(Madras) •

YEMEN
★ Sanaa
• Aden   INDIAN   SRI LANKA
OCEAN   Colombo ★

MALDIVES ★ Male

Legend

★   National capital

km 0 ⊢——⊣——⊣ 500 ⊢——⊣ 1000
mi 0 ⊢——⊣ 500 ⊢——⊣ 1000

© 2000 MapQuest.com, Inc.

15°S

0°   60°E   75°E

90°E 105°E 120°E 135°E 150°E 165°E 180° 165°W 150°W

75°N

NORTH
AMERICA

60°N

R U S S I A

• Novosibirsk

Irkutsk •

45°N

M O N G O L I A   ★ Ulan Bator

Harbin •

Sapporo •

Vladivostok •

NORTH
KOREA

J A P A N

PACIFIC
OCEAN

Beijing ★

★ Pyongyang

Seoul ★ SOUTH
KOREA

Tokyo ★

C H I N A

Osaka •

Chang Jiang

Shanghai •

30°N

Kathmandu
BHUTAN

Taipei ★

Tropic of Cancer

★ NEPAL ★ Thimphu

TAIWAN

BANGLADESH

Guangzhou •

AZER.   — Azerbaijan

Dhaka ★

Macao Hong Kong
(PORT.)

BOS.   — Bosnia and Herzegovina

Calcutta •

CZECH REP.   — Czech Republic

MYANMAR

EST.   — Estonia

LAOS ★ Hanoi

KYRG.   — Kyrgyzstan

Vientiane ★

LAT.   — Latvia

15°N

LIECH.   — Liechtenstein

Rangoon ★

THAILAND

• Da Nang

LITH.   — Lithuania

LUX.   — Luxembourg

Bangkok ★

Manila •

MAC.   — Macedonia

CAMBODIA VIETNAM

PHILIPPINES

PORT.   — Portugal

Phnom ★
Penh • Ho Chi Minh City

RUS.   — Russia

SLOVAK REP.   — Slovak Republic

SWITZ.   — Switzerland

Bandar Seri
Begawan

U.A.E.   — United Arab Emirates

BRUNEI

U.K.   — United Kingdom

Kuala Lumpur

YUG.   — Yugoslavia

★ M A L A Y S I A

SINGAPORE

Singapore

SUMATRA   BORNEO

Equator   0°

CELEBES

★ Jakarta I N D O N E S I A

NEW GUINEA

JAVA

N

W   E

S

15°S

A U S T R A L I A

90°E 105°E

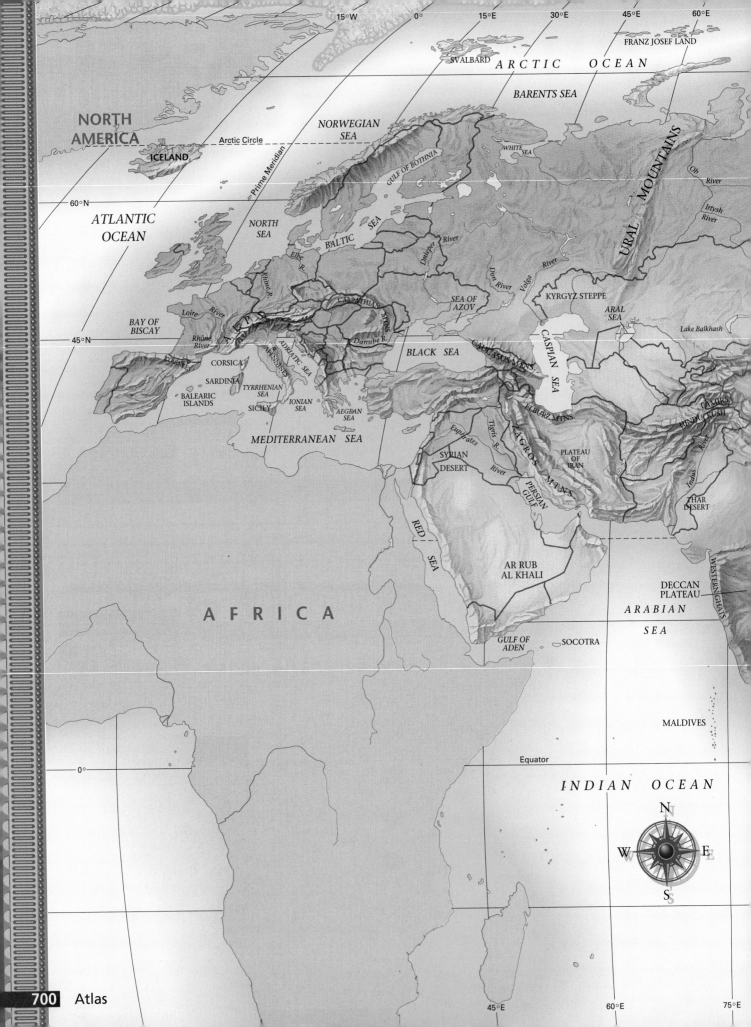

NORTH
AMERICA

Arctic Circle
ICELAND

ATLANTIC
OCEAN

60°N

45°N

Prime Meridian

15°W

0°

15°E

30°E

45°E

60°E

FRANZ JOSEF LAND

SVALBARD

ARCTIC   OCEAN

BARENTS SEA

NORWEGIAN
SEA

WHITE
SEA

Ob
River

URAL MOUNTAINS

Irtysh
River

GULF OF BOTHNIA

BALTIC   SEA

River

NORTH
SEA

Elbe
R.

Rhine R.

Loire   River

Dnieper   River

CARPATHIAN MTNS.

Don River

Volga   River

KYRGYZ STEPPE

ARAL
SEA

Lake Balkhash

BAY OF
BISCAY

Rhône
River

A L P S

Danube R.

SEA OF
AZOV

BLACK SEA

CASPIAN SEA

CAUCASUS MTNS.

PAMIRS

PYRENEES

CORSICA

APENNINES

ADRIATIC SEA

ELBURZ MTNS.

HINDU KUSH

SARDINIA

TYRRHENIAN
SEA

IONIAN
SEA

AEGEAN
SEA

Euphrates
R.

Tigris
R.

ZAGROS MTNS.

PLATEAU
OF
IRAN

Indus River

BALEARIC
ISLANDS

SICILY

MEDITERRANEAN   SEA

SYRIAN
DESERT

River

PERSIAN
GULF

THAR
DESERT

RED
SEA

AR RUB
AL KHALI

DECCAN
PLATEAU

WESTERN GHATS

ARABIAN

SEA

AFRICA

GULF OF
ADEN

SOCOTRA

MALDIVES

0°

Equator

INDIAN OCEAN

N

W   E

S

SIBERIA

Yenisey River

Lena River

Lake Baikal

STANOVOI RANGE

Amur River

ALTAI MTNS.

TIEN SHAN

GOBI (DESERT)

Huang

KUNLUN SHAN

He

PLATEAU OF TIBET

Brahmaputra River

HIMALAYAS

Ganges R.

Chang

Jiang

Mekong River

Irrawaddy River

Xi Jiang

BAY OF BENGAL

GULF OF TONKIN

HAINAN

ANDAMAN IS.

EASTERN GHATS

ANDAMAN SEA

SRI LANKA

SUMATRA

SOUTH CHINA SEA

BORNEO

JAVA SEA

JAVA

CELEBES

SEA OF OKHOTSK

SAKHALIN

KURIL ISLANDS

SEA OF JAPAN

JAPAN

JAPAN TRENCH

PACIFIC OCEAN

BERING SEA

YELLOW SEA

EAST CHINA SEA

Tropic of Cancer

TAIWAN

PHILIPPINE SEA

PHILIPPINES

km 0   500   1000

mi 0   500   1000

© 1996 GEOSYSTEMS GLOBAL CORP.

Equator

NEW GUINEA

ARAFURA SEA

TIMOR SEA

High mountains — Ice cap
Low mountains
Desert
Interior plains
Coastal plains

AUSTRALIA

75°E 90°E 105°E 120°E 135°E 150°E 165°E 180° 165°W 150°W

75°N
60°N
45°N
30°N
15°N
0°
15°S

90°E 105°E 165°E

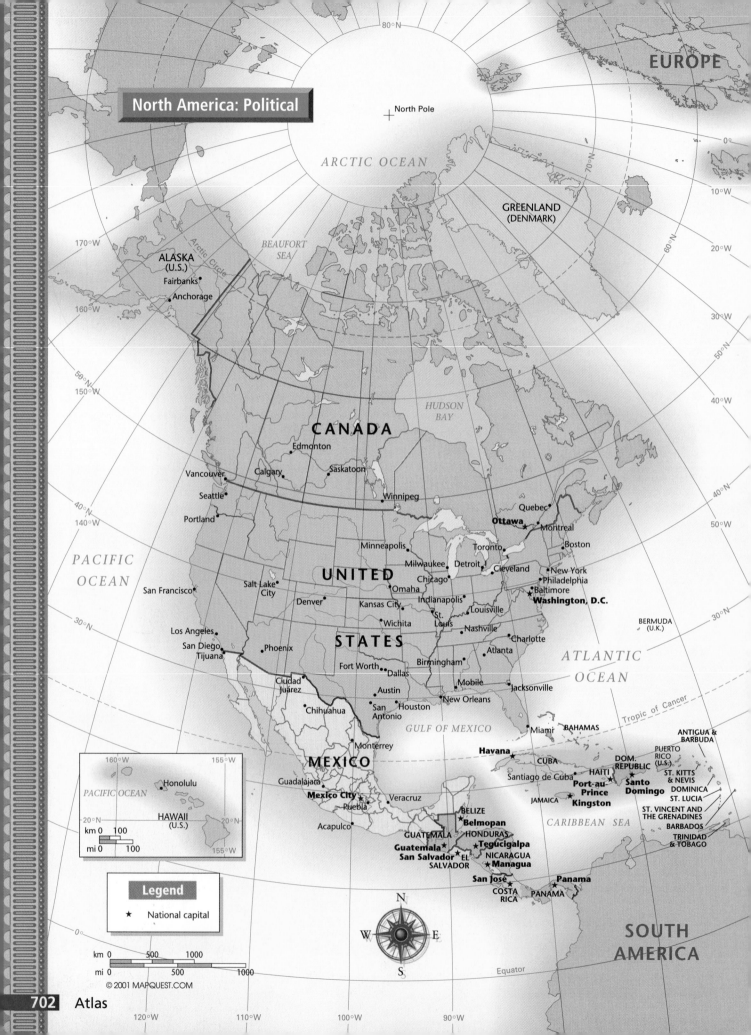

North America: Political

North Pole

ARCTIC OCEAN

EUROPE

GREENLAND
(DENMARK)

BEAUFORT
SEA

ALASKA
(U.S.)
Fairbanks
Anchorage

Arctic Circle

HUDSON
BAY

CANADA

Edmonton
Vancouver   Calgary   Saskatoon
Seattle
Portland   Winnipeg
Quebec
Ottawa ★ Montreal
Boston

PACIFIC
OCEAN

Minneapolis
UNITED   Milwaukee Detroit Toronto Cleveland New York
Chicago   Philadelphia
Salt Lake   Omaha   Baltimore
San Francisco   City   Indianapolis   Washington, D.C.
Denver   Kansas City   Louisville
STATES   Wichita   St.   Nashville   BERMUDA
Los Angeles   Louis   Charlotte   (U.K.)
San Diego   Phoenix   Birmingham   Atlanta   ATLANTIC
Tijuana   Fort Worth   OCEAN
Ciudad   Dallas   Mobile   Jacksonville
Juárez   Austin   New Orleans
Chihuahua   San   Houston
Antonio   GULF OF MEXICO   Tropic of Cancer
Monterrey   Miami   BAHAMAS   ANTIGUA &
MEXICO   Havana   BARBUDA
Guadalajara   CUBA   DOM.   PUERTO
Mexico City ★   Veracruz   Santiago de Cuba   HAITI REPUBLIC   RICO
Puebla   Port-au-   Santo   (U.S.)
Acapulco   BELIZE   JAMAICA Prince Domingo   ST. KITTS
★ Belmopan   Kingston   & NEVIS
GUATEMALA   HONDURAS   CARIBBEAN SEA   DOMINICA
Guatemala ★ ★ Tegucigalpa   ST. LUCIA
San Salvador ★ EL   NICARAGUA   ST. VINCENT AND
SALVADOR ★ Managua   THE GRENADINES
San José   BARBADOS
COSTA   ★ Panama   TRINIDAD
RICA   PANAMA   & TOBAGO

PACIFIC OCEAN

Honolulu
HAWAII
(U.S.)
km 0   100
mi 0   100

Legend
★   National capital

N
W   E
S

SOUTH
AMERICA

Equator

km 0   500   1000
mi 0   500   1000

© 2001 MAPQUEST.COM

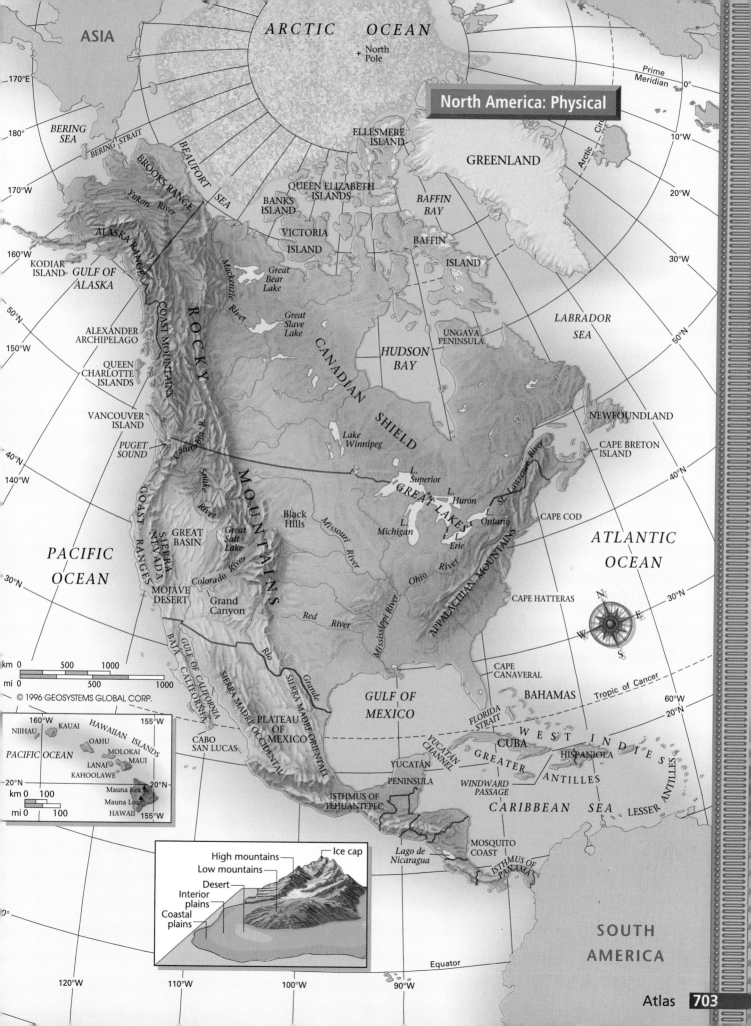

North America: Physical

ASIA

ARCTIC OCEAN

+ North Pole

Prime Meridian

170°E
180°
170°W
160°W
150°W
140°W
120°W
110°W
100°W
90°W
60°W
30°W
20°W
10°W
0°
10°W
20°W
30°W
40°N
50°N
30°N
20°N

BERING SEA
BERING STRAIT
BEAUFORT SEA
BROOKS RANGE
Yukon River
ALASKA RANGE
KODIAK ISLAND
GULF OF ALASKA
ALEXANDER ARCHIPELAGO
QUEEN CHARLOTTE ISLANDS
VANCOUVER ISLAND
PUGET SOUND
COAST MOUNTAINS
COAST RANGES

ELLESMERE ISLAND
GREENLAND
Arctic Circle

QUEEN ELIZABETH ISLANDS
BANKS ISLAND
VICTORIA ISLAND
BAFFIN BAY
BAFFIN ISLAND

Mackenzie River
Great Bear Lake
Great Slave Lake
CANADIAN SHIELD
HUDSON BAY
UNGAVA PENINSULA
LABRADOR SEA

NEWFOUNDLAND
CAPE BRETON ISLAND

ROCKY MOUNTAINS
Columbia R.
Snake River
Lake Winnipeg
L. Superior
GREAT LAKES
L. Huron
L. Michigan
L. Ontario
L. Erie
St. Lawrence River

SIERRA NEVADA
GREAT BASIN
Great Salt Lake
Black Hills
Missouri River
Ohio River
APPALACHIAN MOUNTAINS
CAPE COD
CAPE HATTERAS

PACIFIC OCEAN

MOJAVE DESERT
Colorado River
Grand Canyon
Red River
Mississippi River

ATLANTIC OCEAN

Rio Grande
BAJA CALIFORNIA
GULF OF CALIFORNIA
SIERRA MADRE OCCIDENTAL
SIERRA MADRE ORIENTAL
PLATEAU OF MEXICO
CABO SAN LUCAS
GULF OF MEXICO

CAPE CANAVERAL
BAHAMAS
Tropic of Cancer
FLORIDA STRAIT
YUCATÁN CHANNEL
CUBA
WEST INDIES
GREATER ANTILLES
HISPANIOLA
LESSER ANTILLES

YUCATÁN PENINSULA
WINDWARD PASSAGE
CARIBBEAN SEA
ISTHMUS OF TEHUANTEPEC
Lago de Nicaragua
MOSQUITO COAST
ISTHMUS OF PANAMA

Equator

SOUTH AMERICA

km 0   500   1000
mi 0   500   1000
© 1996 GEOSYSTEMS GLOBAL CORP.

HAWAIIAN ISLANDS
160°W
155°W
NIIHAU
KAUAI
OAHU
MOLOKAI
LANAI
MAUI
KAHOOLAWE
PACIFIC OCEAN
20°N
Mauna Kea
Mauna Loa
HAWAII
155°W
km 0   100
mi 0   100

High mountains
Low mountains
Desert
Interior plains
Coastal plains
Ice cap

Atlas   703

South America: Political

CARIBBEAN SEA

Barranquilla • Maracaibo • Caracas ★

Cartagena •

VENEZUELA

Georgetown ★

Medellín •

GUYANA ★ Paramaribo

Santa Fe
de Bogotá ★

Cayenne

SURINAME

FRENCH
GUIANA
(FR.)

MALPELO
(COLOMBIA)

Cali • COLOMBIA

ATLANTIC
OCEAN

Quito ★

ECUADOR

River

Equator

0°

Guayaquil •

Belém •

GALAPAGOS
ISLANDS
(ECUADOR)

Iquitos •

Amazon

Manaus •

Fortaleza •

Trujillo •

PERU

BRAZIL

Recife •

Lima ★

• Cuzco

10°S

Salvador •

PACIFIC
OCEAN

La Paz ★

★ Brasília

Arequipa •

BOLIVIA

Sucre ★

Paraná River

Belo Horizonte •

20°S

PARAGUAY

Antofagasta •

Tropic of Capricorn

Asunción ★

São Paulo •

Rio de Janeiro

SAN FÉLIX ISLAND
(CHILE)

SAN AMBROSIO
ISLAND
(CHILE)

Salado River

Curitiba •

CHILE

Pôrto Alegre •

JUAN FERNÁNDEZ
ISLANDS
(CHILE)

Córdoba •

30°S

Valparaíso •

Rosario •

URUGUAY

★ Santiago

Buenos Aires ★

★ Montevideo

ATLANTIC
OCEAN

ARGENTINA

Concepción •

Bahía
Blanca •

Valdivia •

Legend

★ National capital

40°S

Comodoro Rivadavia •

N

km 0   300   600

W   E

mi 0   300   600

FALKLAND
ISLANDS
(U.K.)

S

© 1996 GEOSYSTEMS GLOBAL CORP.

TIERRA DEL
FUEGO

50°S

SOUTH GEORGIA
(U.K.)

South America: Physical

CARIBBEAN SEA

ATLANTIC OCEAN

ATLANTIC OCEAN

PACIFIC OCEAN

GULF OF PANAMA

MALPELO

GALAPAGOS ISLANDS

GULF OF GUAYAQUIL

LLANOS

Orinoco River

Angel Falls

GUIANA HIGHLANDS

OCCIDENTAL MTNS.

Cauca River

Magdalena River

Rio Negro

AMAZON BASIN

Solimões River

Amazon River

Madeira River

Tapajós River

Xingu River

Tocantins River

São Francisco River

River

Mt. Huascarán 22,205 ft.

Volcán Misti 19,098 ft.

Lake Titicaca

Mt. Illimani 21,151 ft.

ALTIPLANO

PLATEAU OF MATO GROSSO

BRAZILIAN HIGHLANDS

ATACAMA DESERT

ANDES

Paraguay River

GRAN CHACO

Salado River

Paraná River

Paraná River

SAN FÉLIX I. SAN AMBROSIO I.

JUAN FERNÁNDEZ IS.

Mt. Aconcagua 22,831 ft.

RÍO DE LA PLATA

Colorado R.

PAMPAS

GULF OF SAN MATÍAS

PATAGONIA

GULF OF SAN JORGE

STRAIT OF MAGELLAN

FALKLAND ISLANDS

TIERRA DEL FUEGO

SOUTH GEORGIA

Cape Horn

DRAKE PASSAGE

km 0   300   600

mi 0   300   600

© 1996 GEOSYSTEMS GLOBAL CORP.

Ice cap
High mountains
Low mountains
Desert
Interior plains
Coastal plains

N
W   E
S

Tropic of Cancer

Equator

Tropic of Capricorn

15°N

120°E   135°E   150°E   165°E

NORTHERN
MARIANA IS.
(U.S.)   WAKE I.
(U.S.)

GUAM
(U.S.)

M

PHILIPPINES   I
C
Koror ★   R   ★ Palikir
PALAU   O
N
FEDERATED STATES   E
OF MICRONESIA   S
I
A

M
E
L
A   SOLOMON
N   ISLANDS   ★
Yaren
PAPUA   E   NAURU
NEW GUINEA   N
INDONESIA   CENTRAL   E
NEW   RANGE   ▲ Mt. Wilhelm   S   SOLOMON
GUINEA   14,793 ft.   I   Honiara ● ISLANDS
A

ARAFURA SEA   Port Moresby ★

TIMOR SEA   VANUATU
INDIAN   CAPE   CORAL   Port-Vila
OCEAN   Darwin ●   ARNHEM   GULF OF YORK   ★
LAND   CARPENTARIA PEN.   GREAT   SEA
15°S   BARRIER
KIMBERLEY   BARKLY   REEF   GREAT   NEW
PLATEAU   TABLELAND   DIVIDING   CALEDONIA
RANGE   (FR.)

GREAT
HAMERSLEY   SANDY   GREAT
RANGE   DESERT   AUSTRALIA   ARTESIAN
WESTERN   Mt. Zeil ▲   MACDONNELL BASIN
4,955 ft.   RANGES
GIBSON
DESERT   EYRE
PLATEAU   MUSGRAVE   DEPRESSION
GREAT   RANGES   Brisbane ●
VICTORIA DESERT

30°S   GREAT
NULLARBOR   PLAIN   FLINDERS   DIVIDING
Perth ●   RANGE   Darling R.   RANGE
GREAT AUSTRALIAN   EYRE   ● Sydney
BIGHT   PEN.   Murray   Canberra
Adelaide ●   River   ▲ Mt. Kosciusko
7,310 ft.
Snowy   TASMAN
Melbourne ●   R.
SEA

TASMANIA   SOUTH
● Hobart   ISLAND

45°S

INDIAN OCEAN   N
W ✦ E
S

120°E   135°E   150°E   165°E

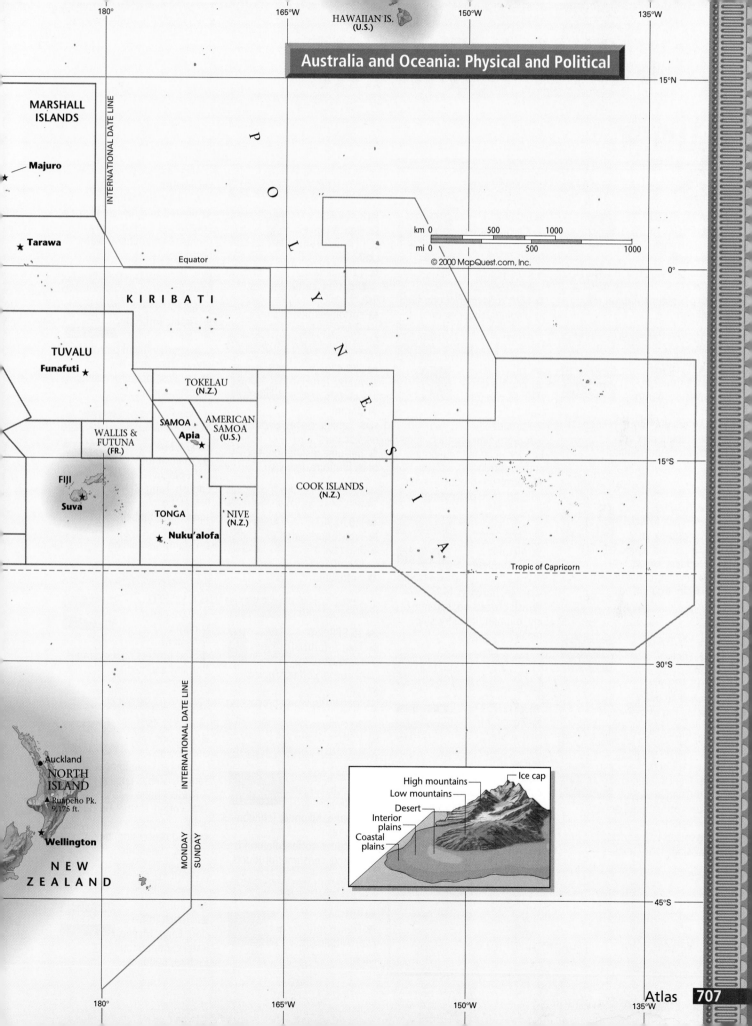

HAWAIIAN IS.
(U.S.)

Australia and Oceania: Physical and Political

MARSHALL
ISLANDS

★ Majuro

INTERNATIONAL DATE LINE

★ Tarawa

Equator

P
O
L
Y
N
E
S
I
A

K I R I B A T I

TUVALU
Funafuti ★

TOKELAU
(N.Z.)

SAMOA
Apia ★

AMERICAN
SAMOA
(U.S.)

WALLIS &
FUTUNA
(FR.)

FIJI
Suva ★

TONGA
★ Nuku'alofa

NIVE
(N.Z.)

COOK ISLANDS
(N.Z.)

Tropic of Capricorn

km 0   500   1000
mi 0   500   1000
© 2000 MapQuest.com, Inc.

180°
165°W
150°W
135°W
15°N
0°
15°S
30°S
45°S

Auckland
NORTH
ISLAND
▲ Ruapehu Pk.
9,175 ft.

★ Wellington

N E W
Z E A L A N D

INTERNATIONAL DATE LINE

MONDAY   SUNDAY

High mountains
Low mountains
Desert
Interior
plains
Coastal
plains

Ice cap

REGIONAL DATABANK

Africa

Algeria

- ⴰⵎ 31,193,917
- 🗣 Arabic (official), French
- ⊛ Algiers
- ⛴ petroleum and natural gas
- ● petroleum, natural gas, mining

Angola

- ⴰⵎ 10,145,267
- 🗣 Portuguese (official), Bantu
- ⊛ Luanda
- ⛴ oil, diamonds, refined petroleum products
- ● petroleum, mining

Benin

- ⴰⵎ 6,395,919
- 🗣 French (official)
- ⊛ Porto-Novo
- ⛴ cotton, crude oil, palm products, cocoa
- ● textiles, construction materials, petroleum

Botswana

- ⴰⵎ 1,576,470
- 🗣 English (official), Setswana
- ⊛ Gaborone
- ⛴ diamonds
- ● mining of diamonds

Burkina Faso

- ⴰⵎ 11,946,065
- 🗣 French (official)
- ⊛ Ouagadougou
- ⛴ cotton, gold, animal products
- ● cotton lint, agricultural processing, soap, textiles

Burundi

- ⴰⵎ 6,054,714
- 🗣 Kirundi (official), French (official)
- ⊛ Bujumbura
- ⛴ coffee
- ● light consumer goods such as blankets, shoes, soap

Cameroon

- ⴰⵎ 15,421,937
- 🗣 English (official), French (official)
- ⊛ Yaoundé
- ⛴ petroleum products, lumber, cocoa beans, aluminum, coffee, cotton
- ● petroleum production and refining, food processing

Cape Verde

- ⴰⵎ 401,343
- 🗣 Portuguese
- ⊛ Praia
- ⛴ fish, bananas, hides
- ● fish processing, salt mining, garment industry, ship repair

Central African Republic

- ⴰⵎ 3,512,751
- 🗣 French (official), Arabic, Hunsa, Swahili, Sangho
- ⊛ Bangui
- ⛴ diamonds, timber, cotton, coffee, tobacco
- ● diamond mining, sawmills

Chad

- ⴰⵎ 8,424,504
- 🗣 French (official), Arabic (official),
- ⊛ N'Djamena
- ⛴ cotton, cattle, textiles, fish
- ● cotton textile mills

Comoros

- ⴰⵎ 578,400
- 🗣 Arabic (official), French (official)
- ⊛ Moroni
- ⛴ vanilla, cloves, perfume, oil, coconut
- ● perfume distillation, textiles, furniture, jewelry

Congo, Republic of

- ⴰⵎ 2,830,961
- 🗣 French (official)
- ⊛ Brazzaville
- ⛴ crude oil
- ● petroleum

Côte d'Ivoire

- ⴰⵎ 15,980,950
- 🗣 French (official)
- ⊛ Yamoussoukro
- ⛴ cocoa, coffee, tropical woods
- ● foodstuffs, wood processing

Democratic Republic of Congo

- ⴰⵎ 51,964,999
- 🗣 French, Lingala, Swahili, Kingwana, Kikongo, Tshiluba
- ⊛ Kinshasa
- ⛴ copper, coffee, diamonds
- ● mining, consumer products

Djibouti

- ⴰⵎ 451,442
- 🗣 French (official), Arabic (official)
- ⊛ Djibouti
- ⛴ hides and skins
- ● limited to a few small-scale enterprises, such as dairy products and mineral-water bottling

Egypt

- ⴰⵎ 68,359,979
- 🗣 Arabic (official)
- ⊛ Cairo
- ⛴ crude oil and petroleum, raw cotton, yarn, textiles
- ● textiles, food processing, tourism, chemicals

Equatorial Guinea

- ⴰⵎ 474,214
- 🗣 Spanish (official), pidgin English, Fang, Bubi, Igbo
- ⊛ Malabo
- ⛴ coffee, timber, cocoa beans
- ● fishing, sawmilling

Eritrea

- ⴰⵎ 4,135,933
- 🗣 Tigre and Kunama
- ⊛ Asmara
- ● food processing, beverages, clothing and textiles

Ethiopia

- ⴰⵎ 64,117,452
- 🗣 Amharic (official), Tigrinya, Orominga, Guaraginga, Somali, Arabic, English
- ⊛ Addis Ababa
- ⛴ coffee, leather products, gold
- ● food processing, beverages, textiles, chemicals

Gabon

- ⴰⵎ 1,208,436
- 🗣 French (official), Fang, Myene, Bateke, Bapounou Eschira, Bandjabi

---

Key

ⴰⵎ Population	⊛ Capital	● Industry
🗣 Language	⛴ Export	

Regional Databank

⊛Libreville
🚢 crude oil
⊕ food and beverages, lumbering and plywood, textiles

Gambia, The

👥 1,367,124
🗣️ English (official), Mandinka, Wolof, Fula
⊛Banjul
🚢 peanuts, fish, cotton lint, palm products
⊕ peanut processing, tourism, beverages

Ghana

👥 19,533,560
🗣️ English (official)
⊛Accra
🚢 cocoa
⊕mining, lumbering

Guinea

👥 7,466,200
🗣️ French (official)
⊛Conakry
🚢 diamonds, aluminum, gold
⊕ mining aluminum, gold, diamonds

Guinea - Bissau

👥 1,285,715
🗣️ Portuguese (official), Criolo
⊛Bissau
🚢 cashews, fish, peanuts, palm kernels
⊕agricultural processing

Kenya

👥 30,339,770
🗣️ English (official), Swahili (official)
⊛Nairobi
🚢 tea, coffee
⊕small-scale consumer goods

Lesotho

👥 2,143,141
🗣️ English (official), Zulu, Xhosa, Sesotho
⊛Maseru

🚢 wool, mohair, wheat, cattle
⊕food, beverages, textiles, handicrafts

Liberia

👥 3,164,156
🗣️ English (official)
⊛Monrovia
🚢 iron ore, rubber
⊕rubber processing, food processing, construction

Libya

👥 5,115,450
🗣️ Arabic, English, Italian
⊛Tripoli
🚢 crude oil, refined petroleum products, natural gas
⊕petroleum, food processing, textiles

Madagascar

👥 15,506,472
🗣️ French (official), Malagasy (official)
⊛Antananarivo
🚢 coffee, vanilla
⊕agricultural processing

Malawi

👥 10,385,849
🗣️ English (official), Chichewa (official)
⊛Lilongwe
🚢 tobacco, tea, sugar, coffee
⊕agricultural processing

Mali

👥 10,685,948
🗣️ French (official), Bambara
⊛Bamako
🚢 cotton, livestock, gold
⊕food processing

Mauritania

👥 2,667,859
Hasaniya Arabic (official), Pular, Soninke, Wolof (official)

⊛Nouakchott
🚢 iron ore, fish products
⊕fish processing, mining of iron ore and gypsum

Mauritius

👥 1,179,368
🗣️ English (official), Creole, French, Hindi, Urdu, Hakka, Bojpoori
⊛Port Louis
🚢 textiles, sugar
⊕food processing, textiles, chemicals

Morocco

👥 30,122,350
🗣️ Arabic
⊛Rabat
🚢 food and beverages, semiprocessed goods
⊕phosphate rock mining and processing, food processing

Mozambique

👥 19,104,696
🗣️ Portuguese
⊛Maputo
🚢 shrimp, cashews, cotton, sugar
⊕food, beverages, chemicals

Namibia

👥 1,771,327
🗣️ English (official), Afrikaans, German
⊛Windhoek
🚢 diamonds, copper, gold, zinc, lead, uranium, cattle
⊕meat packing, fish processing, dairy products

Niger

👥 10,075,511
🗣️ French (official), Hausa, Djerma
⊛Niamey
🚢 uranium ore, livestock
⊕cement, brick, textiles, food processing, chemicals

Nigeria

👥 123,337,822
🗣️ English (official), Hausa, Yoruba, Igbo, Fulani
⊛Abuja
🚢 oil
⊕crude oil and mining

Rwanda

👥 7,229,129
🗣️ Kinyarwanda, French (official)
⊛Kigali
🚢 coffee
⊕mining of tin, agricultural processing

São Tomé and Príncipe

👥 159,883
🗣️ Portuguese (official)
⊛São Tomé
🚢 cocoa
⊕clothing, soap, fisheries, shrimp processing

Senegal

👥 9,987,494
🗣️ French (official), Wolof, Pulaar, Diola, Mandingo
⊛Dakar
🚢 fish, ground nuts, petroleum products
⊕food processing

Seychelles

👥 79,326
🗣️ English, French (official), Creole
⊛Victoria
🚢 fish, cinnamon bark, coconut, petroleum
⊕tourism, processing of coconut and vanilla, fishing

Sierra Leone

👥 5,232,624
🗣️ English, Mende, Temne, Krio
⊛Freetown
🚢 rutile, bauxite
⊕mining

Somalia

👥 7,253,137
🗣 Somali (official), Arabic, Italian, English
✪ Mogadishu
⛴ bananas, animals, fish, hides
● sugar refining, textiles, petroleum refining

South Africa

👥 43,421,021
🗣 Afrikaans, English, Ndebele, Pedi, Sotho, Swazi, Tsonga, Tswana, Venda, Xhosa, Zulu
✪ Pretoria, Cape Town, Bloemfontein
⛴ gold and other minerals
● mining

Sudan

👥 35,079,814
🗣 Arabic (official), Nubian, Sudanic languages, English
✪ Khartoum
⛴ gum arabic, livestock
● textiles, cement

Swaziland

👥 1,083,289
🗣 English, (official), siSwati, (official)
✪ Mbabane (administrative), Lobamba (legislative)
⛴ sugar, wood pulp, cotton
● mining, wood pulp, sugar

Tanzania

👥 35,306,126
🗣 Swahili, English (official)
✪ Dar es Salaam

⛴ coffee, cotton, tobacco, tea
● agricultural processing

Togo

👥 5,018,502
🗣 French
✪ Lomé
⛴ phosphates, cotton, cocoa, coffee
● phosphate mining, agricultural processing

Tunisia

👥 9,593,402
🗣 Arabic (official), French
✪ Tunis
⛴ hydrocarbons, agricultural products
● petroleum, mining

Uganda

👥 23,317,560
🗣 English (official), Luganda, Swahili, Bantu languages
✪ Kampala
⛴ coffee
● sugar, brewing, tobacco

Zambia

👥 9,582,418
🗣 English
✪ Lusaka
⛴ copper, zinc, cobalt, lead
● copper mining, construction

Zimbabwe

👥 11,342,521
🗣 English (official), Shona, Sindebele
✪ Harare
⛴ agricultural products
● mining, steel

Key

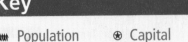

👥 Population   ✪ Capital   ● Industry
🗣 Language   ⛴ Export

Afghanistan

👥 25,888,797
🗣 Pashtu, Afghan Persian, Turkic languages
✪ Kabul
⛴ fruits and nuts, hand-woven carpets, wool, cotton, hides and pelts, precious and semiprecious gems
● soap, furniture, shoes, fertilizer, cement, natural gas

Armenia

👥 3,344,336
🗣 Armenian, Russian
✪ Yerevan
⛴ gold, jewelry, aluminum, transport equipment
● metal-cutting machine tools

Australia

👥 19,164,620
🗣 English
✪ Canberra
⛴ coal, gold, meat, wool, aluminum, wheat, machinery and transport equipment
● mining, industrial and transportation equipment, food processing, chemicals, steel

Azerbaijan

👥 7,748,163
🗣 Azeri, Russian, Armenian
✪ Baku
⛴ oil and gas, chemicals
● petroleum and natural gas

Bahrain

👥 634,137
🗣 Arabic, English, Farsi, Urdu
✪ Manama
⛴ petroleum, aluminum
● petroleum, aluminum, ship repairing

Bangladesh

👥 129,194,224
🗣 Bangla (official), English
✪ Dhaka

⛴ clothing, jute, leather, shrimp
● jute, cotton textiles, food processing, steel, fertilizer

Bhutan

👥 2,005,222
🗣 Dzongkha (official)
✪ Thimphu
⛴ gypsum, timber, handicrafts, cement, fruit, precious stones, spices
● cement, wood products, processed fruits, calcium carbide

Brunei

👥 336,376
🗣 Malay (official), English, Chinese
✪ Bandar Seri Begawan
⛴ crude oil, liquefied natural gas, petroleum products
● petroleum, liquefied natural gas, construction

Cambodia

👥 12,212,306
🗣 Khmer (official), French
✪ Phnom Penh
⛴ timber, rubber, soybeans, sesame
● rice milling, fishing, wood, rubber, cement, gem mining

China

👥 1,261,832,482
🗣 Standard Chinese or Mandarin
✪ Beijing
⛴ textiles, clothing, footwear, toys, machinery and equipment, weapon systems
● iron and steel, coal, machine building, textiles, petroleum, cement

Cyprus

👥 758,363
🗣 Greek, Turkish, English
✪ Nicosia
⛴ citrus, potatoes, grapes, wine, cement, clothing

food, beverages, textiles, chemicals, metal products, tourism, wood products

Fiji

⚏ 832,494
🗣 English (official), Fijian, Hindustani
⊛ Suva
🚢 sugar, clothing, gold, processed fish, lumber
⚙ sugar, tourism, coconut, gold, silver, clothing, lumber

Georgia

⚏ 5,019,538
🗣 Georgian (official), Russian, Armenian, Azeri
⊛ T'bilisi
🚢 citrus, fruits, wine, tea
⚙ heavy industrial products

India

⚏ 1,014,003,817
🗣 Hindi (National Language);
Official Languages: Bengali, Telugu, Marathi, Tamil, Urdu, Gujarati, Malayalam, Kannada, Oriya, Punjabi, Assamese, Kashmiri, Sindhi, Sanskrit
⊛ New Delhi
🚢 clothing, gems and jewelry, engineering goods, cotton yarn, and fabric
⚙ textiles, chemicals, food processing, steel, transportation equipment

Indonesia

⚏ 224,784,210
🗣 Bahasa Indonesia (official), English, Dutch
⊛ Jakarta
🚢 fuel, foodstuffs, raw materials
⚙ petroleum and natural gas, textiles, mining, cement, chemical fertilizers, plywood, food, rubber

Iran

⚏ 65,619,636
🗣 Persian and Persian dialects, Turkic and Turkic dialects
⊛ Tehran
🚢 petroleum, carpets, fruits, nuts, hides
⚙ petroleum, petrochemicals, textiles, cement and building materials, food processing

Iraq

⚏ 22,675,617
🗣 Arabic, Kurdish, Assyrian, Armenian
⊛ Baghdad
🚢 crude oil and refined products, fertilizer, sulfur
⚙ petroleum, chemicals, textiles, construction materials, food processing

Israel

⚏ 5,842,454
🗣 Hebrew (official)
⊛ Jerusalem
🚢 machinery and equipment, cut diamonds, chemicals, textiles and clothing, agricultural products, metals
⚙ food processing, diamond cutting and polishing, textiles and clothing, chemicals, metal products, military equipment, transport equipment, electrical equipment

Japan

⚏ 126,549,976
🗣 Japanese
⊛ Tokyo
🚢 machinery, motor vehicles, consumer electronics
⚙ steel and other metals, heavy electrical equipment, construction and mining equipment, automobiles, textiles, food processing

Jordan

⚏ 4,998,564
🗣 Arabic (official)
⊛ Amman

phosphates, fertilizers, potash, agricultural products
⚙ phosphate mining, petroleum, cement

Kazakhstan

⚏ 16,733,227
🗣 Kazakh (official), Russian
⊛ Astana
🚢 oil, chemicals, grain, wool, meat, coal
⚙ extractive industries (oil, coal, iron ore, manganese, chromite, lead, zinc, copper, titanium, bauxite, gold, silver, phosphates, sulfur), iron and steel

Kiribati

⚏ 91,985
🗣 English (official), Gilbertese
⊛ Tarawa
🚢 coconut
⚙ fishing, handicrafts

Korea, North

⚏ 21,687,550
🗣 Korean
⊛ P'yongyang
🚢 minerals, metal products, agricultural and fishing products
⚙ machine building, military products, electric power, chemicals, mining, metal, textiles, food processing

Korea, South

⚏ 47,470,969
🗣 Korean
⊛ Seoul
🚢 electrical equipment, machinery, steel, automobiles, ships, textiles, clothing, footwear, fish
⚙ electronics, automobiles, chemicals, steel, shipbuilding, textiles, clothing, food processing

Kuwait

⚏ 1,973,572
🗣 Arabic (official) English widely spoken
⊛ Kuwait
🚢 oil
⚙ petroleum, petrochemicals, food processing, building materials, salt, construction

Kyrgyzstan

⚏ 4,685,230
🗣 Kirghiz (Kyrgyz)-official
⊛ Bishkek
🚢 wool, chemicals, cotton, metals, shoes, machinery
⚙ textiles, food processing industries, cement

Laos

⚏ 5,497,459
🗣 Lao (official), French, English
⊛ Vientiane
🚢 electricity, wood products, coffee, tin, clothing
⚙ tin and gypsum mining, timber, electric power, agricultural processing, construction

Lebanon

⚏ 3,578,036
🗣 Arabic (official), French (official), Armenian, English
⊛ Beirut
🚢 agricultural products, chemicals, textiles, metal
⚙ banking, food processing, textiles, cement, oil refining

Malaysia

⚏ 21,793,293
🗣 Malay (official), English
⊛ Kuala Lumpur
🚢 electronic equipment, petroleum, palm oil, wood, rubber, textiles
⚙ rubber and palm oil processing, manufacturing

Maldives

⚏ 301,475
🗣 Divehi
⊛ Male
🚢 fish, clothing
⚙ fishing, tourism, boat building

Marshall Islands

👥 68,126
🗣 English (official), Marshallese, Japanese
⊕ Majuro
🚢 coconut oil, fish, live animals, shells
⦿ coconut, fish, tourism

Micronesia, Federated States of

👥 133,144
🗣 English (official), Trukese, Pohnpeian, Yapese, Kosrean
⊕ Paliker
🚢 fish, coconut, bananas, black pepper
⦿ tourism, construction, fish processing, craft items

Mongolia

👥 2,616,383
🗣 Khalkha Mongol, Turkic, Russian, Chinese
⊕ Ulaanbaatar
🚢 copper, livestock, animal products, cashmere, wool
⦿ copper, animal products, building materials, mining (coal)

Myanmar

👥 41,734,853
🗣 Burmese
⊕ Rangoon
🚢 agricultural and forest products
⦿ agriculture, forestry

Nauru

👥 11,845
🗣 Nauruan (official)
⊕ No official capital; government offices in Yaren District
🚢 phosphates
⦿ phosphate mining, financial services, coconut products

Nepal

👥 24,702,119
🗣 Nepali (official)
⊕ Kathmandu
🚢 carpets, clothing, leather goods, jute, grain
⦿ jute, sugar, and oilseed mills

New Zealand

👥 3,819,762
🗣 English (official), Maori
⊕ Wellington
🚢 wool, lamb, beef, fish, cheese, forestry products
⦿ food processing, wood and paper products, textiles

Oman

👥 2,533,389
🗣 Arabic (official), English, Baluchi, Urdu
⊕ Muscat
🚢 petroleum, re-exports, fish, processed copper, textiles
⦿ crude oil, natural gas production, construction, cement, copper

Pakistan

👥 141,553,775
🗣 Urdu (official), English (official), Punjabi
⊕ Islamabad
🚢 cotton, textiles, clothing, rice, leather, carpets
⦿ textiles, food processing, beverages, construction materials, clothing, paper products, shrimp

Palau

👥 18,766
🗣 English (official), Sonsorolese, Angaur, Japanese, Tobi, Palauan
⊕ Koror
🚢 shellfish, tuna
⦿ tourism, craft items, some commercial fishing and agriculture

Papua New Guinea

👥 4,926,984
🗣 English, pidgin English, Motu
⊕ Port Moresby
🚢 gold, timber
⦿ agriculture, forestry

Philippines

👥 81,159,644
🗣 Pilipino (official), English (official)
⊕ Manila
🚢 electronics, textiles, coconut products, copper, fish
⦿ textiles, pharmaceuticals, chemicals, wood products, food processing, electronics assembly, petroleum refining, fishing

Qatar

👥 744,483
🗣 Arabic (official)
⊕ Doha
🚢 petroleum products, steel, fertilizers
⦿ crude oil, fertilizers, petrochemicals, steel, cement

Saudi Arabia

👥 22,023,506
🗣 Arabic
⊕ Riyadh
🚢 petroleum and petroleum products
⦿ crude oil, petroleum

Singapore

👥 4,151,720
🗣 Chinese (official), Malay (official and national), Tamil (official), English (official)
⊕ Singapore
🚢 computer equipment, rubber, petroleum, telecommunications equipment
⦿ petroleum, electronics, oil drilling equipment, rubber

Solomon Islands

👥 466,194
🗣 Melanesian pidgin
⊕ Honiara
🚢 fish, timber, palm oil, cocoa, coconut
⦿ coconut, fish (tuna)

Sri Lanka

👥 19,238,575
🗣 Sinhala (official and national), Tamil (national)
⊕ Colombo
🚢 clothing and textiles, tea, diamonds, gems, petroleum, rubber products, agricultural products, marine products, graphite
⦿ processing of rubber, tea, coconuts, and other agricultural commodities; clothing, cement, petroleum refining, textiles, tobacco

Syria

👥 16,305,659
🗣 Arabic (official), Kurdish, Armenian, Aramaic, Circassian
⊕ Damascus
🚢 petroleum, textiles, cotton, fruits and vegetables, wheat
⦿ textiles, food processing, beverages, tobacco, phosphate rock mining, petroleum

Key

👥 Population ⊕ Capital ⦿ Industry

🗣 Language 🚢 Export

Taiwan

👪 22,191,087
🗣 Mandarin Chinese (official), Taiwanese
⊛ Taipei
🚢 electrical machinery, electronic products, textiles
⚙ electronics, textiles, chemicals, clothing

Tajikistan

👪 6,440,732
🗣 Tajik (official)
⊛ Dushanbe
🚢 cotton, aluminum, fruits, vegetable oil, textiles
⚙ aluminum, zinc, lead, chemicals and fertilizers, cement, vegetable oil, metal cutting machine tools

Thailand

👪 61,230,874
🗣 Thai
⊛ Bangkok
🚢 machinery and manufactures, agricultural products and fisheries
⚙ tourism, tungsten, tin

Tonga

👪 102,321
🗣 Tongan, English
⊛ Nuku'alofa
🚢 squash, vanilla, fish, root crops, coconut oil
⚙ tourism, fishing

Turkey

👪 65,666,677
🗣 Turkish (official), Kurdish, Arabic
⊛ Ankara
🚢 manufactured products, foodstuffs, mining products
⚙ textiles, food processing, mining, steel, petroleum, construction, lumber, paper

Turkmenistan

👪 4,518,268
🗣 Turkmen, Russian, Uzbek
⊛ Ashgabat
🚢 natural gas, petroleum, cotton, electricity, textiles, carpets
⚙ natural gas, oil, petroleum products, textiles, food processing

Tuvalu

👪 10,838
🗣 Tuvaluan, English
⊛ Funafuti
🚢 coconut
⚙ fishing, tourism, coconut

United Arab Emirates

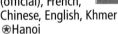

👪 2,369,153
🗣 Arabic (official), Persian, English, Hindi, Urdu
⊛ Abu Dhabi
🚢 crude oil, natural gas, re-exports
⚙ petroleum, fishing, petrochemicals, construction materials, handicrafts, pearling

Uzbekistan

👪 24,755,519
🗣 Uzbek, Russian, Tajik
⊛ Tashkent
🚢 cotton, gold, natural gas, mineral fertilizers, metals, textiles, food products
⚙ textiles, food processing, machine building, natural gas

Vanuatu

👪 189,618
🗣 English (official), French (official)
⊛ Port-Vila
🚢 coconut, beef, cocoa, timber, coffee
⚙ food and fish freezing, wood processing

Vietnam

👪 78,773,873
🗣 Vietnamese (official), French, Chinese, English, Khmer
⊛ Hanoi
🚢 petroleum, rice, agricultural products, marine products, coffee
⚙ food processing, textiles, machine building, mining, cement, chemical fertilizer, glass, tires, oil

Samoa

👪 179,466
🗣 Samoan (Polynesian), English
⊛ Apia
🚢 coconut oil and cream, taro, coconut, cocoa
⚙ timber, tourism, food processing, fishing

Yemen

👪 17,479,206
🗣 Arabic
⊛ Sanaa
🚢 crude oil, cotton, coffee, hides, vegetables, dried and salted fish
⚙ crude oil production, petroleum refining

Central & South America

Argentina

- ♁ 36,955,182
- 🗣 Spanish (official), English, Italian, German, French
- ✪ Buenos Aires
- ⛴ meat, wheat, corn, oilseed
- ◉ food processing, automobiles, textiles

Belize
- ♁ 249,183
- 🗣 English (official), Spanish, Maya
- ✪ Belmopan
- ⛴ sugar, citrus fruits, bananas, clothing
- ◉ clothing production, tourism, construction

Bolivia
- ♁ 8,152,620
- 🗣 Spanish (official), Quechua (official), Aymara (official)
- ✪ La Paz, Sucre
- ⛴ metals, natural gas
- ◉ mining, petroleum, clothing

Brazil
- ♁ 172,860,370
- 🗣 Portuguese (official), Spanish, English, French
- ✪ Brasília
- ⛴ iron ore, soybean bran, orange juice, coffee
- ◉ textiles, shoes, chemicals

Chile
- ♁ 15,153,797
- 🗣 Spanish
- ✪ Santiago
- ⛴ copper
- ◉ copper, fish processing, iron and steel

Colombia
- ♁ 39,685,655
- 🗣 Spanish
- ✪ Santa Fe de Bogotá
- ⛴ petroleum, coffee, coal, bananas
- ◉ textiles, food processing, oil, clothing

Costa Rica
- ♁ 3,710,558
- 🗣 Spanish (official)
- ✪ San José
- ⛴ coffee, bananas, textiles, sugar
- ◉ food processing, textiles, clothing

Ecuador
- ♁ 12,920,092
- 🗣 Spanish (official)
- ✪ Quito
- ⛴ petroleum, bananas, shrimp
- ◉ petroleum, food processing, textiles

El Salvador
- ♁ 6,122,515
- 🗣 Spanish
- ✪ San Salvador
- ⛴ coffee, sugar cane, shrimp
- ◉ food processing, beverages, nonmetal products

Guatemala
- ♁ 12,639,939
- 🗣 Spanish, Indian languages
- ✪ Guatemala
- ⛴ coffee, sugar, bananas
- ◉ sugar, textiles and clothing, furniture

Guyana
- ♁ 697,286
- 🗣 English
- ✪ Georgetown
- ⛴ sugar, aluminum, rice
- ◉ bauxite mining, sugar, rice milling, timber

Honduras
- ♁ 6,249,598
- 🗣 Spanish, Indian dialects
- ✪ Tegucigalpa
- ⛴ bananas, coffee, shrimp, lobster, minerals
- ◉ agricultural processing, textiles, clothing

Nicaragua
- ♁ 4,812,569
- 🗣 Spanish (official)
- ✪ Managua
- ⛴ meat, coffee, cotton, sugar
- ◉ food processing, chemicals, metal products, textiles

Panama
- ♁ 2,808,268
- 🗣 Spanish (official), English
- ✪ Panama
- ⛴ bananas, shrimp
- ◉ manufacturing and construction, petroleum refining

Paraguay
- ♁ 5,585,828
- 🗣 Spanish (official), Guarani
- ✪ Asunción
- ⛴ cotton, soybeans, timber, vegetable oils
- ◉ meat packing, oilseed crushing, milling, textiles

Peru

- ♁ 27,012,899
- 🗣 Spanish (official), Quechua (official), Aymara
- ✪ Lima
- ⛴ copper, zinc, fishmeal, crude petroleum
- ◉ mining of metals, petroleum, fishing, textiles, clothing

Suriname
- ♁ 431,303
- 🗣 Dutch (official), English
- ✪ Paramaribo
- ⛴ aluminum, shrimp, fish, rice
- ◉ bauxite mining, aluminum production, lumbering, food processing

Uruguay
- ♁ 3,334,074
- 🗣 Spanish
- ✪ Montevideo
- ⛴ wool and textile manufactures, beef and other animal products, leather, rice
- ◉ meat processing, wool and hides, sugar, textiles

Venezuela
- ♁ 23,542,649
- 🗣 Spanish (official)
- ✪ Caracas
- ⛴ petroleum
- ◉ petroleum, iron-ore mining, construction materials

Key
- ♁ Population
- 🗣 Language
- ✪ Capital
- ⛴ Export
- ◉ Industry

Europe

Albania

👥 3,490,435
🗣 Albanian
⊛ Tirana
⛏ asphalt, metals, electricity, crude oil
⚙ food processing, textiles and clothing

Andorra

👥 66,824
🗣 Catalan (official), French, Castilian
⊛ Andorra
⛏ electricity, tobacco products
⚙ tourism, sheep, timber

Austria

👥 8,131,111
🗣 German
⊛ Vienna
⛏ machinery and equipment
⚙ food, iron and steel, machinery

Belarus

👥 10,366,719
🗣 Byelorussian, Russian
⊛ Minsk
⛏ machinery and transport equipment
⚙ tractors, metal-cutting machine tools

Belgium

👥 10,241,506
🗣 Dutch, French
⊛ Brussels
⛏ iron and steel, transportation equipment
⚙ engineering and metal products, motor vehicle assembly

Bosnia and Herzegovina

👥 3,835,777
🗣 Serbo-Croatian
⊛ Sarajevo
⚙ steel production, mining

Bulgaria

👥 7,796,694
🗣 Bulgarian
⊛ Sofia
⛏ machinery and equipment
⚙ machine building and metal working

Croatia

👥 4,282,216
🗣 Serbo-Croatian
⊛ Zagreb
⛏ machinery and transport equipment
⚙ chemicals and plastics, machine tools, electronics

Czech Republic

👥 10,272,179
🗣 Czech, Slovak
⊛ Prague
⛏ manufactured goods, machinery and transport equipment
⚙ fuels, metals, machinery and equipment

Denmark

👥 5,336,394
🗣 Danish, Faroese, German
⊛ Copenhagen
⛏ meat, dairy, transport equipment
⚙ food processing, machinery and equipment

Estonia

👥 1,431,471
🗣 Estonian (official), Latvian, Lithuanian, Russian
⊛ Tallinn
⛏ textile, food products
⚙ oil, shipbuilding, phosphates

Finland

👥 5,167,486
🗣 Finnish (official), Swedish (official)
⊛ Helsinki
⛏ paper and pulp, machinery, chemicals
⚙ metal products, shipbuilding, forestry

France

👥 59,329,691
🗣 French
⊛ Paris
⛏ machinery and transportation equipment, chemicals, clothing
⚙ steel, machinery, chemicals, textiles

Germany

👥 82,797,408
🗣 German
⊛ Berlin
⛏ machine and machine tools, chemicals, motor vehicles
⚙ iron, steel, coal, cement, chemicals

Greece

👥 10,601,527
🗣 Greek (official), English, French
⊛ Athens
⛏ manufactured goods
⚙ tourism, food and tobacco processing, textiles

Hungary

👥 10,138,844
🗣 Hungarian
⊛ Budapest
⛏ raw materials and semi-finished goods, machinery and transport equipment
⚙ mining, metals, construction materials

Iceland

👥 276,365
🗣 Icelandic
⊛ Reykjavik
⛏ fish, animal products, aluminum
⚙ fish processing, aluminum

Ireland

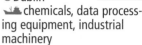

👥 3,797,257
🗣 English, Irish
⊛ Dublin
⛏ chemicals, data processing equipment, industrial machinery
⚙ food products, textiles, chemicals

Italy

👥 57,634,327
🗣 Italian
⊛ Rome
⛏ metals, textiles and clothing
⚙ machinery, iron and steel, chemicals

Latvia

👥 2,404,926
🗣 Lettish (official), Lithuanian, Russian
⊛ Riga
⛏ oil products, metals, timber
⚙ agricultural machinery, electronics

Liechtenstein

👥 32,204
🗣 German (official)
⊛ Vaduz
⛏ small specialty machinery, dental products, stamps
⚙ electronics, metal manufacturing, textiles

Lithuania

👥 3,620,756
🗣 Lithuanian (official), Polish, Russian
⊛ Vilnius
⛏ electronics
⚙ metal-cutting machine tools, electric motors

Luxembourg

- 👥 437,389
- 💬 German, Luxembourgisch, French, English
- ⊛ Luxembourg
- ⚓ finished steel products, chemicals, rubber products
- ⦿ banking, iron and steel, food processing

Macedonia

- 👥 2,041,467
- 💬 Macedonian, Albanian, Russian, Turkish
- ⊛ Skopje
- ⚓ manufactured goods, machinery and transport equipment
- ⦿ oil refining, textiles

Malta

- 👥 391,670
- 💬 Maltese (official), English (official)
- ⊛ Valletta
- ⚓ machinery and transport equipment, clothing
- ⦿ tourism, electronics, ship repair yards, construction

Moldova

- 👥 4,430,654
- 💬 Moldovan (official), Russian
- ⊛ Chisinau
- ⚓ foodstuffs, wine, tobacco, textiles
- ⦿ agricultural machinery, canned foods

Monaco

- 👥 31,693
- 💬 French (official), English, Italian
- ⊛ Monaco

Netherlands

- 👥 15,892,237
- 💬 Dutch
- ⊛ The Hague, Amsterdam
- ⚓ metal products, chemicals, processed food and tobacco
- ⦿ agricultural processing, metal and engineering products

Norway

- 👥 4,481,162
- 💬 Norwegian (official)
- ⊛ Oslo
- ⚓ petroleum, metal and metal products, fish
- ⦿ petroleum, food processing, shipbuilding

Poland

- 👥 38,646,023
- 💬 Polish
- ⊛ Warsaw
- ⚓ intermediate goods, machinery and transport equipment
- ⦿ machine building, iron and steel, chemicals

Portugal

- 👥 10,048,232
- 💬 Portuguese
- ⊛ Lisbon
- ⚓ clothing, machinery, cork and paper products
- ⦿ textiles, wood pulp, paper, and cork

Romania

- 👥 22,411,121
- 💬 Romanian, Hungarian, German
- ⊛ Bucharest
- ⚓ metal, mineral products, textiles, electric machines and equipment
- ⦿ mining, timber, construction materials

Russia

- 👥 146,001,176
- 💬 Russian
- ⊛ Moscow
- ⚓ petroleum, natural gas, wood, metals
- ⦿ mining, chemicals, metal

San Marino

- 👥 26,937
- 💬 Italian
- ⊛ San Marino
- ⚓ building stone, lime, wood, chestnuts, wheat
- ⦿ tourism, textiles, electronics

Slovakia

- 👥 5,407,956
- 💬 Slovak (official), Hungarian
- ⊛ Bratislava
- ⚓ machinery and transport equipment, chemicals, minerals
- ⦿ metal, food and beverages, electricity, gas

Slovenia

- 👥 1,927,593
- 💬 Slovenian, Serbo-Croatian
- ⊛ Ljubljana
- ⚓ machinery and transport equipment
- ⦿ metals and rolling mill products, electronics

Spain

- 👥 39,996,671
- 💬 Castilian Spanish, Catalan, Galician
- ⊛ Madrid
- ⚓ cars and trucks, semifinished manufactured goods
- ⦿ textiles and apparel, food and beverages, metal

Sweden

- 👥 8,873,052
- 💬 Swedish
- ⊛ Stockholm

(United Kingdom, continued)

- ⚓ machinery, motor vehicles, paper products, iron and steel products
- ⦿ iron and steel, precision equipment, wood pulp and paper

Switzerland

- 👥 7,262,372
- 💬 German, French, Italian, Romansch
- ⊛ Bern
- ⚓ machinery and equipment, precision instruments
- ⦿ machinery, chemicals, textiles, watches

Ukraine

- 👥 49,153,027
- 💬 Ukrainian, Russian, Romanian, Polish, Hungarian
- ⊛ Kiev
- ⚓ coal, electric power, metals, chemicals, machinery
- ⦿ coal, electric power, metals, machinery

United Kingdom

- 👥 59,508,382
- 💬 English, Welsh
- ⊛ London
- ⚓ machinery, fuels, chemicals
- ⦿ production machinery, metals, chemicals

Vatican City

- 👥 880
- 💬 Italian, Latin
- ⊛ Vatican City
- ⦿ small amount of printing, banking and financial activities

Yugoslavia

- 👥 10,662,087
- 💬 Serbo-Croatian
- ⊛ Belgrade
- ⚓ machinery and transport equipment, manufactured goods, chemicals, food and live animals
- ⦿ production machinery

Key

- 👥 Population
- 💬 Language
- ⊛ Capital
- ⚓ Export
- ⦿ Industry

North America & Caribbean

Antigua and Barbuda

👥 66,464
🗣 English (official)
⊛ Saint John's
🚢 petroleum products
⬤ tourism, construction

Bahamas

👥 294,982
🗣 English, Creol...

Canada

👥 31,278,097
🗣 English (official), French (official)
⊛ Ottawa
🚢 newsprint, wood pulp, timber, crude petroleum
⬤ minerals, food products, wood and paper products

Cuba

👥 11,141,997
🗣 Spanish
⊛ Havana
🚢 sugar, nickel, shellfish
⬤ sugar milling and refining, petroleum refining

Dominica

👥 71,540
🗣 English (official)
⊛ Roseau
🚢 bananas, soap, bay oil, vegetables
⬤ soap, coconut oil, tourism

Dominican Republic

👥 8,442,533
🗣 Spanish
⊛ Santo Domingo
🚢 sugar, gold, coffee, cocoa
⬤ tourism, sugar processing, mining

Grenada

👥 89,312
🗣 English (official)
⊛ Saint George's
🚢 bananas, cocoa, nutmeg, ...its and vegetables
⬤ food and beverages, textiles

...aiti

👥 ...867,995
🗣 French (official)
⊛ Port-au-Prince
🚢 coffee, agricultural products
⬤ sugar refining, textiles, flour milling, tourism

Jamaica

👥 2,652,689
🗣 English, Creole
⊛ Kingston
🚢 aluminum, bauxite, sugar
⬤ bauxite mining, tourism, textiles

Mexico

👥 100,349,766
🗣 Spanish
⊛ Mexico
🚢 crude oil, oil products, coffee, silver
⬤ food and beverages, chemicals, iron and steel

Saint Kitts and Nevis

👥 38,819
🗣 English
⊛ Basseterre
🚢 machinery, food, electronics
⬤ sugar processing, tourism, cotton, salt, coconut

Saint Lucia

👥 156,260
🗣 English (official)
⊛ Castries
🚢 bananas, clothing, cocoa
⬤ clothing, electronics, tourism

Saint Vincent and the Grenadines

👥 115,461
🗣 English
⊛ Kingstown
🚢 bananas, arrowroot starch
⬤ food processing, cement, furniture, clothing, starch

Trinidad and Tobago

👥 1,175,523
🗣 English (official), French, Hindi, Spanish
⊛ Port-of-Spain
🚢 petroleum, chemicals, steel
⬤ petroleum, chemicals, tourism, food processing

United States

👥 275,562,673
🗣 English
⊛ Washington, DC
🚢 capital goods, automobiles, industrial supplies and raw materials, agricultural products
⬤ petroleum, steel, automobiles, telecommunications, chemicals, electronics

Gazetteer

PLACE	LAT.	LONG.	PAGE
A **Alaska** (the 49th state, the largest U.S. state)	64°N	150°W	**155**
Alexandria, Egypt (city founded by Alexander the Great)	31°N	30°E	**220**
Alps (great mountain chain of south central Europe)	46°N	8°E	**380**
Amazon River (large South American river)	2°S	53°W	**568**
Andes (mountain range in South America)	13°S	75°W	**155**
Angola (country of southwest Africa)	14°S	16°E	**444**
Arabian Sea (northwest part of the Indian ocean)	16°N	65°E	**126**
Arctic Ocean (the smallest ocean)	85°N	170°E	**495**
Argentina (the 2nd-largest nation of South America)	35°S	67°W	**565**
Asia Minor (peninsula of western Asia)	38°N	31°E	**327**
Atacama Desert (dry region in northern Chile)	24°S	69°W	**596**
Athens (capital of Greece)	38°N	23°E	**202**
Australia (nation – continent)	25°S	135°E	**491**
Austria (German-speaking country in central Europe)	47°N	12°E	**415**
Axum (a town in Ethiopia)	13°N	38°E	**322**
B **Babylon** (ancient city-kingdom, capital of Babylonia)	32°N	42°E	**71**
Bay of Bengal (part of Indian Ocean bordering India)	18°N	87°E	**126**

PLACE	LAT.	LONG.	PAGE
Beijing, China (capital of China)	40°N	116°E	**332**
Beringia/Bering Sea (northern part of the Pacific Ocean)	58°N	175°W	**155**
Berlin (capital of Germany)	52°N	13°E	**391**
Bethlehem (city in Israel)	31°N	35°E	**242**
Bombay, India (city in India; now called Mumbai)	19°N	73°E	**367**
Brazil (Portuguese-speaking nation of South America)	9°S	53°W	**578**
British Isles (islands including Great Britain and Ireland)	54°N	4°W	**380**
Buenos Aires (capital of Argentina)	34°S	58°W	**586**
C **Cahokia, Illinois** (an Illinois town east of St. Louis)	38°N	90°W	**165**
Cairo, Egypt (capital of Egypt)	30°N	31°E	**458**
Canaan (biblical name for Israel)	32°N	34°E	**78**
Canada (North American nation)	50°N	100°W	**623**
Cape Town (capital of South Africa)	33°S	18°E	**479**
Caribbean Sea (area of the western Atlantic Ocean)	14°N	75°W	**634**
Carthage (ancient city-state of northern Africa)	37°N	10°E	**228**
Chile (nation in southwestern South America)	35°S	72°W	**597**
China (nation in eastern Asia)	36°N	93°E	**137**

PLACE	LAT.	LONG.	PAGE
Colombia (nation in northwestern South America)	3°N	72°W	**602**
Congo (nation in west central Africa; now called Republic of Congo)	3°S	13°E	**444**
Congo River (African river)	2°S	17°E	**179**
Constantinople (Istanbul) (capital of the Byzantine and Ottoman empires)	41°N	29°E	**297**
Copán (Mesoamerican city)	15°N	89°W	**159**
Costa Rica (nation of Central America)	10°N	84°W	**606**
Crete (island off the coast of Greece)	35°N	24°E	**196**
Cuba (largest nation in the West Indies island group)	22°N	79°W	**644**
Czechoslovakia (former name of the Czech Republic and Slovakia)	49°N	16°E	**391**
D **Danube** (2nd-longest European river)	43°N	24°E	**380**
Deccan Plateau (large plateau covering most of the peninsula of India)	19°N	76°E	**126**
Denmark (nation of northern Europe)	56°N	8°E	**391**
Dominican Republic (nation of the West Indies; shares island of Hispaniola with Haiti)	19°N	70°W	**644**
E **East Indies** (modern-day Indonesia)	4°S	118°E	**365**
Ecuador (nation in northwest South America)	0°N	78°W	**602**
Egypt (Arabic-speaking nation in northeast Africa)	27°N	27°E	**92**

PLACE	LAT.	LONG.	PAGE
English Channel (channel of the Atlantic Ocean between England and France)	50°N	3°W	**380**
Ethiopia (nation of east central Africa)	8°N	38°E	**322**
Euphrates River (Asian river originating in Turkey)	36°N	40°E	**67**
Eurasia (landmass including the continents of Europe and Asia)	50°N	50°E	**299**
F **France** (nation of western Europe)	46°N	1°E	**365**
G **Galilee** (region of Israel)	32°N	34°E	**242**
Ganges River (Asian river originating in the Himalayas)	24°N	89°E	**126**
Gaul (Latin word used by the Romans for the region that is modern-day France)	46°N	0.47°E	**228**
Germany (nation of central Europe)	51°N	10°E	**380**
Ghana (nation of western Africa)	8°N	2°W	**183**
Greece (nation of southern Europe)	39°N	21°E	**228**
Guadalajara (city in western Mexico)	20°N	103°W	**649**
H **Haifa** (city and chief seaport of Israel)	32°N	35°E	**556**
Haiti (nation of the West Indies sharing the island of Hispaniola with the Dominican Republic)	19°N	72°W	**644**

PLACE	LAT.	LONG.	PAGE	PLACE	LAT.	LONG.	PAGE
Harappa (village in Pakistan)	30°N	72°E	**126**	**L** **Lake Texcoco** (largest of the lakes in the Valley of Mexico) .	20°N	99°W	**339**
Himalayas (great mountain chain of South Asia and the Indian subcontinent)	29°N	85°E	**126**	**London, England** (capital of England and the U.K.)	51°N	0.07°W	**379**
Hindu Kush (mountain system of South Asia)	35°N	68°E	**126**	**Luxembourg** (small European nation bordering Belgium, France, and Germany)	49°N	6°E	**391**
Hispaniola (island of the West Indies containing Haiti and the Dominican Republic)	17°N	73°W	**644**	**M** **Macedonia** (region of Greece and nation in southeastern Europe)	41°N	22°E	**228**
Honduras (nation in northern Central America)	14°N	88°W	**565**	**Malaysia** (nation in Southeast Asia)	4°N	101°E	**365**
I **India** (nation in South Asia)	23°N	77°E	**126**	**Mali** (nation in West Africa, lies in the Sahara Desert)	15°N	0.15°W	**270**
Indian Ocean (the third-largest ocean)	10°S	70°E	**126**	**Mecca** (in Saudi Arabia, holiest city of Islam)	21°N	39°E	**256**
Indochina (former French territory containing modern-day Vietnam, Laos, and Cambodia)	17°N	105°E	**365**	**Mediterranean Sea** (sea between Europe and Africa)	36°N	13°E	**186**
Indus River (in Pakistan, the longest of the Himalayan rivers)	26°N	67°E	**126**	**Meroë** (ancient Nubian city and capital)	17°N	33°E	**92**
Israel (nation in Southwest Asia)	32°N	34°E	**556**	**Mesa Verde, CO** (plateau containing ruins of many important Pueblo settlements)	37°N	108°W	**165**
Italy (nation of southern Europe)	43°N	11°E	**387**	**Mesoamerica** (region including the southern part of North America and Central America)	19°N	99°E	**159**
J **Japan** (nation of East Asia on an archipelago on the Pacific Ocean)	36°N	133°E	**495**	**Mesopotamia** (region in southwestern Asia, site of Babylonia and Assyria)	36°N	41°E	**71**
Jerusalem (capital of Israel)	31°N	35°E	**296**	**Mexico** (North American nation)	20°N	100°W	**649**
K **Kenya** (nation of east central Africa)	1°N	36°E	**444**				

PLACE	LAT.	LONG.	PAGE
Middle East (the countries of southwestern Asia)	30°N	38°E	66
Mississippi River (major North American river)	32°N	91°W	165
Missouri River (North American river that feeds the Mississippi)	40°N	96°W	165
Mohenjo-Daro (site of the Indus Valley civilization)	27°N	68°E	126
Mombasa (seaport city in southeast Kenya)	4°N	39°E	467
Montreal (city in Quebec, Canada)	45°N	73°W	654
Mount Everest (mountain in the Himalayas; tallest in the world)	28°N	87°E	126
Mt. Kilimanjaro (mountain in Tanzania; tallest in Africa)	3°S	37°E	175
Myanmar (Burma) nation in Southeast Asia)	21°N	95°E	365
Nairobi (capital of Kenya)	1°S	37°E	467
the Netherlands (nation in northern Europe; also known as Holland)	53°N	4°E	387
Nicaragua (nation in Central America)	13°N	86°W	565
Niger River (river in western Africa)	8°N	6°E	175
Nigeria (nation in West Africa)	9°N	7°E	444
Nile (in Africa, longest river in the world)	28°N	31°E	92
Nok, West Africa (region of important ancient African civilization)	10°N	0°E	179

PLACE	LAT.	LONG.	PAGE
North China Plain (broad area of land in eastern China)	35°N	115°E	137
Norway (Scandinavian nation in northern Europe)	64°N	11°E	391
Nubia (ancient empire in northeastern Africa)	20°N	30°E	92
Ohio River (North American river that feeds the Mississippi)	37°N	88°W	165
Pakistan (nation in western part of the Indian subcontinent)	28°N	68°E	494
Palestine (nation that once occupied the land that is now Israel)	32°N	35°E	556
Persia (ancient empire, now modern-day Iran)	31°N	53°E	333
Persian Gulf (part of the Arabian Sea)	28°N	51°E	67
Perth (city in southwestern Australia)	32°S	116°E	535
Peru (nation in western South America)	10°S	75°W	578
Poland (nation in north central Europe)	53°N	17°E	415
Port-au-Prince (capital of Haiti)	19°N	72°W	644
Pyrenees (mountain range forming boundary between France and Spain)	43°N	0.05°E	380
Quebec (French-speaking province in eastern Canada)	47°N	71°W	654

PLACE	LAT.	LONG.	PAGE	PLACE	LAT.	LONG.	PAGE
R **Red Sea** (sea in the Middle East between Arabian Peninsula and northeast Africa)	23°N	37°E	**322**	**South Africa** (nation on Africa's southern tip)	28°S	25°E	**479**
Rhine River (major river of Europe)	51°N	7°E	**380**	**Spain** (nation in southwestern Europe occupying most of the Iberian Peninsula)	40°N	5°W	**228**
Rio de Janeiro (major seaport city of Brazil)	22°S	43°W	**568**	**Suez Canal** (waterway of northeastern Egypt joining the Mediterranean with the Gulf of Suez)	31°N	32°E	**458**
Río de la Plata (estuary of the Parana and Uruguay rivers in South America)	35°S	58°W	**586**	**Sumer Region** (region of Mesopotamia which had a flourishing ancient civilization)	32°N	46°E	**71**
Rocky Mountains (major mountain system of western North America)	50°N	114°W	**155**	**Sweden** (Scandinavian nation in northern Europe)	60°N	14°E	**415**
Rome (capital of Italy)	42°N	13°E	**226**	**Sydney** (largest city in Australia)	34°S	151°E	**535**
Russia (largest state of the former Soviet Union)	61°N	64°E	**387**	**Syria** (nation in the Middle East)	35°N	37°E	**261**
S **the Sahara** (largest desert on earth, stretches across northern Africa)	24°N	2°W	**175**	**T** **Tarim Basin** (basin in western China occupied largely by desert)	40°N	83°E	**137**
Santiago, Chile (capital of Chile)	33°S	71°W	**597**	**Tel Aviv** (city in western Israel)	32°N	35°E	**556**
Santo Domingo (capital of the Dominican Republic)	18°N	70°W	**644**	**Tennessee River** (major river of the southeastern United States)	36°N	88°W	**165**
Saudi Arabia (nation in Southwest Asia)	22°N	46°W	**551**	**Tenochtitlán** (Aztec capital which later became Mexico City)	19°N	99°W	**339**
Sea of Galilee (freshwater lake on Israel-Jordan border)	33°N	36°E	**242**	**Teotihuacán** (ruins in central Mexico of ancient city and culture of that name)	20°N	99°W	**159**
Serbia (nation in eastern Europe bordering Croatia and Bosnia)	44°N	21°E	**387**	**Tigris River** (in southwestern Asia; site of several ancient civilizations)	35°N	44°E	**67**
Siberia (vast region in Russia covering northern third of Asia)	57°N	97°E	**495**	**Timbuktu** (city in Mali)	17°N	3°W	**270**
Slovakia (nation in eastern Europe)	49°N	20°E	**407**				

PLACE	LAT.	LONG.	PAGE	PLACE	LAT.	LONG.	PAGE
Turkey (nation of Southwest Asia, formerly center of the Ottoman Empire)	40°N	30°W	**326**	**Y** **Yangtze River** (largest river of Asia; flows through China, also known as Chang Jiang)	31°N	117°E	**138**
U **United Kingdom** (kingdom including the countries of the British Isles)	57°N	2°W	**415**	**Yucatán** (peninsula mainly in southeastern Mexico)	21°N	89°W	**159**
Ural Mountains (mountain system of Russia, forming boundary between Europe and Asia)	56°N	58°E	**380**	**Z** **Zaire** (French-speaking nation in Central Africa; now called Democratic Republic of Congo)	1°S	22°E	**444**
V **Vancouver** (largest city of western Canada)	49°N	123°W	**659**	**Zambezi River** (one of Africa's great rivers; in central and southeastern Africa)	16°S	30°E	**179**
Venezuela (nation occupying most of the northern coast of South America)	8°N	65°W	**573**				
Veracruz (city in Mexico)	19°N	96°W	**649**				
Vienna (capital of Austria)	48°N	16°E	**327**				

Geographic Glossary

bay
part of a lake or ocean extending into the land

① butte
a raised, flat area of land with steep cliffs; smaller than a mesa

▼ canyon
a narrow, deep valley with steep sides

▲ cataract
a large, powerful waterfall

cliff
the steep, almost vertical, edge of a hill, mountain, or plain

delta
a triangular area of land formed by deposits at the mouth of a river

② desert
a dry area where few plants grow

▼ flood plain
flat land near the edges of rivers formed by mud and silt deposited by floods

glacier
a large ice mass that moves slowly down a mountain or over land

harbor
a sheltered body of water where ships can safely dock

isthmus
a narrow strip of land connecting two larger bodies of land

3 mesa
a wide, flat-topped mountain with steep sides; found mostly in dry areas

mountain pass
a gap between mountains

mouth (river)
the place where a river flows into a lake or ocean

▲ oasis
a spot of fertile land in a desert, fed by water from wells or underground springs

plain
a large area of flat or nearly flat land

4 plateau
a large area of flat land higher than the surrounding land

▲ tributary
a stream or a river that flows into a larger river

savanna
a region containing scattered trees and vegetation

▼ sea level
the level of the surface of the ocean

strait
a narrow channel of water connecting two larger bodies of water

▼ swamp
an area of land where the ground is soaked with water

valley
low land between hills or mountains

volcano
an opening in the earth, often raised, through which lava and gasses from the earth's interior escape

Biographical Dictionary

The Biographical Dictionary lists many of the people discussed in this book. The page number refers to the place where the person is first mentioned. For more complete references to people, see the Index.

A **Abraham** c. 1800s–1500s B.C., herdsman in the Fertile Crescent who, according to the Bible, became "the father of many nations" (p. 77).

al-Bakri c. A.D. 1067, geographer of early Ghana (p. 184).

Alexander the Great c. 356–323 B.C., king of the Macedonians; one of the greatest generals in history, he conquered much of the ancient world (p. 219).

Alfonsín, Raúl (rah OOL ahl fohn SEEN) elected president of Argentina in 1983; tried to have military officers brought to trial and struggled with a high inflation rate during his term (p. 588).

Archimedes c. 287–212 B.C., an experimenter in physics in ancient Greece; made many important discoveries about the natural world (p. 211).

Aristophanes c. 400s B.C., ancient Athenian playwright known for satirical comedies (p. 211).

Aristotle c. 700s B.C., Greek philosopher who wrote about life and art in the city-state of Athens (p. 199).

Arkamani c. 300s B.C., Nubian king who defied the priests of Amun and moved his capital from Napata to Meroë (p. 117).

Askia Muhammad c. A.D. 1493, he succeeded Sonni Ali as ruler of Africa's Songhai Empire, developing a brilliant system of government (p. 271).

Asoka c. 267 B.C., ruled the Mauryan Empire that was founded by his grandfather, Chandragupta; became famous for putting Buddhist ideas into law (p. 135).

B **Balaguer, Joaquín** (hwah KEEN bah lah GAIR) poet, author of books on Dominican history, president of Dominican Republic seven times (p. 646).

Balboa, Vasco Núñez de 1475–1517, Spanish explorer who, in 1513, was the first European to see the Pacific Ocean (p. 350).

Bolívar, Simón (boh LEE vahr) 1783–1830, Creole who began fighting Spanish rule over Venezuela by 1813; drove Spanish out after nine years (p. 574).

Bonaparte, Napoleon 1769–1821, French general and military hero; seized control of the government in 1799 and became its dictator (p. 363).

Brown, Linda African American who, as a seven-year-old, was not permitted to go to a school in Topeka, Kansas, reserved for white students; Supreme Court decided in her favor in *Brown v. Board of Education*, a landmark case in the U.S. civil rights movement (p. 663).

Brueghel, Pieter (BROY gehl) c. 1525–1569, Flemish painter of the Renaissance who painted *The Peasant Dance* (p. 308).

Brunelleschi, Filippo (broo nuh LEHS kee) 1377–1446, architect who designed a Roman-style dome for the Cathedral of Florence in Italy during the Renaissance (p. 305).

C **Cabot, John** c. 1450–1498, Italian who was an explorer for the British; claimed Canada for England in 1497 (p. 654).

Cabral, Pedro 1467/1468–1520, Portuguese explorer who claimed Brazil for Portugal in 1500 (p. 350).

Caesar, Augustus 63 B.C.–A.D. 14, he was the great-nephew of Julius Caesar and the first great Roman emperor; he eventually had himself declared a god (p. 229).

Caesar, Julius 100 B.C.–44 B.C., first consul of Rome, then dictator for ten years, he was a brilliant general and the first of the long line of Caesars who would rule Rome as emperors (p. 229).

Calles, Plutarco Elías Mexican president who formed the Partido Nacional Revolucionario (National Revolutionary Party) in 1929 (p. 629).

Cartier, Jacques (cart YAY) 1491–1557, French explorer who claimed eastern Canada for France in 1534 (p. 654).

Catherine of Aragon 1485–1536, first wife of Henry VIII, king of England; he asked the Pope to annul their marriage (p. 317).

Champollion, Jean François 1790–1832, the Frenchman who broke the code to understand hieroglyphics (p. 99).

Chandragupta c. 327 B.C., founder of the Mauryan Empire in India; grandfather of Asoka, one of India's greatest leaders (p. 134).

Charlemagne (SHAHR luh mayn) c. 742–814, French king (768–814) who conquered much of western Europe and supported the Christian Church (p. 288).

Cleisthenes 570–508 B.C., Greek statesman who helped reform the government of ancient Athens into a democracy (p. 200).

Columbus, Bartholomew mid 15th c.–1514/15, led Spanish settlers who founded Santo Domingo, now the capital of the Dominican Republic; brother of Christopher Columbus (p. 645).

Columbus, Christopher 1451–1506, explorer who reached the West Indies in 1492 (p. 350).

Confucius b. 551 B.C., founder of a philosophy based on respect for authority and correct behavior (p. 142).

Constantine c. A.D. 312, emperor of the Eastern Roman Empire centered at Byzantium; he was the first such leader to convert to Christianity (p. 246).

Cook, Captain James 1728–1779, discoverer, map-maker, and sailor; Cook helped shape our knowledge of the Pacific (p. 16).

Cortés, Hernando 1485–1547, Spanish conqueror who discovered the Aztec Empire in 1519 and destroyed it in two years (p. 352).

Cranach, Lucas 1472–1553, German painter and friend of Martin Luther (p. 315).

D

d'Este, Isabella (DEHS tay) 1474–1539, noble patron of the city-state of Mantua during the Renaissance (p. 305).

Da Gama, Vasco c. 1460–1524, Portuguese explorer who established a sea route (1497–1498) around the southern tip of Africa to India (p. 350).

Dante Alighieri (DAHN tay) 1265–1321, Florentine writer during the Renaissance; wrote *The Divine Comedy* (p. 306).

Darius c. 400s B.C., Persian king who attempted to conquer Greece and force its inhabitants to live under the rule of force; defeated on the plains of Marathon (p. 202).

David c. 1060–970 B.C., united all twelve tribes and became the second king of Israel (p. 80).

de Courbertin, Baron Pierre c. 1896, organized the modern Olympic Games (p. 206).

Deng Xiaoping (DUHNG SHEE OW PING) 1904–1997, Communist leader who encouraged foreign investment in China; sent in the army to Tiananmen Square in 1989 (p. 528).

Dessalines, Jean-Jacques (zhan zhahk day sa LEEN) c. 1758–1806, leader of a Haitian rebellion that began in 1794; became governor-general and declared Haiti independent in 1804 (p. 628).

Díaz, Bernal c. 1492–1581, European who visited the Aztec city of Tenochtitlán in the early 1500s (p. 341).

Djoser c. 2650–2575 B.C., pharaoh for whom the first pyramid was built (p. 103).

Dubček, Alexander (DOOB chehk) 1921–1992, Communist leader of Czechoslovakia; took office early in 1968 and offered reforms but was forced to resign in August of the same year (p. 406).

Dürer, Albrecht (DUR uhr) 1471–1528, German artist known for his ability to capture the beauty and detail of nature in his paintings (p. 308).

E

Elizabeth I 1533–1603, queen of England (1558–1603), daughter of Henry VIII; sought a shortcut from Europe to Asia; English colonies in the Americas were established during her reign (p. 350).

Elizabeth II 1926–, queen of Great Britain (1952–) who is also queen of independent Canada (p. 655).

Emerson, Ralph Waldo 1803–1882, American poet who referred to "the shot heard round the world" when writing about the Battle of Concord (p. 627).

Erasmus, Desiderius c. 1466–1536, Dutch writer who criticized the Church during the Renaissance (p. 309).

Ezana Abyssinian king (A.D. 300s) who converted to Christianity and made it the official religion of Axum (p. 322).

F

Ferdinand 1452–1516, ruler of Spain who, with his wife Queen Isabella, financed the voyages of Christopher Columbus (p. 350).

Fremiet, Emmanuel (FRUH mee yay) 1824–1910, French sculptor who created a famous statue of Joan of Arc in the 1870s (p. 314).

Fu Hao c. 1300 B.C., wife of an emperor; a general who had great military power during the Han dynasty (p. 141).

G

Galileo Galilei (gal uh LEE oh gal uh LAY) 1564–1642, Italian astronomer who found evidence that the Earth revolved around the sun; the Catholic Church forced him to announce he had changed his mind (p. 356).

Gandhi, Indira 1917–1984, prime minister of India who was assassinated; daughter of Jawaharlal Nehru and mother of Rajiv Gandhi (p. 545).

Gandhi, Mohandas 1869–1948, Indian leader of independence movement against the British; known for his use of nonviolent protest (p. 504).

Genghis Khan (JEHNG gihs KAHN) c. 1162–1227, leader who united Mongol tribes in 1206 (p. 299).

Gutenberg, Johannes c. 1400–1468, German printer; thought to be the first European to use movable type, which created a faster method to print books (p. 316).

H **Hammurabi** 1700s B.C., known as the Lawgiver; ruled Babylon and created a famous code of laws (p. 73).

Hannibal Carthaginian general who crossed the Alps to attack Rome (p. 228).

Henry VIII 1491–1547, king of England (1509–1547) who broke with the Catholic Church and declared himself head of the Church of England so that he could annul his marriage to Catherine of Aragon (p. 317).

Henry (the Navigator) 1394–1460, prince who set up a center for exploration in Sagres, Portugal; correctly believed that Asia could be reached by sailing around the southern tip of Africa (p. 350).

Hesiod c. 700 B.C., Greek poet who told stories about the ancient Greek gods and goddesses (p. 206).

Hidalgo y Costilla, Miguel (ee DAHL go ee kohs TEE yah) 1753–1811, priest and leader of a revolt, who was captured and executed in 1811; gave a famous speech on September 16 (celebrated as Mexican Independence Day), urging his followers to fight Spanish oppression (p. 628).

Hippocrates c. 460–377 B.C., ancient Greek physician who is considered the founder of the scientific approach to medicine (p. 211).

Hitler, Adolf 1889–1945, head of the National Socialist German Workers' Party (Nazi Party), leader of Germany; ordered the killing of millions of Jews and others during World War II (p. 390).

Ho Chi Minh 1890–1969, led Vietnamese Communists who fought the Japanese during World War II (p. 506).

Homer c. 800s B.C., author of the *Iliad* and the *Odyssey*; a Greek poet who worked in the epic style (p. 198).

Hudson, Henry d. 1611, English explorer who sailed up the Hudson River (1609–1611) and claimed the region for the Netherlands (p. 350).

I **Ibn Sina** 979–1037, a Muslim physician who published one of the most popular books on medicine ever written (p. 263).

Imhotep c. 2650 B.C., Egyptian architect, physician, and statesman who built the first pyramid; later worshipped as the god of medicine (p. 103).

Isabella 1451–1504, ruler of Spain who, with her husband King Ferdinand, financed the voyages of Christopher Columbus (p. 350).

J **Jesus** 4 B.C.–A.D. 29/30, a great religious leader called Christ by his followers; believed by most Christians to be the son of God (p. 241).

Joan of Arc c. 1412–1431, French teenager who saved the town of Orléans from English forces; considered a heretic and was executed (p. 314).

John c. 1167–1216, English king who was forced to sign the Magna Carta (p. 293).

Jolliet, Louis 1645–1700, French explorer who, with Marquette, explored the Great Lakes and the Mississippi River valley (p. 350).

K **Kanissai** legendary king of ancient Ghana; known as a "lord of the gold" (p. 184).

Kemal Atatürk 1881–1938, founder of modern Turkey who tried to modernize the country (p. 505).

Kublai Khan (KOO bly KAHN) 1215–1294, grandson of Genghis Khan; made the Mongol Empire more open to trade; was visited by Marco Polo; his death signaled the end of the Mongol Empire (p. 300).

L **Lalibela** (lah lee BAY lah) king of Zagwé dynasty in Ethiopia (late 1100s–early 1200s) who ruled from Roha and was later regarded as a saint; 10 Christian churches carved from volcanic rock were built during his reign (p. 323).

Lao-tzu c. 604-531 B.C., founder of Taoism, a philosophy based on inner harmony achieved through the contemplation of nature (p. 143).

Las Casas, Bartolomé de 1474–1566, a Spanish missionary who wrote about Europeans' treatment of Native Americans during the Age of Exploration (p. 353).

Lavoisier, Antoine (lah vwah ZYAY) 1743–1794, French scientist considered to be the founder of modern chemistry; named oxygen in 1777 (p. 358).

Leeuwenhoek, Antonie van (LAY wuhn hook) 1632–1723, Dutch cloth dealer who made improvements to a device that would lead to the microscope (p. 357).

Lenin, Vladimir 1870–1924, a leader of the Russian Revolution who believed in communism; head of the Bolshevik Party; formed the Union of Soviet Socialist Republics (Soviet Union) (p. 389).

Leonardo da Vinci (duh VIHN chee) 1452–1519, artist, inventor, and scientist; began painting the Mona Lisa in 1503 (p. 306).

Leyster, Judith 1609–1660, Dutch artist; probably the only female member of the painter's guild of Haarlem at the time (p. 309).

Li Po c. A.D. 701–762, lived during China's Tang dynasty and was one of that nation's greatest poets (p. 274).

Louis XVI 1754–1793, king of France, executed during the French Revolution (p. 362).

Luther, Martin 1483–1546, German theologian and leader of the Reformation who posted a list of 95 theses on a church door at Wittenberg in 1517; was excommunicated in 1521 (p. 315).

M **Macmillan, Harold** 1894–1986, British prime minister from 1957 to 1963 (p. 445).

Magellan, Ferdinand c. 1480–1521, commander of the first expedition to sail completely around the world (p. 349).

Malakaye c. 500s B.C., queen who ruled Nubia (p. 117).

Mansa Musa ruled c. A.D. 1312–1337; expanded the empire of Mali created by his great uncle, Sundiata (p. 269).

Mao Zedong (MOW dzuh DOONG) 1893–1976, Communist leader of China who established the People's Republic of China; called for a "Cultural Revolution" in 1966 (p. 505).

Marquette, Jacques 1637–1675, French explorer who, with Jolliet, explored the Great Lakes and the Mississippi River valley (p. 350).

Mbeki, Thabo (TAH boh mm BEHG ee) 1942–, president of South Africa; elected in 1999 (p. 483).

McLuhan, Marshall 1911–1980, university professor turned sociologist; coined the phrase "global village" (p. 44).

Mehmet II Ottoman sultan who stormed Constantinople, capital of the Byzantine Empire, on May 29, 1453, which then fell to Ottoman forces (p. 326).

Menem, Carlos 1930–, elected president of Argentina in 1989; ended state control over wages and prices, pardoned military officers, and reduced the size of the army (p. 588).

Menes c. 3100 B.C., Egyptian king who, according to legend, united Upper and Lower Egypt into one kingdom (p. 95).

Michelangelo Buonarroti (my kuhl AN jah loh) 1475–1564, Italian artist during the Renaissance; painted the ceiling of the Sistine Chapel in Rome, which he completed in 1512 (p. 304).

Montezuma c. 1466–1520, Aztec ruler defeated by Spanish conqueror Hernando Cortés (p. 352).

More, Sir Thomas 1478–1535, English scholar, author of *Utopia*; criticized political and religious problems during the Renaissance (p. 309).

Morelos y Pavón, José María (moh RAY lohz ee pah VOHN) priest who led an army in revolt in Mexico against Spain; controlled most of southern Mexico until he was captured and executed by Spain in 1815 (p. 629).

Moses c. 1400s–1300s B.C., according to the Bible, led the Israelites out of Egypt and to the land God promised to Abraham (p. 78).

Mugabe, Robert (mu GAH bee) 1924–, first president of Zimbabwe, formerly known as Rhodesia (p. 444).

Muhammad Ibn Abd Allah A.D. 570–A.D. 632, a prophet and founder of the religion of Islam (p. 255).

N **Nebuchadnezzar** c. 630–562 B.C., Babylonian king who established his own empire in the Fertile Crescent (p. 75).

Nehru, Jawaharlal (jah WAH hahr lahl NAY roo) 1889–1964, first prime minister of India after it won independence in 1947; father of Indira Gandhi (p. 544).

Nicholas II 1868–1918, Russian czar overthrown by groups of workers in the spring of 1917 (p. 389).

Nkrumah, Kwame (uhn KROO muh) 1909–1972, first African prime minister of Ghana; overthrown in 1966 (p. 444).

O **Ogdai** (AHG dy) d. 1241, ruled Mongols after the death of his father, Genghis Khan, in 1227 (p. 299).

P **Pericles** d. 429 B.C., ruler of Athens who restored the city after its wars with Persia and ordered the construction of the Parthenon (p. 208).

Perón, Juan (peh ROHN) 1895–1974, colonel who was imprisoned and later became president of Argentina (p. 585).

Phidias c. 450s B.C., Greek artist who supervised the building of the Parthenon and the temples that surrounded it (p. 208).

Philip II c. 382–336 B.C., king of Macedonia; father of Alexander the Great (p. 219).

Piye c. 700s B.C., king of Nubia who conquered Egypt (p. 116).

Plato c. 427–347 B.C., philosopher of ancient Athens and student of Socrates; through the writings of Plato we know the teachings of Socrates, whose conversations he recorded in his own works (p. 212).

Polo, Marco 1254–1324, Italian traveler who met and worked for Kublai Khan; published a description of his journeys on the Silk Road (p. 300).

Ponce de León, Juan 1460–1521, Spanish explorer who searched for the "Fountain of Youth" in Florida in 1513 (p. 350).

Ptolemy A.D. 100s, Greek who lived in Egypt and wrote a set of texts which summed up the ancient world's knowledge of geography (p. 351).

Pythagoras c. 500s B.C., a scientist and mathematician of ancient Greece who developed many basic theorems still in use today (p. 211).

R

Raphael 1483–1520, Renaissance artist who completed his painting, *The School of Athens*, in 1511 (p. 306).

Rembrandt van Rijn (REHM brant vahn RYN) 1606–1669, famous Dutch painter of the Renaissance (p. 308).

S

San Martin, José de (deh san mahr TEEN) 1778–1850, led independence movements in areas that are now Argentina, Chile, and Peru (p. 574).

Saud, Abdul Aziz Ibn (AHB dool ah ZEZ IHB uhn sah OOD) c. 1901–1969, leader of the Saudis who captured Mecca and Medina after World War I; united Arab tribes and established the Kingdom of Saudi Arabia in 1932 (p. 552).

Saul c. 1000 B.C., first king of Israel, who led the Israelites in fending off outside invasion (p. 80).

Schliemann, Heinrich c. 1870, German archaeologist and adventurer who discovered the ruins of ancient Troy by reading Homer's poem, the *Iliad* (p. 198).

Senghor, Leopold (sahng GAWR) 1906–, well-known poet and first president of Senegal in 1960 (p. 444).

Shah Jahan 1592–1666, Mughul emperor who, after the death of his wife in 1631, built the Taj Mahal as a tomb in her honor (p. 543).

Shakespeare, William 1564–1616, English playwright of the Renaissance who wrote *Hamlet*, *Macbeth*, and *Romeo and Juliet*; one of the world's most famous writers (p. 308).

Shihuangdi c. 221 B.C., founder of the Qin dynasty in China (p. 144).

Siddhartha Gautama c. 540 B.C., later known as the Buddha, or the Enlightened One, his religious quest became the foundation of the great religion of Buddhism (p.132).

Solomon c. 950 B.C., king of Israel known for his wisdom; the son of David (p. 80).

Solon c. 640–560 B.C., Greek statesman who helped create a legal code for the ancient city-state of Athens (p. 200).

Sonni Ali c. A.D. 1450s, a fierce ruler of Africa's Songhai Empire (p. 270).

Sophocles 496–406 B.C., Greek playwright of Athens who is remembered particularly for his tragedies; among his works are *Oedipus the King*, *Oedipus at Colonnus*, and *Elektra* (p. 210).

Stalin, Josef 1879–1953, Soviet Communist head of government who ruled as a dictator; under his control, the "Eastern Bloc" was created (p. 393).

Suleiman (SOO lay mahn) c. 1494–1566, ruler of the Ottoman Empire (1520–1566) who spread Islamic culture to the northern African coast and across the Middle East to the Persian Gulf; called "the Magnificent" in Europe and "the Lawgiver" by Muslims (p. 326).

Sundiata c. A.D. 1200s, a Mandinka prince who overcame paralysis to found the African empire of Mali (p. 268).

T

Taharqa c. 690–664 B.C., king of Nubia who is mentioned in the Bible; considered the greatest builder of the Kushite dynasty (p. 116).

Tai Zong c. A.D. 589, the first great emperor of the Tang dynasty in China (p. 274).

Tutankhamun c. 1350 B.C., boy-king of Egypt whose magnificent tomb was discovered by Europeans in the 1920s (p. 91).

U

Urban II c. 1042–1099, Pope whose speech in 1095 inspired the first European crusade to take back Jerusalem for Christianity (p. 297).

V

van Eyck, Jan c. 1390–1441, famous Flemish painter during the Renaissance (p. 308).

Vespucci, Amerigo 1454–1512, European explorer of the South American coast (p. 567).

Victoria 1819–1901, queen of England who also later became "Empress of India"; she appointed a viceroy and governors to govern British India (p. 368).

X

Xerxes c. 400s B.C., Persian king who, like his father Darius, tried to conquer Greece; repelled by the Athenians and Spartans at Salamis (p. 203).

Y **Yongle** (YOONG LUH) son of Hongwu (Zhu Yuanzhang); Ming dynasty emperor (1403–1424) who sent seven expeditions, the first in 1405, under Admiral Zheng He to India, Arabia, and Africa (p. 332).

Z **Zhou Enlai** (JOH EN LIE) 1898–1976, first prime minister of China; took more control over the state after the weakening of Mao's power (p. 528).

Zhu Yuanzhang (joo YOO ahn jang) became first emperor of the Ming dynasty of China in 1368 and changed his name to Hongwu; moved the capital to Nanjing (p. 331).

Zumbi leader of Africans living in Palmares in Brazil in the 1600s who were eventually captured by the Portuguese and killed (p. 603).

Glossary

abacus (AB uh kuhs) a counting device made of beads threaded on parallel wires on a frame; invented in ancient China (p. 275).

abdicate (AB dih KAYT) to voluntarily give up a throne or other position of power (p. 323).

aborigines (ab uh RIHJ uh neez) the original inhabitants of Australia (p. 534).

acid rain (AS ihd rayn) rain that has high amounts of acids caused by pollution (p. 624).

afterlife (AF tuhr LYF) in some religious beliefs, a life that follows after death (p. 101).

agriculture (AG rih KUHL chuhr) working the land in order to grow particular things on it (p. 62).

alliance (uh LY uhns) an agreement made between nations for a common cause (p. 339).

allies (AL yz) countries that agree to give military or economic support to one another if necessary (p. 388).

anthropologist (an thruh PAHL uh jihst) a scientist who studies people and their cultures (p. 46).

anti-Semitism (AN tee SEHM ih TIHZ uhm) prejudice or hostility toward Jews (p. 391).

apartheid (uh PAHRT HYT) former official policy of racial separation in the Republic of South Africa (p. 480).

aqueduct (AK wih DUHKT) tunnels and bridges built to transport water; first built in ancient Rome (p. 237).

aquifer (AK wuh fuhr) underground rock where water collects (p. 559).

arable (AR uh buhl) fit or suitable for the planting of crops, as in arable land (p. 624).

archaeologist (AHR kee AHL uh jihst) a scientist who studies past civilizations by examining ancient pottery, buildings, and other remains (p. 46).

aristocracy (ar ih STAHK ruh see) a government controlled by the nobility (p. 199).

artifact (AHR tuh FAKT) objects from the past of historical interest, such as ancient tools and pottery (p. 47).

assassin (uh SAS ihn) a murderer who kills a public figure, usually for political reasons (p. 545).

astronomy (uh STRAHN uh mee) the study of the stars and planets (p. 263).

atmosphere (AT muh SFIHR) a mixture of gases that surrounds the earth (p. 15).

atrium (AY tree uhm) an entrance hall that opens into a larger courtyard (p. 232).

aviary (AY vee EHR ee) a large enclosure for birds (p. 338).

Bantustands (BAN too stans) lands where black South Africans were required to live under a policy of racial separation (p. 480).

basin (BAY sihn) a low area of land surrounded by mountains (p. 137).

bedouin (BEHD oo ihn) a tribe of desert nomads, or wanderers, in North Africa, Syria, or Arabia (p. 552).

beliefs (bih LEEFS) a system of ideas by which people live; ideas in which people have confidence and trust (p. 36).

Bible (BY buhl) a book of ancient writings sacred to Christianity and Judaism (p. 77).

biodiversity (BY oh dih VUR sih tee) a great variety of kinds of plants and animals (p. 606).

biosphere (BY uh SFIHR) the earth's surface and all living things on it (p. 15).

bishop (BIHSH uhp) a high-ranking member of the leadership in the Christian church (p. 249).

border control (BAWR duhr kuhn TROHL) a customs check or border inspection where people must show a passport to go from one country to another (p. 417).

bronze (brahnz) a yellowish-brown metal that combines copper and tin (p. 139).

bureaucracy (burhr AH kraz y) the administration of a government, with many bureaus, or departments, staffed by various officials (p. 146).

caliph (KAH lihf) the head of a Muslim state; a successor to the prophet Muhammad (p. 260).

campesino (KAHM peh SEE noh) a person who lives in the countryside in Mexico (p. 650).

capitalism (KAP ih tl ihz uhm) an economic system of private ownership of factories, businesses, and farms (p. 359).

caravan (KAR uh VAN) a group of people and their vehicles or animals who travel together (p. 114).

cash crop (kash krahp) a crop that is grown to be sold for a profit (p. 438).

caste system (kast SIHS tuhm) a rigid organization of society by levels, or classes, of people (p. 130).

cataract (KAT uh rakt) a dramatic turn or series of waterfalls on a river (p. 93).

cathedral (kuh THEE DRUHL) a large or important house of worship in the Christian faith (p. 292).

chinampa (chee NAHM pah) of Mexican origin, an island of farmland on a lake, created by digging up soil from the lake bottom and piling it into mounds (p. 342).

chivalry (SHIHV uhl ree) a code of honor followed by knights in the Middle Ages (p. 288).

circumnavigate (SUR kuhm NAV ih GAYT) to sail completely around something (p. 349).

city-state (SIHT ee STAYT) an independent state that includes a city and the surrounding area (p. 70).

civil disobedience (SIHV uhl DIHS uh BEE dee uhns) the refusal to obey certain laws because they are thought to be unjust; a form of nonviolent protest (p. 504).

civilization (SIHV uh lih ZAY shuhn) a complex society with a high level of development in government and culture (p. 68).

civil rights (SIHV uhl ryts) rights guaranteed to citizens by their constitution or by laws of government (p. 663).

civil war (SIHV uhl wawr) a war fought between two regions or groups within the same country (p. 145).

class (KLASS) a group of people in society who hold the same social position (p. 71).

climate (KLY miht) the typical weather conditions of a given area over a period of time (p. 24).

cold war, Cold War (kohld wawr) the 40-year period of rivalry between Soviet-bloc and Western-bloc countries after World II (p. 394).

comedy (KAHM ih dee) a lighthearted play, movie, or other work that makes people laugh (p. 211).

commercial farming (kuh MUR shuhl FAHRM ihng) farming that sells goods at competitive prices and is organized to make money (p. 467).

Common Market (KAHM uhn MAHR kiht) an economic union of European countries formed to make trade easier and more profitable (p. 416).

commune (KAHM yoon) a community of people who live and work as a group, sharing responsibilities (p. 527).

communism (KAHM yuh NIHZ uhm) a political system in which the government owns and runs most businesses and often decides where people can live and work (p. 389).

compound (KAHM pownd) a series of rooms built around a courtyard (p. 474).

constitutional monarchy (KAHN stih TOO shuh nuhl MAHN uhr kee) a government led by a king or queen whose power is restricted by a constitution and other laws (p. 362).

consul (KAHN suhl) in ancient Rome, one of two chief government officials; a person appointed by a government to represent its interests in a foreign city (p. 227).

consumerism (kuhn SOO muh RIHZ uhm) the idea that when more goods are consumed, the economy improves (p. 509).

continental climate (KAHN tuh NEHN tl KLY miht) the climate near the interior of a continent; summers are often short and hot and winters are long and cold (p. 382).

Continental Divide (KAHN tuh NEHN tl dih VYD) a stretch of the Rocky Mountains in North America; on the west side of the divide water flows west to the Pacific Ocean; on east side it flows to the Atlantic Ocean (p. 622).

convert (KAHN vurt) a person who changes from one religion to another (p. 322).

covenant (KUHV uh nuhnt) a solemn agreement (p. 77).

Creole (KREE ohl) a dialect of the French language (p. 643).

crucifixion (KROO suh FIHK shuhn) a method of execution in which the victim is nailed or tied on a wooden cross; often used in ancient Rome (p. 244).

crusade (kroo SAYD) a religious war; a military expedition by Christians of the 11th, 12th, or 13th centuries to take the Holy Land away from the Muslims (p. 297).

cuisine (kwih ZEEN) the characteristic style of cooking and preparing food in a particular country (p. 383).

Cultural Revolution (KUHL chur uhl REHV uh LOO shuhn) a period of time in the 1960s and 1970s in China when Mao Zedong enforced strict Communist ideals (p. 527).

culture (KUHL chuhr) the customs, beliefs, and whole way of life of a group of people (p. 35).

cuneiform (KYOO nee uh fawrm) an ancient form of wedge-shaped writing that contained over 800 signs (p. 70).

currency (KUR uhn see) a system of money (p. 415).

D **delta** (DEHL tuh) an area of fertile land formed by mud and sand near the mouth of a river (p. 92).

democracy (dih MAHK ruh see) a government ruled by the people; citizens play an active role (p. 199).

denomination (dih NAHM uh NAY shuhn) a religious group that shares particular beliefs, forms of worship, and government (p. 250).

desalinization (dee sal uh nih ZAY shuhn) the process of removing salt from sea water (p. 554).

desertification (dih ZUR tuh fih KAY shuhn) the expansion of a desert because of overuse by people or livestock, or by natural forces (p. 438).

dialect (DY uh LEHKT) a variation of a language shared by people who live in a particular region (p. 459).

Diaspora (dy AS puhr uh) the scattering of Jews throughout the world since ancient times (p. 81).

dictator (DIHK tay tuhr) a ruler who holds absolute power (p. 575).

disciple (dih SY puhl) a follower who helps spread the ideas and teachings of another; in the Christian faith, a follower of Jesus (p. 243).

discrimination (dih SKRIHM ihn AY shuhn) the unfair treatment of people for unfair reasons, such as religion, race, income, or nationality (p. 662).

dissident (DIHS ih duhnt) a person who disagrees with the government (p. 407).

diversify (dih VUR sih fy) to draw from a variety of sources; in business, to draw income from many products, instead of relying on only one or two (p. 598).

domestication (duh mehs tih KAY shuhn) taming to make useful to people, as in raising wild animals (p. 62).

drip irrigation (drihp IHR ih GAY shuhn) in agriculture, a system of plastic tubes that carries water directly to plants (p. 557).

drought (drowt) an extended dry period with very little rain (p. 438).

dynasty (DY nuh stee) a group of rulers descending from the same family whose power continues for several generations (p. 95).

E **edict** (EE dihkt) a proclamation or law handed down by a ruler (p. 135).

empire (ehm PYR) a state in which a single ruler controls several kingdoms or territories (p. 74).

epic (EHP ihk) a long poem that tells a story about an adventure (p. 195).

estuary (EHS choo EHR ee) the wide area of a river where it meets the ocean and is influenced by tides (p. 586).

Eurasia (yoo RAY zhuh) the combined continents of Europe and Asia (p. 299).

European Union (YUR uh PEE uhn YOON yuhn) an organization that governs political and economic cooperation among member nations in Europe (p. 416).

extinction (ehk STIHNGKT shuhn) completely dying out; the end of a kind of organism (p. 176).

F **fellahin** (FEHL uh HEEN) peasants, or country people, in Egypt (p. 460).

food crop (food krop) a crop grown to be eaten by the grower, instead of being sold (p. 436).

fossil (FAHS uhl) the remains or traces in stone or clay of a plant or animal from an earlier age (p. 47).

free-market economy (free MAHR kiht ih KAHN uh mee) an economy in which farms and factories are privately owned; the owner decides what to produce and what prices to charge (p. 408).

freshwater (FREHSH wah tuhr) relating to rivers and lakes that contain no saltwater (p. 176).

gaucho (GOW choh) a cowboy in South America (p. 577).

geography (jee AHG ruh fee) the study of the earth and its people (p. 15).

geologist (jee AHL uh jihst) a scientist who studies the structure of the earth (p. 553).

glacier (GLAY shuhr) a vast, slow-moving sheet of ice (p. 154).

gladiator (GLAD ee AY tuhr) in ancient Rome, a slave or captive forced to fight another person to the death (p. 235).

global village (GLOH buhl VIHL ihj) a term that compares the world to a small village, where fast, modern communication allows news to travel quickly (p. 44).

glyph (glihf) a carving that represents something, as in a hieroglyph (p. 160).

Gospel (GAHS puhl) a text written after the life of Jesus that records his life, works, and teachings; the four Gospels form part of the New Testament (p. 242).

governor-general (GUHV uhr nuhr JEHN uhr uhl) the personal representative of a king (p. 368).

graziers (GRAY zhuhrz) people who raise cattle, sheep or other grazing livestock (p. 536).

Great Leap Forward (grayt leep FAWR wuhrd) a five-year program to establish communes, launched in China by Mao Zedong in 1958 (p. 526).

guerrilla band (guh RIHL uh band) a small military group that fights against the government in power; military strategy includes sudden acts of violence (p. 504).

guild (gihld) a craft or trade association, formed to give members mutual aid and protection (p. 290).

Gulf Stream (guhlf streem) a warm-water ocean current that starts in the western Caribbean Sea (p. 382).

hacienda (AH see EHN duh) in a Spanish-speaking country, a large estate (p. 576).

Hellenistic (HEHL uh NIHS tihk) having to do with Greek culture; based on the ideas of Greek philosophers, scientists, poets, and playwrights (p. 220).

heretic (HEHR ih tihk) a person who holds opinions and beliefs that are contrary to accepted teachings, especially that are contrary to the teachings of the Church (p. 314).

hieroglyphics (HY uhr uh GLIHF ihks) a method of writing developed in ancient Egypt, in which pictures represent sounds, objects, or ideas (p. 99).

Hijrah (HIHJ ruh) the move from Mecca to Medina by the prophet Muhammad and his followers (p. 257).

Holocaust (HAWL uh KAWST) the massacre of Jews and others by the Nazis during World War II (p. 392).

Homo sapiens (HOH moh SAY pee uhnz) the biological classification of human beings (p. 60).

human region (HYOO muhn REE juhn) an area of human activity; an area where people share the same government or language (p. 26).

hunter-gatherer (HUHN tuhr GATH uhr uhr) an individual or a culture that lives by hunting wild game and fish and gathering plants, fruit, seeds, and honey (p. 61).

hurricane (HUR ih KAYN) a powerful storm with heavy rains and winds over 75 miles per hour (p. 625).

imperialism (ihm PIHR ee uh LIHZ uhm) a policy of extending political and territorial control over other countries, usually by force (p. 365).

indigenous (ihn DIHJ uh nuhs) natural or native to an area, such as an indigenous people (p. 352).

inflation (ihn FLAY shuhn) a sharp and continuing increase in the price of goods and services (p. 587).

irrigation (IHR ih GAY shuhn) supplying water to the land through a system of canals or ditches (p. 67).

isolationism (y suh LAY shuhn ihz uhm) a national policy of not becoming involved with other nations (p. 332).

isthmus (IHS muhs) a narrow neck of land (p. 154).

joint venture (joynt VEHN chuhr) an undertaking in which companies from different countries share the cost of creating and running a business (p. 509).

kibbutz (kih BUTZ) a cooperative settlement where labor, goods, and services are shared by everyone; from the Hebrew word for "gathering" (p. 557).

kiln (kihln) a large oven for hardening and baking clay pottery (p. 335).

kinship (KIHN shihp) ties among family and relatives (p. 180).

knight (nyt) a land-holding noble of the Middle Ages who began training during childhood for a lifetime of duty to his lord (p. 288).

L **labor force** (LAY buhr fohrs) people within a population who are available to work (p. 359).

landform (LAND fawrm) a feature of the earth's surface, such as a mountain or valley (p. 22).

literacy rate (LIHT uhr uh see rayt) the percentage of people who are able to read and write (p. 519).

M **magnetic compass** (mag NEHT ihk KUHM puhs) an instrument that uses a magnetic needle to show direction in relation to the earth's magnetic field (p. 275).

maize (mayz) corn; a grain native to the Americas (p. 154).

mandate (MAN dayt) a command or instruction from a person in authority (p. 142).

marine climate (muh REEN KLY miht) a climate with relatively mild winters and cool summers (p. 382).

maritime (MAR ih tym) having to do with the sea (p. 197).

Marshall Plan (MAHR shuhl plan) an American program that gave and loaned money to Western European countries after WWII (p. 419).

materialism (muh TIHR ee uh LIHZ uhm) the idea that ownership of goods can buy happiness (p. 509).

matrilineage (MAT ruh LIHN ee ihj) tracing ancestry through the mother's side of the family (p. 180).

megalopolis (mehg uh LAHP uh lihs) a large urban area formed by two or more cities and the towns between them (p. 632).

mercenary (MUR suh nehr ee) a soldier hired to fight in a foreign army (p. 339).

mesa (MAY suh) a steep hill with a flat, tablelike top; from the Spanish word for table (p. 167).

mestizo (mehs TEE zoh) a person of mixed Spanish and Native American heritage (p. 578).

middle class (MIH duhl klas) people of average income and position in society; in the Middle Ages, people who ranked between nobles and serfs (p. 290).

millet (MIHL iht) in Turkey, an organized community of religious minorities (p. 327).

monarchy (MAHN uhr kee) a government headed by a king or queen (p. 292).

monopoly (muh NAHP uh lee) a person or group having complete control over a business activity or service (p. 184).

monotheism (MAHN uh thee IHZ uhm) the worship of one all-powerful god (p. 79).

monsoon (mahn SOON) a wind in southern Asia that changes direction with the seasons (p. 126).

mosque (mahsk) a house of worship in Islam (p. 257).

multicultural (MUHL tee KUHL chuhr uhl) associated with many different cultures (p. 534).

multiethnic (MUHL tee EHTH nihk) associated with many different ethnic groups (p. 446).

Muslims (MUHZ luhmz) people who are members of the Islamic faith; those who believe in the teachings of the prophet Muhammad (p. 257).

mysticism (MIHS tih SIHZ uhm) the belief that deep meditation can lead to a direct relationship with God (p. 262).

myth (mihth) a story from the distant past that explains such events as the beginning of the world or the changing seasons (p. 206).

N **NAFTA** the North American Free Trade Agreement, signed in 1992 to create a large trade market (p. 630).

nationalize (NASH uh nuh LYZ) to take a business or service industry away from a private owner and put it under the control of the government (p. 459).

nomad (NOH mad) a person who moves from place to place in search of food and water (p. 78).

O **open-pit mine** (OH puhn piht MYN) a series of steep terraces that have been carved into the earth; raw ore is removed from the pit walls by use of explosives (p. 596).

oracle (AWR uh kuhl) a prophecy, or prediction of the future, usually delivered by a priest or priestess at a religious shrine (p. 207).

oratory (AWR uh tawr ee) the art of public speaking (p. 233).

ore (ohr) a rock that contains a mixture of minerals from which a valuable metal can be taken (p. 119).

orthodox (AWR thuh DAWKS) strict following of established beliefs; a branch of the Christian Church that believes it is closest to the original teachings of Christ (p. 249).

P **pampas** (PAM puhz) an area of grasslands, especially in Argentina (p. 569).

papyrus (puh PY ruhs) a tall water plant of northern Africa and southern Europe, used by ancient Egyptians to make paper (p. 98).

parable (PAR uh buhl) a simple story that illustrates an idea (p. 243).

partition (pahr TISH uhn) the act of dividing or separating, as in a partition between two countries (p. 544).

pass (pas) a gap in a mountain through which people can travel (p. 125).

passport (PAS pawrt) a government document that gives proof of citizenship and permits travel from one country to another (p. 417).

paterfamilias (PAY tuhr fuh MIHL ee uhs) the oldest and most powerful male member of a family, especially in ancient Rome (p. 232).

patrician (puh TRIHSH uhn) in ancient Rome, a wealthy citizen who claimed to be able to trace his or her roots back to the founding of Rome (p. 228).

patrilineage (PAT ruh LIHN ee ihj) tracing ancestry through the father's side of the family (p. 182).

patron (PAY truhn) a wealthy person who gives an artist, or group of artists, money and attention (p. 305).

peninsula (puh NIHN syuh luh) a land surrounded on three sides by water (p. 196).

persecute (PUR sih KYOOT) to harass and annoy another person, often because of differing religious or political beliefs (p. 245).

perspective (puhr SPEHK tihv) a visual technique that allows artists to create the illusion of distance and depth on a flat surface (p. 306).

petrodollars (PEHT roh DAWL uhrz) foreign currency earned by selling oil (p. 553).

pharaoh (FAIR oh) the name given the king in ancient Egypt (p. 95).

philosophy (fih LAWS uh fee) the study of human behavior and of moral truths in the universe (p. 212).

pilgrimage (PIHL gruh mihj) a journey to a religious site (p. 323).

plague (playg) a very contagious disease that strikes and spreads quickly over a large area (p. 300).

planned economy (pland ih KAWN oh mee) an economy planned and owned by the government, which decides what products to make and what prices to set (p. 406).

plantation (plan TAY shun) a large farm or estate (p. 576).

plaza (PLAH zuh) a large public square in a town or city (p. 159).

plebeian (plih BEE uhn) an ordinary working citizen in Rome who had the right to vote but not to hold office (p. 228).

point of view (poynt uhv vyoo) a way of looking at things; an opinion (p. 112).

polis (POH lihs) a city-state in ancient times, governed by small groups of powerful landowners (p. 199).

polytheism (PAWL ee thee IHZ uhm) the worship of many gods (p. 71).

population density (pahp yuh LAY shuhn) the number of people living in a geographic area (p. 469).

porcelain (PAWR suh lihn) a hard white material made from fine clay, invented by the Chinese (p. 336).

prehistoric (pree hih STAW rihk) relating to a period in time before history was written down (p. 60).

propaganda (prahp uh GAN duh) slanted and exaggerated information organized to reflect a particular view or belief (p. 390).

prophet (PRAHF iht) a religious leader thought to be inspired by a god; a person who predicts the future (p. 255).

province (PRAHV ihns) a political region, similar to a state (p. 271).

public housing (PUHB lihk HOWS ihng) housing paid for in part by the government (p. 420).

pueblo (PWEB loh) a village of flat-roofed adobe houses that share adjoining walls and are built in a pattern of steps on many levels (p. 167).

Q quality of life (KWAHL ih tee uhf LYF) the material and spiritual factors that make a life what it is; it includes how people like to live their everyday lives (p. 422).

Qu'ran (kuh RAN) the holy book of Islam (p. 256).

R rabbi (RAB y) a religious scholar or leader in the Jewish faith (p. 81).

rain forest (rayn FAWR ihst) a dense, tropical region near the equator that receives at least 120 inches of rain per year (p. 569).

raj (rahj) in India, power or rulership (p. 368).

reef (reef) a ridge of rock, sand, or coral that rises near the surface of a body of water (p. 498).

reference map (REHF uhr uhns map) a map that shows the location of towns, cities, and geographic features (p. 18).

Reformation (REHF uhr MAY shuhn) a religious movement in Europe that resulted in the separation of the Protestant churches from the Catholic Church (p. 316).

region (REE juhn) an area on the planet's surface that shares a common feature (p. 22).

reincarnation (ree ihn kahr NAY shuhn) in the Hindu religion, a cycle of rebirth in which one is reborn in a human or animal body (p. 131).

Renaissance (rehn ih SAHNS) a period of "rebirth" in art and literature that began in the 14th century, and was characterized by a revival of interest in the cultures of ancient Greece and Rome (p. 305).

republic (rih PUHB lihk) a nation with a constitution and without a monarchy, in which power lies with the citizens (p. 227).

reservation (REHZ uhr VAY shuhn) land set aside by a government for a special purpose, usually for Native American groups (p. 601).

reserve (rih ZURV) an area of protected land where hunting and logging are not allowed (p. 610).

resurrection (REHZ uh REHK shuhn) a rising from the dead, returning to life (p. 244).

revelation (REHV uh LAY shuhn) something that is revealed or disclosed, as in a message from God (p. 256).

ritual (RIHCH oo uhl) a form of ceremony associated with a religious, cultural, or political procedure (p. 37).

rotation (roh TAY shuhn) the circular movement of the earth on its axis (p. 384).

S Sahel (suh HAYL) means "shore"; the southern edge of the Sahara (p. 183).

savanna (suh VAN uh) a hot, grassy plain that has abundant rainfall (p. 24).

scientific method (sy uhn TIHF ihk METH uhd) a way of doing research that first identifies the problem, then gathers evidence, then proposes an explanation, and finally tests the explanation (p. 358).

senate (SEHN iht) a ruling body made up of representatives; the highest decision-making body in the government of ancient Rome (p. 227).

separatism (SEHP uh uh tihz uhm) a policy of separating from an established church, government, or culture (p. 656).

serf (surf) in the Middle Ages, a farmer whose labor, land, and family were owned by a lord (p. 289).

Sharia (shah REE ah) the Holy Law of Islam, which governs every detail of daily life in the Islamic faith (p. 327).

Shi'a (SHEE ah) Muslims who supported Ali, the cousin and son-in-law of the prophet Muhammad (p. 261).

shrine (shryn) a religious site (p. 207).

siege (seej) a battle to capture a city, usually by surrounding the city and establishing a blockade (p. 271).

siege train (seej trayn) a combination of military equipment, including portable towers and ramming devices, used to attack cities (p. 220).

site (syt) a place where scientists search for signs of past human civilization (p. 47).

smelting (smehlt ihng) the process of heating ore to high temperatures to burn away minerals (p. 119).

sorghum (SAWR guhm) a grass that can be made into syrup (p. 174).

sovereignty (SAHV uhr ihn tee) supreme authority or rule; complete independence and self-rule (p. 556).

spartan (SPAHR tn) hard or severe (p. 201).

specialization of labor (SPEHSH uh lih ZAY shuhn uhv LAY buhr) the division of labor among specific, skilled jobs that contribute to the needs of a community (p. 68).

species (SPEE sheez) a basic kind or category of organisms capable of reproducing their own kind (p. 138).

sponsor (SPAHN suhr) a person who pays for an activity or takes responsibility for it (p. 199).

staple (STAY puhl) a basic food consumed by almost all people in a particular culture; a basic item of trade (p. 650).

steppe (step) a vast dry, grassy plain in parts of Europe and Asia (p. 23).

stereotype (STEHR ee uh typ) a widely accepted idea about a place, people, or event that exaggerates some aspects and ignores others (p. 534).

subcontinent (SUHB kahn tuh nuhnt) a vast region that forms the major part of a continent (p. 125).

subsistence farming (suhb SIHS tuhns fahrm ihng) farming that supplies only enough to feed the grower's family, with nothing left to sell (p. 436).

sultan (SUL tuhn) a Muslim ruler (p. 326).

Sunni (SOON ee) the majority of Muslims (p. 261).

surplus (SUR pluhs) an amount or quantity beyond what is needed for immediate use (p. 68).

synagogue (SIHN uh GAHG) a place for worship and study in the Jewish faith (p. 81).

T **tariff** (TAR ihf) fees or taxes on products brought into or out of a country (p. 598).

thematic map (thih MAT ihk map) a map that illustrates a theme or idea (p. 18).

tourism (TUR ihz uhm) the industry of taking care of tourists (p. 466).

tragedy (TRAJ ih dee) a serious story about men and women who meet terrible misfortune (p. 210).

trend (trehnd) a general tendency or pattern of behavior (p. 370).

tributary (TRIHB yuh tehr ee) a stream that flows into a major river (p. 569).

tribute (TRIHB yoot) a kind of payment to the government in exchange for protection (p. 339).

tundra (TUHN druh) an arctic region without trees, having low-growing shrubs and mosses (p. 23).

tyrant (TY ruhnt) a cruel ruler who governs by threat of force (p. 202).

U **underground mine** (UHN duhr grownd myn) a mine with shafts and tunnels to extract minerals from the earth (p. 596).

urbanization (ur buh nih ZAY shuhn) changing or moving from a rural area to an urban area (p. 439).

V **viceroy** (VYS roy) the governor of a country; the representative of the king (p. 368).

W **wildlife preserve** (WYLD lyf prih ZURV) a place where wild animals are protected (p. 466).

work ethic (wurk EHTH ihk) a system of beliefs and ideals about how work should be performed (p. 517).

Y **yoga** (YOH guh) a program of physical exercise and meditation (p. 131).

yucca (YUHK uh) a North American plant used for food and for making rope, baskets and soap (p. 646).

Z **ziggurat** (ZIHG uh rat) huge pyramid-shaped temple of ancient Mesopotamia (p. 71).

Index

Page numbers with *m* before them refer to maps. Page numbers with *p* refer to pictures. Page numbers with *c* refer to charts.

A

Abbasid dynasty, 261, 263, 264
Aborigines, *p515*, *p534*, 534–536, 537, *p537*
Abraham, 77–78, 83, 258
Abu Bakr, 260, 264
Abu Simbel, temples of, 109, 457, *m463*
Abyssinians, 322. *See also* Ethiopia.
Achebe, Chinua, 447
Acropolis, *p190–p191*, *p201*, 208
Adelaide, Australia, 498
Adoration of the Magi (Vivarini), *p241*
Aegean Sea, 197, *m198*
Africa, ancient West
  agriculture, 65, 91–93, 174, 179–180
  daily life, 180–182, *p181*
  maps, *m57*, *m175*, *m179*, *m183*, *m185*, *m186*
  natural resources, 176, *p176*, p187
  rise of cultures, 178–182
  trade, *p173*, 184–187, *m186*
Africa, early
  Carthage, 228
  Muslim kingdoms and empires, 255, 260–265, 268–272
  Roman Empire, *m228*, 231, *m231*, 248, *m248*
  trade, 300–301
Africa, geography, 20, 21, *m57*, 173–176, *m175*, 177, *m322*, *m458*
Africa, maps, *m57*, *m175*, *m179*, *m183*, *m185*, *m186*, *m433*, *m437*, *m441*, *m444*, *m458*, *m467*, *m470*, *m473*
Africa, modern
  agriculture, 436–438, 440–441, 460, 462, 467–468, *m473*
  cities, *p434*, 439, 460. *See also* specific cities.
  climate and geography, 435–439, *m437*, 438, 440, 441, *m441*
  culture and religion, 439, 442–447, 457–461, 472–477
  education, *p435*, 446, p446
  government, 446–447
  imperialism, 350, 365–369, 370–371, *m370*, *m371*, 431, 432, 443, 446
  independence movements, *p435*, 442, *p442–p443*, *m444*, 445–447, *c447*
  languages, *c180*
  natural resources, *p434*, 436–438, 440, *m441*, *m471*
  population, *c345*, *c439*, *m467*, *m470*, 473, *m473*
  urbanization, 439
  World War I, 388
  World War II, 445
Africa, prehistoric, 60, *p60*
African Americans
  desegregation, 660, 663

discrimination, 663
  enslavement, 661
  voting rights, 538, 539
African National Congress, 448, 482–483
Afrikaners, 479, 483. *See also* South Africa.
Agora, *p200–p201*
Agriculture. *See also specific countries, dynasties, empires, or kingdoms.*
  ancient Africa, 65, 91–93, 174, 179–180
  ancient Americas, 64, *p64*, 154, 156–157, 159–161, 166–168, 648
  ancient Asia, 65, 67–68, 126–129, 137–139, 142, 148
  ancient Europe, 196, 226–227
  development of, 61, 64–70, *m65*, 92–93, 126–127, 166–167, 289–290, 342
  livestock, 96, 129, 180, *p181*, 499, 536, *p536*, 608, 650
  medieval Europe, 289–290
  modern Europe, 382–383
  subsistence farming, 436–438, 467–468
  wool production, *c360*
Ahimsa, 131
Ahmose I, Pharaoh, 116
Akhenaten. *See* Amenhotep IV.
Alaska, 153, 622
Aleijadinho, *p605*
Alexander the Great, 125, 129, 133, 134, *p195*, 219–221, *p219*, *m220–m221*
Alexandria, Egypt, 220
Alfonsín, Raúl, 588
Alhambra Palace, *p254*, *p262–p263*
Ali, fourth Rightly Guided Caliph, 261
Allah, 255–259, 260–264. *See also* God.
Almoravids, 184
Alphabets, development of, 31, *c31*, 45, 70, *c70*, 75, 98–100, 118, *c118*, *c145*, 169, 276, 277, 340, 528, 529
Alps, *p378*, 380
Alsace-Lorraine, 387
Amanishakheto, pyramid of, 120
el-Amarna, Egypt, 108
Amarna Letters, 112
Amazon rain forest, 569, 601
Amazon River, 566, *p568*, 569
Amenhotep I, Pharaoh, 111
Amenhotep IV, Pharaoh, *p108*
American colonies, 50, 366
American Revolution, 50–51, 63, 361, 629, 633
Americas. *See also* Caribbean Islands, Central America, North America, *and* South America.
  ancient agriculture, 64, *p64*, 154, 156–157, 159–161, 166–168
  early civilizations, 154–157, *p154*, *m155*, *p156*, *c156*, *p157*, 163
  geography, 153–154
Amsterdam, Netherlands, *p405*, 419–423, *m421*, 424–425, *m425*

Amun, 116–117, *p116*
Anasazi people, 153, *c156*, 164, 166–168, *p166*, *p168*
Andes, *m17*, 153, 154, 156, 162, *p162*, *p566*, 568, *p569*, 572, *m573*, 579, *m677*
Angelou, Maya, 616
Angola, 371, 445
Antarctica, 21, 355, *m695*
Anthony and Cleopatra (Shakespeare), 312
Anthropologists, *p35*, 46–47, 48
Anti-Semitism, 390–392, 395–401, 555
Antigua and Barbuda, *c629*
Anubis, *p100*
Apache ceremonies, *p34*, 38, *p38*
Apartheid, 448, *p457*, 480–483, 484–485
Apedemak, 118
Aphrodite, 215, 217, 239
Apollo, 217
Apollo 13: The Junior Novelization (Anastasio), 636–639
Appian Way, 231
Aquarius, Apollo 13 lunar module, 637
Aqueduct, *p224*, 236–237, *p236*
Arabia, *m256*. *See also* Southwest Asia *and specific countries.*
Arabian Peninsula, 255, 256, 257, 260
Arabic language, *c31*, *p257*
Arabic numbers, 263
Aramaic language, 75
Arawak people, 644
Archaeologists, 35, 46, 47–48, *p47*, *p48*
Archaeology, 46–48, 59–61, 104–111, 118, 120–121, 140, 144–145, 162, 165, 173–174, 176, 178–179, 186, 198, 232
Archimedes, 211
Architecture, 36–37, 40–42. *See also specific cultures and locations.*
  ancient, *p72*, *p81*, *p83*, *p97*, *p102–p103*, *p118*, *p120*, *p127*, *p130*, *p135*, *p136*, *p158*, *p160*, *p161*, *p162*, *p164*, *p166*, *p190–p191*, *p201*, *p207*, 208–209, *p210*, *p224*, *p233*, *p235*, *p236*, *p237*, *p238*, 240, *p240*, *p242*, *p246*, *p247*
  early, *p258*, *p262*, *p263*, *p269*, *p282–p283*, *p286*, *p289*, *p291*, *p292*, *p306*, *p328–p329*
  European Renaissance, *p304*, *p305*, *p306*, *p324–p325*, *p330*, *p334–p335*, *p340–p341*, *p409*, *p542*
  modern, *p374–p375*, *p378*, *p430–p431*, *p460*, *p461*, *p465*, *p468*, *p488*, *p489*, *p492*, *p508*, *p509*, *p514*, *p562*, *p584*, *p605*, *p616–p617*, *p631*, *p642*, *p646*, *p652*, *p658*
Arctic, 344, 622, *m694*
Ardèche, France, cave paintings, *p58*, 59–60, *p60*, 62, 63
Ares, *c239*
Argentina. *See also specific cities.*
  democracy movement, *p584*, 585, 587–588, *p588*, 589, *p589*
  economics, 584, 586, 587, 588–589

(r) Werner Forman Archive/Art Resource **173** (t) Erich Lessing/Art Resource; (r) Volkmar Wentzel/National Geographic Society Image Collection **174** James Morris/PANOS Pictures **175** (l) Wendy Watriss/Woodfin Camp & Assoc.; (m) Tim Davis/Tony Stone Images; (tr) Warren Jacobs/Tony Stone Images; (br) Jo Daniell/Black Star **176** (r) F. Jackson/Robert Harding Picture Library; (l) Clem Haagner/ARDEA, London **178** Werner Forman Archive/Art Resource **179** Robert Caputo/Aurora **185** (t) Volkmar Wentzel/National Geographic Society Image Collection; (b) T. Abercrombie/National Geographic Society Image Collection **187** ZEFA Germany/The Stock Market **190-191** Koji Yamashita/Panoramic Images **192** (t) Francis Bartlett Fund. Courtesy of Museum of Fine Arts, Boston (13.189); (l) (r) Robert Frerck/Woodfin Camp & Assoc. **193** (m) (r) Laurie Platt Winfrey, Inc. **194** Francis Bartlett Fund. Courtesy of Museum of Fine Arts, Boston (13.189); (m) Rolf Ronove/ Globe Photos; (l) Courtesy of Museum of Fine Arts, Boston (61.195); (r) Scala/Art Resource **195** (t) (l) Ron Sheridan/A.A.& A.; (m) (r) Michael Holford **196** Bildarchiv Preussischer Kulturbesitz **197** David Peter/Globe Photos **199** Courtesy of Museum of Fine Arts, Boston (61.195) **201** Douglas Waugh/Peter Arnold **203** Mike Andrews/A.A.& A. **204-205** (bk) Jeff Hunter/The Image Bank **204** Ronald Sheridan/A. A.& A. **205** Nimatallah/Art Resource **206** Courtesy of Museum of Fine Arts, Boston (04.12) **207** (l) Robert Frerck/Woodfin Camp & Assoc.; (r) Bildarchiv Preussischer Kulturbesitz **208** (l) (r) Ron Sheridan/A.A.& A. **209** (l) Greg Pease/Tony Stone Images; (r) Michael Holford **210** (t) F.H.C. Birch/Bruce Coleman; (b) Reproduced courtesy of the Trustees of the British Museum, London **211** Ron Sheridan/A.A. & A. **212** The Metropolitan Museum of Art, Catharine Lorillard Wolfe Collection, Wolfe Fund, 1931 (31.45) **218** Scala/Art Resource **219** Erich Lessing/Art Resource **224** Bob Abraham/The Stock Market; (l) Scala/Art Resource; (m) Adam Woolfitt/Woodfin Camp & Assoc.; (r) Alinari/Art Resource **225** (t) Scala/Art Resource; (l) SuperStock; (m) Erich Lessing/Art Resource; (r) SuperStock **226** Scala/Art Resource **227** UPPA/Photoreporters, Inc. **228** Scala/Art Resource **229** SuperStock **230** (l) Sonia Halliday Photographs; (r) Erich Lessing/Art Resource **231** (t) Adam Woolfitt/Robert Harding Picture Library; (b) SEF/Art Resource **232** Rolf Adlercreutz/Gamma-Liaison **234** (t) Luiz C. Marigo/Peter Arnold; (b) Scala/Art Resource **235** Huber/Marka/ZUMA **236** Adam Woolfitt/Woodfin Camp & Assoc. **237** (t) Hoerst Schafer/Peter Arnold, Inc.; (b) Erich Lessing/Art Resource **238** (t) National Gallery of Art, Washington. Samuel H. Kress Collection. Photo by Richard Carafelli.; (b) Robert Frerck/Woodfin Camp & Assoc. **240** Hubertus Kanus/Photo Researchers **241** SuperStock **242** (t)SuperStock; (b)Ray Goodburn/Windrush Photos **243** © Richard T. Nowitz **244** Scala/Art Resource **245** Scala/Art Resource **246** Scala/Art Resource **247** (l) Steve Berman/Gamma-Liaison; (r) Sidali-Djenidi/Gamma-Liaison **249** (t) Giraudon/Art Resource; (b) SuperStock **250** Scala/Art Resource **254** Robert Mackinlay/Peter Arnold, Inc.; (l) Nabeel Turner/Tony Stone Images; (m) Hilarie Kavanagh/Tony Stone Images; (r) Cary Cralle/The Image Bank **255** (t) Raga/The Stock Market; (l) Klaus Paysan/Peter Arnold, Inc.; (m) SuperStock; (r) Joe Viesti/Viesti Associates **256** Nabeel Turner/Tony Stone Images **257** Visual Arts Library **258** The Metropolitan Museum of Art, Harris Brisbane Dick Fund, 1939 (39.20) **259** ARAMCO World **260** Reproduced courtesy of the Trustees of the British Museum, London **263** Mark Romanelli/The Image Bank **265** (cover) James L. Stanfield/National Geographic Society Image Collection **266** Mehmet Biber/National Geographic Society Image Collection **269** Klaus Paysan/Peter Arnold, Inc. **270** Bibliotheque Nationale, Paris **271** Laurie Platt Winfrey, Inc. **272** Wendy V. Watriss/Woodfin Camp & Assoc.; (l) Robert Young Pelton/Westlight **273** Laurie Platt Winfrey, Inc. **275** The Freer Gallery of Art **276** SuperStock **277** Joe Viesti/Viesti Associates **278** Scala/Art Resource **282-283** Terry Williams/The Stock Market **284** (t) Charly Franklin/FPG; (l) Scala/Art Resource (r) Sonia Halliday Photographs **285** (l) © Dennis Cox/China Stock; (m) John Bigelow Taylor/Art Resource; (r) Reproduced courtesy of the Trustees of the British Museum, London **286** Charly Franklin/FPG; (l) Bilderarchiv Preussischer Kulturbesitz; (m) Sylvain Grandadam/Tony Stone Images; (r) National Palace Museum, Taipei, Taiwan, Republic of China **287** (t) Dallas & John Heaton/Westlight; (l) The Bettmann Archive; (m) National Gallery of Art, Washington. Gift of Mr. & Mrs. Robert Woods Bliss; (r) Scala/Art Resource **288** (t) Giraudon/Art Resource; (bl) The Board of Trustees of the Royal Armouries; (br) Heidelberg University Library from Manesse Liederhandschrist 14c. (MS 848,fol. 149) **289** Musee Conde, Chantilly, France. Giraudon/Art Resource **290** (t) Public Record Office, London; (b) Bibliotheque Nationale, Paris **291** (t) (l) © Museum of London; (r) Charles Best Photography **292** Travelpix/FPG **293** The Walters Art Gallery, Baltimore **294-295** (bk) Jeff Hunter/The Image Bank **295** Benn Mitchell/The Image Bank **296** British Library **298** British Library **299** National Palace Museum, Taipei, Taiwan, Republic of China **300** (t) © United Nations Educational and Cultural Organization, Paris; (l) Dr. Tony Brain/Science Photo Library/Photo Researchers; (r) Stephen Dalton/Photo Researchers **302** (r) Visual Arts Library **304** (l) Scala/Art Resource; (r) Nippon Television Network Corporation **305** (t) Erich Lessing/Art Resource; (l) Scala/Art Resource; (r) Edovard Berne/Tony Stone Images **306** (t) Scala/Art Resource; (b) Erich Lessing/Art Resource **307** (l) Scala/Art Resource; (tr) Tetra Associates; (br) © Her Majesty Queen Elizabeth II. Not to be reproduced without written permission from Royal Collections Enterprises Ltd. **308** (t) Erich Lessing/Art Resource (b) Bridgeman/Art Resource **309** National Gallery of Art, Washington. Gift of Mr. & Mrs. Robert Woods Bliss. **314** R. Kord/H. Armstrong Roberts **315** (l) Foto Stadtarchiv Worms; (r) Scala/Art Resource **316** (l) © Concept & Bild; (r) The Metropolitan Museum of Art, Rogers Fund, 1913 **317** Scala/Art Resource **320** Tony Stone Images; (l) Kal Muller/Woodfin Camp & Assoc.; (m) Wan-go Weng, Inc.; (r) The Metropolitan Museum of Art, Gift of Robert E. Tod, 1937. (37.191.1) **321** (t) Dr. George Gerster/Comstock; (l) Robert Harding Picture Library; (r) D. Donne Bryant/DDB Stock Photo; (r) James A. Stanfield/ National Geographic Society Image Collection **323** Robert Caputo/Aurora **324** (l) Reproduced by courtesy of the Trustees of the British Museum, London; (r) Robert Caputo/Aurora **325** (l) Kal Muller/Woodfin Camp & Assoc.; (r) Chester Higgins, Jr./Photo Researchers **326** (l) The Metropolitan Museum of Art, Rogers Fund, 1938. (38.149.1); (r) Sonia Halliday Photographs **328** Ankara Universitesi To Mer **329** R & S Michaud/Woodfin Camp & Assoc. **330** James A.Stanfield/National Geographic Society Image Collection **331** (l) ©Dennis Cox/China Stock; (r) George P. Koshollek/Woodfin Camp & Assoc. **332** Wan-go Weng, Inc. **333** Stuart Westmorland/Tony Stone Images **335** (t) © Don Hamilton; (b) Susan Van Etten/Picture Cube **336** Mike Yamashita/Woodfin Camp & Assoc. **337** (l) The Asia Society, New York, Mr. & Mrs. John D. Rockefeller 3rd Collection. Photo: Lynton Gardiner; (r) The Metropolitan Museum of Art, Gift of Robert E. Tod, 1937. (37.191.1) **338** Robert Harding Picture Library **339** Bodleian Library (MS. Arch, Seld. A. 1 Fol. 47 Recto) **340** John Bigelow Taylor/Art Resource **341** The Granger Collection **342** David Hiser/Photographers/Aspen **343** Robert Harding Picture Library **348** e.t. Archive; (l) Giraudon/Art Resource; (m) Courtesy of the Trustees of the Victoria & Albert Museum; (r) Mansell Collection Ltd. **349** (t) National Maritime Museum Picture Library; (l) Photo Bulloz; (m) SuperStock; (r) Harvey Lloyd/The Stock Market **350** Giraudon/Art Resource **351** Courtesy of the Trustees of the Victoria & Albert Museum **352** (l) © G. Dagli Orti, Paris; (r) © George H. H. Huey **354** (bl) (br) National Maritime Museum Picture Library; (m) John Banagan/The Image Bank **354-355** National Maritime Museum Picture Library **355** (tr) Walter Iooss, Jr./The Image Bank; (bl) Jeff Hunter/The Image Bank **357** (l) (r) Museum Boerhaave, Leiden; (m) Royal Society **358** (t) Bridgeman/Art Resource; (bl) Scala/Art Resource; (br) The Science Museum/Science & Society Picture Library **359** (tl) Spectrum Colour Library; (tr) (br) The Science Museum/Science & Society Picture Library; (bl) The Bridgeman Art Library **361** Mansell Collection Ltd. **362** Photo Bulloz **363** Photo Bulloz **364** Reproduced by courtesy of the Trustees of the British Museum, London **366** Cooper-Hewitt, National Design Museum, Smithsonian Inst./Art Resource **367** David Sutherland/Tony Stone Images **368** (t) The Royal Archives © Her Majesty Queen Elizabeth II; (b) The British Library **369** Camera Press/Renta Ltd. **370** Michael Holford **371** The Science Museum/Science & Society Picture Library **374-375** Allen Prier/ Panoramic Images **376** (t) Koji Yamashita/Panoramic Images; (l) AKG, London; (r) Brad Markel/Gamma Liaison **377** (r) R. Bossu/Sygma; (m) Chris Niedenthal/Black Star; (r) Henk van der Leeden/Benelux Press **378** Koji Yamashita/Panoramic Images; (l) Luis Castaneda/The Image Bank; (m) Alain Choisnet/The Image Bank; (r) Hulton Deutsch Collection Ltd. **379** (l) Courtesy Carole Frohlich; (m) Hulton Deutsch Collection Ltd.; (r) Photo AKG, London **381** Alain Choisnet/The Image Bank **386** (l) R. Bossu/Sygma; (r) J. Langevin/Sygma **388** Brooklyn Eagle **389** (t) Hulton Deutsch Collection Ltd.; (b) e.t. Archive **390** (t) Courtesy Carole Frohlich; (b) Hugo Jaeger/Life Picture Service **391** (l) Arnold Kramer, United States Holocaust Memorial Museum; (r) Photo AKG, London **392** (t) AKG, London; (b) PHOTRI **393** Hulton Deutsch Collection Ltd. **394** Brad Markel/Gamma-Liaison **395** © Corbus/Hulton-Deutsch Collection **396** Corbis **397** Corbis **400-401** (bk) Jeff Hunter/The Image Bank **400** © Reportagebild **404** Bullaty Lomeo/The Image Bank; **404** (l) D. Hudson/Sygma; (m) James L. Stanfield/National Geographic Society Image Collection; (r) Fievee/Sipa Press **405** (l) J. M. Turpin/Sygma; (m) B & U International Picture Service; (r) Truus van Gog/HH **406** Josef Koudelka/Magnum Photos **407** D. Hudson/Sygma **408** Chip Hires/Gamma-Liaison **409** Chris Niedenthal/Black Star **410** James L. Stanfield/National Geographic Society Image Collection **411** Layne Murdoch **414** (r) REA/SABA; (l) Patrick Durand/Sygma **416** B. Rheims/Sygma **417** Raphael Gaillarde/Gamma-Liaison **418** Charlier/Sipa **419** Hulton Deutsch Collection Ltd. **420** Rijksmuseum Foundation **421** (l) Rijksmuseum Foundation; (r) Photo KLM **422** (r) Mike Wilkinson/REX Features, London; (tr) Henk van der Leeden/Benelux Press; (br) Thijs Hoefnagels/Benelux Press **424** (t) Tjeerd Moolhuysen/WVF/Tony Stone Images; (b) Harald Sund/The Image Bank **425** (t) Grant Faint/The Image Bank; (m) Visbach/Benelux Press; (b) Rentmeester/The Image Bank **430-431** Tony Stone Images **432** (t) Ian Murphy/Tony Stone Images; (l) Lori Grinker/Contact Press Images; (r) Tony Stone Images **433** (l) Tibor Bognar/The Stock Market; (m) Robert Frerck/Odyssey; (r) Jeffrey Aaronson/Network Aspen **434** Ian Murphy/Tony Stone Images; (l) Lori Grinker/Contact Press Images; (m) Mark Petersen/Tony Stone Images; (r) Uniphoto **435** (t) John Garrett/Tony Stone Images; (l) UPI/Bettmann; (m) (r) Jeffrey Aaronson/Network Aspen **436** (t) William Campbell/Peter Arnold Inc.; (b) Lori Grinker/Contact Press Images **437** (tl) Lorne Resnick/Tony Stone Images; (tm) Travelpix/FPG International; (tr) S. Purdy Matthew/Tony Stone Images (bl) ZEFA/The Stock Market; (bm) Frederick Myers/Tony Stone Images; (br) Uniphoto **440** (t) Steve McCurry/Magnum Photos; (m) Larry C. Price/Contact Press Images; (b) Lars Ternblad/The Image Bank **441** Tom Owen Edmunds/The Image Bank **442-443** Jeffrey Aaronson/Network Aspen **443** John Moss/Black Star **444** (l) P. Jordan/Gamma Liaison; (m) (r) UPI/Bettmann **446** (t) Wendy Stone/Gamma-Liaison; (b) Piero Guerrini/Gamma-Liaison **456** Robert Frerck/Tony Stone Images; (l) Bruno Barbey/Magnum Photos; (m) Dennis Stone/Tony Stone Images; (r) Jeffrey Aaronson/Network Aspen **457** (t) Adam Woolfitt/Robert Harding Picture Library; (l) Sally Mayman/Tony Stone Images; (m) David Turnley/Black Star; (r) Gideon Mendel/Magnum Photos **459** (t) Bruno Barbey/Magnum Photos; (b) Tracie Pierce/SABA **461** Guido Alberto Rossi/The Image Bank **462** Tor Eigeland/Black Star **462-463** Tor Eigeland/Black Star **463** (t) Tor Eigeland/Black Star; (b) Giuliand Colliva/The Image Bank **464** Camerapix **465** (t) Dennis Stone/Tony Stone Images; (b) Alon Reininger/Contact Press Images **466** (l) BKA/Network Aspen; (ml) Nicholas Parfitt/Tony Stone Images; (mr) Mitch Reardon/Tony Stone Images; (r) Mark Newman/Adventure Photo **468** Ron Watts/Westlight **470** (t) Laurence Hughes/The Image Bank; (b) Andrea Pistolesi/The Image Bank **471** Travelpix/FPG International **472** Sally Mayman/Tony Stone Images **474** © Jason Laure **475** Robert Frerck/Odyssey Productions **476** © Jason Laure **477** Andersen/Gaillarde/Gamma Liaison **479** Roger de la Harpe/ABPL **480-481** Ian Berry/Magnum Photos **481** David Turnley/Black Star **482** Jeffrey Aaronson/Network Aspen **483** AP/WideWorld **484-485** (bk) Jeff Hunter/The Image Bank **484** Gideon Mendel/Magnum Photos **488-489** R. Ian Lloyd/Westlight **490** (t) Peter Charlesworth/SABA; (l) Uniphoto; (r) Jean Miele/The Stock Market **491** (l) Cathlyn Melloan/Tony Stone Images; (m) Nabeel Turner/Tony Stone Images; (r) Ricki Rosen/SABA **492** Peter Charlesworth/SABA; (l) Uniphoto; (m) Mike Langford/Auscape Int.; (r) © Bill Bachman **493** (t) John Noble/Tony Stone Images; (m) Robert E. Murowchick; (l) National Archives; (r) R. Ian Lloyd/Westlight **494** (t) Orion Press; (m) © Dennis Cox/ChinaStock; (b) Martyn Colbeck/Earth Scenes **495** (t) Paul Harris/Tony Stone Images; (m) (b) Uniphoto **496** Mike Langford/Auscape Int. **497** Mike Langford/Auscape Int. **498** (t) Simeone Huber/Tony Stone Images; (m) Peter Stone/Pacific Stock; (b) Australian Picture Library/Westlight **499** (t) R. Ian Lloyd/Westlight; (b) Carl Roessler/Tony Stone Images **500-501** Gregory G. Dimuian/Photo Researchers **501** (t) Greg Davis/*TIME* Magazine; (l) Guido Alberto Rossi/The Image Bank; (r) Darryl Torckler/Tony Stone Images **502** (l) Don Smetzer/Tony Stone Images; (r) Jean Miele/The Stock Market **504** (t) Robert E. Murowchick; (l) Photo Source, Ltd., London; (m) National Archives **505** (t) Sygma; (m) U.S. Army Photograph; (b) Sygma, Paris **506** Stanford Zalburg **507** Tony Stone Images **508** R. Ian Lloyd/Westlight **510** P. & G. Bowater/The Image Bank **510-511** P. & G. Bowater/The Image Bank **511** (l) Kevin Forest/The Image Bank; (r) Naomi Duguid/Asia Access **514** Harvey Lloyd/The Stock Market; (l) Charles Gupton/Tony Stone Images; (m) Larry Dale Gordon/The Image Bank; (r) Keren Su/Pacific Stock **515** (t) Jose Fuste Raga/The Stock Market; (l) Peter Turnley/Black Star; (m) John Cancalosi/Auscape Int.; (r) Jean-Paul Ferrero/Auscape Int. **517** (t) Alan Levenson/Tony Stone Images; (l) Raga/The Stock Market; (r) Stangler/Uniphoto **518** Charles Gupton/Tony Stone Images **519** Lou Jones/The Image Bank **527** Manfred Morgenstern **528** Greg Girard/Contact Press Images **529** (t) Peter Turnley/Black Star; (b) Jean Higgins/Aristock **530** (t) Mike McQueen/Tony Stone Images; (b) Greg Girard/The Stock Market **532** Jean-Paul Ferrero/ARDEA, London **533** (t) The Image Bank; (b) Ralph A. Reinhold/Animals Animals **534** Jeffrey Aaronson/Network Aspen **536** (t) Bill Bachman; (b) Ken Straiton/The Stock Market **537** Auscape Int. **538-539** (bk) Jeff Hunter/The Image Bank **538** Pictorial Library, Australian Department of Foreign Affairs and trade **542** Earl Bronsteen/Panoramic Images; (l) The Stock Market; (m) Dinodia/Uniphoto; (r) Baldelli/Contrasto/SABA **543** (t) Ben Simmons/The Stock Market; (l) Nabeel Turner/Tony Stone Images; (m) Baitel-Benianuus/Gamma Liaison; (r) Uzi Keren/REA/SABA **545** (t) Crispin Rodwell/Gamma Liaison; (b) Cathlyn Melloan/Tony Stone Images **546** Jay Ullal/STERN/Black Star **547** Jay Ullal/STERN/Black Star **548** Steve McCurry/Magnum Photos **549** Steve McCurry/Magnum Photos **550** SuperStock **551** Nabeel Turner/Tony Stone Images **552** Baldelli/Contrasto/SABA **555** Baitel-Benianuus/Gamma Liaison **557** (t) Stephane Compoint/Sygma; (l) Ricki Rosen/SABA; (r) D. Aubert/Sygma **558** Tor Eigeland/Black Star **559** Rosen/SABA **562-563** David Pollitck/The Stock Market **564** (t) Mark Moffett/Minden Pictures; (l) Tony Morrison/South American Pictures; (r) Don Boroughs **565** (l) Eduardo Gil; (m) Carlos Humberto/Contact Press Images; (r) Michael & Patricia Fogden **566** Mark Moffett/Minden Pictures; (l) Tony Morrison/South American Pictures; (m) Thomas Stephan/Black Star; (r) Wolfgang Kaehler/Gamma-Liaison **567** (t) Stuart Westmorland/Tony Stone Images; (l)Carlos Humberto/Contact Press Images; (m) Pascal Perret/The Image Bank; (r) © Steven Rubin **568** Tony Morrison/South American Pictures **569** (t) Bethwald/Network Aspen; (b) Tony Morrison/South American Pictures **570-571** The Bettmann Archive **574** Stuart Franklin/Magnum Photos **576** Gary Apyne/Gamma-Liaison **577** (t) The Bettmann Archive; (b) Claudio Edinger/Gamma Liaison **578** © Steven Rubin **580** (l) Clive Brunskill/Allsport; (b) Ben Radford/Allsport; (m) Tom Ettinger **580-581** Focus On Sports **581** (cover) Walter Iooss, Jr.; (b) Tim Davis/Photo Researchers **584** Eduardo Gil/Black Star **584** (l) Walter Bibikow/The Image Bank; (m) Eduardo Gil/Black Star; (r) Eduardo Gil **585** (t) Bettmann Archive; (l) Peter Feibert/Gamma Liaison; (m) R. Andrew Odum/Peter Arnold; (r) Beth Wald/Network Aspen **586** Carlos Goldin/DDB Stock Photo **587** (t) Rafael Wollmann/Gamma Liaison; (b) Eduardo Gil **588** Don Boroughs **589** Eduardo Gil/Black Star **595** Chris Anderson/Aurora **596** (l) Eduardo Gil; (r) L.B. Bastlan/DDB Stock Photo **598** Philip & Karen Smith/Tony Stone Images **600** Carlos Humberto/Contact Press Images **601** (c) Conservation International **602** Vautier de Nanxe **603** Daniel Augusto Jr./Pulsar **604** Luiz Alberto/Gamma Liaison **605** (l) Peter Frey/The Image Bank; (r) Fernando Bueno/The Image Bank **607** (l) S.J. Kraseman/Peter Arnold; (m) Kevin Schafer/Peter Arnold; (r) (b) Michael Fogden/Animals Animals **608** Michael & Patricia Fogden **610** Beth Wald/Network Aspen **612-613** (bk) Jeff Hunter/The Image Bank **612** (l) Jacques Jangoux/Tony Stone Images; (r) Sue Cunningham/Tony Stone Images **613** Koji Yamashita/Panoramic Images **616-617** Mark Segal/Panoramic Images **618** (t) NASA/Mark Marten/Photo Researchers; (l) Jurgen Vogt/The Image Bank; (r) Max & Bea Hunn/DDB Stock Photo **619** (l) ALTI Publishing/M. Calderwood; (m) George S. Zimbel; (r) Harald Sund/The Image Bank **620** NASA/Mark Marten/Photo Researchers, Inc.; (l) Tom Bean/Tony Stone Images; (m) Terjerakke/The Image Bank; (r) Warren Faidley/International Stock **621** (t) Capt. Clay H. Wiseman/Animals Animals; (l) Dunwell/The Image Bank; (m) Nigel Atherton/Tony Stone Images; (r) David W. Hamilton/The Image Bank **622** (l) Rob Boudreau/Tony Stone Images; (r) Larry Ulrich/Tony Stone Images **625** Paul Chesley/Tony Stone Images **626** Angel Franco/NYT Pictures **628** The Bettmann Archive **629** Don Klumpp/The Image Bank **631** AP Photo/ Doug Mills **633** (cover) Jane Burton/Bruce Coleman Ltd. **642** Robert Frerck/Odyssey; (l) SuperStock; (m) Kathleen Marie Rohr/DDB Stock Photo; (r) The Granger Collection **643** (t) Murray & Assoc./Tony Stone Images; (l) George Zimbel; (m) Harald Sund/The Image Bank; (r) The Bettmann Archive **645** Jurgen Vogt/The Image Bank **646** Max & Bea Hunn/DDB Stock Photo **647** Martha Cooper/Viesti Associates **648** Robert Frerck/Tony Stone Images **649** (l) Will & Demi McIntyre/Photo Researchers; (r) Robert Frerck/Tony Stone Images **650** The Stock Market **651** (t) Paul Thompson/FPG Int.; (b) ALTI Publishing/M. Calderwood **652** ALTI Publishing/M. Calderwood **655** National Archives of Canada (54105) **656** George Zimbel **658** Janeart/The Image Bank **658-659** Steve Niedorf/The Image Bank **659** (t) Gary Cralle/The Image Bank; (m) Dave Watters/Tony Stone Images; (b) Jeffrey Aaronson/Network Aspen **660** Harald Sund/The Image Bank **661** (l) Bettmann; (r) California Dept. of Parks and Recreation **662** (l) The Bettmann Archive; (r) FPG Int. **663** (t) Bettmann; (ml) Archive Photos; (mr) © Junebug Clark; (bl) Carl Iwasaki/Life Magazine © Time Warner Inc.; (br) A. Grace/Sygma **664** Earth Imaging/Tony Stone Images **666-667** (bk) Jeff Hunter/The Image Bank **667** Will & Deni McIntyre/Photo Researchers **676-677** Ira Block/The Image Bank **680** Steve Dunwell **687** Library of Congress **724-725** J. Cowlin 1993/Panoramic Images **724** (m) Wernher Krutein/Gamma-Liaison; (r) Luis Garrido/Gamma Liaison; (l) Manuel Rodriguez/The Image Bank **725** (tr) Jordan Francois/Photo Researchers; (l) Jacky Gucia/The Image Bank; (r) Wesley Hitt/Gamma Liaison; (b) Andrea Pistolesi/The Image Bank

Assignment Photo Credits

Dave Desroches: 20, 21, 49 (tl, bl), 51, 205, 539, 613, 691 (background); FayFoto: 295, 635; Ilene Perlman: 36-37; Tony Scarpetta: 47, 82, 121, 600, 604, 611, 627, 645, 650 (background); Dorey Sparre: 690 (tl, m), 691; Tracey Wheeler: 49 (m), 121 (inset), 401, 485, 539 (inset)

Illustrations

Francis Back: 351; Glasgow & Associates: 381, 553, 572-573, 624, 625; Robert Hynes: 23, 67, 608-609; Hank Iken: 289, 438; Nenad Jakesevic: 102, 333; Matthew Pippin: 291; 687; Jared Schneidman: 103, 107, 258, 341, 500; Mark Siedler: 384-385, 385; Wood Ronsaville Harlin, Inc.: 72, 97, 139, 181, 200-201; 233, 235, 262, 329, 334-335

Maps

David Mackay Ballard: 501; Susan Carlson: 196, 339; DLF Group: 45, 202, 220-221, 261, 264, 333, 681; © 1996 GeoSystems Global Corp.: 12-13, 56-57, 192-193, 284-285, 376-377, 432-433, 490-491, 564, 565, 618-619, 692-707; GeoSystems Corp.: 17, 20-21, 26, 29, 61, 65, 67, 71, 79, 80, 92, 114, 126, 137, 155, 158, 159, 165, 175, 183, 185, 198, 228, 230, 242, 248, 250, 256, 276, 297, 299, 301-303, 322, 327, 334, 355, 365, 370-371, 380, 387, 391, 407, 409, 415, 425, 437, 441, 444, 458, 463, 467, 470, 471, 473, 494-495, 498, 503, 516, 520, 521, 535, 544, 546, 548, 549, 552, 556, 568, 571, 573, 578, 586, 597, 602, 606, 623, 644, 649, 659, 672, 673 left, 674-680; Glasgow and Associates: 673 right; Nenad Jakesevic: 179; Ellen J. Kuzdro: 18, 186; Joe LeMonier: 226, 275; Ortelius Design: 270, 634; Mike Reagan: 367